T0092159

Alice 3 and Java: Learning Creative Programming Through Storytelling and Gaming

Alice 3 and Java: Learning Creative Programming Through Storytelling and Gaming

Wanda P. Dann
Don Slater
Laura Paoletti
Dave Culyba
Carnegie Mellon University

 Pearson

330 Hudson Street, NY NY 10013

Director, Portfolio Management: Engineering, Computer Science & Global Editions: *Julian Partridge*
Specialist, Higher Ed Portfolio Management: *Tracy Johnson*
Portfolio Management Assistant: *Kristy Alaura*
Managing Content Producer: *Scott Disanno*
Content Producer: *Carole Snyder*
Web Developer: *Steve Wright*
Rights and Permissions Manager: *Ben Ferrini*
Manufacturing Buyer, Higher Ed, Lake Side Communications Inc (LSC): *Maura Zaldivar-Garcia*
Inventory Manager: *Ann Lam*
Product Marketing Manager: *Yvonne Vannatta*
Field Marketing Manager: *Demetrius Hall*
Marketing Assistant: *Jon Bryant*
Cover Designer: *Laura Paoletti*
Full-Service Project Manager: *Revathi Viswanathan, Cenveo Publisher Services*
Project Management: *Rose Kernan, RPK Editorial Services, Inc.*

Credits and acknowledgments borrowed from other sources and reproduced, with permission, in this textbook appears on page.

Copyright © 2018 Pearson Education, Inc. All rights reserved. Manufactured in the United States of America. This publication is protected by Copyright, and permission should be obtained from the publisher prior to any prohibited reproduction, storage in a retrieval system, or transmission in any form or by any means, electronic, mechanical, photocopying, recording, or likewise. For information regarding permissions, request forms and the appropriate contacts within the Pearson Education Global Rights & Permissions department, please visit http://www.pearsoned.com/permissions/

Many of the designations by manufacturers and sellers to distinguish their products are claimed as trademarks. Where those designations appear in this book, and the publisher was aware of a trademark claim, the designations have been printed in initial caps or all caps.

Screenshots © 2017 by Oracle Corporation. Reprinted with permission.

Library of Congress Cataloging-in-Publication Data
Names: Dann, Wanda P. author.
Title: Alice 3 and Java : learning creative programming through storytelling and gaming
    / Wanda P. Dann, Don Slater, Laura Paoletti, Dave Culyba.
Description: First edition. | Boston : Pearson Education, Inc., [2017] |
    Includes index.
Identifiers: LCCN 2016025489| ISBN 9780136156741 | ISBN 0136156746
Subjects: LCSH: Object-oriented programs (Computer programs) | Digital
    storytelling. | Alice (Computer file) | Java (Computer program language)
Classification: LCC QA76.64 .D3576 2017 | DDC 005.1/17—dc23
    LC record available at https://lccn.loc.gov/2016025489

www.pearsonhighered.com

ISBN 10:   0-13-615674-6
ISBN 13: 978-0-13-615674-1

Contents

Preface *xvii*

Prologue: Lawrence Prenderghast's Haunted Circus *1*

Episode 1 • March 1, 1910: Larry *4*

1 • Introduction *7*

1.1   **Program and Programming** *8*

1.2   **A Problem-Solving Approach** *8*

1.3   **A First Program Task** *9*

1.4   **Analyze the Task** *10*

    Summary 11
    Terms 11
    Concept Questions 11

2 • Design *13*

2.1   **Design Thinking** *14*

2.2   **Set Design** *15*

2.3   **Algorithm Development** *18*

2.4   **Translate the Set Design into an Alice Scene** *18*

    2.4.1 Add an object to the scene *21*

    2.4.2 Position an object using the cursor and one-shots *23*

2.5   **Saving a Project** *26*

2.6   **Creating a Sense of Place** *27*

    Summary 29
    Terms 29
    Concept Questions 29
    Exercises 30

v

3 • Implementation in Alice 35

3.1 **Open a Saved Project** 36

3.2 **The Code Editor** 39

3.3 **Creating (Writing) a Code Statement** 40

3.4 **Run the Program** 43

    3.4.1 Calling a method with a detail parameter 44

    3.4.2 A quick look at what happens behind the scene (optional) 44

3.5 **View Alice Code with Java Syntax** (optional) 46

Summary 47
Terms 47
Concept Questions 48
Exercises 48

4 • Implement and Test 49

4.1 **Implementation with Incremental Development** 51

4.2 **Creating Documentation with Comments** 52

4.3 **Testing** 54

4.4 **Translating Algorithm to Code** 54

    4.4.1 Moving with a vehicle 55

    4.4.2 Turning a subpart 59

4.5 **Bugs and Debugging** 60

4.6 **Design Revision** 64

Summary 67
Terms 67
Concept Questions 67
Exercises 70

Episode 2 • The Train Engine 73

5 • Procedures, *do together,* and Count Loops 77

5.1 **Story Analysis** 78

5.2 **Design** 78

5.3 **Implement and Test** *80*

5.4 **Declare a Custom Procedure** *81*

5.4.1 Name a custom procedure *82*

5.4.2 Code editor panels and *this* *83*

5.5 **Writing Code to Define a Custom Procedure** *84*

5.6 **Calling a Custom Procedure** *85*

5.7 *do together* *86*

5.8 **Multiple Calls to a Custom Procedure** *87*

5.9 **Nested Code Blocks** *88*

5.10 **Repetition with a *Count* Loop** *90*

Summary 91
Terms 91
Concept Questions 92
Exercises 93
Projects 95

Episode 3 • The Tunnel *97*

6 • Stepwise Refinement and Inheritance *101*

6.1 **Story Analysis** *102*

6.2 **Design** *102*

6.3 **Implement and Test with Stepwise Refinement** *104*

6.3.1 Camera and object markers in a scene *104*

6.3.2 Comment documentation *105*

6.3.3 Stepwise refinement—decomposition, again and again *106*

6.3.4 Use a camera marker to view objects inside the cabin *107*

6.3.5 Declare and implement a procedure in the Scene class *109*

6.3.6 Stepwise refinement with camera and object markers *112*

6.4 **When to Use Stepwise Refinement** *116*

6.4.1 Stepwise refinement: Setting an object's skin resource? *116*

6.4.2 Stepwise refinement: Visualizing an invisible action? *117*

6.4.3 Stepwise refinement: Sound effect and lengthy dialog? *118*

6.5 **Inheritance** *121*

6.5.1 Writing a custom procedure for a parent class *122*

6.6 Exporting *126*

Summary 128
Terms 129
Concept Questions 129
Exercises 130

7 • Implementation in Java *133*

7.1 The NetBeans IDE *134*

7.2 Create a New Java Project *135*

7.3 Syntax-Sensitive Text Editor *137*

7.3.1 TODO *138*

7.4 Writing Java Code *139*

7.4.1 System.out for Text Output *140*

7.4.2 NetBeans Keyboard Shortcuts *141*

7.5 Run *142*

7.6 What Happens When the Run Button Is Clicked *142*

7.7 Comparison: Graphics- vs. Text-based Editors *144*

Summary 147
Terms 147
Concept Questions 147
Exercises 147

8 • Importing: Alice 3 to Java and Code Templates *149*

8.1 Alice and Java, Side by Side *150*

8.2 Import an Alice Project into NetBeans *151*

8.3 Organization of Classes and Code Components in the NetBeans IDE *155*

8.3.1 Class Menus *155*

8.3.2 Edit Tabs *155*

8.4 Code Component Organization Scheme in a Class *156*

8.4.1 Transfer of the properties component *157*

8.4.2 Transfer of procedure components *158*

8.4.3 Transfer of Alice's hidden code to NetBeans *160*

8.5 Writing Code for 3D Graphics Animation in Java *161*

8.5.1 Use code completion to add an argument (detail) for an optional parameter *161*

8.5.2 Using code completion to write code statements with required parameters *163*

8.6 Using a Code Palette *165*

8.6.1 *doTogether* Code Template *165*

8.6.2 Lambda expressions in Java 8 *167*

8.6.3 *do in order* is assumed within a thread *168*

8.6.4 Using the Counted For Loop Template *169*

Summary 170
Terms 171
Concept Questions 171
Exercises 172

Episode 4 • The Forest Cabin *173*

9 • Code Reuse, Parameters, Data Types, Variables, and Arithmetic Expressions *177*

9.1 Analyze the Story *178*

9.2 Design *179*

9.3 Starter World *180*

9.4 Implementation: Camera Illusion Technique *182*

9.5 Implementation: Spine Bending Animation Technique *184*

9.6 Implementation: Code Reuse *185*

9.6.1 Importing previously saved code *187*

9.6.2 Reusing imported code *188*

9.7 A Custom Procedure with a Parameter *190*

9.8 Compute a Value, Using Variables and Arithmetic Expressions *195*

9.8.1 Declaring and initializing a variable *195*

9.8.2 Creating an arithmetic expression *197*

9.9 Using a Variable as a *count* Loop Control *199*

9.10 Data Types in Alice *202*

Summary 203
Terms 204
Concept Questions 204
Exercises 205

10 • Java: Parameters, Data Types, Variables, Expressions, and Loop Control 209

10.1 Data Types in Alice and Java *211*

10.1.1 Primitive data types in Java *212*

10.1.2 Built-in, legal operations on primitive data types *213*

10.2 Writing Code with Parameters and Variables in Java *214*

10.2.1 Add parameters to the header *215*

10.2.2 Variables and arithmetic expressions in Java *215*

10.3 Writing Code with *doTogether* in Java *216*

10.4 Using a Variable as a *for* Loop Limit *219*

10.5 Testing Code in Java *221*

Summary 222
Terms 223
Concept Questions 223
Exercises 224

Episode 5 • The Ringmaster Coat 225

11 • Interactivity with Events, If/Else, Conditions, and Built-in Functions 229

11.1 From Animation to Game *230*

11.2 Story Analysis and Adaptation *230*

11.3 Design *231*

11.3.1 Algorithm *232*

11.3.2 Starter world *233*

11.4 Implementation: UI to Display Instructions on a Billboard *235*

11.5 Implementation: Event Listener for Mouse-Click on an Object *238*

11.6 Object Mover Listener *242*

11.7 An Event Listener for Changing the Point of View *243*

11.8 If/Else and Conditional Expressions *245*

11.8.1 Conditional Expressions *246*

11.8.2 Conditional expressions with built-in functions *246*

11.8.3 Code within *if* and *else* segments of the *if/else* code block *249*

11.8.4 Preventing repeated event listener firing *250*

11.9 Event Listener for Mouse-Click with Multiple Target Objects *251*

11.10 A Tracking Variable for Game Condition *254*

11.11 Design Revisited *258*

Summary 259
Terms 259
Concept Questions 260
Exercises 261
Project 262

Episode 6 • March 1, 1910: Nicholas 263
....

12 • Custom Functions, While Loops, Random Values, Input, and a Game Algorithm 269
....

12.1 Story Analysis *270*

12.2 Design *271*

12.3 Starter World *272*

12.3.1 Create an internal pivot point *272*

12.3.2 Test with a temporary statement *275*

12.3.3 Reposition for cutscene *276*

12.3.4 Pre-made procedures in the starter world *276*

12.4 Implementation: Cutscene *277*

12.4.1 Using an external pivot *279*

12.4.2 Using an internal pivot *280*

12.4.3 Using a marker object as an argument *281*

12.5 Decomposition and Implementation: Game *283*

12.6 Repetition with a *while* Loop *286*

12.7 Swap with Pivot Markers *287*

12.8 Shuffle with Random Selection of Swap Objects *289*

12.8.1 Randomly choose one of three possible values *290*

12.9 Writing a Custom Function *291*

12.10 Player (User) Input *294*

12.10.1 Get the input *294*

12.10.2 Use the input *296*

12.11 Check the Game State: End Conditions *297*

12.12 Generalizing a Game Algorithm *299*

Summary 300
Terms 300
Concept Questions 300
Exercises 301
Project 303

Episode 7 • March 1, 1910: Esther *305*

13 • Built-in Arrays, Poses, More Events, and Interactive Controls *311*

13.1 Story Analysis for Demo *312*

13.2 Design for Demo *312*

13.2.1 Algorithm for demo *313*

13.2.2 Demo starter world *313*

13.3 Implement and Test the Demo *314*

13.3.1 Built-in array of skeletal joints *315*

13.3.2 Iteration with *for each in* *316*

13.3.3 *straightenOutJoints* *319*

13.3.4 Iteration with *each in together* *320*

13.4 Story Analysis for an Interactive Game *321*

13.4.1 Adapting for an interactive game *322*

13.4.2 Game starter world *323*

13.4.3 Pre-made custom procedures *324*

13.5 High-Level Structure *325*

13.6 Opening Cutscene *325*

13.7 Animating with Poses *326*

13.8 Play Game Decomposition *330*

13.9 Implementation: Stairs Animation *332*

13.9.1 Stair-twisting helper procedure *333*

13.9.2 Using an infinite *while* loop *333*

13.10   Implementation: Main Flow of the Game *335*

13.10.1 Set up the game *336*

13.10.2 The main game loop *336*

13.10.3 Updates *337*

13.10.4 Interactive control with Binary Operators *341*

13.10.5 Testing and debugging interactivity *346*

13.11   Check Game End Conditions *348*

13.12   Feedback for Win or Loss *349*

Summary 350
Terms 350
Concept Questions 350
Exercises 351
Project (Open Ended) 353

Episode 8 • March 1, 1910: Adelaide *355*

14 • Custom Arrays and Functions *361*

14.1   Demo: Basic Operations with a Custom Array *362*

14.1.1 Create and initialize a custom array of objects *363*

14.1.2 Iterate through a custom array *365*

14.1.3 Access an item in an array *367*

14.2   Program Example Story Analysis and Design *370*

14.2.1 Design *371*

14.2.2 Starter world *372*

14.3   Implementation with a Custom Array *375*

14.3.1 Writing a procedure with an array parameter *376*

14.3.2 Calling a procedure with an array argument *378*

14.3.3 Writing a procedure with a custom array but no parameter *378*

14.3.4 Pre-made procedures for Adelaide encounter *382*

14.4   Visual Alignment of a Custom Array (Horizontal) *382*

14.5   Linear Search of an Array *386*

14.5.1 A *compareTo* Custom Function *387*

14.6   Visual Alignment of an Array (Vertical) *389*

Summary 391
Terms 392
Concept Questions 392

Exercises 393
Projects 394

15 • Java: Custom Arrays and Sort 397

15.1 **Arrays in Java** 399

15.1.1 Java array declaration 400

15.1.2 Java array initialization 401

15.1.3 Access an individual element in an array 402

15.2 **Sorting an Array** 404

15.2.1 The selection sort algorithm 404

15.2.2 Implementation: select sort 406

15.2.3 A function helper method: *findLargestAfterIndex* 407

15.2.4 Calling the helper function 409

15.2.5 A procedure helper method: *swap* 409

15.2.6 Using the Integer class *compareTo* function 411

15.2.7 Calling *sort* 412

15.3 **Visual Representation of the Sort Mechanism** 413

15.3.1 Modifying the *swap* procedural method for visualization 413

15.3.2 Modify the call to *sort* 414

Summary 416
Terms 416
Concept Questions 416
Exercises 417

Episode 9 • March 1, 1910: Gideon 419

16 • Event-Driven Programming and Advanced Game Controls 425

16.1 **Analyze the Story** 426

16.2 **Design** 427

16.3 **Implementation: The Opening Cutscene** 429

16.4 **Implementation: Game with an Implied Loop** 430

16.4.1 Game analysis and design 431

16.4.2 Game setup 432

16.5   Event Listener: keyPress *435*

16.6   Debugging: TextString Output for Feedback *439*

16.6.1 Setup for text display *440*

16.6.2 Tracking and updating the text string display *442*

16.6.3 Testing *444*

16.6.4 Debug to restrict multiple event triggers *445*

16.7   Event Listeners for Speed Updates *446*

16.7.1 Time-elapsed event *447*

16.7.2 Rounding error *448*

16.7.3 Format output to display with two decimal places *448*

16.7.4 Collision Event Listener *449*

16.8   Event Listeners for End Conditions *451*

16.8.1 Win condition: collisionStarted event listener *451*

16.8.2 Loss condition: viewExited Listener *452*

Summary 453
Terms 454
Concept Questions 454
Exercises 454
Open-Ended Project 455

Epilogue *457*

Epilogue Capstone Project *461*

Index *471*

Preface

Alice is an educational software tool intended for teaching and learning fundamental concepts of computer programming with animation, storytelling, and gaming as the context. This book, and the Alice 3 software, builds on and extends the innovative approach introduced with Alice 2 and the *Learning to Program with Alice* textbook (written by Dann, Cooper and Pausch and first published in 2004). Formal studies have proven the effectiveness of this approach in attracting a diverse population, as well as increasing the retention rate of students in introductory levels in both high school and early college courses. This success and the highly positive feedback from hundreds of thousands of instructors and students inspired the Alice team at Carnegie Mellon University to continue Alice system development and provide strong support for instructors.

Teaching Approach

Creative Problem Solving

A creative problem-solving approach is used throughout the book. Each chapter begins with a new problem, which is basically: "Design and create a program that animates the story of (or simulates, or plays the game of) ...." Our problem-solving approach is an adaptation of a well-known approach developed by George Polya and published in his book, *How to Solve It*. A quick summary of Polya's problem-solving approach is

- Understand the problem.
- Devise a plan.
- Carry out the plan.
- Look back.

In computer programming, problem solving involves many of the same steps but is more dynamic and often involves repeated steps, frequent testing, and revision. Therefore, we have adapted the problem-solving approach to a cyclic model with a focus on the problem task, creating a design, implementing code, and testing the code. This approach incorporates some elements of *design thinking* that starts with understanding and analyzing a problem (a challenging task), involves experimentation, and expects design and implementation changes. These elements of design thinking are highly complementary to traditional decomposition and stepwise refinement used in programming.

Teaching Classes and Methods in the Context of Animation

A major feature, in terms of **student engagement**, is the enhanced animation capability provided by Alice 3 through a library of built-in classes, visually embodied by unique 3D models. These characters and props cover a wide range of stories and cultures. They are designed to capture the storytelling imagination of students and evoke the creation of animations inspired by the works of professional animation and gaming studios such as Disney, **Pixar**, DreamWorks, Electronic Arts, and others. In addition to their visual appeal, Alice's Gallery classes provide features to jumpstart student animation programming, including built-in animation **methods**. For example, the bird class includes pre-made methods for unfolding and folding a bird's wings. These built-in animation methods provide for rapid production of student story animations. And although these pre-made animations make it easy for students to get started, they are merely an inspirational beginning. Alice provides a powerful, intuitive interface for students to create their own customized methods and animations from the programmatically simple to the complex. Students can even create their own custom classes complete with **inheritance** features. Alice's emphasis on visualizing classes of characters and props eases students into **object-oriented** thinking.

Learning Programming Through Storytelling and Gaming

In between the chapters of the textbook are **episodes** of an unfolding story about a mysterious, haunted circus train, a cast of unique characters, and the adventurous task of lifting a magic spell from a troupe of circus performers. This story is meant to be the creative backdrop for an Alice 3 programming course. Throughout the book, the main narrative leads students through the creation of animations and interactive games adapted from episodes of *Lawrence Prenderghast's Haunted Circus* story.

Episode 1 introduces the *Haunted Circus* story and the two main characters: a yeti and a haunted circus ringmaster. After the Prologue and Episode 1, additional episodes of *The Haunted Circus* story appear at intervals between the text chapters.

An important turning point in *The Haunted Circus* story occurs in Chapters 9 and 10, where the yeti and the circus ringmaster encounter the storyteller in the woods and set out on an adventure to reunite the circus friends. At this point, the path through the story episodes is somewhat flexible, and the chapter sequence may be selected as desired by the instructor.

Transitioning from Alice 3 to Java

A significant innovation in this textbook is software features and instructional material that support transition to a production-level language (Java). This is in response to the requests of hundreds of instructors who participate in our online Alice Educators List. The request is: "Alice has been great for engaging my students and helping me teach the fundamental programming concepts. Now, how do I make the transition to Java (or C++, or Python)?" In this book, several chapters are devoted to providing assistance to the instructor and students for building on the concepts learned in Alice to make a successful transition to Java.

We believe, however, that it isn't enough to just add a few chapters on Java. For this reason, the groundwork is carefully laid within the Alice chapters and then built upon in the Java chapters to mediate a transition from Alice to Java. Some features of Alice 3 have been improved to provide a close correlation between Alice and Java's object-oriented concepts. For example, the Alice 3 gallery models are organized in a hierarchy of classes, which enables using inheritance in Alice in a manner that is more faithful to the way it is used in Java, C++, and other object-oriented languages.

Audience

. . . .

We understand that instructors will use this text to implement and support curriculum and objectives that meet the needs and requirements of students in their own specific educational institutions. In other words, we expect instructors will use the textbook in many different ways. Nonetheless, the following provides a short description of the target population and courses we taught, and others we envisioned, as this book was written.

In a semester-long course for introductory programming for non-majors, with an interdisciplinary focus: The programming examples presented in this text have a story-telling and animation context that is well suited to courses with an interdisciplinary focus. Preliminary testing with non-majors in liberal arts schools and in curricula for media arts, gaming, communications, and other programs of study has been highly successful.

In a semester-long introductory programming course for majors who have little or no programming experience: In many colleges, thirty to fifty percent of incoming majors have experience in personal productivity with computers, but not in programming. Students with little or no previous programming experience are at a disadvantage in a rigorous CS101 course and are at risk of dropping out or changing their major. Alice has been shown to significantly increase retention and achievement of these students.

As a primary component in the AP Computer Science Principles course: This book encompasses the span of computational thinking practices: connecting computing, creating computational artifacts, abstracting, analyzing problems and artifacts, communicating, and collaborating. The animation problem-solving context exemplifies most of the big ideas in the CS Principles curriculum, including creativity, abstraction, algorithms, and programming.

As a preparatory course prior to an AP Computer Science (Java) course: Alice 3 can be displayed in Java mode. This allows students to create program code in a gentle drag-and-drop programming environment where typing code with the details of syntax is not the major focus. This approach was used in Seymour Papert's *Logo* and Rich Pattis's *Karel the Robot*, which were inspirations for the Alice project.

Concept Order and Chapter Sequence

Pedagogic Features

- When a new term is introduced, it is printed in **bold blue**.
- A list of new terms is provided at the end of each chapter and are in the index.
- A summary is presented at the end of each chapter.
- A set of concept questions is provided in each chapter.
- Exercises are provided in each chapter. In most chapters, exercises are included for extending and enriching the example problem task for that chapter.
- Projects ideas are provided for later chapters, after students have experience with the Alice and NetBeans IDEs.
- An optional capstone project is presented in the Epilogue.

Note: Over time, exercises and projects become more free-form and open ended. For this reason, the number of exercises and projects included in the chapters are numerous at the beginning but decrease in the latter half of the book.

The following is a quick overview of the programming concepts introduced by chapter. See the Table of Contents for a list of chapter titles and a more detailed description of chapter content.

Table   Concepts by Chapter

Chapter	Concepts
1	Overview of problem solving approach, adapting a story for a program task, program task analysis, basic introduction to classes & objects
2	Design techniques (scene setup, storyboard, algorithm), saving a project world
3	An Alice tutorial project, *do in order*, code statements, running an Alice program
4	Decomposition and implementation, comments, testing, bugs & debugging
5	Designing, naming, and implementing a custom procedure, *do together*, code reuse by calling a procedure many times, nested code blocks, repetition with a *count* loop
6	Stepwise refinement, marker objects, inheritance (parent & child classes), exporting code
7 (Java)	A Java tutorial project, writing Java code statements, running a Java program
8 (Java)	Importing an Alice project into Java (NetBeans), code organization – Alice vs. Java, using code completion in NetBeans, using *doTogether* (equivalent to Alice's *do together*) and counted *for* loop code templates
9	Code reuse by importing saved code, using parameters with custom procedures, variables and data types, arithmetic expressions, using a computed value as a count loop control
10 (Java)	Data types in Java (wrapper classes and primitive values), using parameters with custom procedures, declaring and initializing variables, arithmetic expressions, using a computed value as a *for* loop control, testing Java code
11	Interactivity with event listeners, If/Else and conditional expressions, built-in functions, game components, tracking a game condition
12	Repetition with a *while* loop, random values, writing a custom function, a general game algorithm with player input and game end conditions
13	Built-in arrays, cutscene, game interactive controls, Boolean operators
14	Implementing a custom array, basic array operations, linear search of an array
15 (Java)	Declaring and initializing a custom array in Java, selection sort, array visualization
16	Game implementation with an implied loop (within event listeners), text string output for feedback, rounding errors and output formatting, collision events

The first three or four chapters of the book are meant to be covered in quick succession, ideally in the first week of class meetings/lab. Remaining chapters vary in length and may take two to five class meeting/lab days each. The pathway through chapters, topic selection, and sequence can be modified at the instructor's discretion to meet specific needs and goals. The following dependency chart may assist in plotting a path.

The chapters highlighted in yellow are Java chapters and those in white are Alice 3 chapters.

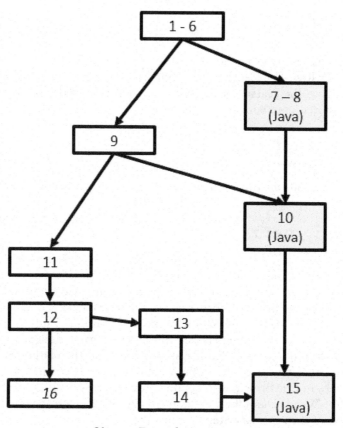

Chapter Dependency Diagram

A Few Suggested Custom Sequences

- For an "all Alice" path, the Java chapters may be omitted by using a sequence such as 1-2-3-4-5-6-9-11-12-14-15 and 16, as time allows.
- For younger students, a path that avoids both arrays and Java is possible by following the sequence 1-2-3-4-5-6-9-11-12.
- For a two-week introduction at the beginning of a traditional CS1 course in Java, a possible sequence is 1-2-3-4-7-8 and the use of the provided Starter worlds to transition to Java.

The Alice 3 Software

The Alice 3 software is free and is available for download at **www.alice.org**. We recommend downloading the latest version for your computer (PC, Mac, or Linux). The Alice website also provides instructions for installation and an FAQ, with links for providing bug reports. The Alice 3 system is 3D graphics and runs using Java's OpenGL graphics library. Please note that some tablets do not run Java and, therefore, will not run Alice.

Alice works well with most digital projection systems for classroom presentations, including high resolution.

Instructor Resources

The instructor resources are available to instructors who adopt this book by logging into Pearson's Instructor Resource Center at www.pearsonhighered.com/Dann. If you do not already have access to the Pearson IRC, contact your Pearson sales representative or visit www.pearsonhighered.com/educator/replocator.

Student Resources

Student support materials for this book are available at www.alice.org/Alice3ToJava.

Acknowledgments

Alice 3 lives in the heart and soul of the dedicated people in the Alice team. The primary engineers and architects of the Alice 3 software were Dennis Cosgrove and Dave Culyba. Dennis contributed to the original Alice and was the lead architect and software engineer for Alice during the early days of Alice development with Randy Pausch.

Particular thanks go to Sabrina Haskell, professional game designer at Schell Games. Sabrina contributed to the design thinking used throughout the textbook and specifically to the game design and structure in the chapters where game examples are used.

A huge thanks to Eric Brown, who assumed the Director position of the Alice Project upon retirement of Wanda Dann. Eric maintained team focus with the textbook authors to insure completion of the necessary graphics, manuscript, and software revisions.

We are most grateful to Electronic Arts for their contribution of the Sims 2 artwork to the Alice 3 Gallery. The 3D models from the Sims 2 artwork is the foundation of the gallery. An incredible collection of 3D models has been added to Alice 3 to create cultural diversity. These models were created by an Alice team of character artists and summer interns, under the leadership and direction of Laura Paoletti. The original design of the 3D models was developed in consultation with John DeRiggi, Senior Character Artist at Schell Games. We owe much gratitude to the contributions of Pei Hong, staff character artist, and summer interns including: Austin Booker, Matthew Kline, Yuan (Dorothy) Sheng, and Gregory Mirles.

Our deep gratitude goes to early testers and users of Alice 3 and this textbook for their helpful feedback, suggestions, and comments: Stephen Cooper at Stanford University, William Taylor, Anita Wright, and RoseMary Boiano at Camden County College, Eileen Wrigley and Don Smith at Allegheny Community College, Tebring Daly at Collin College, Cristy Charters at Florida International University, and Leslie Spivey at Edison Community College. Jeisson Hidalgo-Cespedes, in residence at Carnegie Mellon as a visiting scholar from the University of Costa Rica, reviewed the first five chapters and prepared many questions and examples used in these chapters.

Sincere thanks to Tracy Johnson of Pearson for supporting this effort. A huge thank you to the editorial staff at Pearson who helped bring this textbook to life, particularly Kristy Alaura, Carole Snyder, Rose Kernan, and Revathi Viswanathan. We gratefully acknowledge the reviewers of this textbook Tim Gallagher—Winter Springs High School, Teresa Elmore—Libertyville High School Saquib Razak—Carnegie Mellon University Qatar, Anita Wright Camden County College, Leslie Spivey—Edison Community College, Laine Agee—White Station High School, William Taylor—Camden County College.

This material is based upon work partially supported by the National Science Foundation under Grant Numbers 0894104 and 0903271. Any opinions, findings, conclusions, or recommendations expressed in this material are those of the authors and do not necessarily reflect the views of the National Science Foundation.

We are most grateful for funding to support the development of Alice 3 with a transition to Java and faculty development workshops. Over the last decade, this funding has been provided by: Oracle, the Sun Microsystems Foundation, Electronic Arts, Hyperion, Google, the Payne Family Foundation, the Hearst Foundation, and the National Science Foundation.

Wanda Dann
Don Slater
Laura Paoletti
Dave Culyba

Notes to the Student

This book is all about learning to write a computer program. Taking a programming course can be challenging and time consuming. In fact, there are times when it can be downright frustrating. As authors and educators, we want to stand up and say there is a better way to learn real computer programming. This book is designed to introduce programming in a creative context. We want to make it more engaging and less complicated, but still cover all the essential concepts expected in an introductory programming course curriculum.

In this book, you will step into the world of creating 3D animations. Each chapter presents the concepts of programming with hands-on examples that illustrate creating a short animation or game for *Lawrence Prenderghast's Haunted Circus*, an original story written by Laura Paoletti. In the example animation and gaming projects, you will be bringing the story to life by creating programs that illustrate portions of the and games presented in the chapters and exercises. Alice was originally developed as a tool for creating prototype animations for use with head-mounted devices in virtual reality research. Alice is similar to professional software tools used by animators in animation and gaming studios (Pixar, Disney, DreamWorks, Nickelodeon, Electronic Arts, and many others). In animation and gaming studios, a project team is often composed of artists, animators, designers, and programmers who work together to create short animated segments that evolve and are combined into the final product. Likewise, your instructor may ask you to work on a project with a team.

Depending on your goals, you may also transfer your work from Alice to Java. Java is a production-level programming language used by professionals to create real-world software applications. For example, Alice itself is written in Java. The Java chapters in this book provide examples that apply the concepts learned in Alice to write code in Java. This experience is most helpful to students who plan to continue developing their programming skills by taking an AP Computer Science or CS1 (or CS 101) college or university-level programming course.

Supplementary materials for this textbook are at **www.alice.org/Alice3ToJava**.

Lawrence Prenderghast's Haunted Circus

Prologue

. . . .

Early in the year 1910, Lawrence Prenderghast took his train and his circus to visit a tiny ghost town at the base of the Windy Mountain. His troupe grumbled about the fool's errand their leader was on. Everyone knew the town's mill had been abandoned since 1904, and no train stopped there anymore. No one believed Prenderghast would find what he was looking for. The troupe came round a bend and entered a picturesque valley forest. With the snow-covered mountain looming above them, they began to wonder, even when Prenderghast led them away from the tracks to explore.

As they walked through the woods, tiny clapboard houses winked in and out between the sturdy trunks of the fir trees. One cabin in the center of the valley appeared decrepit. But after another step, as the view of the cabin shifted between the next two trees, it filtered through time. The paint was bright and the wooden beams sturdy, as new as when first built. While walking, the dual images of the cabin combined together, flickering through the trees like a zoetrope.

Inside the cabin, a storyteller awaited anyone brave enough to face the wilderness. She is the reason Prenderghast came. "Leave a token, and stay forever, or leave and accept impermanence," the witch intoned with a smile. The witch unearthed from the moss an old shay locomotive, left behind by the logging company, and gifted it to Prenderghast. And he gave her something in return. He and his troupe spent the next few days restoring the engine to working order.

In the last week of February, it started to snow. It snowed for six days, over three feet of snow per day. And, worried they'd never make it over the mountain, the circus train left the ghost town and drove through the storm. The train was forced to stop before entering the tunnel through the Windy Mountain. Two other trains were also waiting to pass. There was no way of knowing if the tunnel was clear or if avalanches on the western side blocked the exit, and to end up stuck in the tunnel would mean either suffocation from running the engine for heat, or freezing to death slowly. Mountaineers claimed the spot where the trains waited was the safest on the slopes. No avalanche had happened here in recorded history.

None until the early hours of that morning, before sunrise, when the storm switched from snow to warm rain. A single lightning bolt struck the mountain peak and sent a wall of snow cascading towards the tracks. The snow swept all three trains off the ledge and

1

down the slope, carrying trees and debris along the way. The trains crumpled like toys, and only a few people survived the wreck. The disaster made newspaper headlines: the deadliest avalanche in history.

The storm let up in the days that followed, but when rescue operators finally dug their way to the wreckage, they found the remains of only two trains. The third, the Prenderghast Circus train, was nowhere to be seen.

March 1, 1910: Larry

The Ice Block

Larry sees the moment the snow strikes his beloved train, because he is outside oiling the lubrication points in the process of starting the engine. The snow hits the metal with a kind of "splat" noise, and then hits him. And from there his awareness stops. For the first time in his life, the circus ringmaster isn't hyperaware of his body. In fact, he can't feel it at all. He can't move, either. The stillness is peaceful and quiet and leaves a lot of room for thinking. One train of thought leads to another, and he finds himself sorting through memories and stories. If he's stuck here for the time being, he may as well organize his life.

It takes him a while. One hundred years to be exact. His thoughts are finally interrupted a century after the disaster by a baby yeti hunting in the Arctic mountains on her snowboard.

The yeti's stomach growls almost as loudly as the wind howling through the glaciers. This is a bad winter, and the food stores at home are empty. When she complains about her rumbling tummy, her mother hands her a salvaged snowboard and sends her off to find whatever can be scrounged up among the ice floes.

So far, no luck.

Until she spots a single pale yellow bone sticking out of a snow cliff. Sliding her snowboard closer to the wall of snow, she scrapes off the top layer to reveal a frozen block of ice. Attached to the end of the bone is a skeletal hand. A human hand. The hand wiggles ever so slightly and then waves.

An entire body may be hidden underneath the slowly eroding ice, if there was only some way of getting to it. But she is so hungry that without even thinking she clomps her mouth over the arm bone and starts gnawing with her large fangs.

A blood-curdling scream issues from within the ice. Cracks begin to form, spreading like spider webs from the point where bone meets ice. The arm starts wriggling and twisting. She hangs on by her teeth for dear life. The dull roar of a yell grows louder and louder until finally the ice shatters completely. An entire skeleton stumbles out of the cavity. The screaming abruptly stops. The skeleton stands frozen in place.

The skeleton cautiously lifts his arm to locate the source of the pain and sees what is biting him. Screaming again, the skeleton stumbles backwards, flailing his arms. With a loud snap, the arm the yeti is attached to breaks off. She's still clinging to it when the arm soars through the air and lands in a snow drift. She suddenly finds herself buried in snow with nothing but her feet wriggling in the cold air. Bending her tiny legs and kicking up, she jumps to her feet and shakes the wet snowflakes off her fur like a dog. Picking the arm out of the snow, she turns to look at the skeleton.

The skeleton's entire body recoils; he falls back gracefully and lands on his tail bone. He stares at her in horror. She stares back, casually walking closer and chewing on his arm bone like it was a turkey leg.

The skeleton's gaze transfers to the bone, makes the connection, and lifts the stump of his left arm. He lifts his right arm too, stretching the rattling collection of bones and flexing his working hand in front of his face. This is exactly what the skeleton expects to see, so this time he manages not to cry out. Instead the skeleton swallows. Or, at least, he makes the muscle movements his brain remembers swallowing requires. When he looks down at his chest nothing actually happens. No lungs, no throat, no stomach.

"I think I'm dead," he concludes, looking at the ice surrounding him, "I was frozen. In snow . . . " he trails off, "I'm dead, but I'm still alive. As a skeleton," he continues, "And talking to myself. As usual."

He looks back at the creature. She's still chomping on his arm. "What are you?" he wonders aloud.

The yeti simply stares, wide eyed and blinking. She is still so hungry she's unwilling to stop chewing even for a second of conversation.

"You're like . . . an itty bitty yeti," the skeleton observes, noting the fact that she barely comes up to his waist and is covered in a fluffy pale blue fur.

"Am not," she says.

The skeleton screams and flounders backward in the snow.

"Not itty bitty," the baby yeti explains, "I'll grow. I'm just a late bloomer is all."

"A talking baby yeti," the skeleton repeats in disbelief, "you're impossible. A creature of myth."

"My name is Tashi. And you're a talking skeleton."

The skeleton blinks, shuts his mouth, and nods, "In that case, may I have my arm back?"

"No."

"No?!"

"I'm hungry," Tashi shrugs.

"But I'm a living, talking skeleton. Named Larry," he scrambles to his feet, "and that's my arm."

"And I eat living, talking things for lunch every day," Tashi explains casually.

"How barbaric," Larry looks horrified.

"Are you a vegetarian?"

"What?"

"Do you eat meat?"

"Yes," Larry says slowly, confused, "Well, used to . . ."

Tashi pulls the arm out of her mouth and shrugs again as if to say "Well then."

Larry glares, "Are all itty bitty yeti this intelligent?"

"No, I'm weird. I like human things. The other kids make fun of me." Tashi tilts her head innocently, "Are you going to make fun of me?"

"No," says Larry darkly, "I strongly suspect if I make fun of you, you'll be chewing on my dislocated head next."

Tashi stops chewing to laugh, "I like you. You're funny," and tosses the arm back to Larry.

"Thank you," Larry replies. He stands and tries to regain his dignity. He holds the arm in his functional hand and waves the stub of the other, "I wonder how I put myself back together."

Tashi shrugs and looks bored.

Larry slowly brings the two bones together and connects them. For a second he worries nothing will happen. He nearly decides to give up and start searching for medicinal tape when a blue light begins to glow around the joint. The light flares for a half-second and then fades to nothing. He releases his hand around the bone and moves the arm gently to discover it successfully reconnected.

"That's a relief!" Larry stands tall, feeling elegant once more. Despite his lack of a proper suit and ". . . where is my hat?" He dives for the ice crevice, trying to see inside.

"You mean this?" Tashi pulls a hat from behind her back and pops it on her head. She smiles beguilingly up at the skeleton.

"Where did you get that?" Larry asks.

"From the train," Tashi's smile widens.

"The . . . the train?" Larry asks, "Where is the train?"

"In the cave."

"And where is the cave?"

"I dunno."

"But you said . . ."

"Why should I tell you?"

"Because it's my train!"

"But I found it!"

"You itty bitty . . . ingrate! Give me my hat!" Larry lunges, but Tashi expertly dodges and the skeleton eats snow instead. With a gleeful laugh the baby yeti runs off. Larry scrambles to his feet and chases after her, leaping over the snow in great strides.

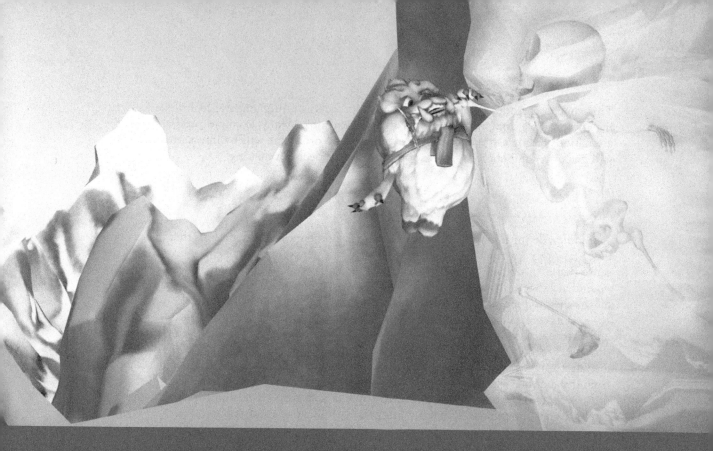

][

Introduction

Concept Objectives

- Define program and programming
- A problem-solving approach
- Adapting a story narrative to a task statement
- Analyzing a task statement
- Background details
- Objects and actions

This chapter introduces a problem-solving approach as a fundamental technique for writing the example computer programs in this textbook. Many example programs will be animations telling a story or playing a game. Some programs will be interactive and some will perform computations for random actions and decision making.

1.1 Program and Programming

A common definition of a computer **program** is a sequence of instructions that tells a computer how to perform a specific **task**. We refer to a programming task as a **problem** in the sense that a "problem" is "a creative and challenging task." The challenge is that the computer hardware only performs the actions/instructions described in the program. This means the program instructions must be effective.

At its core, **computer programming** designs and implements creative solutions to address human needs. For example, computers facilitate communication through complex systems such as Facebook™ or Twitter™. Computer-controlled robots are used in everything from manufacturing to surgery. Art galleries hold interactive installations that gather information from the audience with cameras or sensors, process the data, and give live feedback. Programming provides the software tools used to animate and create three-dimensional models for games. And a programmer ultimately brings those animations and games to life.

1.2 A Problem-Solving Approach

In computer programming, problem solving begins with the goal of writing code to perform a task and often involves repeated steps. Newly written code requires frequent testing, and it is possible that revisions will be needed along the way. Therefore, the problem-solving approach used in this book is represented in a cyclic model. The cycle includes four major steps: analyze and understand the task, design a plan, implement the design, and test. Figure 1.1 is a

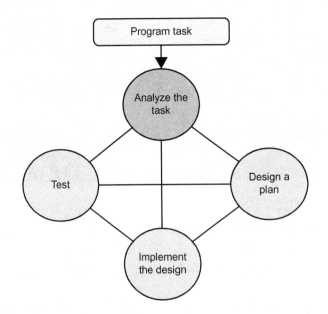

Figure 1.1   *A problem-solving approach*

diagram that represents the steps in this problem-solving process. There is a clockwise progression from analyzing and understanding, to design, to implement, and then test. However, lines also connect each step to each of the other steps because it is likely that the programmer will repeat many of the steps again and again. In this way, the diagram represents a cyclic process.

1.3 A First Program Task

Episode 1 of Lawrence Prenderghast's Haunted Circus story introduces two leading characters, Tashi and Larry. Tashi is a 30 year-old yeti. She is still a "baby" in the Yeti's extraordinary lifespan, but is rapidly growing up. Tashi yearns for independence and adventure in the world beyond her cave. In this episode, Tashi discovers Larry, a human skeleton buried in snow and ice. Larry was the ringmaster of a circus sideshow that once traveled up and down the coastal towns and rugged mountains of the Pacific Northwest. Larry's circus train and all the troupe members were caught in an avalanche a hundred years ago. Our first program task is to create an animation for an excerpt of the first episode of the story.

In the entertainment industry's production of animated films, the narrative of a story is typically adapted to the capabilities and needs of animation software and film media. Not every detail from the original writing will be included and some parts will be modified in a visual telling of the story. Below is a summary of the first excerpt of the *Haunted Circus* to be used as a program example. In this adaptation, you will notice that many details have been omitted and some have been modified.

> When the avalanche hits the train, Larry becomes encased in ice. He is still alive, but unable to move, leaving him only to his thoughts. A hundred years pass, and a baby yeti discovers an unusual ice block while out hunting. Tashi, the yeti, grows weary of the same old barren snowfields around her cave home and daydreams about finding better food and adventure elsewhere. To her surprise, as she gets closer Tashi sees a skeletal hand sticking out of a crack in the ice. The hand wiggles, and she realizes something could be alive inside. Tashi hops on her snowboard, pushes off, and crashes into the ice block. The block splits neatly in two and reveals a full human skeleton. Larry screams in shock at discovering he's become a skeleton, but also in fear of Tashi. Until he sees she has his top hat. He figures she must have stolen his hat from his train, so he chases after the thieving yeti, hoping to find the remains of his circus troupe.

Adaptation of a written story for an animation requires a focus on the essential aspects of plot and character development. One way to focus is to create a summary breakdown of the plot that can be programmed as actions (instructions). Consider the limitations of complexity and make any changes to the plot that might make it easier to program. For example, in the original story Tashi bites the skeleton's hand. But, in our summary, Tashi runs her snowboard into the block of ice. This is to shorten and simplify the actions for a first program example. Our summary breakdown is as follows:

> Tashi is out hunting for food.
>
> She sees a strange block of ice covered in snow with a skeleton hand hanging out of a crack in the ice.
>
> The skeleton hand wiggles, and whatever is inside is clearly not as dead as it appears.
>
> She runs into the block of ice with her snowboard.
>
> The fissure splits further until the block falls apart to reveal the full skeleton.

1.4 Analyze the Task

The first step is to analyze and understand the program task. In tasks where a graphics display is a major concern, the analysis includes identification of (1) background details and (2) objects and actions (Figure 1.2).

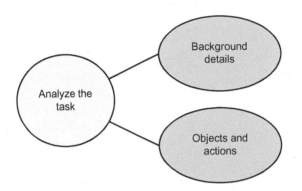

Figure 1.2   *Two techniques used in analyzing and understanding the program task*

In the case of story adaptations, an excerpt often includes a description of the setting, which is based on background information. Background information includes environment descriptions and the motivations behind a character's actions. Background information is useful for setting up the scene for an animation or gaming task. The objects and actions are needed for outlining the steps to be performed in carrying out the task. The challenge is to recognize which part of the problem statement is background information and which part is a description of the objects and actions to be performed.

To recognize background information, ask if this describes the setting in terms of:

- the scene (e.g., grassy, mountains, trees, chairs, sofa, or television)?
- the appearance of an object (e.g., cute, clever, young, old, white, or green)?
- the personality of an object (e.g., happy, joyful, sad, sarcastic, or shy)?
- an attitude and motivation (e.g., positive, negative, or friendly)?
- in the case of a game, how the game is played?

The background information in this excerpt from Episode 1 describes an arctic mountain scene with a snow cliff, glaciers, snow, and ice. Tashi's motivation is that she is hungry. The skeleton's motivation is to attract Tashi's attention.

To recognize a task description, ask if this describes the plot directly in the form of:

- objects and actions (e.g., penguin skates)?
- information about how an action is performed (e.g., penguin skates slowly)?

In the example shown below, the objects (nouns) are highlighted in blue and the actions (verbs) in red. Note that not all nouns and verbs are highlighted. We have highlighted only those that are essential to creating the animation.

Tashi is out **hunting** for food.

She **sees** a strange **block of ice** covered in snow with a **skeleton hand** hanging out of a crack in the ice.

The **skeleton hand wiggles**, and whatever is inside is clearly not as dead as it appears.

She **runs** into the block of ice with her snowboard.

The **fissure splits** further until the ice **block falls apart** to reveal the skeleton.

Summary

This chapter introduces a problem-solving approach to creative programming. Many different kinds of programming tasks are possible. In this book, the program tasks involve creating animations and games to bring to life successive episodes of the *Lawrence Prenderghast's Haunted Circus* story. The first example is a program task from Episode 1. The narrative of Episode 1 is first adapted to create a task statement. Then, the task is *analyzed* to identify (1) the background information (which will be used for setting up the scene in a graphics display) and (2) the objects and actions the objects will perform to complete the task.

Terms

computer programming	problem	task
object	program	

Concept Questions

1. Describe the four steps of the problem-solving approach used in creating a computer program (as used in this textbook).

2. Briefly describe the difference between background and object-action information in a task statement for an animation.

3. Each of the following is a typical program exercise found in Alice programming textbooks. Describe the (a) background information and (b) objects and actions (if any).

   (a) A penguin has a soccer ball and is practicing kicking the ball. The target is an open water hole in the ice. Create an animation where the penguin kicks the ball toward the water. If the ball goes into the water, have the penguin celebrate this success.

   (b) Open the Moon star world, which contains outpost buildings, a satellite, and a space ship. Create an animation where the space ship hovers and then circles the outpost. Then, the ship lands near the outpost stage. To land, the space ship must move forward and down, again and again, until it is less than three feet above the ground surface.

4. Identify a story or book that you have read and a movie version of the story. Describe at least two ways the movie version was different from the book. Why do you think the movie version was different?

2
Design

Concept Objectives

- Design thinking
- Set design
- Develop an algorithm

- Translating set design to an Alice scene
- Saving a project
- Creating a sense of place

2.1 Design Thinking

Design thinking is an integral part of successful programming. The amount of time taken to *design a plan* (Figure 2.1) reduces implementation time and helps keep a production schedule on track.

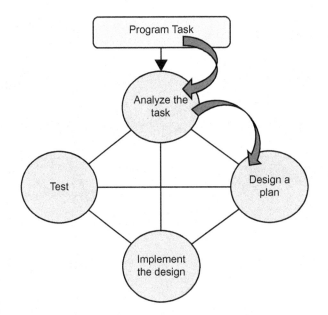

Figure 2.1   *Next step: Design a plan*

VIDEO ALERT!

Before reading this chapter, we highly recommend viewing:

- Video: Adding Objects to an Alice 3 Project

This video is available at: **http://www.alice.org/3.1/materials_videos.php**

To design a plan for animating our story, we combine set design with algorithms (Figure 2.2). Ultimately, the set design will be translated into the 3D scene of an Alice world and the algorithm will be translated into program code Planning the story in a visual shorthand helps determine the sequence of actions, the progression of motivation, and how the animation will appear on screen to the viewer. An **algorithm** consists of a step-by-step list of actions that provides a description of how to perform the task. A design plan can be broad and generalized to span an entire task, or it can be a segment of a larger whole. For example, the adaptation of Episode 1 is only one segment of the entire story in this textbook.

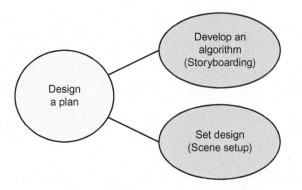

Figure 2.2 • *Design in Alice programming*

2.2 Set Design

....

Adapting text to animation requires figuring out visual aspects writing cannot describe. To do this easily and allow for experimentation without significant coding changes, we start with a storyboard. In animation, a sequence of frames representing the screen is called a **storyboard**, which depicts the action, expressions, and camera changes over time. Each frame is sketched by hand, and sometimes includes a caption describing the intention of the frame. The details of the sketches are minimal, with only enough to convey key story bits. These include a character's emotions or reactions, prop placement, movement of objects, and the layout of the scene. The goal is to tell the entire story in the simplest visuals possible. A basic storyboard consists of:

- frames, where each frame represents a significant action in a story
- the sequence of individual frames connecting the actions together to form the plot

To create a storyboard, start with a step-by-step list of object-action pairs, determined in the task analysis (described earlier in Chapter 1). Some steps may take more frames than others, but the goal is to keep the total sequence as small as possible. The following list is for the adaptation of Episode 1:

- **Tashi** is out **hunting** for food.
- **she sees** a strange **block of ice** covered in snow with a **skeleton hand** hanging out of a crack in the ice.
- the **skeleton hand wiggles**, and whatever is inside is clearly not as dead as it appears.
- **she runs into the block of ice** with her **snowboard**.
- the **fissure splits** further until the **ice block falls apart** to reveal the skeleton.

Take a look at the basic storyboard in (Figure 2.3). The storyboard focuses on the character's body movement, the placement of the characters on screen, and the main action. In this case, we positioned the yeti and skeleton first and then built the world around them. A sequence of actions is planned, ending with the snowboard hitting the ice block and the ice block falling apart.

Figure 2.3 *Basic character placement and action storyboard*

NOTE: The storyboards in this textbook were sketched by an artist. To create your own storyboards, you may use sketches, Alice screen shots, or create storyboards with the art and drawing tools in a word processor or presentation slides.

The level of detail in a storyboard is directly proportional to the amount of information being shown. Storyboards should be done quickly, include everything that needs to be seen, and tell the story. When beginning a complex painting, an artist will do thumbnail sketches to test out different compositions. These sketches take minutes compared to the hours that the final painting will take, but the artist uses these sketches to iterate quickly until they decide on the final painting composition. Without the sketches, they may get halfway through the final painting only to realize they aren't happy with its composition.

Similarly, we can do a series of short storyboards to iterate on details such as which direction a character moves on screen or the comedic timing of a visual gag. Storyboards save a lot of time before spending hours animating and programming the final segment.

Each frame of a storyboard illustrates what will be seen through the lens of the camera at that step in the animation. When the frame shows a different view of the scene, this implies the camera has been moved to zoom in, zoom out, or pan some portion of the scene. Adding in more dynamic camera angles changes the mood or feel of the scene and helps to tell the story or play a game.

The basic storyboard illustrated earlier decides the position of the characters and sequence of actions. In the storyboard, the background can be filled in behind the characters to complete the composition of the scene (Figure 2.4). In this example, the scene features a snow-covered mountain with a cave. The icicles hanging off the cave mouth frame the curve of a train frozen in ice. The frozen train provides both a backdrop to the action and a hint at the next segment.

Figure 2.4   *Add background scene details in the storyboard.*

The scene provides context and setting, similar to a theater stage or a movie backdrop. **Set design** uses background information to envision the environment, props, and atmosphere needed to tell the story. A quality set will give the story a sense of place and history. Each prop needs a reason for being included, whether to describe location or show aspects of a character's personality.

2.3 Algorithm Development

A storyboard visualization allows us to think about steps that can be written as statements that the computer can perform to animate the story. The list of steps is an algorithm, where each step in the algorithm can be translated into one or more code **statements** (or **instructions**) the computer can perform (Figure 2.5). The *Do in order* at the beginning of the algorithm indicates the instructions are to be performed (or **executed**) in sequence. The ordering of steps is based on the sequence in the storyboard.

Do in order
Tashi snowboards into the scene
Skeleton's hand wiggles
Tashi snowboards forward
Snowboard crashes into the ice Block
iceBlock splits apart

Figure 2.5   *Algorithm*

As mentioned earlier, ultimately the set design will be translated into the 3D scene of an Alice world and the algorithm will be translated into program code. In the remainder of this chapter, we will explore translating the set design shown above into an Alice scene. The next chapter will illustrate translating the algorithm into program code.

2.4 Translate the Set Design into an Alice Scene

Begin by starting Alice. A Select Project dialog box is automatically displayed. Follow these steps to create a snow-covered scene (Figure 2.6):

(1) Select the Blank Slates tab.
(2) Select the snow-covered scene button.
(3) Click OK.

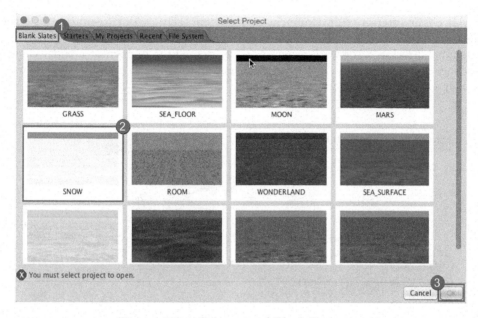

Figure 2.6 · *Snow-covered Blank Slate scene*

When Alice opens with the selected snow template, it automatically opens in the Code editor (Figure 2.7). The Code editor has four panels: Camera view, Methods panel, Editor, and Controls panel.

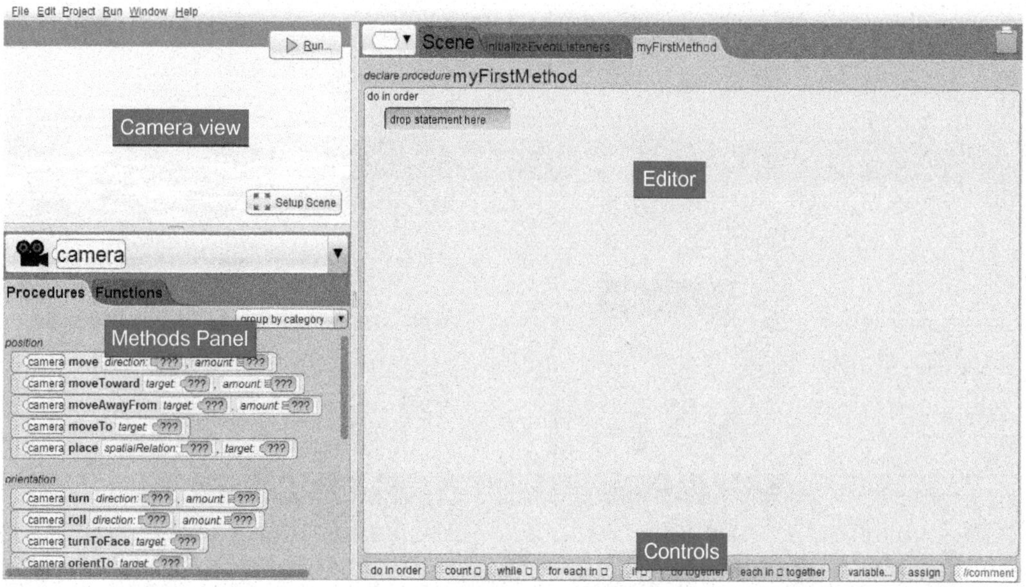

Figure 2.7 · *The Code editor*

Alice is an interactive development environment (**IDE**) with two editors: a Code editor and a Scene editor. An IDE is a graphic, interactive environment designed to help the programmer develop a software program. Only one editor is open at a time. Click the Setup Scene button (Figure 2.8) to open the Scene editor. (The Code editor will be used in later chapters for writing program code.)

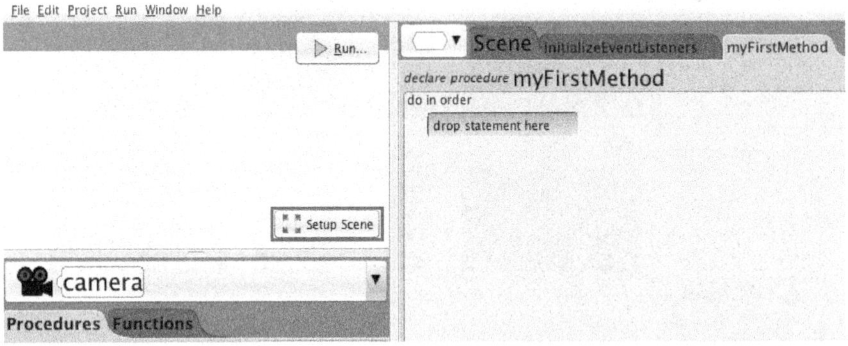

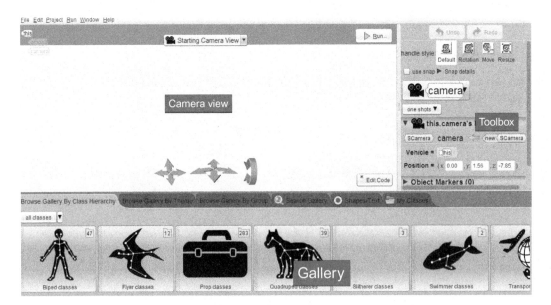

Figure 2.8   *Click the Setup Scene button.*

The Scene editor (Figure 2.9) has three panels: Camera view, Toolbox, and Gallery. The Camera view panel is where a scene is constructed. The Gallery provides **3D models** for adding objects to the scene. The Toolbox is used for positioning and orienting objects in the scene and for creating **markers**. A marker is like a piece of tape on the set of a stage for filming or theater production. The marker remembers the "spot" where the camera or another object will be positioned during the animation.

Figure 2.9   *The Scene editor*

In the upper left of the scene in the Camera view panel is an Object tree. The Object tree (Figure 2.10) contains a list of tiles. The list of tiles begins with *this* (this scene). *This* scene contains a *ground* surface tile and a *camera* tile. The highlighted tile (*camera*) corresponds to the selected object in the Toolbox (to the right of the scene).

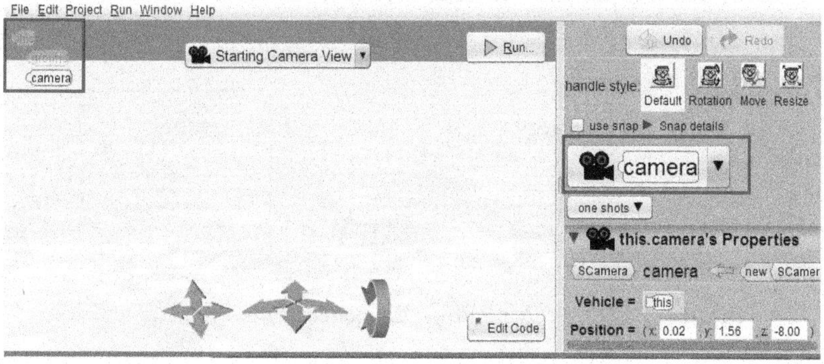

Figure 2.10 • *The selected object is highlighted in the Object tree.*

2.4.1 Add an object to the scene

Other objects may be added to the scene using the 3D model classes from the Gallery, located at the bottom of the Scene editor (Figure 2.11). A **class** is a computer file containing instructions that tell Alice how to construct and display a specific type of **object**. An object is an entity that has an identity and a state (defined by one or more properties). A **property** is an item of information or an attribute that is associated with an object. For example, most objects in Alice have name, color, and location properties). A class also defines actions (behaviors) that this type of object knows how to perform.

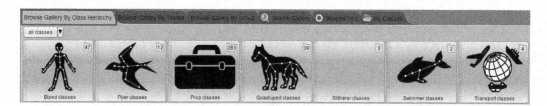

Figure 2.11 • *The Gallery in the Scene editor*

The Gallery has six tabs in which the classes are organized to make it easier to locate a specific type of object. The first tab on the left, the Class Hierarchy tab, is open by **default**. In computer programming, the term default is used to describe a built-in, preselected value. The Class Hierarchy tab will be used in this chapter. Other Gallery tabs will be illustrated, as needed, in later chapters.

Classes in the Class Hierarchy tab are further organized into categories, based on mode of mobility. Bipeds move around with two legs, Flyers with wings, Quadrupeds with four legs, Swimmers with fins, and Transports with wheels on the ground or sails or motors in water or air. The Props category contains classes of objects that, typically, do not move around from one place to another unless pushed or carried by some external force.

In this example, let's add a snow-covered, icy mountain to the scene. A mountain is a Prop, so click the Prop category button. Scroll to the right to locate the IceMountain (Figure 2.12). The label for each class begins with the word *new* and the name of the class is capitalized. The word *new* is a **keyword** that may be used to tell Alice to construct a new object of this type. A keyword is a reserved word in a programming language with a predefined meaning.

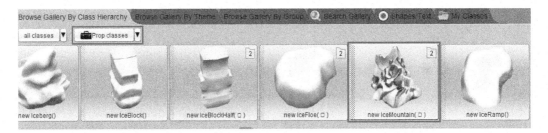

Figure 2.12   *IceMountain 3D model in the Prop classes*

Click on the IceMountain button. When the button is clicked, Alice displays a selection of two IceMountain model variations default and flipped (Figure 2.13).

Figure 2.13   *Two variations of the IceMountain model*

Click once on the IceMountain (DEFAULT) button. An Add Scene Property dialog box is displayed (Figure 2.14). Alice automatically enters the name, *iceMountain*, in the name textbox. This is the default name for the object. The default name is the same as the name of the class except that it begins with a lowercase letter. You may accept this name or enter a different name. Near the top of the dialog box is a preview **declaration**. In this example, the declaration is a **code**

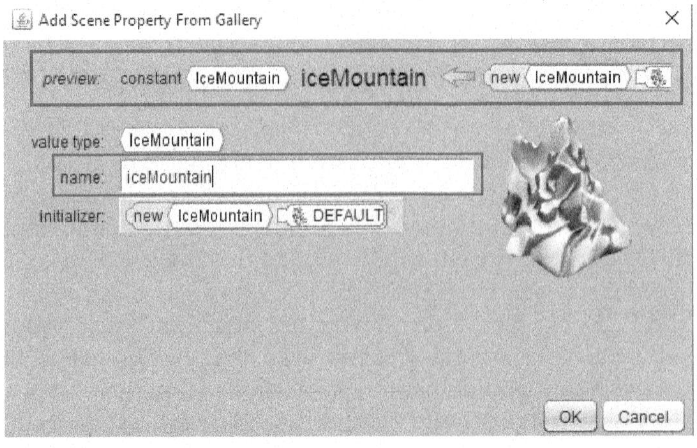

Figure 2.14   *Add an iceMountain object to the scene.*

statement (an instruction) that uses the keyword *new* to tell Alice to create an object and add it to the scene. Other kinds of declarations will be illustrated, as needed, in later chapters.

Click the OK button and Alice will add a mountain object to the scene in a **default location**, usually at the center of the ground surface. Figure 2.15 is a screen capture of the iceMountain object that is now in the scene. Notice a tile for the iceMountain object has been added to the Object tree in the upper left of the Scene editor. In essence, this means the iceMountain now "belongs to" or "is a **property of**" this scene.

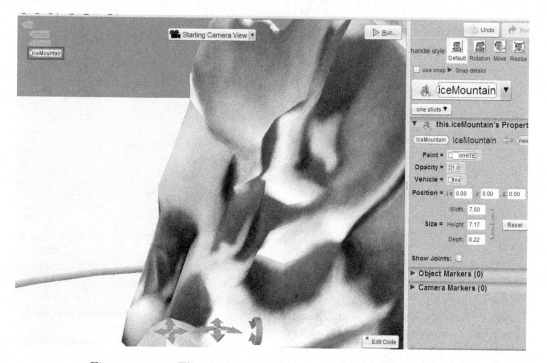

Figure 2.15 *The iceMountain object has been added to the scene.*

VIDEO ALERT!

Before reading the next section, we highly recommend viewing:

- Video: One-Shot Procedures in Alice 3
- Video: One-Shot Procedures and Sub-Parts in Alice 3

Videos are available at: **http://www.alice.org/Alice3ToJava**

2.4.2 Position an object using the cursor and one-shots

Positioning objects is an important part of translating a set design into an Alice scene. Because the iceMountain object is very large, its default position in the scene is very close to the camera. In fact, the mountain is so close to the camera that only a small portion of the mountain can be seen. For example, we cannot see that the mountain has a cave with icicles hanging over the cave entrance. Two techniques may be used to position an object: (1) use the cursor to drag and rotate the object, or (2) use **one-shots** (a menu of positioning actions in the Toolbox).

First, try using the cursor to drag the mountain away from the camera, toward the back of the scene. As the cursor drags the mountain, you will see a 3D set of axes with its origin marking the center point of the mountain (Figure 2.16).

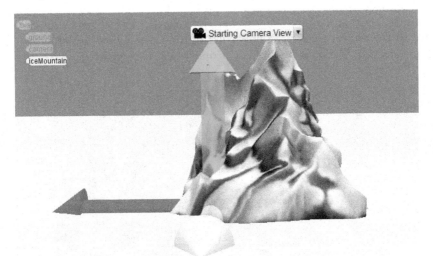

Figure 2.16   *3D axes mark the center point of an object as it is dragged around the scene.*

When you release the cursor, a ring handle is displayed surrounding the mountain (Figure 2.17). The center of the ring is at the center point of the mountain. We want the cave in the mountain to face the front of the scene (that is, face the camera). To change the direction the iceMountain is facing, use the cursor to select and drag the ring handle to turn it until the cave is visible to the camera.

Figure 2.17   *Select and drag the ring handle to turn the mountain.*

When the cursor selects the ring, the ring is activated. Wait until the ring is high-lighted before using the cursor to turn the object. On some computer systems, the cursor may not actively select the mountain or the ring handle. If this happens on your computer, hold down the CTRL key on Windows or Option on Mac and then use the cursor to directly move and turn the mountain until the cave is visible (Figure 2.18).

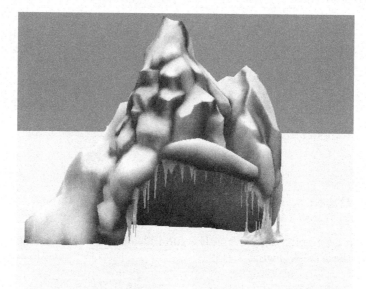

Figure 2.18   *The iceMountain's cave is facing the camera.*

One-shots may be used for more precise positioning. Select the camera in the Toolbox panel on the far right of the Scene editor (Figure 2.19). Then click the one-shots button in the Toolbox. The one-shots menu will be displayed immediately below the Object selector.

Figure 2.19   *Select the camera and then click the one-shots menu button.*

In the one-shots menu, select procedures (Figure 2.20). Cascading menus display a list of actions that can be performed on/by an object. In this example, we selected *move*, FORWARD (a direction), and 2.0 (an amount). When the menu selections are completed, the camera should immediately move forward 2.0 meters. Note that the amount you move the camera forward in your scene may be larger or smaller, depending on how close you wish to move the camera to view the cave.

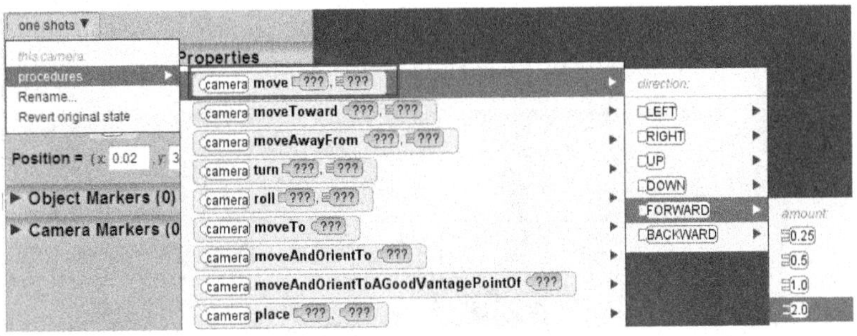

Figure 2.20   *Cascading menus to select a one-shot action*

2.5 Saving a Project

As you work on developing a project, it is a good idea to periodically save it. To save your project, follow these steps (Figure 2.21):

(1) Use Alice's File menu and select **Save As**. Alice will display a navigation dialog box with the MyProjects folder as the default location for saving your project. If you wish to save the project in a different location (desktop, file folder, server account, or thumb drive), use the Save As dialog box to navigate to the desired location.

(2) Enter a name for the project in the File name textbox—for example, **FirstWorld**. Do not include special characters (for example, %, $, #) or blank spaces in the name.

(3) Click the **Save** button. When saved, the project file will automatically have a ".a3p" file name extension for "Alice 3 project." Do not enter the extension; Alice will automatically add it.

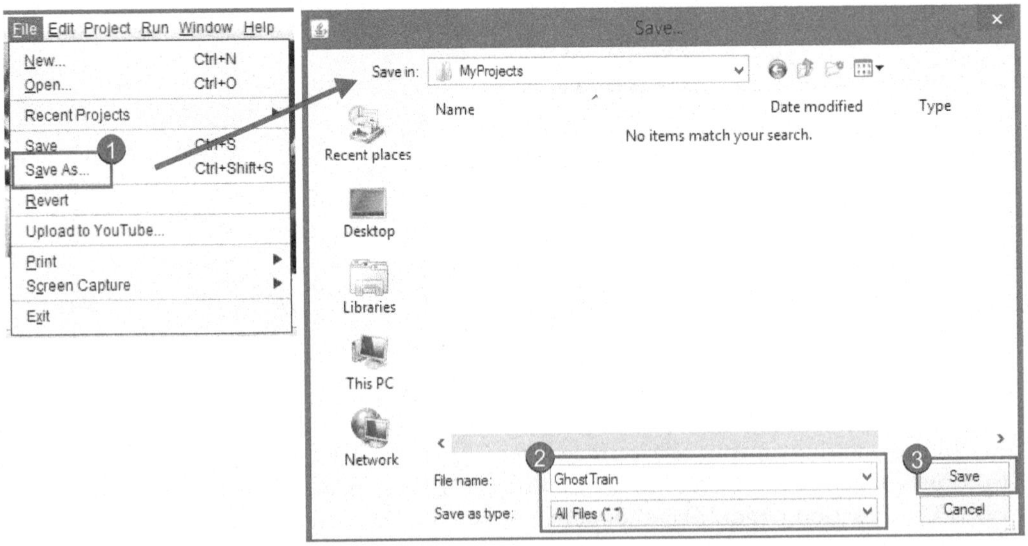

Figure 2.21   *Saving a project*

Source: © Microsoft Corporation.

We recommend saving your project every 20 to 30 minutes as you work. We also recommend successive saves with version numbers—for example, FirstWorld-V1.a3p, First-World-V2.a3p, FirstWorld-V3.a3p, etc. Saving successive versions is a standard operations protocol in professional workplaces. The idea is to avoid losing your work. If the latest version fails somewhere in the development process, you can always go back to the previous version and resume work without great loss of time.

2.6 Creating a Sense of Place

Tashi is supposed to be snowboarding in an arctic mountain range, but the basic background scene created above only has a single mountain on a flat plane. The large expanse of blue sky behind the mountain and the flat horizon line behind it fails to create a sense of place. To fill in the background environment, rotate, resize, and connect additional iceMountain objects. Consider the many rotation options for iceMountain objects (Figure 2.22). The first mountain is the one used for the cave. The next three are all various views of each side. The flipped version of the mountain may be used for further visual variety (Figure 2.23).

Figure 2.22   *Rotated mountain peak showing the different sides*

Figure 2.23   *The flipped mountain peak offers further visual variety.*

To create a mountain range, select one mountain and resize it larger than the rest. Push a smaller mountain into the bigger one to create a ridge that appears seamless (Figure 2.24).

Figure 2.24 *A mountain ridge created by resizing and pushing objects into each other*

The handle style buttons (top right) are used for rotating, resizing, and moving, Figure 2.25. The goal is to create a non-uniform mountain range that provides an interesting background and hides the harsh horizon line (Figure 2.26).

Figure 2.25 *Handle style buttons select the cursor's action*

Figure 2.26 • *Resulting mountain ridge*

Summary

To design a plan for the program that animates our story, we combine set design with an algorithm. Set design uses background information to envision the environment, props, and atmosphere needed to tell the story. A storyboard is a design technique used to aid in designing the sequence of actions, character expression, and camera angles in a visual shorthand. An algorithm consists of a step-by-step list of actions that provides a description of how to perform the task. Ultimately the set design is translated into the 3D scene of an Alice world and then the algorithm is translated into code statements (instructions the computer can perform). This chapter illustrated translating the set design into an Alice world, where objects are added to the scene and positioned in the scene. The next chapter will illustrate translating the algorithm into code.

Terms

3D model	executed	property
algorithm	instructions	resource (in a 3D model)
class	IDE	set design
code statement	keyword	statement
declaration	marker	storyboard
default	object	
default location	one-shot	

Concept Questions

1. (a) What is the purpose of set design? (b) What is the purpose of an algorithm?
2. Suppose you are to build a scene where a dead fish is supposed to be floating near the sea surface. Give two different one-shot actions that could be used to have the fish float belly up.

3. What is the purpose of saving your project every 20 to 30 minutes?

4. What is the purpose of saving your project using successive version names?

5. Are culinary recipes algorithms? Explain your answer.

6. Write an algorithm for changing the batteries in a flashlight. Is the order of the steps important? Why?

Exercises

The exercises in this chapter provide practice in design and scene setup in Alice 3. The Search tab in the Alice Gallery may be helpful. **Reminder:** Remember to save your work when creating a scene and/or writing code.

1. Deep underwater a shipwreck hides a treasure chest full of pirate gold. The gold has lain on the ocean floor for over a century, and finally a modern-day diving crew has discovered the location of the sunken ship and is planning an expedition. Using the storyboard depicting what they might find at the site, create your own underwater scene in Alice. Use the SEA_FLOOR template from the Blank Slates tab of the Project dialog box and then add objects using the Scene editor.

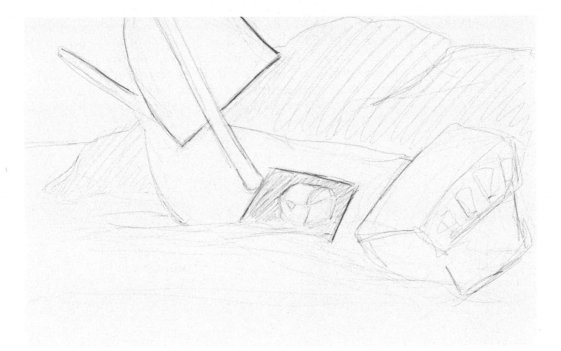

2. This storyboard is for a story where a lone seagull traveled too far away from shore and got lost. Create an algorithm for this basic storyboard and then set up the scene in Alice. Begin with the Ocean Template Starter world and add the rocks, seagull, and palm tree. When writing the algorithm, keep in mind the sub-actions that are not necessarily described in the captions, for example, camera movement and the appearance or disappearance of objects. When setting up the scene, how would you create a reflection of a seagull object in the water?

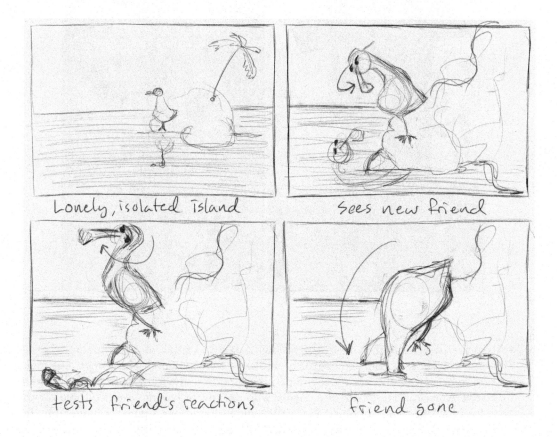

Lonely, isolated island   Sees new friend

tests friend's reactions   friend gone

3. Some classes in the Alice Gallery are provided in construction sets. One of the construction sets is for creating a castle. Start a new world in Alice, and add a camera marker for the original position of the camera in the scene. Then, use the classes in the Castle Tower construction set to create a castle tower. The middle and top components should be positioned on top of the base vertically, as shown here. Try using one-shots to move the camera around so you can confirm the pieces of the tower are in stable positions. (You can use the Undo button in the Toolbox to return the camera to its original position.)

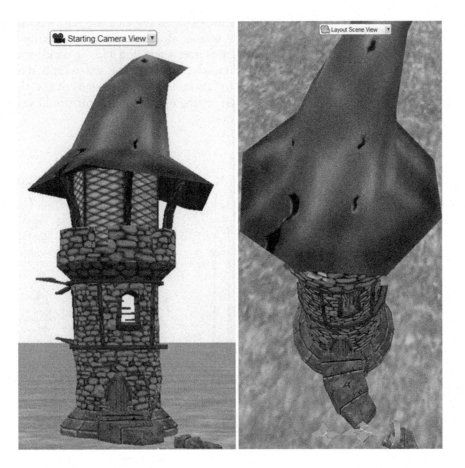

4. Use the object-action pairs in the following tale to create, at a minimum, a seven-frame storyboard. Some steps can be broken down into multiple frames, but make sure to briefly explain your reasoning in the captions. The folklore of a Southwestern Native American tribe tells of a coyote who dreamt of having beautiful blue fur the color of a lake. He watched a bird bathe in the lake four times every morning for four days, and on the fifth morning the bird emerged from the lake with blue feathers. The coyote begged the bluebird to teach him the secret. The bird told him to do exactly as she did and sing, "There's a blue water. It lies there. I went in. I am all blue," each morning while in the lake. The coyote follows the instructions and earns his vibrant blue coat. But he was so proud of his new colors that he was too busy admiring himself to watch where he was walking. He tripped and rolled into the ground, covering himself with dust, which is why coyotes are the color of dirt.

5. Complete a storyboard and algorithm, and set up a scene for the following short tale: Roc, a little polar bear, grew up in a land devoid of mountains. Her father wouldn't let her stray far from the sea ice. And although Roc could see the distant jagged shapes and she knew mountains must exist somewhere, she couldn't reach them. When she found a sled half-buried in snow, she discovered the wooden runners slid very well across ice. But she also discovered that running and jumping on the sled only gave her enough momentum to last a few minutes. She dreamed of climbing the mountains and sledding down. One day a traveling yak, very far from his home, walked across Roc's path with a small, strange creature on his back. The friendly creature introduced herself and explained they'd been looking for the sled *everywhere*. Roc offered to give it back, but on one condition: the yak must pull the sled across the ice floes so Roc could experience the speed of sledding downhill. Everyone was in agreement with this, and for a minute Roc's dreams came true until they reached the end of the ice and were going too fast, and they all ended up in the water, bedraggled and undignified.

3

Implementation in Alice

Concept Objectives

- Open a saved project
- Alice has two kinds of methods: procedures and functions
- Writing a code statement, calling a method
- Sending an argument to a parameter

- Basic syntax in Alice statements
- Running an Alice program
- Calling a procedure with a detail (optional) parameter
- Display code in Java mode

Chapters 1 and 2 introduced a problem-solving approach for computer programming, as used in this textbook. Thus far, two components have been described and illustrated: "Analyze the task" and "Design a plan." The next component in the problem-solving process is "Implement the design" (Figure 3.1). **Implementation** is the process of translating a design algorithm into program code.

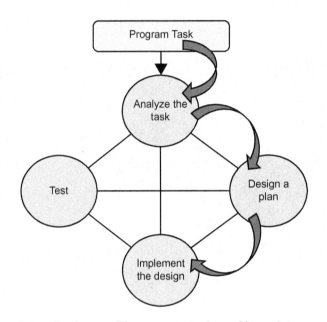

Figure 3.1   *Implement: The next step in the problem-solving approach*

We will use the Alice Code editor for implementation. This chapter is a quick tutorial for the Code editor. The tutorial example will be created using the FirstWorld scene, created in Chapter 2. If you did not create your own copy of the world in Chapter 2, you may do so now or obtain a copy from your instructor. If you are taking a course, your instructor may ask you to use this chapter as part of a lab. Even if you are studying on your own, the authors encourage you to use this chapter as a tutorial. Sit at a computer, open the Alice 3 software, and follow along. Use Alice's Code editor to build the code in a step-by-step "active learning" style.

3.1 Open a Saved Project

Open Alice on your computer. In the Select Project dialog box, follow these steps to open the project (Figure 3.2):

(1) Click the **File System** tab.

(2) Click the **Browse** button. A file navigation box will be displayed.

(3) Use the file navigation box to navigate to the location on your computer where the project has been saved. Click once on the file name.

(4) Click the **Open** button in the lower right of the file navigation box.

(5) Click **OK** in the Select Project/File System tab. Be patient—the project file is compressed and it may take several seconds to decompress the file.

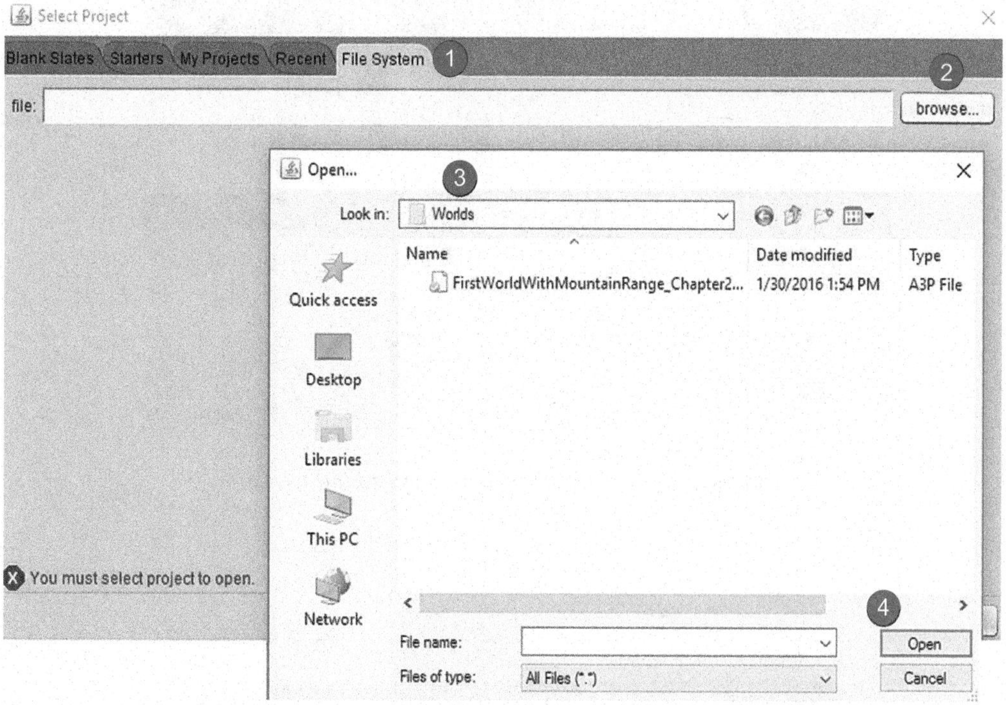

Figure 3.2 • *Open the FirstWorld project file from Chapter 2.*
Source: © Microsoft Corporation.

In this tutorial, Tashi, the little yeti in the *Haunted Circus* story, will say "Hello, World!" This simple example pays homage to a traditional first test-program in Computer Science, first introduced by Brian Kernighan in his book, *The C Programming Language*, published in the 1970s.

In the Scene editor, find the YetiBaby 3D model in the gallery. Select the one that has a scarf and drag it into the scene (Figure 3.3). Then, in the popup dialog box (Figure 3.4), enter "Tashi" (without the quotes) in the name box.

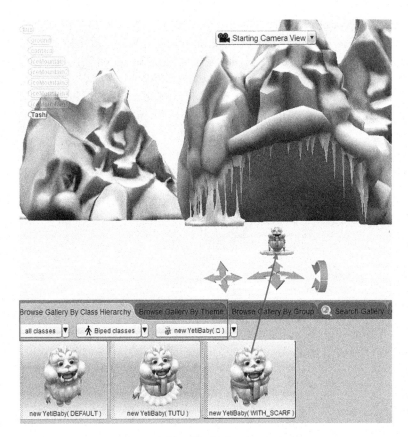

Figure 3.3   *Add a YetiBaby object to the scene.*

Figure 3.4   *Popup dialog box for creating and naming a new YetiBaby object.*

3.2 The Code Editor

Return to the Code editor by clicking the Edit Code button in the Scene editor. Now that you have created an initial scene, the scene is displayed in the Camera view panel (upper left of Figure 3.5). The tabs on the right are editor tabs, where code statements may be written. Alice automatically displays a tab for *Scene*, which is the **active class** (the currently open class). Two additional tabs, *initializeEventListeners* and *myFirstMethod*, are also automatically displayed. The *myFirstMethod* tab is displayed on top of the other tabs, which means *myFirstMethod* is the **active method** (the method currently open for editing). The background color of a class tab is yellow-green but a method tab is slate-blue.

Figure 3.5   *Camera view (left) and Code editor panel (right)
with active class and method tabs*

(1) Click on the *myFirstMethod* tab in the Code editor. (2) In the Methods panel (lower left), click the **Object selector** box to select *this* (Figure 3.6). The word *this* is a keyword that refers to *this* scene. (A **keyword** is a word that has a special meaning in a programming language.)

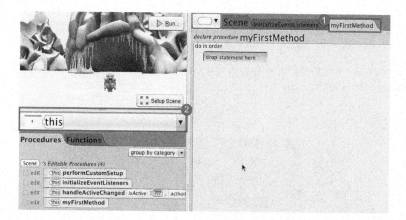

Figure 3.6   *Select* this *in the Object selector*

Click on the **Scene** tab to open the Scene class tab (Figure 3.7). The Scene class is a blueprint that tells Alice (1) what actions (**procedures** and **functions**) a scene can perform and (2) what components (**properties**) a scene contains.

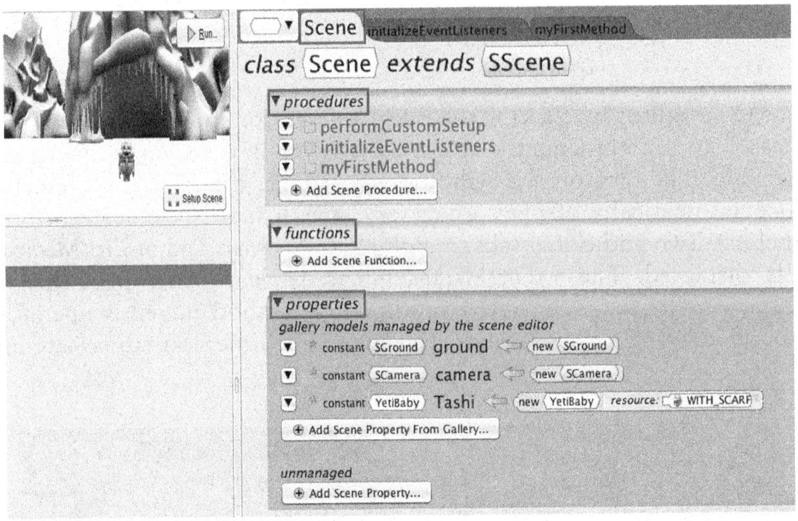

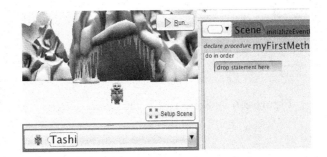

Figure 3.7   *The Scene class tab*

Procedures and functions are two different forms of **methods**. Procedural methods are actions that can be performed by or on an object. Functional methods are actions that compute or retrieve information about an object.

The Properties section contains the declaration statements for the objects belonging to a scene. The Scene class always has two built-in properties (*ground* and *camera*). In the initial scene created earlier, Tashi was added to the scene. In Alice programming terms, Tashi is now a property of the scene. Additional properties may be added in the Properties sub-section labeled "unmanaged."

3.3 Creating (Writing) a Code Statement

Once again, click the *myFirstMethod* tab in the Code editor. Then click on the Object selector and select Tashi (Figure 3.8).

Figure 3.8   *Select Tashi in the Object selector box.*

The Methods panel (immediately below the Object selector) has two tabs, one containing Procedures (procedural methods) and the other containing Functions (functional methods) (Figure 3.9).

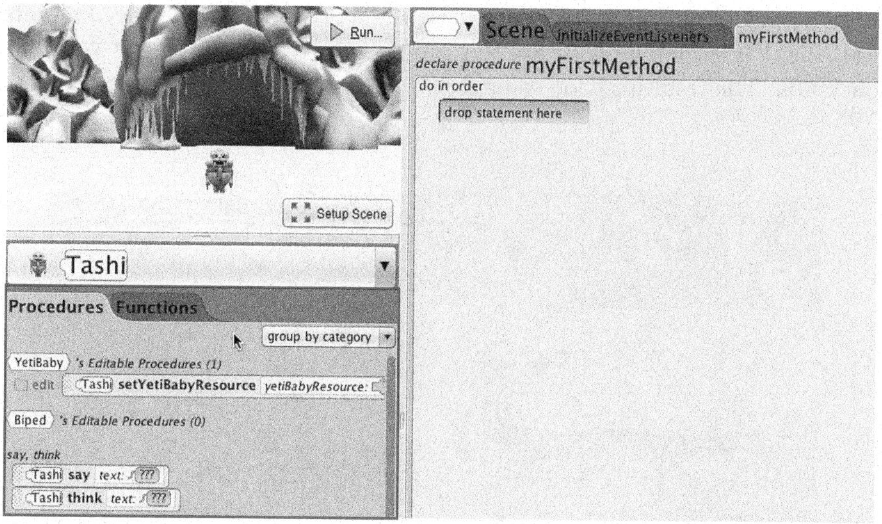

Figure 3.9 *Procedures and Functions tabs in the Methods panel*

With Tashi selected in the Object selector, the Procedures and Functions tabs now contain tiles that represent actions Tashi "knows" how to perform (Figure 3.10). For example, *say* and *think* are verbal expression actions and *move*, *moveToward*, *moveAwayFrom*, *moveTo*, and *place* are positioning actions. A code statement is created (written) by dragging a tile into the editor and supplying any information (data) needed to perform the action.

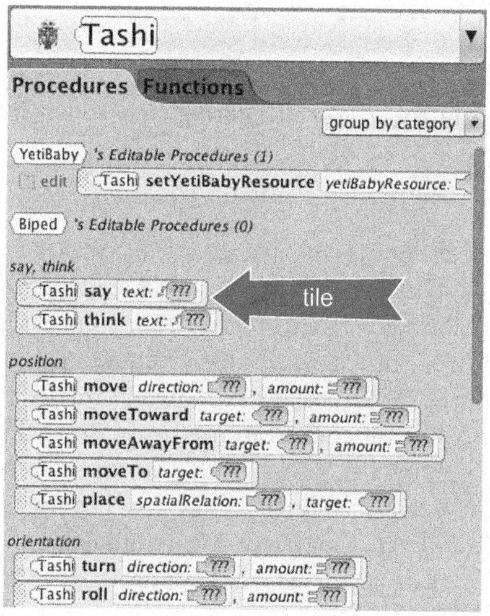

Figure 3.10 *Procedure tiles for Tashi*

Follow these steps to write a *say* statement (Figure 3.11):

(1) Use the cursor to drag the *say* procedure tile into *myFirstMethod's* editor tab. When the cursor is released, the *say* tile is "dropped" into the editor.

(2) Alice displays a dropdown menu. Select **Custom TextString**.

(3) In the popup input box, enter the text Hello, World!. You do not need to enter quote marks—Alice automatically adds quote marks around the text you enter.

(4) Click **OK**. The resulting code statement is shown in Figure 3.12.

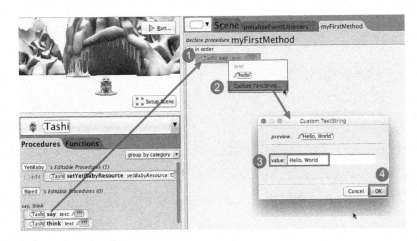

Figure 3.11   *A menu requesting information*

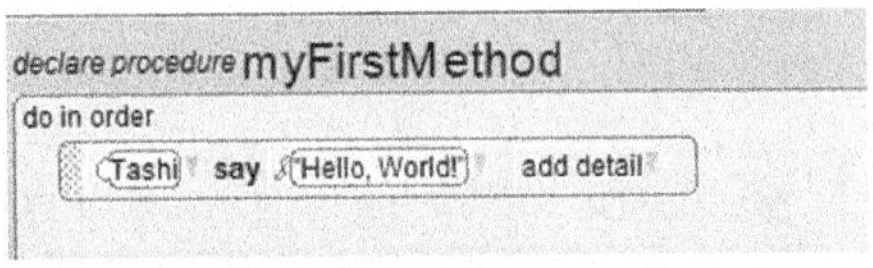

declare procedure myFirstMethod
do in order
    (Tashi) **say** ("Hello, World!")   add detail

Figure 3.12   *Resulting code statement*

When the *say* procedure tile was dragged into the editor tab, Alice asked for some information in a dropdown menu. This is because the *say* procedure has a parameter, named *text*. A **parameter** refers to information (data) required in order to perform its task. The string of text we entered, "Hello, World!", is known as an **argument** (a data value sent to the parameter). Many of the built-in procedures in Alice have parameters that expect to be sent an argument.

As shown above, the resulting code statement in Figure 3.12 is composed of the name of the object (Tashi), followed by the name of the action (a procedure), and then information needed to perform the action. The order of the components in a code statement is determined by Alice **syntax**. In a programming language, syntax is the set of rules that govern the arrangement of words, phrases, and symbols in code statements.

Before continuing, please remember use SaveAs to save the project file. We used the name *HelloWorld*, but a different name is fine.

3.4 Run the Program

Test the code by clicking the Run button (Figure 3.13). When Run is clicked, the program creates a **runtime window** in which the initial scene is displayed. When the scene is displayed, we say the scene has been (**activated**). When the scene is activated, the code statements in *myFirstMethod* are executed.

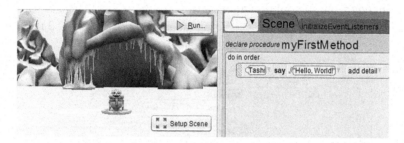

Figure 3.13   *Click Run to test the code.*

The *do in order* at the beginning of *myFirstMethod* tells Alice to execute the code statements in **sequence**, one after the other. In this example, there is only one statement. The statement codes a **call** to the *say* procedure. To call a method (either procedure or function) means to tell the computer, at runtime, to perform the action defined by that procedure. In this example, Tashi says, "Hello World!" (Figure 3.14). Remember to close the runtime window (X on PC, red dot on Mac) after viewing the animation.

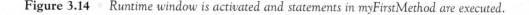

Figure 3.14   *Runtime window is activated and statements in myFirstMethod are executed.*

3.4.1 Calling a method with a detail parameter (optional)

Some procedures also have **detail parameters** that have default values. If we do not specify a value for a detail parameter, Alice will use the default value. For example, each procedure has a default *duration* of one second. If we do not specify a different duration, Alice will perform the procedure in one second. If you wish to specify a different duration, follow these steps (Figure 3.15):

(1) Click the *add detail* menu at the end of the statement tile.
(2) Select *duration* from the pulldown menu.
(3) Select a *duration* value from the cascading menu—in this example, 2.0 seconds.

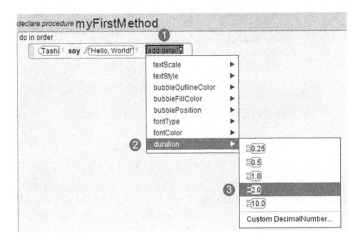

Figure 3.15   *Select an argument for a detail parameter.*

3.4.2 A quick look at what happens behind the scene (optional)

The Run button in the Alice IDE hides much of the code within the Alice system that produces the graphics output for animation. Let's take a quick look at how some of the graphics output is actually created. Knowing how the graphics output is actually produced will help you later in understanding how to write your own program code.

First, click the Class menu button in the Code editor and then select Program in the cascading menu (Figure 3.16). If the Program class is not listed in the Class menu, see the following *Tip* to enable its display.

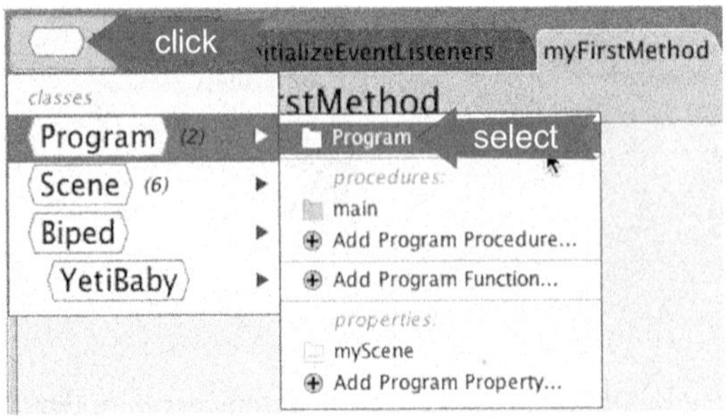

Figure 3.16   *Select the Program class in the Class menu.*

TIP: *Enable Display of the Program Class:*

If the *Program* class is not listed in the Class menu, select Window/Preferences in the Alice menu bar, and then enable the display of the Main Program class in the cascading menus (Figure 3.17).

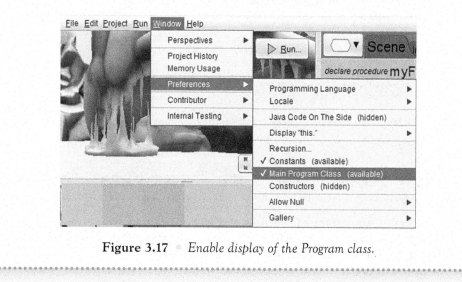

Figure 3.17 ● *Enable display of the Program class.*

When Program is selected in the Class menu, a new tab opens in the Code editor (Figure 3.18). The *Program* class defines a procedure named *main* and declares an object, named *myScene*, which is the actual scene displayed in the Camera view window.

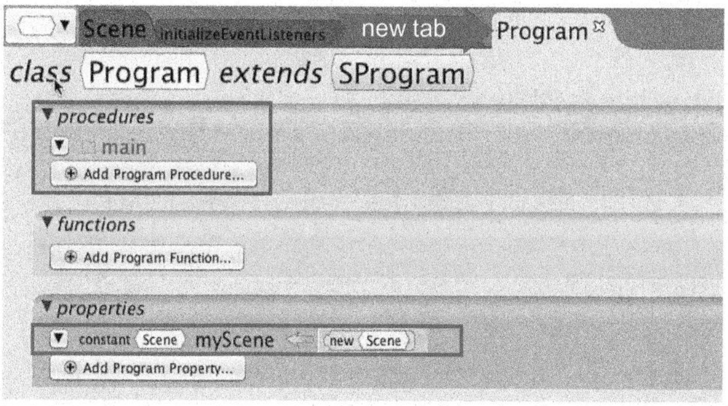

Figure 3.18 ● *Program class tab*

To see the code in the *main* procedure, click on *main*. A new *main* editor tab is opened where the code is displayed (Figure 3.19). A lot of details are involved in this code, which is beyond the scope of a first introduction. For simplification, let's just pay attention to two actions:

(1) In the second code statement *initializeInFrame* is called, which creates and displays a runtime window (a frame).

(2) In the third code statement, *setActiveScene* is called, which **activates the scene** (sets the scene as active, paints the scene in the runtime window, and calls the scene's *myFirstMethod*).

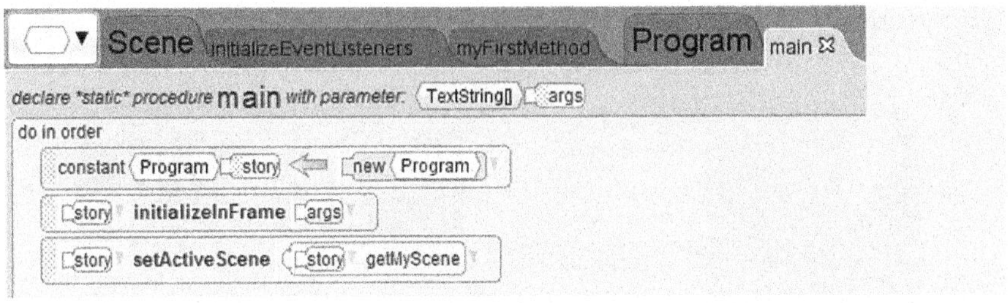

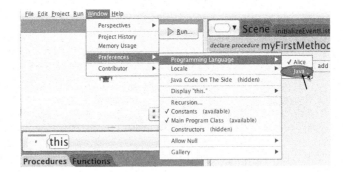

Figure 3.19   *When Run is clicked, the runtime window is displayed and activated*

3.5 View Alice Code with Java Syntax (optional)

Now that the example program has been implemented, you may have an interest in seeing what the code looks like in Java. Alice has a simple syntax, with a minimal number of quote marks, parentheses, semicolons, and other symbols.

For those who prefer a more production-level-language look and feel, Alice provides an option in the Preferences menu for Java syntax code display. Your instructor may prefer to use the Java syntax display. To change to Java syntax, select the Window menu and then Preferences/Programming Language. Then, in the cascading menu, select Java (Figure 3.20). Program statements in the Code editor will now be displayed with greater fidelity to Java syntax than the default Alice syntax. Note that this setting only affects the display of code statements, not other elements of the Alice IDE.

Figure 3.20   *Setting the programming language preference to Java*

For comparison purposes, Figure 3.21 shows the example code used in this chapter in Alice syntax mode. Figure 3.22 shows the exact same code in Java syntax mode. Differences in corresponding statements are highlighted in blue and red in the two figures.

The **red boxes** highlight differences in words and phrases. In Alice, a procedural method begins with the words *declare procedure*. In Java, a procedural method is specified using the word *void*. A procedure is considered *void* because a value is not computed and passed along to some other component in the program code.

The **blue ovals** highlight differences in punctuation marks and symbols. The general lack of punctuation marks in Alice code is possible because the graphic tiles visually separate the components in a statement. Java syntax uses parentheses, commas, semicolons, and other symbols to separate statement components.

Figure 3.21   *Alice code displayed with the Alice syntax setting*

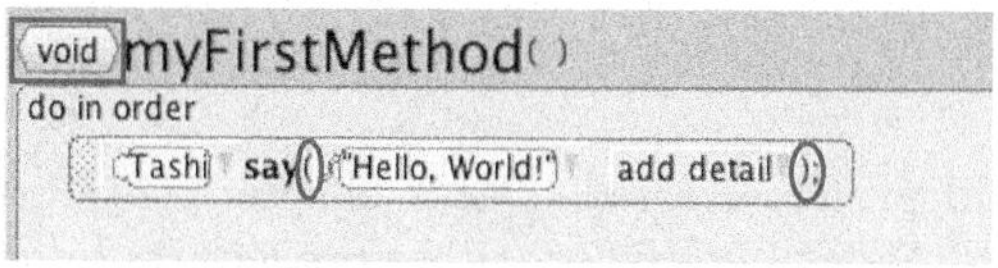

Figure 3.22   *Alice code displayed with the Java syntax setting*

Summary

This chapter is a tutorial for learning to write code statements in Alice's Code editor. The editor provides a methods panel containing tiles that may be dragged into the editor tab to create a code statement. Methods are actions that may be either procedures or functions. The general format (syntax) of an Alice statement is the name of an object followed by the name of a method that is to be performed. In this chapter, we used procedural methods.

Many procedures require arguments for one or more parameters (information the procedure needs in order to perform the action). For example, a *say* procedure requires a text string argument to specify the words to be displayed in a text bubble. A detail parameter has a default value, which may be replaced. For example, a *say* statement has a detail parameter for duration with a default one-second value, which may be replaced.

Terms

activate the scene	declaration statement	procedure
active class	detail parameter	property
active method	function	runtime window
activated	implementation	sequence
argument	keyword	syntax
call	method	
data	parameter	

Concept Questions

. . . .

1. What is the relationship of "code implementation" to a "design algorithm"?
2. What are the two different kinds of tabs in the editor panel of the Code editor?
3. A method can be either a procedure or a function. What is the primary difference?
4. How is an argument related to a parameter?
5. Some parameters are described as "detail" parameters. Why?
6. What is the purpose of a property declaration statement?
7. Explain, as a list of steps, what really happens "behind the scene" when the Run button is clicked in Alice.
8. When Java syntax is enabled in the Alice IDE, a procedure may be labeled "void." What does void mean in this context?

Exercises

. . . .

1. In the HelloWorld project created in this chapter, only one statement was created (Tashi says, "Hello, World!"). Explore other procedures by writing statements to have Tashi:
   (a) *think* "What a great scene!"
   (b) *move* forward 1 meter (you may assume she is sliding on the ice and snow)
   (c) *turn* right one complete revolution
   (d) *turn* backward a quarter of a revolution
   (e) *roll* forward complete revolution
   (f) change color—try yellow or green.
2. Select one of the worlds you created for the exercises at the end of Chapter 2. Write statements to have one of the objects in the scene perform *move*, *turn*, and *roll* actions in sequence and then *say* something. For example, if you select the world for Chapter 2, Exercise 2, you might write code to have the seagull float by moving forward, then turning around twice, roll forward one revolution, and then say, "The water is cold today."
3. Modify exercise 1, above, by changing the order of the two *turn* statements in the code. Now, run again. Compare the new animation action to the action that was performed in exercise 1. Explain why the order of the code statements makes a difference.
4. Add two characters to an Alice scene. Have one character tell a joke and then have the other character respond in some way.

4 Implement and Test

Concept Objectives

- Implementation using incremental development.
- Using comments for documentation
- Translating an algorithm to code statements
- Finding bugs and debugging
- Revising an algorithm

In this chapter, the algorithm for an adaptation of a selected excerpt of Episode 1 will be implemented. The algorithm was previously developed in Chapter 2. Each step of the algorithm will be translated into one or more code statements and then tested. The end product will be an animation similar to a film short.

VIDEO ALERT!

Highly recommended videos to accompany this chapter include

- Video: Animation of Objects in Alice 3
- Video: Understanding Move, Turn, and Roll in Alice 3

Videos are available at: www.alice.org/Alice3ToJava

A starter world, named *Episode1Starter.a3p*, has been prepared for this chapter. The starter world may be downloaded from www.alice.org/Alice3ToJava. Start Alice and open the Episode1Starter.a3p file (Figure 4.1).

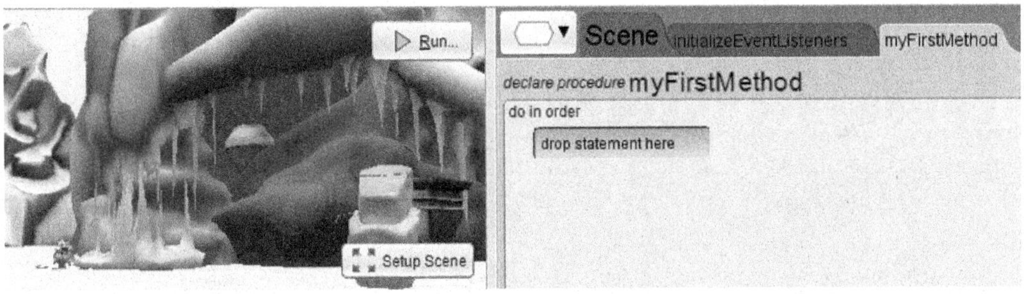

Figure 4.1   *Opening view of starter world in the Code editor*

Click the Setup Scene button to open the Scene editor for a larger view of the scene (Figure 4.2). The starter world setup is based on the set design in storyboards presented previously in Chapter 2. The major characters include Tashi standing on a snowboard and Larry, the skeleton, frozen in an ice block. The starter world scene also includes an arctic mountain range and a train engine covered with ice.

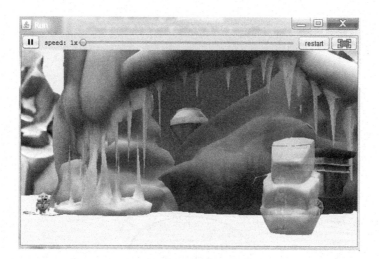

Figure 4.2 *View of the scene in the Scene editor*

4.1 Implementation with Incremental Development

We will use an **incremental development** process for implementation, in which a few lines of code are written, then saved, and a test run is performed. If the code executes as expected, a few more lines of code are written and then the program is saved and tested again. If the code does not work as expected, the code is revised so as to fix the problem before continuing. Figure 4.3 illustrates the cyclic nature of incremental development.

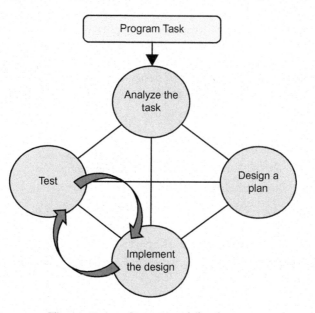

Figure 4.3 *Incremental development*

Click on the Edit code button to return to the Code editor. Then click on the *myFirst-Method* tab. The Scene's *myFirstMethod* tab is the editor space where our code implementation will begin. Three operations are typically part of the implementation process (Figure 4.4): (1) creating documentation with comments, (2) decomposing complex actions into simple steps, and (3) translating the algorithm steps into one or more code statements.

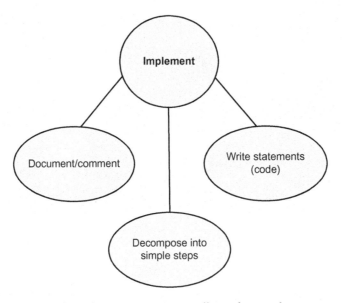

Figure 4.4   *Three operations typically used in implementation*

4.2 Creating Documentation with Comments

Begin by adding at least some documentation to your program using comments. A **comment** is one or more lines of text intended for the human reader. Comments are not executable code statements, but are added for the purpose of providing information to the person who is reading and possibly modifying the code. Software developers typically write comments that include items such as: name of the programmer who wrote the code, date, and a description of what the code is intended to accomplish. If you are taking a course, check with your instructor for documentation requirements. In this example, the design algorithm will be used to document what the code is intended to accomplish. The algorithm, created earlier in Chapter 2, is repeated here (Figure 4.5).

Do in order

> Tashi snowboards into the scene
> Skeleton's hand wiggles
> Tashi snowboards forward
> Snowboard crashes into the iceBlock
> IceBlock splits apart

Figure 4.5   *Design algorithm for Episode 1, Haunted Circus*

The first line in the algorithm, *do in order*, is a control structure. A **control structure** determines the order in which statements are **executed** (performed) when the code runs. *Do in order* tells Alice to execute the statements in sequence. In Figure 4.6, notice *myFirstMethod* already has *do in order* in the editor tab. The next line of the algorithm is "Tashi snowboards into the scene." Select the *comment* tile in the Controls panel and drag it into the editor (Figure 4.6).

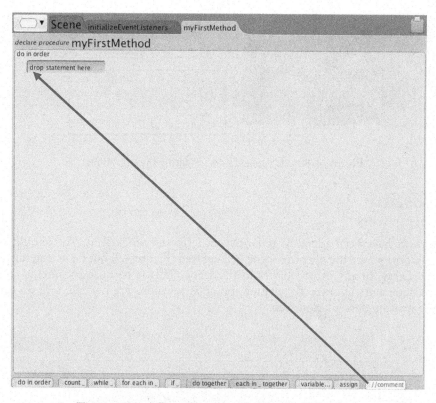

Figure 4.6 • *Drag comment tile into the Code editor*

When the cursor is released, a textbox is created in the editor. Enter the comment in the textbox, beginning with two right-slash characters, the "//" symbol (Figure 4.7). The "//" is a **symbol** that tells the Alice system this line is a comment.

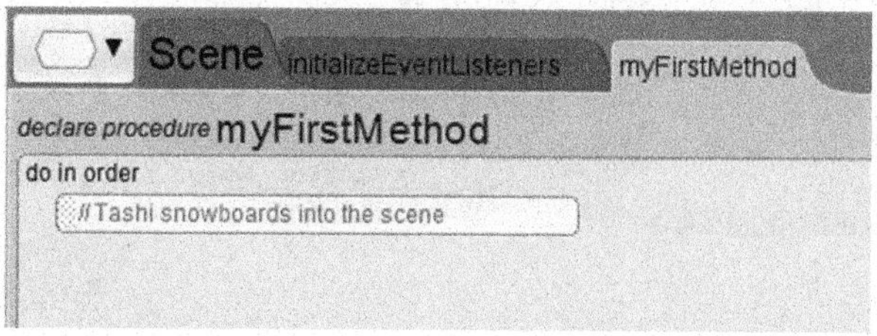

Figure 4.7 • *Enter a comment using the keyboard.*

Using this technique, add a comment for each line listed in the algorithm, as shown in Figure 4.8. In this example, each line is written in a separate comment box. Separate comment lines will allow you to add program code statements between the comments. Other comments may be added later, but this is a good start.

Figure 4.8   *Comments documenting the algorithm*

4.3 Testing

Five comments have been added to *myFirstMethod*. To test, click Run. You should see the runtime window where the opening scene is displayed (Figure 4.9) but no action takes place with Tashi, Larry, or any other objects in the scene. This is because comments are NOT executable statements. If correctly written, no code revisions are needed, and we can proceed to the next implementation step.

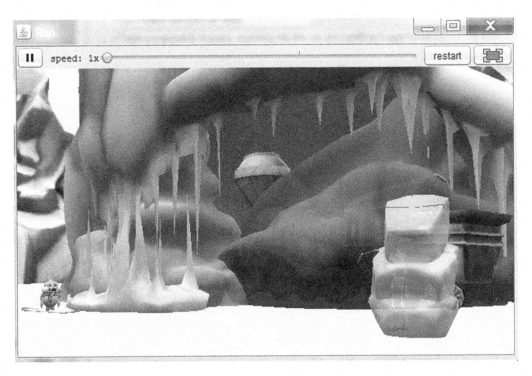

Figure 4.9   *A runtime window displays the opening scene.*

4.4 Translating Algorithm to Code

The first object-action step is Tashi snowboarding into the scene. We want to translate this step into a statement. Begin by selecting Tashi in the Object selector (Figure 4.10). The Procedures tab now displays tiles for the built-in procedures for Tashi.

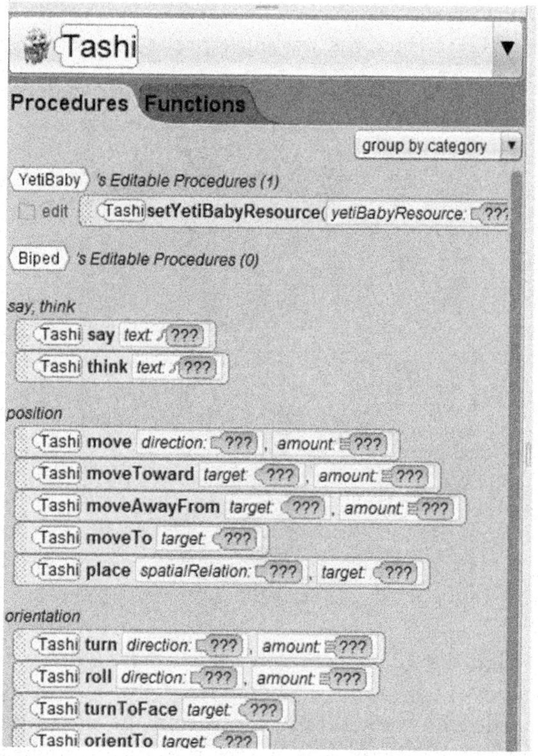

Figure 4.10   *Tiles for Tashi's built-in procedural methods*

If you scroll through the Procedures tab searching for a tile that represents a snow-boarding action, you will not find it. This is because snowboarding is a complex action involving two objects: the snowboard and Tashi. When an algorithm step is a complex action, it must be broken down into two or more simpler actions. The technique of breaking down a complex action into several simpler actions is known as **decomposition**, one of the three operations in implementation, illustrated earlier in Figure 4.4.

4.4.1 Moving with a vehicle

To decompose this complex action, think about what happens when Tashi rides on her snow-board. Basically, the snowboard moves and Tashi moves along with it. The snowboard is acting as her vehicle. All objects in an Alice scene have a **vehicle** property. If an object has a vehicle set, then it will move with that object as though physically attached to it.

By default, the vehicle of a newly created object is pre-set to the scene. The vehicle property may be reset, either in the Scene Editor's Toolbox or in a code statement. We will set the vehicle as a code statement, as part of the decomposition for the snowboarding action. Figure 4.11 illustrates the decomposition: first set Tashi's vehicle to be the snowboard, then move the snowboard. When the snowboard moves, Tashi will automatically move with it.

> *Do in order*
>
> > Set Tashi's vehicle to the snowboard
> > Snowboard move forward

Figure 4.11   *Decomposition of a snowboarding action*

To write a statement to reset Tashi's vehicle, scroll down in the Procedures tab to find the *setVehicle* tile (Figure 4.12). Notice the *setVehicle* procedure requires an **argument** for its parameter, named *vehicle*.

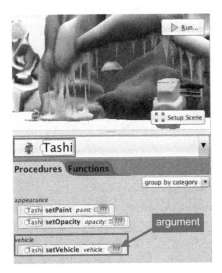

Figure 4.12   *Tashi's setVehicle procedure tile*

Drag the *setVehicle* tile into the editor and position the tile immediately after the first comment (Figure 4.13). (A highlighted line marks the location where the code statement will be created when the cursor is released.)

When the cursor is released, a dropdown menu is displayed where a target vehicle can be selected. In this example, we selected snowboard (Figure 4.14). The resulting code statement is shown in Figure 4.15.

Figure 4.13   *Drag the* setVehicle *tile into the editor and drop after the first comment*

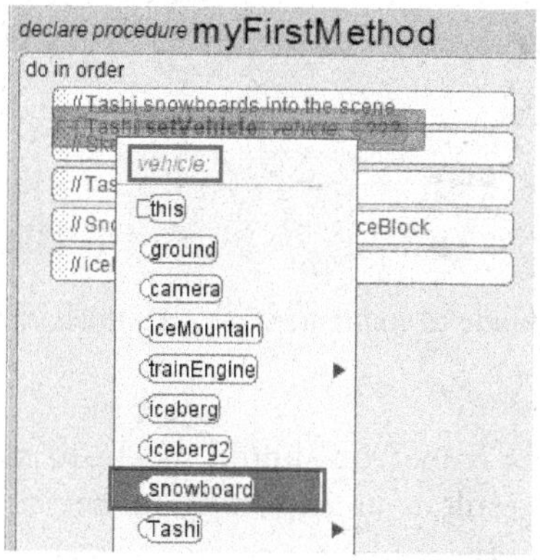

Figure 4.14 • *Select an argument value for vehicle.*

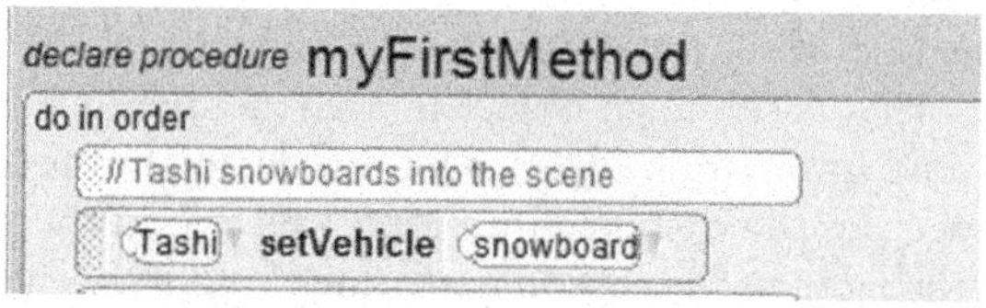

Figure 4.15 • *A code statement to set Tashi's vehicle to the snowboard*

Next, create a statement to have the snowboard move forward. Select the snowboard in the Object selector and then drag its *move* tile into the editor, immediately beneath the *setVehicle* statement (Figure 4.16). When the cursor is released, select FORWARD as the direction and Custom Decimal Number as the amount. In the popup number pad, enter 1.5. The resulting code is shown in Figure 4.17.

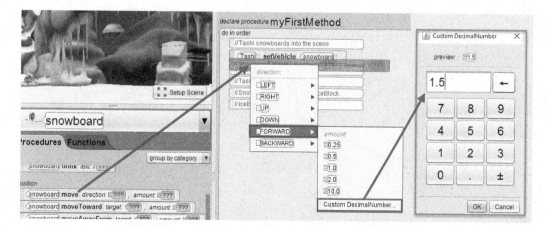

Figure 4.16 • *Drag* move *tile, select FORWARD, and enter custom amount.*

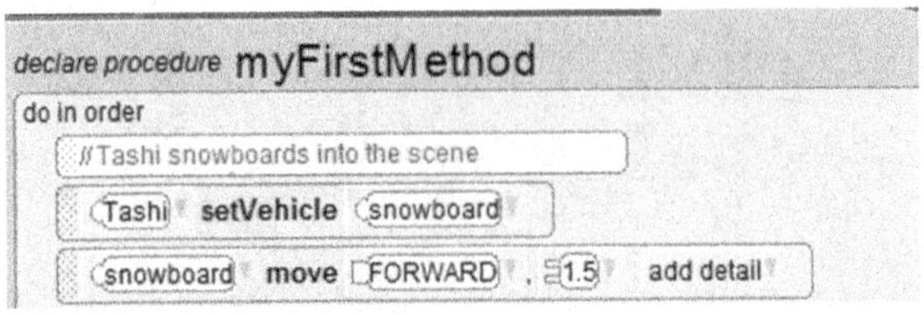

```
declare procedure myFirstMethod
do in order
    // Tashi snowboards into the scene
    Tashi  setVehicle  snowboard
    snowboard  move  FORWARD  , 1.5  add detail
```

Figure 4.17   *Code to implement Tashi snowboarding into the scene*

Test the code by clicking Run. You should see Tashi moving forward with the snowboard. Assuming your test result is as expected, no revisions are necessary and we can proceed with the next step.

TIP: **Arguments in a move Statement**

Direction may be any one of six possible values: LEFT, RIGHT, FORWARD, BACKWARD, UP, or DOWN. Each object in a virtual world has its own sense of direction, as illustrated in Figure 4.18. *Amount* is a decimal number (also known as a *real* number) that specifies the distance in meters (relative to the scale of the virtual world). By default, the *move* procedure is performed in a self-centric manner, based on the object's own orientation. That is, if an object is told to *move* FORWARD, it will move forward in the direction it is currently facing. An object's sense of left, right, forward, back, up, and down is not the same as your sense of left, right (and so on...) as you view the screen.

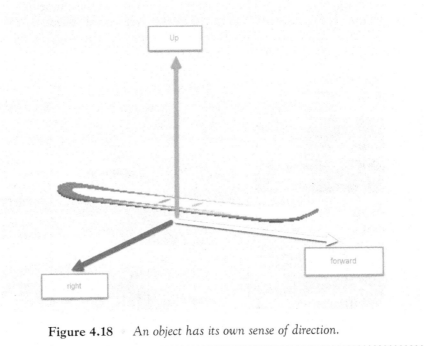

Figure 4.18   *An object has its own sense of direction.*

4.4.2 Turning a subpart

In the next step, the skeleton (Larry), trapped in an iceBlock, wriggles his hand. As with Tashi's snowboarding, there is no built-in procedure for a wriggle action. Figure 4.19 illustrates a decomposition with a sequence of *turn* statements to rotate backward, then forward, and backward again. (A more sophisticated action could be implemented. But this is okay as a first example.)

Do in order

turn backward
turn forward
turn backward

Figure 4.19 *Decomposition: a sequence of actions for wriggling a hand*

TIP: *Arguments for a Turn Procedure*

A *turn* is a rotational action requiring two arguments: *direction* and *amount*. The *direction* may be LEFT, RIGHT, FORWARD, or BACKWARD. The direction of a *turn* is self-centric, based on the orientation of the object, regardless of the position of the camera. This means that when an object turns left, the turn is to the object's left. When an object turns right, it is to the object's right. The *amount* of rotational motion is measured in revolutions, with one complete revolution equivalent to 360 degrees.

To create the statement, select Larry in the Object selector and then drag Larry's *turn* procedure tile into the editor (Figure 4.20). When the cursor is released, select BACK-WARD as the *direction* and 0.25 revolutions as the *amount*.

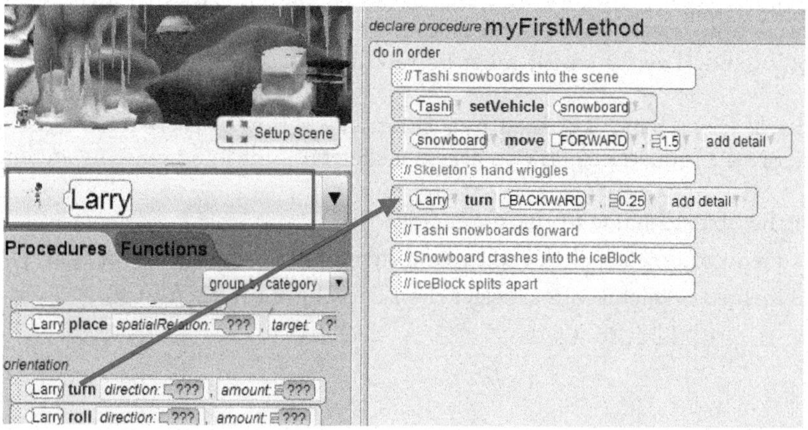

Figure 4.20 *The first turn statement for the wriggle action*

4.5 Bugs and Debugging

Run the project to test the statement. When the statement is executed, the entire Larry object *turns* backward (Figure 4.21). This is a **bug** in our code. A bug is an error, which can be an error in grammar, punctuation, or logic; or it might simply be an error of intention. In this example, it is an error of intention because Larry's hand was intended to turn but instead our code turns Larry's entire body.

Figure 4.21   *The entire object turns*

To **debug** (remove the error), consider what the statement tells Alice to do. The statement begins with the name of the object followed by the name of the action to be performed (an object/action pair). As written, the statement tells Alice to turn Larry—that is, the whole skeleton object. There is no clue in the statement that tells Alice to turn only the skeleton's hand. The statement must be rewritten to specify a subpart of the skeleton object.

As in real life, a hand is turned by a rotational action of the hand's wrist joint. The image in Figure 4.22 illustrates how to access a skeletal joint in an existing statement:

(1) Select the object's name in the statement.
(2) In the menu of objects, click the expand menu arrow for the object (Larry).
(3) In the menu of skeletal joints, select the skeletal joint (*getLeftWrist*).

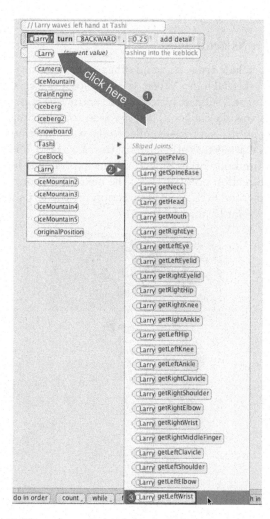

Figure 4.22 • *Accessing a skeletal joint in an existing statement*

The debugged statement is shown in Figure 4.23. Run to test the modified statement. You should see Larry's hand turn backward (relative to the wrist joint).

Figure 4.23 • *Debugged statement*

TIP: *Actions of a Skeletal Joint*

Subparts of an object include arms, legs, and other extremities that are connected to the torso of the body by a skeletal joint. When we say "a joint is accessed," we mean a skeletal joint is used to animate a subpart instead of the entire object. A procedure gets a **joint-reference** (a link to a skeletal joint) that is connected to a subpart. A joint-reference is used to *turn*, *roll*, or *orient* a subpart—similar to the way a wire on a marionette is used to *turn*, *roll*, or *orient* a marionette's arms, hands, legs, feet, head, and other subparts.

As with the entire body of an object, a joint has its own sense of direction. A joint's FORWARD direction points toward the next joint linked to it in the skeletal hierarchy. For example, the FORWARD direction for the left shoulder joint points toward his left elbow joint (Figure 4.24).

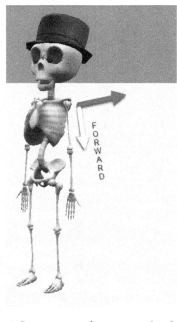

Figure 4.24   *Orientation of a joint in the skeletal hierarchy*

Two additional statements are needed, as indicated in the algorithm for wriggling Larry's hand. Instead of writing the statements to have the entire skeleton object perform the turn action and then modifying the statements to access the left wrist skeletal joint, let's select the skeletal joint at the beginning so no further modifications are needed. To access a skeletal joint in the Object selector, follow these steps (Figure 4.25):

(1) Click the down menu arrow in the Object selector.
(2) Click the menu expansion arrow for the object in the dropdown menu.
(3) Select the joint from the menu of skeletal joints in the object.

Figure 4.25 ⊙ *Accessing a skeletal joint for creating a new statement*

Drag the *turn* tile into the editor to create the remaining two statements for a wriggling action (Figure 4.26). Test-run. You will see the hand wriggle, but it happens much too slowly. Increase the speed of the actions by specifying a *duration* for each statement, as shown in Figure 4.27.

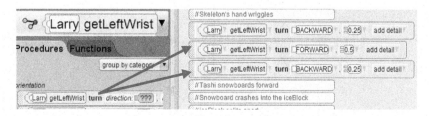

Figure 4.26 ⊙ *Sequence of three statements to create a hand-waving action*

```
// Skeleton's hand wriggles
(Larry) getLeftWrist  turn [BACKWARD] , ⊟0.25 , duration ⊟0.5  add detail
(Larry) getLeftWrist  turn [FORWARD] , ⊟0.5 , duration ⊟1.0  add detail
(Larry) getLeftWrist  turn [BACKWARD] , ⊟0.25 , duration ⊟0.5  add detail
```

Figure 4.27   *Revised code for waving Larry's hand faster (shorter duration)*

As you endeavor to create realistic animations, you will often find it necessary to adjust the timing of different actions by resetting the **duration**. In the previous example, the duration of each backward turn was reset to 0.5 seconds, but the duration of the forward turn is set at 1 second. This is because the forward rotation angle is twice that of a backward rotation and should, therefore, be given twice as much time to execute.

4.6 Design Revision

The next step in the algorithm is "Tashi snowboards forward." This is similar to the action implemented earlier where Tashi snowboards into the scene. However, it is not necessary to set Tashi's vehicle to the snowboard again. Once an object's vehicle has been set, it remains until purposely reset. All we really need to do is have Tashi provide some motion to push the snowboard forward a specified distance. One way to do this is to have Tashi lean left and right, thereby giving the appearance of using her legs to push the snowboard forward.

Let's give some consideration to the amount that should be specified for the distance the snowboard should move forward. Looking ahead, the next step in the algorithm is to have the snowboard crash into the iceBlock. Implementation would be easier if we combine these two steps of the algorithm into one object-action. This is a design revision. The cyclic nature of a design revision is shown in (Figure 4.28).

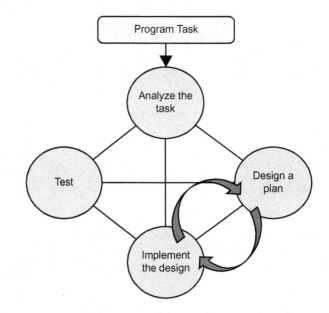

Figure 4.28   *Cyclic nature of design revision and implementation*

A decomposition for the combined steps is shown in Figure 4.29.

Do in order

> Tashi roll left (provides visual appearance of Tashi pushing the snowboard forward)
> snowboard move forward (use the necessary distance to crash into the iceBlock)
> Tashi roll right (return to upright position)

Figure 4.29 *Decomposition of the snowboard crashing into the iceBlock*

A practical technique for estimating the horizontal distance between the snowboard and the ice block is to temporarily turn on the snap grid in the Scene Editor's Toolbox (Figure 4.30). In this example, the "use snap" checkbox was selected in the Toolbox and the grid spacing set at 1. This sets each grid block to 1 meter on a side (an area of 1 square m.). Counting the number of blocks between the two objects gives an estimate of distance. In this example, we counted six blocks between the front edge of the snowboard and the nearest edge of the iceBlock object.

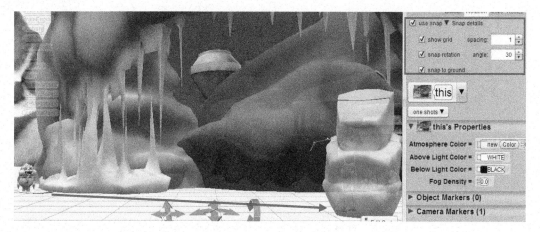

Figure 4.30 *A snap grid drawn on the ground surface*

Write statements to have Tashi *roll* left (as she pushes the snowboard) and then have the snowboard *move* forward an estimated 6 meters. Then, a statement to have Tashi *roll* right (back into an upright position on the snowboard) after the snowboard crashes into the iceBlock object (Figure 4.31). Note these statements are written after two comments because the code is for the two combined steps.

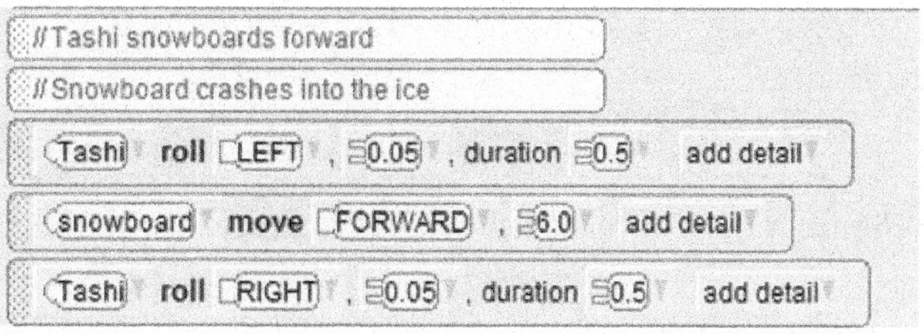

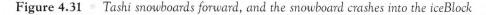

Figure 4.31 *Tashi snowboards forward, and the snowboard crashes into the iceBlock*

The snowboard's collision with the ice block should cause the iceBlock object to split apart and reveal the entire skeleton. A decomposition of this action is shown in Figure 4.32.

Do in order

iceBlock front half turn forward

iceBlock back half turn backward

Figure 4.32 *Decomposition of the iceBlock split*

Add code statements to implement the ice block split (Figure 4.33). The code in *myFirstMethod* is now complete. Now we can step back and look at the overall structure of the code (Figure 4.35). Note that the code is enclosed in a shadow-edged box in *myFirst-Method*. The graphic box is Alice's visual representation of a *do in order* code block. A **code block** is a segment of executable program code, enclosed in a control structure, that performs a specific task.

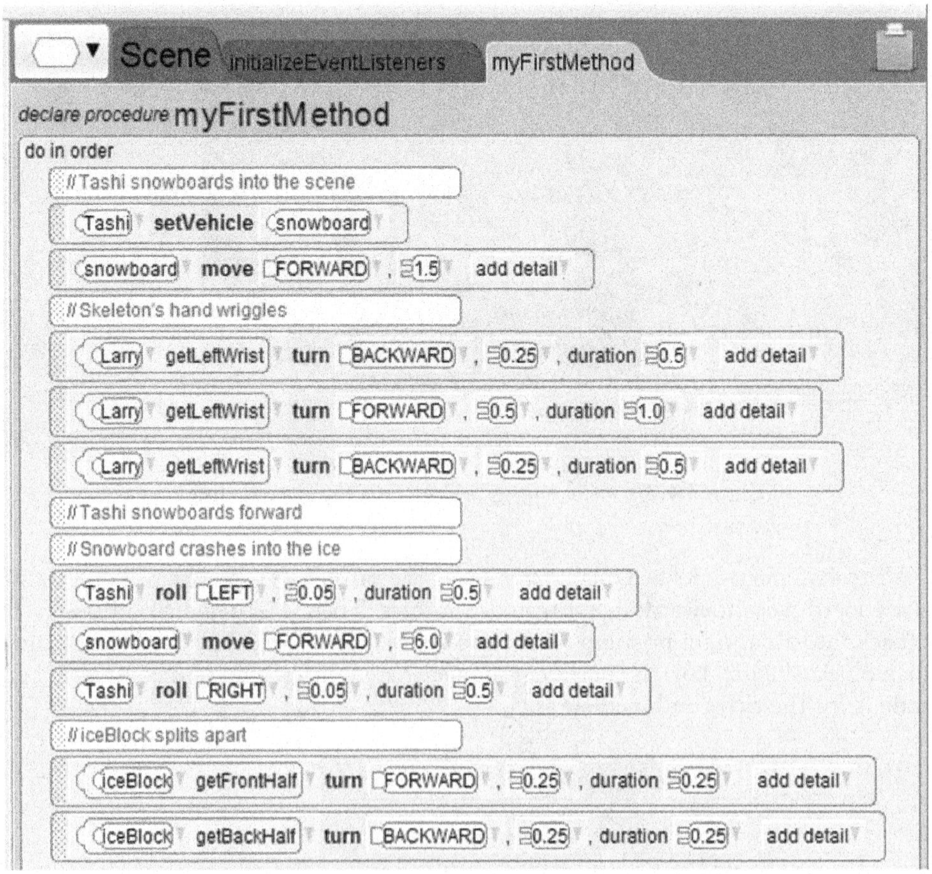

Figure 4.33 *Completed code block in* myFirstMethod

Test-run. You should see the completed animation, ending with the ice block splitting to show the skeleton (Figure 4.34).

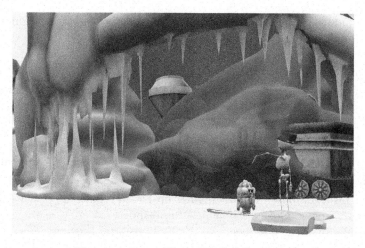

Figure 4.34 • *The iceBlock splits open.*

Summary

The example program in this chapter animates an adapted selection of Episode 1 of the *Haunted Circus* story. The algorithm for the program was previously developed in the design process illustrated in Chapter 2. The algorithm was implemented by translating each algorithm step into code statements, using incremental development, in which a few lines of code are written and then immediately tested. Only when the code has been tested and revised, as needed, do we proceed to the next step in the algorithm. A major advantage of incremental development is easier debugging (removing errors from code). Comments are added during the implementation process to document such items as: the programmer who wrote the code, the date it was written, and a description of what the code is intended to accomplish.

Terms

argument	debug	incremental development
bug	decomposition	joint-reference
code block	duration	the // symbol
comment	execute	vehicle
control structure	implementation	

Concept Questions

1. What does it mean to "implement" a program?
2. What is the difference between "design" and "implementation"?
3. If a comment is not executable code, why bother to include it in your program?

4. A line of code is recognized as a comment in Alice because: (select one)
    (a) It is in *myFirstMethod*
    (b) It begins with //
    (c) It is preceded by a *do in order* control structure

5. What control structure is used to tell Alice that a control block contains code that will be executed in sequence?

6. Why is incremental development described as an "iterative" process?

7. What is the difference, if any, between "run" and "execute" code?

8. What is the meaning of "decomposition," as used in computer programming?

9. Which of the following situations is an example of decomposition? (select one)
    (a) Make Tashi jump by first moving her up 1 meter and then down 1 meter.
    (b) Make the snowboard be the vehicle for Tashi.
    (c) Add a comment to a sequence of instructions after they have been tested.

10. What does it mean to "call" a procedure?

11. In a procedure call, what is the purpose of an argument?

12. What happens in a move statement if the distance parameter is sent an argument that is a negative value?

13. Each of the *move*, *turn*, and *roll* procedures in Alice requires an argument for *direction*. List the possible directions for each procedure:
    (a) *move*
    (b) *turn*
    (c) *roll*

14. When an object *moves*, what properties of the object change (one or more changes)?

15. When an object *turns*, what properties of the object change (one or more changes)?

16. What happens if an object is set as the vehicle for two different objects? (select one)
    (a) All three objects move together when the vehicle moves.
    (b) It is not possible; the *setVehicle* procedure only accepts one argument.
    (c) The second object replaces the first one in the vehicle.
    (d) The second object is ignored and the first one is held in the vehicle.

17. Is it required for an object to be physically touching its vehicle to have the vehicle action work as expected?

18. Describe how to reset an object's vehicle in the Scene editor.

19. Let's suppose two code statements were added to the end of *myFirstMethod* in the textbook example. The first added statement has Tashi step off snowboard. The second added statement has Tashi kick the snowboard.
    (a) What happens when the program is tested?
    (b) What revision would be needed to correct this problem?

20. According to the code shown here, which one of the following is true?
    (a) Duration of statement (2) is 0.5 seconds because Alice applies the same duration as the previous statement.
    (b) Duration of statement (2) is 0 seconds, because no duration is specified.
    (c) Duration of statement (2) is 1 second, because Alice assumes this value when it is not otherwise specified.
    (d) The program is incomplete. The programmer must provide the duration in statement (2).

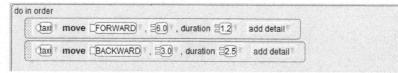

21. Assume an animation where a pedestrian signals to a taxi for a ride. The code shown here is intended to have the taxi arrive quickly but stop 3 meters past the pedestrian. And then the taxi should move backward slowly until reaching the pedestrian. How does the code shown below actually work?

```
do in order
    taxi  move  FORWARD , 6.0 , duration 1.2  add detail
    taxi  move  BACKWARD , 3.0 , duration 2.5  add detail
```

    (a) The taxi moves forward fast and then moves backward slowly, which is the expected behavior.
    (b) The taxi moves forward slowly and then moves back quickly. The durations must be swapped.
    (c) The taxi moves forward and backward at the same speed.

22. Other than duration, what parameters have default values that might be given arguments for a *move* statement?

23. Assume you are creating an animation in which a police car is driving south (relative to the local geographic region). Suddenly, the driver receives a radio communication to pursue a car that is 500 meters to the north. Of course, the police car must make a U-turn and then drive north. Consider the following code:

```
declare procedure myFirstMethod
do in order
    policeCar  move  FORWARD , 5.0 , add detail
    policeCar  turn  LEFT , 1.0  add detail
    policeCar  move  BACKWARD , 5.0  add detail
```

    When the code is tested, which of the following occurs?
    (a) The car makes a U turn and then drives north in an appropriate manner.
    (b) It has a bug. The car makes a 360-degree turn, instead of a 180-degree turn.
    (c) It has a bug. The car turns left and then drives east.
    (d) It has two bugs: The car makes a 360-degree turn and continues driving south.

24. Tashi is dancing. Match each set of Alice statements with the best movement description. Not all descriptive matches are used.

```
    Tashi  getHead  turn  BACKWARD , 0.07  add detail
    Tashi  getHead  turn  FORWARD , 0.07  add detail
```
1.

```
    Tashi  getRightHip  turn  BACKWARD , 0.07  add detail
    Tashi  getRightHip  turn  FORWARD , 0.07  add detail
```
2.

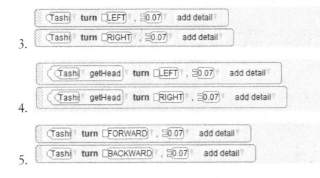

3.

4.

5.

Descriptions:

a. Tashi jumps   e. Tashi raises hand
b. Tashi says "no" with head   f. Tashi levitates
c. Tashi bows   g. Tashi kicks
d. Tashi says "yes" with head   h. Tashi dances

25. Match each phrase on the left with a term on the right.

A decimal number contains a(n)   sequentially
To debug is to   an iterative process
Comments are intended for   revolutions
Incremental development is   a human reader
A turn is measured in   simple steps
A text string is enclosed within   decimal point
A duration is a(n)   fix a bug
A move amount is measured in   optional argument
A *do in order* executes code   to execute code
To run is the same as   quote marks
To decompose is to divide into   meters

Exercises

....

1. If not already done, re-create the code in the Episode 1 project, as illustrated in the narrative of this chapter. The starting world (Episode1Starter.a3p) may be downloaded at:

   https://www.alice.org/AliceToJava

   Modify the code to provide a more dramatic hand wriggle and have Tashi jump (quickly move up and down) when she sees the hand's motion.

2. Trit the toucan doesn't have enough money to afford a gym membership, but he likes to swing on century plant branches. Create the scene shown here and then write code for an animation where Trit swings around the branch three times (*turn*). Each swing should have a shorter duration than the previous one. After three swings, Trit gets dizzy and falls from the branch to the ground (*moveTo*).

3. Create an underwater scene with a cave, snail house, dolphin, and pajama fish (Ocean theme). The dolphin is facing away from the pajama fish, as shown.

Write code to have the pajama fish and dolphin play a game of "hide and seek," where the fish hides in the snail house and the dolphin swims around the cave and snail house looking for her fishy friend. Use a *turnToFace* statement to have the fish face the snail house before moving forward to hide in the house. Also, have the dolphin swim in a rectangular path around the snail house and cave, as illustrated in this diagram:

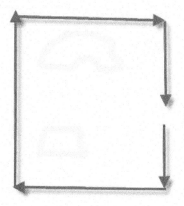

4. Using the scene setup as in Exercise 3, add a starfish to the scene, positioned between the cave and the snail house. Once again, write code to have the pajama fish and dolphin play a game of "hide and seek," where the fish hides in the snail house and the dolphin swims around looking for her fishy friend. In this version, however, do not have the dolphin swim in a rectangular path around the snail house. Instead, use a statement to have the dolphin turn one complete revolution around the cave and snail house, *asSeenBy* the starfish. *asSeenBy* is a detail parameter that causes an object to perform an action using another object as its center of rotation. In this example, the dolphin should swim a large circle around the house and cave, as if the starfish was the dolphin's center of rotation.

The Train Engine

Tashi disappears behind a snow drift. Larry rattles around the corner to discover nothing but fresh, pristine snow, glistening in the setting sun. He stops suddenly, his leg going through the snow up to his thigh. Trying to walk in this with his legs in their current state is worse than walking on stilts. He trudges through the deep snow for a few more steps until, without warning, instead of hitting solid ground his foot hits empty air. He drops through the hole hidden by a snow drift and hits ice. The bones making up his body split apart and clatter to the floor in a pile.

Falling apart is a surprisingly painless experience.

"Having trouble?" Tashi mocks, calmly swinging around a stalagmite.

Frustration burns through the skeleton. He can feel a strange sort of blush heat the white of his skull. The anger makes his bones rattle and hum, and with a snap, every piece pops back in place.

Tashi stops twirling about and stares.

"Aha!" Larry yells, pouncing on Tashi and wrestling his hat away from the creature's icy claws. Larry straightens up grandly, rolling his hat back onto his head, feeling properly himself again. And for the first time, he takes a good look around the cave. His jaw dislocates and drops open far wider than humanly possible.

His precious steam engine lies before him, half-buried in the snow and covered in a thick layer of frost. He skedaddles toward it and runs his hands along the boiler. His body goes cold, the freezing temperature of the metal quickly seeping into his bones. But his mind hardly registers the change.

"Do you know how to make it work?" Tashi asks curiously.

"Of course," Larry replies, "Surely you know how to work a simple steam engine."

"Yeah, but. This one looks like it was dug out of a scrap heap," Tashi explains.

"It was," Larry says, grinning, "dug out of moss and brought back to life."

"Can you show me?"

"The moss I unearthed it from is somewhere far away ..." Larry says quietly.

"No, show me how the engine runs!" Tashi demands.

"Yes," an idea begins to form in the skeleton's skull, "Yes, I'll get it running for you."

Tashi claps her hands excitedly, her ivory nails clacking together.

Larry climbs into the cabin and pries the fire box door open.

"Are you going to help me?" he asks, sticking his head out the door.

"I can't," Tashi holds up her hands apologetically, "the metal is too cold to touch."

"I guess there are advantages to being a living skeleton, then," he responds, "hand me up any wood you can find."

"I'll ask to borrow some firewood," Tashi runs off deeper into the cave.

When the baby yeti returns, instead of giving Larry the firewood, she starts stacking it into a pit and then lights it. The metal begins to heat, and the snow and ice melt, filling the cave with steam.

"Baby!" a loud, low, growling voice calls from around the corner. "Baby, what are you doing with that wood?"

Tashi gulps and looks guilty, "nothing, mother."

Larry pokes his head out of the cabin window. A huge, ten-foot-tall, full-grown yeti stands with hands on hips, glaring at the shorter yeti below. Mama's foot could neatly squash baby without hardly any trouble.

"Look who I brought home!" Tashi announces, exuding false cheer and gesturing towards the skeleton.

"Oh, honey," the mother yeti sighs. "You're not befriending the food again are you?"

"Awwww, mom ..."

"Baby," the mother scolds, "surely you remember the lecture about Stockholm syndrome ..."

"I know, I know," Tashi whines.

"A creature of prey befriended by a predator ...," the mother starts.

"... is not a friend at all because hostages often empathize and identify with the captor in order to make them seem less a threat ..." Tashi recites in a sing-song voice as if hearing this lecture often.

"Pardon me," Larry interrupts, waving at the mother, "but I don't empathize or identify with your child at all. And an already dead skeleton would make a very poor meal, so technically none of those theories apply to our situation."

The mother yeti stares at Larry for a full minute with unblinking, intense eyes above her fanged mouth. Then a small gust of hot air steams from her thin lips. She closes her eyes as if burdened by a lower life form frustratingly more intelligent than her and she's too tired to do anything about it and says, "Fine," her eyes flutter open and turn to the baby yeti, "Don't stay up too late." And with that done, she retreats further into the cave.

"Yes!" Tashi punches her fist in the air and turns back to the train.

5

Procedures, *do together,* and Count Loops

Concept Objectives

- Declaring a custom procedure for a class of objects
  - Select the class
  - Create a declaration statement
  - Naming conventions
  - Code editor panels and *this*
- Writing code to define a custom procedure

- Calling a custom procedure
- Using *do together* for simultaneous execution
- Write procedure once, call many times
- Using nested code blocks
- Using a count loop for repetition

In this chapter, **custom procedures**, *do together*, and the *count loop* control structure will be introduced. A custom procedure is a procedure written by the programmer, as opposed to a built-in procedure in the Alice software system. The *do together* control structure creates a code block and tells Alice to execute code statements within that block concurrently (simultaneously). A *count* loop is a control structure that creates a code block for repetition. At runtime, Alice executes the code statements within a *count* loop a counted number of times.

The concepts and techniques of writing code with custom procedures, *do together* and *count* loops will be illustrated with a programming example to animate a script based on a selected segment of the *Haunted Circus* Episode 2, *The Train Engine*. In this episode, Larry discovers the frozen circus train steam engine in Tashi's cave. The train is Larry's most prized possession—It was "home" for him and members of the circus troupe. Tashi is intrigued by the engine and wants to see it run. The same problem-solving steps described and illustrated in Chapters 1 through 4 will be applied in this and other chapter examples in this textbook.

5.1 Story Analysis

The first step is to read and analyze the story to determine its background components and select the objects and actions for an animation script. A part of *The Train Engine* episode, selected and adapted for an animation example (the program task) in this chapter, is summarized here:

> Larry's train turns out to have been frozen inside the baby yeti's cave all along. To melt the ice off his train, Larry asks Tashi if she knows where he could find wood to start a fire. But when Tashi leaves and returns with an armful of firewood, she ignores Larry and starts assembling her own fire pit. Larry climbs down from the cab and watches, skeptical that an itty bitty yeti can melt the ice off his train if he can't do it himself. Tashi succeeds in lighting the wood and yells "fire!" boastfully. The ice on the train melts in seconds. Surprised, Larry begins to take Tashi a little more seriously. Tashi herself is smug; she knew her value all along.

As in the first programming example, this example selects and adapts a small portion of the episode for the purpose of creating an animation. Not every detail from the original writing is included, and some details are changed. The background information in Episode 2 is the same as in Episode 1: a snow-covered mountain scene where the skeleton and yeti are standing beside a train engine that is buried in ice. One analysis of the selected story excerpt could be

> **Larry rejects** Tashi's offer to help melt the ice from the train.
> **Larry scoffs** at Tashi.
> Insulted, **Tashi starts a flame** to prove Larry wrong.
> **Tashi gets excited** and is a bit pleasantly surprised that her plan actually works.
> The **flame grows and melts** the ice.

5.2 Design

The story analysis above provides a starting point for design. Based on the story analysis, props can be selected for the background and the characters and actions selected for animating a segment of the story. Then the flow of the actions can be designed with a full storyboard. First, take the time to draw a basic composition shot of the initial scene. The storyboard shown (Figure 5.1) has six frames. The first frame (upper left) depicts the initial scene.

Figure 5.1 • *Storyboard with six frames*

An *algorithm* for the task, derived from the storyboard, is shown in Figure 5.2. Note that the flow of steps in the algorithm is closely related to the storyboard, though some variation is likely.

> *Do in order*
>
> > Larry says "You can't melt the ice off my train."
> > Larry says "You're nothing but an itty bitty Yeti."
> > Tashi jumps and yells "FIRE!"
> > flames appear and grow larger
> > flames flicker and the ice melts away from the engine

Figure 5.2 • *Algorithm for the* Thaw *animation*

Based on the set design in the first frame of the storyboard, an Alice project world named *ThawStarter.a3p* has been prepared as a starter world for this example. The name of the starter world reflects the major action in the animation, thawing the ice from the train. The starter world may be downloaded from **www.alice.org/Alice3ToJava**.

Download the project. Then start Alice 3 and open the downloaded world. If successfully downloaded, the initial scene should appear as shown in Figure 5.3. A logs object is positioned between Tashi and Larry, who are standing in front of the ice-covered train engine. Two objects are hidden in this scene: flames (located below ground, beneath the logs) and a non-iced train engine (same location as the iced train engine). These objects are used in exercises at the end of the chapter.

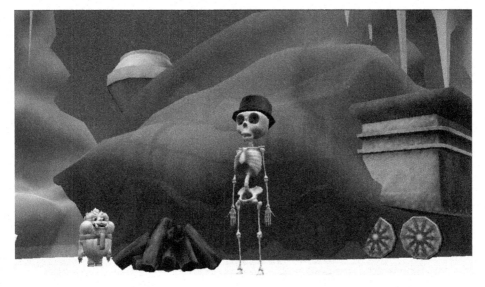

Figure 5.3   *The initial scene in the* ThawStarter.a3p *project world*

5.3 Implement and Test

The next step is to implement the code. Click on the *myFirstMethod* tab in the Code editor. Notice comments have already been entered to document the algorithm (Figure 5.4).

Figure 5.4   *Comments in* myFirstMethod

The entire first half of the algorithm is a conversation between Tashi and Larry. When the story script begins, Tashi has offered to help Larry melt the ice from his train, but Larry doubts her ability to help. Create a statement to have Larry say, "You can't melt the ice off my train." Position the *say* statement immediately below the first comment and add a *duration* of 2.5 seconds (Figure 5.5).

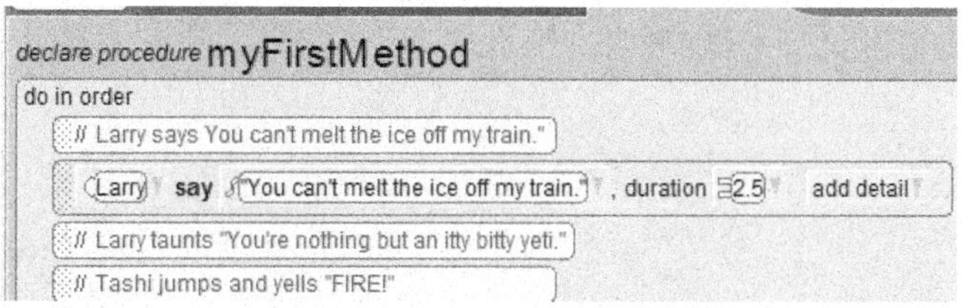

Figure 5.5 A say *statement with a 2.5-second* duration

Click the Run button to test the *say* statement. A *duration* of 2.5 seconds was selected to allow the human reader time to read the words in the speech bubble.

The *say* statement makes a speech bubble appear above a character's head, but typically when a character says something, the mouth moves in a talking motion. Larry doesn't have a "talk" procedure to simulate a talking action.

5.4 Declare a Custom Procedure

Talking is a common action in storytelling animations, so let's write a custom *talk* procedure that could be reused in this and other projects. A decomposition for simulating a talking action is shown in Figure 5.6.

```
Do in order

    mouth turn forward 0.15 revolutions
    mouth turn backward 0.15 revolutions
```

Figure 5.6 *Decomposition for* talk

A custom procedure must be declared and defined as a method in a class. A procedure is declared by writing a **procedure header**, a procedure declaration statement that gives a name to the procedure. Then, in the procedure's code block, statements are written that tell Alice how to perform the action. In Alice, general guidelines for declaring a custom procedure include

- If only one type of object performs actions in the decomposition steps, declare the procedure in the class that defines that type of object.
- If more than one object performs actions in the decomposition steps and the objects are of different types, declare the procedure in the Scene class.

Note: These guidelines will be revisited and expanded in later chapters. In this example, Larry is the object doing the talking. Larry is an instance of the Skeleton class, so a *talk* procedure will be declared and defined in the Skeleton class. To declare a custom procedure in Alice, follow the steps in Figure 5.7.

(1) Select the Class menu in the Code editor.

(2) Select the Skeleton class in the menu of classes.

(3) Click Add Skeleton Procedure in the cascading menu.

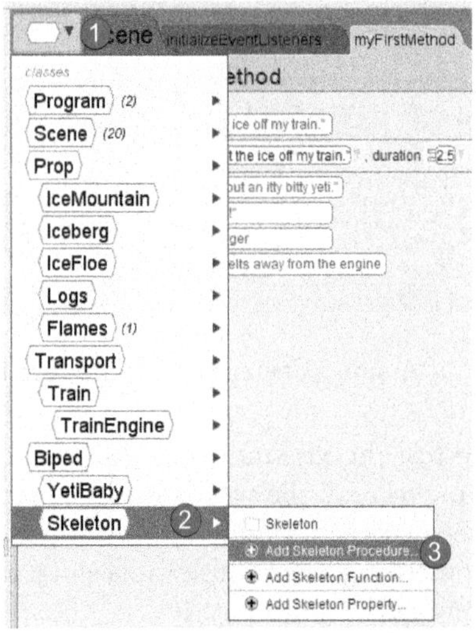

Figure 5.7   *Add a custom procedure to the Skeleton class.*

5.4.1 Name a custom procedure

A dialog box is displayed where the name of the procedure must be entered (Figure 5.8). Enter *talk* and then click the **OK** button.

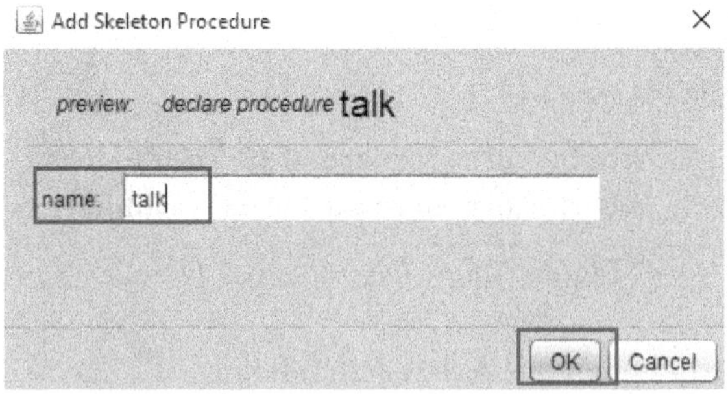

Figure 5.8   *Naming a custom procedure*

The name of a procedure is expected to be self-documenting. A name is self-documenting if it sufficiently describes the action performed by the procedure. In this example, the name *talk* is more self-documenting than a generic name such as *procedure1* or *xyz*. Programming languages often have conventions for naming procedures, functions, and other identifying components. A naming convention is a set of rules, agreed upon and typically used by programmers for naming objects, files, and data elements. Alice conventions for naming methods and objects include

- Begin a name with a lowercase letter, from *a* to *z*.
- The rest of the name may include lowercase and uppercase letters and digits. Do not use special characters such as +, −, %, !, or quote marks.
- Write the name as all one word, with no spaces. If multiple words are desired, use camelCase, beginning the first word in lowercase and additional words beginning

with an uppercase letter. This convention is known as camelCase because capital letters within the name resemble the humps on the back of a camel.

When the OK button is clicked, new tabs are displayed in the Code editor. In this example, the Skeleton class tab is automatically added to the Code editor, and a procedure tab for *talk* is automatically inserted just to the right of the Skeleton class tab. The Skeleton class is now the active class, and the *talk* procedure is now the active editor tab in the Code editor (Figure 5.9). At the top of the new *talk* editing tab, Alice displays the procedure header—a line of code that declares the procedure, giving it a name. The rest of the *talk* tab is the editing space, where the code for the custom procedure will be implemented.

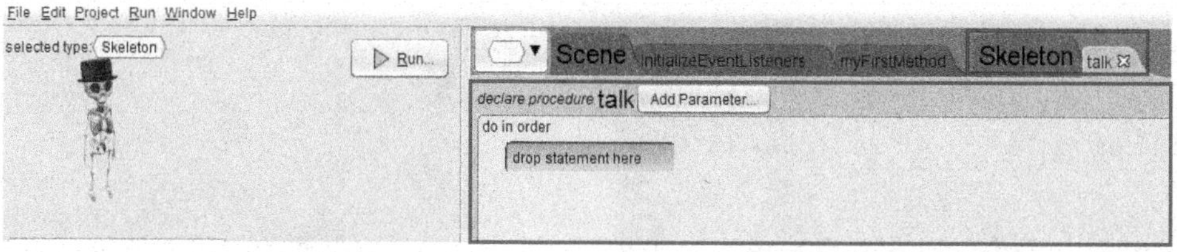

Figure 5.9 *New editor tabs are displayed when a custom procedure is declared.*

5.4.2 Code editor panels and *this*

To the left of the editor tabs, the Camera view panel now displays an image of a typical object belonging to the Skeleton class. The Object selector displays a miniature image of a skeleton object and the name *this*. And *talk* is now listed in the Procedures tab, within the list of procedure tiles for the Skeleton class (Figure 5.10).

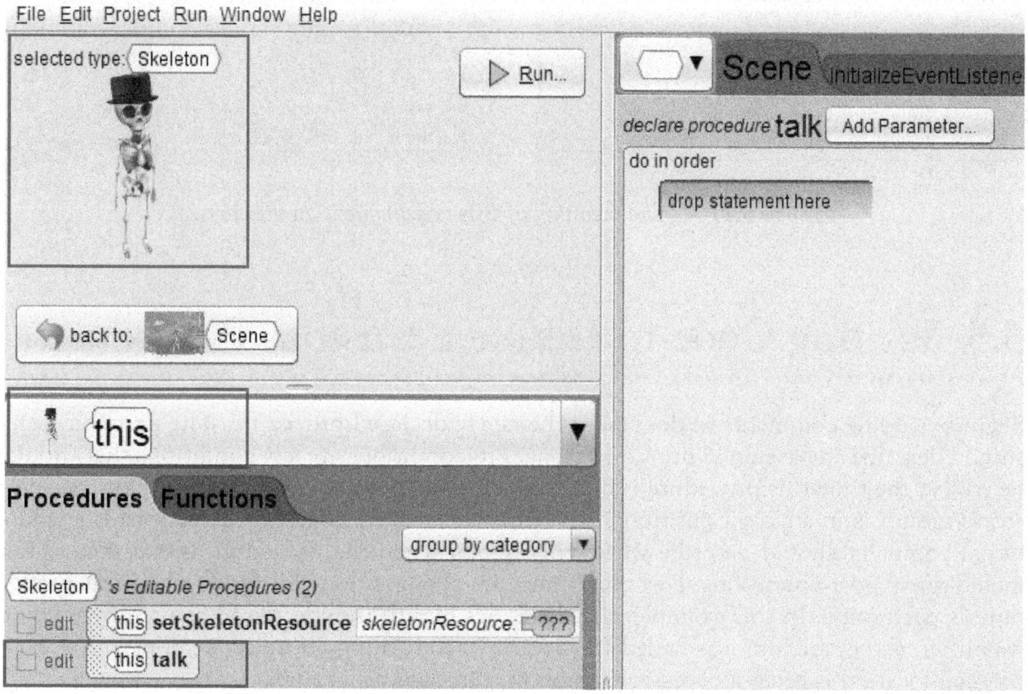

Figure 5.10 *The* talk *procedure is declared in the Skeleton class.*

Just as in our everyday conversations, the word "this" is dependent on the context in which it is used. For example, you might say, "This is my coat" when taking a coat from a coat rack. Or, you might say, "I need to answer this," when receiving a call on your cell phone. When a method (procedure or function) of the Scene class is selected, *this* refers to "this scene" (Figure 5.11, left). When a method of a class other than Scene is declared, *this* refers to any object of that class (Figure 5.11, right). In the case of the Skeleton class, *this* refers to any "this skeleton." In this example, Larry is the only skeleton, but if two or three skeletons were in the world, each would be able to talk.

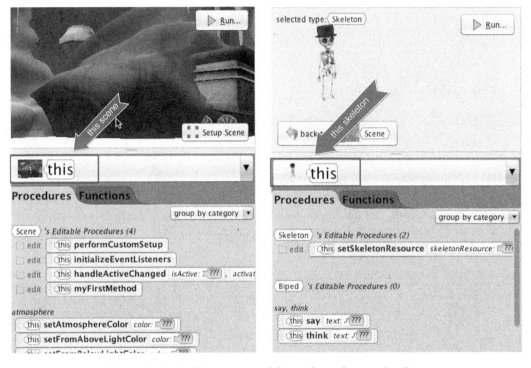

Figure 5.11   *The meaning of* this *is dependent on the class.*

5.5 Writing Code to Define a Custom Procedure

Begin by adding comments to document the newly declared procedure. The first comment should describe any **assumed pre-conditions**. Pre-conditions are any conditions that should be true at the time this procedure is called. In this example, we are assuming that the skeleton's mouth is in a closed position at the time the procedure is called. At least one additional comment should describe what will happen when the procedure is executed. This includes any **post-conditions**. Post-conditions are changes that will result when this procedure is performed. In this example, the skeleton's mouth is expected to return to where it was when the procedure was called (Figure 5.12). Returning an object's subparts to their original location is often a necessary action in a custom procedure.

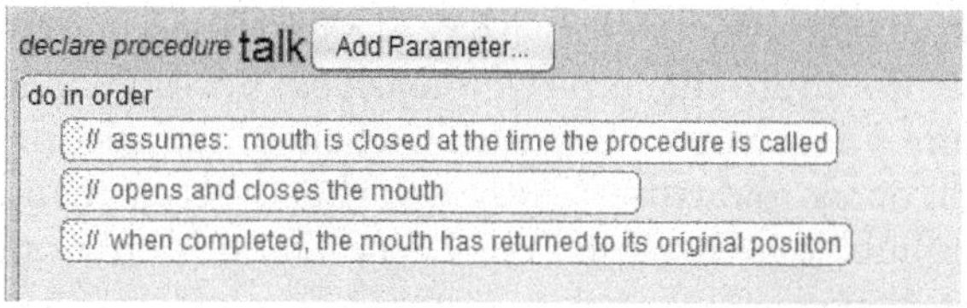

declare procedure **talk** Add Parameter...
do in order
// assumes: mouth is closed at the time the procedure is called
// opens and closes the mouth
// when completed, the mouth has returned to its original posiiton

Figure 5.12 *Assumptions and changes in object state should be documented.*

Next, translate the design decomposition into code statements. For convenience, the design decomposition for *talk* is repeated here in Figure 5.13.

Do in order

mouth turn forward 0.15 revolutions
mouth turn backward 0.15 revolutions

Figure 5.13 *Decomposition for talk*

Select this skeleton's mouth in the Object selector of the Methods panel. Then, drag the *turn* procedure into the editor to create two *turn* statements, one that turns the mouth FORWARD and a second that turns the mouth BACKWARD 0.15 revolutions. Set the duration to 0.25 seconds for each statement, for a total of 0.5 seconds (Figure 5.14).

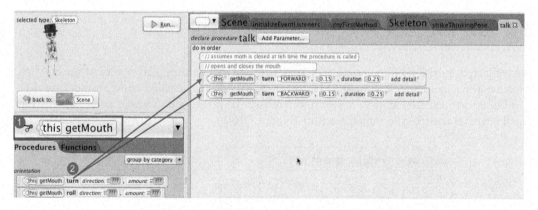

Figure 5.14 *Calls to the mouth's* turn *procedure*

5.6 Calling a Custom Procedure

If you have not done so recently, we suggest you save the project and then test-run. When the project runs, the scene appears in the runtime window and the speech bubble is displayed, but Larry's mouth does not open and close.

Think about what happens when the Run button is clicked. The scene is activated and displayed in the runtime window and then *myFirstMethod* is called. *myFirstMethod* is executed but the code we have written is in the *talk* procedure, not in *myFirstMethod*. A procedure only executes when it is called. A statement is needed to call (tell Alice to execute) the *talk* procedure. Defining the procedure (writing the code statements in the procedure) is not a call to the procedure.

To resolve this issue, click the tab for *myFirstMethod*. Select Larry in the Object selector. Then, drag the *talk* procedure tile into *myFirstMethod*, positioning it immediately under the *say* statement (Figure 5.15). Now, when Run is clicked, the speech bubble is displayed and then Larry's mouth opens and closes. Although this is better than before, we still have a problem. The speech bubble is displayed but Larry's mouth only opens and closes after the speech bubble goes away.

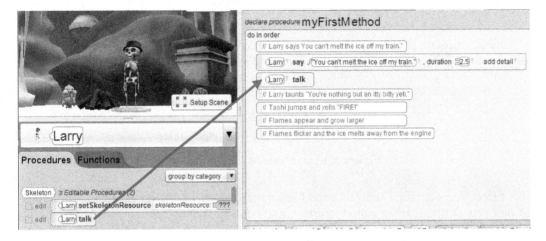

Figure 5.15   *Create a statement in* myFirstMethod *that calls the* talk *procedure.*

5.7 *do together*

As indicated by the *do in order* control structure at the beginning of *myFirstMethod*, Alice executes the statements in sequence. However, Alice has a *do together* control structure that can be used to execute statements simultaneously. To create a *do together* code block, drag the *do together* control tile into the editor (Figure 5.16).

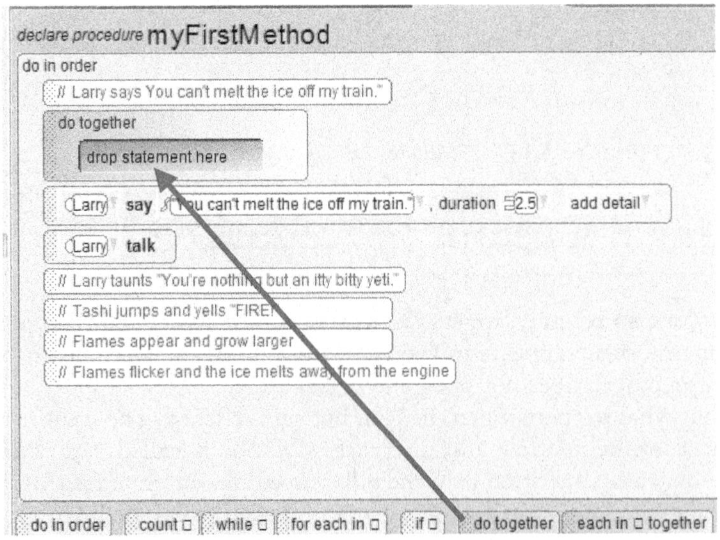

Figure 5.16   *Drag the* do together *tile into the editor tab.*

Next, drag the *say* and *talk* statements into the *do together* code block. The result is shown in Figure 5.17. Test-run the code.

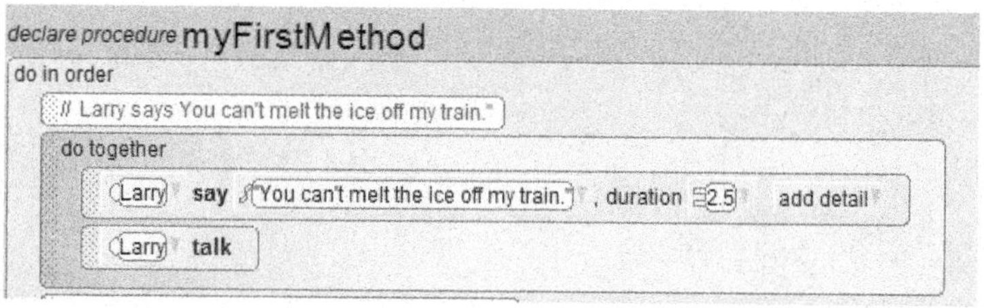

Figure 5.17 • *Resulting* do together *code block*

5.8 Multiple Calls to a Custom Procedure

When the code is tested, you will notice that Larry's mouth opens and closes only once, but there are many words in the sentence. A good imitation of talking should have the mouth open and close several times while the speech bubble remains on the screen (2.5 seconds). Because one execution of *talk* takes only 0.5 seconds, the *talk* action should be executed five (2.5/0.5 = 5) times.

This is a major advantage in writing a custom procedure: **code reuse**. Once the *talk* procedure has been written, it can be called again and again in many places in the program. In other words, the *talk* procedure becomes a building-block for creating animations in the same way as built-in Alice procedures (*move, turn, roll, say,* etc.). The goal of writing a custom procedure is to "write once, use many times."

One way to create repeated calls to a procedure is to drag the tile from the procedures tab into the editor again and again. However, Alice has a **copy-and-paste** keyboard shortcut you may find convenient. To use the copy-and-paste shortcut, press and hold the keyboard CTRL key (OPTION/ALT on Mac) and use the cursor to drag and drop a copy of the statement. Notice in Figure 5.18 the copied tile is displayed with a shadow/grid until it is dropped into position. Continue to hold the cursor down until the CTRL key is released.

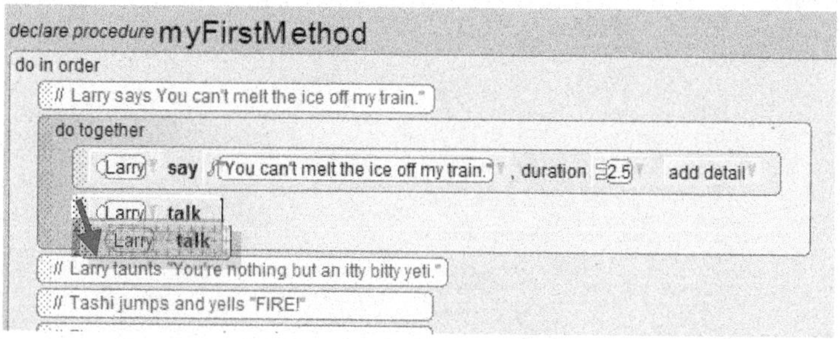

Figure 5.18 • *Use a copy-and-paste keyboard shortcut.*

Use the copy-and-paste shortcut to create five statements that repeatedly call the *talk* procedure (Figure 5.19).

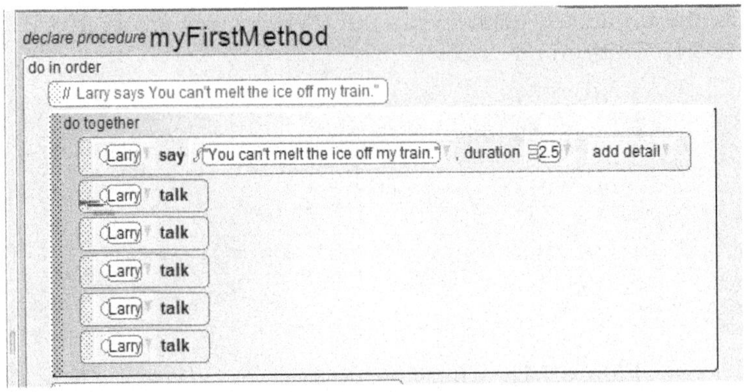

Figure 5.19   *Five calls to the* talk *procedure*

5.9 Nested Code Blocks

After creating the five *talk* statements, test-run. You will see that Larry still opens and closes his mouth only once! This is because the five statements are all within the *do together* code block and are, therefore, executed at the same time. Although we want the repeated *talk* procedure calls to be executed at the same time as the speech bubble is displayed, we also want the five *talk* procedure calls to be executed in sequence.

One way to resolve this issue is to make use of a **nested code block**. A nested code block is one code block totally enclosed within another code block. Create a *do in order* code block and nest it within the *do together* code block. Then, drag the five *talk* statements into the *do in order* (Figure 5.20). Now, when tested, you should see the *say* speech bubble display on screen for 2.5 seconds and, at the same time, Larry's mouth open and close five times in sequence.

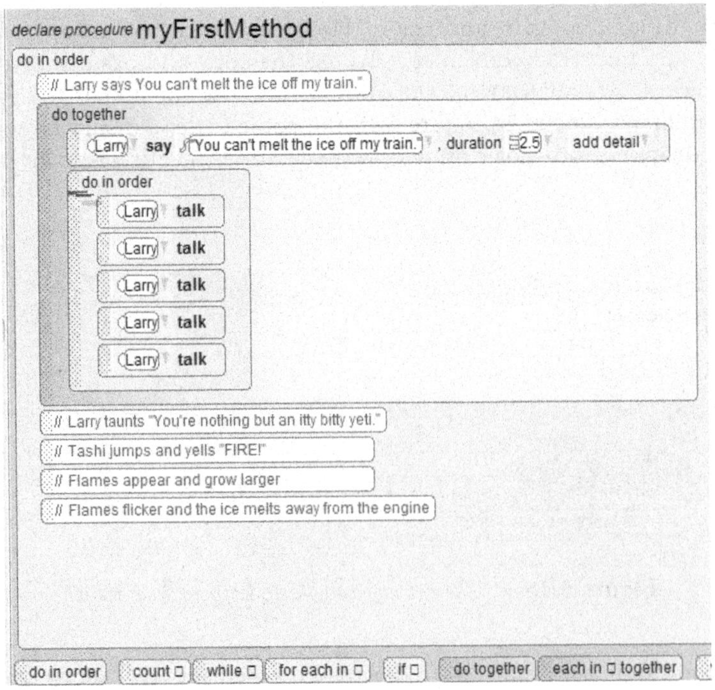

Figure 5.20   *Repeated calls to* talk *in a nested* do in order

Conversation is needed to tell the story, but animated body actions are also needed to convey the emotions and motivations of the characters in a story or game. For example, an important component in this episode of the Haunted Circus story is Larry's doubt that Tashi can help in melting the ice and snow from the train engine. The code above implements Larry's verbal expression. But Larry's doubt could be more strongly communicated by body actions that would convey some of the emotion of Larry's doubt. Such statements provide **body language** that helps tell the story. For inspiration, look again at the top right frame in the storyboard (Figure 5.21). The sketch in the storyboard shows Larry with his body turned and his torso bent forward to look at Tashi.

Figure 5.21   *Use body language to communicate emotion.*

Statements to implement Larry turning his body and bending forward to look at Tashi may be added in a *do together* code block (Figure 5.22).

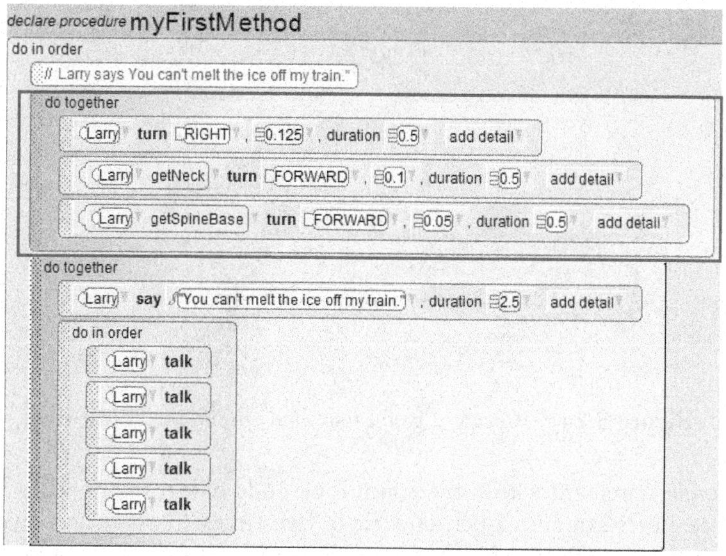

Figure 5.22   *Statements added in a* do together *code block*

5.10 Repetition with a *Count* Loop

Repeated writing of the same *talk* statement five times in the *do in order* code block may seem a bit tedious. It would be even more annoying if it were ten, twenty, or even a hundred statements. To provide a quick and easy way to handle repetition, Alice has a *count* code structure. A count code structure repeats execution of a code block a counted number of times. Because count is repetitive, it is known as a **count loop**. Many programming languages have count loops, often referred to as a **for loop** because it repeats **for** a counted number of times.

To illustrate how the repetition works, let's remove the *do in order* code block and replace it with a count loop. Right-click on the left margin of the *do in order* code block and then select Delete from the pop-up menu, (Figure 5.23).

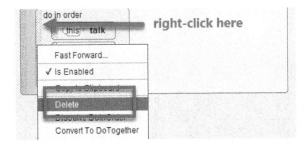

Figure 5.23   *Deleting a code block*

Now, (1) drag the count tile from the Control panel into the code editor and drop it where the *do in order* was previously located. A popup menu prompts for a loop control value that determines the number of repetitions. In this example, choose (2) Custom WholeNumber. (3) In the pop-up number pad, enter 5 as the number of repetitions, and (4) click OK (Figure 5.24).

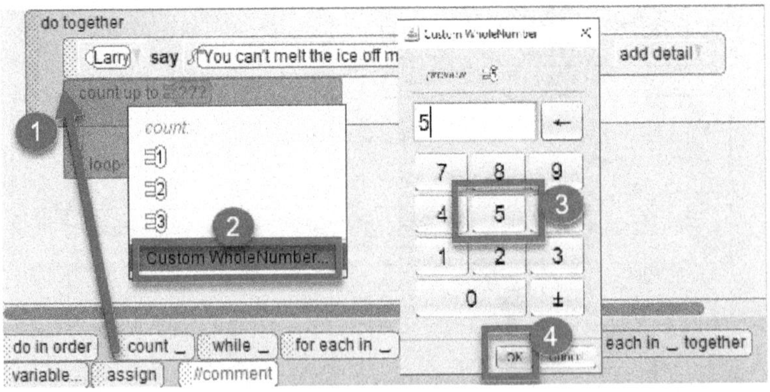

Figure 5.24   *Create a count loop and specify the* count *value*

Create a *talk* statement within the count loop code block, Figure 5.25. Test run again. You should see Larry's mouth open and close five times in sequence. Even though the count code block is nested within a *do together*, the count loop executes five times in sequence.

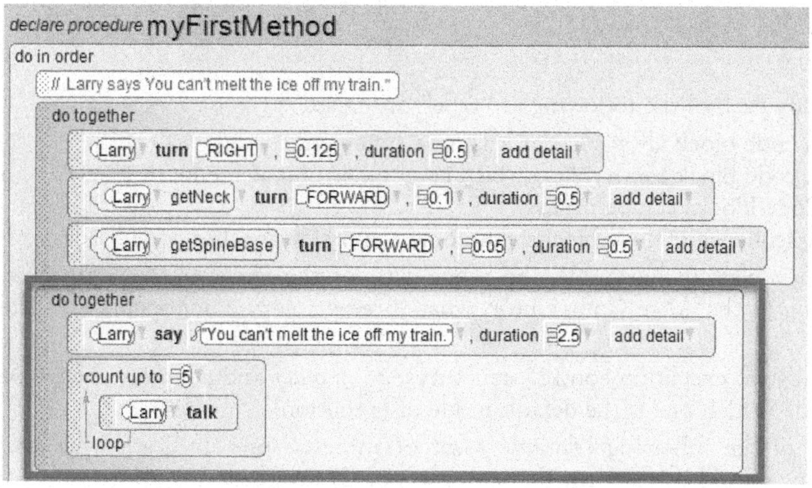

Figure 5.25 • *Completed* count loop, *nested within a* do together

In the second step of the algorithm, Larry taunts Tashi and insults her by saying, "You're nothing but an itty bitty yeti." Statements may be added with "body language" animated actions to help convey Larry's message. For example, he might extend his arms and wave "No" with his hands. Completion of the remaining steps in the algorithm is left as exercises. The exercises are intended to provide an opportunity for you to practice and experiment with writing custom procedures and using *do together*.

Summary

In this chapter, the programming example animates an adaptation of a segment of Episode 2 in the *Haunted Circus* story. The animation provides a context for introducing the fundamentals of writing your own custom procedure for a class of objects and using the *do together* control structure. To define your own custom procedure, the procedure must be declared for a specific class of objects, given a name, and then defined by writing code statements within the procedure. In Alice, a procedure defined for a class may then be used by any object of that type. For example, the *talk* procedure illustrated in this chapter was written for the Skeleton class. Therefore, any skeleton object in the scene would be able to talk. An important goal of writing custom procedures is code reuse: write once and call many times.

Adding a *do together* control structure creates a code block in your code. Statements within a *do together* code block are executed simultaneously. A *do in order* code block and a *do together* code block may be nested, one inside the other, to allow some actions to occur sequentially while other actions occur simultaneously.

Terms

assumed pre-condition	copy-and-paste keyboard	nested code block
body language	shortcut	procedure declaration
call a procedure	custom procedure	procedure header
camelCase	*do together*	post-condition
code reuse	naming convention	self-documenting name

Concept Questions

1. Identify each of the following as "true" or "false."
   (a) A code block always has at least one statement.
   (b) A code block can have an arbitrary number of statements.
   (c) Code blocks can be nested.
   (d) A sequence of code blocks can be nested inside another code block.

2. When a class (for example, the Scene class or the Skeleton class) tab is opened for editing in the Alice Code editor, what three primary components are listed on the tab?

3. So far, two execution control structures, *do in order* and *do together*, have been introduced. Which one is the default mode of execution?

4. Each of the following contains a set of three actions. Indicate whether the three actions should be performed (1) in order, or (2) together.
   (a) Pedal a bike, steer a bike, and whistle (biking).
   (b) Chop an onion, turn on the stove, and break an egg (cook with a recipe).
   (c) Wash hands, brush teeth, and dry hands (after eating a meal).
   (d) Sing, move limbs, and move body (dancing).
   (e) Dig a hole in the ground, place a seed into the hole, and cover the hole.
   (f) Hold an umbrella, walk, and listen to your friend's voice message on a cell phone.
   (g) Cover eyes, count, and listen (playing hide and seek game).

5. Group the following concepts by their equivalence: do in order, do together, simultaneous, sequential, concurrent, parallel, and series. Explain the differences between the groups you create.

6. (a) Is the order of the statements relevant in a *do in order* code block? (b) Is the order of the statements relevant in a *do together* code block? Explain your answers.

7. A 1-second statement and a 2-second statement comprise a code block. What is the total block duration if it is:
   (a) a *do in order* block.
   (b) a *do together* block.

8. What is meant when we describe a procedure as "custom" as opposed to saying a procedure is "built in"?

9. When writing a custom procedure:
   (a) What is documented by a pre-condition comment?
   (b) What is documented by a post-condition comment?

10. A custom procedure is proposed for Larry in which he will raise his arms toward his face to protect himself from a snowball. Which of the following potential names is most self-documenting?
    (a) protect
    (b) xyz
    (c) protectFace
    (d) protectFaceWithArms

11. In the following list, select all the names that adhere to camelCase conventions for naming procedures.
    (a) pickBackpackUp
    (b) mAkEAphOnecAll
    (c) HitTheCeiling
    (d) eat
    (e) 2hit3UFOs
    (f) sleep_and_snork
    (g) oopsOuchEek

12. Does adhering to a naming convention, such as camelCase, ensure that your procedure names will always be meaningful?

13. Why does Scene remain the active class when Larry is selected in the Object selector?

14. What is the difference between *defining* a procedure and *calling* a procedure?

15. How many times is a procedure defined in a class?

16. Each of the following describes a custom procedure that might be written for the example code in this chapter. For each one, indicate the class (*Scene, Skeleton, YetiBaby, TrainEngine, Logs,* or *Flames*) where the procedure would best be written.
    (a) The fire gradually dies.
    (b) The fire dies, and the logs sink into the ground.
    (c) A skeleton performs a hip-hop dance move.
    (d) A tunnel appears in an *iceMountain*, and a train engine moves through it.

17. What advantage do programmers gain from writing custom procedures?

18. An object's *resize* procedure requires a factor argument (a decimal number). What is the visible effect on the object if the factor is:
    (a) higher than 1.0?
    (b) 1.0?
    (c) greater than 0.0 but less than 1.0?
    (d) 0.0?
    (e) less than 0.0?

19. In the animation example shown in this chapter, Larry can call the *talk* procedure, but Tashi cannot. Explain why this is so.

20. What is the purpose of a count loop?

Exercises

· · · · · · · · · · · · · · · · · · · ·

If you did not create the *Thaw.a3p* project as presented in this chapter, you may do so now or perhaps obtain a copy from your instructor. Exercises 2 though 6 describe custom procedures that may be written to complete the implementation of the algorithm for the *Thaw* project. In each exercise, create a custom procedure for the action, then call the procedure from *myFirstMethod* to test-run. If any bugs are found, debug so the code runs as expected. When the procedures are properly implemented, the train engine should be visible with no snow and ice around it.

1. In *myFirstMethod*, add code to implement the step where Larry insults Tashi by saying she is nothing but an itti bitti yeti. Use a count loop to have Larry's mouth talk at the same time as the speech bubble is displayed.

2. Create a simple *jump* custom procedure in the *YetiBaby* class. The *jump* procedure should have Tashi quickly move up and then down a short distance. Test the procedure by calling it from myFirstMethod and have Tashi yell "FIRE!!!" at the same time.

3. Revise the *jump* custom procedure to have Tashi extend her arms upward at the same time as she jumps up and return her arms to their original position as she moves back down. Hint: Extending the arms upward uses both *turn* and *roll* for the shoulder joints.

4. The starter scene has a flames object (an instance of the Flames class) hidden about 0.3 m. below the logs. Add statements to *myFirstMethod* to have the flames appear after Tashi jumps and yells, "FIRE!" To make the flames appear, the flames must *move* upward and grow larger (*resize*) at the same time. **Hint:** Experiment with using the *flame* object's built-in *resize* procedure. Notice that the *resize* procedure has a parameter named *factor*. Use a factor greater than 1 to make an object increase in size.

5. Create a custom procedure to have the flames object *flicker*—that is, alternately grow larger and fade and then grow smaller and brighten. **Hint:** Experiment with using the *flame* object's built-in *opacity* procedure to fade and brighten. Test by calling *flicker* several times while the flames object appears (combine with Exercise 3).

6. The Iceberg class in the starter world has a pre-written *melt* procedure. Create a custom procedure that melts the two iceberg objects at the same time as the *trainEngine* object gradually fades away and the *trainEngine2* object gradually appears.

7. When Tashi fires the logs, have Larry throw up his arms in front of his face to protect his face from the heat of the flames. Then write code to have Larry return his body to its original position.

8. In this project, Wia the witch has realized she is missing an ingredient for the brew she is creating in her cauldron. She needs to fly to the nearest herb shop to find the ingredient. Add a small Cone object at the top-left corner of the scene and make it invisible. The cone will be a target for Wia's flight. Then create a custom procedure (named *diagonalFlight*) for the Scene class, in which Wia will fly off the screen in a diagonal motion with the cone as the target. A Witch Airlines starter world is available for download at **www.alice.org/Alice3ToJava**.

Projects

1. Create an Alice animation for the following story: A child, named Jack, has an alien friend. Jack is teaching his alien friend how to dance a "Moonwalk" step. First, Jack does the Moonwalk dance movement, and then the alien tries to replicate it. Jack is a very good dancer, but the poor alien has trouble learning all the quick leg and foot motions. Write procedures to have Jack do a Moonwalk dance movement and then have the alien do the exact same movements, but one step at a time.

2. Create an Alice animation for a story segment of your own selection. The project must include nested code blocks, custom procedures, and *do together*.

The Tunnel

In the cab, Larry cleans the debris from the bottom of the firebox. Scraping the leftover hardened ice off the grate would normally be impossible, but he seems to have acquired superhuman strength along with his sort of half-life state. Tashi lifts several extra pieces of wood up to him, and one by one he fills the grate. Larry reaches down for the last piece of wood and winds up holding a strange little red box instead. He looks to the baby yeti for explanation.

"A matchbox," Tashi says, "to start the fire. Take a match out, strike it against the rough side, and toss it in."

Larry does as instructed. The sudden ignition of the little wooden sticks into flame surprises him so much that each time he accidentally drops them on the wet ice where they fizzle out in seconds. Eventually he manages to light a match and carefully fling it onto the logs. Gradually, the fire starts to roar. Larry breaks up the ice covering the coal box hatch, digs deep to find relatively dry coal, and shovels it in on the right, left, back, and front to cover the entire box.

Tashi climbs into the cab and scoots closer to the firebox. She places her hands flat against the metal, "I can touch it! Ooooh, it's warm." Her hands wander up toward the steam pipe and she recoils when she hits it. "Hot! Very hot!" She slaps her hands against her fur and looks up at Larry in consternation.

Larry is sorely tempted to say in a very derisive drawl, "Of course."

But he doesn't get the chance because in that instant a metallic clank shakes the frozen stalactites hanging overhead, and the entire train engine jerks downward. The rumbling, grinding noise is loud and sudden and knocks both the skeleton and the baby yeti off their feet.

"What was that?" Tashi asks.

Without answering, Larry slides across the cab floor, still slick with melting ice, and drops out the door. The engine, which had previously been stuck crooked in the snowy ground, now rests easily on all ten wheels, facing the back wall of the cave. His mind starts to race, calculating the odds. There are no tracks. He grabs the oil can and administers it to the wheels. With the ground frozen, it would take an insurmountable amount of luck to steer the train straight. Larry adjusts the steam to full speed ... but the cave wall—a perfect flat surface, so smooth with ice he can see his emaciated reflection—the cave wall will work.

He grabs on to the engine bell's cord and drags down hard. It clangs once, then twice.

"What are you doing?" Tashi asks, pitching her voice high enough to be heard over the booming bell.

"Leaving!" Larry roars back. He pulls down again. Three.

"Where are you leaving?" Tashi asks.

"I don't know," he replies.

"You've nowhere to go except smashed against solid rock."

"Wrong," Larry says as the bell clangs for the fifth time. He holds his breath. Or he would hold his breath if he had any. At any rate, his rib cage goes still.

There is a false sense of calm before the storm, because his mind is racing and his nerves are at attention, waiting. A white flash of memory surfaces and the answer comes to him: this was the point when everything broke apart. "I'm going to look for the rest of my train."

"Well," Tashi considers this information, "then where are they?"

"I don't know," he yells.

"Take me with you," Tashi screams back, "you need me."

"No, I don't," he hollers back and yanks on the bell again.

"Do too!"

"Do not!" The seventh bell clang echoes on the cave walls. One more and then ... yellow light illuminates the cave. Tashi leans closer to the window to watch as, one by one, popcorn lights flicker into life all along the boiler and metal machinery of the train and the entire engine sparkles as if covered in fairy dust.

The wind hits next.

The gust comes from the opposite direction of what one might imagine when traveling on a train. It surges in behind Tashi and Larry and pushes them both forward insistently until they are smushed flush up against the front windows of the cab, like two umbrellas caught in a gale. Tashi's puffy cheeks flatten against the glass and force her eyes into a squint. Her nose pinches her forehead painfully. But she still manages to widen her eyes as the strong wind gusts swirl together in front of the cave wall and form strange grey clouds. The clouds harden like raw lamb's wool being teased into dryer lint until the strange substance looks stiff and hard as solid rock. The rocks seem to have formed a sort of three-quarter circle. Looking exactly like the entrance to ...

"A tunnel!" Tashi tries to say, except it comes out as "mwr tummeh" thanks to her face still pressed against the window with her breath fogging up the glass.

A bony hand grabs the scruff of her neck and yanks her off the window with a "smuck!" Larry holds her steady, bracing his own rattling bones with a foot against the brake.

"That's right," he says, "a tunnel. Last chance to get off."

"Never!" Tashi exclaims excitedly, breaking into a large smile.

"Be careful what you wish for," Larry warns bitterly. But a wry grin escapes him as he nudges the brake loose. The engine shudders and then lurches forward an inch. The wind speed increases, blowing all of Tashi's fur nearly horizontal, and the engine leaps forward another foot. And then it keeps going, and chugging, with the wind pushing, until finally it's seething forward in a fluid motion. And starts to veer to the right, ever so slightly, the wheels skidding on the ice.

"No, no, no, no," Larry mutters, throwing his body to the left as if his string of bones would be of any help. Tashi gets pulled after him. She flops onto the bench on the left side of the car. The train lists horribly—another half a foot and it will plow into the side of the tunnel instead of going through. Tashi crouches on the bench, braces her feet against the metal side, and, with a great "heeuuuaaaarrrghh" of effort, kicks off the wall and flies into the air. The force behind the baby yeti's inhuman strength rights the course of the train in an instant. Larry is flung onto the floor of the cab and thrown up against the coal box. The wind catches Tashi halfway through her flight and sweeps her into the window where she clings to the ledge and closes her eyes.

And in this way, neither Tashi nor Larry actually sees the train disappear through the tunnel. But the mother yeti, who comes plodding slowly toward the cave room to complain about the noise, watches in shock as the substance of the metal engine appears to dissolve until only the lights are visible and then it slides through a swirling tunnel of wind.

6

Stepwise Refinement and Inheritance

Concept Objectives

- Using stepwise refinement
- Using marker objects (to reposition the camera, characters, and props)
- Writing a custom procedure for the Scene class
- Working with inheritance, a custom procedure for a parent class

This chapter further explores custom procedures, extending the concepts and techniques of writing custom procedures to include **stepwise refinement** and **inheritance**. Stepwise refinement is a design technique that repeatedly decomposes a complex action again and again into smaller and smaller pieces, until the steps are straightforward and the code can be implemented by calling built-in procedures. Inheritance is a feature of object-oriented programming languages (for example, Alice, Java, and C++) that allows objects of a class to reuse methods (both procedures and functions) and properties defined in another class, based on a class hierarchy relationship.

The concepts and techniques for using stepwise refinement and inheritance will be illustrated using an example program to animate a script adapted from a selected segment of the *Haunted Circus* Episode 3, *The Tunnel*. In this episode, Tashi and Larry fire up the steam engine and ring the magic bell. The bell opens a tunnel—an energy vortex with a portal. Larry and Tashi ride the train into the portal and the journey begins.

6.1 Story Analysis

The first step in our problem-solving approach is to read and analyze the story to determine the background components of the story and select the objects and actions for an animation script. The part of the *The Tunnel* episode selected for an animation example in this chapter is summarized here:

> Although confused, Larry still is certain of a few things. He knows that if he remains some semblance of a living being, the rest of his troupe might have survived the avalanche too. He knows the train has a magical ability to transport through tunnel portals, although he isn't quite sure how to control it yet. He knows the train will go somewhere but not exactly where. While Tashi watches, Larry fills the firebox with coal, stokes the engine, and releases the brake. Just as he is about to ring the bell, he notices Tashi sitting on the bench across from him. He tells her this is her last chance to get off the train before he leaves. She takes it as a challenge and, eager for adventure, responds with "never!" Larry rings the bell eight times, a wind tunnel arises to create a portal vortex, and the entire train disappears through it.

As in previous episodes, the narrative of the story is adapted for the purpose of creating an animation. Not every detail from the writing is included, and a few details are changed. To turn the story into a short animation, one analysis of this episode could be

> shovel coal **into the firebox** as Tashi observes
> coal burns in the engine
> steam **pressure** in the engine **increases**
> engine **bell rings** — a signal for departure
> Larry and Tashi **talk** about Tashi wanting to go along on the train
> **train lights turn on** and the **wind howls** as the **train departs** through the portal

6.2 Design

The analysis provides a starting point for design using a storyboard. Once the props for the background and the characters that will perform actions have been established, you can then figure out the flow of the animation with a full storyboard. The following storyboard has five frames (Figure 6.1). Notice the top row is actually one frame that includes camera cuts to different views of the scene (turning one way to view the coal box and another way to view the firebox). This is important because, eventually, you will need to write code statements that move and orient the camera for different viewpoints in the scene.

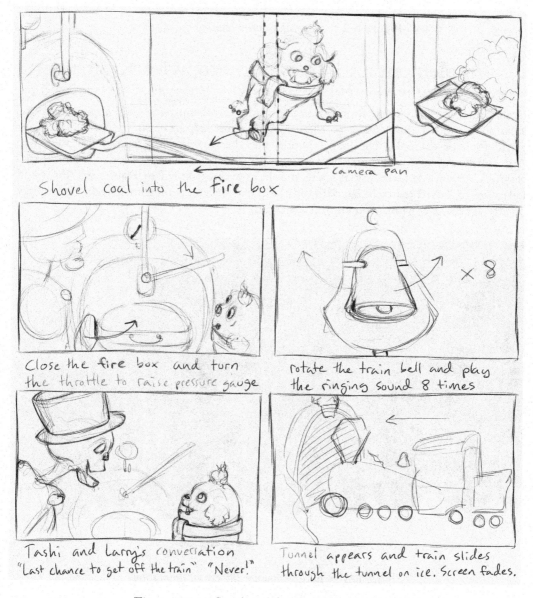

Figure 6.1 • *Storyboard for* The Tunnel *excerpt*

From the task analysis and the storyboard, a possible algorithm for the task is shown in Figure 6.2.

do in order

      shovel moves coal from coal box to fire box, as Tashi observes

      coal burns

      steam pressure builds in the engine

      bell rings (again and again), as Larry and Tashi talk

      train lights turn on and the train departs through the tunnel

Figure 6.2   *Algorithm for animating the script*

6.3 Implement and Test with Stepwise Refinement

In the *Haunted Circus* story, tunnels act as portals to transport the train engine from one location to another. An Alice project named *PortalStarter.a3p* has been prepared as a starter world for this example. The starter world may be downloaded from **www.alice.org/Alice3ToJava**. Download the project. Start Alice and open the downloaded world. If successfully downloaded, the initial scene should appear as shown in Figure 6.3. Tashi and Larry are on board the train, standing in the cabin. Several semi-transparent, camera-like objects are floating within and around the cabin.

Figure 6.3   *Initial scene for the portal animation*

6.3.1 Camera and object markers in a scene

The floating objects in and around the cabin are markers. A **marker** is a special type of object that remembers a location and orientation for the camera or other types of objects in the scene. In this example, the markers will be used for close-up views of the coal box, the shovel, and the firebox in the interior of the cabin.

A pre-made custom procedure, named *cameraMarkerTour*, is included in the starter world to provide a quick demo of using camera markers. (A custom procedure is considered "pre-made" if it is included in a starter world but is not part of the Alice code library.) To view the demo first select *this* in the Object selector and then drag the tile for the custom-built *cameraMarkerTour* into *myFirstMethod* (Figure 6.4).

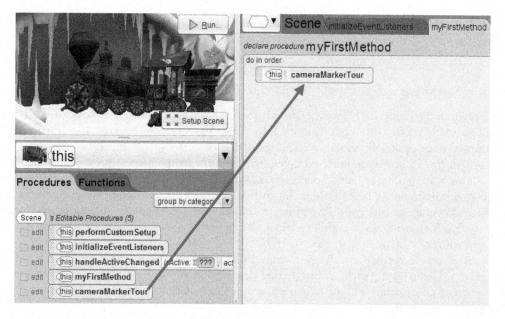

Figure 6.4 • A *statement to test-run* cameraMarkerTour

Next, test-run. You should see the camera reposition in sequence to six different camera markers. Each camera marker provides a different view of the interior of the cabin, except for the last marker. The last marker returns the camera to its original position.

You may wish to run the project several times to get a sense of the position of objects within the cabin. Notice Larry is on one side of the cabin and Tashi is on the other, facing Larry. Toward the front of the cabin is a firebox where the steam is created that runs the engine. At the back of the cabin is the coal car that trails along behind the engine. You may also wish to view the code in the *cameraMarkerTour* procedure. If so, click *edit* next to the *cameraMarkerTour* tile in the procedures panel.

After viewing the camera marker demo, delete the *cameraMarkerTour* statement in *myFirstMethod*. Also, if you viewed the *cameraMarkerTour* procedure code, close the tab for the procedure in the Code editor.

> ## VIDEO ALERT!
>
> You may find it helpful to view video 10, Creating Camera Markers for Recording Camera Positions, at: http://www.alice.org/3.1/materials_videos.

6.3.2 Comment documentation

Begin by adding comments in *myFirstMethod* to document the steps in the algorithm (Figure 6.5).

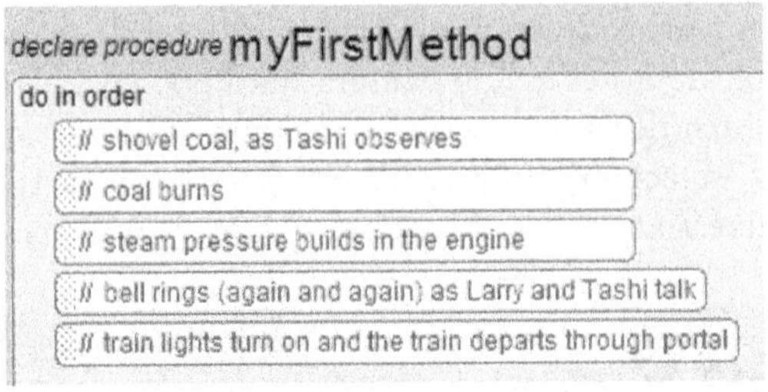

declare procedure myFirstMethod
do in order
// shovel coal, as Tashi observes
// coal burns
// steam pressure builds in the engine
// bell rings (again and again) as Larry and Tashi talk
// train lights turn on and the train departs through portal

Figure 6.5 *Comments that reflect the design*

6.3.3 Stepwise refinement—decomposition, again and again

In previous chapters, each step of the algorithm was decomposed, if needed, and then implemented, writing the code line by line. This was possible because the introductory examples were relatively short and the sequence of actions was intuitive. However, the actions in this example are more complex, which makes implementation more challenging.

One way to simplify a complex, challenging algorithm is to use stepwise refinement. Stepwise refinement is repeated decomposition for a step in the algorithm. The action is broken down again and again into smaller and smaller pieces until the decomposed steps are straightforward and the code can be implemented by creating statements that call built-in procedures.

A **stepwise refinement diagram** may be used (Figure 6.6). The first iteration of the diagram is basically the same as the textual description earlier, but shows *myFirstMethod* as the starting point, and each line of the algorithm in a box that represents an action that will be implemented, in order, from top to bottom.

Shovel coal as Tashi observes
Coal burns and steam pressure builds
myFirstMethod
Bell rings (repeatedly) Larry & Tashi talk
Train lights turn on and train leaves through portal

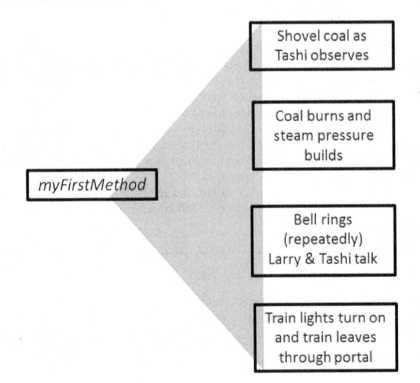

Figure 6.6 *Overall design diagram that represents stepwise refinement*

The first action is "Shovel coal, as Tashi observes." This shoveling action is complex because the shovel must retrieve the coal from the coal box, carry it, and then deposit it in the firebox. In addition to the movement of shovel and coal, two other issues add to the complexity: (1) Who is shoveling the coal? (2) How do we show Tashi's excitement as she observes?

One stepwise refinement technique is to decompose a highly complex action into several procedures, instead of just one procedure. The shoveling action naturally decomposes into three procedures: (1) one to shovel the coal out of the coal box (*fromCoalBox*), (2) one to turn the shovel toward the firebox (*turnTowardFirebox*), and (3) one to put the coal into the firebox (*toFirebox*) (Figure 6.7).

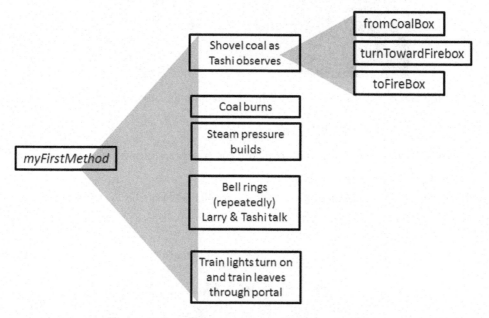

Figure 6.7   *Decomposition to multiple procedures*

Once again, note that the stepwise refinement diagram implies the three procedures for the shoveling coal action will be performed top-down. Each of these sub-procedures will now be decomposed, implemented, and tested, in order.

First, the *fromCoalBox* procedure will be decomposed. Thinking about the steps needed to retrieve a clump of coal from the coal box would be easier if we could see the relative position of the shovel to the coal box. When you look at the initial scene, it is difficult to see the shovel and the coal box because they are inside the train engine's cabin but the camera is positioned outside and some distance away.

6.3.4 Use a camera marker to view objects inside the cabin

We can use one of the camera markers to gain a view of the shovel and the coal box. Click Setup Scene to open the Scene editor. The first step in using a camera marker is to view the list of camera markers in the Toolbox. Follow these steps (Figure 6.8):

(1) Select camera in the Object selector.
(2) Expand the Camera Markers menu.

Figure 6.8   *View the Camera Markers menu in the Scene editor's Toolbox.*

To use a camera marker for the shovel and the coal box, follow these steps (Figure 6.9):

(1) Click the shovelCoalShot button.
(2) Click the camera reposition button, at the top-left side of the markers menu.

Figure 6.9   *Reset the camera in the Scene editor.*

When the camera reposition button is clicked, the camera will move and orient to the *shovelCoalShot* marker. You should now see a close-up shot of the shovel in the Camera view panel (Figure 6.10).

Figure 6.10 *A view of the shovel with the blade facing the coal box, inside the cabin*

This close-up camera shot in the Scene editor is partially obscured by the camera and object markers. To view the close-up shot without the markers, click Run. The close-up shot (Figure 6.11) reveals that the shovel in the starter world was purposely positioned in front of the coal box, with the blade end facing the coal box.

Now that we know more about where the shovel is located relative to the coal box, the camera should be returned to its original, starting position. Nothing was changed in the scene and no code statements were written, so just click the Undo button at the top of the Toolbox.

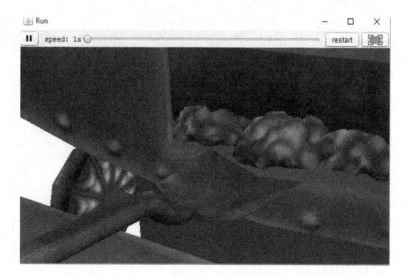

Figure 6.11 *Close-up shot in the runtime window; markers are not visible*

6.3.5 Declare and implement a procedure in the Scene class

With knowledge of where the shovel is positioned, the *fromCoalBox* procedure can now be decomposed (Figure 6.12) and then implemented.

do in order

> camera move and orient to a close-up view of the shovel (shovelCoalShot)
> shovel move to position the blade under a clump of coal
> set coal vehicle to the shovel
> shovel return to its original location

Figure 6.12   fromCoalBox *decomposition*

To implement the decomposition as code statements, begin by declaring the *fromCoal-Box* procedure. Recall the guidelines for declaring a custom procedure are

- **If only one type of object performs actions in the decomposition steps, declare the procedure in the class that defines that type of object.**
- **If more than one object performs actions in the decomposition steps and the objects are of different types, declare the procedure in the Scene class.**

In this example, the camera, shovel, and coal perform actions; therefore, this procedure should be declared for the Scene class (Figure 6.13).

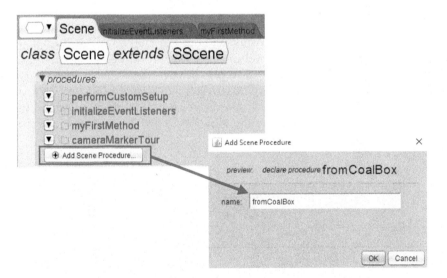

Figure 6.13   *Declare the* fromCoalBox *procedure for the Scene class.*

Alice creates a new tab in the Code editor, immediately to the right of *myFirstMethod*. In the *fromCoalBox* editor tab, add comments to document assumptions (shovel is positioned in front of and with the blade toward the coal box), the actions that occur (the shovel moves into the coal box and picks up a clump of coal), and the post-condition (the shovel is back in its original position and has a clump of coal on the blade) (Figure 6.14).

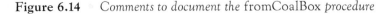

Figure 6.14   *Comments to document the* fromCoalBox *procedure*

The first decomposition step is to reposition the camera into a close-up view of the shovel within the cabin. Drag a *moveAndOrientTo* procedure tile into the editor and select *shovelCoalShot* as the target camera marker (Figure 6.15).

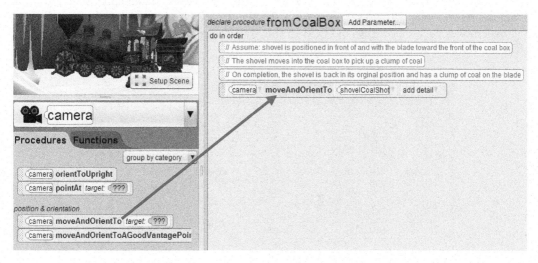

Figure 6.15   *Create a* moveAndOrientTo *statement.*

Go ahead and test this action. In *myFirstMethod*, create a statement to call *fromCoalBox* (Figure 6.16). Then test-run. You should see the camera move into the same position as was done earlier, in the Scene editor's Toolbox.

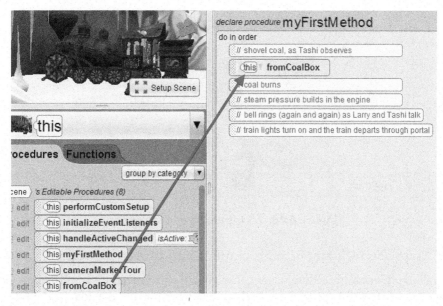

Figure 6.16   *Create a statement to call* fromCoalBox.

As you view the runtime window, note that this action positions the camera in front of Larry. In other words, the camera is showing the scene from Larry's point of view. This position was purposely selected to give the illusion that Larry is shoveling the coal, without having to write code to animate Larry's upper body, particularly the arms and hands, to hold and move the shovel.

Return to the editor tab for the *fromCoalBox* procedure to create statements for the remainder of the decomposition. These are simple procedure statements similar to code written in previous examples (Figure 6.17). The coal's vehicle is set to the shovel before the shovel moves back out of the coal box. In this way, the coal will ride on the shovel blade as the shovel moves.

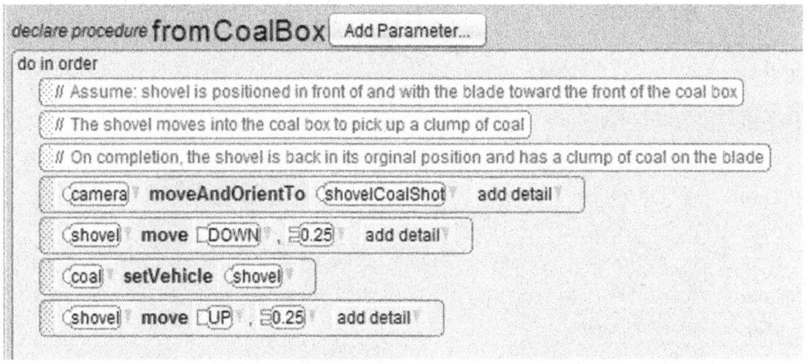

Figure 6.17   *Completed* fromCoalBox *procedure*

Recall that an object moves relative to its own sense of direction. In this example, UP and DOWN directions are used in the shovel's *move* statements because a shovel's *UP* direction (green arrow) is through the handle and its *DOWN* direction is through the blade (Figure 6.18).

Figure 6.18   *Orientation of a shovel object*

6.3.6 Stepwise refinement with camera and object markers

The *turnTowardFirebox* procedure is next. The goal in this procedure is to turn the shovel so its blade (and the coal) is toward the firebox (ready for putting the coal in the fire box). In the same way as a camera marker is used to reposition the camera, an object marker may be used to reposition an object such as a shovel. The Portal starter world already has an object marker, *shovelTurnPosition*. In addition, the starter world has a camera marker, *shovelCoalTurnShot*, that will be used to provide an up-close view of the shovel moving into position. A decomposition for *turnTowardFirebox* is shown in Figure 6.19.

do together

    camera move and orient to shovelCoalTurnShot
    shovel move and orient to shovelTurnPosition

Figure 6.19 ◦ turnTowardFirebox *decomposition*

Declare a new procedure for the Scene class and name it *turnTowardFirebox*. Then, in the *turnTowardFirebox* editor tab, add comments to document assumptions, actions, and post conditions. To have the camera and shovel actions occur at the same time, create a *do together* code block and write the statements within it (Figure 6.20).

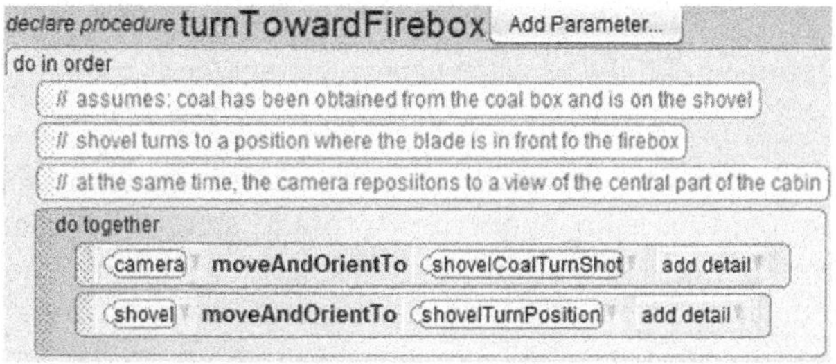

Figure 6.20 ◦ *Code statements to reposition camera and shovel*

Return to *myFirstMethod* and add a statement to call the procedure (Figure 6.21).

Figure 6.21 ◦ *Call the two procedures in sequence in* myFirstMethod.

Test-run the project. You should see the shovel get coal from the coal box and then turn. While the shovel turns, the camera is also repositioning. Run and view the animation again. If you carefully watch the shovel's handle as it turns, you will see that nobody's hands are holding the handle. In other words, the illusion is lost. It is clear that Larry is not actually shoveling the coal.

One way to solve this problem is to delay repositioning the camera, giving the shovel a short amount of time to start turning before the camera starts repositioning. Return to the *turnTowardFirebox* tab and add a *do in order* code block, nesting it within the *do together* code block. Drag the camera *moveAndOrient* statement into the *do in order* code block and set its duration of 0.5 seconds. Then add a *delay* 0.5-second statement immediately before the camera *moveAndOrientTo* (Figure 6.22). Test-run again. Adjusting the timing allows the shovel to complete part of its turn before the camera starts to reposition.

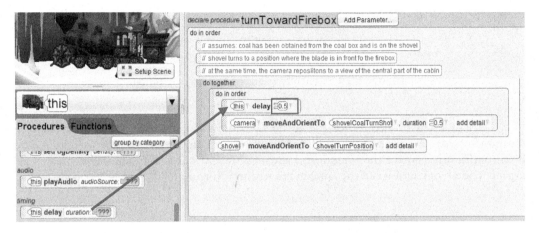

Figure 6.22   *Delay the camera's* moveAndOrientTo.

Note that the new camera view clearly shows Tashi watching the shovel. Because Tashi is in view of the camera, this is an opportunity to add statements that create some body language to communicate Tashi's reaction to watching the coal being shoveled. As shown in Figure 6.23, a *do in order* code block is added with statements to have Tashi tip her head when the shovel is in front of her, which conveys her interest in the action.

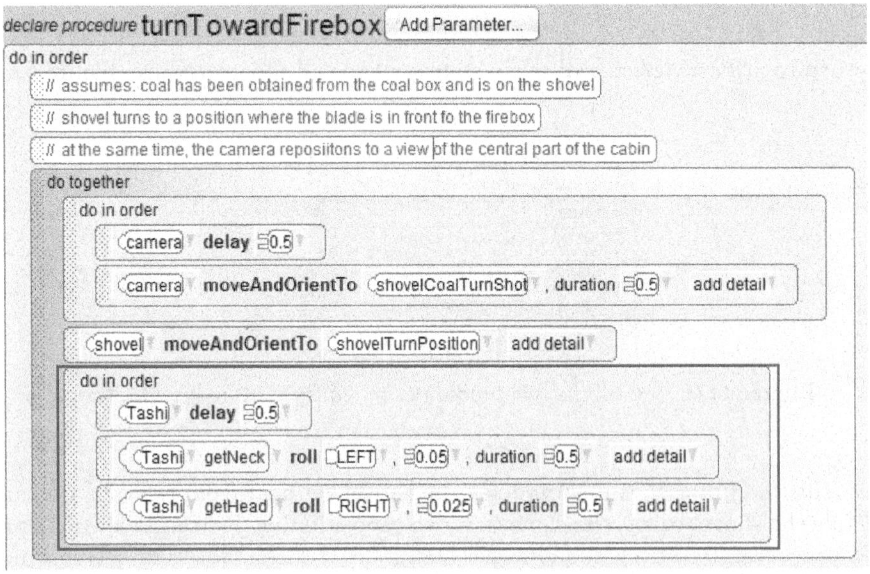

Figure 6.23   *Added statements to show Tashi's emotion*

The *toFirebox* procedure is next. The goal of the *toFirebox* procedure is to have the shovel carry the coal into the firebox and then remove the shovel. A decomposition for the *toFirebox* procedure is shown in Figure 6.24. First, the shovel must be moved into a position in front of the firebox and then moved to push the blade into the firebox. To leave the coal in the firebox, the coal's vehicle must be reset (this time, to the train) before the shovel can be removed.

> *do in order*
> > *do together*
> >
> > > camera move and orient to a close-up view of the firebox
> > > shovel move and orient to a position in front of the fire box
> >
> > coal's vehicle set to train
> >
> > remove shovel from firebox

Figure 6.24 ● *Design for the* toFirebox *procedure*

Declare a new procedure for the Scene class and name it *toFirebox*. Add comments to document assumptions, actions, and post-conditions. A camera marker, *shovelCoalEndShot*, will be used to reposition the camera for a close-up view of the firebox. An object marker, *shovelEndPosition*, will be used to move the shovel into position in front of the firebox.

To start the implementation, create a *do together* code block and add statements to move and turn the camera to the *shovelCoalEndShot* marker and the shovel to the *shovelEnd-Position* marker (Figure 6.25). Once again, nest a *do in order* within the *do together* code block and add a *delay* statement to delay the start of the camera repositioning.

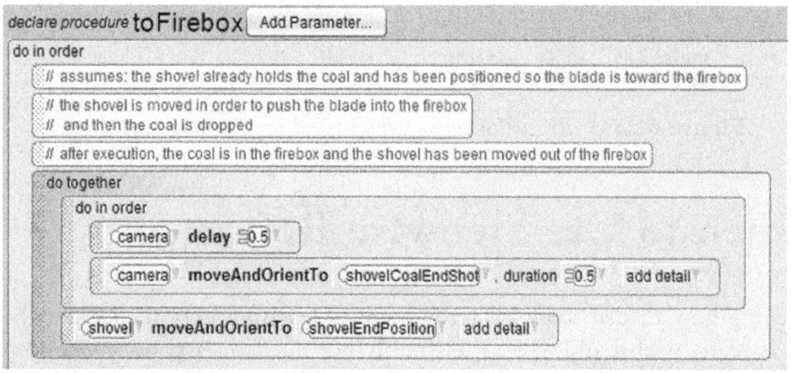

Figure 6.25 ● *The* toFirebox *procedure with comments and the first* do together *code block*

Although the procedure is not yet fully implemented, go ahead and test-run it. Return to *myFirstMethod* and add a statement to call the *toFirebox* procedure, positioning the statement immediately after the statement that calls *turnTowardFirebox* (Figure 6.26). Test-run the project. You should see the shovel get coal from the coal box, turn, and move into position in front of the firebox as expected.

Figure 6.26 ● *Call the procedure in* myFirstMethod.

In the previous two procedures, the clump of coal travels with the shovel at every *move*, *turn*, or *roll* because the coal's vehicle was set to the shovel in the *fromCoalBox* procedure. Now, the coal must separate from the shovel, remaining in the firebox when the shovel is removed. To implement this action, add code (Figure 6.27) to set the coal's vehicle to the train and then a statement to move the shovel out of the firebox.

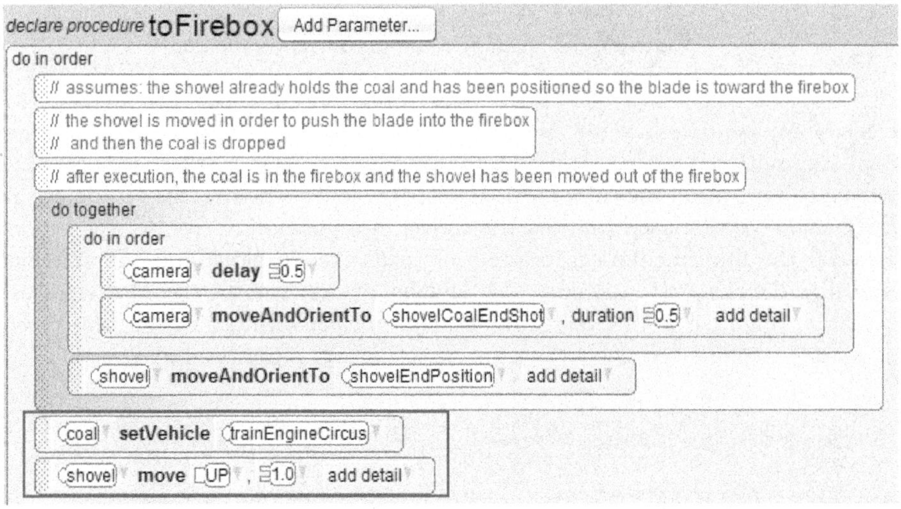

Figure 6.27   *Reset the coal's vehicle and then remove the shovel.*

6.4 When to Use Stepwise Refinement

Part of learning how to use stepwise refinement is learning how to decide when stepwise refinement is really useful and when it is simply not needed. A good question to ask yourself is: "Is this a highly complex action that needs repeated decompositions to enable writing code for animation?" If so, then the decision to use stepwise refinement is reasonable. Otherwise, the decision should be to keep it as simple as possible. The next few steps for the example algorithm will be used to illustrate.

6.4.1 Stepwise refinement: Setting an object's skin resource?

Now that the coal is in the firebox, the next step in the algorithm is to make the coal appear to catch fire and burn. Is this a highly complex action that needs a lot of decomposition in order to write code to animate burning the coal? In nature, a clump of coal is a black or dark-brown mineral substance. When coal burns, a chemical reaction occurs in which atoms in the coal combine with oxygen from the air to create water molecules. This combustion process releases large amounts of energy in the form of heat and light, which causes the coal to glow a red-orange color.

The underlying combustion process is indeed a highly complex action. However, for the purpose of animation all we really want to do is visually capture the change in appearance—the color of the coal changes from its natural color to a red-orange glow. Fortunately, the Coal class in the Alice gallery is one of many classes that have been developed with more than one **resource**. A resource is a paint object (color and texture) that gives an object its **skin** (an outside coating). A coal object has two resources, one for the natural mineral skin and one for a skin that makes the coal look like it is burning. The skin can be changed by writing a statement to set the resource. This is a simple action, not requiring stepwise refinement.

To reset the coal object's skin to the burning resource, first return to *myFirstMethod* in the Code editor. In the Object selector on the left, select the coal object. You will see a list of procedure tiles in the Procedures tab, one of which is *setCoalResource*. Use the cursor to drag the *setCoalResource* tile into the editor. When the cursor is released, select BURN-ING from the cascading menu (Figure 6.28) of possible resources.

Test-run the project. You should see the coal start to burn after it has been dropped into the firebox and the shovel removed.

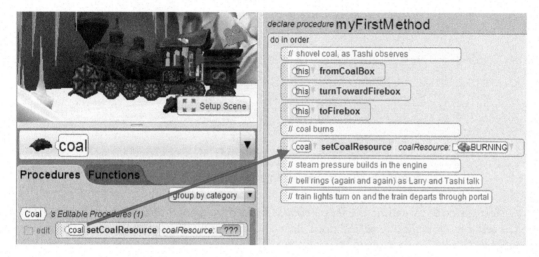

Figure 6.28   *Set the coal's resource to BURNING.*

6.4.2 Stepwise refinement: Visualizing an invisible action?

Now that the coal is burning, the next step in the algorithm is "steam pressure builds in the engine." But, pressure buildup happens within the steam engine, which means we can't see it happening. It is an invisible action. One way to visualize an invisible action is to provide a mechanical or electronic device that measures the change and provides a dial or gauge as evidence of change. Is this a highly complex action that needs stepwise refinement?

To visualize the engine pressure buildup, the train engine's equipment includes a pres-sure gauge with a hand that turn clockwise as the pressure increases and counter-clockwise as it decreases. An initial decomposition for using the pressure gauge is shown in Figure 6.29.

> *do in order*
>> firebox door closes
>> camera move and orient to view the pressure gauge (camera marker)
>> gauge hand turns clockwise on the dial (2 seconds)
>> throttle kicks in (rolls to its left)
>> delay 1 sec

Figure 6.29   *Decomposition for using the pressure gauge*

Each line of the decomposition may be translated into code using built-in Alice procedures. No further decomposition is needed for this procedure, so we can proceed without stepwise refinement.

Declare a custom procedure for the Scene class and name it *pressureBuilds*. In the *pressureBuilds* editor tab, add comments to document assumptions, actions, and post-conditions. Then, create statements to implement the actions (Figure 6.30). Note that the pressure gauge and the throttle are sub-parts of the train engine and, in each case, a joint must be used to roll it.

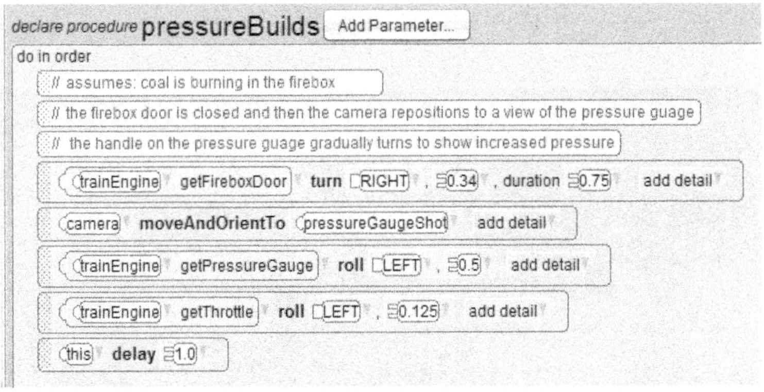

Figure 6.30   *Completed* pressureBuilds *procedure*

Test the code by calling the *pressureBuilds* procedure from *myFirstMethod* (Figure 6.31). In the test run, you should see the door close and a close-up view of the pressure rising on the gauge.

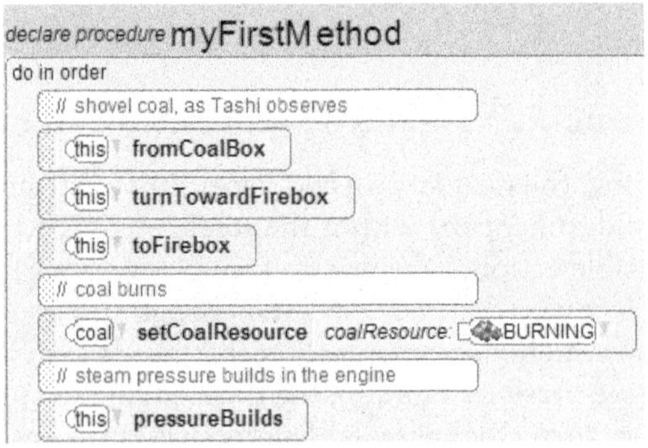

Figure 6.31   *Test by calling* pressureBuilds *in* myFirstMethod.

6.4.3 Stepwise refinement: Sound effect and lengthy dialog?

In the next algorithm step, the train's bell is to ring repeatedly. While the bell is ringing, Tashi and Larry engage in a conversation about why the bell is ringing, where the train is going, and whether Tashi will go along on the adventure. This is a complex action involving a sound effect and a lengthy conversation (a dialog) between Larry and Tashi. Ringing a bell and characters talking are not built-in procedures. Stepwise refinement will be useful for breaking this action into simpler steps. The stepwise refinement diagram (Figure 6.32) shows a breakdown into two procedures, *ringBell* and *dialog*.

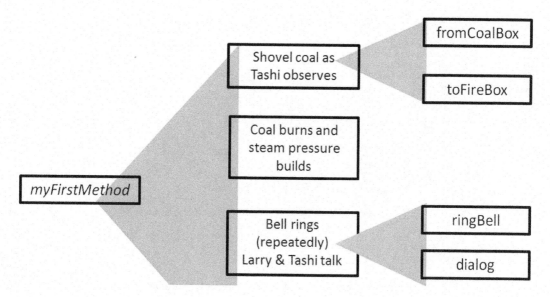

Figure 6.32 • *Design using stepwise refinement on third step.*

Let's begin with *ringBell*. A procedure to ring the train's bell has been pre-made and is included in the *Portal.a3p* world that you downloaded for this chapter. Select *trainEngineCircus* in the Object selector of the Code editor. The *ringBell* procedure is listed in the Procedures tab (Figure 6.33). Although the *ringBell* procedure is pre-made, let's view the code that plays the sound. Click *edit* to the left of the *ringBell* tile in the Procedures tab. The code should be displayed as shown in Figure 6.34.

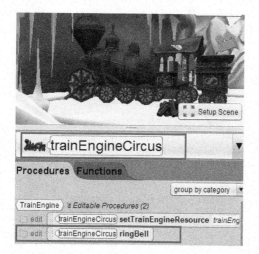

Figure 6.33 • *The* trainEngineCircus *has a pre-made* ringBell *procedure.*

Two statements in *ringBell* call *playAudio*, a built-in procedure. The *playAudio* procedure requires an *audioSource* argument. An audio source is a digital sound recording. In this example, *bell3.mp3*, a recording of an old fashioned locomotive bell, was selected. The *tips* segment, at the end of this chapter, illustrates how to import an audio file.

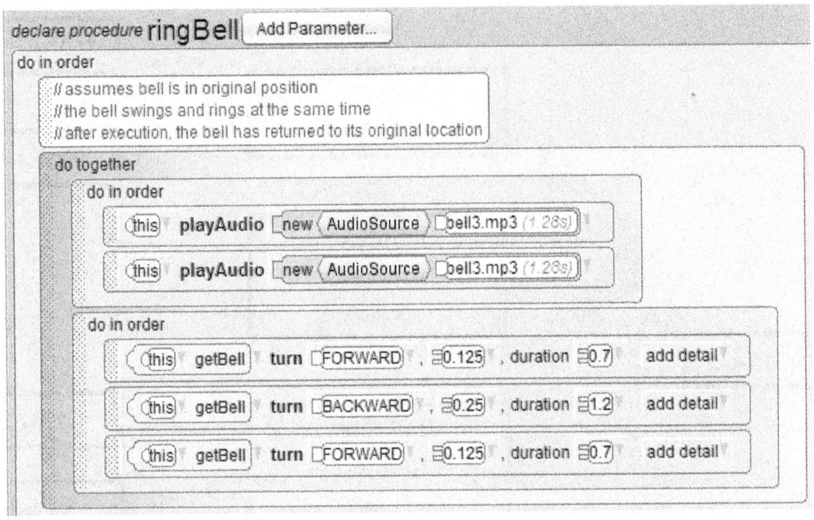

Figure 6.34   *The code in the* ringBell *procedure*

In the *ringBell* procedure, each *playAudio* statement is in a *do together* code block with statements that *turn* the bell forward and backward. It is important that the turn statements be written so as to return the bell to its original position when the procedure ends. This is because the bell is expected to ring several times and each time it rings it should start, again, in its original position.

To test the *ringBell* procedure, select *myFirstMethod*. For a close-up view of the ringing bell, first add a statement to move and orient the camera to the *bellShot* camera marker and then a statement that calls *ringBell* (Figure 6.35). Test-run. You should hear the bell ring once.

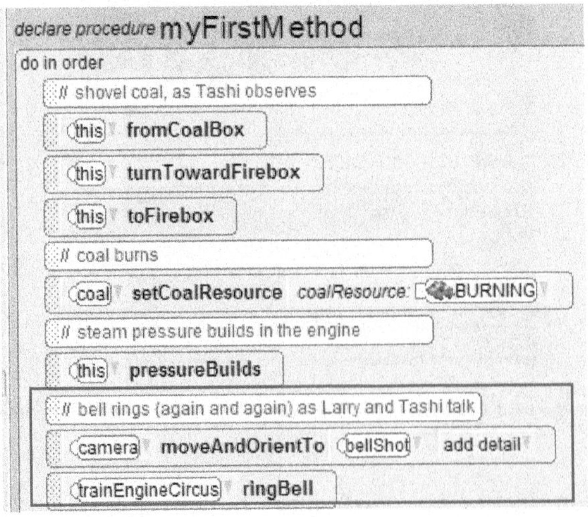

Figure 6.35   *Test the* ringBell *procedure.*

6.5 Inheritance
....

As described above, the bell should ring repeatedly and at the same time as Larry and Tashi are talking. To make this happen, we will write a *dialog* procedure to animate a conversation between Larry and Tashi. Then, the *dialog* procedure can be called at the same time as the *bellRing* procedure is called, repeatedly.

A possible decomposition for a *dialog* procedure is shown in Figure 6.36. The focus in this decomposition is a conversation between the two characters. Adding statements to communicate the emotions of the characters through body language is left to you. See the end-of-chapter exercises.

> *do in order*
>
> > *Tashi say "What are you doing?"*
> > *Larry say "The train is leaving"*
> > *Larry say "I am going to look for the rest of my train!"*
> > *Larry say "I remember at least four cars."*
> > *Tashi say "Take me with you"*
> > *Larry say "Last chance to get off."*
> > *Tashi say "Never!"*

Figure 6.36   *Decomposition for* dialog *procedure*

An implementation can be accomplished by creating a sequence of *say* statements. We know, however, that a *say* statement makes a speech bubble appear above a character's head, but does not also move the mouth in a talking motion. In Chapter 5, a *talk* procedure was defined for the Skeleton class.

The skeleton's *talk* procedure may only be used by objects belonging to the Skeleton class. This was fine in the *Thaw* animation because the *talk* procedure was only used to have Larry talk. But in this *Portal* animation, the *dialog* procedure has both Larry and Tashi talking. Larry and Tashi are objects of different types, defined by different classes (Skeleton and YetiBaby). A talk procedure is needed for both Skeleton and YetiBaby classes.

Looking forward to future animation projects, other characters belonging to other classes will also be expected to talk. In most cases, talking characters in the *Haunted Circus* story are objects belonging to classes in the Biped **family** (Figure 6.37).

Figure 6.37   *A few of the classes in the Biped family*

A family of classes in the Alice gallery is a set of 3D models that share some common characteristics. In the Biped family, classes share a basic internal skeletal joint system with a spine that connects to a head, two arms, and two legs, and stand upright with feet on the ground. Procedures written to animate the skeletal joints of a bipedal object may be expected to work for objects of any class in the family. For example, if *talk* works for a *Skeleton* object, *talk* might be expected to also reasonably work for a *YetiBaby* object. In fact, *talk* might be expected to reasonably work for objects of most other classes in the Biped family, such as *Snowman or WhiteRabbit*.

The organization of the Alice gallery implements a family-based hierarchy of classes. Biped is a **parent class**. Each class belonging to the Biped family is a **child class** of the Biped class. Child classes inherit methods (procedures and functions) and properties from their parent class. For example, if a *talk* procedure is written for the Biped class, all child classes in the Biped family will inherit the *talk* procedure from the Biped parent. Inheritance is a programming language feature that allows child classes to reuse code written in its parent, grandparent, and other classes in its ancestry. Inheritance is a primary feature of object-oriented programming languages such as Alice 3 and Java.

6.5.1 Writing a custom procedure for a parent class

Let's explore how inheritance works. Create a *talk* procedure for the Biped class and then call *talk* for both Larry and Tashi. For your convenience, the decomposition for the *talk* procedure is shown again (Figure 6.38).

```
do in order

    mouth turn forward 0.15 revolutions
    mouth turn backward 0.15 revolutions
```

Figure 6.38   *Decomposition for* talk

First, open the Biped class tab in the Code editor by clicking the Classes menu button and then selecting Biped in the cascading menus (Figure 6.39).

Figure 6.39   *Open the Biped class tab.*

As shown in Figure 6.40, the first line of code in the Biped class is: "class Biped *extends* SBiped". The keyword *extends* means that Biped is a child class of a built-in Alice class named SBiped. That is, SBiped is the parent class of Biped. Writing a *talk* procedure in Biped will extend (add to) the procedures already written in SBiped. To create the new *talk* procedure, follow these steps:

(1) Click the Add Biped Procedure button.
(2) Enter the name *talk* in the popup dialog box.
(3) Click OK.

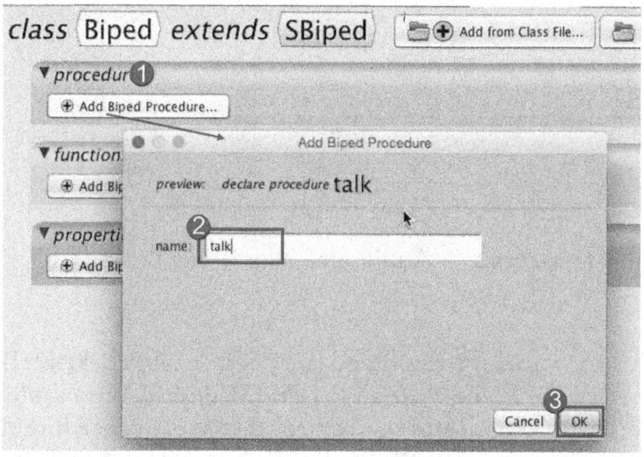

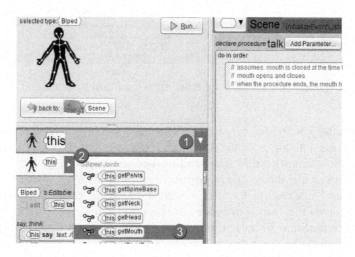

Figure 6.40   *Add a procedure named* talk *to the Biped class.*

A *talk* editor tab is now displayed in the Code editor. In the new *talk* editor tab, add comments to document assumptions, actions, and post-conditions.

Now, in the Methods panel, follow these steps to access the skeletal joint for the Biped's *mouth* (Figure 6.41).

Figure 6.41   *Select* mouth *in the Biped skeletal joint system.*

(1) Click the Object selector menu button.

(2) Select *this*.

(3) Select *getMouth* in the cascading menu.

Then, drag the *turn* procedure tile into the editor to create two statements: one to turn the mouth forward and a second to turn the mouth backward. Use 0.15 revolutions for the amount and a duration of 0.25 seconds (Figure 6.42). Note that the *talk* procedure has a total duration of 0.5 seconds.

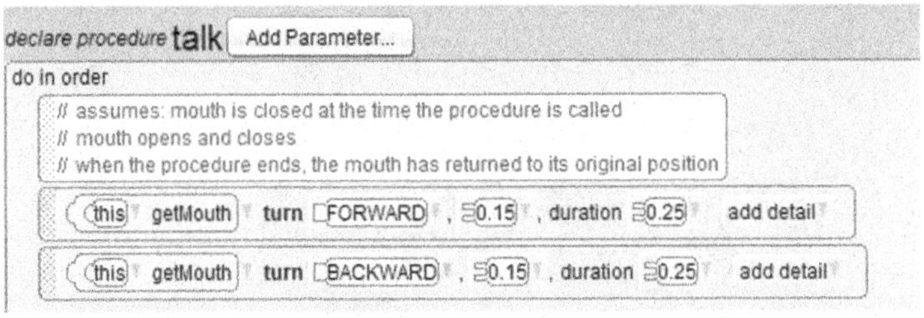

Figure 6.42   A talk *procedure for the Biped class*

In the camera view panel for the Biped class editor tab, click the Back to Scene button. Alice will return to the Scene class and *myFirstMethod* is, once again, the active editor tab. Select Tashi in the Object selector to confirm that a *talk* procedure tile is listed on the Procedures tab, as inherited from the Biped class (Figure 6.44, left). Now, do the same steps with Larry to confirm that a talk procedure tile is now listed on Larry's procedure as well (Figure 6.43, right).

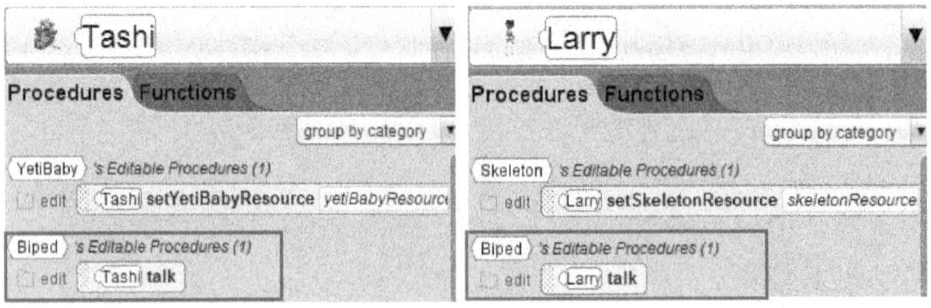

Figure 6.43   talk *is inherited from the Biped parent class.*

Now, the *dialog* procedure can be implemented. Declare a new procedure for the Scene class and name it *dialog*. A *dialog* editor tab is displayed in the Code editor. Add comments to document assumptions, actions, and post-conditions.

The first steps in the *dialog* decomposition are Tashi asking, "What are you doing?" and Larry's answer, "The train is leaving." Create a *do together* code block containing both *say* and *talk* statements for Tashi's question. In the *say* statement, use a *duration* of 1.5 seconds and 1.5 as the *textScale*. Because the *say* duration is 1.5 seconds, a *do in order* sequence of three *talk* statements (0.5 seconds each) is needed. Then, do the same for Larry's answer (Figure 6.44).

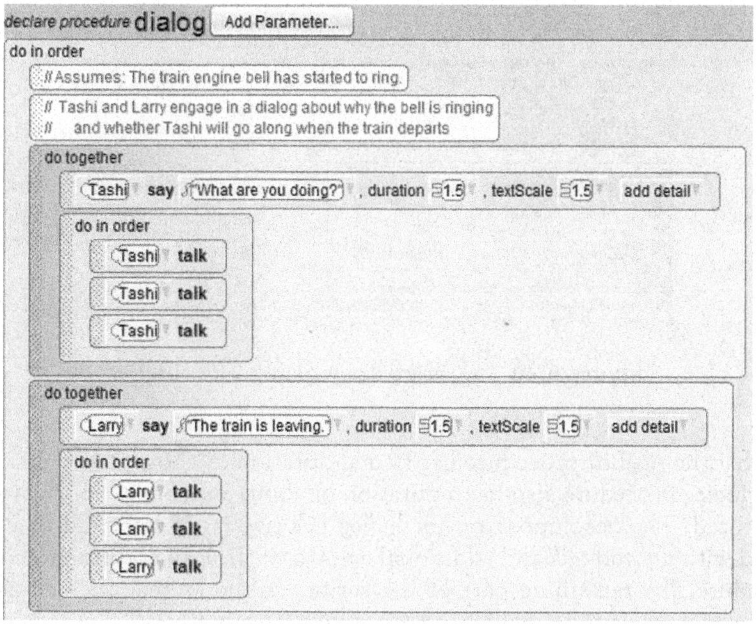

Figure 6.44   *First two steps in dialog procedure*

Although the *dialog* procedure is not complete, let's go ahead and do a test run. This will allow you to check how well the *talk* and *say* are working together. Return to *myFirstMethod* and add a statement to move and orient the camera back to the *pressureGaugeShot* camera marker, so Larry and Tashi will be in the camera's view. Then call *dialog* (Figure 6.45).

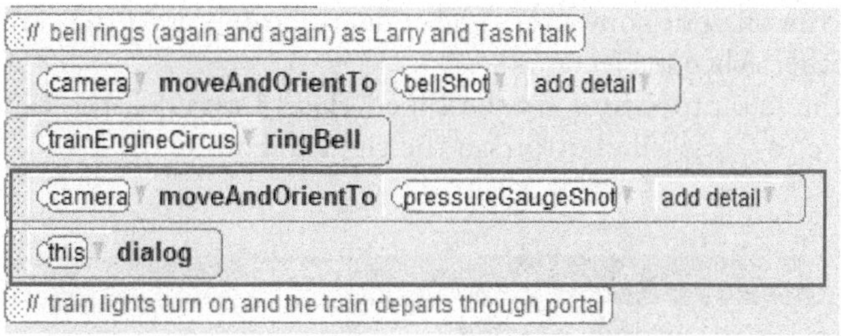

Figure 6.45   *Statements in* myFirstMethod *to reposition the camera and call* dialog

When the code runs, the bell rings, then Tashi talks, then Larry talks. However, the bell does not ring at the same time as Tashi and Larry are talking. To fix this bug, add a *do together* code block in *myFirstMethod* and drag the statement that calls *dialog* inside it. Then add a statement that calls *ringBell* (Figure 6.46).

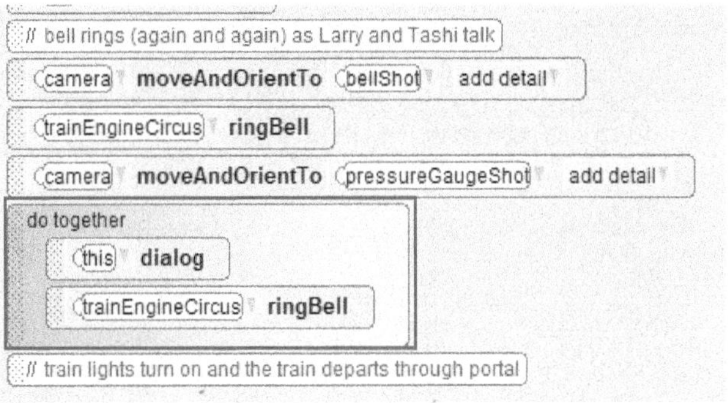

Figure 6.46   *Synchronizing* dialog *with* ringBell

Note that the *ringBell* procedure has a total duration of about 3 seconds. As currently written, the *dialog* procedure also has a duration of about 3 seconds. So, right now, the two are synchronized. The decomposition for *dialog* has five more steps, all of which may be implemented with *say* and *talk* and additional calls to *ringBell*. In addition to completing the *dialog* procedure, the remaining part of the script for the animation includes the train's departure through the tunnel, which acts as a mysterious portal. Completing the dialog procedure and the departure of the train through the portal is left as an exercise for you. See the exercises at the end of this chapter.

6.6 Exporting

Now that *talk* has been written and tested, it is easy to envision how it would be useful for other projects. In this and other episodes of the *Haunted Circus*, conversation between characters is a primary component in storytelling. Alice provides a feature that allows for exporting code for reuse in other animation projects. To **export** means to save the custom-written code to a file on your computer. The code in the exported file can then be **imported** (retrieved) in another Alice project.

To export the *talk* procedure for the Biped class, first click the Biped editor tab and then click the Save to Class File button on the right (Figure 6.47).

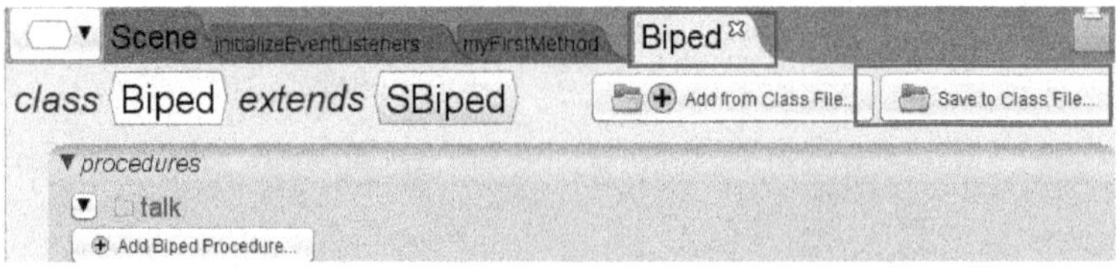

Figure 6.47   *Click the Save to Class File button on the Biped editor tab.*

Alice automatically displays a Save dialog box. By default, the folder to which the file will be saved is MyClasses. MyClasses is a folder that was created on your computer when Alice 3 was installed (Figure 6.48). You may navigate to a different folder on your computer or save on a USB drive, if you wish.

To save a file, a name must be entered in the File name box. In this example, we used the name *BipedTalk.a3c* to identify the relevant class and procedure names. Notice the file name extension is *.a3c* to indicate this is an Alice 3 file containing custom code for a specific class. After a file name has been entered, click the Save button.

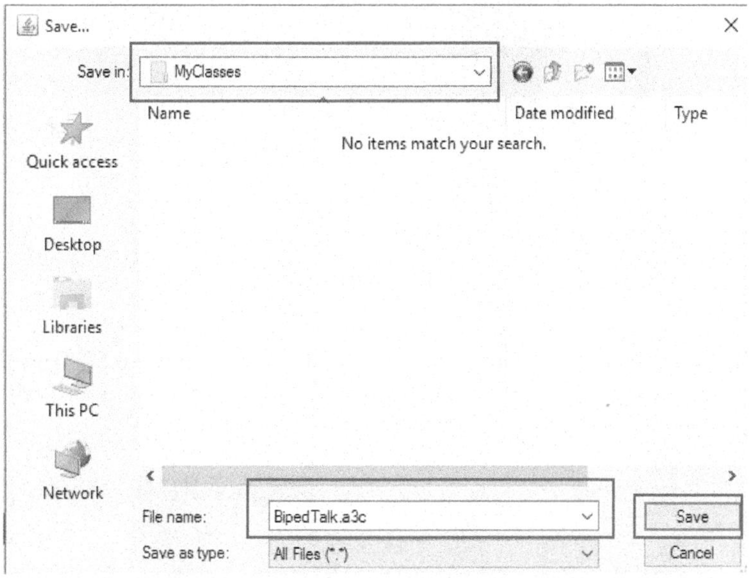

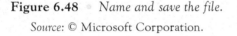

Figure 6.48 • *Name and save the file.*

Source: © Microsoft Corporation.

TIPS: **3D Model Internal Skeletal Joint System**

The *talk* procedure, above, relies on the consistency of the internal skeletal joint system of the Biped family of classes in the Alice Gallery. In general, a common internal skeletal joint system is a reliable basis for creating procedures in a parent class such that any child class may inherit and use the code. Be aware, however, that some variations do exist. For example, in the Quadruped family the Elephant class defines a 3D model that has a trunk. The joints in an elephant's trunk are *not* part of the common internal skeleton. Dogs, cats, lizards, and other quadrupeds do not have trunks. For this reason, any procedure written specifically for the elephant's trunk should *not* be defined in the Quadruped class for inheritance by other classes in the family.

TIPS: *Importing an Audio Source File*

Before an audio source file is selected in a *playAudio* statement, it must be imported into your project from the Alice sound gallery or your own digital sound file. To import an audio file, click Project in the menu bar and then select Resource Manager in the drop-down menu (Figure 6.49).

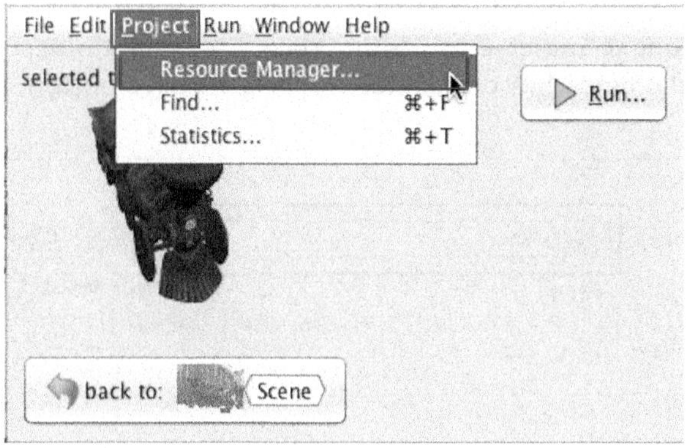

Figure 6.49   *Open Project/Resource Manager.*

A Resource Manager dialog box will be displayed (Figure 6.50). In the Resource Manager dialog box, click the Import Audio button, which will display an Import Audio file selection/navigator dialog box in its own window.

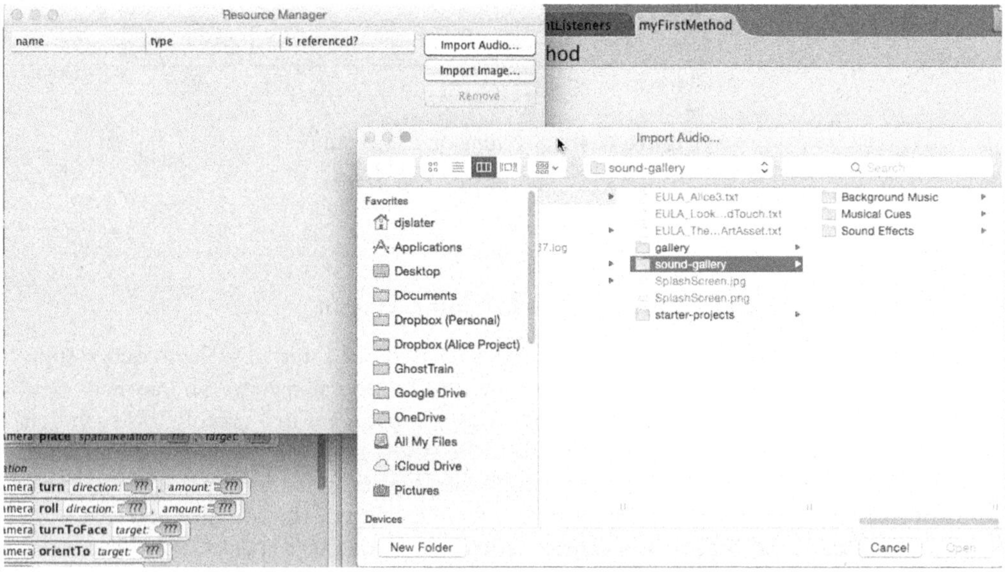

Figure 6.50   *Importing an audio resource file*
Source: © Microsoft Corporation.

Summary

In this chapter, the *Portal* animation example includes tasks that are more complex than in previous chapters. One strategy for designing an algorithm for a highly complex task is stepwise refinement, where some steps are decomposed again and again into smaller and smaller pieces until the steps can be implemented by calling built-in procedures.

One of the challenges in the *Portal* animation is that many of the actions take place within an enclosed area, the interior of the train engine's cabin. Camera markers were created in the scene at the time the scene was created. Then, *move and orient* statements were used to reposition the camera at runtime to view actions such as the shovel carrying coal from the coal box to the firebox. Object markers were used to reposition other objects, particularly for actions such as creating the illusion that Larry was shoveling the coal. Resetting a skin resource for a coal lump was also used to create the appearance of burning.

In this chapter, some custom procedures involved more than one object of different class types. For example, *fromCoalBox* involves actions performed by the camera, the shovel, and a clump of coal. Such procedures were implemented in the Scene class.

Also in this chapter, a custom procedure was written for the Biped class, the parent class of the Biped family. A procedure written for a parent class is inherited and may be performed by objects of the child classes in that family. In this case, *talk* was written for the Biped class and then used by Tashi (YetiBaby) and Larry (Skeleton). Alice provides a feature for exporting custom procedures written for a specific class. The exported code may then be reused in other projects, which will be demonstrated in later chapters.

Terms

audio resource	family	parent class
camera marker	import	resource
child class	inheritance	skin
export	object marker	stepwise refinement

Concept Questions

1. What is the relationship between stepwise refinement and decomposition?
2. A highly complex action is to be implemented. Which of the following techniques is the approach illustrated in this text?
   (a) Reduce the number of procedures. Each procedure requires effort to be created and maintained. It's better to have a few long procedures than many short ones.
   (b) Use lots and lots of procedures. We can decide the name of each procedure, and it helps to make the code more readable. It does not matter if these procedures have just one statement.
   (c) An intermediate between the previous two options.
3. Which of the following procedures is likely to have a duration of 0.0 seconds? Explain your choice. More than one answer is possible.
   (a) *move*
   (b) *turn*
   (c) *resize*
   (d) *setOpacity*
4. Which of the following situations indicate that stepwise refinement would be useful in creating a design algorithm for a project?
   (a) When all steps can be implemented by calling built-in procedures.
   (b) When one or more steps cannot easily be implemented with a single decomposition.

(c) When there are only comments in a procedure.

(d) When optional arguments are required, such as *asSeenBy* or *setCoalResource*.

5. Sometimes it makes sense to use a *delay* statement inside a *do together* code block. Why? Give an example in your answer.

6. The *ringBell* procedure was written for the TrainEngine class. Why is this a better choice than writing a *ringBell* procedure for the Scene class?

7. The *dialog* procedure was written for the Scene class. Why is this a better choice than writing a *dialog* procedure for the Skeleton class?

8. Let's suppose a new procedure, named *laugh*, is going to be defined. In the *laugh* procedure, an object will open and close its mouth while its eyes close. In the following table, each row is a class in which the *laugh* procedure could be written. In each column, mark with a Y the objects that are able to call *laugh*, and with an N the objects that are not able to call *laugh*. The first row has been done as an example.

	Larry	Tashi
Skeleton	Y	N
YetiBaby		
Biped		
Scene		

9. (a) What procedure is called to reposition the camera in a scene?

(b) What type of argument must be supplied in this statement?

10. Which of the following imported file types are managed by Alice's Resource Manager? (Select all that apply.)

(a) audio files

(b) video files

(c) image files

11. Create a diagram showing the class hierarchy of all classes in Alice's Swimmer Gallery.

12. Tashi is an object of type *YetiBaby* and Larry is an object of type *Skeleton*, but both are Bipeds. Explain why both are Bipeds.

13. What is the parent class of each of the following classes in the Alice Gallery?

(a) BlueTang

(b) Walrus

(c) Bus

(d) Sailboat

14. How can the size of the text in a speech bubble be changed, when displayed by a *say* statement?

Exercises

1. In the Alice code presented in this chapter, the *dialog* procedure is incomplete in that only the first two steps in the decomposition for *dialog* have been implemented. Create your own version of the *dialog* procedure so the entire conversation is implemented.

2. A conversation between two characters in a story is more effective if some body movements are included to convey the emotions and motivations of the characters doing the talking. Add at least three actions to *dialog* that accompany different lines

of conversation. For example, have Larry turn his head to look at Tashi when he tells her he is going to look for the rest of his train. Or, to emphasize Tashi's determination to go along on the train, have Tashi jump up and down when she says, "Never!"

3. Implement a *departure* procedure for the final step in the *Through the Portal* animation example. Here are some hints:

   (a) To view the train departing through the portal, reposition the camera to the *originalPosition* camera marker, which provides an exterior view of the train engine and the side of an ice mountain.

   (b) The role of the portal in our story is played by a tunnel object, embedded into the side of one of the ice mountains in the scene. At the time the scene was created, the portal was made invisible by setting its opacity property to 0.0. Before the train begins to move, gradually make the tunnel visible again.

   (c) As the tunnel appears, play a howling wind sound effect. You will need to import an audio file for this purpose.

   (d) The moving train should have its lights turned on. See the CIRCUS_LIGHTS resource for the engine.

   (e) The train is about 6 meters in front of the portal.

   (f) A fade-away effect can be created by gradually reducing the size of the tunnel and increasing the Scene's fog density as the train moves into the tunnel.

4. Create a simple snow-covered scene with a Cheshire cat and an Alien object. Experiment with inheritance by writing a custom procedure named *waveArm* that has a Biped object wave its right arm. Test the inheritance by writing code in *myFirstMethod* to have the cat and the alien objects wave and say hello to one another.

5. Create a scene with a tall mountain. Place several camera marker objects around the mountain. Use the scene in a world where the animation begins with the camera originally positioned at the top of the mountain. As the animation plays, the camera moves from the top of the mountain to the mountain's base by repositioning to successive camera markers, one by one, down the mountain side.

6. Create a project with a movie-style scene set, where a Southwestern desert mock-up and a watering hole are on the left and an African savannah mock-up is on the right. Next, add an elephant and a mandrill monkey to the African side of the scene. Create two different paths, one for the elephant and one for the monkey, using object markers between the two scene mock-ups. Each animal should have a path consisting of at least three markers. Once the scene and markers are ready, write code to create an animation where the elephant and monkey wander from the African savannah to the watering hole in the Southwestern desert, each following its own path.

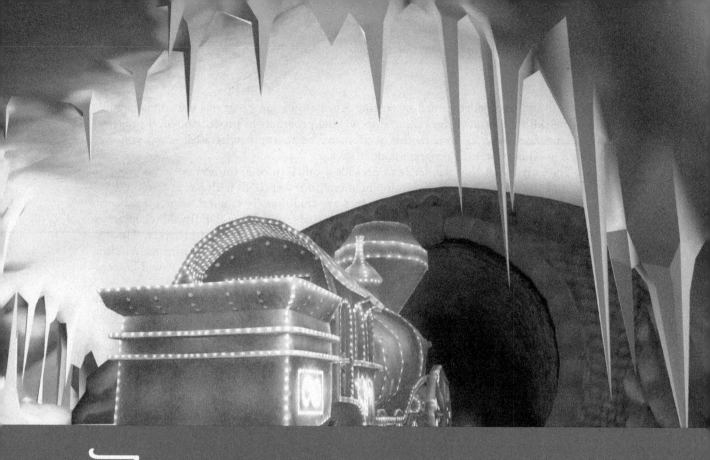

7

Implementation in Java

Concept Objectives

- Writing a code statement in Java
- Basic syntax in Alice statements
- Sending an argument to a parameter
- Using code completion
- What happens when a program runs in Java, as compared with Alice

133

The skills and knowledge gained in writing Alice animation programs are fundamentally the same skills and knowledge essential to writing programs in production-level programming languages, such as Java. In this section, we begin applying strategies and concepts learned in Alice to writing program code in Java.

The purpose of this chapter is to provide a quick tutorial on how to write program code in NetBeans, an integrated development environment (IDE) with a **text-based editor**. A text-based editor is where code statements are traditionally entered using a keyboard, instead of a drag-and-drop, **graphics-based** editor such as the Alice IDE. In this chapter, we will work in NetBeans to create a text-based version of the *HelloWorld* program. The version created in this chapter will display the output in text, instead of in a runtime window, with a graphics animation. Once the text-based program has been written, it will be compared to the graphics-based *HelloWorld* program from Chapter 3.

As with the tutorial on writing program code in Alice's IDE (presented earlier, in Chapter 3), we encourage you to sit at a computer, open NetBeans, and follow along. Use the NetBeans Code editor to build the code, step by step, in an "active learning" style.

This chapter assumes you have NetBeans installed on your computer. If not, please download from **https://netbeans.org/downloads** and install. Detailed instructions for downloading and installing NetBeans may be found at: **http://www.alice.org/Alice3ToJava**.

7.1 The NetBeans IDE

Open NetBeans. Although NetBeans is an editor for creating text-based programs, it is an IDE in a window environment with several graphic components, such as buttons, panels, and tabs. If this is the first time NetBeans has been opened on your computer, the window display will look similar to that shown in Figure 7.1. If NetBeans is displaying its Start page, click the X on the Start page tab to close it.

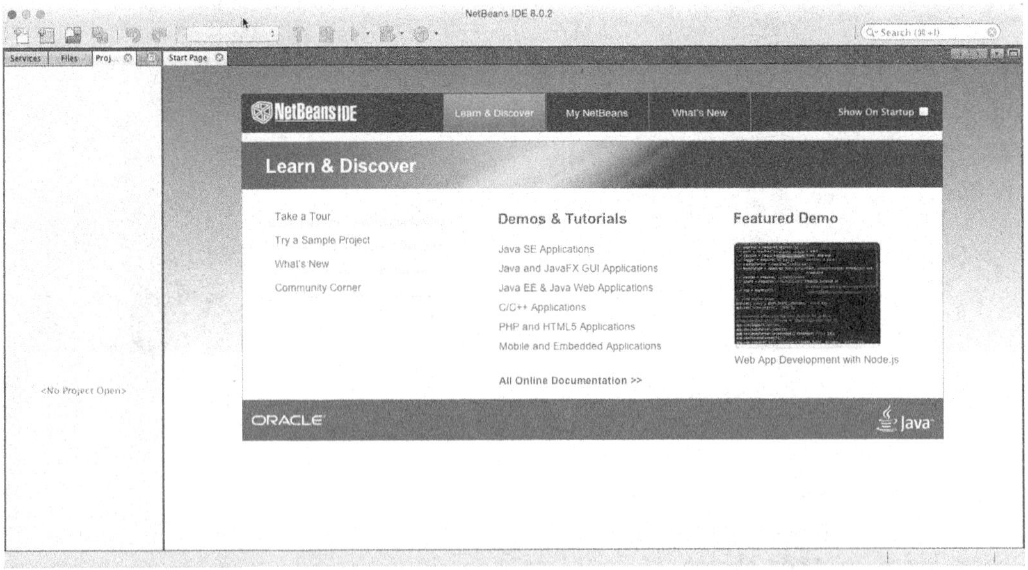

Figure 7.1   *The NetBeans Start page*

Much like Alice, the NetBeans window is subdivided into a set of four panels: Projects, Editor, Palette, and Navigator (Figure 7.2).

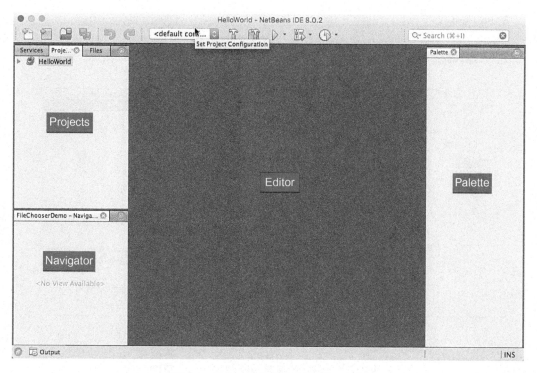

Figure 7.2 · *NetBeans IDE panels*

The Projects panel lists the project(s) currently open, including component files. The Editor panel has tabs, where each tab provides an editing space for a selected class file. The Navigator displays a list of the methods and variables in the currently selected project. The Palette panel provides drag-and-drop templates for code blocks. Additional details about each panel will be provided, as needed, in later chapters.

7.2 Create a New Java Project

To create a new Java project, (1) click the **File** menu in the menu bar at the top left of the NetBeans window. Then, (2) select **New Project** from the pull-down menu (Figure 7.3).

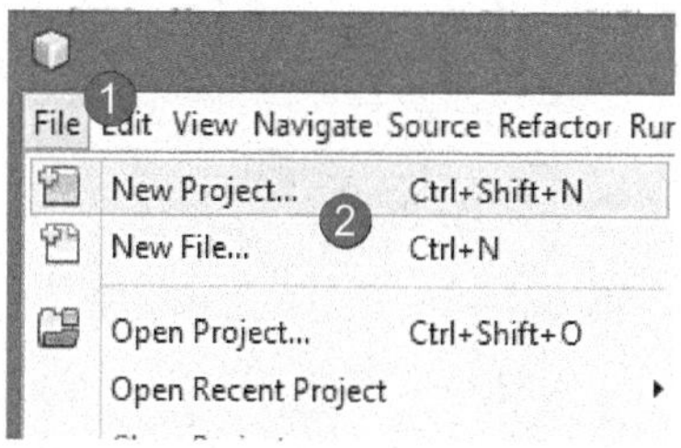

Figure 7.3 · *Select File/New Project.*

A New Project dialog box is displayed with two selection panels: (1) Select **Java** in the Categories panel, and (2) then select **Java Application** in the Projects panel. Then, (3) click **Next** (Figure 7.4).

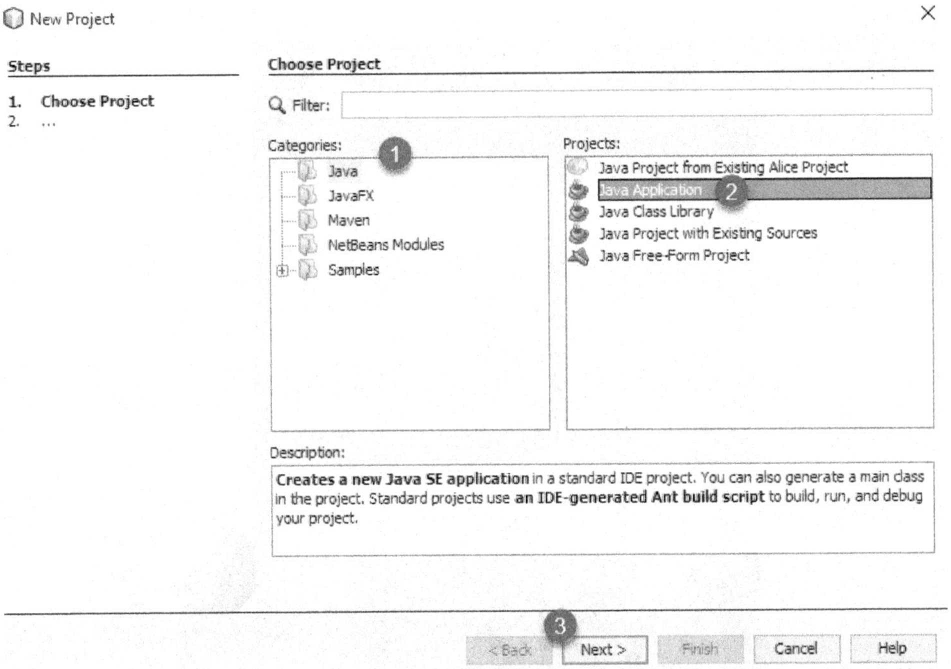

Figure 7.4   *Select Java and Java Application.*

A second dialog box, New Java Application, will be displayed. In this box, (1) enter a Project Name and (2) a name for the Main class, which contains the *main* method (Figure 7.5). In this example, we entered *HelloWorld* as the name of the project and *Program* as a name for the class that will contain the *main* method. **Note**: *camelCase* was used for naming the

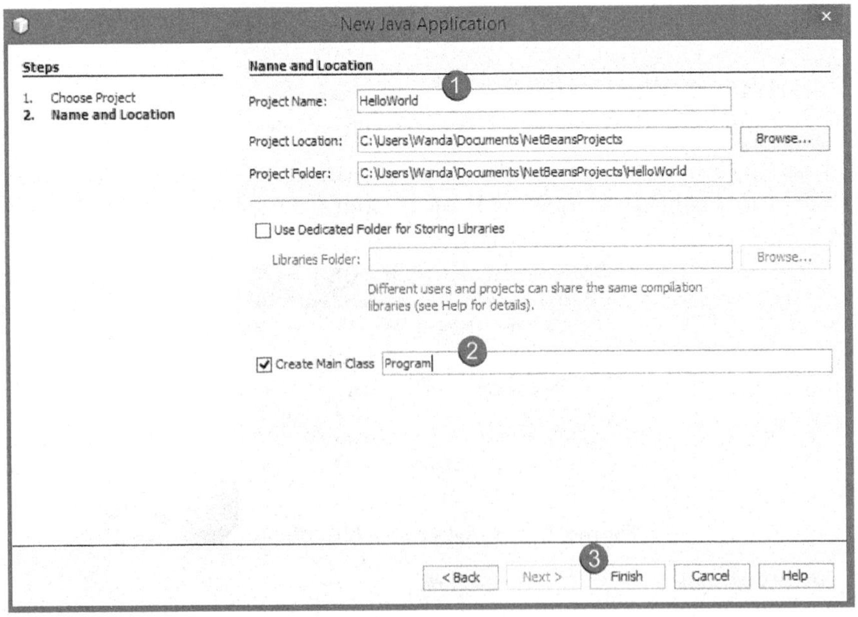

Figure 7.5   *Enter a project name and a main class name, and click Finish.*

project to avoid spaces in the filename. This follows the rules of Java naming conventions, in which the name of a file is a single word, with no space or special symbols such as %, &, or *. (3) Click the **Finish** button.

NetBeans now displays the name of the project (*HelloWorld*) in the Projects panel (on the left of the IDE) and the Program class with a *main* method is displayed in the editor (in the center of the IDE; Figure 7.6).

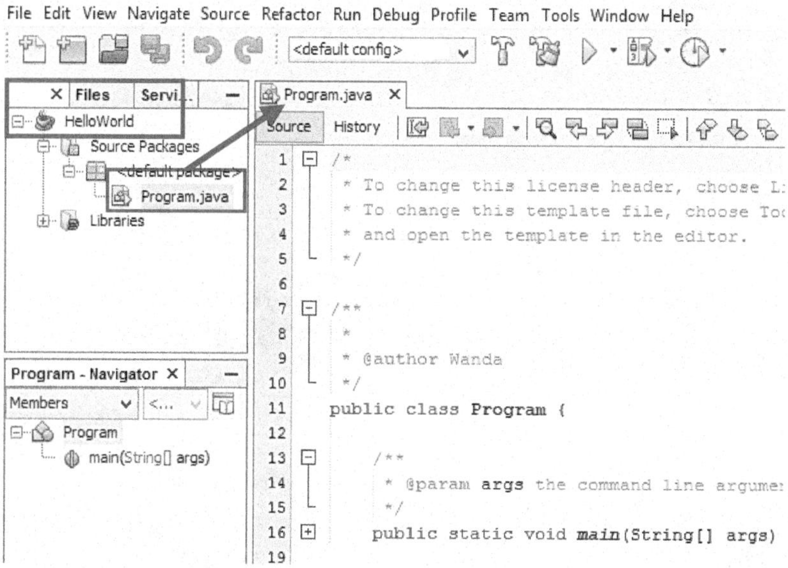

Figure 7.6 ● HelloWorld *project in NetBeans*

7.3 Syntax-Sensitive Text Editor

The *Program.java* file is a class file that automatically displays a template for creating code statements, including a *main* method. Different syntactic components in the code are displayed in different colors to make it easier to read and debug the code. Keywords (predefined words in Java) are blue, names of objects are green, and class and method names are black. Comments are displayed in light gray. Comments are also distinguished using two different symbolic notations:

```
/*
 * This is one type of comment symbol, which may
 * enclose several lines in one comment.
 */
// This is a single-line comment.
```

You may modify the comments and add more comments to suit your own purposes. For example, programmers frequently add a program description comment and document the authorship of the code near the top of the file (Figure 7.7).

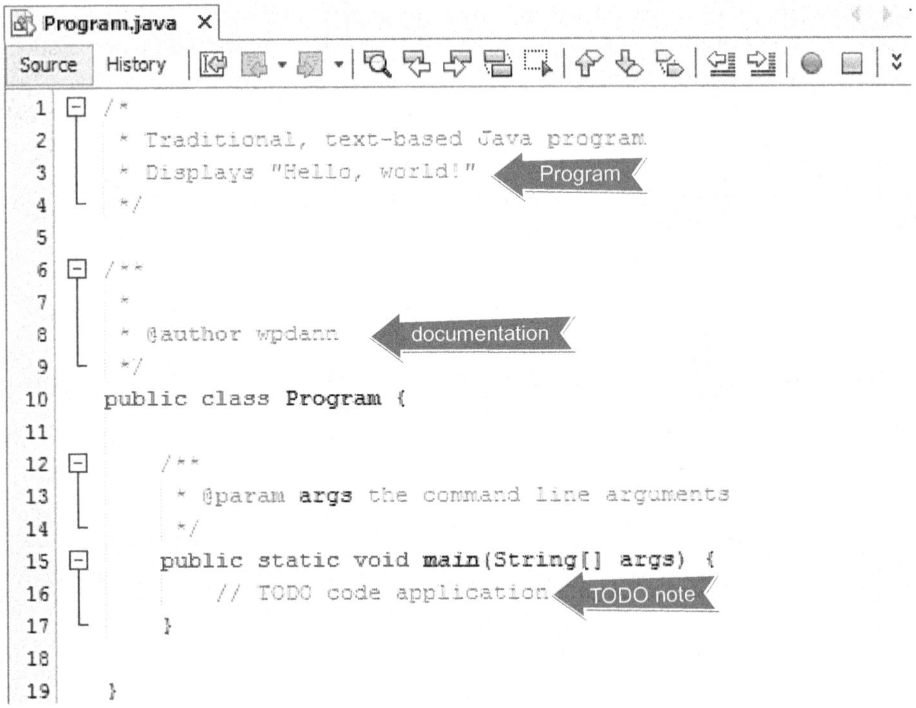

Figure 7.7 *Comments are gray in color.*

7.3.1 TODO

In some places in the project's code, NetBeans automatically generates a TODO note, a comment that reminds the human programmer to add code in a specific place for some particular purpose. The TODO note in the *main* method shown in Figure 7.8 indicates that

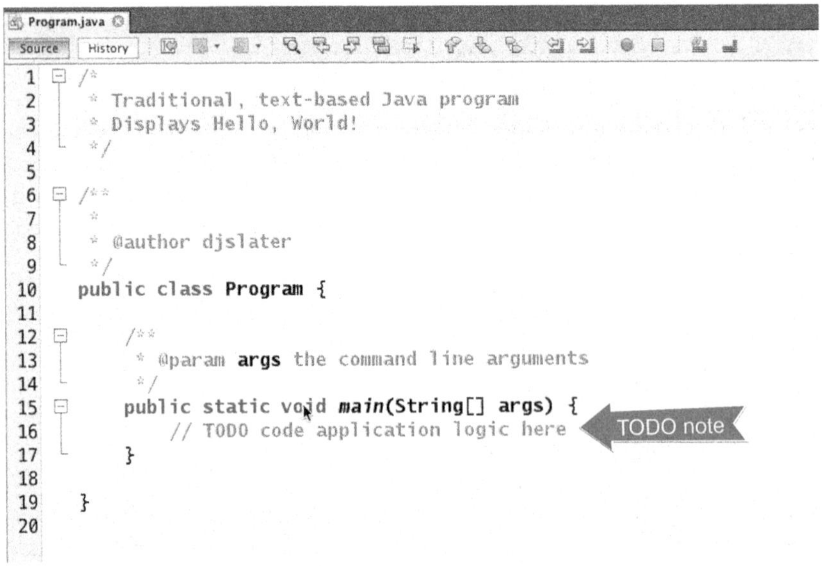

Figure 7.8 *TODO ... a reminder to add or modify code here*

application logic code statements should be written in *main*. When a Java program runs, the *main* method in the controlling class executes first because the code in *main* is generally expected to manage the overall operation of the program application (the application's "logic").

The same project components are used in Alice, where Alice automatically creates a Program class with a *main* method for each new project you create. As in Alice, *main* is a procedural method. In Java, a procedural method is always labeled *void*. Functional methods have other labels, which will be described in later chapters as needed.

7.4 Writing Java Code

Let's begin by replacing the TODO reminder in *main*. First, delete the TODO comment and then position the cursor in the blank line between the two curly braces (Figure 7.9). Be careful to leave the left and right curly braces.

```
public static void main(String[] args) {

}
```

Figure 7.9   *Curly braces enclose a code block.*

A convenient way to get started writing Java code is to use an Alice example as a guideline. For convenience, the code from the Alice *HelloWorld* program is shown in Figure 7.10.

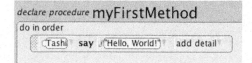

Figure 7.10   *A statement that tells Tashi to say "Hello, World!"*

Alice code statements are generally composed of a sequence of syntactic elements in a specific order:

```
object action <argument details, if any>
```

Java uses the same general syntax format, but adds punctuation marks (dots, parentheses, and a semicolon):

```
object.action (<argument details, if any>);
```

Important things to know about a Java code statement:

• A dot, known as a **dot operator**, is used to connect the object and action words. You may interpret the dot as "belonging to." In other words, *object.action* is interpreted as "the *action* method belonging to this *object*." In Alice, the statement tile does the same thing. As shown in Figure 7.10, an Alice statement tile connects the object (Tashi) with the action (*say*) and is interpreted as "call the *say* procedure belonging to Tashi."

- Parentheses are used to enclose arguments when a method (procedure or function) is called. If no arguments are needed, the parentheses are empty but still there.
- A semicolon marks the end of a statement.

When typing Java code, it is very important to pay attention to capitalization and punctuation, such as the semicolon at the end of a statement. Also, be certain to enter the statements in the *main* method within the curly braces, { }.

7.4.1 System.out for Text Output

In Alice, we used the name of a graphic model (for example, Tashi) as an object name in a code statement to create a graphics display in a runtime window. But in this text-based Java program, we will write code that uses text as the output.

In Java, **System.out** is an object commonly used for displaying text. Just as Tashi is the name of a *YetiBaby* object declared in the Scene class, **out** is the name of an *Output* object declared in Java's built-in System class.

Position the cursor within the *main* method and start typing, as shown here:

```
System.
```

Pause after typing the dot. NetBeans has a **code completion** feature that attempts to interpret what you are typing as you type it. A pop-up dialog box will appear and suggest various options for completing your code (Figure 7.11).

```
/**...3 lines */
public static void main(String[] args)
{
    System.|
}       err
        in
        out
        arraycopy(Object src, int srcPos, Object dest, int d
        clearProperty(String key)
```

Figure 7.11   *Code completion: select **out***

Select **out** in the code completion dialog box (this requires a double-click). Then type another dot and pause. Your code should now look like this:

```
System.out.
```

Another code completion drop-down menu is displayed, listing procedural methods that an **out** object can perform (Figure 7.12).

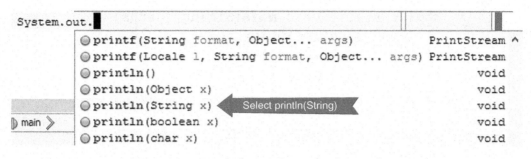

Figure 7.12 • *Code completion for the **out** object*

Scroll through the drop-down menu to find the **println** procedure. Select **println(String x).** Your code statement should now look like this:

```
System.out.println(x);
```

In this case, NetBeans is using *x* inside the parentheses as a placeholder for a String argument. String is a Java class that defines a text string consisting of a sequence of keyboard characters, which may include the digit keys. A string is enclosed in double quotes. Replace *x* with "Hello, World!" Be sure to include the quote marks. Figure 7.13 illustrates the completed statement.

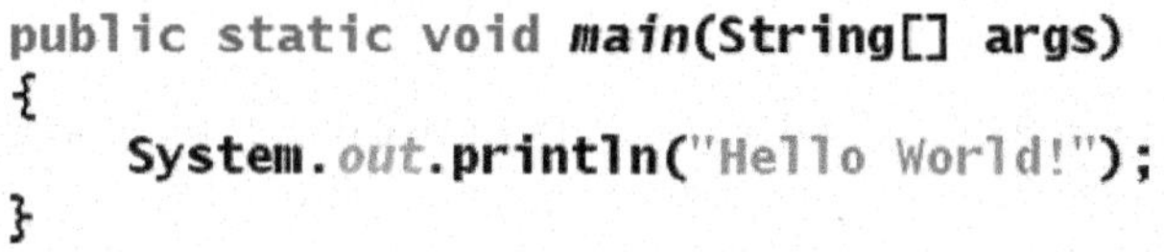

```
public static void main(String[] args)
{
        System.out.println("Hello World!");
}
```

Figure 7.13 • *A Java code statement that outputs the text string, "Hello, World!"*

7.4.2 NetBeans Keyboard Shortcuts

NetBeans has a large number of keyboard shortcuts that can be used to make typing in the code much easier. A printable list of keyboard shortcuts is at *wiki.netbeans.org/ Keyboard_Shortcuts*.

One of our favorite keyboard shortcuts is to position the cursor at the beginning of a blank line in the editor and type **sout** and then press the TAB key. NetBeans expands **sout** into **System.out.println("");** and positions the cursor between the double quotes, ready for entering a String argument.

Try it: Enter **sout** on a line in *main* and then press the TAB key (Figure 7.14).

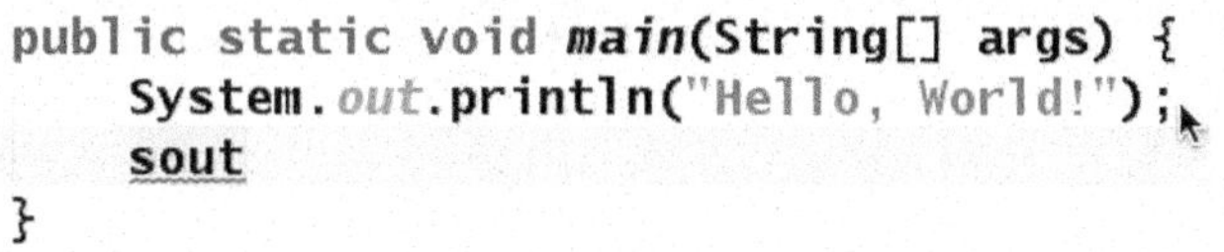

```
public static void main(String[] args) {
    System.out.println("Hello, World!");
    sout
}
```

Figure 7.14 • *Enter a keyboard shortcut on a blank line and then press TAB.*

The result is shown in Figure 7.15. If nothing is entered within the quote marks, the statement will output a blank line.

```
public static void main(String[] args) {
    System.out.println("Hello, World!");
    System.out.println("");
}
```

Figure 7.15   *The code template is expanded when the TAB key is pressed.*

7.5 Run

To test the code, click the Run button in the NetBeans menu bar (Figure 7.16).

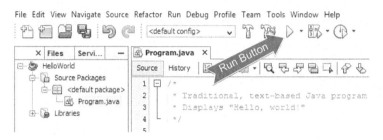

Figure 7.16   *Run button in NetBeans*

The execution results are displayed in an Output panel at the lower right of the IDE (Figure 7.17). A successful run of the program outputs a line of text, "Hello, World!" Notice that the quote marks are not part of the output.

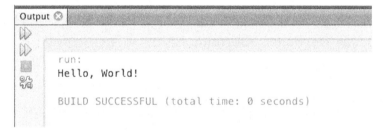

Figure 7.17   *Execution results are displayed in the Output panel.*

7.6 What Happens When the Run Button Is Clicked

Notice in Figure 7.17 that a green line in the Output panel says BUILD SUCCESSFUL (total time: 0 seconds). To explain what this means, let's take a look back a few decades to a time before modern computers were developed with graphics and windows interfaces. The monitor displayed a text-based console where users entered **command lines,** which were instructions to the underlying computer operating system. Today's computer systems still have a console box where command lines can still be entered (Figure 7.18). For example, you could enter *dir* to tell the computer to list the names of the files in the current folder.

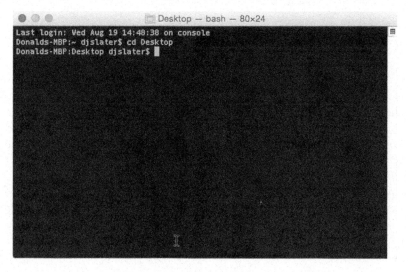

Figure 7.18 *Command-line console box*

The console box could also be used to enter commands to run a program. For example, you could enter *javac HelloWorld.java*. Running the program begins by translating the program code (the source) into simpler instructions that the computer can execute. In order to be successfully translated, the code must have a format that meets the rules of the programming language, known as the **syntax**. You don't have to use the console box to enter commands to translate the code and then run the program. When you click the Run button, NetBeans automatically does all the commands for you. The source code goes through a **build** (several steps of translation) before actually running (Figure 7.19). The translation steps are beyond the scope of this textbook, but Figure 7.19 illustrates the overall build process. The build process includes interpreting the code for the specific underlying operating system (platform).

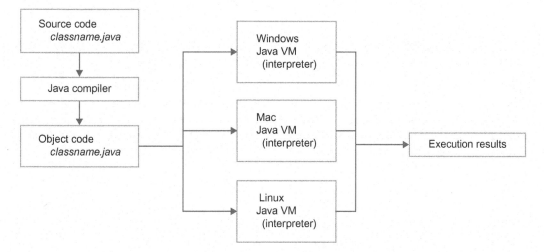

Figure 7.19 *Build and run a Java program.*

After a successful build, the computer's underlying operating system (for example, Windows on a PC, the Mac OS, or Linux) calls the Program class's *main* method. This is why the header for the *main* method is written like this:

```
public static void main(String [] args)
```

The syntax of Java requires the three words—public, static, and void—which are modifiers that tell Java how the method executes. In the context of a method header, the term public indicates a method that may be called from anywhere outside the file. (As in real life, the term "public" means "available to all.") This allows *main* to be called by the operating system. In the context of a method header, static allows *main* to be executed without creating an object of type *Program*. Void, as mentioned earlier, indicates *main* is a procedural method, which does not return a value when executed. The meaning of these terms will be described in greater detail and in different contexts in later chapters.

The *main* method header in the *HelloWorld* example code, shown again in Figure 7.20, has a parameter named *args*. The *args* parameter expects to be sent a text string containing command-line arguments, if there are any. The [ ] symbol allows for zero or more command-line arguments. (The [ ] symbol will be discussed in greater detail in a later chapter.)

```
public class Program {

    /**
     * @param args the command line arguments
     */
    public static void main(String[] args) {
        System.out.println("Hello, World!");
        System.out.println("");
    }
}
```

Figure 7.20   args *allows for a text string containing command-line arguments.*

7.7 Comparison: Graphics- vs. Text-based Editors

For comparison purposes, the *HelloWorld* Alice code is shown again in Figure 7.21 and the Java code version in Figure 7.22. In Alice's IDE, the overall Program class is displayed in one tab and the code for *main* in a separate tab. This arrangement is convenient for a drag-and-drop graphics environment. In NetBeans' text-based IDE, however, the Program class and the code for *main* are all on one tab.

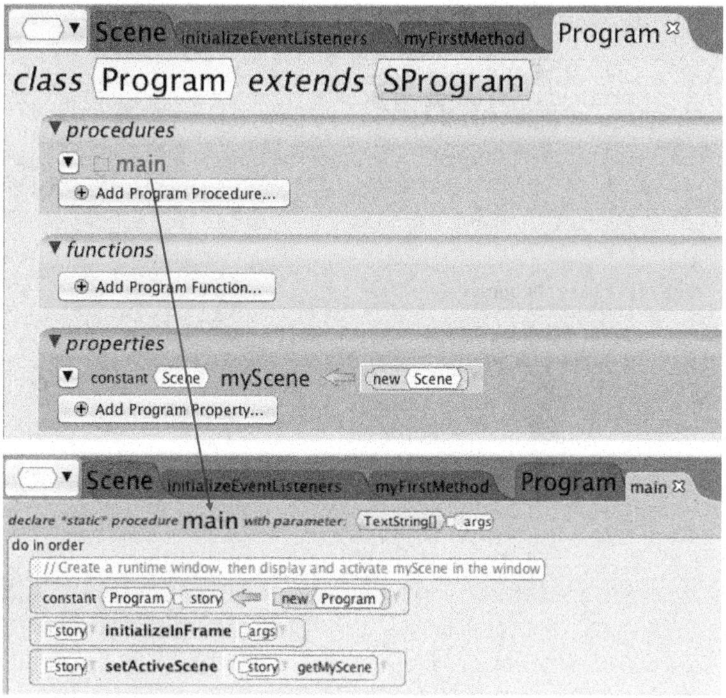

Figure 7.21 *Alice Program class with* main

Figure 7.22 *Java Program class with* main

A significant difference between these two Program classes is the generated output. In Java, the output to NetBeans' Output panel is shown in Figure 7.23.

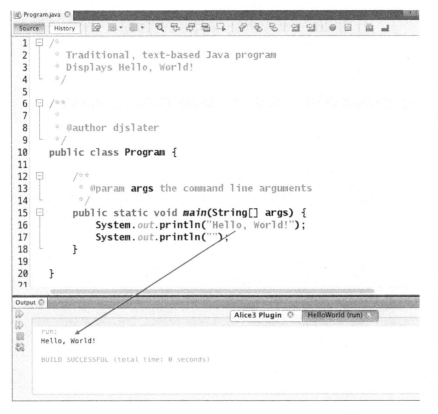

```java
1   /*
2    * Traditional, text-based Java program
3    * Displays Hello, World!
4    */
5
6   /**
7    *
8    * @author djslater
9    */
10  public class Program {
11
12      /**
13       * @param args the command line arguments
14       */
15      public static void main(String[] args) {
16          System.out.println("Hello, World!");
17          System.out.println("");
18      }
19
20  }
21
```

```
Output

                                        Alice3 Plugin    HelloWorld (run)
    run:
    Hello, World!

    BUILD SUCCESSFUL (total time: 0 seconds)
```

Figure 7.23   *Text display to Output panel*

In Alice, the output is displayed in a graphic scene in a runtime window. The scene's *myFirstMethod* is called, where the objects' actions are visually represented (Figure 7.24).

Figure 7.24   *Graphics output to a runtime window*

Summary

In this chapter, the example program is created in NetBeans. Code statements were written to create a text output and were compared to statements written in Alice to create graphics output. The basic syntax of Alice statements is the same as that of Java statements because Alice is implemented in Java. However, Alice statements use graphic tiles instead of the punctuation marks (semicolons, parentheses, and dots) used in Java. The NetBeans editor provides a code completion feature that helps in selecting arguments for parameters and meeting syntax requirements.

Both Alice and Java have a "main class"—a class that contains a *main* method. The *main* method is the basic starting point when the program executes. In Alice, the Program class is the main class. In Java programming examples in this textbook, the main class is also named Program (for consistency). However, as you browse Java programs online and in other textbooks, you will often find the main class has been given a different name.

Terms

application logic	keyboard shortcut	syntax
build	modifier	system
code completion	public	text-based editor
command line	source code	TODO note
dot operator	static	void
graphics-based	String	

Concept Questions

1. In the Alice IDE, each class has a class tab and one or more method tabs. How many tabs does each class have in the NetBeans IDE?
2. What is the purpose of the *main* method in a Java program?
3. What is the purpose of the *main* method in an Alice program?
4. Java is sometimes described as a "multiplatform" programming language. Why?

Exercises

1. Create a Java project with a Program class containing *main*. In the *main* method, write code to print your first name vertically in the Output panel; for example:

   A
   l
   i
   c
   e

2. Create a Java project with a Program class containing *main*. In the *main* method, write code to print a poem in the Output panel. Your poem should have at least two verses.

3. Create a Java project with a Program class containing *main*. In the *main* method, write code to print the following.

    (a) I'm learning how to use Java strings.

    (b) Double quotes are used, like this: "Hello, Joe" Hint: To enclose a double quote in a text string, precede the quote mark with a backslash, like this: \"

    (c) Are numbers, like 15.8, actual numeric values?

4. Create a Java project with a Program class containing *main*. Add code to *main* that outputs one of the following patterns. Then, create one of your own design.

    (a)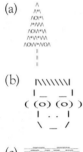

    (b)

    (c)

8

Importing: Alice 3 to Java and Code Templates

Concept Objectives

- Import an Alice project into NetBeans
- Using the NetBeans IDE to work with project components (menus and tabs)
- Relating class code components in Alice to the same components in Java
    - properties → fields

- procedures and functions, by task performed
- components in the Scene class for setting up the scene
- Writing code for 3D graphics animation in Java (code completion, arguments)
- Writing code for *do together* in Java (lambda expression, threads)

The programming example in this chapter illustrates how to import an Alice project into NetBeans and then write code statements in Java to modify or create a new animation. Learning to program with Java is typically included in Computer Science and Computer Information Systems programs of study. The Java programming language is a global standard for developing embedded and mobile applications, games, business software, and web-based content.

We will use an Alice plug-in for NetBeans to import an Alice project and provide a library of Java classes for creating 3D graphics animation. NetBeans does not have an interactive drag-and-drop Scene editor for creating a scene. However, a scene can be created in Alice and then imported into NetBeans, where Java code statements can be written to create 3D graphics animation. You will find the syntax of Java code familiar because Alice is implemented in Java.

> ## VIDEO ALERT!
>
> Before continuing, we highly recommend viewing:
>
> * video #25, *From Alice 3 to the NetBeans IDE*
>
> Available at **http://www.alice.org/3.1/materials_videos.php**

As an example for demonstrating an Alice to Java import, the completed *HelloWorld .a3p* project from Chapter 3 will be used. If you did not create this project as you studied Chapter 3, you may wish to do so now, or you may obtain a copy from your instructor if taking a course.

8.1 Alice and Java, Side by Side

Start Alice and open the *HelloWorld.a3p* project. Enable a side-by-side view and select Window in the menu bar. Then, select Preferences/Java Code On The Side from the cascading menus (Figure 8.1).

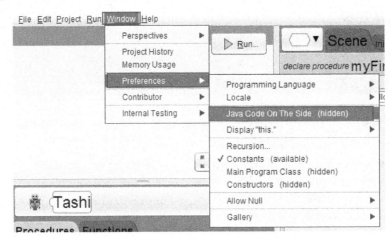

Figure 8.1   *Preference setting for Java code on the side*

The code in *myFirstMethod* should now be displayed side by side, Alice on the left and the equivalent Java on the right (Figure 8.2).

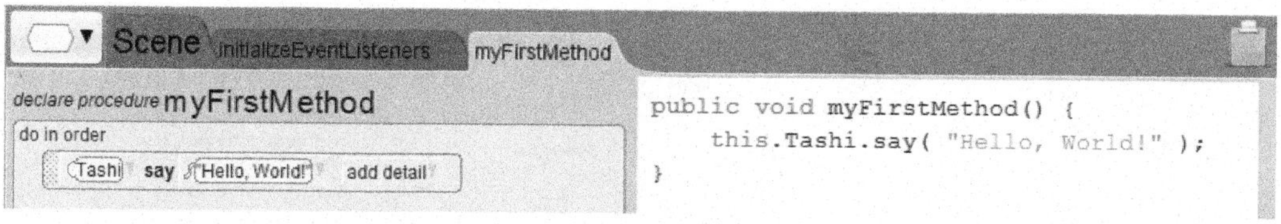

Figure 8.2 • *Alice and Java side-by-side code panels*

The Java code in the side-by-side view appears very much the same as in a Java Code editor. For example, curly braces enclose a code block, instead of the *do in order* graphic box used in Alice (Figure 8.3).

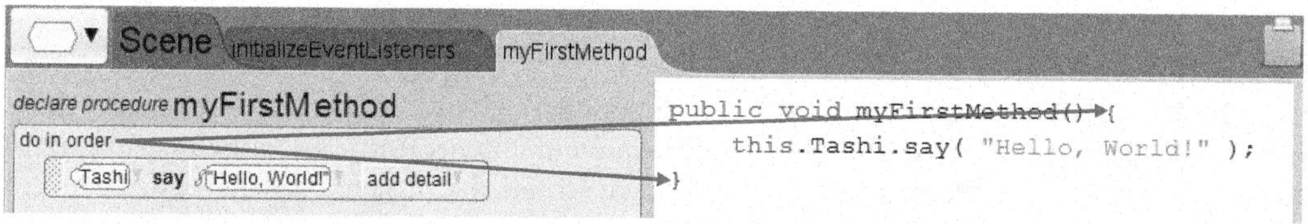

Figure 8.3 • *In Java, curly braces enclose a code block.*

If changes are made to the code in the Alice Code editor, the changes are automatically reflected in the Java panel. However, at the time of this writing, the code in the Java panel on the right *cannot* be directly edited. To work directly with the Java code, the project must be transferred to a Java integrated development environment (IDE). The next section of this chapter provides a quick tutorial on how to import an Alice project into Java. For a more detailed illustration, please consult the *Alice 3 How to Guide*, available at: http://www .alice.org/3.1/Materials/HowToGuide/HowToGuide5.pdf.

8.2 Import an Alice Project into NetBeans
....

Start NetBeans. In NetBeans, select the **File** menu in the menu bar and then **New Project** in the drop-down menu (Figure 8.4). In the New Project dialog box that appears, select **Java** in the Categories panel and **Java Project from Existing Alice Project** in the Projects panel. Then click the **Next** button.

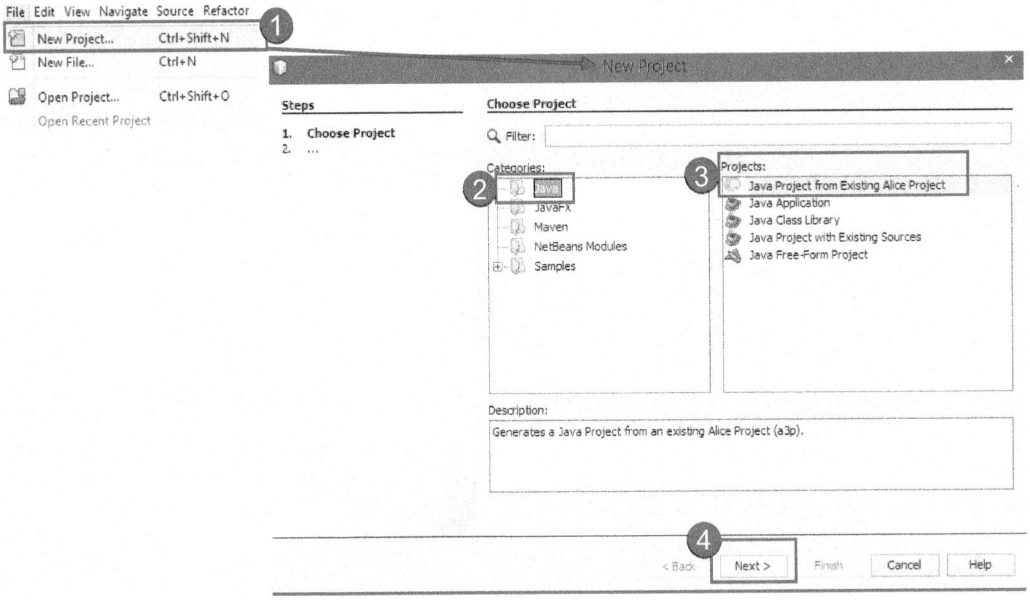

Figure 8.4   *Create a new project from an existing Alice project.*

A second dialog box will be displayed (Figure 8.5). Click the **Browse** button and then use the navigator box to find and select the *HelloWorld.a3p* project file. NetBeans automatically opens Alice's MyProjects folder. If you have stored the project elsewhere, navigate to that directory. When you have selected the file, click the **Open** button.

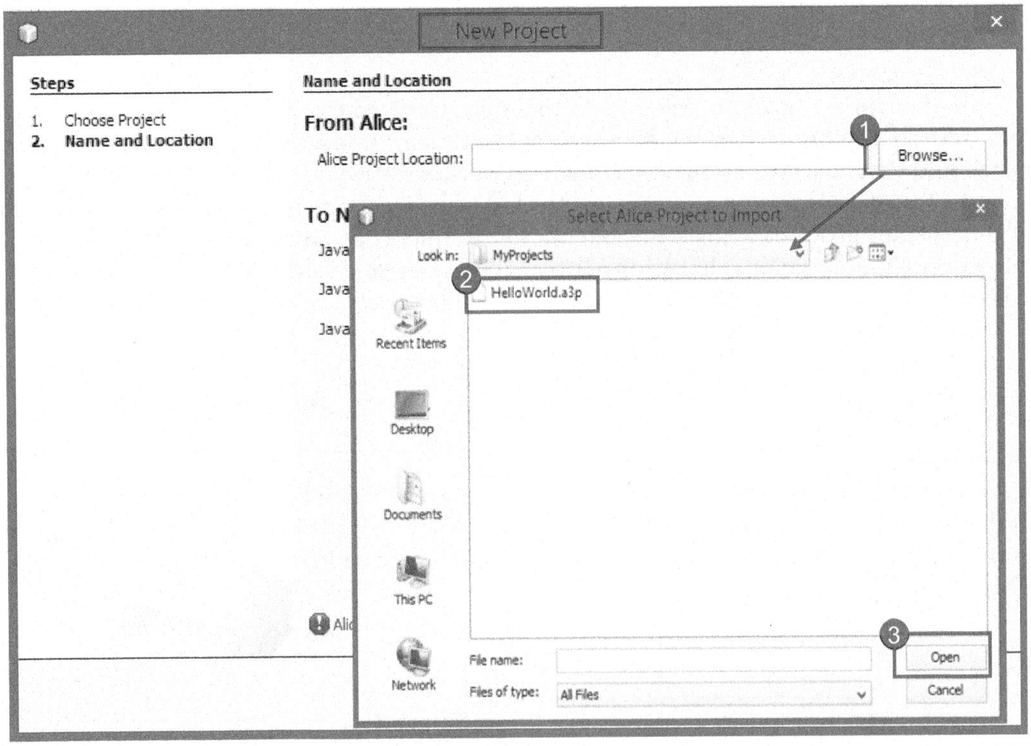

Figure 8.5   *Browse to locate and select the Alice 3 project.*

When the Open button is clicked, the navigation box closes and focus returns to the previous New Project dialog box. Two sets of directory paths are displayed. The first, labeled "From Alice:" indicates the location of the file to be imported (Figure 8.6). The second one, labeled "To NetBeans" has a textbox labeled Java Project Name. In this text-box, enter a name for the new Java project. (We entered *HelloWorld3DGraphics*.) Finally, click the **Finish** button. The import process should begin immediately, but may take several seconds, depending on the size of the Alice project being imported.

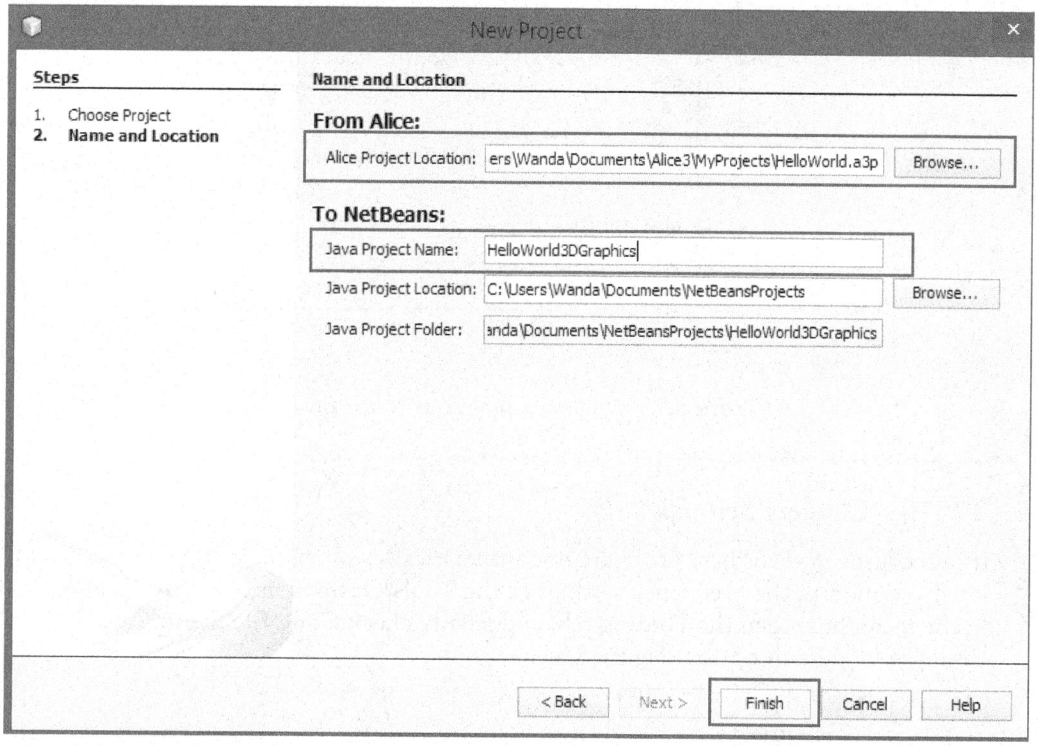

Figure 8.6 • *Name and location for storing the imported project*

TIPS: *NetBeans Files, Storage, and Edited Code*

NetBeans automatically adds *.nbm* as a filename extension. The file is then stored in a directory for NetBeans projects. **When you edit code in the NetBeans version of the project, the new code is saved in the NetBeans project but not in the original Alice project.**

Figure 8.7 shows the NetBeans IDE with the imported project. The name of the project should be displayed in the Projects panel. In the Source Packages part of the project, the *Scene.java* file has been selected. The Scene.java tab is now active in the Editor panel. In the editor tab, the procedures are collapsed, by default. The code statements in a procedure may be viewed and edited by clicking the expand box (a box with a + symbol) to the left of the procedure header.

To confirm that the project has been successfully imported, click **Run** in NetBeans. If the project was not successfully imported, check that the correct version of the Alice plug-in has been installed.

File Edit View Navigate Source Refactor Run Debug Profile Team Tools Window Help

```
 1 ⊞ imports
 8
 9     class Scene extends SScene {
10
11         /* Construct new Scene */
12 ⊞      public Scene()  {...3 lines }
15
16         /* Event listeners */
17 ⊞      private void initializeEventListeners()  {...5 lines }
22
23         /* Procedures and functions for this scene */
24 ⊞      public void myFirstMethod()  {...3 lines }
27         /* End procedures and functions for this scene */
28
29 ⊞      /* Scene fields  */
34
35 ⊞      /* Scene setup  */
71
72 ⊞      /* Procedures and functions to handle multiple scenes */
100    }
```

Figure 8.7   *Imported project in NetBeans IDE*

TIPS: *Options Settings*

If procedures in the Editor panel are not automatically collapsed, you may wish to set this option in the preference settings in the **Tools/Options** menu. Select Editor in the menu box, then the **Folding** tab, and finally check **Code Blocks** in the **Collapse by default** option (Figure 8.8).

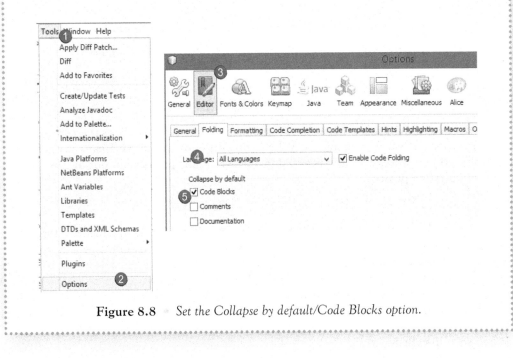

Figure 8.8   *Set the Collapse by default/Code Blocks option.*

8.3 Organization of Classes and Code Components in the NetBeans IDE

When an Alice project is imported to NetBeans, the Alice classes are transferred and reorganized into a standard organization pattern. In other words, some "housekeeping" takes place during the import process. The overall appearance of the major components in the Alice IDE and the NetBeans IDE is similar, each having a menu bar at the top and two small panels to the left of large editor tabs on the right. However, the content displayed in the panels and tabs is different. The following describes the organization pattern, and illustrates where you will find Alice classes and the code components within a class, in the NetBeans IDE.

8.3.1 Class Menus

Figure 8.9 presents a side-by-side comparison of the Class menus in Alice and Java projects. The image on the left shows the class menu as displayed in Alice. The image on the right shows the Class menu in the NetBeans Project panel.

One major difference between the two menus is: the Alice menu is organized by class hierarchy. For example, in Alice the Program and Scene classes are listed first. In NetBeans, the classes are listed alphabetically. Also, in NetBeans each class is listed as a file with a *.java* filename extension. For example, the Scene class is in a file named *Scene.java*.

Although the Class menus are organized differently, they work the same way. A click on a class name in the menu opens (if not already open) the appropriate class editor tab and activates that tab for editing. More than one class can be open at the same time, but only one class at a time is being actively edited (the edit tab displayed on top of the stack of tabs is the active tab).

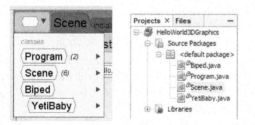

Figure 8.9 *Class menu in Alice (left); class menu in NetBeans (right)*

8.3.2 Edit Tabs

In both Alice and NetBeans, the edit tabs are where the code is written. In Alice, an opened class has a Class tab and methods belonging to that class are each given a separate editing tab immediately to the right of the class's tab (Figure 8.10). Colors distinguish the Class tab (yellow-green) from the methods tab (gray). The active editing method tab (displayed on top of the stack of edit tabs) is displayed in a bright lavender color. In Figure 8.10, the active editor tab is *myFirstMethod*.

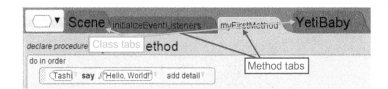

Figure 8.10   *Class tabs and method tabs in the Alice 3 Code editor*

Separate tabs for each class method allows an easy drag-n-drop of statement tiles when writing code in Alice's graphic user interface. Writing code in NetBeans, however, is performed by keyboard entry. This allows NetBeans to display just one edit tab for a class—there are no separate method tabs (Figure 8.11). Methods and properties of a class are written within the one edit tab for each class.

Figure 8.11   *Class tabs in NetBeans*

8.4 Code Component Organization Scheme in a Class

As mentioned above, importing classes and code from an Alice project to a Java project requires a bit of "housekeeping." To avoid unexpected bugs, the Alice plug-in uses a standard scheme for organizing the code within a class edit tab during the import process. The most commonly imported class in an Alice project is the Scene class. So, the Scene class will be used as an example in this section.

Figure 8.12 is a side-by-side screen capture of the Scene class editor tab in Alice (left side) with the Scene class editor tab in NetBeans (right side). Alice organizes the content in the class edit tab into component sections in a standard order:

- Procedures
- Functions
- Properties

The Alice plug-in organizes the content into component sections in a standard order:

- Imports (classes used from the Alice class library)
- Constructors (for creating an instance of this class)

- Event listeners
- Other custom methods (procedures and functions)
- Fields (properties)
- Setup methods (only in the Scene class)
- Procedures and functions for multiple scenes (only in the Scene class)

Alice's simpler code component scheme is possible because the code for methods (both procedures and functions) are defined on separate edit tabs. Also, Alice hides some code "behind the scene" so the graphic interface is less cluttered. Some of the hidden code is non-editable.

In NetBeans, all components in a class are included on the one class edit tab. This includes code that was hidden in Alice and automatically generated code, some of which may have been non-editable in Alice. The Scene class is likely to have all of the components listed above. The Scene class is the only class that will have the last two components (setup and multiple scenes methods). Most other classes will have only a few of the components in the list. Any included components, however, will be in the order listed above.

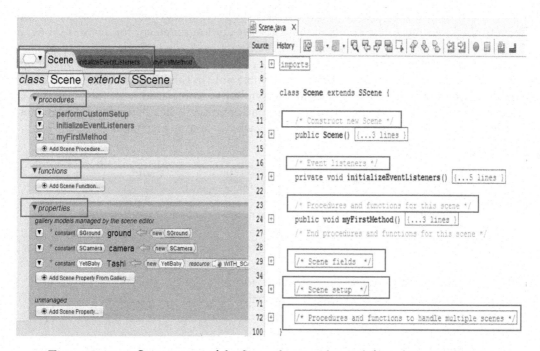

Figure 8.12 *Organization of the Scene class in Alice 3 (left) and NetBeans (right)*

8.4.1 Transfer of the properties component

Figure 8.13 shows the transfer of Alice's properties code block to NetBeans' **Fields** code block.

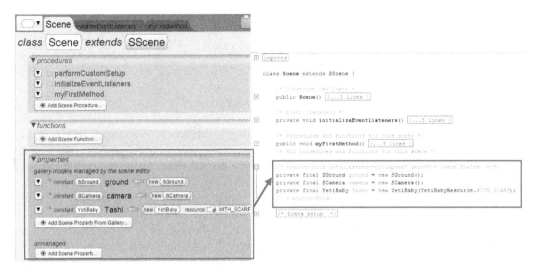

Figure 8.13   *Transfer: properties to fields*

In this transfer, the syntax in the property declaration statements is modified to conform to the Java syntax. For example, the Alice declaration statement for Tashi is shown in Figure 8.14; it is modified when transferred to NetBeans, as shown in Figure 8.15. The primary modification is the replacement of Alice's keyword *constant* with Java's keywords *private* and *final*. Private means the object is directly accessible only in this class. Final is Java's equivalent of Alice's constant. Also, Alice's arrow symbol ← is replaced with the = symbol in Java. Both symbols are known as an **assignment operator**. Alice has no end-of-statement symbol, so a semicolon is added to the end of each declaration statement.

Figure 8.14   *Tashi declaration statement in the Scene class Editor tab*

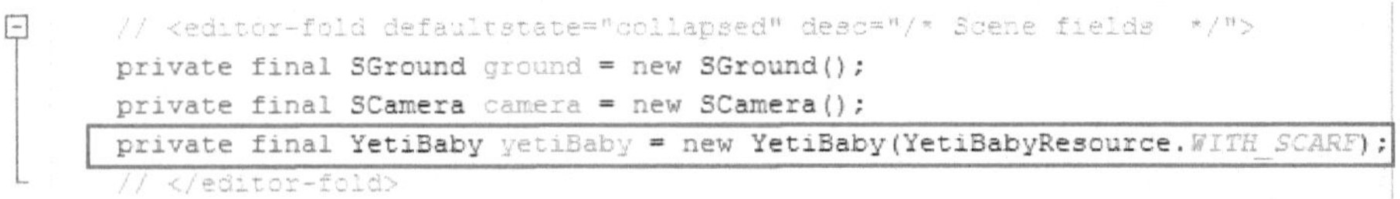

Figure 8.15   *Baby Yeti declaration statement in the* Scene.java *class file*

8.4.2 Transfer of procedure components

The Alice plug-in transfers procedures based on the kind of task the procedure performs: **Constructor, Event listener, Scene setup**. In this example, the *performCustomSetup* procedure is transferred to the Scene setup category and the *intializeEventListeners* procedure is transferred to the **Event listener** component (Figure 8.16). The **Event listener** component is found only in the Scene class.

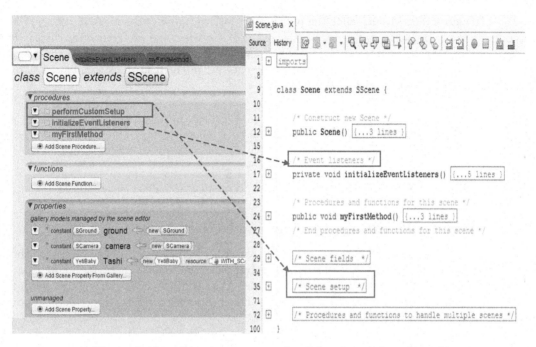

Figure 8.16 • *Procedures are transferred based on task performed.*

If the procedure doesn't perform one of those three tasks, then it is transferred to the
Procedures and functions component (a generic component for custom procedures
designed for some other task). In this example, *myFirstMethod* (Figure 8.17) is transferred to
the Procedures and functions component

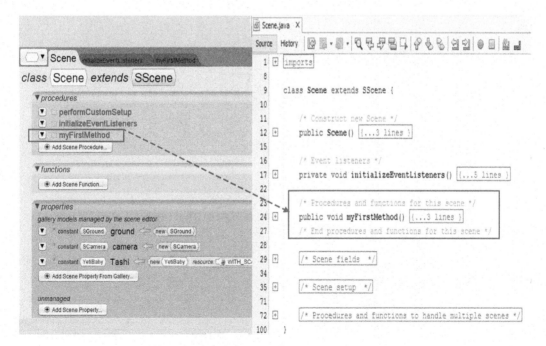

Figure 8.17 • myFirstMethod *transfers to Procedures and functions for this scene.*

To view *myFirstMethod*, click the plus box at the beginning of the method header. The code is exactly the same as the code displayed in Alice when the preference for display in Java syntax mode is enabled (Figure 8.18). Because *myFirstMethod* is defined in the Scene class, the keyword *this* represents any scene object. We might read the statement as "This scene's Tashi object says 'Hello, World!'"

```
/* Procedures and functions for this scene */
public void myFirstMethod() {
    this.Tashi.say("Hello, World!");
}
```

Figure 8.18   *Display of* myFirstMethod *in Alice, with Java mode enabled*

8.4.3 Transfer of Alice's hidden code to NetBeans

The three highlighted red boxes in Figure 8.19 are components in a NetBeans class tab that are typically hidden in Alice. The first is the **Imports** component. Import statements are needed in Java to provide access to classes in the Alice and Java code libraries, as needed. For now, you can rely on the Alice project to have properly transferred necessary import statements. In later projects, instructions will be provided for adding import statements to this component.

The second highlighted component is the **Constructor** code block. In the Alice IDE, objects are added to the scene used in the Scene editor. The Alice plug-in automatically creates the constructor component needed to create the scene in the imported project in Java.

A third highlighted box is the **Procedures and functions to handle multiple scenes** component. This is because multiple scene capability is not yet fully implemented in Alice 3. However, experimentation with creating multiple scenes is possible in Java. This component is found only in the Scene class.

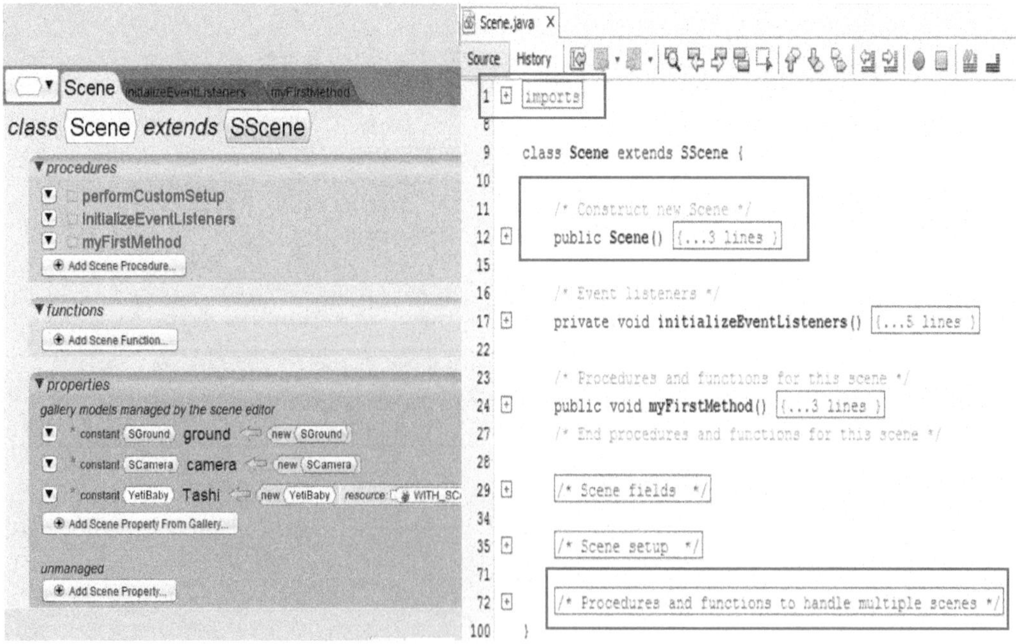

Figure 8.19   *Scene class components not typically displayed in the Alice IDE*

The **Scene setup** component (Figure 8.20) automatically contains a procedure named *performGeneratedSetup*. The *performGeneratedSetup* procedure holds auto-generated code, based on a "snapshot" of the scene that was in Alice's Scene editor, just prior to the last time the project was saved. The Alice plug-in transfers this procedure to the Scene class in NetBeans because NetBeans has no Scene editor and relies on the scene as it was originally created in Alice. This component is found only in the Scene class.

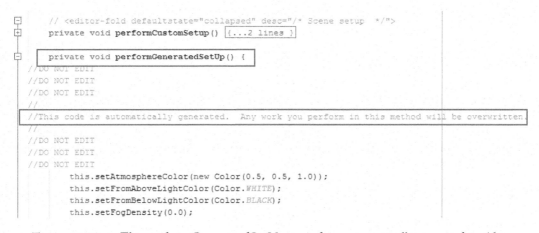

Figure 8.20 ● *The* performGeneratedSetUp *procedure automatically generated in Alice*

8.5 Writing Code for 3D Graphics Animation in Java

Now that the organization of code components in the Scene class has been introduced, you are ready to actually write some code of your own in the imported project. First, we will look at how to modify an existing code statement. Then, we will write additional code statements. Regardless of whether code is being modified or written "from scratch," your attention should be focused on using NetBeans' drop-down menus for code completion and the necessary symbols (parentheses, commas, semicolons, etc.) that must be entered to meet the rules of Java syntax.

8.5.1 Use code completion to add an argument (detail) for an optional parameter

The imported *HelloWorld* project has a *say* statement that has a **required parameter** (a text string that will be displayed in a speech bubble when the program runs). A required parameter means you must supply an argument for that parameter when writing the statement. In this example, the argument we supplied was "Hello, World!"

By default, "Hello, World!" is displayed for just one second when the program runs. However, a *say* statement does have an **optional parameter**, *duration*, that allows you to set the number of seconds. An optional parameter has a default value, but you may, if you wish, supply a different value for the parameter when writing the statement. Let's modify the *say* statement in Java, adding an argument (2.0 sec.) for the optional parameter, *duration*.

Prompt NetBeans for an optional parameter by positioning the cursor at the end of the text string, just before the right parenthesis (Figure 8.21).

```
/* Procedures and functions for this scene */
public void myFirstMethod() {
    this.Tashi.say("Hello, World!");
}
```

Figure 8.21   *Position the cursor just before the right parenthesis.*

With the cursor in position, type a comma and then enter **Say.** and pause typing. (Note that, for this prompt, you must type the name of the built-in procedure with a capital letter instead of lowercase.) The capitalized named of the built-in procedure prompts Net-Beans to display a drop-down (code completion) menu with a list of optional parameters (Figure 8.22) for this procedure. (If the drop-down menu disappears. Just delete the dot and retype it. The menu will be displayed again.)

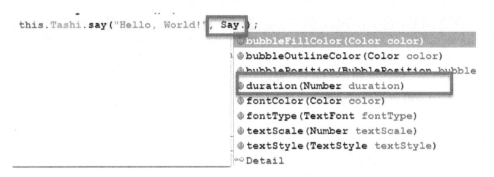

```
this.Tashi.say("Hello, World!", Say.);
                                  bubbleFillColor(Color color)
                                  bubbleOutlineColor(Color color)
                                  bubblePosition(BubblePosition bubble
                                  duration(Number duration)
                                  fontColor(Color color)
                                  fontType(TextFont fontType)
                                  textScale(Number textScale)
                                  textStyle(TextStyle textStyle)
                                  Detail
```

Figure 8.22   *Code completion menu shows a list of optional parameters.*

Actually, Say is a class in the Alice library that defines optional parameters (*bubbleFill-Color, bubbleOutlineColor, duration, fontColor, fontType, TextScale,* and *TextStyle*) for the *say* procedure. Select (double-click) *duration*, and NetBeans automatically enters *Say.duration(null)* as shown in Figure 8.23.

```
public void myFirstMethod()  {                        Number duration
    this.yetiBaby.say("Hello, World!" , Say.duration(null)  );
}
```

Figure 8.23   *The* duration *argument with a null placeholder*

In *Say.duration,* the term *null* is a placeholder for an argument value, which must be a decimal number. Replace *null* with 2.0. The resulting statement is shown in Figure 8.24.

```
/* Procedures and functions for this scene */
public void myFirstMethod() {
    this.Tashi.say("Hello, World!", Say.duration(2.0));


}
```

Figure 8.24 ● *Modified* say *statement*

The *say* built-in procedure and its corresponding Say class is just one example. Many built-in Alice procedures have a corresponding class that defines optional parameters for that class. If you are unsure whether a built-in procedure has optional parameters, just position the cursor as shown in the example above and then type a comma, the capitalized name of the procedure, a dot, and then pause to see if a drop-down code completion menu is displayed.

8.5.2 Using code completion to write code statements with required parameters

NetBeans' code completion feature can be helpful in writing code with required parameters as well. For example, some Alice built-in procedures, such as *move, turn,* and *roll,* have required parameters, for which an argument must be supplied but the value is restricted to a small set of values. For example, a *move* statement has a required *direction* parameter but the value is restricted to LEFT, RIGHT, UP, DOWN, FORWARD, or BACKWARD. No other value may be used.

To restrict the values that may be entered for a required argument, the Alice library of classes includes **Enum classes.** An Enum class enumerates a specific list of possible values. For example, the *move* statement has a corresponding Enum class, named MoveDirection, that defines a list of possible values for *move, turn* has a TurnDirection class, and *roll* has a RollDirection class.

```
MoveDirection values: LEFT, RIGHT, UP, DOWN, FORWARD, BACKWARD
TurnDirection values: LEFT, RIGHT, FORWARD, BACKWARD
RollDirection values: LEFT, RIGHT
```

In a code statement, an optional argument is specified by starting with the name of the optional argument class, then a dot., followed by the value. For example, you might write a statement to have Tashi move forward 1.5 meters, in 0.5 seconds like this:

```
Tashi.move(MoveDirection.FORWARD,1.5, Move.duration(0.5));
```

You may be wondering why the statement above is written without the keyword *this* at the beginning. This statement uses an **implicit** *this.* Tashi is an object that was declared as belonging to a scene, as defined by the Scene class. In NetBeans, *this* may be implicit when the object performing an action in a statement has been declared as belonging to the class where the code is written. Instead of writing **this.Tashi**, we can just write **Tashi**, and Java will assume the statement is defined for the Tashi object in the scene where *myFirstMethod* is executing.

To create the statement in *myFirstMethod*, first click the mouse cursor at the end of the *say* statement, after the semicolon., Then, press the ENTER key to insert a new line between the first line of code and the closing curly brace: } (Figure 8.25).

```
public void myFirstMethod() {
    this.Tashi.say("Hello, World!", Say.duration(2.0));
```

position cursor here

```
}
```

Figure 8.25   *Position the cursor on a blank line, before the right curly brace.*

Enter **Tashi.m** and pause typing. (When typing the code, be careful to note that Java is case sensitive, so uppercase and lowercase letters must be typed correctly.)

You will see a drop-down menu of possible methods beginning with the letter m (*move, moveAndOrientTo, moveAwayFrom, moveTo, moveToward*) (Figure 8.26).

```
public void myFirstMethod() {
    this.Tashi.say("Hello, World!", Say.duration(2.0));
    Tashi.move
}
```

⊚ move(MoveDirection direction, Number amount, Detail... details)	void
⊚ moveAndOrientTo(SThing target, Detail... details)	void
⊚ moveAwayFrom(SThing target, Number amount, Detail... details)	void
⊚ moveTo(SThing target, Detail... details)	void
⊚ moveToward(SThing target, Number amount, Detail... details)	void

Figure 8.26   *Pop-up menu of possible options*

Select the *move* statement (double-click). NetBeans automatically fills in the rest of the statement with a *move* statement template and placeholder components. Figure 8.27 shows the statement.

```
/* Procedures and functions for this scene */
    public void myFirstMethod() {
        this.Tashi.say("Hello, World!", Say.duration(2.0));
        Tashi.move(MoveDirection.LEFT, null, details);
    }
```

Figure 8.27   *Resulting* move *statement template*

MoveDirection.LEFT is a placeholder for *direction* and *null* is a placeholder for *amount*. Replace LEFT with FORWARD and replace *null* with 1.5.

Replace the word *details* by typing **Move.**—be sure to type the dot—and then pause typing (Figure 8.28). Select duration and then replace the *null* placeholder with 0.5 as the value. The completed statement is shown in Figure 8.29.

```
Tashi.move(MoveDirection.FORWARD, 1.5, Move.);
```

◍ animationStyle(AnimationStyle animationStyle)
◍ asSeenBy(SThing entity)
◍ duration(Number duration)
∞ Detail
⚯ class

←→🗔🖾

```
org.lgna.story.
DurationAnimationStyleArgumentFactory

public static AnimationStyle animationStyle
(AnimationStyle animationStyle)
```

Figure 8.28   *Replacing the optional argument placeholder*

```
public void myFirstMethod() {

    this.Tashi.say("Hello, World!", Say.duration(2.0));
    Tashi.move(MoveDirection.FORWARD, 1.5, Move.duration(0.5));
}
```

Figure 8.29   *Resulting* move *statement with optional argument*

If any red error marks appear in the newly written statement, correct any typing errors. Test-run. If you have successfully added the *move* statement, the animation should show Tashi saying "Hello, World!" and then moving forward 1.5 meters in 0.5 seconds.

In case an optional argument is not wanted, the *details* placeholder may simply be erased from the statement. (Note: Be sure to remove the comma immediately preceding *details*.) Figure 8.30 illustrates the statement with required arguments only.

```
public void myFirstMethod() {
    this.Tashi.say("Hello, World!", Say.duration(2.0));
    Tashi.move(MoveDirection.FORWARD, 1.5 );
}
```

Figure 8.30   A move *statement with required parameters only*

8.6 Using a Code Palette

Alice's *do in order* is equivalent to Java's set of curly braces that enclose a sequential code block. Alice's *do together* code block does not have a built-in Java equivalent. This section will explore how to create a *do together* code block, using *doTogether* (a Java version of Alice's *do together* control structure, installed by the Alice plug-in for NetBeans). As an example, let's modify the code in *myFirstMethod* to have Tashi say hello and move forward at the same time.

8.6.1 *doTogether* Code Template

On the far right of the NetBeans IDE is a code palette (Figure 8.31). A code palette is a panel that contains a set of code templates that can be dragged into the Code editor. The code palette installed by the Alice plug-in contains code templates for the control structures commonly used in Alice, one of which is *do together*. (If the panel does not appear in NetBeans on your machine, use NetBeans' Tools/Palette menu to display it.)

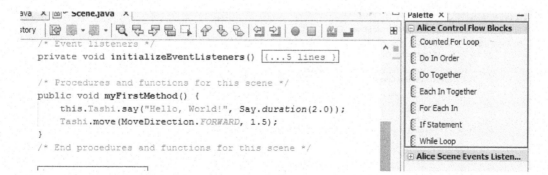

Figure 8.31   *Control statements palette*

To use the palette, first create a blank line in the code block to make space for a code template. In the example shown in Figure 8.32, the cursor is positioned just to the left of the first line, where Tashi says hello. With the cursor in position, press the ENTER key. A blank line should be created (Figure 8.33).

```
public void myFirstMethod() {
    this.Tashi.say("Hello, World!", Say.duration(2.0));
    Tashi.move(MoveDirection.FORWARD, 1.5 );

}
```

Figure 8.32   *Position cursor to the left of this statement*

```
public void myFirstMethod() {
    |                              blank line
    this.Tashi.say("Hello, World!", Say.duration(2.0));
    Tashi.move(MoveDirection.FORWARD, 1.5 );

}
```

Figure 8.33   *Blank line has been prepared*

Drag the *do together* code template and drop it onto the blank line (Figure 8.34). A Do Together dialog box is automatically displayed where a value must be selected to specify the number of things (actions) that will be performed simultaneously. In this example, two statements are to be performed at the same time, so enter **2** and click **OK**. When OK is clicked, you should see a *doTogether* code template inserted (Figure 8.35).

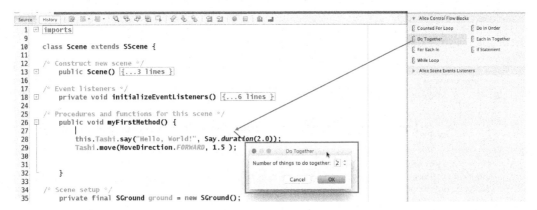

Figure 8.34   *Drag in the code template, drop it, select 2, click OK.*

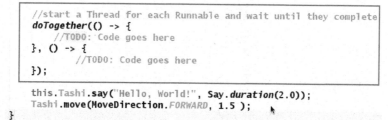

```
public void myFirstMethod() {

    //start a Thread for each Runnable and wait until they complete
    doTogether(() -> {
        //TODO: Code goes here
    }, () -> {
        //TODO: Code goes here
    });

    this.Tashi.say("Hello, World!", Say.duration(2.0));
    Tashi.move(MoveDirection.FORWARD, 1.5 );
}
```

Figure 8.35 • *Resulting* doTogether *template inserted in* myFirstMethod

The *doTogether* code template makes use of a lambda expression, which was introduced in the Java programming language with the release of Java 1.8 (often referred to as Java 8). If you experience errors with the *doTogether* code template, you may need to update your Java Development Kit (JDK) installation to Java 1.8 (or later version).

8.6.2 Lambda expressions in Java 8

An important detail to notice is the Java version of the *doTogether* code block is the same structure as the *do together* in Alice but requires more detailed symbolic notation. The code block begins with *doTogether* followed by a left parenthesis (and ending with a right parenthesis and a semicolon); as shown in Figure 8.36.

```
doTogether(
    // code statements are here, within the parentheses
);
```

Figure 8.36 • *The basic structure of a* doTogether *code block*

Code statements within a *doTogether* code block are enclosed in one or more lambda expressions (Figure 8.37). Each lambda expression begins with () -> { and ends with }. The lambda expression is a **lambda code block**, nested within the *doTogether* code block.

```
doTogether( () -> {
    // TODO: code goes here
} );
```

Figure 8.37 • *A lambda expression encloses one or more code statements.*

Two or more lambda expressions may be in a *doTogether* code block and are separated by a comma (Figure 8.38).

```
doTogether( () -> {
    //TODO: code goes here
}, () -> {
    //TODO: code goes here
} );
```

Figure 8.38 *Two lambda statements, separated by a comma*

In the first lambda code block, replace the TODO comment with the *say* statement, and in the second lambda code block, replace the TODO comment with the *move* statement (Figure 8.39).

```
public void myFirstMethod() {

    //start a Thread for each Runnable and wait until they complete
    doTogether(() -> {
        this.Tashi.say("Hello, World!", Say.duration(2.0));
    }, () -> {
            Tashi.move(MoveDirection.FORWARD, 1.5);
    });


}
```

Figure 8.39 *Threads in a Java* doTogether

Test by clicking **Run**. The lambda code blocks execute at the same time because the **lambda expression** symbol, () →, tells Java to create a **thread**. A thread is runnable—an independent path of execution that allows for running two or more threads at the same time. In a *doTogether*, the threads start at the same time and run concurrently until all the code in each thread has finished. As an analogy, think of a race where all the participants in the race start at the same time and they each follow their own path until they reach the finish line. The race is not over until all the participants have reached the finish line.

8.6.3 *do in order* is assumed within a thread

Threads within a *doTogether* are executed at the same time, but statements within each thread are executed in sequence. If a single lambda code block contains more than one statement, the statements within that thread will be executed in sequence. For example, as shown in Figure 8.40, add a turn statement in the second thread to have Tashi turn right, 1 revolution in 0.25 seconds. Test run again. Notice that the *move* forward and the *turn* right are executed in sequence, but these actions occur at the same time as the speech bubble is displayed on screen.

```
doTogether(() -> {
        this.Tashi.say("Hello, World!", Say.duration(2.0));
}, () -> {
        Tashi.move(MoveDirection.FORWARD, 1.5 );
        Tashi.turn(TurnDirection.RIGHT, 1.0, Turn.duration(0.25));
});
```

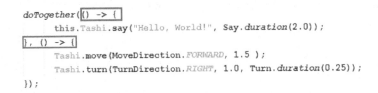

Figure 8.40 *Statements within a single lambda expression execute sequentially.*

8.6.4 Using the Counted For Loop Template

In Chapter 5, Alice's *count* loop was introduced for repetitive actions. Java has a *for* loop that may be used in the same way as Alice' *count* loop. The Code palette in NetBeans includes *Counted For Loop*, a template that implements Java's *for* loop. A Java *for* loop has syntax elements that support a wide range of code flexibility, some of which are presented here and others will be presented in Chapter 10.

In this example, we will add a *for* loop to have Tashi turn around four times. Delete the *turn* statement within the *doTogether* code block. Then, drag the *Counted For Loop* template from the Code palette into the second thread, as shown in Figure 8.41.

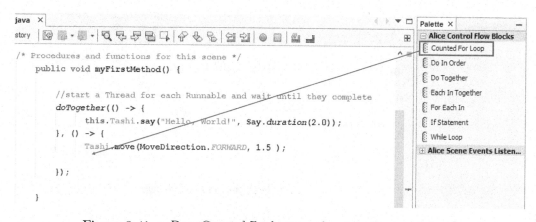

Figure 8.41   *Drag Counted For loop template into the second thread*

A pop-up dialog box asks you to enter a name for the loop control variable. In this example, we entered *count*. When OK is clicked, the *Counted For loop* template is copied into the editor (Figure 8.42).

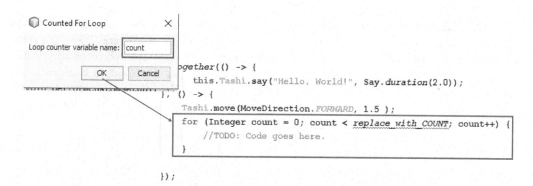

Figure 8.42   *Enter a name for the loop control variable and click OK to create template*

The template begins with the keyword *for*, followed by a set of parentheses containing three components, separated by semicolons. The first component declares the loop control variable (*count*) and automatically initializes it to zero. The second component compares the count variable to a limit value and stops the loop when the limit is reached. The third component increases the count by 1, with each repetition.

The template already has the first and third components completed. Your job is to finish the second component by removing "replace_with_COUNT" and entering an integer (whole number, only) in its place. In Figure 8.44, "**replace_with_COUNT**" is replaced with 4 to have the *turn* statement repeat four times. Now, a *turn* statement is entered (in place of //**TODO: Code goes here**). Test again. You should see the Tashi *move* forward and then *turn* four times.

```
//start a Thread for each Runnable and wait until they complete
doTogether(() -> {
     this.Tashi.say("Hello, World!", Say.duration(2.0));
}, () -> {
    Tashi.move(MoveDirection.FORWARD, 1.5 );
    for (Integer count = 0; count < 4; count++) {
        Tashi.turn(TurnDirection.RIGHT, 1, Turn.duration(0.25));
    }

});
```

Figure 8.43   *Completed for loop code block*

Summary

This chapter illustrates how to import an Alice project into NetBeans. A NetBeans plug-in allows for importing and provides a library of Alice classes, including the Alice Gallery. An imported project contains all of the components seen in Alice, but the organization of the components is somewhat different. For example, the Class menu in NetBeans is organized alphabetically, but in Alice the Class menu is organized by hierarchy of classes. In the Alice IDE, each method (procedure or function) in a class gets its own editor tab. In NetBeans, each class has just one editor tab, and all methods for that class are defined on that tab.

Once an Alice project is imported, you may modify the code and write your own code statements to animate the characters and props in the imported scene. The code statements are very much the same as the code statements written in Alice, with the addition of curly braces to enclose code blocks, parentheses to enclose arguments, and a semicolon at the end of each statement. NetBeans provides a code completion feature that assists in selecting arguments for parameters. A details menu is typically provided for optional parameters.

The plug-in installs a palette of code templates for writing code using control structures. Each entry in the code palette is similar to a control tile in Alice and provides assistance in handling the use of curly braces to enclose code blocks. One of the most helpful code templates is the *doTogether* code block, where Java's lambda expression, () →, is used to nest lambda code blocks within a *doTogether*. Each lambda code block is a thread that can run independently. Because a thread can run independently (in its own track), multiple threads in a *doTogether* are executed at the same time.

Terms

. . . .

assignment operator	final	non-editable code
code completion	for loop	optional parameter
code palette	implicit *this*	private
constant	lambda code block	required parameter
doTogether	lambda expression	thread
Enum class	method	

Concept Questions

. . . .

1. If an Alice project named *Avalanche.a3p* were imported to NetBeans and you did not specify a different name, what would the name of the project be in NetBeans (including the file name extension)?

2. In Alice's Class menu, classes are listed in order in which objects were added to the scene and some classes are listed by families in a class hierarchy. How are classes listed in NetBeans' Project panel?

3. Compare the way class code is displayed in Alice with class code display in NetBeans.

4. What is the purpose of a property declaration statement in the Scene class in Alice? In Java?

5. What is the difference in symbolic notation for an assignment operator in Alice and Java?

6. In the Scene class, what is the purpose of each of the following procedural methods:
   (a) *myFirstMethod*
   (b) *performGeneratedSetUp*
   (c) *performCustomSetup*

7. In general terms, what action is an event listener expected to perform?

8. Some code blocks appear in Java classes (for example, in the Scene and Program classes) that are not displayed in the same classes in the Alice IDE? Explain why this is so.

9. Compare the way optional parameter arguments are supplied in Alice with how they are supplied in NetBeans.

10. Which of the following define optional arguments?
    (a) *Say.duration*
    (b) *MoveDirection*
    (c) *Turn.asSeenBy*
    (d) *TurnDirection*
    (e) *Roll.animationStyle*

11. Which of the following restrict values that may be used as arguments for required parameters?
    (a) *Say.duration*
    (b) *MoveDirection*
    (c) *Turn.asSeenBy*
    (d) *TurnDirection*
    (e) *Roll.animationStyle*

12. Write the following Alice statements as each would appear in the NetBeans editor.

(a)   `snowboard` **move** `FORWARD` , `6.0` add detail

(b)   `Tashi` **setVehicle** `snowboard`

(c)   `IceBlock` **turn** `FORWARD` , `0.05` , duration `0.25` add detail

13. What is the purpose of the code palette in NetBeans?

14. What is the Java equivalent of each of the following Alice control tiles:
    (a) *do in order*
    (b) *do together*

Exercises

. . . .

Exercises 1 and 2 require the *Thaw.a3p* project (presented in Chapter 5) be imported into NetBeans. If you did not create the *Thaw.a3p* project as you studied Chapter 5, you may create the project first, or obtain a copy from your instructor if taking a course.

1. In the imported *Thaw* project, modify the statement in which Tashi says "FIRE!" to display the text with a 25 percent larger font size.

2. In the imported *Thaw* project, add new statements at the end of *myFirstMethod* (after the ice has melted) to have Tashi jump and Larry say "Wow, that was cool!" so that Tashi's jump and Larry's response are executed at the same time.

3. The *Thaw* project is an adaptation of the story in Episode 2, *The Train Engine*. For purposes of animation, the adaptation removes and changes many details of the story. Review the episode again and add two or three statements to the imported *Thaw* project to enrich the animation by adding some detail that was omitted.

Episode 4

The Forest Cabin

The train emerges out the opposite end of the tunnel with uncontrollable speed, but at least on the proper train tracks this time. Larry throws himself on the brake and drags until the train starts to slow down. Right before they come to a stop, the train bumps and rattles as if there is something on the tracks. Larry is incredibly grateful when everything finally stops.

He stands shakily. And unhinges Tashi's jaw from his ankle and sets the creature lightly on her feet.

"But, I'm hungry!" Tashi complains, "Travel is exhausting."

"We'll find you proper food," Larry says and sticks his head out the window, "as soon as we figure out where we are."

He says it as if he doesn't know. But as soon as he steps out the door and off the train's metal wheel well, Larry knows. Surrounded by tree-lined mountain ridges in the middle of a forest, there is only one place this could be.

"Follow me," the skeleton gestures behind him, only to discover that he's alone, "Baby yeti?"

Figuring the savage beast could take care of itself, Larry shrugs his shoulders and stoops down in front of the train. He rips some of the thick moss up from the path to reveal a metal rail. The ground cover explains the bumpy ride—from here on, not a single patch of the railroad tracks looks clear of brush. Looking ahead along the narrow path through the forest, he can see uniform bumps in the ground where the railroad ties lie underneath the growth. Careful to keep alongside one of the rails, the skeleton follows the path. Every once in a while he glances back to make sure the tunnel and train are still there, but after a last bend in the road even that small assurance is gone.

Eventually he finds what he's looking for. The first sign is a rotting board nailed to a tree, the words obscured years ago. Then wooden dwellings come in and out of focus between the trees—crumbling single-room shacks, half-green with moss and mold, no bigger than the cabin of his train engine. And in the center of the clearing, where the tracks come to an abrupt end, is the tiniest hut of all. Larry places his hand on the door and gives it a small push.

"You're late," a refined voice admonishes.

Larry looks aghast at the old woman sipping tea in the middle of the room. Across the table is Tashi, her claws hooked in her own teacup, casually drinking as if this was something she did every day.

"I wasn't aware there was a time to keep," Larry stutters.

"One hundred years late," the old woman continues. "What kept you?"

"I was frozen."

"Ah, yes, that can happen," she sighs and pours a third cup of tea. "No matter. Have a seat."

Larry sits on a nearby log, feeling a little out of place. Or, more accurately, feeling the fine porcelain china and lace tablecloth and the very act of taking tea are out of place in this stinking, weatherworn hovel. He picks up his cup and sips. The hot water slithers down the backsides of his teeth and drips off his chin. Larry hastily puts the cup back down again and dabs at the mess with one of the embroidered cloth napkins.

"Have you done it, then?" the woman asks.

Tashi raises a knowing eyebrow at the skeleton.

"Done what?" Larry asks, glaring at Tashi and feeling like he's missing something.

"Collected your train," the woman says simply, as if it were obvious.

Tashi nods sagely.

"How could you have possibly known that?" Larry snaps at Tashi and ignores the storyteller.

"You haven't done it, then," the storyteller sighs heavily, looking terribly put upon.

"I bet it was you who broke it up!" Larry accuses, standing and upending his tea. The steaming liquid spills onto the tablecloth, staining the white lace brown.

The storyteller hardly seems to notice.

"The avalanche, the blinding white light, and then suddenly frozen in the side of a mountain—it was all you!" Larry continues, "And my friends ... gone ..."

"You must find them, of course," the storyteller nods.

"I already have some ideas about where to start looking," Tashi adds sagely.

"You?" Larry blinks.

"You're going to need help," Tashi states, "and I'm all you've got."

"Tashi is right," the old woman says, "it fits that you should help each other."

"Nothing is fitting; this wasn't what you promised me." Larry crosses his arms petulantly.

The storyteller sighs, "Is it not?"

Larry sits silently, glaring, and feeling utterly in over his head.

9

Code Reuse, Parameters, Data Types, Variables, and Arithmetic Expressions

Concept Objectives

- Using animation techniques
  - View illusion
  - Spinal bend
- Importing and reusing saved procedure code
- Declaring a custom procedure with a parameter

- Calling a custom procedure with an argument
- Declaring a variable to store a value
- Using an arithmetic expression
- Using a variable as a loop control
- Specifying a data type for a variable or parameter

The program example in this chapter extends and builds on animation techniques and programming concepts presented in the first half of this textbook. Along the way, this chapter lays the groundwork necessary for interactive and games programming presented in the second half of this textbook.

Animation techniques are extended by using a path (a sequence of markers) for smooth camera movement through a densely populated area (a forest of trees), spine bending in an object's body, and cuts to view different parts of the scene. A camera cut is an abrupt repositioning (0.0 seconds) of the camera.

Programming concepts are extended by adding parameters to custom procedures. Adding parameters to custom procedures allows for sending objects and items of data to the procedure at runtime. Variables are introduced for storing data and arithmetic expressions for computing data values. In addition, a count loop control structure is introduced for managing repetition of statements in a code block.

9.1 Analyze the Story

The programming example animates a selected segment of Episode 4 of the *Haunted Circus* story. This episode begins when the portal opens into a mountain forest scene where the train has just emerged from the portal. Larry and Tashi get off the train and wander through a ghost town of cabins in the woods. They encounter a gnarled old woman, who is the storyteller. Larry remembers her from 100 years ago and is angered when he makes the connection—the storyteller was the one who cast a magic spell that scattered his train and his circus friends when the avalanche hit.

Begin by reading and analyzing the episode, named *The Forest Cabin*, to determine the background components and select objects and actions for an animation script. The selected segment is summarized here:

> The tunnel rematerializes in a forest, and the train steams through on tracks that are at first clear but quickly become overgrown with moss and ferns. As the train slows down and rolls to a stop because of the blocked tracks, Larry hops out and explores the forest. He's distracted by memories of the last time he came here with his circus troupe and doesn't notice Tashi quietly disappear behind him. He follows the tracks and then a walking path through the forest to the same old town he stayed in 100 years ago. The storyteller's cabin is exactly where he remembered it. Larry peeks inside, nervous about what he will find. The storyteller is older than he expected, but still alive, and sitting right next to her is Tashi, looking very friendly. The old woman directs Larry to find his circus friends, who were also on the train and trapped by the avalanche.

As in previous episodes, the narrative of the story will be adapted for the purpose of creating an animation. Not every detail from the writing will be included, and a few details may be changed. Let's start with the actions that occur after the train has arrived through the portal, the train has already stopped, and Larry has jumped off the train. A possible story analysis of the episode could be

> Larry follows the path to the storyteller's cabin
> Larry sneaks a peek into the storyteller's cabin
> Larry enters the cabin to encounter Tashi already with the storyteller
> Tashi and Larry talk with the storyteller
> The storyteller tells Larry he must find his circus friends

9.2 Design

The design storyboard begins with a basic composition shot of the scene with an initial camera position and has six frames (Figure 9.1) Note that Larry starts walking, but is distracted and doesn't notice that Tashi has jumped off the train and disappears on her own. Some frames in the storyboard have camera action notations. The third storyboard frame illustrates a camera action intended to provide an illusion that the viewer (the person watching the animation) will be seeing what Larry sees as he walks through the forest. Eventually, the camera (and Larry) arrives at a cabin. Then, the camera cuts to show Larry cautiously peeking in the door. The last frame of the storyboard shows the camera repositioning to view the interior of the cabin where Larry encounters Tashi and the storyteller sitting at a table, having tea.

Figure 9.1 *Storyboard for* Forest Cabin *episode*

With the task analysis and the storyboard completed, a possible algorithm for the task may be summarized as shown in Figure 9.2.

do in order

> Larry walks a path through the woods toward the storyteller's cabin
>
> Larry stands by the door and peeks into the cabin
>
> Larry enters the cabin and encounters Tashi, who is already with the storyteller
>
> Tashi and Larry talk with the storyteller who sends them on an adventure (to find Larry's circus friends)

Figure 9.2   *Algorithm for Forest Cabin*

9.3 Starter World

Using the set design in the first frame of the storyboard as a guide, an Alice project named *GhostTownStarter*.a3p has been prepared as a starter world for this example. The starter world may be downloaded from **www.alice.org/Alice3ToJava**.

Download the project. Then start Alice and open the downloaded world. If successfully downloaded, the initial scene should appear as shown in Figure 9.3. In the initial scene setup, the train engine is shown riding on train tracks that run through in the middle of a forest. Old wood cabins are nestled between the trees in an old, abandoned ghost town. Larry has already hopped down from the train and is standing near the center of the scene, as seen by the camera.

Figure 9.3   *Initial scene for the GhostTown animation*

Open the Scene editor and select *this* scene in the Toolbox. In the Toolbox, notice that this scene has both camera and object markers (Figure 9.4). In this example, the object markers will be used for positioning Larry and Tashi at different locations in and around the storyteller's cabin.

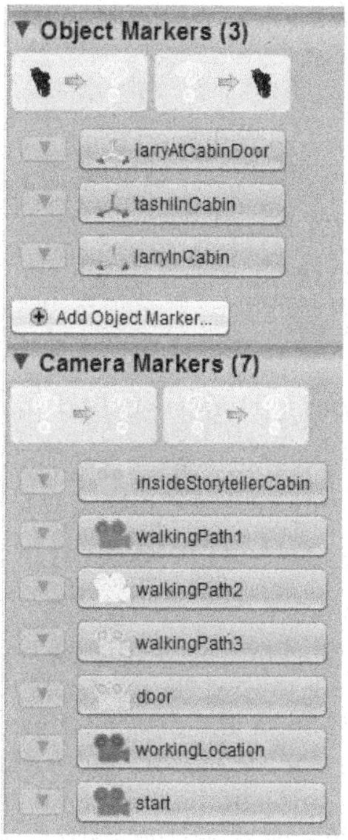

Figure 9.4 • *Object and camera markers in the GhostTown scene*

Three camera markers are used to track a walking path from the train engine to the storyteller's cabin (Figure 9.5).

Figure 9.5 • *A view of the walking path with camera markers*

Comments have already been added to *myFirstMethod* to document the algorithm (Figure 9.6).

declare procedure **myFirstMethod**

do in order

// Larry walks a path toward the storyteller's cabin

// Larry stands by the door and cautiously peeks into the cabin

// Larry enters the cabin and encounters Tashi already with the storyteller

// Tashi and Larry talk with the storyteller and the storyteller reveals Larry must find his circus friends

Figure 9.6   *Comments in* myFirstMethod *document the algorithm.*

9.4 Implementation: Camera Illusion Technique

When the train arrives in the forest, Larry immediately recognizes the old ghost town. He hops off the train and starts to walk toward the storyteller's cabin. He is so distracted that he doesn't notice Tashi hop off the train and disappear into the forest on her own.

We want to create an illusion for the person who is viewing the animation (the viewer) to see what Larry sees as he walks through the forest. An animation technique will be used to have the camera "become Larry's eyes." In the starter world, the camera is already positioned behind Larry, so you will be able to see Larry start walking into the woods.

To begin, Larry and the camera will start to move forward at the same time. Then, the camera will gradually move forward a distance that positions the camera in front of Larry's eyes. In this way, the camera viewpoint is what Larry sees, thereby creating the illusion. Camera markers will be used to reposition the camera along the path, first to *walkingPath1*, then to *walkingPath2*, and finally to *walkingPath3*. A decomposition for Larry walking through the forest, using the camera illusion technique, is shown in Figure 9.7.

> *do in order*
>
>> *do together*
>> Larry move forward 0.75 m.
>> camera move forward 0.75 m.
>> *do together*
>> camera reposition to walkingPath1 (marker)
>> Larry move forward 3 m.
>> camera reposition to walkingPath2 (marker)
>> camera reposition to walkingPath3 (marker)
>> delay 1 sec.

Figure 9.7   *Decomposition using a camera illusion technique*

In the Scene class, declare a custom procedure, named *walkPath*. Add comments to document assumptions, actions, and post-conditions. Then add statements to implement code (Figure 9.8).

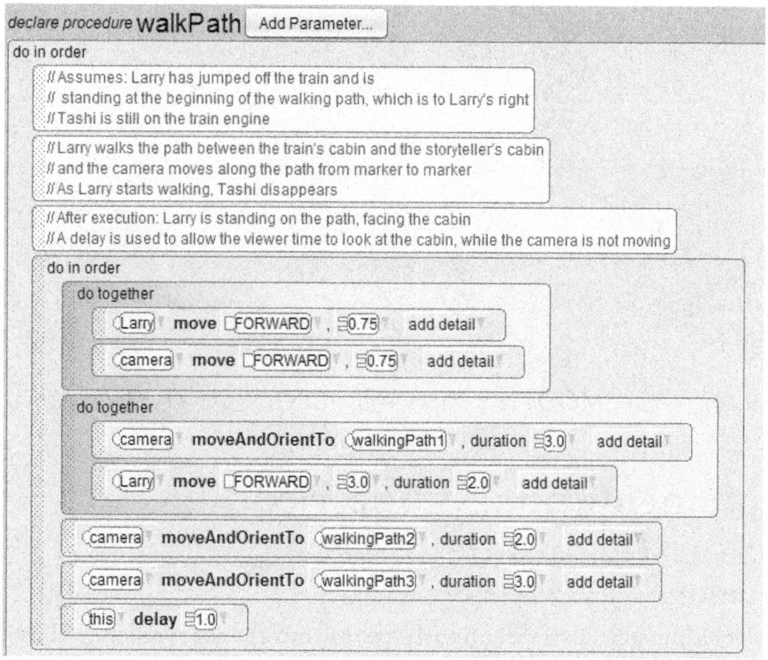

Figure 9.8 walkPath *procedure*

Add two statements to *myFirstMethod*: First a *delay* of 0.5 seconds, and then a call to the *walkPath* procedure (Figure 9.9).

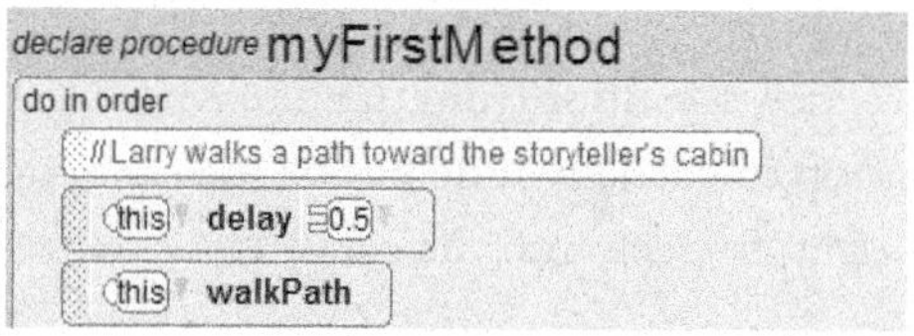

Figure 9.9 *Call* walkPath, *after a short* delay

Test-run. A *delay* statement ensures that you will see Larry and the camera move forward at the beginning of the walk. Otherwise, Alice's 0.5-second "fade in from black" (automatically begins every Run) will decrease the effectiveness of the beginning walk that sets up the illusion. You will see Larry and the camera start to move forward along the path. Then, the camera moves forward to the first marker, *walkingPath1*, a distance of about 3.1 meters. At the same time, Larry moves forward 3 meters. Because the camera moves forward a greater distance than Larry, the camera is now in front of Larry, allowing the human viewer to see the path ahead as if through Larry's eyes.

As you watch the animation, you may notice a slight hesitancy as the camera moves from marker to marker. This occurs on some computer systems but not on others. If this happens on your computer, you can make the path walk animation smoother by adding arguments for *animationStyle* and *pathStyle* optional parameters (Figure 9.10). The *animationStyle* determines whether the action begins/ends gently or at full speed (abruptly). The *pathStyle* determines whether the path is traveled bee_line (straight line from marker to marker) or is smoothed (curved).

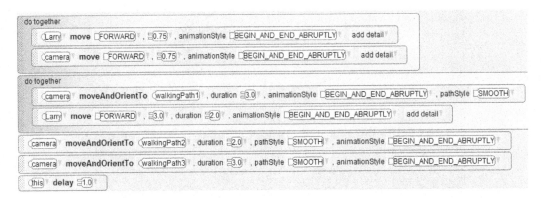

Figure 9.10   *Add SMOOTH* pathStyle *and BEGIN_AND_END_ABRUPTLY* animationStyle.

9.5 Implementation: Spine Bending Animation Technique

In the next algorithm step, Larry cautiously peeks into the storyteller's cabin. In order to peek into the cabin, Larry must be standing close to the cabin door. An object marker, *larryAtCabinDoor.* will be used to position Larry at the edge of the door so he is partially hidden by the door frame. A cut to *door* camera marker will also help in repositioning the camera's viewpoint. Then, statements will be added to have Larry cautiously bend at the waist to peek into the cabin. A decomposition for *sneakPeek* is shown in Figure 9.11.

> *do in order*
>
> >camera cut to view the door from the interior of the cabin (marker)
> >
> >Larry reposition to partially hide beside the cabin door (marker)
> >
> >Larry bend right, to peek into the cabin
> >
> >delay 1 sec.
> >
> >Larry bend left to stand upright

Figure 9.11   *Decomposition for a* sneakPeek *procedure*

Declare a custom procedure, *sneakPeek,* in the Scene class. Add comments to document assumptions, actions, and post-conditions. First, add a camera cut statement to reposition the camera in 0.0 seconds. Next, add a statement to move and orient Larry to the *larryAtCabinDoor* marker. Once again, use 0.0 seconds as the *duration* (Figure 9.12).

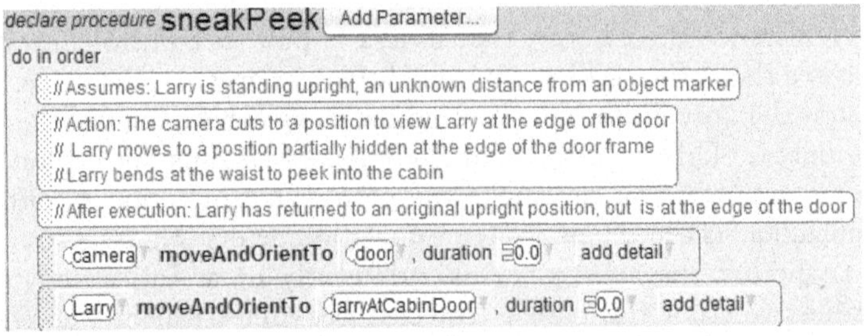

Figure 9.12   *Code statements for a camera cut and object positioning*

The next step in the decomposition is to have Larry bend his body in such a way as to cautiously peek into the cabin. A technique for bending the body of a Biped is to turn a joint in the middle of the spine, as shown in the code statements added in Figure 9.13.

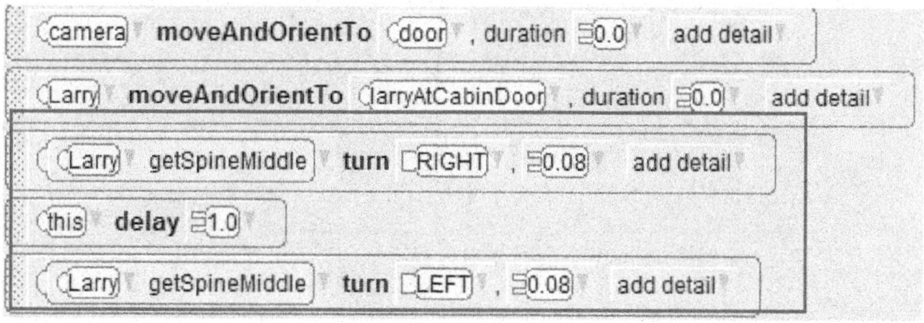

```
camera  moveAndOrientTo  door , duration ≡0.0    add detail

Larry  moveAndOrientTo  larryAtCabinDoor , duration ≡0.0    add detail

  Larry  getSpineMiddle   turn  RIGHT , ≡0.08    add detail

  this  delay ≡1.0

  Larry  getSpineMiddle   turn  LEFT , ≡0.08    add detail
```

Figure 9.13   *Bending at the middle of the spine*

Create a statement in *myFirstMethod* to call the *sneakPeek* procedure (Figure 9.14). Then run the program to test it. You should see Larry standing at the door of the cabin, where he bends at the waist and then returns to an upright position.

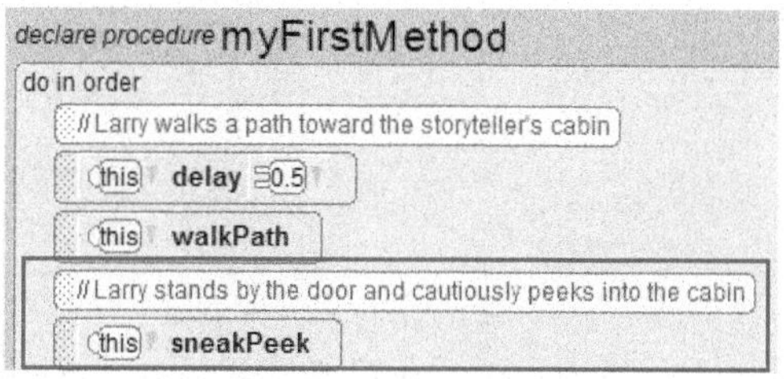

```
declare procedure myFirstMethod
do in order
  // Larry walks a path toward the storyteller's cabin
  this  delay ≡0.5
  this  walkPath
  // Larry stands by the door and cautiously peeks into the cabin
  this  sneakPeek
```

Figure 9.14   *Call* sneakPeek *from* myFirstMethod.

9.6 Implementation: Code Reuse

The last two steps in the *GhostTown* algorithm are first, Larry's encounter with the storyteller; and second, the storyteller revealing her expectation that Larry will collect the cars belonging to the haunted circus train and search for his circus friends (a trek-style adventure). The primary action is a conversation (dialog) between the storyteller, Larry, and Tashi. A storyboard may be used to illustrate the dialog. Figure 9.15 is a storyboard for the last step in the algorithm, where the storyteller reveals the adventure that lies ahead.

An added benefit of a storyboard is its illustration of the setting. In this example, the illustration shows Larry, Tashi, and the storyteller inside the cabin, sitting around a table. The starter world already has the storyteller in position at the table. After peeking into the cabin, however, Larry is still standing outside the cabin, by the door. Also, code is not yet written to move Tashi, who disappeared from the camera's view at the beginning of the animation. For Larry's encounter with the storyteller, code is needed for a camera cut to view the interior of the cabin. Also, Tashi and Larry must be moved into positions at the table. The starter has a camera marker, *insideStorytellerCabin*, for a cut to view the interior and object markers, *tashiInCabin* and *larryInCabin*, for Tashi and Larry's anticipated positions at the table.

Add a procedure to the Scene class, and name it *storytellerEncounter*. Add comments to document any assumptions, actions, and post-conditions. Next, add a statement to cut the

"Have you done it yet, then?."
"Done what?"

"Collected your train."

"It was you who broke it up."

"All my friends... gone..."
"You must find them, of course."

"I have some ideas about where to start looking"

"You're going to need help, and I'm all you've got"

Figure 9.15   *Storyboard for the dialog in* storytellerEncounter *and* revealTrek

camera to the *insideStorytellerCabin* camera marker. Then add statements to position Tashi at the *tashiInCabin* and Larry at the *larryInCabin* object markers (Figure 9.16).

```
declare procedure storytellerEncounter   Add Parameter...
do in order
    // Assumptions: Larry and Tashi are outside the cabin
    // Larry and Tashi enter the cabin and the storyteller greets Larry

    camera   moveAndOrientTo   insideStorytellerCabin  , duration ⌐0.0    add detail

    Tashi   moveAndOrientTo   tashiInCabin  , duration ⌐0.0    add detail

    Larry   moveAndOrientTo   larryInCabin    add detail
```

Figure 9.16   *Camera cut and object positioning for* storytellerEncounter

Now, statements may be added to implement the encounter dialog. The storyteller greets Larry, saying "You're late ... a hundred years late. What kept you?" Larry responds, "I was frozen." The storyteller says, "Ah yes, that can happen."

9.6.1 Importing previously saved code

Thinking about writing code for the story's dialog prompts a reminder of the *talk* procedure written for the Biped class in Chapter 6. At that time, the *talk* procedure was exported as a class file named *BipedTalk*. Instead of writing the *talk* procedure again, we can reuse *talk* by importing it into this project.

Because *talk* was originally written for the Biped class, it will be imported into the Biped class in this project. First, open the Biped class editor tab. Then, click the Add from Class File button in the upper right of the Biped editor tab. A dialog box will automatically display. Select the *TalkingBiped.a3c* file in the *MyClasses* folder on your computer and then click Open (Figure 9.17). Note that if you previously exported the *Biped's talk* file to a different folder or a USB drive, the dialog box may be used to navigate to that folder or USB drive to find the file for import.

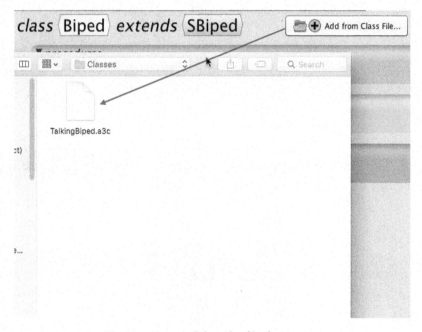

Figure 9.17 *Select the file for import.*

An Add Procedures, Functions, and Properties dialog box is displayed (Figure 9.18). Click the Next button to view the *talk* code that will be imported (Figure 9.19). Then, click the Finish button. The Biped class tab should now have the imported *talk* procedure (Figure 9.20).

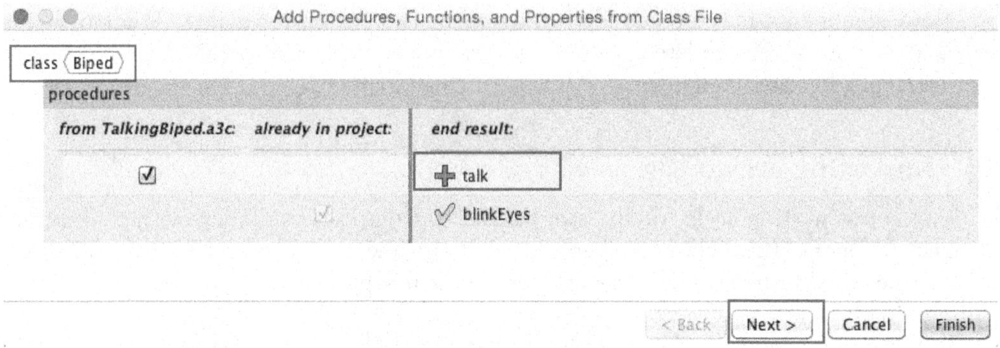

Figure 9.18   *Selecting the* talk *procedure for the Biped class*

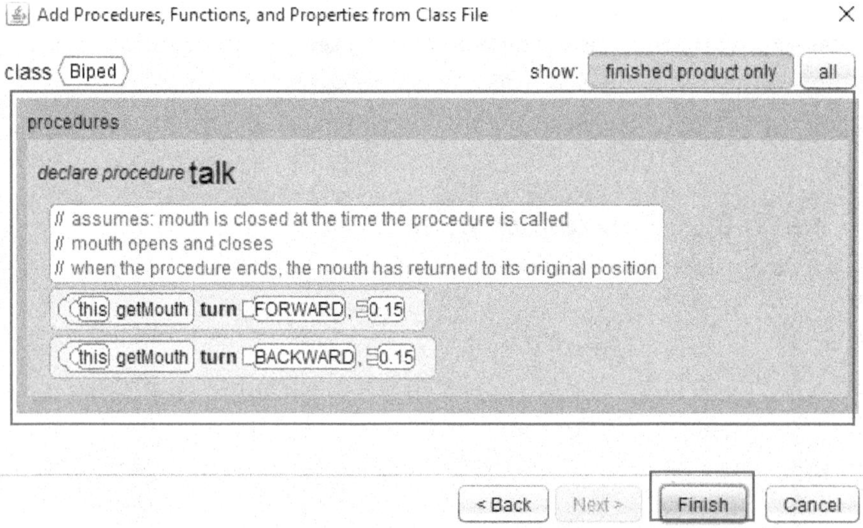

Figure 9.19   *The* talk *procedure code to be imported*

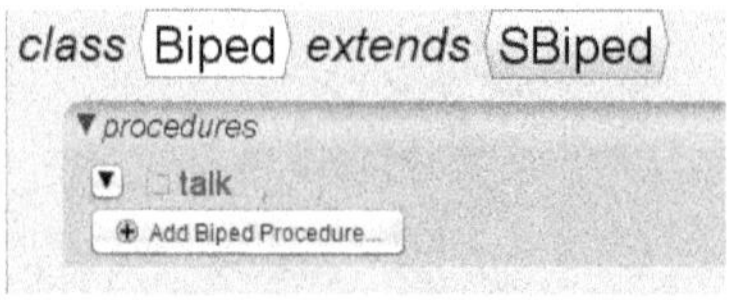

Figure 9.20   *The* talk *procedure is now in the Biped class.*

9.6.2 Reusing imported code

Larry, Tashi, and the storyteller are instances of different child classes in the Biped family. Therefore, statements may be written to call the *talk* procedure for any of the three characters, as needed. Remember that the *talk* procedure works in coordination with a *say* statement. The *say* statement displays the line of text in a speech bubble and *talk* animates the mouth with a turn forward/backward action to simulate talking.

To coordinate the actions of *say* and *talk*, add a *do together* code block with a *say* statement for the storyteller: "You're late ... a hundred years late." Add a nested *do in order* code block and four statements to call the *talk* procedure in sequence. In this example (Figure 9.21), *say* has a *duration* of 2.0 seconds. The *talk* procedure has a *duration* of 0.5 seconds. Four talks are needed to synchronize *talk* and *say*.

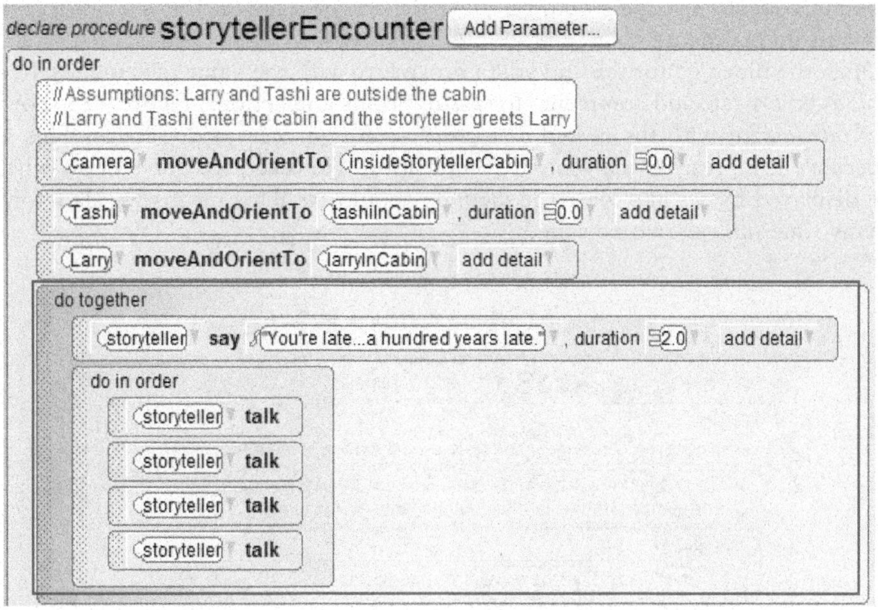

Figure 9.21 ● Do together *with a nested* do in order *to coordinate* say *and* talk

Return to *myFirstMethod* and create a statement to call *storytellerEncounter* (Figure 9.22). Test-run the program. Carefully watch the synchronization of *talk* and *say*.

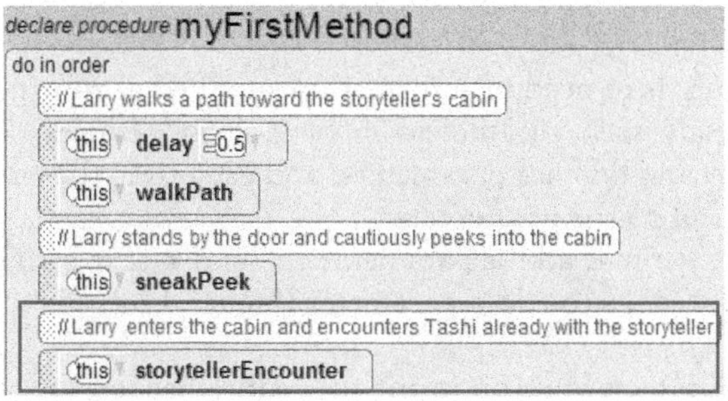

Figure 9.22 ● *Call the* storytellerEncounter *procedure.*

9.7 A Custom Procedure with a Parameter

Before adding the remaining statements in the dialog, stop to consider the code written to synchronize *talk* and *say* in nested *do together* and *do in order* code blocks. The effort is minimal for just a few lines of dialog. However, in projects with a large number of *say* statements, writing the synchronized code becomes tedious and prone to error. In addition, the code becomes increasingly more difficult to read and debug. Because the *talk* and *say* combination is frequently used, it would be convenient to package the two actions together into a single custom procedure.

Open the Biped editor tab and add a procedure with the name *talkAndSay*. In the new *talkAndSay* editor tab, add comments for assumptions and actions. Figure 9.23 shows a first draft of *talkAndSay* with the nested *do together* and *do in order* code blocks. This is a first draft because it represents the general composition. However, we don't know what words will be displayed by *say* and what the *duration* should be. This means we also don't know how many times *talk* should be called.

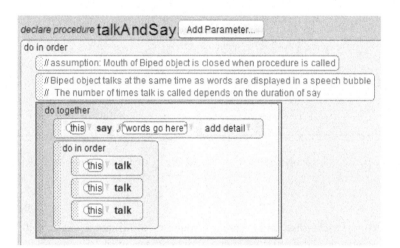

Figure 9.23   *First draft of code statements in the* do together

When a procedure is in need of information supplied at runtime, a parameter may be added. You have already seen parameters in built-in procedures. For example, the *move* procedure has *direction* and *distance* parameters, and each time the *move* procedure is called, argument values are sent to the parameters.

In this example, we will add a parameter to send a text string argument to the *say* statement. Follow these steps to add a parameter (Figure 9.24).

(1) Click the Add Parameter button in the procedure header.
(2) Click the value type menu.
(3) In the dropdown menu, select *TextString* as the type of data. When the data type is selected, Alice closes this menu.

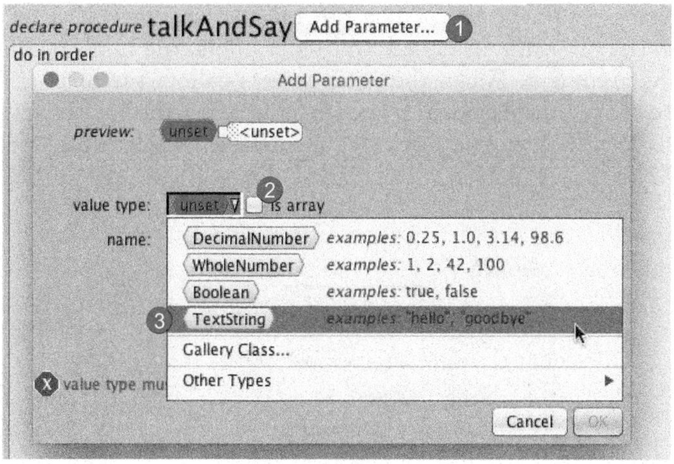

Figure 9.24 • *Add a parameter of type* TextString.

Now enter a name, *words*, for the parameter. Finally, click OK (Figure 9.25).

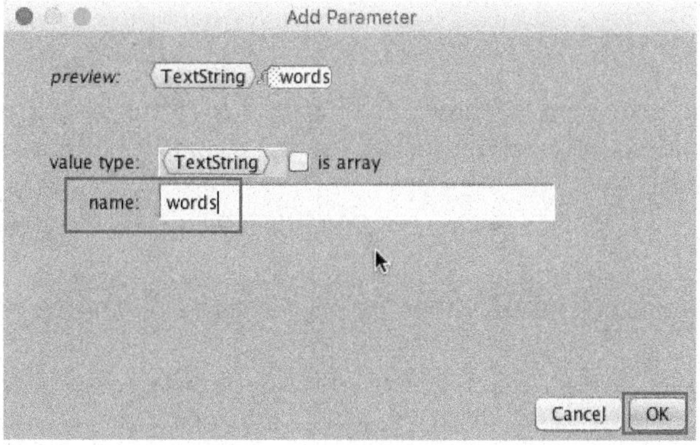

Figure 9.25 • *Enter a name for the parameter.*

You should now see *words*, of type *TextString*, listed as a parameter in the procedure header (Figure 9.26).

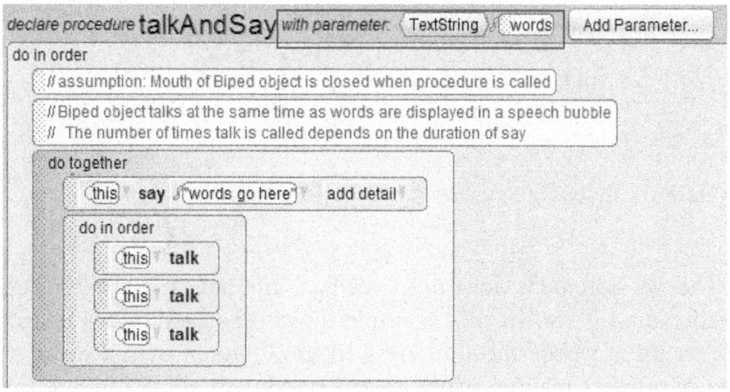

Figure 9.26 • talkAndSay *now has a parameter named* words *of type* TextString.

A parameter's data type tells Alice the kind of argument that can be sent to the parameter when the procedure is called. In this example, the *words* parameter can only be sent a text string argument. When the procedure is called, the text string is intended to supply the words to be displayed in a speech bubble by the *say* statement. Click on the "Words go here" placeholder in the *say* statement. Then, select *words* from the dropdown menu (Figure 9.27).

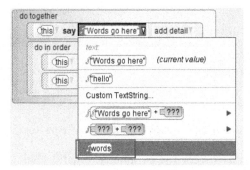

Figure 9.27   *Select the* words *parameter as the text string for the* say *statement.*

The resulting statement is shown in Figure 9.28. In effect, the *words* parameter is acting as a placeholder, representing the text string that will be sent as an argument when *talkAndSay* is called.

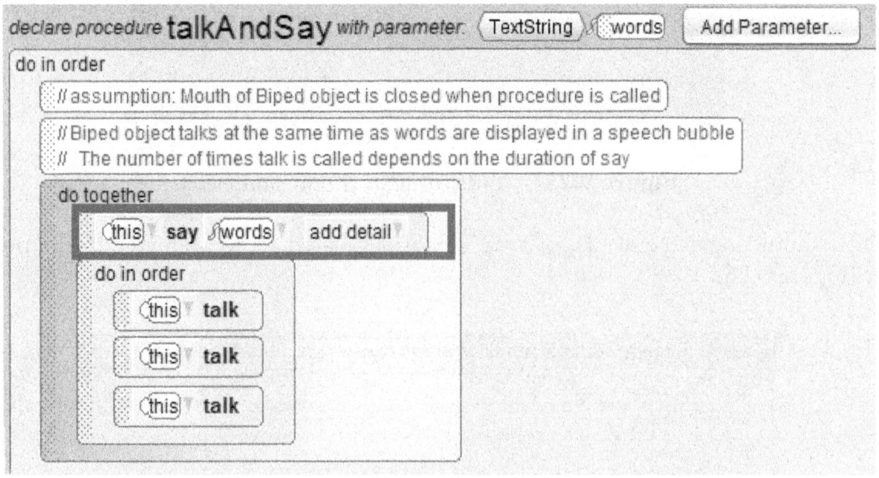

Figure 9.28   *Resulting* say *statement with the* words *parameter as the text string*

Because the *say* statement does not specify a *duration*, the speech bubble will be displayed for the default 1.0 sec. In this example, however, the *duration* should be allowed to vary. A longer string of words should have a longer *duration* than a short string of words.

A second parameter may be added to *talkAndSay* to allow for sending the number of seconds for the *say* statement's *duration*. Once again, click the Add Parameter button. A duration value is a decimal number (has digits before and after a decimal point). Click the value type menu and select *DecimalNumber* as the type (Figure 9.29). Then enter *seconds* as the name (Figure 9.30). Finally, click OK.

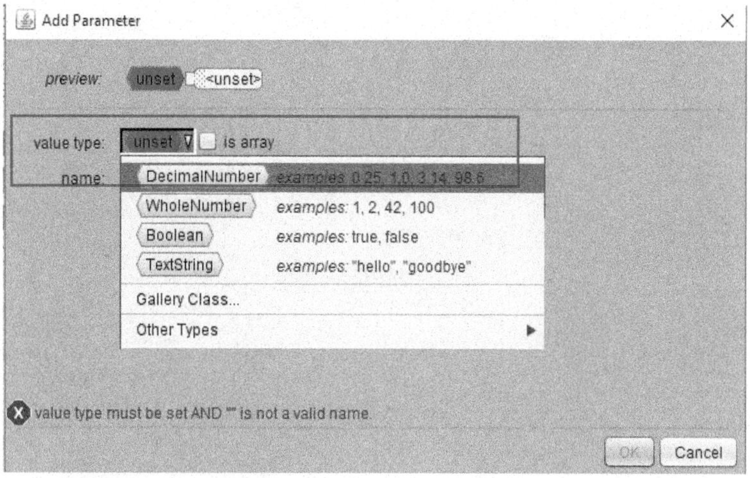

Figure 9.29 ◦ *Select* DecimalNumber *as the data type.*

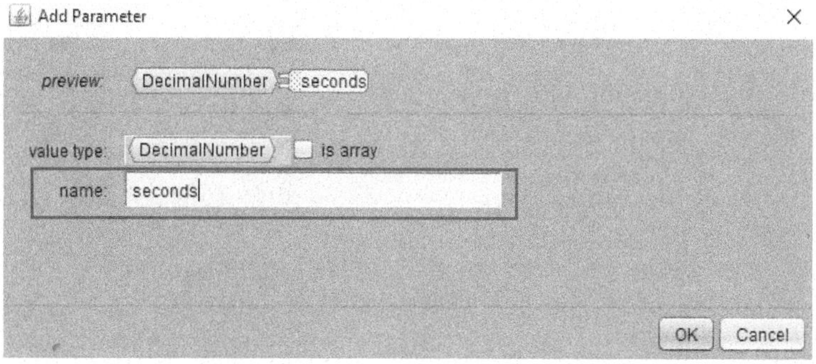

Figure 9.30 ◦ *Enter the name,* seconds.

The *talkAndSay* procedure should now have two parameters, *words* of type *TextString* and *seconds* of type *DecimalNumber* (Figure 9.31).

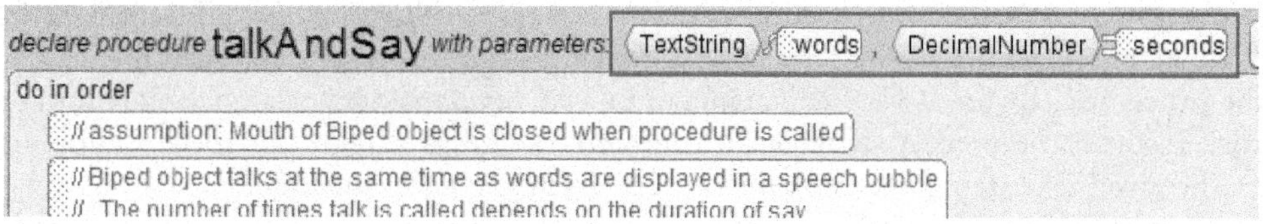

Figure 9.31 ◦ *Two parameters of different data types*

To use the argument sent to the *seconds* parameter as the duration of *say*, click the add detail button in the statement tile, select *duration* in the pulldown menu, and then *seconds* in the cascading menu (Figure 9.32). The resulting code is shown in Figure 9.33.

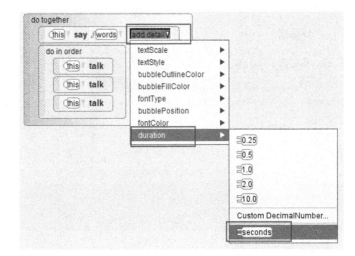

Figure 9.32   *Use the* seconds *parameter to set the duration of* say.

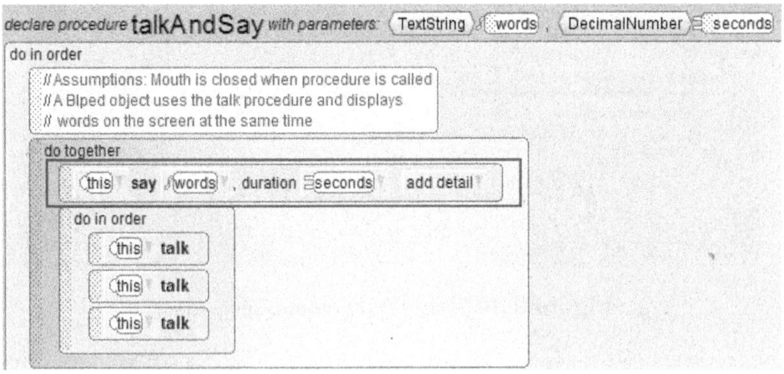

Figure 9.33   *The* say *statement uses arguments sent to* words *and* seconds *parameters.*

To test the *talkAndSay* procedure, return to the *storytellerEncounter* editor tab and add the statements that call *talkAndSay*. Four statements are needed, one for each line of dialog in the procedure (Figure 9.34). Each statement has a *duration* appropriate for the number of words. Test-run the project. Now, each time *talkAndSay* is called, the speech bubble displays the given text string and remains on screen for the given *duration*.

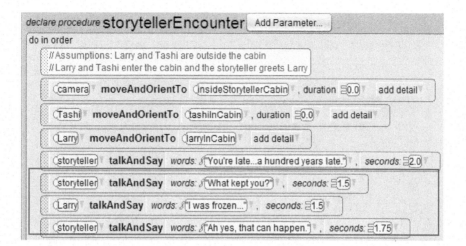

Figure 9.34 • *Dialog statements call* talkAndSay *with arguments for two parameters.*

9.8 Compute a Value, Using Variables and Arithmetic Expressions

Each time *talkAndSay* is called, the *talk* action is executed three times no matter how many words are in the text string and how long the speech bubble is displayed. However, the number of times the mouth opens and closes should be synchronized with the *duration* of the *say* statement.

A simple computation may be used to help resolve this problem. As you know, the *talk duration* is 0.5 sec. Therefore, if a *say* statement has a *duration* of 1.0 sec, *talk* should be called twice. If the *say duration* is 1.5 seconds, *talk* should be called three times. If 2 seconds, *talk* should be called four times. This pattern is simple: the number of talks equals two times the number of seconds in the *duration*.

Of course, you can easily compute two times the number of seconds in your head. But in a computer program, a code statement is needed that gives instructions to the computer for computing the value. One way to give instructions for computing a value is to create a variable that will store the result, then do the arithmetic operation to obtain the value. First, declare a **variable**. A variable is a named storage location in your computer's memory where a data item of a specific type may be stored.

9.8.1 Declaring and initializing a variable

Step 1. In the *talkAndSay* editor tab, declare a variable by dragging the *variable* tile from the Controls panel and dropping it on a line just before the *do together* code block (Figure 9.35).

Step 2. In the Insert Variable popup box, enter *numTalks* as the name for the variable (Figure 9.36).

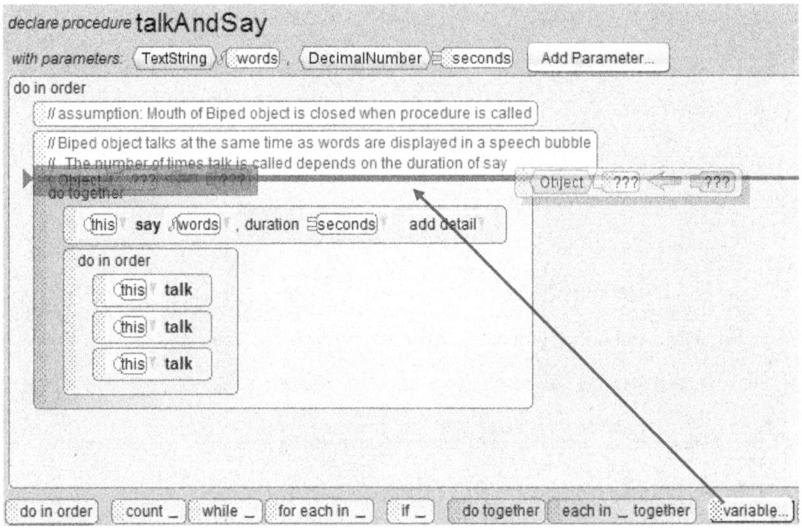

Figure 9.35   *Drag the* variable *tile to the editor tab.*

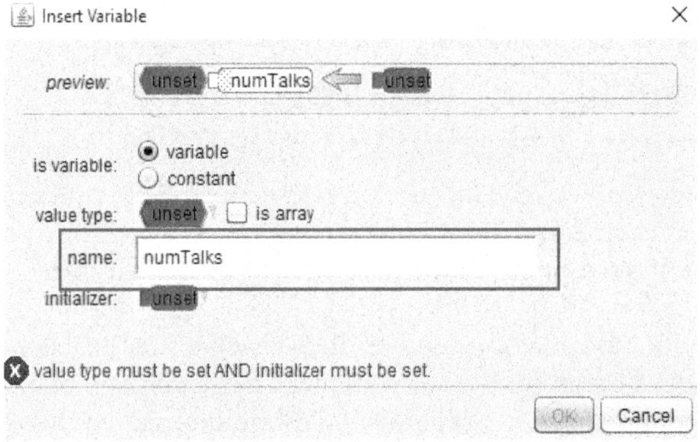

Figure 9.36   *Enter the variable name.*

Step 3. Select the type. In this example, select *DecimalNumber* because the calculation involves *seconds*, which is a decimal number (Figure 9.37).

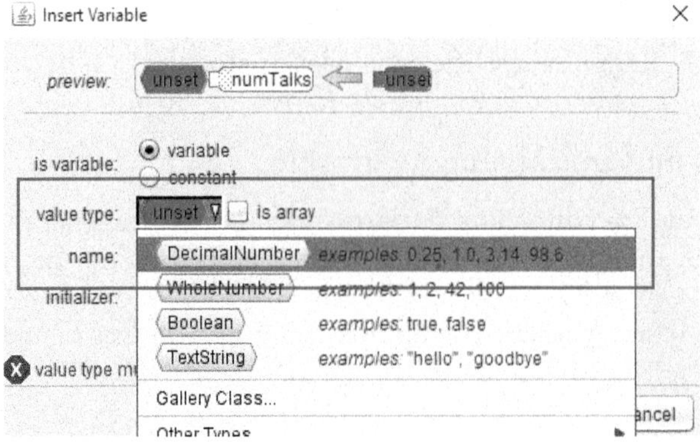

Figure 9.37   *Select the type.*

Step 4. Select an initial value for the variable. In this example, select 1.0 as an initial value (Figure 9.38). (In this example, this is a placeholder value that will be replaced.) Finally, click OK.

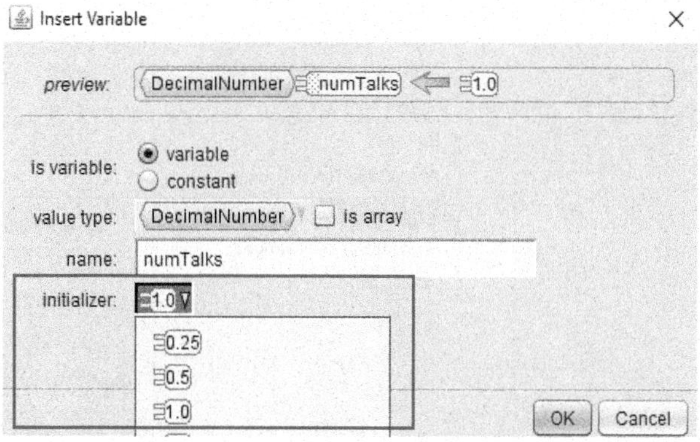

Figure 9.38   *Select an initial value.*

The resulting statement is shown in Figure 9.39. This statement tells Alice to obtain a storage location in the computer's memory. In this example, the variable's storage location is given the name *numTalks* and the first data item stored in it is 1.0. Variables are sized and labeled for storing a specific kind of data. In this example, *numTalks* will store a decimal number. This means it cannot store some other type of value.

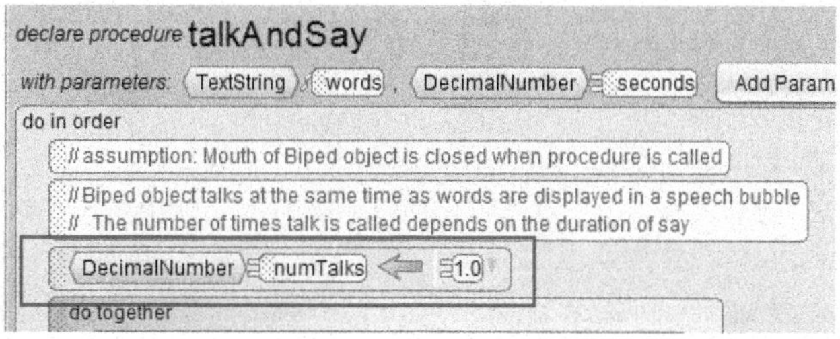

Figure 9.39   *Declaration and initialization statement for* numTalks *variable*

9.8.2 Creating an arithmetic expression

Variables are not always initialized to a placeholder value. But, in this example, the initial value for *numTalks* is a placeholder. The placeholder will be replaced with an arithmetic expression that computes the number of times *talk* should be called. To create the arithmetic expression, follow these steps (Figure 9.40):

(1) Click the initial value in the variable statement.
(2) Select Math in the dropdown menu.
(3) A cascading menu contains tiles for basic arithmetic operations (+ addition, – subtraction, * multiplication, and / division). Select multiplication in the cascading menu.

The menus will cascade further for selection of the two operands (the two values that will multiplied). Select 2.0 and *seconds* (Figure 9.41). The resulting statement is shown in Figure 9.42.

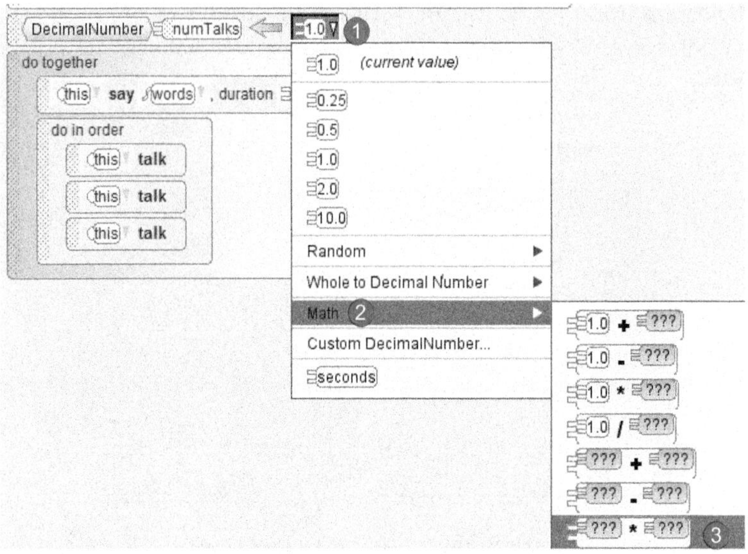

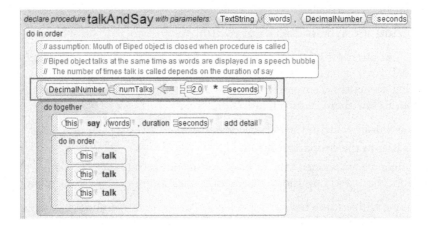

Figure 9.40   *Replace the placeholder with an arithmetic expression (multiplication).*

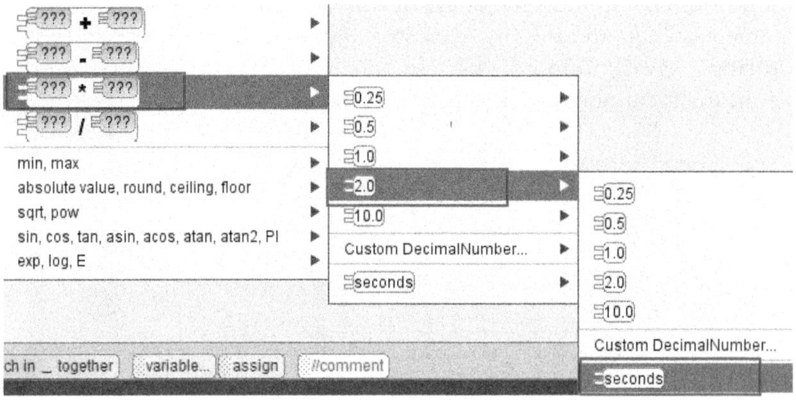

Figure 9.41   *Select two operands for multiplication.*

Figure 9.42   *Compute and store the number of times* talk *will be called.*

9.9 Using a Variable as a *count* Loop Control

Now, the computed value in *numTalks* can be used to control the number of times *talk* is called. The *do in order* control structure will be replaced by a **count** control structure. A count control structure repeats execution of a code block a counted number of times. Because *count* is repetitive, it is often referred to as a **count loop**.

To remove *do in order*, right-click on the left margin of the *do in order* code block, then select Delete from the popup menu (Figure 9.43).

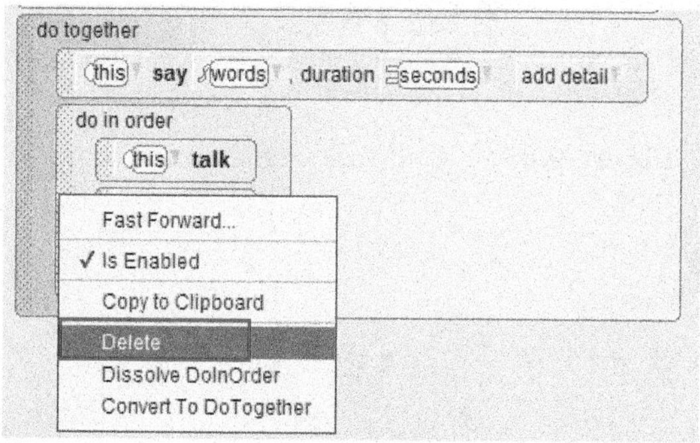

Figure 9.43   *Right-click* do in order *and select* Delete.

Next, drag the *count* tile from the Control panel into *talkAndSay* (Figure 9.44) and drop it where the *do in order* was previously located. A popup menu prompts for a **loop control value** that determines the number of repetitions. In this example, we selected 1 (a placeholder value).

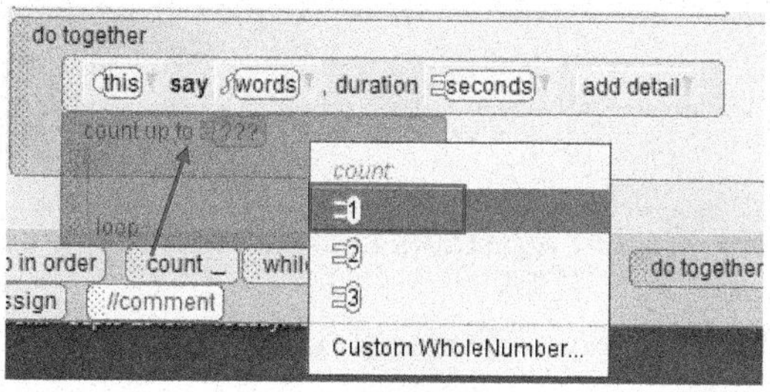

Figure 9.44   *Drag the* count *tile into the editor and select a placeholder value.*

Next, add a *talk* statement within the *count loop* code block (Figure 9.45). Because *talkAndSay* is a custom procedure for the Biped class, "`this`" in the statement "`this.talk`" refers to any Biped object.

Now, the placeholder value (1) in the *count* control structure should be replaced by the variable *numTalks*, which holds the computed number of repetitions. This is a problem in that *numTalks* stores a Decimal number but the count control structure counts using a Whole (Integer) number value. In other words, the count control structure repeats 1, 2, 3, 4, . . . times.

The Decimal value in *numTalks* must be converted to a Whole number (Integer) value. A quick and easy way to convert the value is to round the value. To round the value, follow these steps (Figure 9.46):

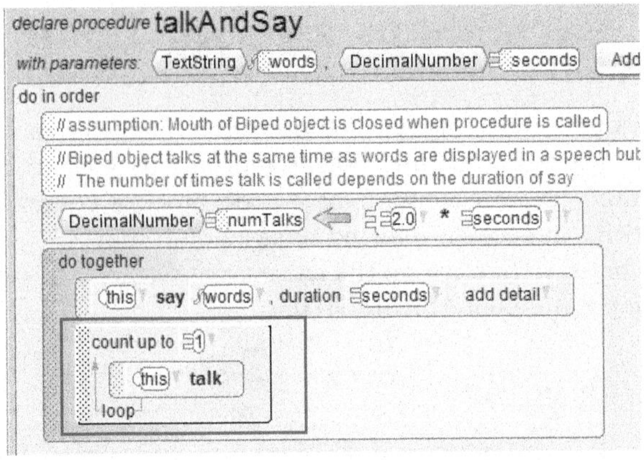

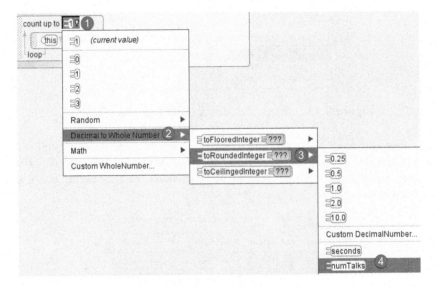

Figure 9.45 *Call* talk *in the* count loop.

Figure 9.46 *Convert* numTalks *Decimal value to a Whole number.*

(1) Click the placeholder loop control value (1, in this example).

(2) Select Decimal to Whole Number in the pulldown menu.

(3) A cascading menu contains tiles for *floor* (nearest integer down), *round* (nearest integer up or down depending on decimal value), and *ceiling* (nearest integer up). Select *toRoundedInteger* (rounds a decimal to an integer number)

(4) Select *numTalks* in the cascading menu.

The completed *talkAndSay* procedure is shown in Figure 9.47. Test-run the project again. When testing, watch the talking actions by the storyteller and Larry. Each time the *talkAndSay* statement is executed, the speaker's mouth should keep *talking* as long as the *say* speech bubble is displayed.

The last algorithm step is the storyteller revealing the trek-style adventure that Larry and Tashi will now carry out. The storyteller asks Larry, "Have you done it then?" and Larry responds, "Done what?" When the storyteller says, "Collected your train," Larry blames the storyteller for the avalanche and the demise of his circus train and his friends.

TIP: *Order of Operations:*

The example above is a simple arithmetic expression that multiplies two numbers. Of course, an arithmetic operation may be complex. As an example, we might have computed the loop control value using the formula: $2.0 * seconds - 1$ which, in Alice code, looks like this:

> DecimalNumber numTalks ⟵ 2.0 * seconds - 1.0

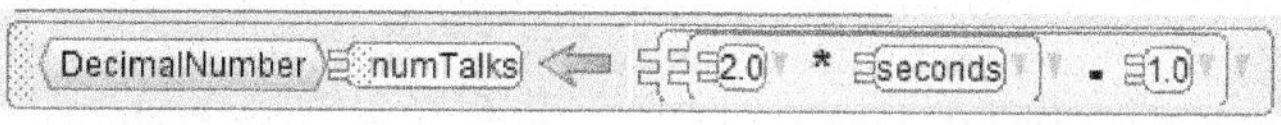

In Alice, multiplication and division operations are performed before addition and subtraction. Let's say that *seconds* is 3.5. The multiplication would be performed first and then subtraction, like this:

$$2.0 * 3.5 - 1$$
$$7.0 - 1$$
$$6.0$$

Parentheses may be used to modify the order of operations. The formula could be rewritten as:

$2.0 * (seconds - 1)$ which, in Alice code, looks like this:

> DecimalNumber numTalks ⟵ 2.0 * seconds - 1.0

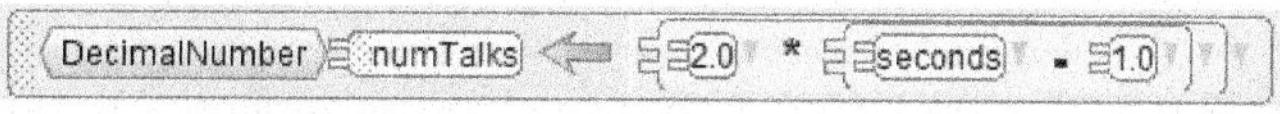

Notice that Alice uses a nested tile to represent a part of the expression enclosed in parentheses. The part of the expression enclosed in parentheses is evaluated first. Now, the evaluation will be performed like this:

$$2.0 * (3.5 - 1)$$
$$2.0 * 2.5$$
$$5.0$$

The storyboard shown previously in Figure 9.15 provides an illustration of the dialog to be created in the *revealTrek* procedure. The *revealTrek* procedure is left as an exercise for you. See the end of chapter exercises.

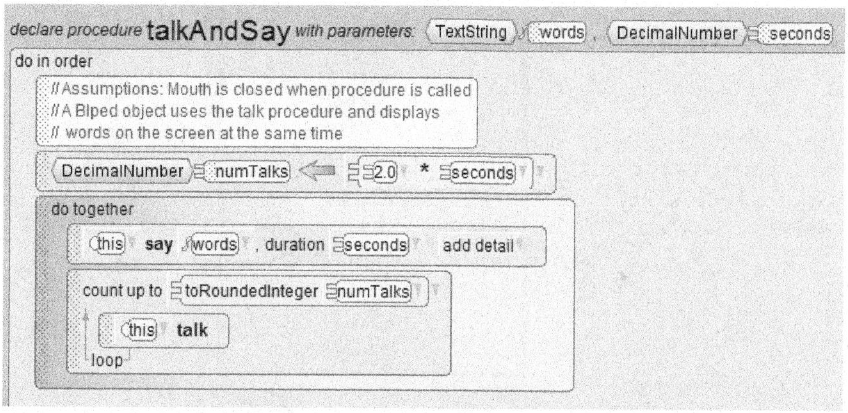

Figure 9.47   *Completed* talkAndSay *procedure*

9.10 Data Types in Alice

The data type of a variable or parameter may be any one of the listed data types in the dropdown menu (Figure 9.48). In Alice, standard data types are defined by classes, such as *DecimalNumber*, *WholeNumber*, *Boolean*, or *TextString*. *DecimalNumber* is a number having a decimal point and digits before and after the decimal point. *WholeNumber* is a number that does not have a decimal point. In mathematics, a *DecimalNumber* is a **real** value and *Whole-Number* is an **integer** value. A *Boolean* has only two possible values: *true* or *false*. A *Text-String* is a sequence of alphabetic letters, digits, and special symbols, enclosed in quotes.

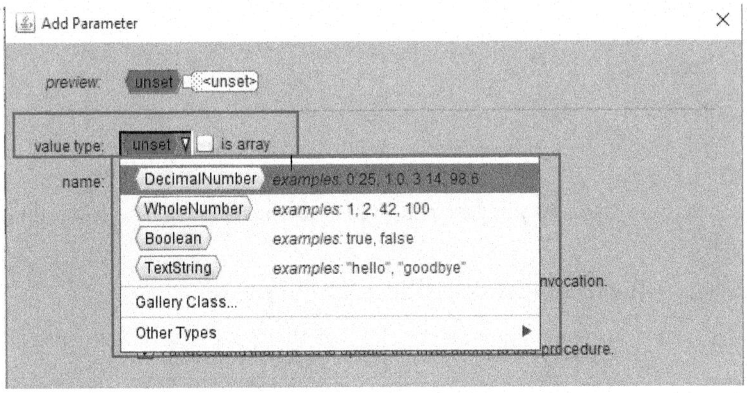

Figure 9.48   *The menu of data types*

In addition to the standard types, Alice has a Gallery of 3D models. Each 3D model is defined by a class and is a data type. If Gallery Class is selected in the pulldown menu, a Gallery Class dialog box is displayed (Figure 9.49). The Gallery Class dialog box contains a menu of classes that can be selected as a variable or a parameter's data type.

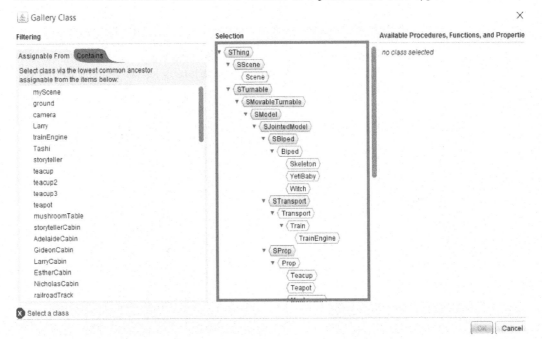

Figure 9.49   *Center panel is a menu of data types for Gallery models.*

Alice has other data types such as *SJoint*, *Color*, and *Enum* types for *move*, *turn* and *roll* directions. Figure 9.50 provides an overview reference for data types in Alice.

Type	Contains	Examples
DecimalNumber	Floating point number (Double)	1.0, 6.0289, -2.0001
WholeNumber	Integer (no decimal)	0, -1, 15, -2001
Boolean	Truth value	true, false
TextString	A string of characters	"Hello", "Name: "
Gallery class	Instances of 3D models	Larry (Skeleton), Tashi (YetiBaby)
SJoint	Joint in model skeletal system	neck, rightShoulder
Color	RGB color code	(0, 0, 255) Blue (0, 0, 0) Black (255, 0, 0) Red
MoveDirection	Direction for *move*	LEFT, RIGHT, FORWARD, UP, DOWN, BACKWARD,
TurnDirection	Direction for *turn*	LEFT, RIGHT, FORWARD, BACKWARD
RollDirection	Direction for *roll*	LEFT, RIGHT

Figure 9.50 *Frequently used Alice data types*

Summary

This chapter is a bridge from the first half to the second half of this textbook. The concepts presented in this chapter extend and build on the animation techniques and programming techniques presented in the previous chapters and lays the groundwork for interactive and games programming in the remaining chapters. Animation techniques for camera cuts, camera view illusions, movement through a path of markers, and spine bending provide special effects and increase interest for the viewer.

Adding a parameter to a custom procedure was introduced for the purpose of sending information to the procedure at runtime. Adding a parameter requires the specification of a data type—the kind of information that may be sent as an argument to the parameter. Likewise, declaring a variable requires data type specification. In Alice, data types include *DecimalNumber*, *WholeNumber*, *Boolean*, *TextString*, and objects of classes, such as a 3D model class from the Gallery.

A parameter may be used for more than one purpose in a procedure. For example, in the *talkAndSay* procedure, *seconds* is used for the *duration* in the *say* statement and is also used to compute the number of times *talk* should be called. An arithmetic expression may be used to compute a value of a numeric type. If a variable is used to store the computed value, the variable must be declared as having a specific data type. In cases where a value is not of the required data type, it is sometimes possible to convert the value to another type. For example, a *DecimalNumber* may be converted to a *WholeNumber* using *toRoundedInteger*.

Terms

arithmetic expression	data value	real
camera cut	Enum class	repetition
count	Gallery class	*toRoundedInteger*
count loop	integer	variable
data type	loop control value	

Concept Questions

1. Assume a procedure has been written for the TeaTray class with the header:
   declare procedure spin (Biped who, WholeNumber numTimes)
   Which of the following calls to the *spin* procedure have a bug? For each answer that you identify as having a bug, describe the bug.
   (a) teaTray.spin (falcon, 1)
   (b) teaTray.spin (YetiBaby, 1)
   (c) teaTray.spin (yetiBaby, 2.0)
   (d) teaTray.spin (bowlingPin, 3)
   (e) teaTray.spin (skeleton, 3)

2. The formula for computing the number of seconds before a dropped object will hit the ground is:
   time = squareRoot ((2 * distance) / acceleration)
   Write a line of code that declares a variable named *time* and includes an arithmetic expression to compute the *time*. Note that the distance must be in meters because the acceleration is due to Earth's gravity (9.8 m/sec^2).

3. Identify the data type of each of the following values:
   (a) 2.12125
   (b) −256
   (c) 0
   (d) 0.0
   (e) true
   (f) "My name is:"
   (g) "seven"

4. In each of the following arithmetic expressions, what is the resulting value?
   (a) 11 * 2
   (b) 11 INTEGER_DIVIDE 2
   (c) 11.0/2.0
   (d) 11 INTEGER_REMAINDER 2
   (e) 11.0/new DecimalNumber(2)
   (f) 11 * 2 − 5
   (g) 11 * (2 − 5)
   (h) 11.0 /2.0 * 5.0

5. Given the following code, how many times does the penguin sing?

   WholeNumber happy ← 5
   WholeNumber numTimes ← happy + 1 * 3
         count up to numTimes
             penguin.sing
   loop

6. From the programmer's perspective, what benefit is gained by writing and calling the *talkAndSay* procedure in a program?

7. In Alice, a placeholder value is sometimes selected from a menu of possible values (instead of the value we actually want in the statement). Why is the use of a placeholder value a common occurrence when creating code in the Alice IDE?

Exercises

....

1. In the *GhostTown* example illustrated in this chapter, the code for the last step in the algorithm was not implemented. However, the storyboard presented in Figure 9.15 provides a decomposition for the dialog where the storyteller informs Larry of the need to collect the cars belonging to the circus train and find his friends. Implement the *revealTrek* procedure based on the storyboard. Experiment with varying durations for text strings of different lengths.

2. Review the ending of Episode 4, *Forest Cabin*, which provides greater detail for the dialog and emotions of Larry, Tashi, and the storyteller as the storyteller directs Larry to collect the train cars and search for his friends. Add statements to the *revealTrek* procedure to complete the dialog. Also, add at least two statements to create body language that conveys some of the emotions of the characters.

3. In the *GhostTown* example illustrated in this chapter, Larry walks a path to the storyteller's cabin. Then, Larry cautiously peeks into the cabin. In the original episode, when Larry peeks into the cabin, he is surprised that Tashi has already moved into the cabin and is sitting at the table with the storyteller, having tea as if they were old friends. To animate Larry's surprise, write a *blinkEyes* procedure for the Skeleton class and then call *blinkEyes* from the *sneakPeek* procedure. Hint: Turn both the eyelid and the eye joints for each eye.

4. A favorite attraction for a Safari company is a hot air balloon ride over the savannah. Create a short animation that might be used for a web page banner. Start with a scene containing a hot air balloon (Transports/Aircraft) and several tall trees (Props), as shown here. Other objects may be added to create a more savannah-like appearance. Be sure the balloon's basket is initially on the ground. Write a *rise* procedure for the HotAirBalloon class, having a *WholeNumber* parameter named *height*, for the number of meters the balloon should rise above the ground. In the *rise* procedure, use a count loop to have the balloon move upward one meter at a time, swaying left and right as it moves upward. The count loop should execute *height* times.

5. You are working on a project to create an underwater game. The first task in creating the project is to create an underwater scene with background props and fish that are constantly swimming. To create the environment for your underwater game, begin with the UnderWater Full starter world. Add four fish objects (Swimmer/Fish) of at least two different Fish classes, as shown here. Create a *swim* method for the Fish class, in which the fish's tail turns right 1/8, then left 1/4, and then right 1/8 rev, with synchronized durations and moves forward 0.5 meters at the same time. Test by calling the *swim* procedure such that the four fish are swimming forward, all at the same time. Check that each fish's tail motion is synchronized with its forward motion. That is, the tail should stop flapping side to side at the same time as the fish stops moving forward.

6. You are working on a team to create an animation project for a veterinarian. The vet plans to play the animation on a computer in the waiting room at the vet's office. Part of the plan for the animation is to have different animals "speak" to their owners about good health care. Alice doesn't have a built-in "speak" for Quadrupeds. So, create a "speak" procedure for the Quadruped class. Create a test scene with at least two Quadruped objects of different classes and text with appropriate audio clips. In each case, when the procedure is called, the animal's mouth should be appropriately animated at the same time as the sound plays. Be sure to sync the animated motion with the duration of the sound playing.

7. Create an Alice scene containing a cylinder, a cone, and a sphere (Shapes gallery). For each shape, create a variable to store its volume as a decimal number. Then, use the formulas shown below to compute the volume of the shape and store it in the variable. Display the shape's volume by having the shape say the volume.

Cylinder: $V = \pi r^2 h$

Cone: $V = \frac{1}{3}\pi r^2 h$

Sphere: $V = \frac{4}{3}\pi r^3$

10

Java: Parameters, Data Types, Variables, Expressions, and Loop Control

Concept Objectives

- Using data types in Java
- Creating a custom procedure with a parameter in Java
- Using variables and arithmetic expressions in Java

- Writing code with *doTogether* in Java
- Using a variable limit value in a for loop
- Using a Boolean expression with relational operators in Java
- Calling a custom procedure with arguments in Java

The purpose of this chapter is to continue the exploration of parameters, variables, and data types—this time in Java. We will do this by re-creating, on the Java side, one of the methods previously created in Alice. Along the way, Java syntax requirements for these code components will be presented.

The example used in this chapter is *GhostTownExportToNetbeans.a3p*, a modified version of the *GhostTown* project presented in Chapter 9. The file may be downloaded from **www.alice.org/Alice3ToJava**, or you may obtain a copy from your instructor, if you are taking a course.

The presentation in this chapter assumes you already know the details of how to import an Alice project into NetBeans. (If you need a reminder, please review the instructions in Chapter 8.) Start NetBeans, and import *GhostTownExportToNetbeans.a3p* as a new Java project from an existing Alice project (Figure 10.1).

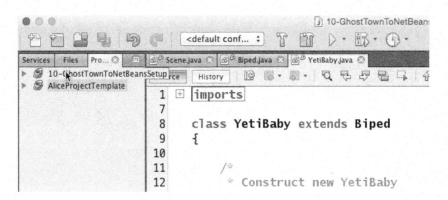

Figure 10.1   *Selecting the* GhostTrainToNetBeansSetup.a3p *project to import*

After import, the display in NetBeans should look something like that shown in Figure 10.2. In the image shown here, the YetiBaby class tab is active in the editor, but you may have a different active class tab displayed on your computer.

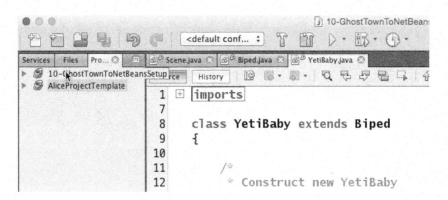

Figure 10.2   GhostTownToNetBeansSetup *project in NetBeans*

Click Run to test that the import was successful. You will see much of the same animation as in the Alice version of the *GhostTown* project (Figure 10.3). However, a key element of the animation is missing: the *talkAndSay* procedural method was removed. In this chapter, *talkAndSay* will be rewritten in Java. Re-creating Java code based on what you have seen before in Alice is an effective way to learn how to write Java code.

Figure 10.3 ● GhostTownToNetBeansSetup *project running in NetBeans*

10.1 Data Types in Alice and Java

The *talkAndSay* custom procedure has two parameters. When a parameter is declared for a custom procedure, it must have a specific data type. Writing *talkAndSay* as a custom procedure in Java has the same data type requirement. To create custom procedures with parameters in Java, you must be able to specify a Java data type for each parameter.

Alice uses classes to define four standard data types: *DecimalNumber*, *WholeNumber*, *Boolean*, and *TextString*. Java classes that define standard data types are shown in Table 10.1. *Double* and *Float* in Java both define decimal number types, but to a different degree of

Table 10.1 ● *Data Types in Java*

Type - Alice	Type - Java	Contains	Examples
DecimalNumber	Double, Float	Floating point number	1.0, 6.0289, -2.0001
WholeNumber	Integer, Short, Long, Byte	Integer (no decimal)	0, -1, 15, -2001
Boolean	Boolean	Truth value	true, false
TextString	String	A string of characters	"Hello", "Name: "
	Character	A single character (number, letter, symbol)	'a', '1', '@'

precision. *Integer, Short, Long,* and *Byte* define whole number types, but each has a different range of whole number values. Notice that Java not only has a String type but also has a type for a single character, the Character class.

10.1.1 Primitive data types in Java

The data types listed in Table 10.1, above, are known as **wrapper classes** because each class defines a type of object that contains a built-in, **primitive** data item (similar to wrapping a gift in a box). A wrapper class also defines methods for that type of data (similar to including a gift card and a return slip in the gift box). We say the wrapper object **encapsulates** the primitive value and methods.

To better understand what is meant by the term "primitive data," consider the different representations of the value 6 in Figure 10.4. Each representation is understandable by the way it is used in a sentence, equation, scoreboard, or some other context.

Figure 10.4   *Different representations of the value 6*

Humans are very good at using context to help determine the meaning of a value's representation and are able to determine if the attempted use of that representation makes sense. For example, in Figure 10.5, we see a Roman numeral representation in what looks like a long division operation (the context). However, there is no easy way to perform this operation. A human would realize that the use of Roman numerals in this context doesn't make much sense.

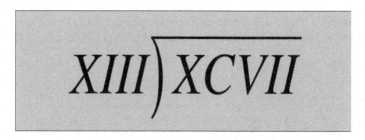

Figure 10.5   *An attempted long division operation*

Computers are not very good, on their own, at determining appropriate use of a data representation in a specific context. So computer programming languages have built-in primitive data types and operations that can be performed with a type of value. Java's primitive data types are listed in Table 10.2. Notice that, other than *int* and *char*, the names of primitive types and the names of Java wrapper classes are the same except wrapper class names are capitalized.

Table 10.2 • *Java Primitive Types*

Alice Classes	Java Classes	Primitive types	Contains	Examples
DecimalNumber	Double, Float, Byte, Char	double, float, byte, char	Floating point number	1.0, 6.0289, -2.0001
WholeNumber	Integer, Short	int, short	Integer (no decimal)	0, -1, 15, -2001
Boolean	Boolean	boolean	Truth value	true, false
TextString	String		A string of characters	"Hello", "Name: "
	Character	char	A single character (number, letter, symbol)	'a', '1', '@'

A primitive data item is stored directly as a binary representation of the value in the computer's memory. In fact, storage in memory is a major distinction between different primitive types of the same kind of value. For example, Java's primitive representation of a whole number may be an *int* or a *short*, which are distinguished by an *int* stored directly in memory using 32 bits (4 bytes), whereas a *short* is stored using 16 bits (2 bytes). By comparison, a *double* number is stored directly in memory using 64 bits (8 bytes). A **bit** (shorthand for **b**inary dig**it**) is the smallest unit of data in the memory, holding either 0 or 1. A **byte** is eight bits.

10.1.2 Built-in, legal operations on primitive data types

Each primitive data type has built-in **legal operators** that define exactly the context in which it may be used. Table 10.3 shows the arithmetic legal operators for addition, subtraction, multiplication, and division.

Table 10.3 • *Java Arithmetic Operators*

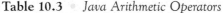

Operation	Operator
Addition	+
Subtraction	-
Multiplication	*
Division	/
Modulus	%

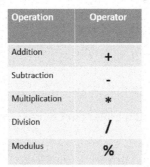

You may be unfamiliar with %, known as the modulus operator. Modulus computes the remainder when two numbers are divided. For example if the value 17 is divided by 5, the quotient is 3 and the remainder is 2. Modulus computes and returns the remainder value, 2. In Java, the modulus operation may be used with either whole number or floating point values.

10.2 Writing Code with Parameters and Variables in Java

Tables 10.1, 10.2, and 10.3, earlier, are a helpful reference for specifying the data types of parameters in a Java version of the *talkAndSay* procedural method. Open the Biped editor tab, either by clicking on Biped.java in the Projects panel. If already open, click on the Biped.java tab in the editor Figure 10.6.

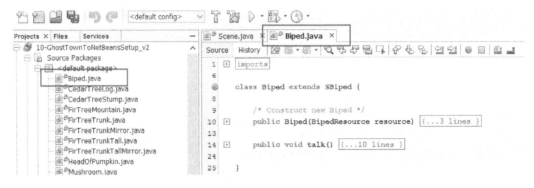

Figure 10.6   *Open Biped.java class tab in NetBeans*

As imported from the Alice project, the Biped class contains a constructor and the *talk* procedure. Position the cursor in a new blank line immediately after the *talk* method code block and before the closing curly brace for the class. In the blank line, type a header for *talkAndSay*, as shown in Figure 10.7.

```
class Biped extends SBiped
{

    /*
     * Construct new Biped
     */
    public Biped(BipedResource resource)
    {...3 lines }

    public void talk()
    {...12 lines }

    public void talkAndSay() {

    }

}
```

Figure 10.7   *A code block to declare the* talkAndSay *procedure in the Biped class*

Add appropriate comments for assumptions and actions (Figure 10.8). After execution, the Biped object's mouth is back in its original position.

```
public void talkAndSay () {
    //Assumptions: Mouth of the Biped object is closed when the procedure is called
    // Biped talks at the same time as text is displayed in a speech bubble
```

Figure 10.8   *Add comments for documentation.*

10.2.1 Add parameters to the header

Recall the Alice version of *talkAndSay* has two parameters: *words* of type *TextString* and *seconds* of type *DecimalNumber* (Figure 10.9).

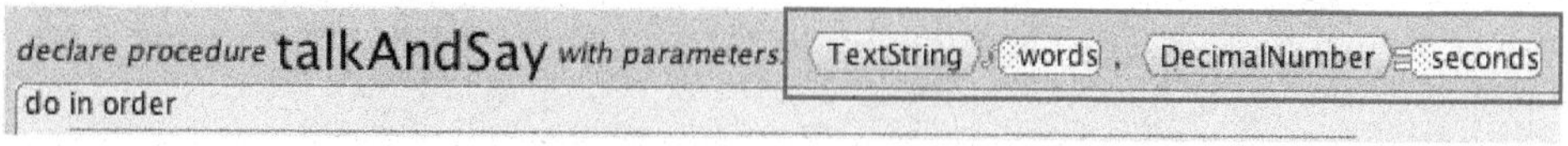

Figure 10.9   *Parameters for the* talkAndSay *method in Alice*

The Java class *String* corresponds to the Alice class *TextString*. Within the parentheses in the *talkAndSay* header, enter **String** for the type and **words** for the name, as shown in Figure 10.10.

```
public void talkAndSay(String words) {
    //Assumptions:  Mouth of the Biped object is closed when the procedure is called
    // Biped talks at the same time as text is displayed in a speech bubble
}
```

Figure 10.10   *Declaring* words *parameter with Java's* String *data type*

Enter *seconds* with Java's *Double* data type, as shown in Figure 10.11. Be sure to type a comma between the two parameter entries.

```
public void talkAndSay(String words, Double seconds) {
    //Assumptions:  Mouth of the Biped object is closed when the procedure is called
    // Biped talks at the same time as text is displayed in a speech bubble
}
```

Figure 10.11   *Parameter* seconds *using Java's* Double *class as the data type*

10.2.2 Variables and arithmetic expressions in Java

In the Alice version of this procedure, the *seconds* parameter value is used in two ways: to specify the duration for a *say* statement, and to compute the number of times the *talk* procedure will be called in sync with the speech bubble display. In preparation for writing a code block that calls *say* and *talk* in sync, let's go ahead and write a statement to compute the number of times *talk* will be called. The formula for computing the number of times talk will be called is illustrated in Figure 10.12. This formula has two parts: a variable on the left of the assignment operator (in Java, the = symbol) and an arithmetic expression on the right of the assignment operator).

variable   **= arithmetic expression**

numberOfCalls   =   2 * seconds

Figure 10.12   *Formula for computing number of times to call* talk

Once again, look at Alice's side-by-side view of the corresponding Alice and Java statements for this computation (Figure 10.13).

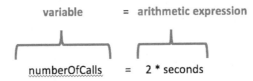

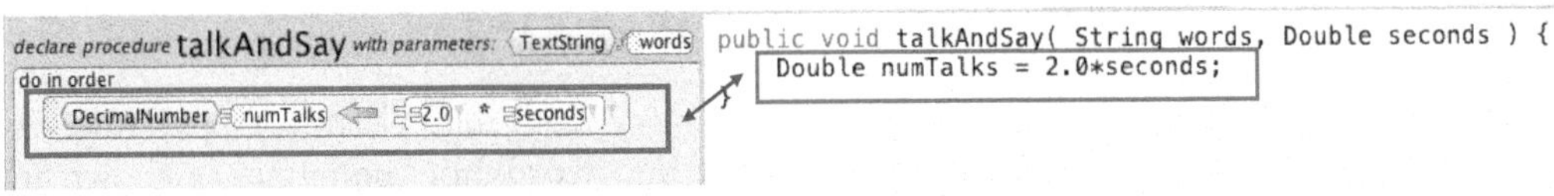

Figure 10.13   *"Java Code on the Side" view of arithmetic expressions*

The *numTalks* variable, which is of type *DecimalNumber* in Alice, will be declared as type *Double* in Java. Enter the statement in the procedure, as shown in Figure 10.14.

```
public void talkAndSay(String words, Double seconds){
    //Assumptions:  Mouth of the Biped object is closed when the procedure is called
    // Biped talks at the same time as text is displayed in a speech bubble

    Double numTalks = 2 * seconds;
}
```

Figure 10.14   *Declaration and initialization of* numTalks *variable*

10.3 Writing Code with *doTogether* in Java

In the Alice version of *talkAndSay*, a *do together* code block is used to synchronize *say* and *talk* statements (Figure 10.15).

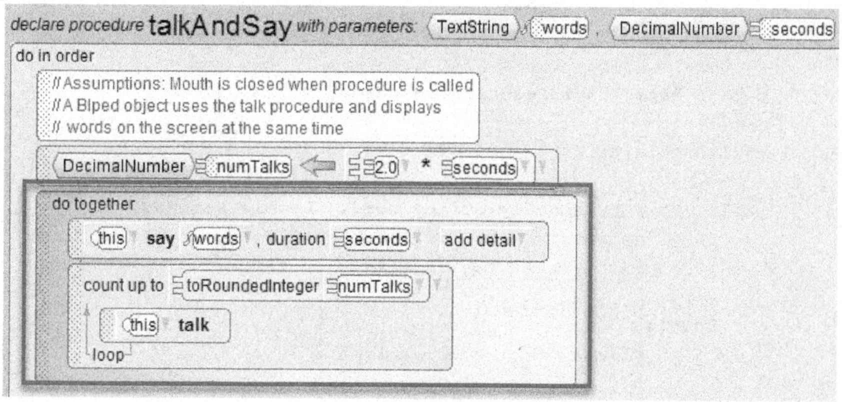

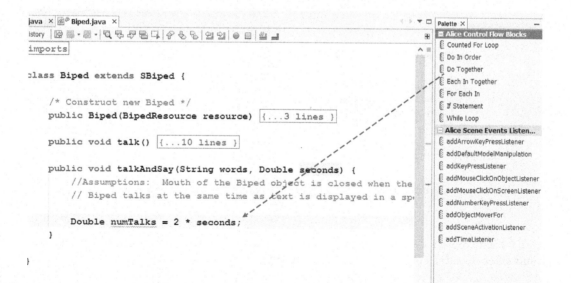

Figure 10.15   Do together *code block in Alice version of* talkAndSay

The plugin's *doTogether* code template will be used to create a *doTogether* code block. Use the cursor to drag Do Together from the Palette into the *talkAndSay* procedure. Release the cursor in a blank link immediately following the *numTalks* statement, as shown in Figure 10.16. (If the Alice Palette is not showing, select Windows in NetBeans' menu bar and IDE Tools/Palette in the cascading menus to display the Palette.)

Figure 10.16   *Dragging the* Do Together *code block into the* talkAndSay *procedure*

When you release the cursor in the editor, a dialog box will appear to ask how many threads ("things to do together") for the *doTogether* block. In this example, two threads (one for *say* and one for *talk*) are needed. Select 2 and click OK (Figure 10.17).

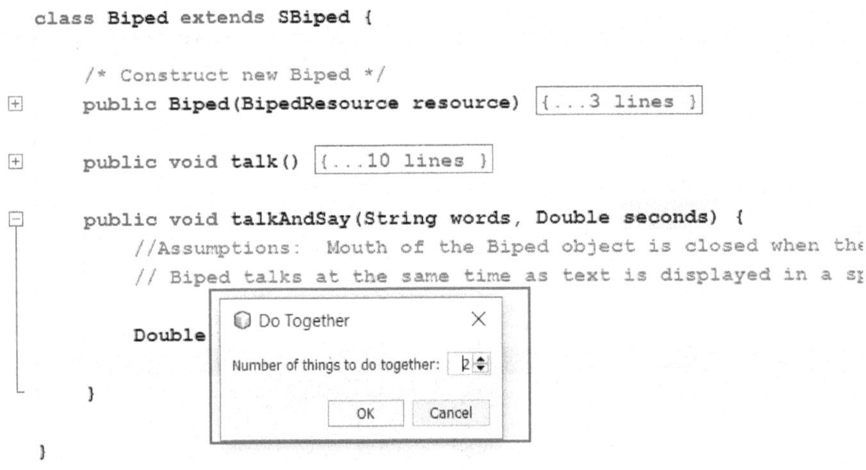

```
class Biped extends SBiped {

    /* Construct new Biped */
 ⊞  public Biped(BipedResource resource) {...3 lines }

 ⊞  public void talk() {...10 lines }

 ⊟  public void talkAndSay(String words, Double seconds) {
        //Assumptions:  Mouth of the Biped object is closed when the
        // Biped talks at the same time as text is displayed in a sp

        Double
    }

}
```

Figure 10.17   Do Together *dialog box specifying the number of threads*

In the first thread (first lambda code block), add a *say* statement for *this* Biped. Use *words* as the argument for the String (Figure 10.18). (Reminder: Lambda expressions were previously described in Chapter 8 as a syntax that can be used for implementing a thread.)

```
public void talkAndSay(String words, Double seconds){
    //Assumptions:  Mouth of the Biped object is closed when the procedure is called
    // Biped talks at the same time as text is displayed in a speech bubble

    Double numTalks = 2 * seconds;

    //start a Thread for each Runnable and wait until they complete
    doTogether(() ->
    {
        this.say(words, details);
    }, () ->
    {
        //TODO: Code goes here
    });
}
```

Figure 10.18   *Using the* words *parameter in a* say *statement*

Next, replace *details* in the *say* statement with *Say.duration* as an optional parameter and enter *seconds* as the argument (Figure 10.19).

```
    //start a Thread for each Runnable and wait until they compl
    doTogether(() ->
    {
        this.say(words, Say.duration(seconds));
    }, () ->
    {
        //TODO: Code goes here
    });
```

Figure 10.19   *Completed* say *statement with* seconds *as* duration *in the first thread*

10.4 Using a Variable as a *for* Loop Limit

The talking motion can now be added to the second thread. To add a *Counted For loop* in the second thread of the *doTogether*, return to the Biped class tab in NetBeans. Drag a *Counted For loop* control structure from the Palette into the second thread, as shown in Figure 10.20.

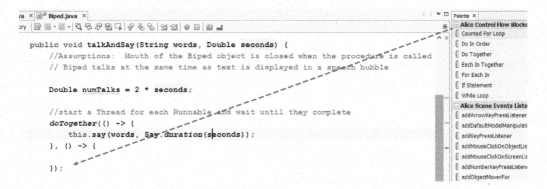

Figure 10.20 • *Drag a* Counted For loop *into position in the* doTogether

In the pop-up dialog box, enter *count* as the name of the loop control variable and then click OK. The result is shown in Figure 10.21.

```
//start a Thread for each Runnable and wait until they complete
doTogether(() ->
{
    this.say(words, Say.duration(time));
}, () ->
{
        //TODO: Code goes here

    for (Integer count = 0; count < replace_with_COUNT; count++)
    {
//TODO: Code goes here.
    }

});
```

Figure 10.21 • Counted For loop *template*

The template begins with *for* followed by a set of parentheses and then a set of curly braces where the code statements will be written. Within the parentheses are three components, separated by commas: an initialized loop control variable, a **Boolean expression**, and an arithmetic expression. A Boolean expression compares two values and evaluates to *true* or *false*.

The first component declares a **loop control variable**, of type Integer. The loop control variable counts the number of times the loop executes. The name you entered in the dialog box is automatically initialized to zero (Figure 10.22). You can enter a different number to modify the initial count, but it must be an integer value.

```
doTogether(() -> {
    this.say(words, Say.duration(seconds));
}, () -> {
    for (Integer count = 0; count < replace_with_COUNT; count++) {
        //TODO: Code goes here.
    }

});
```

Figure 10.22   *Loop control variable, initialized to 0*

The second component is a Boolean expression that compares two values: the value of count and the number of times the loop should repeat. To compare two values, a Boolean expression contains a **relational operator** between the two values. Relational operators are listed in Figure 10.23.

==	equal to
!=	not equal to
<	less than
<=	less than or equal to
>=	greater than or equal to

Figure 10.23   *Relational operators used in Boolean expressions*

The *for loop* is intended to repeat again and again until the value of *count* reaches some limit value. The *replace_with_COUNT* is a placeholder for the limit value. In this example, we plan to start with a count of 0 and repeat until *talk* has been called *numTalks* number of times. So, the less than operator (<) is correct and *numTalks* is the limit value. Enter *numTalks* as the limit value, in place of *replace_with_COUNT*, as illustrated in Figure 10.24.

```
//start a Thread for each Runnable and wait until they complete
doTogether(() ->
{
    this.say(words, Say.duration(seconds));
}, () ->
{

    for (Integer count = 0; count < numTalks; count++)
    {
//TODO: Code goes here.
    }

});
```

Figure 10.24   numTalks *variable replaces the placeholder in Boolean expression.*

The third component is an arithmetic expression that either **increments** or **decrements** the counter (the *count* variable). NetBeans has automatically generated the expression, *count++*. The ++ symbol is an increment operator, which means "add 1" to the counter. (The expression might be modified by using the −− operator, a decrement that would subtract 1 from the counter.)

In this example, the first time the loop executes, the value of *count* is 0. At the end of the first execution, *count* is incremented so it has a value of 1. Then the Boolean expression (*count* < *numTalks*) is evaluated. If *true*, the loop executes again. At the end of this execution, *count* is incremented again so it has a value of 2. Again, the Boolean expression (*count* < *numTalks*) is evaluated. If *true*, the loop executes yet again. This execute-increment-evaluate cycle repeats again and again until the Boolean expression (*count* < *numTalks*) becomes *false*. Then, the *for* loop ends and execution proceeds to the next statement in the program.

Now that we have examined the three components within the parentheses belonging to the *for* loop control structure, it is time to add code within the code block. Add a statement to call the *talk* procedure inside the code block, as shown in Figure 10.25.

```
//start a Thread for each Runnable and wait until they complete
doTogether(() ->
{
    this.say(words, Say.duration(seconds));
}, () ->
{
    for (Integer count = 0; count < numTalks; count++)
    {
        this.talk();
    }
});
```

Figure 10.25   *Completed* for *loop code block*

10.5 Testing Code in Java

To test-run *talkAndSay*, code statements must be entered that call the procedure. Return to the *storytellerEncounter* procedure in the Scene class. In the imported version of the *Ghost-Town* project, any Alice statements that called *talkAndSay* have been removed and replaced with TODO comments. The TODO comments show where you are to write the statements in Java Figure 10.26.

```
    public void storytellerEncounter() {
//Assumptions: Larry and Tashi are outside the cabin
//Larry and Tashi enter the cabin and the storyteller greets Larry
        this.camera.moveAndOrientTo(this.insideStorytellerCabin, MoveAndOrientTo.duration(0.0));
        this.Tashi.moveAndOrientTo(this.tashiInCabin, MoveAndOrientTo.duration(0.0));
        this.Larry.moveAndOrientTo(this.larryInCabin, MoveAndOrientTo.duration(0.0));
//
//*** TODO: a call to talkAndSay goes here:  storyTeller -> "You're late... a hundred years late" 6 words
//
//*** TODO: a call to talkAndSay goes here:  storyTeller -> "What kept you?" 3 words ***
//
    }
```

Figure 10.26   *TODO statements in* storytellerEncounter

Replace the two *TODO* comments with statements to call *talkAndSay* (Figure 10.27). The first statement is to have the storyteller say "You're late … a hundred years late." The second statement is to have the storyteller say "What kept you?" Be sure to enter the quote marks. Because the first text string has 6 words, send 2.0 as the argument for the *seconds* parameter. The second text string is shorter, so send 1.5 as the argument for *seconds*.

```
public void storytellerEncounter()
{
    //Assumptions: Larry and Tashi are outside the cabin
    //Larry and Tashi enter the cabin and the storyteller greets Larry
    this.camera.moveAndOrientTo(this.insideStorytellerCabin, MoveAndOrientTo.dura
    this.Tashi.moveAndOrientTo(this.tashiInCabin, MoveAndOrientTo.duration(0.0));
    this.Larry.moveAndOrientTo(this.larryInCabin);

    storyteller.talkAndSay("You're late... a hundred years late.", 2.0);
    storyteller.talkAndSay("What kept you?", 1.5);
}
```

Figure 10.27   *The* storyTellerEncounter *procedure with* talkAndSay *statements*

Run the program and watch the storyteller's talking action. Each time the *talkAndSay* statement is executed, the storyteller's jaw should *talk* as many times as needed to sync with the speech bubble's display.

Completing the *GhostTown* project in Java is left as an exercise for you. See the exercises at the end of this chapter.

Summary

In both Alice and Java, the data type of an object is defined by a class. The 3D models in Alice's Gallery are each defined by a class. Directions for *move, turn,* and *roll* instructions in Alice are defined by Enum classes. Other types of information (numbers, Booleans, and strings of text) in Alice are defined by Decimal Number, WholeNumber, Boolean, and TextString classes, respectively. When an Alice project is imported into NetBeans, the data types in the Alice code are automatically converted to Java data types in the Java code. This can be accomplished because, in most cases, Alice data types and Java data types correspond. Be aware, however, that Java has a larger and more diverse library of classes than does Alice. For example, Java has a Character class for a single character, but Alice does not. Review Table 10.1 for Alice and Java data type correspondence.

Some Java data types are known as wrapper classes because each class wraps a built-in, primitive data element in an object and defines special methods for that data element. Primitive data type names (other than *int* and *char*) are the same as the corresponding wrapper class names, except the names start with a lower case letter. Review Table 10.2 for a list of primitive data element names and types of values. Note that *String* does not have a primitive data type because a text string is actually a sequence of characters (primitive type *char*). Each primitive data type has built-in legal operators that define exactly the kinds of operations that may be performed on that data. For example, a modulus operation (% operator) may be performed on an *int* primitive data element. Review Table 10.3 for the legal operators associated with each primitive type.

As in Alice, a variable is a named location in memory that stores a value of a specific data type. A variable can be assigned a value by writing a code statement with a variable on the left, an assignment operator in the middle, and an arithmetic expression on the right. Java's assignment operator is '=' (as compared to the '←' assignment operator in Alice).

NetBeans has a plugin Code Palette (illustrated previously, in Chapter 8). A variable value may be used to provide a limit for Java's counted *for* loop. The example in this chapter used a variable of type Integer (a wrapper class) to control the number of times a *for* loop executes to have Tashi repeatedly turn.

Terms

bit	*float*	modulus
Boolean expression	*for* loop	primitive data
byte	increment	relational operator
decrement	*int*	*short*
double	legal operator (for a type)	wrapper class
encapsulate	loop control variable	

Concept Questions

1. For each of the following data items, indicate its data type in terms of Java classes: Double, Integer, Boolean, String, or Character.
   (a) true
   (b) 'a'
   (c) 75.3682
   (d) 75
   (e) "Hello"
   (f) '?'
   (g) "Why not?"
   (h) 0.0
   (i) 0

2. For each of the following data items, indicate its data type in terms of primitive type: double, int, boolean, or char.
   (a) true
   (b) 'a'
   (c) 75.3682
   (d) 75
   (e) '?'
   (f) 0.0
   (g) 0

3. In question 2, data items such as "Hello" and "Why not?" are not included. Why not?

4. Each of the following Java statements has an error. Indicate what the error is and describe why it is an error.
   (a) Integer value = true;
   (b) Double value = "Hello";
   (c) String str = Hello;
   (d) Character letter = x;
   (e) Double result = 54.87 % 17.1;
   (f) int value = 8;

5. What is the difference between *Double* and *double* as Java data types?

6. What is the result when each of the following computations is evaluated in Java?
   (a) 22 / 7
   (b) 22 % 7
   (c) 22.0 / 7

7. In the following code, what sequence of symbols begin a lambda code block?

```
doTogether(()-> {
    {
        this.say(words);
    }, ()->
    {
        this.talk(4);
    }
    } );
```

8. When the *do together* template is dragged into the text editor from the Palette, what information must be entered before the *doTogether* code block will be displayed?

9. When the *Counted For loop* template is dragged into the text editor from the Palette, what information must be entered before a *for loop* code block will be displayed?

10. What placeholder is displayed in Java's *for loop* code block when the *Counted For loop* template is dragged into the text editor from the Palette?

Exercises

1. If you have not already done so, download the *GhostTownExportToNetbeans.a3p* project (or obtain a copy from your instructor). Import the project into NetBeans.
   (a) Complete the Java code re-creation for *talkAndSay*, belonging to the Biped class, as described in this chapter's narrative. Then rewrite all the calling statements in *storytellerEncounter*, as was done Chapter 9.
   (b) Re-create and test the *sneakPeak* method.
   (c) Re-create and test the *revealTrek* method.

2. Import the *Thaw*.a3p project, created in Chapter 5, into NetBeans. Create a *talkAnd-Say* method in the Biped class of the Thaw project. (Hint: You can use NetBeans text editor to simply copy and paste from one project to another.) In the Scene's *myFirst-Method*, find the *doTogether* code block where Larry says "You can't melt the ice off my train. You're nothing but an itty bitty yeti." Then, replace the *doTogether* code block in *myFirstMethod* with a call to *talkAndSay*.

The Ringmaster Coat

"Start by exploring the cabins first," the storyteller prods gently, "You remember living here for a while, don't you?"

Larry abruptly stands. Without another word, he leaves the little cottage and walks into the middle of the clearing, trying to remember which log cabin he used the last time he was here. There were about ten cabins scattered in the near vicinity. He pushes the door open to the first one, throwing his shoulder against it to get the creaky hinges to move. Inside is as clean as he left it, the moss and vines covering the outside of the house didn't flourish here.

In the middle of the one-room cottage rests an old iron dress form. And hanging on the dress form, looking neat and crisp, is Larry's red and white striped ringmaster coat. He runs his hand along the fabric, hesitant to pull it off. He doesn't have to. Instead the fabric dissolves under his fingertips in shimmering light, like dust. The entire coat starts to shrivel into nothing, as if a fire is spreading from the point he touched it, until the fabric is gone completely. Larry takes a step back in surprise.

And realizes the coat is on him now. He twists from side to side, and the coat bumps against his bones. The swing and the heft of the fabric feel familiar, and the coat fits perfectly, as always. He flattens his collar and jerks the sleeves straight. The only difference is a few missing buttons.

"Very stylish," Tashi pipes up from behind him sarcastically.

Larry turns to her, "Relic from my circus days."

"Are the missing buttons the ones in your glasses?" Tashi observes.

Larry takes his glasses off and turns them around. And discovers he is looking at his own skull. A very strange, out-of-body experience. "I don't know," he confesses, "If they are, they seem to be my eyes now. So I can't tell."

"At least if you lose your glasses, you'll be able to see exactly where they are," Tashi jokes, "Mother is always losing her reading glasses. And I have to find them."

"I'd rather have eyes," Larry says sourly. He puts the glasses back on. It's a relief to see properly again. He watches Tashi stare out one of the cabin windows at another hut across the way.

"What's in the other cabin?" Tashi asks.

"I don't know," Larry says.

"Want to go find out?" Tashi asks mischievously.

Larry chuckles and shrugs, still skeptical about the storyteller's typical prophetic double-talk and vague hints.

They begin to search the cabins mixed among the trees. Most of the little wooden huts come up empty. But the third one contains a single bright orange pumpkin. A morbid grin and eyes are carved into the side of the pumpkin, its guts scooped clean. The flesh of the squash should be rotten and brown, but it's as fresh and juicy as the day it was cut.

Tashi's stomach rumbles, "Looks good enough to eat."

226

"Nicholas' mask," Larry says reverently, "Our clown. He'd take it off and recite Shakespearean quotations as if the pumpkin head was a skull. The crowd thought it was hilarious. Nicholas considered it art."

"I bet it'd still make a great snack," Tashi jokes, "even if it has been magically preserved." Tashi steps forward and lightly touches the pumpkin. It dissolves exactly as the coat did. It's what he expected, but Larry still stares silently, watching his friend's personal token crumble away.

"Let's move on, there should be three more," Larry says.

They hear the next cabin before they see it. A light silver tinkling through the trees, the kind of noise made when an angel gets its wings. They follow the sound and discover a gigantic bell inside the next decaying cabin. Outside the cabin, the ringing is quiet, muffled as if under heavy blankets. But as soon as they step over the threshold, the full booming clang of the bell shakes the very foundation of the cabin.

"That bell came from Esther's tower," Larry says, "She always said if every belfry needs bats, every bat needs a belfry."

"It's loud!" Tashi whines above the noise. She covers her ears with her hands, "Quick, touch the thing so it goes away."

Larry does and the bell dissolves. The silence is sudden and deadening, and a bit alarming. The absence of the bell is a lot more tangible than the pumpkin. The loss makes Larry's memories of the avalanche feel more real.

"Where do you think these things are going?" Tashi asks curiously.

Larry shrugs, "If I had to guess, I'd say they're reappearing wherever my friends are, or wherever whatever is left of my friends is."

The next cabin they find contains dead cats, which is rather ominous for the state of the circus troupe.

"At least they don't smell," Tashi says as she and Larry stare, stunned at the group of decaying cats. There are 18 of them, and they all stare with reflective dull yellow eyes set inside black fur that blends into the shadows so well that it's almost impossible to tell what they are, like a multieyed monster.

Larry bends down and brushes a tuft of hair half fallen off a cat's shoulder, "Why are these showing their age, when the pumpkin was fine?"

"I imagine something about how nonliving things can be preserved, but these cats clearly couldn't be frozen in time and kept alive at the same time," Tashi says.

The cats are certainly frozen, their joints stuck in a permanent pose of fright with arched backs and stick-straight legs and tails up in alarm.

"But I'm alive," Larry hesitantly rests his hand on the head of the nearest cat, it starts to crumble and blow away, and in a sweeping wind they all dissolve into thin air.

"Adelaide is going to be devastated," Larry says sadly, "She was always the mother hen to those kittens."

Even Tashi looks a little regretful.

The wind carries with it an intense smell of lemon and cloves. Larry immediately follows. The smell grows stronger and then overwhelms them the minute they enter the next cabin. The cabin also contains the less intrusive scent of leather and damp wool. In the center of the floor lie two oven mitts, yellowed from use.

Tashi coughs, "Eurgh, rank. It's like someone spilled a perfume bottle and left it for ..."

"One hundred years and no one ever opened a window?" Larry almost laughs.

"Yeah, leave that door open behind you," Tashi squints at the oven mitts.

Larry bends down, picks up a mitt in each hand, and watches as they dissolve through his fingers.

"Gideon's favorite oven mitts," Larry says, "He wore these constantly, even when not baking, I kept having to replace the knitted inner lining. It was a challenge getting him to take them off for the amount of time it took me to fix them."

"Yet he left them behind ..." Tashi says.

"Must not have been planning to cook much anymore," Larry says. He leaves the cabin hastily. Tashi follows, still wanting to talk.

"If Adelaide loved those kittens, and Gideon needed these mitts, why would they forget them? The pumpkin I can understand—new ones grow every season, and the bell obviously is more symbolic than sentimental, but these last two are irreplaceable. So, why?"

"I don't know," Larry says curtly. He makes a beeline for the train engine.

"Do you think they knew something would happen?"

"No, we had maybe 15 minutes of warning before the storm changed," Larry argues.

"Then what made them ..."

"They had to!" Larry turns around and glares at the baby yeti, "That was the deal, got it?" He swings himself up into the train cab and starts the engine, "See this?" he rings the bell eight times and waits impatiently while the tunnel appears, "I asked the witch for a train that could travel anywhere I wanted, whenever I wanted, without the limitation of needing tracks. She granted my wish, but I had to leave something in exchange. She asked for my coat." He tugs on his sleeve.

"So what did your friends ask for?" Tashi prompts.

"I don't know," Larry reluctantly admits.

They both eye the tunnel. Unlike how it was when they arrived, the train tracks running behind the engine are now moss covered and broken. The old tracks in front of them leading to the tunnel are new and clear.

"Then where will this take us next?" Tashi asks.

"It goes anywhere, wherever you intend to go, as long as you already know how to get there," Larry explains, "That's what the witch said."

"So it can follow things, like a dog tracking a fox," Tashi concludes.

"That's one way of looking at it," Larry agrees.

"Then it'll follow the tokens, because we knew where to get the tokens, and the tokens know where to get your friends," Tashi says excitedly.

Larry nods. He grins, "All right. Where do you want to go first?"

traveling halloween sideshow

1904 - 1910

"the woman who lives as a bat"

"the #6 lifed enchantress"

"skinniest person alive"

"the boneless wonder"

"the headless clown"

II

Interactivity with Events, If/Else, Conditions, and Built-in Functions

Concept Objectives

- Creating a UI to display instructions for an interactive game
- Creating event listeners: mouse-click, object mover (arrow keys), point of view change
- Writing code to handle an event, when a listener fires
- Using an *if/else* control structure for conditional execution
- Creating a conditional expression in an if/else control statement
- Calling a built-in function (also known as a functional method)
- Using a tracking variable for game conditions (win/lose)

A primary focus in this chapter is an exploration of programming for **interactivity**. Until now, we have assumed that code blocks in a program will execute in a pre-planned sequence to create an animation similar to a video or film-short. An interactive program, however, expects the user to perform some action that may affect the sequence. For example, a person may interact with a program by clicking the mouse, touching the screen, or pressing keys on the keyboard. A mouse click, screen touch, or keypress is known as an **event**, which is "something that happens." A special kind of procedure, known as an **event listener** is used in interactive programming. An event listener waits for an event and then responds in such a way as to "handle the event."

Integral to programming for interactivity is decision making, which is often implemented using *if-else* control structures and **conditional expressions**. An *if-else* control structure depends on the current condition of an object (or multiple objects) as the program is running. For example, a condition could be: "Is the skeleton within 5 meters of the cabin in the woods?" Determining a condition is often performed by calling a built-in **function**. A function **is a** method that retrieves or computes a value and returns the value to the calling statement.

To illustrate interactivity, *if/else*, conditionals, event listeners, and built-in functions, the programming task in this chapter will animate a selected segment of Episode 5, *The Ringmaster Coat*, of the *Haunted Circus* story, in the form of a simple, interactive game. In this episode, Larry and Tashi search the cabins in the ghost town, seeking clues for finding the missing members of the circus.

11.1 From Animation to Game

Animations progress on their own and do not require interaction from the user. Games, on the other hand, generally require input and decision making on the part of the user, called the **player** in games. We will use "player" and "user" interchangeably in our discussion of interactive programs. A common use of input in digital games is navigation of the player's character through the game world. This input is referred to as the **controls** of the game. Games often have **user interfaces (UIs)** that display information and/or allow players to control parts of the game.

Games have **goals** that the player must achieve to progress in the game. As the player gains or loses progress, a game provides **feedback** to help them understand how well they are doing. This feedback can take many forms, including a numerical score, character dialog, or visual effects.

Finally, games also usually have **end conditions**. These are rules that determine if the game is over and if a player won or lost. More specifically, games may have **win conditions** that indicate when the game is won by a player, and **fail conditions** that indicate when the player has failed, resulting in the player losing the game entirely or losing progress.

11.2 Story Analysis and Adaptation

To adapt *The Ringmaster Coat* episode to an interactive game, begin, as usual, by reading and analyzing the story to determine the background components and select the objects and actions. The selected episode segment for this example is summarized here:

Larry leaves the storyteller's cabin frustrated, and Tashi follows. The last time
Larry stayed in the ghost town, he left a very sentimental object in the care of the

storyteller, and he is curious if the object is still intact. He finds his own cabin among the trees and sees a red-and-white striped coat, worthy of a circus ringmaster, inside. The coat is pristine, clean, and exactly as he last wore it, as if it's been preserved in glass instead of sitting in a decrepit shack for a century. The minute Larry touches the fabric it starts to glow and dissolves in front of his eyes. When the coat reappears on Larry, it feels and sits just like it used to when he had muscle and skin to cover his bones. Feeling much more like himself, Larry guides Tashi toward one of the other cabins to see if his friends left anything behind themselves. When they touch the next token (a pumpkin head, a bell, a litter of taxidermy black kittens, or a pair of oven mitts), it too seems to disappear. With haste, Larry and Tashi scramble for the train, ring the bell to trigger the tunnel, and take off after one of the tokens. Presumably, if the first token went to Larry, they can follow another token to one of the lost circus members.

As in previous episodes, the narrative of the story will be adapted. Not every detail from the writing will be included, and a few details may be changed. To this end, one analysis of this episode could be:

Larry and Tashi begin their search, wandering through the woods

    <u>When Larry gets near to his old cabin,</u>

        his old ringmaster **coat** briefly appears then **magically dissolves,** and **reappears** on Larry's shoulders

    <u>When a token is found,</u>

        The token is collected

    <u>After the tokens are found,</u>

        Larry and **Tashi board the train**

            Larry and **Tashi** realize the tokens will lead them to other circus members

            The **train departs** through the portal (following one of the tokens)

This analysis looks similar to story analyses presented in previous chapters. A subtle difference is that some lines are underlined and begin with the word "when" or "after." The underlined phrase emphasizes that the action to be performed depends on a condition or an event. For example, the coat only moves from the coat rack to Larry's shoulders when Larry gets really close to his old cabin. Conditions are very important in interactive programs because they allow the program to respond based on player input. Conditions are related to the game's goals and end conditions. In this case, the player's goals are to collect the tokens and Larry's ringmaster coat. The win condition that ends the game is when the player collects the tokens.

11.3 Design

In terms of sequence, we know the beginning and the end: the game begins with Larry and Tashi starting a search of cabins in the woods and ends after the tokens have been collected. However, once the ringmaster's coat is found, there is no specified sequence in which the tokens should be collected. Instead, the game will allow the player to interactively guide Larry and Tashi through the woods to collect the port tokens in any order. Once the player has collected all four tokens, the win condition is triggered and the game ends. Note that there is no fail condition for this game.

11.3.1 Algorithm

A game often begins with a UI screen that displays instructions to the player, including the controls used in the game and the goals of the game. After the user has read the instructions, the game begins. When the win condition of the game has been accomplished, the game ends. Using this basic game structure, a possible algorithm is shown in Figure 11.1.

do in order

> display game instructions
> wait for the user to find the ringmaster's coat and all four tokens
> unlock a portal and depart

Figure 11.1   *Possible algorithm for the* GhostTrainHub *game*

Although this basic algorithm format was successful in previous chapters, it does not capture the interactivity of a game. An algorithm for a game must include the different kinds of actions expected from the user. In this example, mouse-clicks and keypresses are expected. Each mouse-click or keypress is an event. So, the algorithm must also contain a design for event listeners (listen for the action) and a response to the event. For example, when the player clicks on the instructions screen, the instructions should be hidden and the camera repositioned for starting the game. One way to represent the overall game structure and event listeners is an interactivity diagram (Figure 11.2).

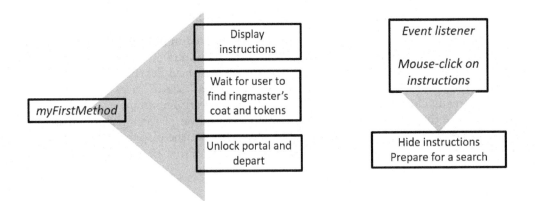

Figure 11.2   *Game design with an event listener*

Note that a click on the instructions screen is not mentioned in the boxes on the left of the diagram. This is because the boxes on the left represent the sequential flow of execution of code in *myFirstMethod*. The boxes on the right represent an event listener and the event listener's response. You can read the listener on the right as "in the event" that the player clicks the instructions screen, the instructions screen will be hidden and action will be taken to start the interactive search for tokens. The event listener's response is an event handler.

We don't know exactly when the event will occur, so the event listener begins execution when the Run button is clicked. An event listener is a **thread**, a process that runs at the same time as the program's *main* process. As an analogy, think of threads as similar to athletes in a race during a track meet. Each athlete runs the race in their own lane at the same time as their competitors. The design in Figure 11.2, above, has two threads: the main thread containing *myFirstMethod* and an event-driven thread containing the event listener for a mouse-click on the instructions screen.

11.3.2 Starter World

A starter project, named *GhostTrainHubStarter.a3p*, and a Billboard image, named *instructionsBillboard.png*, have been created for this chapter. A Billboard is a 2D image that may be imported and displayed in an Alice world. Unlike Gallery objects, a 2D image is a flat object having only two sides (front and back). The files are zipped together in a file named *GhostTrainHub*.zip that is available for download at **www.alice.org/Alice3ToJava**. Download and unzip the file. Then, save the starter world and image file in a location on your computer where you can easily find them.

Start Alice and open the downloaded *GhostTrainHubStarter.a3p* project file. When the project starts, you will see comments documenting the algorithm already added to *myFirstMethod*. The forest scene is dark, so open the Scene editor to view the scene, Figure 11.3. The train engine can be seen on the tracks in the old ghost town.

Figure 11.3 • *Opening view of* GhostTrainHubSetUp *in the Code editor*

The old town has two portals (tunnels): the first is an arrival portal and the second is a departure portal to other locations. You can think of it as a transport hub. Years ago, when the Prenderghast circus was on tour, the train stopped at a train station in this old town. Each member of the circus stayed in a cabin in the forested area around the old station. The view-from-the top image in Figure 11.4 is missing a few trees, in order to provide an overview of the cabins' locations.

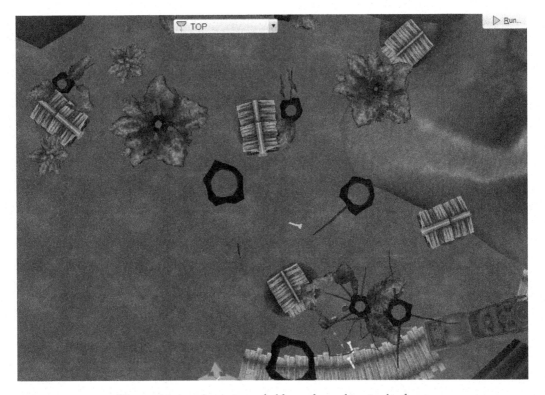

Figure 11.4 • *Locations of old wooden cabins in the forest*

Object markers and camera markers are shown in Figure 11.5. Two object markers, named *LarryInTrain* and *TashiInTrain*, are positions for boarding the train. A third marker, *instructionsLocation*, is for game instructions. Five camera markers are camera viewpoints: *start*, *instructionsShot*, *portalView*, *followView*, and the *trainCabinView*. Object markers, and how they differ from camera markers, were discussed previously in Chapter 6.

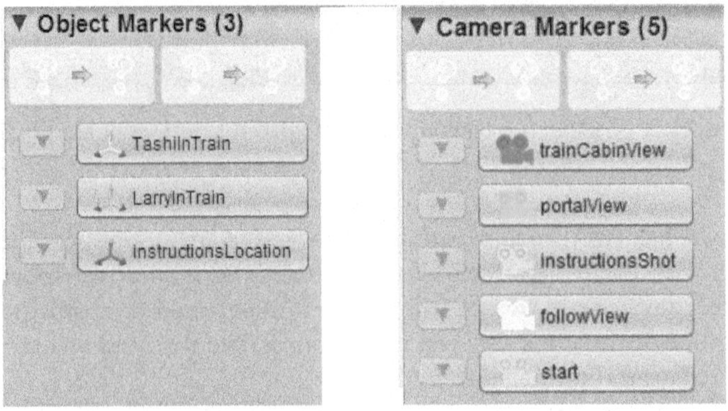

▼ Object Markers (3)

TashiInTrain
LarryInTrain
instructionsLocation

▼ Camera Markers (5)

trainCabinView
portalView
instructionsShot
followView
start

Figure 11.5 • *Object and camera markers in the Ghost Train hub scene*

11.4 Implementation: UI to Display Instructions on a Billboard

The first algorithm step is to create a UI to display instructions for the game. The instructions for the game have been prepared in a text editor and then captured as an image file. The file is named *InstructionsBillboard.png* and was downloaded with the starter world.

In Alice, an image file may be imported into a project. To import the image, first select the Resource Manager from the Project menu (Figure 11.6).

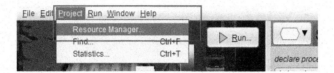

Figure 11.6 ● *Select Resource Manager from the Project menu.*

A Resource Manager dialog box is displayed. In the example shown in Figure 11.7, two resources have already been imported in the Starter world. To import the *Instructions-Billboard* image, select the Import Image button.

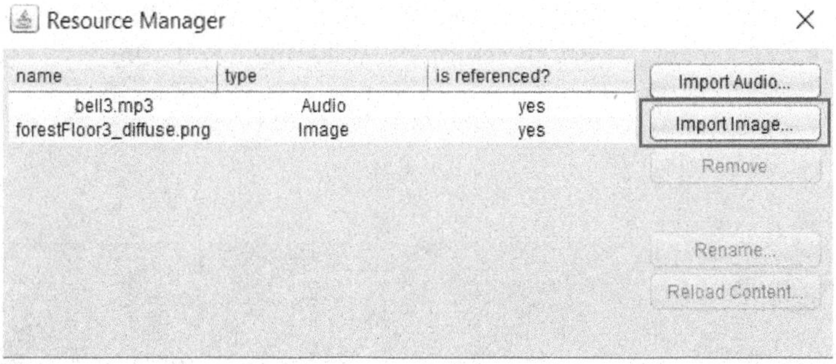

Figure 11.7 ● *Click the Import Image button in the Resource Manager.*

Navigate to the location on your computer where the *InstructionsBillboard.png* file has been stored and then select the file for import (Figure 11.7). When imported, the image file will be added to the list of imported items (Figure 11.8) in the Resource Manager. Note the imported *InstructionsBillboard* image is not yet "referenced." This means the image has not been displayed in the scene.

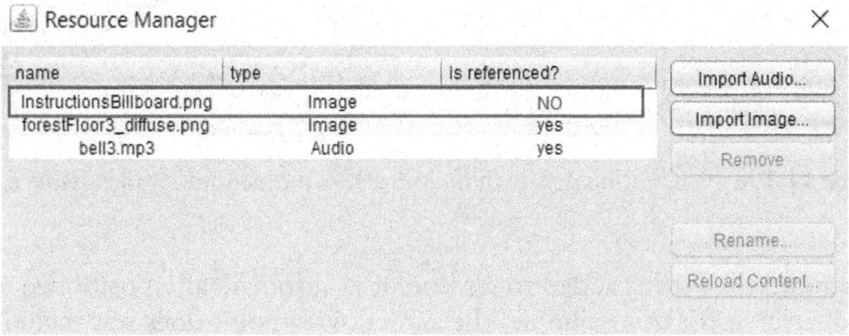

Figure 11.8 ● InstructionsBillboard *image file has been imported.*

To display the image, a Billboard object must be created and the image painted onto the front (or back) of the billboard. To create a Billboard object, in the Scene editor, select the Shapes/Text tab of the Gallery and select the new Billboard button (Figure 11.9).

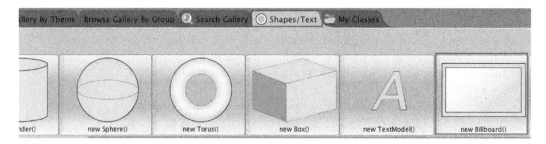

Figure 11.9   *Select the new Billboard button in the Shapes/Text Gallery.*

A Billboard dialog box is displayed. Name and paint the billboard following these steps (Figures 11.10a and b):

(1) Enter a name. In this example, the billboard is named *instructions*.
(2) In the front paint menu, select the *InstructionsBillboard.png* image (Figure 11.10a).
(3) In the back paint menu, select the color BLACK (Figure 11.10b).
(4) Click OK.

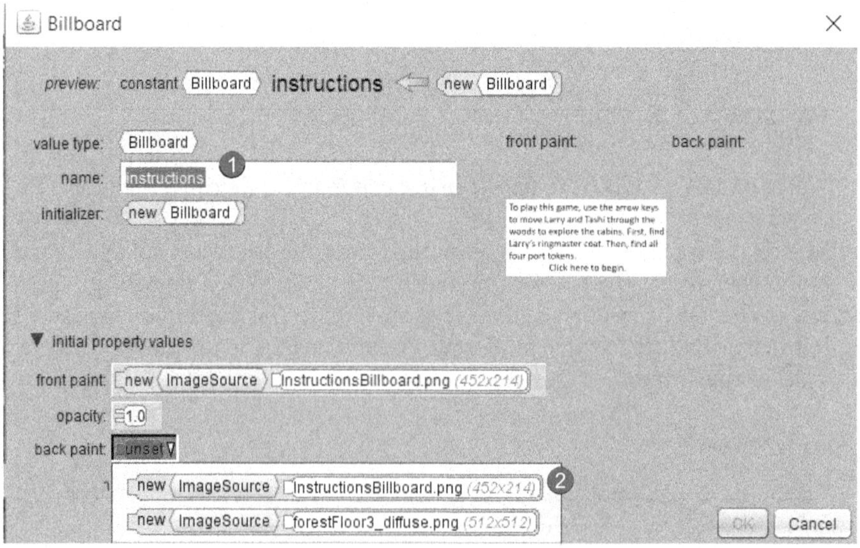

Figure 11.10a   *Creating a new billboard with a name and a front paint image*

When a new billboard is added to a scene, it is automatically positioned at the center of the ground surface. (In this example, the camera viewpoint does not include the center of the ground surface, so the billboard will not be visible to you.) In anticipation of this

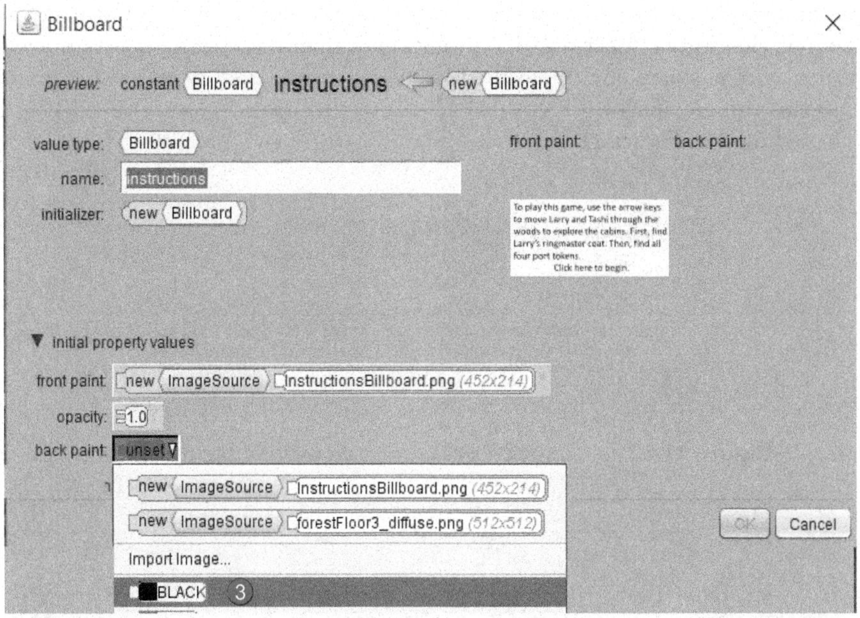

Figure 11.10b • *Select a paint color for the back of the billboard.*

situation, the starter world already contains an object marker, named *instructionsLocation*. Select the *instructions* billboard in the Object Selector (Figure 11.11). Then, use a one-shot procedure to move and orient the billboard to the *instructionsLocation* marker.

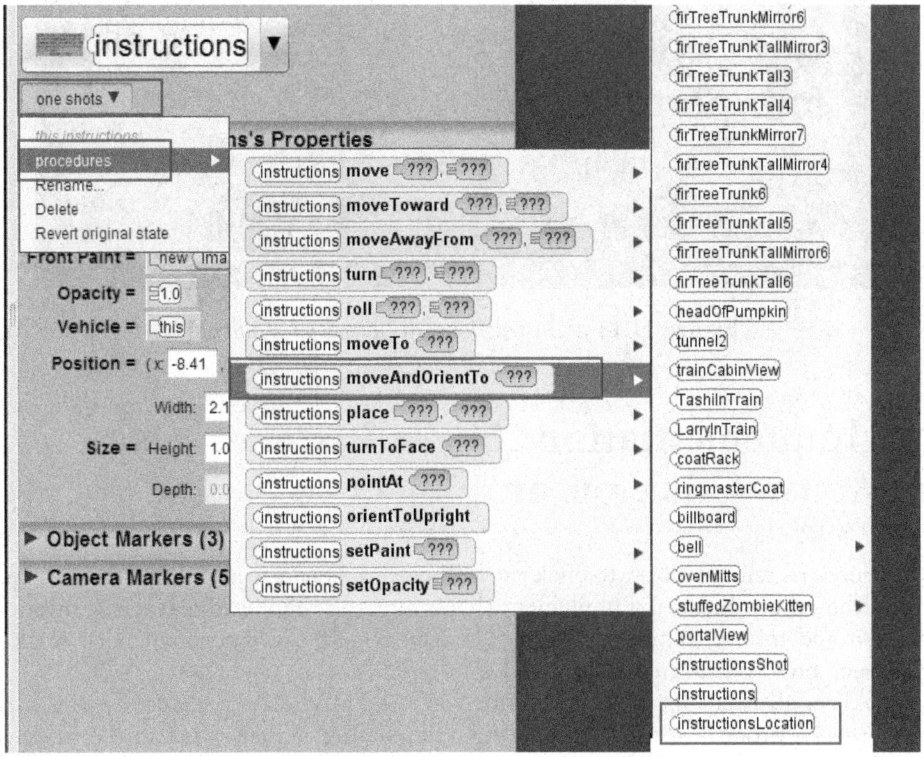

Figure 11.11 • *Use a one-shot procedure to reposition the billboard to a marked location.*

The billboard is now in an appropriate location in the scene, but still not visible to the camera in its initial location. To zoom the camera in for a close-up view of the instructions, add a statement in *myFirstMethod* to move and orient the camera to the *instructionsShot* camera marker (Figure 11.12). Test run again. Now, the billboard should be visible as shown in Figure 11.13.

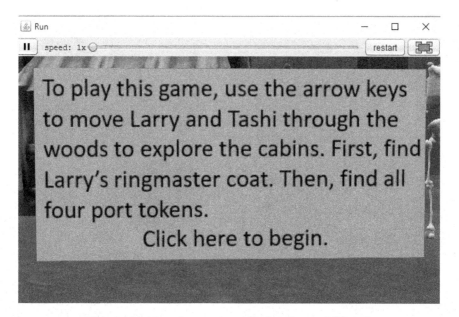

Figure 11.12   *Camera zoom in for a close-up of the instructions*

Figure 11.13   *Instructions, displayed on a billboard*

11.5 Implementation: Event Listener for Mouse-Click on an Object

The instructions tell the player to click the billboard to start the search for the ringmaster's coat and the other tokens. To implement this interactive step, a **mouse-click** listener will be written and tested. (Although known as a mouse-click event, it will also work for a screen touch on a touch-sensitive screen.)

In Alice, all event listeners are defined in the Scene class, using the built-in *initializeEventListeners* procedure. Select the Scene's *initializeEventListeners* tab in the Code editor (Figure 11.14).

Figure 11.14   *initializeEventListener editor tab*

To create a new mouse-click listener, follow these steps (Figure 11.15):

(1) Click the Add Event Listener button.
(2) Select Mouse from the dropdown menu.
(3) Select *addMouseClickOnObjectListener*.

Figure 11.15   *Add a mouse-click on object listener.*

The resulting code block is shown in Figure 11.16. Within the code block is a procedure declaration for the *mouseClicked* listener. By default, the *mouseClicked* listener responds to a click on any object in the scene, including the ground surface.

Figure 11.16   *addMouseClickOnObjectListener event code block*

In this case, we only want to respond to a click on the instructions billboard object. To specify a particular object (or objects) that will trigger this event (Figure 11.17):

(1) Click the *add detail* button at the top of the code block.
(2) Select *setOfVisuals* from the pulldown menu.
(3) Select Custom Array from the cascading menu. (An array is an arrangement of a set of objects or values.)

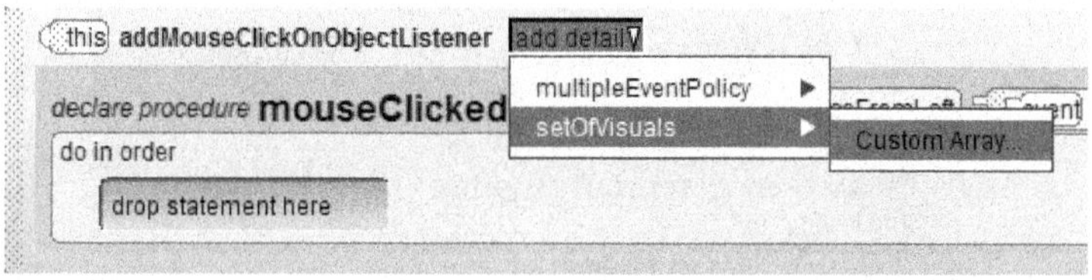

Figure 11.17   *Select* setOfVisuals *for the mouse-click listener.*

A dialog box is displayed (Figure 11.18). The selected object name(s) will be stored in an array named Visual[]. An **array** is an ordered set of items of a particular data type. In this example, the array will contain only the *instructions* billboard. Click the add button and then select the *instructions* billboard

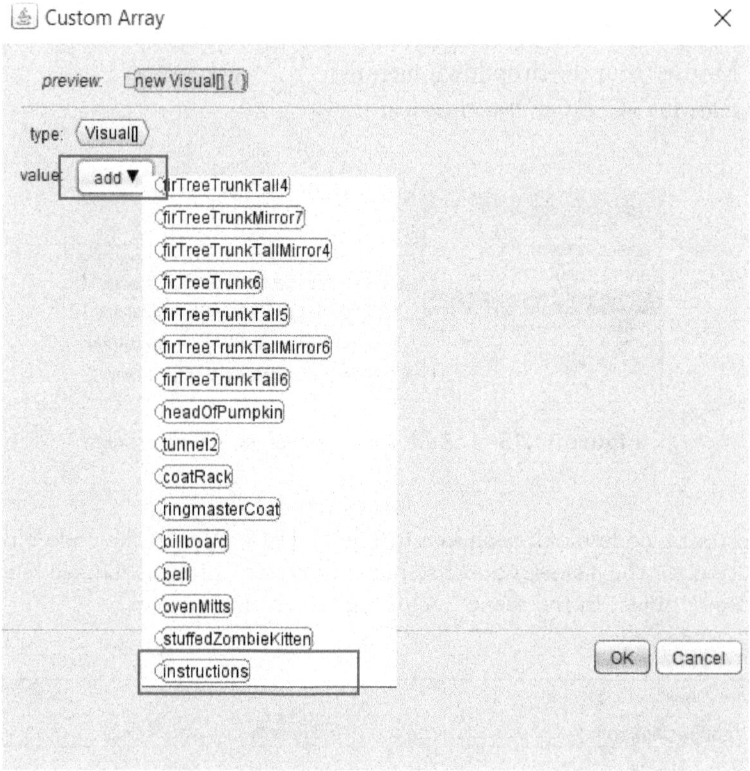

Figure 11.18   *Add the* instructions *billboard to the custom array.*

The result is shown in Figure 11.19. Now, the listener will respond to a mouse-click on the *instructions* billboard only.

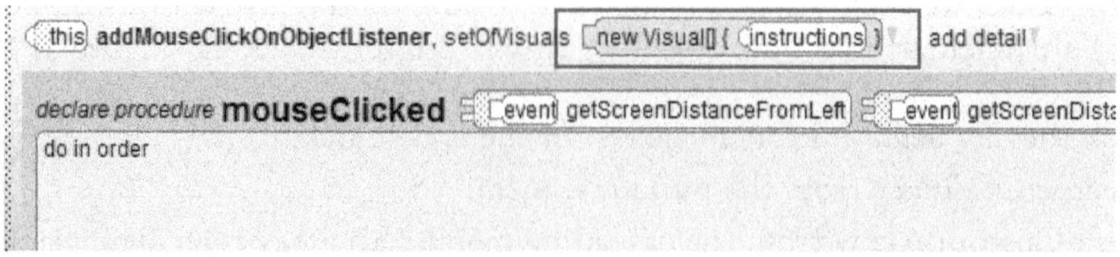

Figure 11.19   *Listen for mouse-click on* instructions *billboard.*

Typical of procedures in Alice, the *mouseClicked* procedure begins with the *do in order* control structure. The *do in order* code block is where code will be written to respond to a click on the billboard. In other words, this code block handles the mouse-click event.

As shown earlier (Figure 11.2), the response is to hide the billboard and prepare for the game. First, hide the billboard and reposition the camera (currently in a close-up shot of the billboard.) Add a *do together* control structure. Within the *do together* code block, add a statement to *move* the billboard out of sight, 10 m below ground level. Use a duration of 0.0 seconds so it just vanishes. Next, add a statement to reposition the camera to its original *start* position (Figure 11.20).

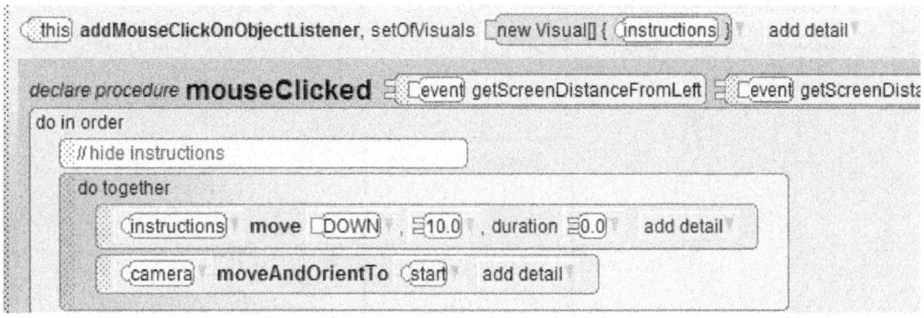

Figure 11.20   *Hiding the* instructions *billboard*

The game is played by allowing the player to navigate Larry and Tashi through the woods to find the ringmaster's coat and other tokens. Allowing the player to navigate characters in the scene requires some preparation. One character (Larry) will be directly navigated by the player, and Tashi and the camera will follow along, making all the same moves and turns as Larry.

To implement this navigation strategy, add a *do together* control structure. Within the *do together* code block, add a statement to gradually move and orient the camera to a marked position, named *followView*, immediately behind Tashi. In gaming terminology, a **follow camera** follows behind a character. Then, set the vehicle of the camera and Tashi to Larry (Figure 11.21).

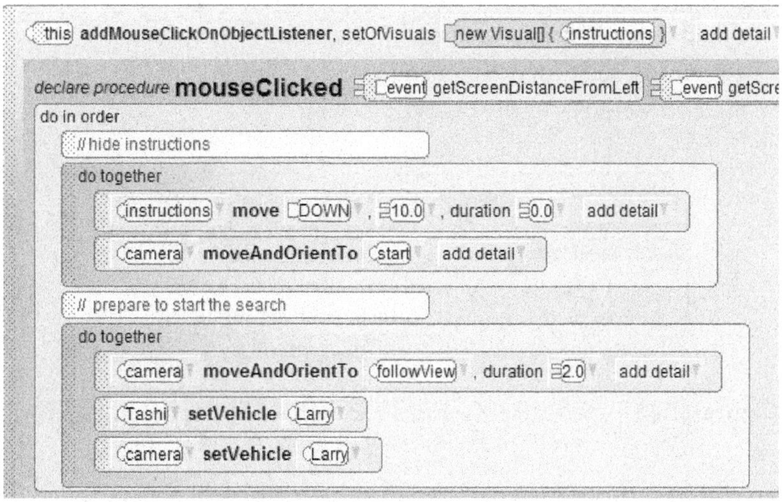

Figure 11.21   *Completed* mouseClicked *listener*

Test run. When the runtime window is displayed, click on the *instructions* billboard. The billboard should disappear. The camera should then move into position, ready to follow Larry and Tashi as the player navigates through the woods.

11.6 Object Mover Listener

Now that the camera is in follow position and vehicles have been set for the camera and Tashi, it is time to set up our game's controls. A listener is needed to allow the player to control Larry's movement through the woods. Arrow keys will be used to move and turn Larry. This is known as an **object mover** listener. A design diagram for the listener is shown in Figure 11.22.

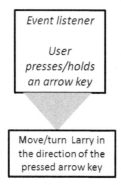

Figure 11.22   *Design for event listener to control Larry's movement*

Player navigation of a character is common in a game. So, Alice has a built-in *Object-Mover* listener in which the arrow keys are pre-programmed. The forward and backward arrow keys move the target object forward or backward as long as the user holds the key. The left and right arrow keys turn the object left or right as long as the user holds the key.

To create a new *ObjectMover* listener (Figure 11.23):

(1) Click the Add Event Listener button.
(2) Select Keyboard in the dropdown menu.
(3) Select *addObjectMoverFor* in the cascading menu.

Figure 11.23   *Select the Keyboard's* addObjectMoverFor *in the menu.*

A menu will be displayed for selecting the object that will be controlled by the arrow keys. In this example, select Larry. The resulting *addObjectMover* listener statement (Figure 11.24) does not have a code block.

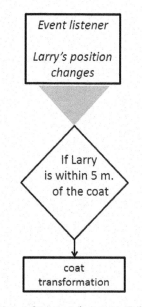

Figure 11.24   *ObjectMover event listener statement*

Test the *ObjectMover* listener by running the project. After the billboard is hidden and preparations are made for the search, use the arrow keys to steer Larry around the scene. Try each arrow key to be sure the listener is responding to each keypress. Also, try holding the key for a short time. Finally, try holding two arrow keys at the same time.

11.7 An Event Listener for Changing the Point of View

Now that the player can control Larry and Tashi's walk through the woods, it is time to think about collecting Larry's ringmaster coat and then other tokens. When Larry gets "near to" his old cabin, his ringmaster's coat suddenly appears, hanging on a coat rack in the cabin.

A possible event listener is Alice's *pointOfViewChange* listener. An object's "point of view" includes the object's position and its orientation. The *pointOfViewChange* will signal each time Larry changes position. A design diagram for the listener is shown in Figure 11.25. Statements in the event handler will check if Larry has moved to a position that is now within five meters of the coat rack. If so, the coat will transform (dissolve and reappear on Larry's shoulders).

Figure 11.25   *Design diagram for* pointOfViewChange *listener*

To create a new *pointOfViewChange* listener, click the Add Event Listener button. Then, follow these steps (Figure 11.26):

(1) Select Position/Orientation in the dropdown menu.
(2) Select addPointOfViewChangeListener in the cascading menu.
(3) Select Custom Array.

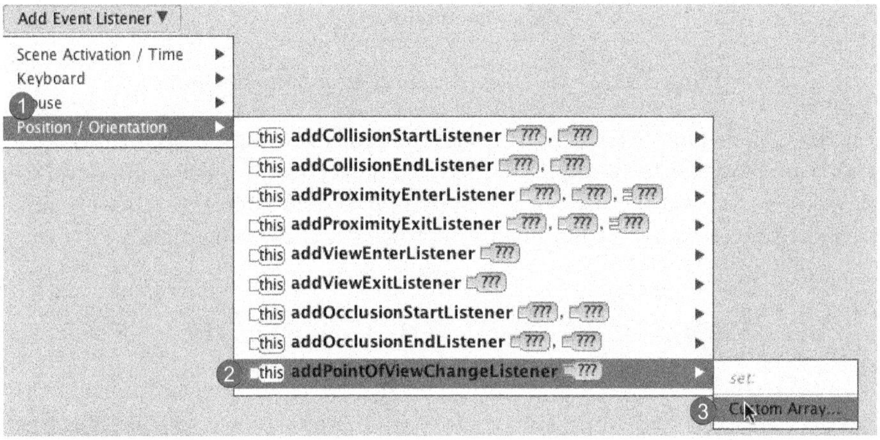

Figure 11.26   *Select options for a* pointOfViewChange *listener.*

When the Custom Array menu option is selected, a dialog box is displayed where an object (or several objects) may be selected. Click the add button (Figure 11.27). In this example, select Larry. Larry is the only object to be tracked, so click OK to close the box. The resulting listener code block is shown in Figure 11.28.

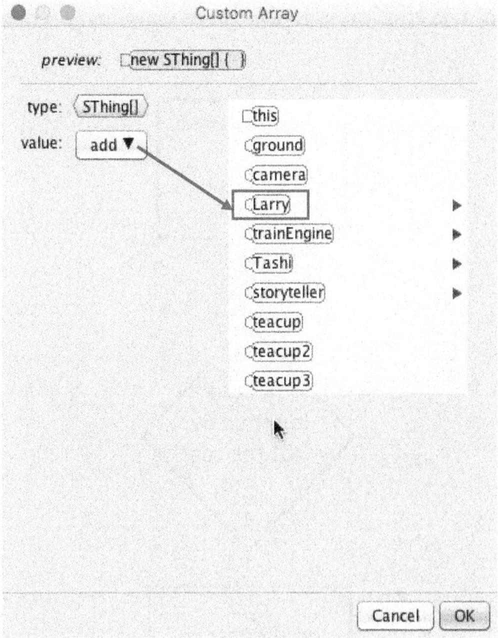

Figure 11.27   *Add Larry as the object that will be tracked.*

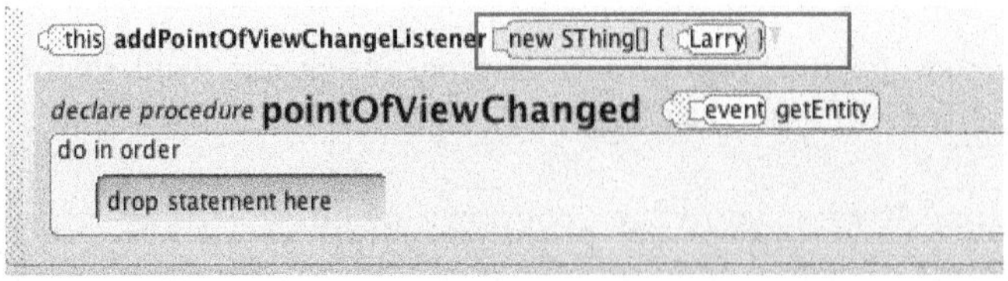

Figure 11.28   pointOfViewChanged *event listener*

11.8 If/Else and Conditional Expressions

Each time the player uses an arrow key to navigate Larry and Tashi around in the wooded area, Larry changes position, which causes the *PointOfViewChanged* listener to fire, that is, to signal the event. When the event fires, the *pointOfViewChanged* procedure executes. Code must be written within the *PointOfViewChanged* code block to handle the event.

The Alice programming language has an *if/else* control structure that can be used to check the condition that Larry has moved to a position within five meters of the coat rack. As illustrated in Figure 11.29, the condition evaluates to either *true* or *false*. If the value is *true*, the statements within the *if* part of the code block are performed. Otherwise, the statements in the *else* part of the code block are performed.

Figure 11.29 ● if/else *control structure*

To create an *if/else* control structure (1) drag the *if_* tile from the Code editor's control panel into the editor, as shown in Figure 11.30. From the popup menu of options, (2) select *true* as a placeholder value. The resulting *if/else* code block is shown in Figure 11.31.

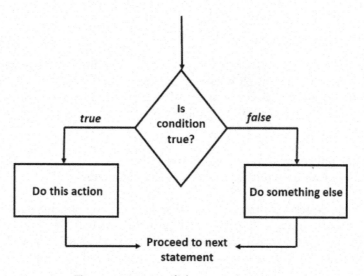

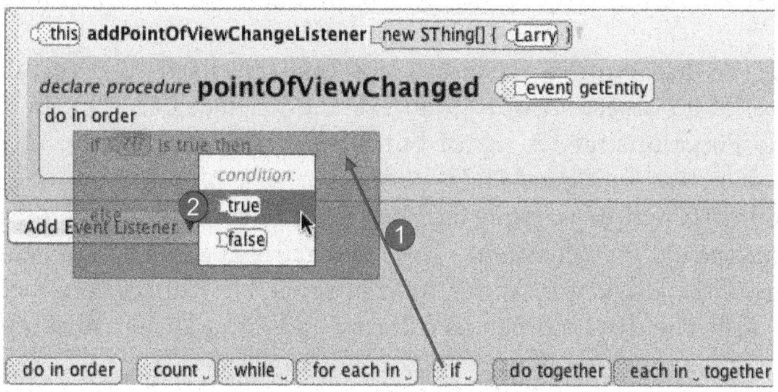

Figure 11.30 ● *Create an* if/else *control structure by dragging the* if_ *tile into the editor.*

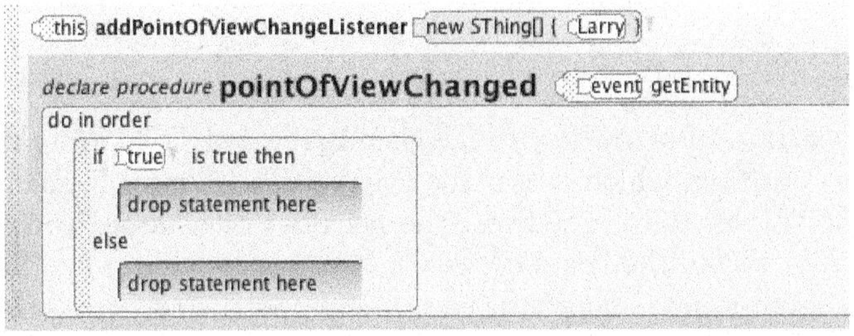

Figure 11.31   *Resulting* if/else *code block*

11.8.1 Conditional Expressions

The *true* placeholder condition must be replaced with a conditional expression that determines whether Larry has moved to within five meters of the coat on the rack. A conditional expression is evaluated as *true* or *false*. We use conditional expressions every day as we talk about current conditions and relationships. For example, we might say or write something like this:

> **A ten-dollar bill is equal to ten one-dollar bills.**
> **The distance from here to the river is less than 50 meters.**

A conditional expression often contains one or more components such as values (for example, 3.25 or 100), variables, and relational operators (such as == or >). Because a conditional expression may contain several components, the expression is typically enclosed in parentheses. For example, each of the following is a conditional expression:

```
(tenDollar == 10 * oneDollar)
(distance < 50)
```

11.8.2 Conditional expressions with built-in functions

In this example, a conditional expression is needed to check Larry's distance to the coat rack. As the program executes, Larry is moving around, so the distance is changing. In other words, the skeleton object's condition is changing, which is also known as a **change in state**.

Each Alice class has **built-in functions** that may be used to determine the current condition (or state) of an object as a program executes. Select Larry in the Object selector and then click the Functions tab. A list of built-in functions for Larry, an instance of the Skeleton class, is displayed in Figure 11.32.

When called, a function is expected to compute/retrieve the requested value and return the value to the calling statement. The returned value has a data type (for example, *Boolean*, *TextString*, *DecimalNumber*, and *WholeNumber*). The function named *getDistanceTo* computes and returns the distance between Larry and some other object, specified by an argument. The distance returned is of type *DecimalNumber*.

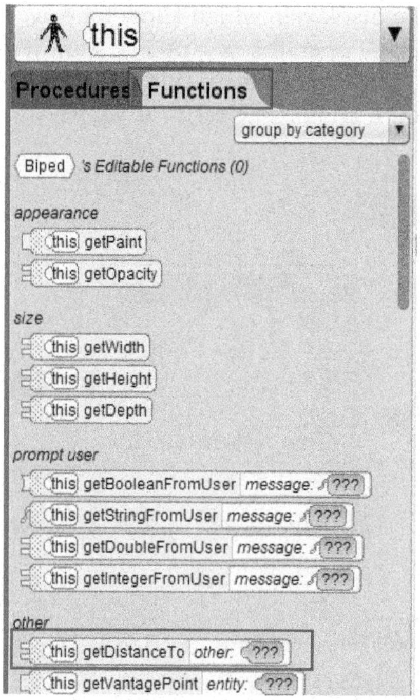

Figure 11.32 • *Built-in functions for Larry*

We will replace the *true* placeholder in the *if/else* code block with a conditional expression that calls the *getDistanceTo* function and compares the returned distance value to five meters. Click on *true* (Figure 11.33). In the popup menu, select Relational (DecimalNumber) {==,!=,<,<=, >=, >}. *DecimalNumber* was selected as the data type because the distance returned by the function is a decimal number.

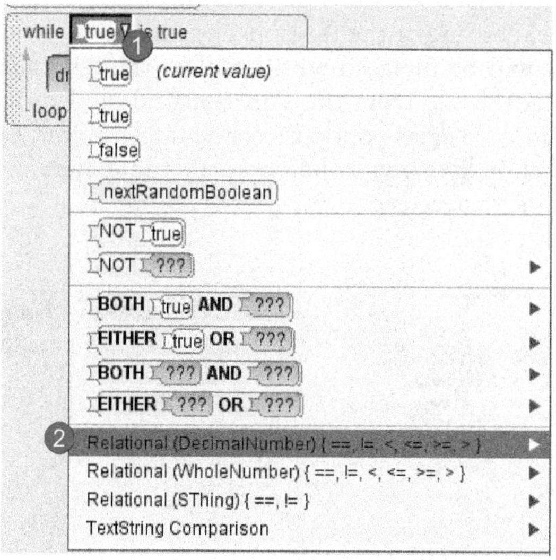

Figure 11.33 • *Replace true with a Relational (DecimalNumber) expression.*

Cascading menus will be displayed, which allow for selection of an operator and two operands. Select the less than (<) operator because we want to know if the distance is less than five meters. Then, select two operands. In this example, we selected 0.25 as placeholders for the two operands (Figure 11.34). The result is shown in Figure 11.35.

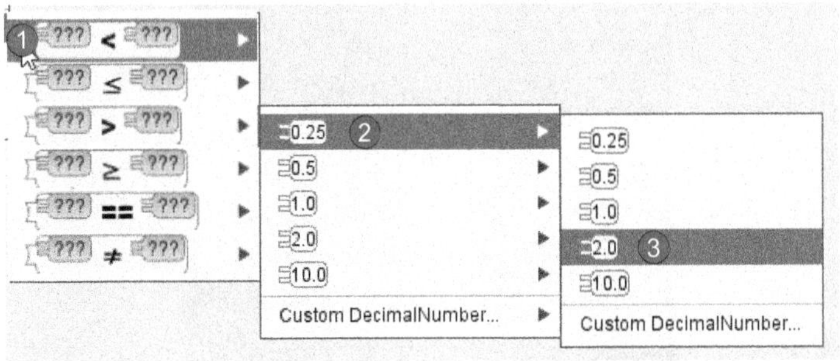

Figure 11.34   *Cascading menus to select operator and operands*

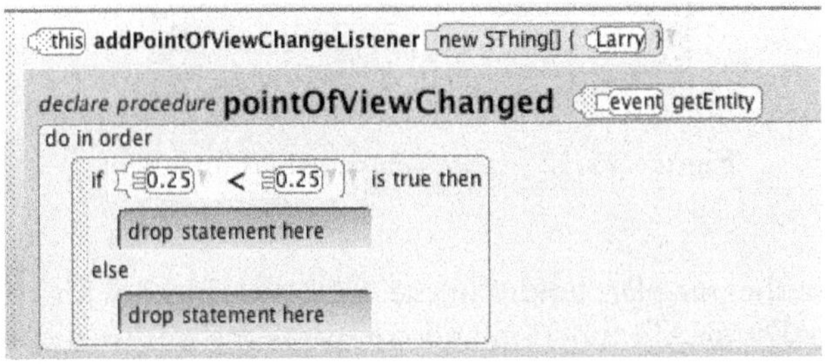

Figure 11.35   if/else *code block with a conditional expression having two placeholders*

The *if/else* code block's *true* has now been replaced by a conditional expression containing a less than (<) relational operator. This is an intermediate step because we must now select the operands on either side of the relational operator.

The first operand will be replaced with a call to the *getDistanceTo* function. Figure 11.36 illustrates dragging the tile from the Functions tab and dropping it onto the first operand. A dropdown menu displays options for the target object. Select the *coatRack* (not the *coat*). The coat is eventually going to be on Larry's shoulders, which would make this condition continually *true*, thereafter.

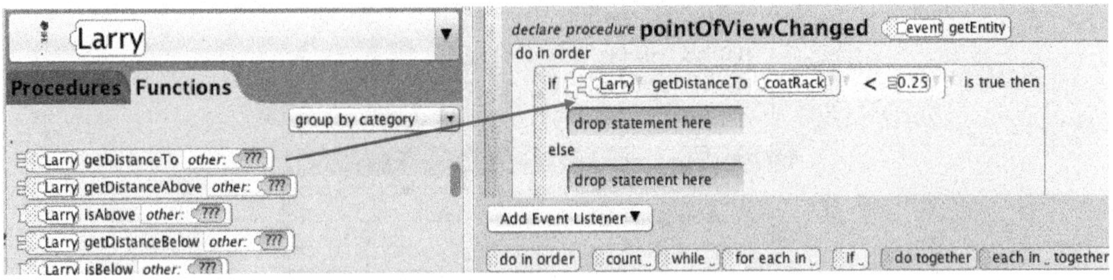

Figure 11.36   *Drag in* getDistanceTo *tile and select* coatRack *as an argument.*

Now, replace the second operand with 5.0. The completed conditional expression is shown in Figure 11.37.

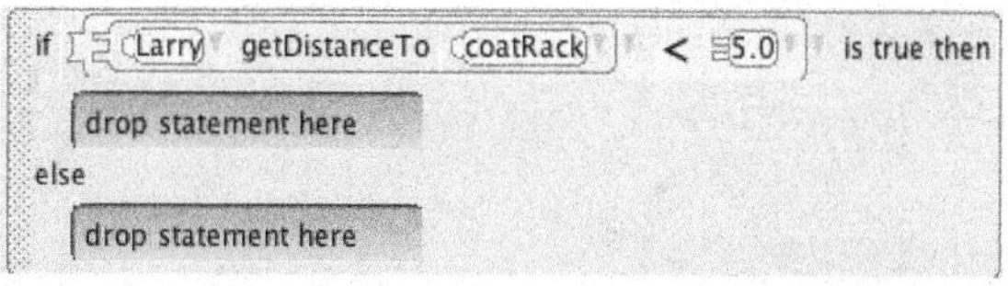

```
if [    Larry   getDistanceTo   coatRack   ] < 5.0   is true then
       drop statement here
else
       drop statement here
```

Figure 11.37   if/else *code block with a conditional expression*

11.8.3 Code within *if* and *else* segments of the *if/else* code block

Now that the conditional expression has been coded, it is time to add statements within the *if/else* code block to handle the event. The *if* segment of the *if/else* code block should call a procedure to transform the coat, and the *else* segment should do nothing. That is, if the condition is *true*, the coat should become visible, then dissolve, and then reappear on Larry's shoulders in such a way that he is wearing the coat. If the condition is *false*, no action is needed. A decomposition for a *coatTransformation* procedure is shown in Figure 11.38.

> coatRack and coat become visible
>
> Larry say "Look, my coat!"
>
> ringmasterCoat appears on Larry's shoulders

Figure 11.38   *Decomposition for a* coatTransformation *procedure*

More than one object is involved in the action, so return to the Scene class tab and declare *coatTransformation* as a new procedure. In the new *coatTransformation* editor tab, add *do together* code block. In the *do together*, add statements to set the opacity of the coatRack and ringmasterCoat to 1.0. Then, add a statement to have Larry say "Look, my coat!" This animation and dialog is an example of how the game gives feedback to the player to let them know they have achieved one of the game's goals (Figure 11.39).

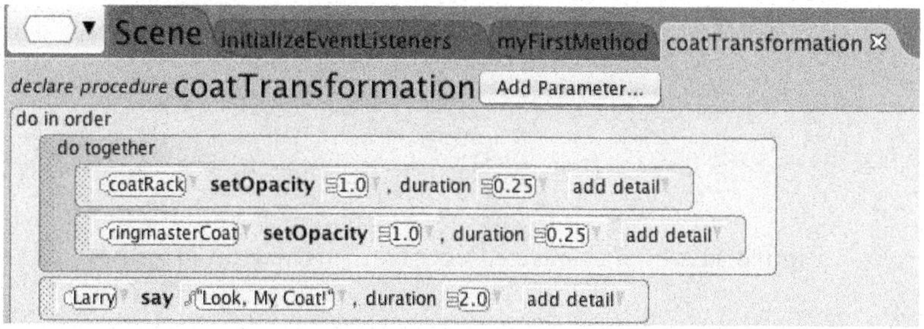

```
Scene  initializeEventListeners   myFirstMethod  coatTransformation ⊠
declare procedure coatTransformation   Add Parameter...
do in order
    do together
        coatRack   setOpacity  1.0  , duration  0.25   add detail
        ringmasterCoat   setOpacity  1.0  , duration  0.25   add detail
    Larry   say  "Look, My Coat!"  , duration  2.0   add detail
```

Figure 11.39   *Make the coat and coat rack visible in* coatTransformation.

To make the coat appear on Larry's shoulders, add a statement to set Larry's skin texture to the Skeleton resource, WITH_COAT (Figure 11.40). Note that this is an illusion—the coat that Larry will wear is a painted skin on the Skeleton object, not the coat object that was hanging on the coat rack.

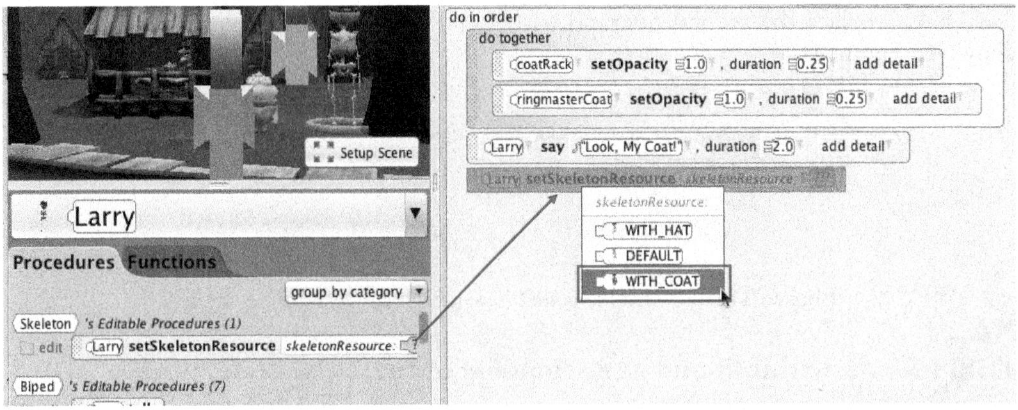

Figure 11.40   *Set a coat resource for Larry.*

11.8.4 Preventing repeated event listener firing

It is the "nature of the beast" that listeners will fire repeatedly, each time the event occurs. So, if Larry moves and is still within five meters of the coatRack, the coat and coat rack will appear again, and again. One way to prevent repeated listener firing is to prevent the condition from occurring again. In this example, add a statement to move the coat rack 30 meters below ground with a 0.0-second *duration*. The coat's vehicle is the coatRack, so moving the coatRack also moves the coat object that was hanging on the rack. The completed code for *coatTransformation* is shown in Figure 11.41.

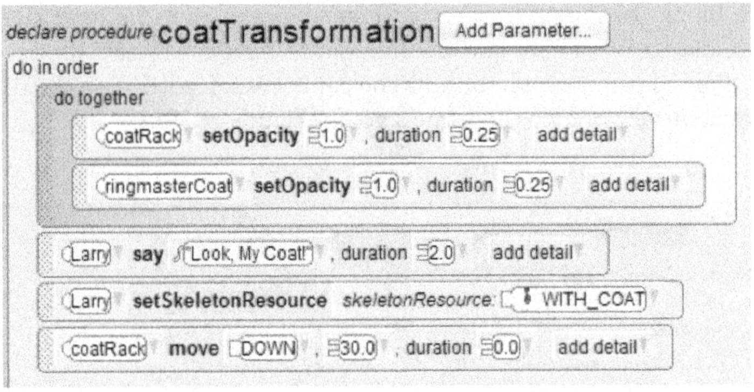

Figure 11.41   *Completed* coatTransformation *procedure*

Now, return to the *pointOfViewChangeEventListener* on the *initializeEventListener* edit tab. Add a statement to call *coatTransformation* in the *if* part of the *if/else* code block (Figure 11.42). Note that no statement is added to the *else* part of the *if/else* code block.

To test the listener and the *coatTransformation* procedure, run the program and use the arrow keys to move Larry forward toward his old cabin.

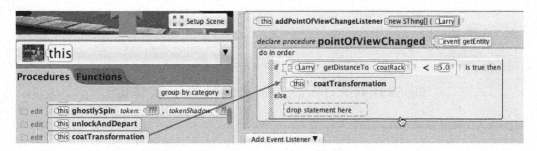

Figure 11.42 ● *Completed code to handle the* pointOfViewChange *event*

11.9 Event Listener for Mouse-Click with Multiple Target Objects

In addition to the ringmaster's coat, the player is looking to collect four tokens, each in a different cabin. When a portal token is found, a click on the token will be used to collect it. A mouse-click listener was created earlier, for a click on the game *instructions* billboard. A second mouse-click listener is needed to listen for a click on any of the four tokens. A design for the listener is shown in Figure 11.43.

Figure 11.43 ● *Design diagram for mouse-click on a token*

Add a second *mouseClicked* listener (Figure 11.44). (Refer back to Section 11.4 for step-by-step instructions, if needed.)

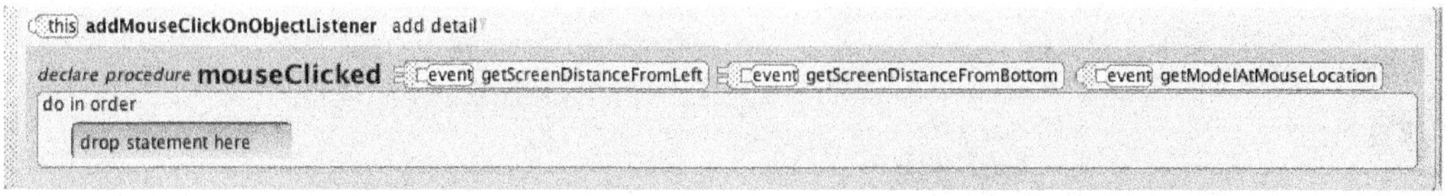

Figure 11.44   *Another* mouseClicked *event code block*

In the new *addMouseClickOnObject* listener code block, click the add detail button at the top of the code block, select setOfVisuals and then Custom Array. In the Custom Array dialog box, add *headOfPumpkin* as one of the tokens (Figure 11.45). Click the add button three more times to add *bell*, *ovenMitts*, and *stuffedZombieKitten*.

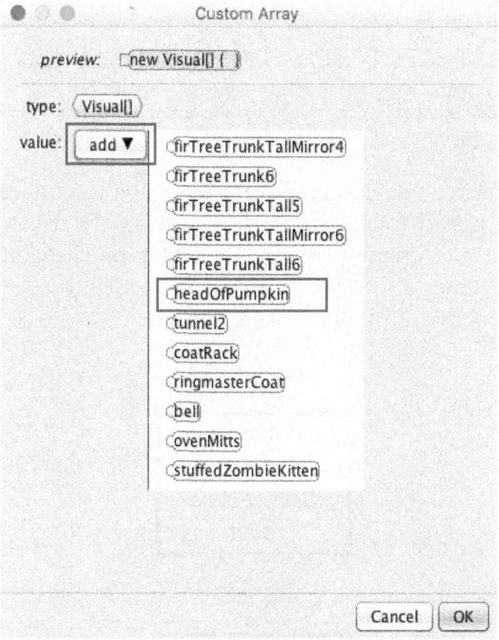

Figure 11.45   *Add the* headOfPumpkin *token to the custom array.*

The Visual[] array is shown in (Figure 11.46). Click OK. The resulting mouse-click listener code block is shown in Figure 11.47.

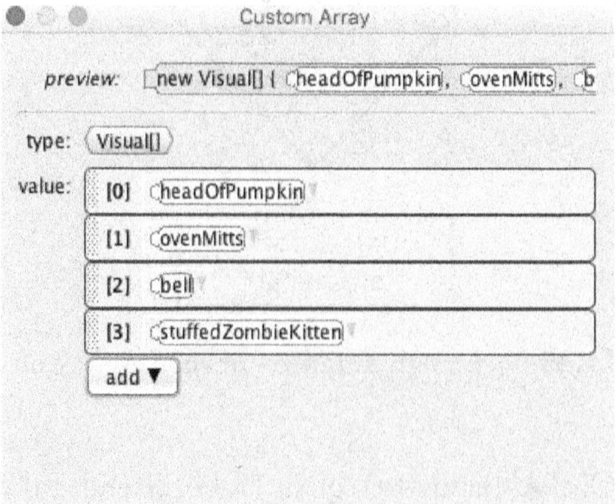

Figure 11.46   *Four token objects added in the Visual set*

this addMouseClickOnObjectListener, setOfVisuals ⌈new Visual[] { ⌈headOfPumpkin, ⌈ovenMitts, ⌈bell, ⌈stuffedZombieKitten }   add detail

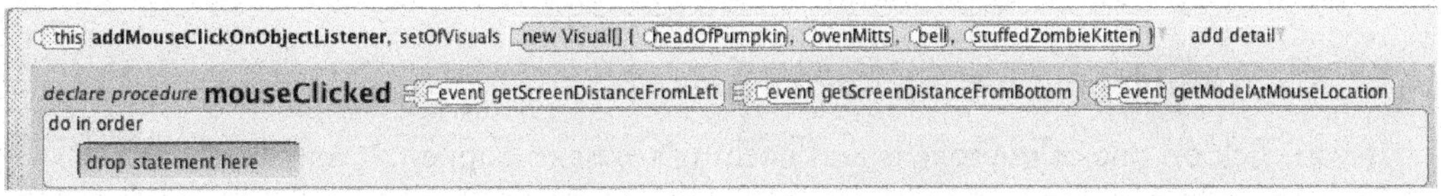

declare procedure **mouseClicked** ⌈event getScreenDistanceFromLeft ⌈event getScreenDistanceFromBottom ⌈event getModelAtMouseLocation
do in order
    drop statement here

Figure 11.47 • *Resulting* mouseClickedOnObject *listener code block*

Now, code statements may be added to the *mouseClicked* procedure to handle the event when the player clicks on a token. In the design diagram, the handler action is to collect the token. In this example, the collection action will be the token moving toward the train engine and quickly dissolving into thin air. Add a *do together* and then two statements: one to move the token toward the engine and one to change the token's opacity. In order to write statements for the token, we first need to know which of the four tokens was clicked.

The clicked token object can be accessed by selecting *this* in the Object selector and then event.*getModelAtMouseLocation* (Figure 11.48). Note that the second mouse-click object in the menu is the one you want (the first mouse-click object would be the instructions billboard). With the clicked token in the Object selector, you can now add statements to collect the token (Figure 11.49)

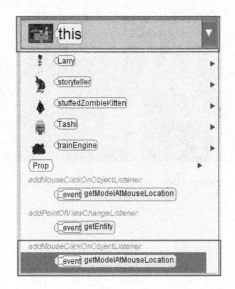

Figure 11.48 • *Select the clicked token in the Object selector.*

⌈event getModelAtMouseLocation ▼

Procedures Functions

group by category ▼

position
⌈event getModelAtMouseLocation move direction: ⌈??? , amount:
⌈event getModelAtMouseLocation moveToward target: ⌈??? , a

this addMouseClickOnObjectListener, setOfVisuals ⌈new Visual[] { ⌈headOfPumpkin, ⌈ovenMitts, ⌈bell, ⌈stu
declare procedure **mouseClicked** ⌈event getScreenDistanceFromLeft ⌈event getScreenDistance
do in order
    do together
        ⌈event getModelAtMouseLocation setOpacity ⌈0.0 add detail
        ⌈event getModelAtMouseLocation moveToward ⌈trainEngine ⌈1.0 add detail

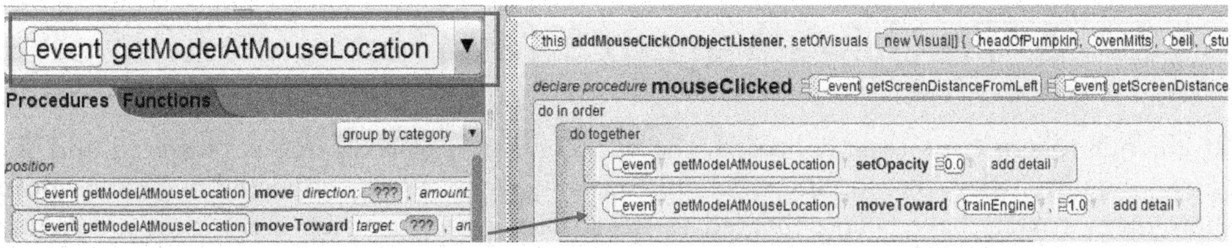

Figure 11.49 • *Create statements to collect the clicked token object.*

Test-run the project to determine whether clicking on a token causes the token to move toward the engine and disappear. Try collecting more than one token.

TIP: *Troubleshooting interactive code*

If you click on one of the tokens and nothing seems to happen, it may be that the "bounding boxes" for objects in the scene overlap. In 3D graphics, a bounding box is the smallest geometric box that surrounds an object in a scene. If the bounding boxes of objects overlap, Alice may incorrectly identify which object is clicked by the cursor. To troubleshoot this problem, use the arrow keys to move the camera around slightly so as to get a close view of the cabin with the token fully visible, as shown in Figure 11.50. Then, click again. Usually, one or two small adjustments do the trick.

Figure 11.50   *Use arrow keys to obtain a close view with the token fully visible.*

If Alice has been running for several hours and you have been testing and retesting the arrow keys, it is possible the arrow keys will get "sticky"—either not responding or continuing to respond even when you release the key. Save your project, exit Alice, then restart Alice. A restart should clear the sticky key issue.

11.10 A Tracking Variable for Game Condition

If all four tokens have been collected, the win condition of the game is triggered and the game ends. In order to recognize when all four tokens have been collected, we must count how many tokens have been collected as we go along, step by step. Each time a token is collected, increase the count and then stop the game when the count reaches four.

A variable can be used to track the count. Start the variable with a value of 0 and add 1 to it each time a token is collected. A variable that tracks the count is known as a **counter**. The tokens belong to the scene, and listeners are defined in *initializeEventListeners*, which belongs to the Scene class. So, it makes sense to declare a counter variable as a property of the Scene class. Open the Scene class tab and scroll down to the unmanaged properties section. Add a Scene Property, named *portTokenCount*, of type *WholeNumber* (Figure 11.51). Initialize the variable to 0. Declaring a variable and assigning a value to a variable was discussed previously in Chapter 9.

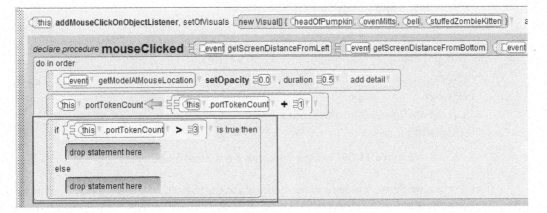

Figure 11.51 *Declare a variable named* portTokenCount *of type* WholeNumber.

Now return to the *mouseClicked* procedure. Create a statement that adds 1 to the *portTokenCount* (Figure 11.52) each time a token is clicked.

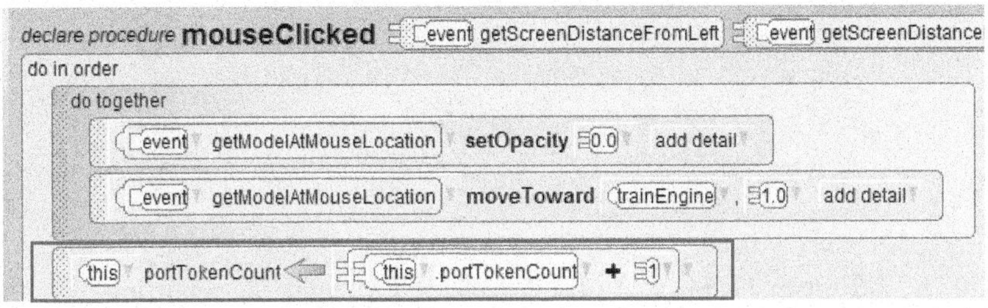

Figure 11.52 *Add 1 to the* portTokenCount *each time a token is clicked.*

After the count has been updated, an *if/else* statement can be used to check the count to see if all tokens have been collected. Drag an *if/else* control tile into the editor and create a conditional expression that evaluates whether the *portTokenCount* is greater than 3 (Figure 11.53).

Figure 11.53 If/else *with conditional statement to check count greater than 3*

If the *portTokenCount* is greater than 3, then the tokens have all been collected and the game is over. Larry and Tashi board the train, realizing the tokens will guide their journey to find the other circus members. In the *if* segment of the *if/else* code block, add a statement to unlink the camera so it will no longer follow Larry. Then, add statements to have Larry and Tashi board the train in preparation for departure. Use the object markers to reposition them on the train, as shown in Figure 11.54. Also add statements to set their vehicles to the train engine so when the train moves, they will move with it.

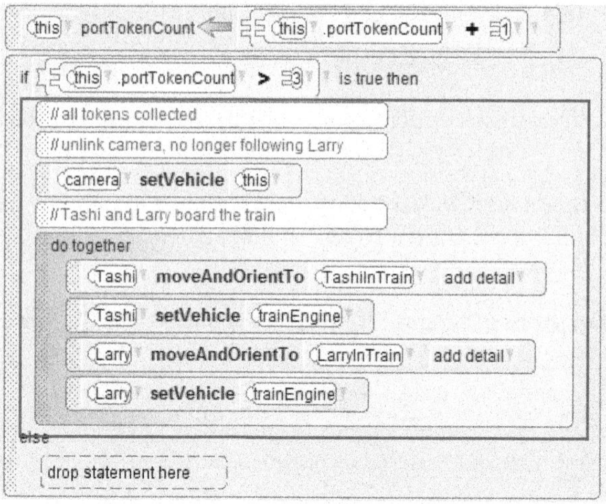

Figure 11.54   *All tokens collected, prepare for departure.*

Now, an *unlockAndDepart* procedure may be created to handle the departure. A decomposition for the *unlockAndDepart* procedure is shown in Figure 11.55.

do in order
  do together
    Camera move to train portal view
    Unlock the portal by setting its opacity to 1.0
  Camera move to train cabin view
  Larry and Tashi dialog – realization that they can use the tokens to lead the train to the circus members
  do together
    bell rings
    train moves forward (into the tunnel)
    fog density increases

Figure 11.55   *Decomposition for* unlockAndDepart

Declare a new Scene procedure, named *unlockAndDepart*, and enter code statements to implement the actions in the decomposition. Figure 11.56 illustrates the beginning of the procedure and the dialog. Note the *portalView* camera marker is used for viewing the tunnel as it appears and the *trainCabinView* camera marker for viewing the interior of the train cabin where the dialog occurs between Larry and Tashi. The dialog is implemented using *talkAndSay*, imported for the Biped class. Importing a procedure from a saved class was discussed earlier, in Chapter 9.

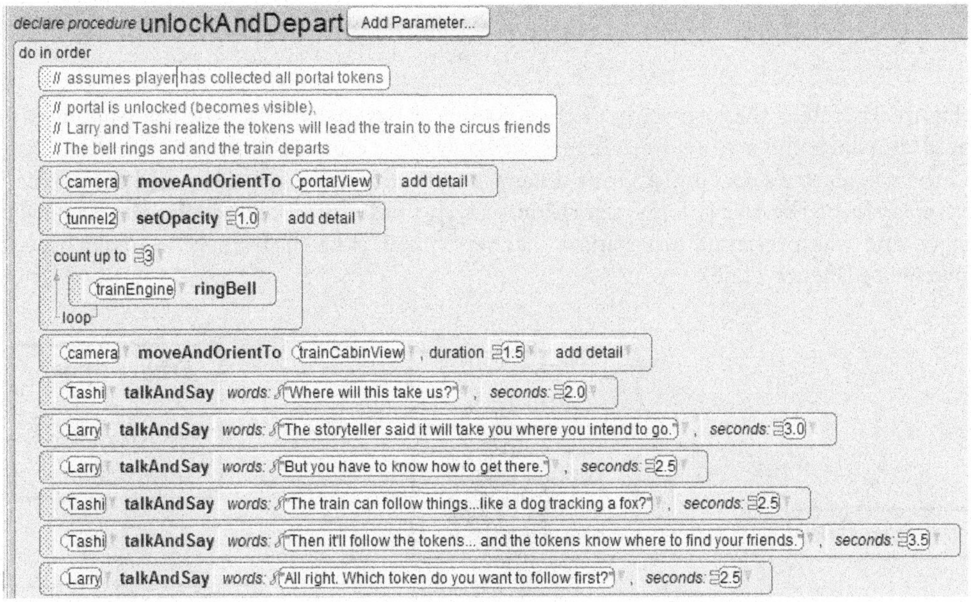

Figure 11.56   *An implementation of* unlockAndDepart

The last part of the *unlockAndDepart* procedure, where the bell continues to ring as the train engine pulls into the tunnel and the fog increases for a fade-out, has not been implemented. This part of the procedure is left as an exercise for you. See the end of chapter exercises.

Return to the *mouseClicked* listener and add a statement to call *unlockAndDepart* in the *if* segment of the *if/else* statement (Figure 11.57). No statement is needed in the *else* part of the *if/else* statement.

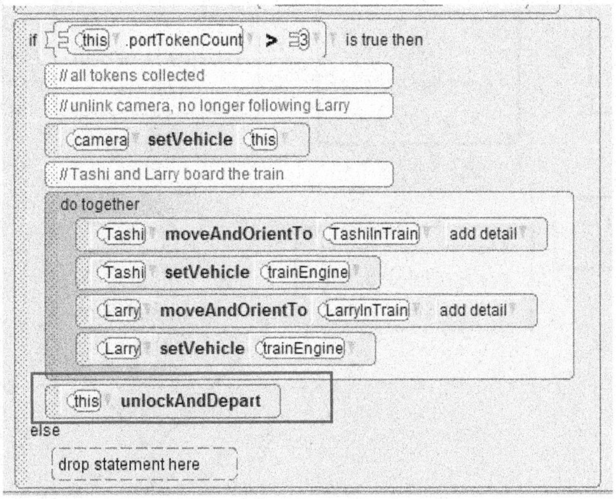

Figure 11.57   *Call* unlockAndDepart *if the* portTokenCount *is greater than 3.*

To test the *mouseClicked* and *unlockAndDepart* procedures, run the animation several times to find different tokens in different cabins in different sequences.

11.11 Design Revisited

In Figure 11.1, near the beginning of this chapter, a basic algorithm for the game was pre-sented, in which the actions were listed as: display game instructions, wait for the user to find the ringmaster's coat and all four tokens, and finally unlock a portal and depart for the next episode of the story. This algorithm was the basis of a design diagram for *myFirst-Method* and was presented alongside a listener thread. The diagram is repeated here, for convenience (Figure 11.58).

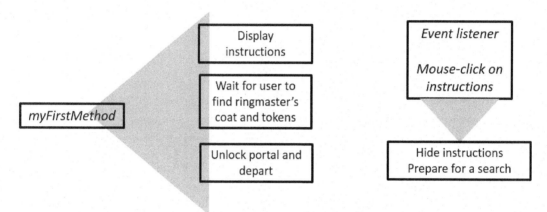

Figure 11.58   *Game design with a listener*

As the game was developed in this chapter, additional listeners were designed and implemented (Figure 11.59).

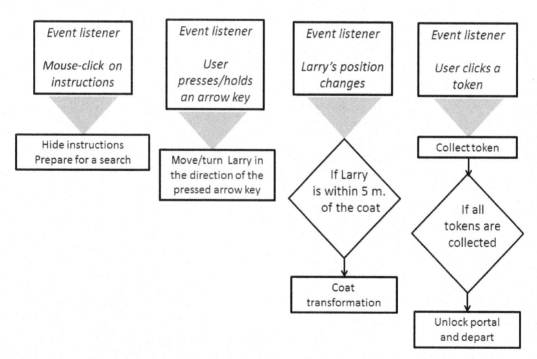

Figure 11.59   *Event listeners in the Ghost Train Hub game*

Compare the *myFirstMethod* diagram, leftmost in Figure 11.57, with the listener for a mouse-click on a token—, rightmost diagram in Figure 11.58. In essence, the listener is where the code is implemented to collect and count the tokens. The listener also detects when all tokens have been collected and calls a procedure for unlocking the portal and train departure, effectively ending the game.

The only code written in *myFirstMethod* was a statement to move and orient the camera for a close-up shot of the *instructions* billboard at the start of the game. Typical of interactive, event-driven programming, event listeners are "where the action is."

Summary

This chapter introduces interactivity and event-driven programming. An event is something that happens and is detected by event listeners as the program runs. For example, an event may be a mouse-click or a keypress. Listeners are threads—processes that run at the same time as the *main* process that is activated when the Run key is clicked. In this chapter, mouse-click and object mover keypress listeners were illustrated. Other listeners will be illustrated in later chapters, as needed.

In an interactive program such as a game, the player controls the flow of execution (the path of execution through the code). Through the game's controls, the player interacts with the program as it runs, which determines the game's outcome, including the sequence in which some actions take place. In this example, the order in which the tokens are collected is determined by the player using the arrow keys to navigate the characters through the woods in a search for tokens. As the program runs, conditions (such as the position of an object or the camera) change. Such changes are known as state changes.

An *if-else* control structure is often used to check on the current state of an object while the program is running. An *if-else* control structure evaluates a condition and then branches to execute one of two parts (an *if true* segment, or an *else false* segment). Only one segment is executed, the other is skipped. In this example, an *if/else* control is used to check whether the skeleton was within five meters of the ringmaster's coat on a coat rack. An *if/else* control is also used to check whether all tokens have been collected.

The condition in an *if-else* control structure is a conditional expression that results in either a *true* or a *false* value. Conditional expressions often call built-in functions. A function computes or retrieves a value and returns it to the calling statement. In this example, a built-in *distanceTo* function was called to determine Larry's distance to the coat, each time his position changed.

In games, conditions are often used to determine if and when a player has achieved a goal in the game. In response to player progress on a goal, the game provides feedback to the player. Game completion is determined by game end conditions, including win conditions and fail conditions.

Terms

array	controls	event fire
built-in function	end condition	event handler
conditional expression	event	event listener

fail condition   mouse-click   user
feedback   object mover   user input
follow camera   player   user interface (UI)
goals   state   win condition
if/else control structure   tracking variable
interactivity   thread

Concept Questions

1. What is the difference between a traditional, sequential program and an interactive program from the perspective of:
   (a) The user
   (b) The programmer

2. If a program has a *main* process and two mouse-click listeners, how many threads does it have at runtime?

3. Conditions play a major role in games. What kinds of conditions are known as "end conditions" for a game? Describe each.

4. In what way are the goals of a game related to feedback in the game?

5. If an elephant is located 50.33 meters from the center of a river that is 15.75 meters wide, evaluate each of the following conditional expressions:
   (a) (elephant.getDistanceTo(river) > river.getWidth())
   (b) (elephant.getDistanceTo(river) < river.getWidth())
   (c) (elephant.getDistanceTo(river) != river.getWidth())
   (d) (elephant.getDistanceTo(river) = = river.getWidth())

6. Based on the elephant and river setting described in Question 5, write a code segment that declares a variable named *distanceInFrontOf* and initialize it to an arithmetic expression that computes the distance between the front of the elephant's trunk (assuming the trunk is in a non-extended position at the front of the animal) and the closest edge of the river.

7. Based on the elephant and river setting described in Question 5, which segment of the following *if/else* statement is executed?

   if (elephant.getDistanceTo(river) > river.getWidth())
       elephant.playAudio(trumpet1)
   else
       elephant.playAudio(trumpet2)

8. Assuming it is not nested within a loop, how many times does a particular *if/else* statement in a program execute?

9. What is the effect of an *if/else* control structure on the execution path of a program?

10. What is the purpose of a follow camera in a game?

11. Is it possible to have a billboard object that has different images on the front and back? Explain your answer.

12. Explain why there is no editable code block for the *ObjectMover* listener.

13. A *MouseClickOnObject* listener is a thread that is alert for a click on a specific object. Describe how the object is specified in the listener code.

14. In what way are event listeners related to the controls of a game?

Exercises

. . . .

The following exercises are modifications for the example program in this chapter.

1. The second mouse-click listener handles the event by having the clicked token move toward the train and fade away as its opacity is set to 0.0. A mouse-click on a token would be much more gratifying if a dramatic animation were to occur.

    (a) Add a ghostly spin procedure for the Prop class. Name it *specialEffect* and define it for the class of that token. To create a ghostly spin, add a shadow token just behind the token and have the shadow be partially transparent. Then in response to the mouse click, have the token and its ghostly shadow resize and spin to create a ghost-like effect before fading away. A decomposition for the ghostly spin *specialEffect* procedure is shown here.

           do together
               tokenShadow resize (larger then smaller)
               token spin

    (b) Because the *specialEffect* procedure is written for the Prop class, you should be able to call it for more than one type of token. Is there any token for which *specialEffect* does not work?

2. Complete the implementation of the *unlockAndDepart* procedure, as per the decomposition shown in Figure 11.54

3. Add statements to the *unlockAndDepart* procedure to convey Tashi and Larry's excitement and enthusiasm when they realize the tokens can be used to take them to the circus members.

4. Start with Alice's African starter scene. Add an elephant and sections of a river to create a scene similar to that shown below. Make the animation interactive to allow the user to move the elephant. When the elephant arrives at the river, display a billboard that says "hakuna kuogelea" ("no swimming" in Swahili).

Project
....

Create an experimental prototype for an interactive game: In this prototype, try having 10 balloons float upward from the ground at different speeds. (Within two seconds, all balloons should have floated off screen.) When the player clicks a balloon, the balloon should disappear. Use a counter variable to track the number of balloons the player successfully clicks before the balloons float off the screen. Display the result as feedback to the player.

March 1, 1910: Nicholas

The Pumpkin Head

For a very long time during the avalanche all Nicholas knows is dark and cold. The dull roar approaching from the south grows louder until his ears are full of it, and then the circus wagon jerks sideways against the train car. The cover flattens within seconds, and that's when the cold hits, pushing in from all sides. The wagon tumbles over itself, and Nicholas is thrown like a rag doll from floor to ceiling and back again. On the twenty-eighth wagon roll, Nicholas feels a sudden snap and his eyesight fails. His body goes numb from the cold.

It isn't until the temperature starts to rise that Nicholas even realizes the world outside his head still exists. But soon the heat grows sticky and the air humid, and the floppy position he's lying in slowly becomes uncomfortable. He sits up.

And notices he can't open his eyes. Nicholas realizes his mask must have been shaken off his head. The pumpkin-shaped mask has a face and bionic eyes. Without the mask, he has no sense of vision. He shrugs his shoulders and pulls up the turtleneck of his shirt to cover his small head.

When Nicholas stands, he nearly steps on a book. His entire collection fell off the shelves. He carefully arranges them back into their designated spots, based on the embossed leather spines. He forces the crooked door open and steps outside. The wagon feels mostly intact, except for the wheels, and the entire thing seems to be stuck in a very large tree.

Never one to panic, Nicholas measures the situation. He's been in similar situations; fixing broken equipment is his specialty. He pulls out his toolbox from underneath his bed. Everything is intact, including the large packet of pumpkin seeds he always keeps tucked in the corner.

He quietly sets to work.

After a long while, Nicholas wonders why he is no more tired or hungry than when he began. He opens the toolbox again and hefts the packet of seeds into his palm. He isn't hungry now. He might be later, although he doubts it.

Nicholas gingerly climbs down the tree. It's a beautifully laid out tree, with a cascade of rocks leading down, like stairs, to a pool of fertile soil. He prepares the soil in a small plot and starts laying the seeds. Planting pumpkins is a skill buried in his muscle memory, something he can't forget no matter how many times he tries to. His body falls into heavy, dull routine.

Once finished, he sits dejectedly beside his miniature plot of dirt, digs his hand in the soil, and curls his fingers around one of the seeds. He holds it there, letting the familiarity comfort him while trying not to think of how alone he appears to be after the crash. Nicholas tries to lift his hand out of the dirt, but something sticks, as if another hand is wrapped around his own and holding him down. He panics, dragging his arm backward, shoving with his feet. He twists his wrist and feels the rough roots wrapped around it, roots far too mature for a

264

plant that should still be a seed. Nicholas snaps a few roots off until he can yank his hand free. He jerks backward and plops onto the ground.

"Wow," a low, impish voice says, sounding begrudgingly impressed, "only five minutes and already you have a full-grown vine there."

Nicholas twitches in the direction of the noise.

"I must admit, even with all my tricks, I can't make plants grow that quickly," the voice says. The sound comes closer, as if the speaker is advancing on Nicholas. "What're your intentions in this jungle, exactly? I've been watching you," the voice says. "Are you here, perhaps, on accident?"

Nicholas jabs his finger in the direction of the voice, his shoulders shaking in a mock form of nodding "yes."

"Okay," the voice says, "not many people show up in a metal machine, lie unconscious for weeks, and then start growing squash once they wake up. I'll trust your answer." The voice turns significantly kinder, "By the way, did you know you're missing your head?"

After that the mysterious voice doesn't appear much, except as a watchful presence on occasion. Nicholas spends a week rebuilding the wagon. He isn't even sure how great the final result looks, but the structure feels strong. He tends to the pumpkin patch out of habit, although he knows he doesn't need them. Nicholas experiments with growing things. He combines plant species, tries to measure the rate of accelerated growth. For a while he begins to believe it's all he's good for, once again.

Nicholas tries to read a book. He opens it. He runs his hands across the page. He can feel someone watching him.

"I need your help," the voice says. "A baby peccary is in trouble, caught above a waterfall."

A cold hand takes hold of Nicholas's wrist and leads him through the forest swiftly.

"I need you to make this grow," the voice pushes Nicholas's hand to the ground.

Nicholas digs through the dirt until he hits the roots of the vine. It takes a minute of concentration before the energy flows forward, and he can hear the shifting of leaves. Nicholas can feel the plant, as if it's an extension of himself. The voice gives him directions about where to grow the vine.

They save the peccary. From the quiet grunts issuing behind them as they walk, Nicholas can tell the peccary follows them home.

"You stupid peccary, don't you see my tracks are facing the opposite direction. Follow those, go away," the voice says, annoyed, "I don't keep pets. I'm undying and pets die."

But when Nicholas sits on his bed that night, a snoring, farting ball of fur sleeps next to him, and like that, Nicholas has a pet. Sometimes Nicholas hears the voice talking and the peccary answering in grunts and he realizes the two are having a conversation.

"We'll call him Ubiratan," the voice announces to Nicholas, "My name, by the way, is Curupira."

Nicholas scratches his own name in the dirt. But it doesn't do any good, because Curupira can't read the writing.

Curupira starts taking Nicholas on hunts for loggers. Ubiratan follows Curupira, Nicholas rides on the peccary's back, and the peccary becomes Nicholas' eyes. Nicholas disables the machinery. He compels vines or trees to grow around the metal, to break wheel axles and deaden gears. And from the screams and ripping noises, Nicholas is fairly certain the human loggers meet a similar fate at the hands of Curupira.

They deserve it—they invaded the forest.

In return for fighting the loggers, Curupira fixes Nicholas's books. Curupira embosses the letters on each page with tree sap and then Nicholas reads by feel. He does math problems on leaves, punching out diagrams and equations. He measures time by the number of pages Curupira's translated relative to the number of books he knows are in his collection.

Years pass; Ubiratan ages. The old peccary loses his own eyesight, and soon both he and Nicholas confine themselves to the wagon. Nicholas stretches his ability to reach plants farther and farther away. He no longer has to be with Curupira to disable logging machines. So he's slightly confused when Curupira comes to him again.

"I found another machine," Curupira warns quietly, "This one's different."

Curupira leaves to deal with the loggers while Nicholas stretches his awareness for any unusual metal in the jungle. He finds it, and as the vines twist around the machine he can sense the shape, and it feels vaguely familiar, as ingrained in his muscle memory as knowing how to plant pumpkins. His memories are interrupted when Curupira swings in through the open-back canvas and lands on the bed next to Nicholas.

"Two of them escaped from the machine before the vines encroached!" Curupira exclaims, "They followed me. They weren't fooled at all by my backwards feet. The little one is some kind of expert hunter. It could tell which direction my tracks were really going by the indentation of the mud. And one of them is a skeleton! I can't eat a skeleton!"

"Wait ..." Curupira interrupts himself, "Is that one of our pumpkins?" The bed shifts slightly and Nicholas senses Curupira crouching in the center of the wagon. "Maybe this is what they've come for," Curupira carries the mysterious pumpkin outside.

Curupira leaves the door ajar—Nicholas can tell because of the cooler air wafting in. Nicholas hears two voices discussing something at the base of the tree. One voice is unnervingly familiar, and the other high and squeaky.

"Well, we're getting close because there's a pumpkin patch. Do any of them have faces?" the squeaky voice says.

"No luck," the familiar voice says dejectedly.

"Looking for something?" Curupira asks just outside the wagon door. There's a dull thud of Curupira's foot connecting with a pumpkin, and a loud thump of the pumpkin landing several feet below at the base of the tree. "Guess which pumpkin out of these three is the head," Curupira announces, "and it's yours."

"What happens if we guess wrong?" the familiar voice asks, uncertain and nervous.

Silence. Although Nicholas is fairly certain he knows the answer.

He also now knows who the voice belongs to. He'd recognize Lawrence Prenderghast's distinct overdramatic tone anywhere.

"I guess the first pumpkin," Lawrence states confidently.

"Correct," Curupira says, sounding disappointed, "Now take your pumpkin and get out of my forest before I change my mind about being lenient."

"One more request," Lawrence says, "May we see inside the wagon stuck in your tree?"

"Why?" Curupira asks, suspicious.

"It once belonged to a friend," Lawrence says gravely, "I think you might know him."

"No," Curupira insists, "My tricks have no effect on you, you saw through my backwards trail, you beat my game, and for that I'm letting you live. But don't think I won't still devour you if you continue to encroach on my forest. Take your metal machine and leave!"

"First take this pumpkin head to our friend and tell us what he says," Lawrence says calmly.

"He can't say anything," Curupira retorts, "or see. He doesn't have a head."

Silence, as Curupira ponders this. In a moment he realizes, and says quietly, "Okay. I'll permit it."

Someone pushes the wagon door farther open.

Nicholas tries to concentrate on his reading. He's comfortable, he knows what to expect here, he has utmost faith in Curupira's ability to tackle the conflict outside without his help. Nicholas has other concerns. A specific math problem is giving him trouble. It's hard to calculate the arch of a projectile object if one can't see the diagram on the page. Pages rustle by the wind from the open door. Nicholas tries to ignore it.

"I believe you lost this, my friend," Lawrence says.

Nicholas sits up straight, still turned toward his book.

A heavy weight suddenly falls on his shoulders. He stands, turns, opens his eyes, and comes face to face with a skeleton. A skeleton wearing a top hat and red striped coat.

"Larry?" Nicholas asks.

The skeleton smiles.

And in an instant, Nicholas, the circus wagon, and his personal train car disappear. He's transported to a very familiar cabin in the middle of a pine forest, and once again he's all alone.

12

Custom Functions, While Loops, Random Values, Input, and a Game Algorithm

Concept Objectives

- Creating an internal pivot for rotating an object
- Writing code that uses external/internal pivot markers for rotating an object
- Using a *while* loop
- Calling a built-in function to generate a random value
- Creating a custom function
- Calling a built-in input function
- Using variables to track and check game state

An exploration of games programming continues in this chapter with a classic game that swaps and shuffles objects in an ordered row (numbered positions, left to right on the screen). Objects will be randomly selected from the row for the swap and shuffle actions. Internal pivot and external pivot points and markers will be used to perform the rotational actions in swap and shuffle procedures. A custom function will be written to identify the location of objects in the row after a shuffle. A *while* loop will be introduced for repetition in a game where the player has a limited number of tries to win the game. The player will be asked to use the keyboard to input a text value, and local variables (variables declared in a procedure) will be used to track the state of the game.

To illustrate pivots for rotation, custom functions, *while* loops, random actions, and user input, the programming task in this chapter will continue with Episode 6, *The Pumpkin Head*. In this episode, the portal opens in a South American rain forest, where Larry and Tashi encounter Curupira, a popular creature of Brazilian folklore. Curupira plays tricks on poachers and hunters and preys on loggers who devastate the forest. The example program will implement a cutscene and a game. In games programming, a cutscene is a short animation that tells part of the story before the game begins.

12.1 Story Analysis

Begin by reading and analyzing the story to determine the background components and select the objects and actions for the opening cutscene and game. In this episode, Larry and Tashi travel through the portal to find Nicholas, the "headless circus clown." He had a pumpkin-shaped mask with bionic eyes that provide a sense of sight. Nicholas was Larry's best friend and had a love of learning, especially math and engineering. The segment of Episode 6 selected for this chapter is summarized here:

> The train has traveled through a portal and re-materialized in a rainforest in South America. Tashi and Larry have wandered away from the train, through the dense forest of trees and exotic plants. Tashi and Larry are standing near a pumpkin patch. They remember the pumpkin head token had a face. None of the pumpkins in this pumpkin patch, however, has a face.
>
> They are startled by the sudden appearance of Curupira, who is standing at the top of a pile of rocks, near the old Prenderghast circus wagon. Curupira seems to know Larry and Tashi are trying to find Nicholas, the former circus clown.
>
> Curupira kicks a pumpkin to the ground where it rolls toward Larry. Curupira then jumps down, rock by rock. He challenges Larry and Tashi to play a version of the old shell game. He will shuffle the pumpkins and if they can guess which pumpkin is the one with a face, they get the pumpkin and can leave the forest, alive. Larry guesses correctly and gets the pumpkin. Larry recognizes the pumpkin as the mask and asks that it be given to Nicholas, who is in the circus wagon.

To turn this segment of the *The Pumpkin Head* episode into an interactive program, one summary analysis of the episode could be:

> Larry and Tashi are in a rain forest, looking for the pumpkin head token
> Curupira appears at the top of a rock pile and kicks a pumpkin head to the ground
> Curupira jumps down the rock pile, landing on the ground
> Curupira plays a shell game with Larry and Tashi

When the **pumpkin head is guessed**, Larry and Tashi win the pumpkin

The **pumpkin head is returned** to Nicholas

12.2 Design

Based on the summary analysis, a possible **high-level algorithm** for the task is shown in Figure 12.1. This algorithm is described as "high level" because we are aware that further decomposition will be needed. The first three lines in the algorithm represent the opening cutscene and the remaining lines represent the interactive game portion.

do in order

> Larry and Tashi explore the pumpkin patch for a pumpkin with a face
> Curupira suddenly appears and kicks a pumpkin down the rock pile
> Curupira jumps down the rock pile, rock-by-rock (like a set of steps in a staircase)
> Curupira plays a version of an old game with Larry and Tashi
> If Larry and Tashi win within three guesses,
>> Larry and Tashi win the pumpkin head
>> Larry asks that the pumpkin head be returned to Nicholas

Figure 12.1 • *Algorithm for the cutscene and game*

The set design must include an initial scene for the cutscene but must also have a pre-planned starting scene for when the game begins. One way to handle the need for two scene designs is to start with the second scene and then work your way backward to the first scene. So, the scene for the start of the game (Figure 12.2) is set up first. Markers are dropped to remember the positions of objects for the start of the game. Then, objects are repositioned to their locations for the beginning of the cutscene. Later, after code is written for the cutscene, the objects will be repositioned to the markers, ready for the start of the game.

Figure 12.2 • *A storyboard-style illustration of a starting scene for the game*

12.3 Starter World

A startup project file, *FindingNicholasStarter.a3p*, may be downloaded from **www.alice.org/Alice3ToJava**. Download the file and open it in Alice 3. Click the Scene Setup button to view the scene in the Scene editor (Figure 12.3). The starter world is setup for the cutscene but also includes the markers for setting up the scene for the game. Larry and Tashi are positioned near a pumpkin patch in the rainforest. Curupira and Nicholas are both off-screen. Curupira is standing beside the old Prenderghast circus wagon, at the top of a tall rock pile. Nicholas is hidden within the circus wagon.

Figure 12.3   *Actual setup scene in the editor*

Select camera in the Object Selector and view the object and camera markers (Figure 12.4). The large number of object and camera markers in this scene is typical of a scene where a cutscene precedes an interactive game. Also, objects in this scene are positioned at varying levels above the ground surface. Several objects are located above the ground on a rock pile that creates a hillside. Markers will make it much easier to write code that moves objects up and down the hillside, especially to transition from the cutscene to the game.

12.3.1 Create an internal pivot point

The initial scene for this starter world is still in need of one last setup step. We left this last step for you because we want to illustrate an animation technique that makes use of an

Figure 12.4 • *Object and camera markers in the initial scene*

internal pivot point. The following provides instructions for creating an internal pivot, but more information can be found online in the Alice 3 User's Guide at **www.alice.org**.

The pumpkin head that has a face is named *pumpkinWithFace*. Like most Alice objects, *pumpkinWithFace* has a **pivot point** at the base of the object, where it sits on the ground. A pivot point is a reference point around which an object rotates. To illustrate, select *pumpkinWithFace* in the Toolbox and use a one-shot to *turn pumpkinWithFace FORWARD 0.25 revolution*. The result is that *pumpkinWithFace* ends up with its face buried in the ground (Figure 12.5). (Remember to Undo to return *pumpkinWithFace* to an upright position.)

Figure 12.5 • *Pumpkin object turns around a pivot point at its base.*

In most instances, rotation around a pivot point at the base of an object makes sense. However, as you will see later, when Curupira kicks *pumpkinWithFace* down the hill and it lands on the ground, it is supposed to roll across the ground toward Larry. The pumpkin should roll like a soccer ball, not dig into the ground with every turn. To have *pumpkinWith-Face* roll across the ground, a pivot point is needed in the center of the pumpkin. We can't change the built-in pivot point but we can create our own internal pivot point.

To create an internal pivot, select the Axes class in the Shapes/Text tab of the Gallery, and add an *axes* object to the scene. You are unlikely to see the *axes* object (it sinks into the thick cover on the rainforest floor). Select the newly added *axes* object in the Toolbox object selector. Then, use a one-shot to *moveAndOrient* the *axes* object to *pumpkinWithFace*. The axes will now be positioned with the center point at the bottom of the pumpkin, as shown in Figure 12.6. You can see the red X-axis extends to the right and the green Y-axis extends upward, through the top, of the pumpkin.

Figure 12.6 *Added* axes *object is now centered at the bottom of the pumpkin.*

The *pumpkinWithFace* object's height is about 0.4 m. To position the axes in the middle of the pumpkin, use a one-shot to move the axes up 0.2 m. The result should be similar to that in Figure 12.7, where the white axis now extends outward between the eyes.

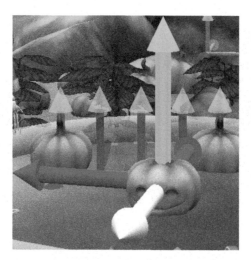

Figure 12.7 *Center of* axes *object is now in the middle of the pumpkin.*

Now hide the axes by shrinking its height to 0.02 (Figure 12.8). The *axes* object now sits in the middle of the pumpkin like a pumpkin seed. Finally, set the axes' vehicle to *pumpkinWithFace*, as shown in Figure 12.8.

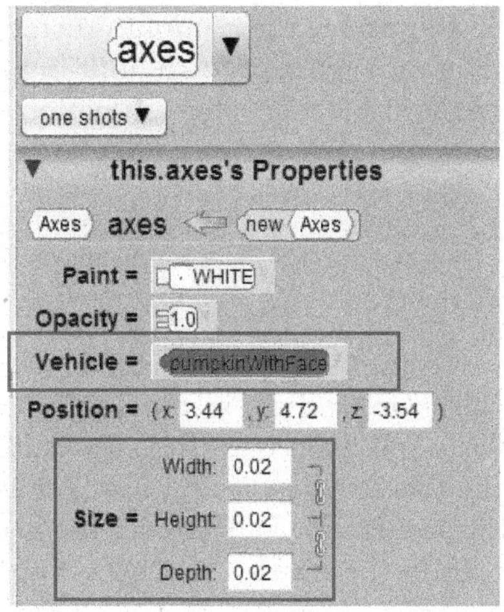

Figure 12.8 ● *Set size to 0.02 and vehicle to* pumpkinWithFace.

12.3.2 Test with a temporary statement

Return to the code editor and click on the *myFirstMethod* editor tab (Figure 12.9). You will see comments that document the algorithm has already been added.

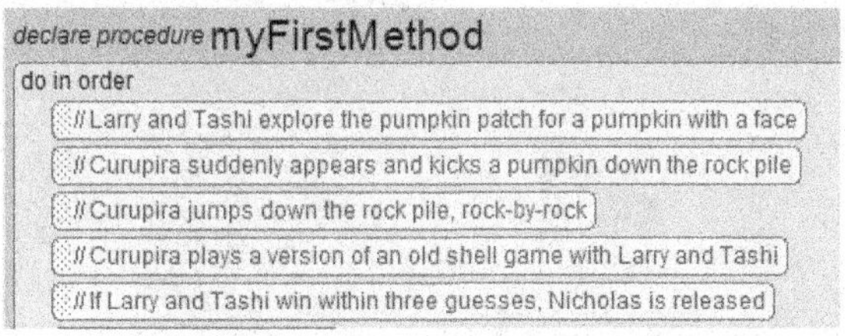

Figure 12.9 ● myFirstMethod *in starter world*

Create a temporary test statement: Select *pumpkinWithFace* in the Object selector and drag a *turn* tile into the editor. Select FORWARD as the direction and 0.25 as the revolution. Now, click the add detail menu button and select *asSeenBy* and *axes* as the pivot. The resulting statement is shown in Figure 12.10.

Figure 12.10 ● myFirstMethod *with* turn *statement*

Test-run the project. You should see the pumpkin turn on top of the ground surface. Turning an object around a pivot other than its own built-in pivot is a highly useful animation technique and a skill worthy of practice. The animation example in this chapter uses both internal and external pivots. **Before continuing, delete the temporary test statement in** *myFirstMethod.*

12.3.3 Reposition for cutscene

Now that *pumpkinWithFace* has an internal pivot point, it can be moved to a starting position for the cutscene. Select *pumpkinWithFace* in the Toolbox object selector. Then, use a one-shot to *moveAndOrient pumpkinWithFace* to the *pumpkinHeadStart* marker. The pumpkin will move upward (onto the rocks, near Curupira), which is its starting position. Figure 12.11 shows the resulting initial scene. *pumpkinWithFace* has been repositioned to the top of the rock pile and cannot be seen in the starting camera viewpoint.

Figure 12.11   *Initial scene for the cutscene*

12.3.4 Pre-made procedures in the starter world

Three classes in the starter world have **pre-made procedures**. Pre-made procedures are custom procedures that were written by the authors, specifically for examples in this textbook. The code in pre-made procedures uses animation techniques and programming concepts illustrated in previous chapters. In this chapter example, pre-made procedures are used to enable a rapid presentation of the cutscene. However, some code constructs for special effects will be highlighted in the chapter discussion.

The Scene class has *lookingForPumpkinWithFace*, *CurupiraKickPumpkin*, and *Curupira-JumpRockPath* (Figure 12.12, top left). The Biped class has *startle* and *kick* (Figure 12.12, top right). Note the Biped class also has *talk* and *talkAndSay*, imported for reuse. The Curupira class has *turnAndJump* and *rollAndJump* (Figure 12.12, bottom).

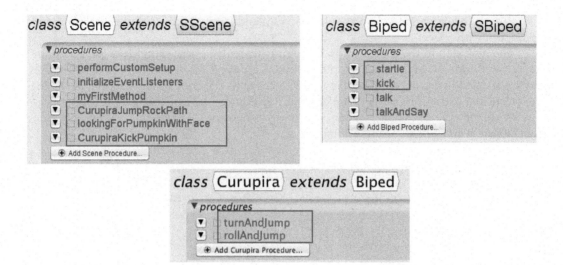

Figure 12.12 *Pre-made procedures in the Scene and Biped classes*

12.4 Implementation: Cutscene

The first algorithm step is a short dialog between Larry and Tashi, who are talking about looking in the pumpkin patch for the pumpkin that has a face. As shown in Figure 12.13, Tashi and Larry's conversation is implemented in the *lookingForPumpkinWithFace* procedure.

```
declare procedure lookingForPumpkinWithFace   Add Parameter...
do in order
    //Assumptions: Tashi and Larry are standing near the pumpkin patch
    //Tashi and Larry talk about looking for the pumpkin that has a face

    Tashi  turn  LEFT , 0.05 , duration 0.5   add detail

    Tashi  talkAndSay  words: "Well, we found pumpkins." , seconds: 2.0

    Tashi  talkAndSay  words: "Do any of them have a face?" , seconds: 2.5

    Larry  getHead  roll  RIGHT , 0.04 , duration 1.5   add detail
```

Figure 12.13 *Implementation of* lookingForPumpkinWithFace

Immediately following the first comment in *myFirstMethod*, add a *delay* statement and then a call to *lookingForPumpkinWithFace* (Figure 12.14). The code here consists of animation techniques and programming concepts already covered in previous code examples, so is used here with little explanation.

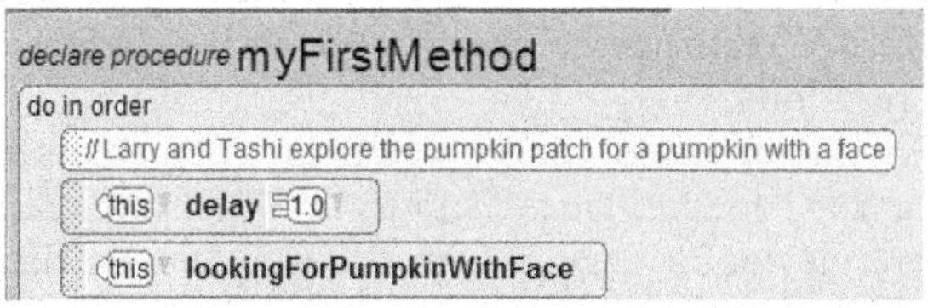

```
declare procedure myFirstMethod
do in order
    //Larry and Tashi explore the pumpkin patch for a pumpkin with a face
    this  delay 1.0
    this  lookingForPumpkinWithFace
```

Figure 12.14 *A call to the* lookingForPumpkinWithFace *procedure*

Run the project to test. You should see Tashi and Larry talking about their search for a pumpkin with a face.

The next step in the algorithm is: Curupira suddenly appears and kicks the pumpkin down the hillside, where it lands on the ground. Larry and Tashi hadn't noticed Curupira and are startled by his appearance. Figure 12.15 contains the code for this action, as implemented in the pre-made *CurupiraKickPumpkin* procedure. Most of the code in this procedure is very much the same as code you have seen before. However, a couple of code elements are worthy of some attention.

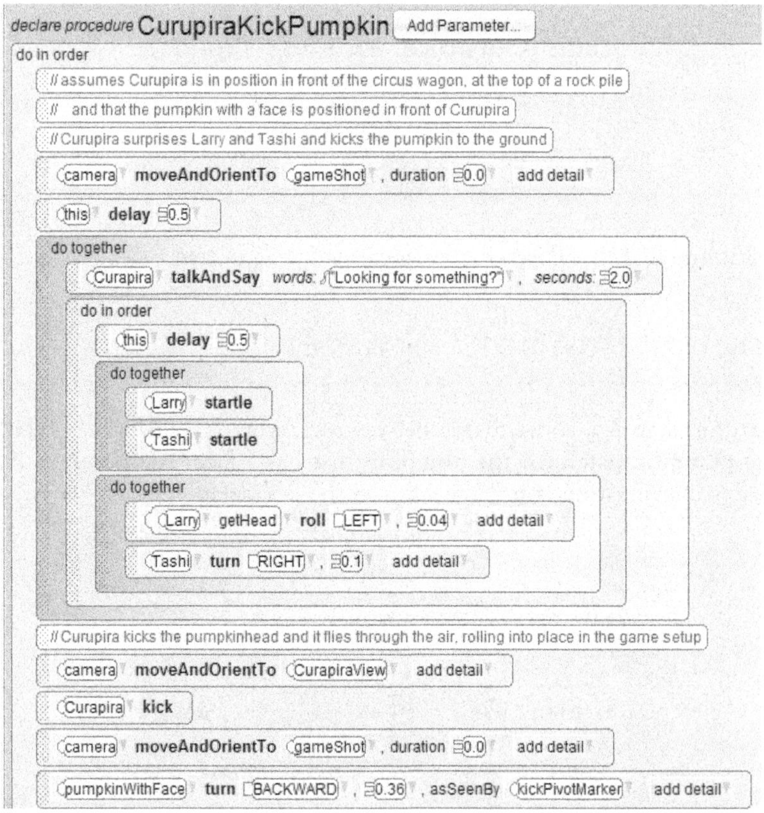

Figure 12.15   *Curupira startles Larry and Tashi when he kicks the pumpkin to the ground.*

Notice a *do in order* is nested within a *do together* and the *do in order* begins with a short *delay*. The nested code blocks allow for Curupira to *say* something and the speech bubble remains on screen at the same time as Tashi and Larry's startled reactions. (The *startle* pre-made procedure was written for the Biped class. Therefore, both Tashi and Larry inherit, and can perform, the *startle* procedure.)

To view the effect of this technique, add a statement in *myFirstMethod* to call *CurupiraKickPumpkin* (Figure 12.16). Test-run the project. Watch for the speech bubble on screen with Tashi and Larry's reactions.

Test-run, again. As the animation runs, watch for the camera to move to different viewpoints. Then look at the code in Figure 12.15 to find the statements that reposition the camera. The first camera viewpoint change is to the *gameShot* marker to view Curupira's surprising appearance. The second viewpoint change is to the *CurupiraView* marker to view the pumpkin being kicked to the ground.

```
declare procedure myFirstMethod
do in order
    // Larry and Tashi explore the pumpkin patch for a pumpkin with a face
    this   delay  1.0
    this   lookingForPumpkinWithFace
    // Curupira suddenly appears and kicks a pumpkin down the rock pile
    this   CurupiraKickPumpkin
```

Figure 12.16 • *Call* CurupiraKickPumpkin *in* myFirstMethod.

12.4.1 Using an external pivot

Run the animation one more time! This time, carefully watch Curupira's foot hit the pumpkin and the pumpkin's flight to the ground. Now, look again at the code in Figure 12.15, above, to find the statements that kick the pumpkin. Actually, kicking the pumpkin requires two statements:

(1) Curupira performs the *kick* procedure so his foot hits the pumpkin. The *kick* procedure is defined in the Biped class. Curupira is a Biped and inherits *kick*.

(2) The pumpkin *turns* through the air (the last statement in the *CurupiraKickPumpkin* procedure).

If you watch the pumpkin carefully as it flies through the air, you will see that it moves through a curved path. We could have simply moved the pumpkin from the top of the rock pile to the ground by using a *moveAndOrientTo* statement. This would have caused the pumpkin to travel in a straight-line path, illustrated on the left in Figure 12.17. Instead, to achieve a more realistic projection, an external pivot marker named *kickPivotMarker* was added (illustrated on the right in Figure 12.17). Then, a *turn* statement is used with *asSeenBy* *kickPivotMarker*. The *asSeenBy* parameter makes *kickPivotMarker* the center of rotation (Figure 12.18).

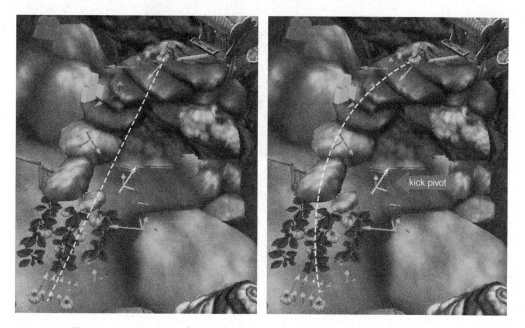

Figure 12.17 • *(Left) straight-line path, (right) with external kick pivot*

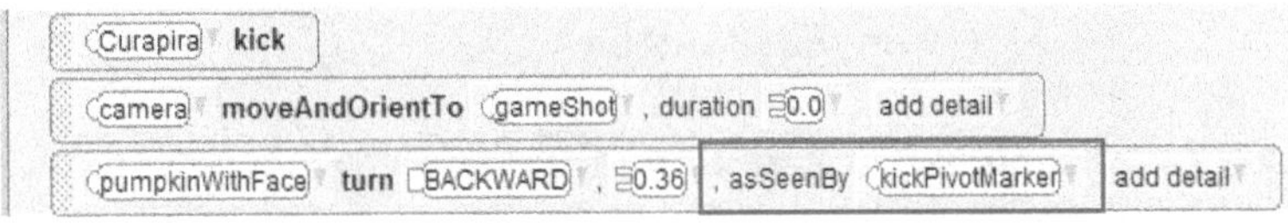

```
Curapira  kick
   camera  moveAndOrientTo  gameShot , duration ≡0.0    add detail
   pumpkinWithFace  turn  BACKWARD , ≡0.36 , asSeenBy  kickPivotMarker   add detail
```

Figure 12.18   *Using asSeenBy with an external pivot marker gives an arc to the flight.*

12.4.2 Using an internal pivot

The *turn* statement with an external pivot creates a realistic projectile path and the pumpkin lands on the ground near the pumpkin patch. As shown by the red arrow in Figure 12.19, the game-play location for the pumpkin is in the middle of the row, between the two pumpkins already in position for playing the shell game.

Figure 12.19   *The pumpkin lands short of the desired location.*

To transition to the game-play position, the pumpkin should now turn forward, along the ground like a soccer ball, and move into the row at a marked position, *spot2* (Figure 12.20). The first pumpkin on the left is at *spot1* and the third pumpkin on the right is at *spot3*. When the pumpkins are all at the markers (*spot1, spot2, spot3*), all three pumpkins will be in a linear row, and each pumpkin will be 0.6 m from its nearest pumpkin neighbor.

Figure 12.20 • *Three spot markers for a row of three pumpkins, 0.6 meters apart*

Modify the *CurupiraKickPumpkin* procedure. Add a *do together* code block at the bottom of the procedure (Figure 12.21). Then, add a statement to *turn* the pumpkin *forward*. To make the pumpkin turn but stay on the surface of the ground (rather than dig into the ground), use *asSeenBy* with the internal pivot, named *axes*. Add a second statement in the *do together* that *moves* the pumpkin to the *spot2* marker position (Figure 12.21).

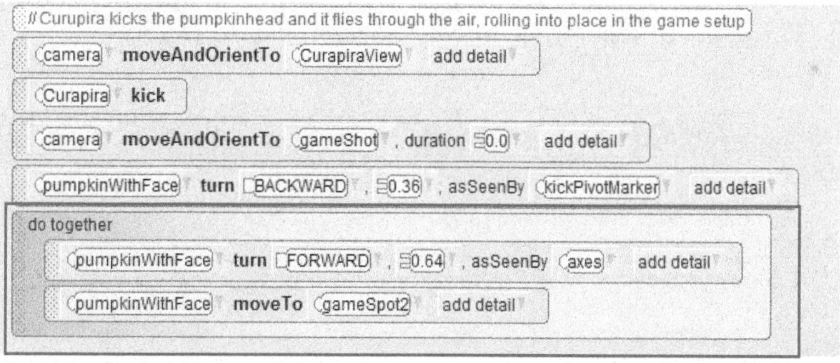

```
// Curupira kicks the pumpkinhead and it flies through the air, rolling into place in the game setup
camera  moveAndOrientTo  CurapiraView  add detail
Curapira  kick
camera  moveAndOrientTo  gameShot , duration 0.0  add detail
pumpkinWithFace  turn BACKWARD , 0.36 , asSeenBy kickPivotMarker  add detail
do together
    pumpkinWithFace  turn FORWARD , 0.64 , asSeenBy axes  add detail
    pumpkinWithFace  moveTo gameSpot2  add detail
```

Figure 12.21 • *The pumpkin with a face turns and moves into game position.*

Test-run again. At the end, you should see the pumpkin roll into position between the two other pumpkins. The pumpkin's face should be visible when it is in the row position.

12.4.3 Using a marker object as an argument

The next step in the algorithm is: Curupira travels down the side of the rock pile to meet Larry and Tashi on the ground. Traveling down the rock pile requires jumps from step to step. This action is implemented using a path of object markers. (You have seen code for a path of markers before, in the *GhostTown* project in Chapter 9.) The sequence of markers for this example world is shown in Figure 12.22. Four markers (*jump1*, *jump2*, *jump3*, and *jump4*) create a path from the top to the bottom of the rock pile. A final marker is on the ground (*gameMarker*).

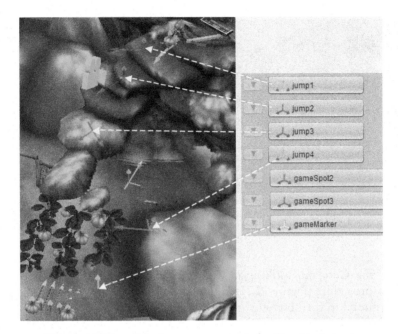

Figure 12.22 *Markers create a path for Curupira's jump.*

The Curupira class has two pre-made procedures for a jump action: *turnAndJump* and *rollAndJump*. The code for each procedure is shown in Figure 12.23.

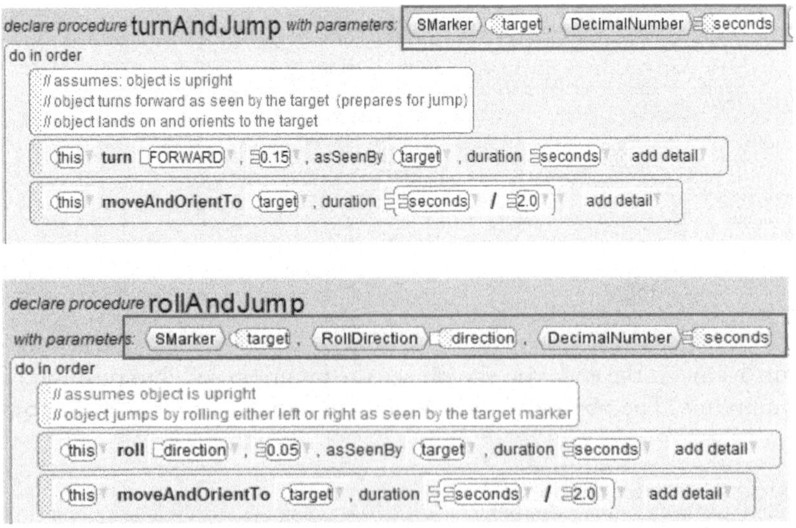

Figure 12.23 *Two pre-made procedures for Curupira's jumps*

Notice that each *jump* procedure has a parameter for a target object marker (of type *SMarker*) and seconds for duration (of type *DecimalNumber*). The *rollAndJump* procedure has a third parameter for selecting a direction (of type *RollDirection*) for *roll* (either LEFT or RIGHT).

The Scene class has a pre-made procedure, named *CurupiraJumpRockPath*, which is implemented as a sequence of calls to Curupira's *jump* procedures (Figure 12.24). Three jumps are forward turns and two jump rolls, one right and one left.

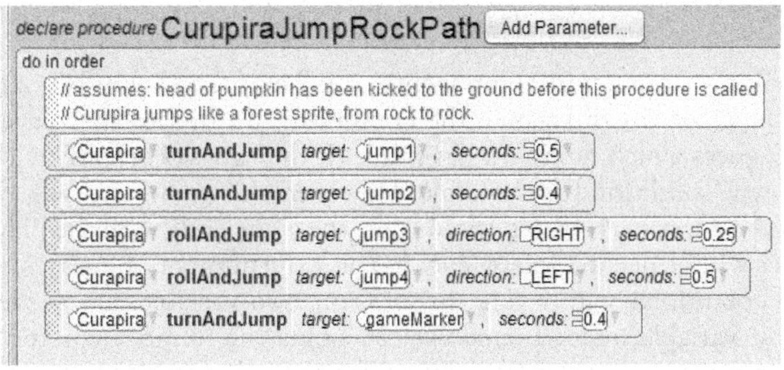

Figure 12.24   *Implementation of* jumpRockPath

Test the procedure by calling *CurupiraJumpRockPath* in *myFirstMethod*, as shown in Figure 12.25.

Figure 12.25   *Call to* jumpRockPath

12.5 Decomposition and Implementation: Game

The remaining steps in the algorithm are for implementing the game:

> Curupira plays a version of an old shell game with Larry and Tashi
> If Larry and Tashi win within three guesses,
>> Larry and Tashi win the game
>> Larry asks that the pumpkin head be returned to Nicholas

The shell game (also known as "thimble rig") is ancient, dating back to ancient Greece and Rome. The game involves three identical shells (for example, walnut shells, thimbles, or cups). A small ball or a peanut is hidden under one of the three shells and then the shells are shuffled around quickly. Then the observer is asked to guess which shell the ball is under. The game is infamous because of its common use as a dishonest gambling game. In the game illustrated here, no cheating or betting is involved.

Based on the description of the game, we know that playing the shell game is too complex to be decomposed and implemented in just one procedure. The game mechanism should be broken down into components that provide a specific action or track the game state. For example, the pumpkins will be shuffled, which requires swapping their positions. Another example is the player will have three guesses, which requires tracking the number of guesses.

When breaking a game into components, it is helpful to begin by clarifying the end conditions for the game. In this game, the conditions are tied to the player having three tries to correctly guess which pumpkin has a face. If they guess correctly within three tries, they trigger the win condition for the game. However, this game also has a fail condition. If the player fails to guess correctly in three tries, the game ends with the player losing. Two tracking variables will be needed: *guessCount* to track the number of guesses, and *gameActive* to track the end conditions (win or fail). In addition, two variables are needed for the player's guess. A first variable, named *inputNumber*, holds the number entered by the player, selecting a game spot in the row of pumpkins. The second variable, named *selectedPumpkin*, identifies the pumpkin at that game spot. The end conditions and tracking variables are listed at the beginning of the decomposition (Figure 12.26).

do in order

    Tracking variables
        guessCount (the number of guesses, initially 0)
        gameActive (game is active, initially true)
        inputNumber (the game spot guessed by the player)
        selectedPumpkin (the pumpkin located at the game spot guessed by the player)

Curupira looks at Larry and says "Guess which pumpkin has a face and you win the pumpkin."
repeat as long as the game is active
    shuffle the pumpkins
    ask the player to guess which pumpkin has a face (enter game spot: 1, 2, or 3)
    increase guessCount by 1
    if the selected pumpkin is pumpkinWithFace
        gameActive set to false, player wins
    else
        if guessCount is 3
            gameActive set to false, player loses
        else
            //game is still active

Figure 12.26   *Decomposition for playing the game*

Begin implementation by declaring a custom procedure, named *playGame*, in the Scene class. Add comments that document the assumptions (all objects in the scene are now in the start positions for the game, but the pumpkin's face is still showing) and actions (The pumpkins are shuffled, the pumpkin's face cannot be seen, and then the player gets three guesses).

In the *playGame* editor tab, Figure 12.27, declare the tracking variables and variables that will be used to obtain the player's input:

- Boolean variable, named *gameActive* and initialized to *true*.
- WholeNumber variable, named *guessCount* and initialized to 0.
- WholeNumber variable, named *inputLocation* and initialized to 0.
- Prop variable, named *selectedPumpkin* and initialized to pumpkin3: (a placeholder).

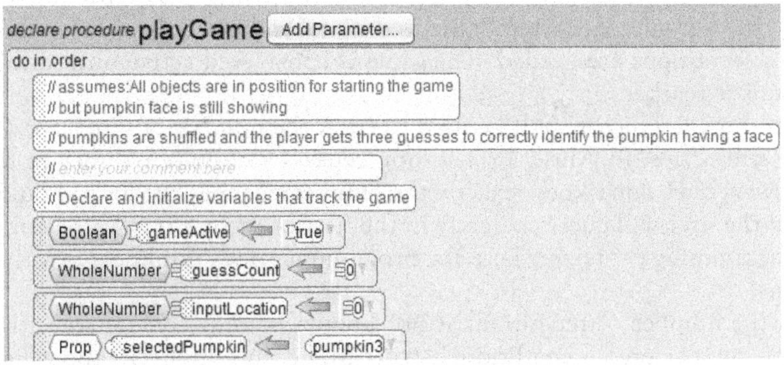

Figure 12.27   *Declare and initialize local variables to track game values.*

The first action in the game is Curupira's challenge to Larry and Tashi. Add a *do together* code block and statements within (Figure 12.28).

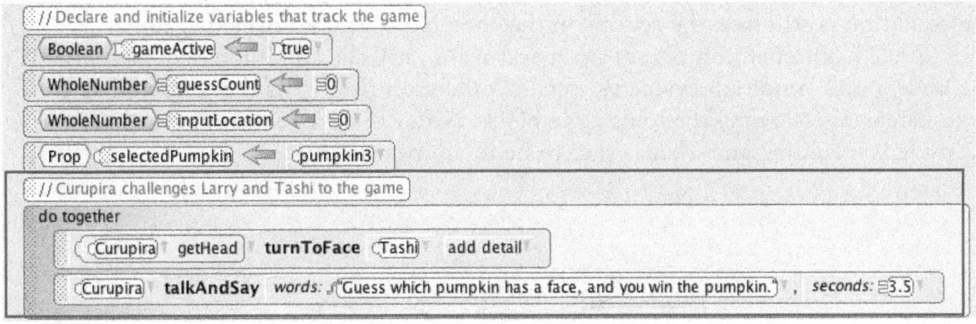

Figure 12.28   *Curupira challenges Larry and Tashi to play a shell game.*

Now is a good time to test-run the project again. Return to *myFirstMethod*. Beneath the statement that calls *CurupiraJumpRockPath*, add a call to the *playGame* procedure (Figure 12.29).

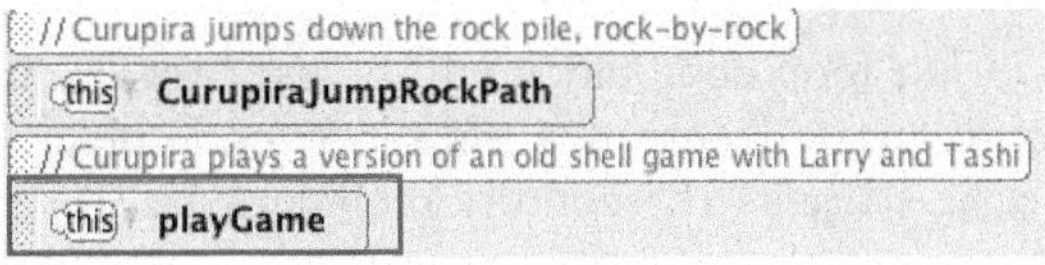

Figure 12.29   *In* myFirstMethod, *add a call to* playGame.

12.6 Repetition with a *while* Loop

The next step in the decomposition is to repeatedly shuffle the pumpkins and ask the player to guess which pumpkin has a face. The player will enter a number (1, 2, or 3) to select the first, second, or third pumpkin in the row (numbered left to right). Because the player has three tries to guess the correct pumpkin, this action may repeat up to three times. However, if the user guesses correctly the first or second time, the game ends immediately and no more repetitions are needed. The game is considered active until one of these two end conditions is reached.

A loop control structure will be used to track the number of repetitions and whether the game is still active. In Alice, a *count* loop repeats a definite number of times. In this example, however, we don't know exactly the number of times the loop should repeat. It is possible that the user will guess correctly in the first or second try. This example is typical of many programming contexts where the programmer does not know exactly the number of repetitions.

When the number of repetitions is not known, a *while* control structure is used. A *while* control is considered a conditional structure because it checks the value of a conditional expression. In this example, the condition is that the game is active (a Boolean condition, which is either *true* or *false*).

As illustrated in Figure 12.30, a *while* statement evaluates a conditional expression and if the value is *true*, the instructions within the code block are performed. This is similar to an *if/else* statement where a condition is checked before instructions may or may not be performed. However, an *if/else* statement executes just once and then the flow of execution continues on to the statement following the *if/else* code block. In a *while* loop, the flow of execution returns to the top of the *while* code block and the condition is checked again. If the condition is still *true*, the actions in the code block are performed again.

While loop repetition occurs again and again until the condition becomes *false*. When the *while* loop's condition evaluates to *false*, execution flow exits the loop and skips to the next statement following the *while* code block. **Note:** If the condition never becomes *false*, the cycle is unending and *while* is said to be in an infinite loop.

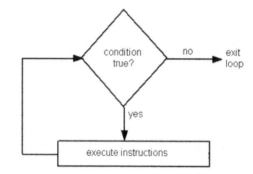

Figure 12.30   A while *loop executes repeatedly until the condition becomes false.*

In this example, a *while* loop code block will be used to repeatedly shuffle the pumpkins and ask the player to guess. To create a *while* loop code block, drag the *while* tile into the editor and select *gameActive* as the condition (Figure 12.31). At the beginning of the procedure, the *gameActive* variable was initialized to *true*, so we know the loop will execute at least once.

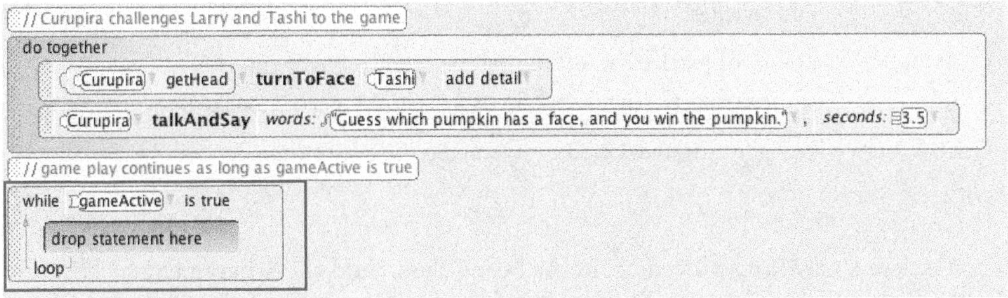

// Curupira challenges Larry and Tashi to the game
do together
Curupira getHead turnToFace Tashi add detail
Curupira talkAndSay words: "Guess which pumpkin has a face, and you win the pumpkin." , seconds: 3.5
// game play continues as long as gameActive is true
while gameActive is true
drop statement here
loop

Figure 12.31 *The* while *loop condition is "while the game is active."*

The first action inside the *while* loop is to shuffle the pumpkins. A shuffle is performed by swapping two pumpkins at a time. We will write two **helper procedures**: one named *swap* to swap two pumpkins, and the second named *shuffle* to call *swap* 12 times with randomly selected pumpkins. A helper procedure is a procedure that helps another procedure carry out its task.

12.7 Swap with Pivot Markers

The *swap* procedure will use object markers as pivot points for exchanging the locations of the pumpkins in the row. Three pivot markers are needed: *leftPivot*, *centerPivot*, and *rightPivot*. As illustrated in Figure 12.32, the *leftPivot* will be used to swap pumpkins in positions 1 and 2, the *rightPivot* for pumpkins in positions 2 and 3, and the *centerPivot* for the outside pumpkins, in positions 1 and 3.

left pivot
center pivot
right pivot
1
2
3

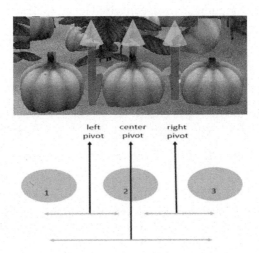

Figure 12.32 *Pivot points for swapping positions of two pumpkins at a time*

A decomposition for *swap* is shown in Figure 12.33. The decomposition is generic in that *obj1* and *obj2* represent any two pumpkin objects and *pivot* represents any one of the pivot markers.

do together

object1 turn left 0.5 rev. as seen by pivot (marker)

object2 turn left 0.5 rev. as seen by pivot (marker)

Figure 12.33   *Decomposition for swap*

Declare a new *swap* procedure in the Scene class. Add three parameters: *obj1* and *obj2* of type *Prop*, and *pivot* of type *SMarker*, as shown in Figure 12.34. In the *swap* editor tab, enter the code statements to implement the design.

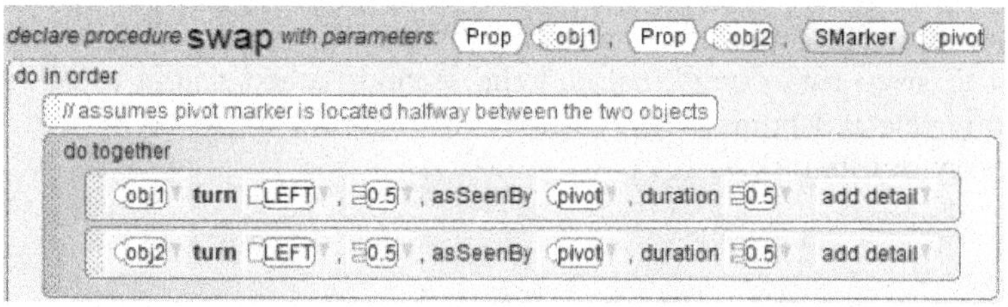

Figure 12.34   *Implementation of swap*

For testing purposes, let's swap the pumpkins in spots 1 and 2 in the row. At the beginning of the game, *pumpkin1* is in spot 1 and *pumpkinWithFace* is in spot 2. The pivot marker between them is *leftPivot*. Within the *while* code block, add a statement to hide the pumpkin's face. Then, add a temporary test statement to call *swap* with *pumpkin1*, *pumpkin-WithFace*, and *leftPivot* as arguments, respectively (Figure 12.35).

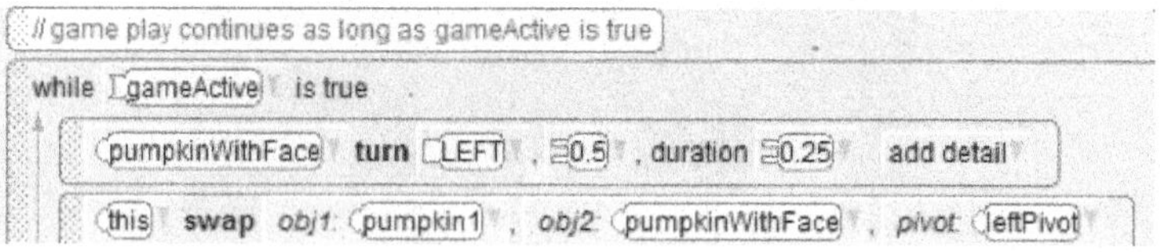

Figure 12.35   *A call to test the swap procedure*

Test-run the project. You should see *pumpkinWithFace* turn to hide its face. Then, *pumpkin1* (originally in position 1) and *pumpkinWithFace* (originally in position 2) swap places. The result is shown in Figure 12.36.

Notice the *pumpkinWithFace* object has turned so the face can be seen, again. This is because *swap* turns the pumpkins 0.5 revolutions. To keep the face hidden, revise the *swap* procedure by adding a second statement for each object, in which the object *turns* the opposite direction, with no *asSeenBy* argument, as shown in Figure 12.37.

Figure 12.36   pumpkin1 *and* pumpkinWithFace *swapped places.*

```
declare procedure swap with parameters: ( Prop )( obj1 ) , ( Prop )( obj2 ) , ( SMarker )( pivot )
do in order
    // assumes pivot marker is located halfway between the two objects
    do together
        obj1  turn  LEFT  , 0.5 , asSeenBy  pivot , duration 0.5    add detail
        obj1  turn  RIGHT  , 0.5 , duration 0.5    add detail
        obj2  turn  LEFT  , 0.5 , asSeenBy  pivot , duration 0.5    add detail
        obj2  turn  RIGHT  , 0.5 , duration 0.5    add detail
```

Figure 12.37   *Turning the opposite direction around its own center point*

Test-run the project again. Because the object is now *turning one direction* around its own center point at the same time as it *turns* the *opposite direction* around the pivot marker, the face now remains toward the back of the scene. The *swap* procedure is intentionally slow for testing and debugging purposes. When the testing is complete, decrease the duration of all statements in *swap* to a smaller value, for example 0.3 or 0.35 seconds.

Before continuing, return to *myFirstMethod* **and remove the temporary test statement that calls** *swap.*

12.8 Shuffle with Random Selection of Swap Objects

To play the game, the pumpkins should be swapped many times before the player is asked to guess. Rapid, multiple swaps is known as a shuffle. A shuffle should be rapid so the player really has to pay attention to visually track the object. Importantly, after the swaps, the location of *pumpkinWithFace* should not be the same with every shuffle.

Declare a custom *shuffle* procedure in the Scene class. Add comments for assumptions (pumpkins are in a row, located at the *gameSpot* markers) and actions (randomly selects a pair of pumpkins and swaps them). The shuffle procedure will call *swap* a counted number of times. Each call to *swap* will randomly choose a pair of pumpkins.

12.8.1 Randomly choose one of three possible values

There are three choices for random selection: swap the two pumpkins on the outside, swap the two pumpkins on the left, or swap the two pumpkins on the right. One way to implement a random selection of one of three choices is to generate a random number value of 1, 2, or 3 (like pulling a number out of a hat. If the number is 1, swap the two end pumpkins around the center pivot. If the number is 2, swap the two on the left around the left pivot. Otherwise, the number has to be 3, so swap the two pumpkins on the right around the right pivot. A decomposition for the random selection is shown in Figure 12.38.

> *do in order*
>
> Generate a random number in the range of 1..3
> If the number equals 1
>   Swap the two end pumpkins
>   Else
>   If the number equals 2
>   Swap the two pumpkins on the left
>   Else
>   Swap the two pumpkins on the right

Figure 12.38   *Decomposition for a random selection*

The first action in the decomposition is to generate a random number—1, 2, or 3. To hold the random number, first add a variable of type *WholeNumber* to the procedure, name it *randomValue*, and initialize to 0 as a placeholder. Now, click the placeholder, select *Random* from the dropdown menu, and then *NextRandomIntegerFromAUpToAndIncludingB*, 1, and 3 from the cascading menus, as shown in Figure 12.39.

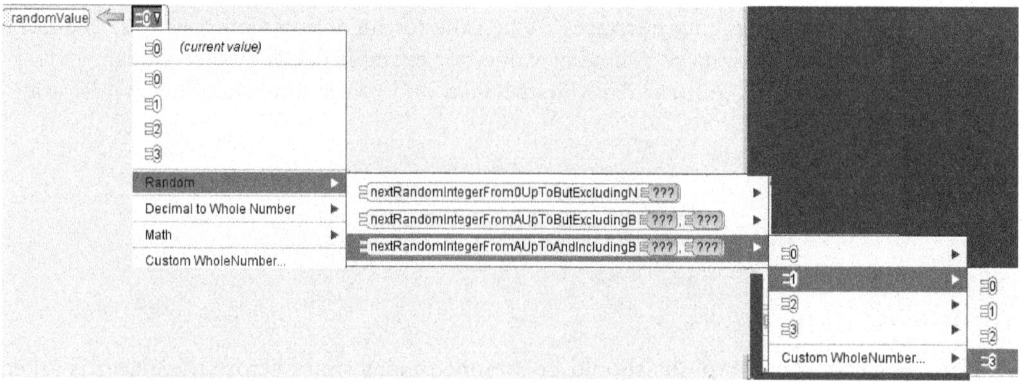

Figure 12.39   *Generating a random value between 1 and 3, inclusive*

Now, add two *if/else* code blocks, one nested inside the other, each checking the value of the random number. The logic of the nested *if/else* code blocks is shown in Figure 12.40.

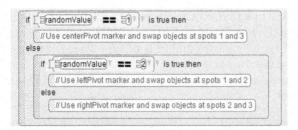

Figure 12.40   *Two* if/else *code blocks, one nested inside the other*

12.9 Writing a Custom Function

The *if* and *else* segments are where the calls to *swap* will be written. For example, in the first *if* segment (if *randomValue* equals 1), the *swap* statement should look something like this:

```
this.swap (pumpkin at spot1, pumpkin at spot3, center pivot)
```

To write this call to *swap*, the name of the pumpkin at spot1, the pumpkin at spot3, and the pivot are needed as arguments. We know the name of the pivot *(centerPivot)*. But, except for the first time *swap* is called, we don't know the names of the pumpkins at spot1 and spot3. We need a method to identify which pumpkin is at a specific spot.

Methods can be either procedures or functions. Procedures perform an action but do not compute and return a value. Functions retrieve or compute a value and return it to the calling statement. Alice has built-in functions (introduced previously, in Chapter 11). In this example, however, the Scene class does not have a built-in function that returns the name of an object, given the spot at which it is located. We will write our own **custom function** to return the name of a pumpkin at a given game spot in the row of pumpkins. To declare a new custom function for the Scene class, open the Scene class tab and follow these steps (Figure 12.41):

(1) Click the Add Scene Function button.

(2) In the popup dialog box, select *Prop* as the **return type** (the data type of the value to be returned by the function).

(3) Enter a name for the function, *getPumpkin*.

(4) Click OK.

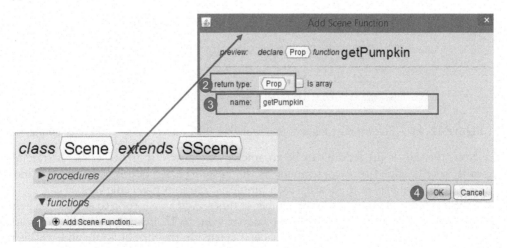

Figure 12.41   *Steps to declare a new function in the Scene class*

A new *getPumpkin* function editor tab will be displayed, as shown in Figure 12.42. Notice the declaration, *Prop getPumpkin*. This tells Alice that the function will return a reference to an object of type *Prop* (a pumpkin is of type *Prop*). In the *getPumpkin* code block, add comments for assumptions and actions. We want to send the name of a game spot as an argument to the function. In the function header, add a parameter, named *spot*, of type SMarker (Figure 12.42).

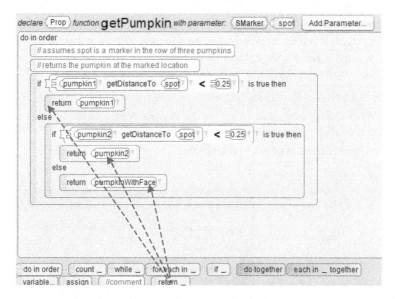

Figure 12.42   *New* getPumpkin *function with an SMarker parameter named* spot

To identify the pumpkin at a specific spot in the row of pumpkins, *getPumpkin* must check three possible choices: *pumpkin1*, *pumpkin2*, or *pumpkinWithFace*. The identification is made based on the distance between each pumpkin and the *spot* marker. We know each pumpkin in the row is 0.6 meters from a neighboring pumpkin. So, if a pumpkin's distance to the *spot* marker is less than 0.25 m. (less than half the distance to a neighboring pumpkin and its marker), the pumpkin must be located at *spot*. When the comparison yields a *true* result, a **return statement** is used to send the identified pumpkin's name back to the calling statement (Figure 12.43). A function must have at least one *return* statement. When a *return* statement is executed, control returns to the code statement that called the function. When control returns, the value specified by the *return* statement is used in place of the function call.

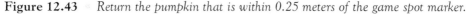

Figure 12.43   *Return the pumpkin that is within 0.25 meters of the game spot marker.*

Now, the *shuffle* procedure can be completed, as shown in Figure 12.44. A statement that calls *swap* is added to each segment of the nested *if/else* code block. The arguments include calls to *getPumpkin* to identify the pumpkins' random pivot markers.

Shuffle should call *swap* a counted number of times. Add a *count* loop to enclose the nested *if/else* code blocks (Figure 12.45). Set the loop control value to 12. Leave the variable declaration for *randomValue* outside the loop, so the variable is created in the memory only once. Inside the loop, include the statement that generates a new random value each time the loop repeats.

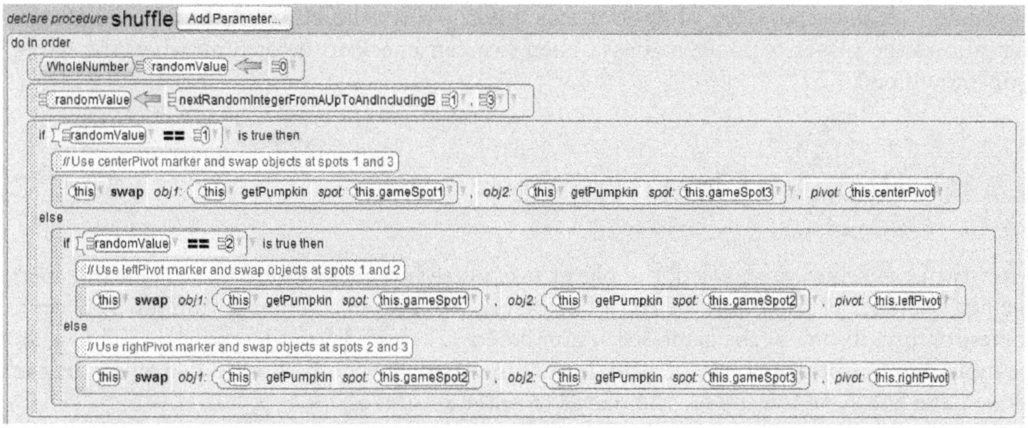

Figure 12.44 • *Two pumpkins are swapped about a randomly selected pivot marker.*

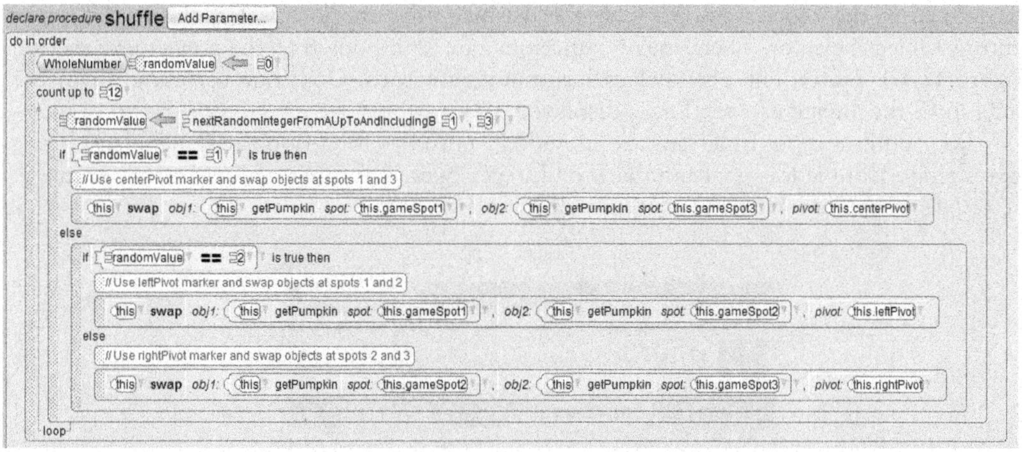

Figure 12.45 • *A count loop is used to repeat the shuffle a counted number of times.*

To test the *shuffle* procedure, return to the *playGame* procedure tab in the editor. Add a statement to the *while* loop to call *shuffle* (Figure 12.46).

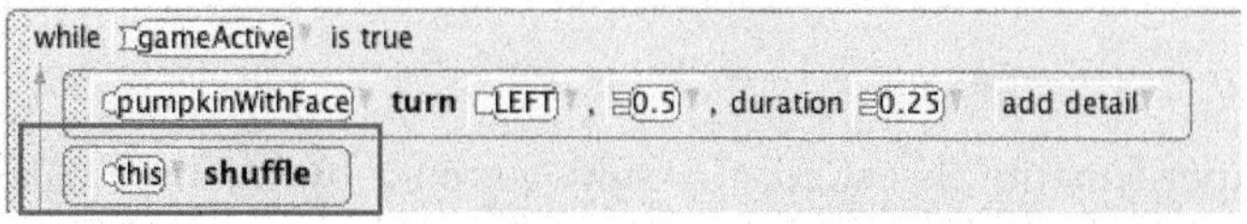

Figure 12.46 • *A call to* shuffle *in the* gamePlay *procedure*

Test-run the project. You should see the pumpkins swap positions, again and again, in random sequence. *Shuffle's count* loop is written to *swap* the pumpkins 12 times. However, you will see the *swaps* continue until you shut down the runtime window. The continued swapping occurs because the while loop has a bug. To fix the bug, we need to write code that allows the player to input a guess. Then, we can check to determine when the while loop should end.

12.10 Player (User) Input

After the pumpkins are shuffled, the player is expected to guess where (at which game *spot*) *pumpkinWithFace* is located in the row. The player is expected to enter a number, 1, 2, or 3, corresponding to one of the game *spots*, numbered 1, 2, and 3 from left to right. This is an example of a traditional form of **user input**. In Alice, a **prompt** box is displayed on the screen, and the system waits for the player to enter a number.

12.10.1 Get the input

A prompt box is displayed as part of a call to an **input function**. In Alice, input functions are defined in the Scene class. To view the list of input functions, select *this* in the Scene Editor's Object Selector. Then, in the Functions tab, scroll down to the *prompt user* section (Figure 12.47). **Note:** The Scene class has many funcitons. Continue scrolling down the panel until the *prompt user* section is displayed.

Four built-in input functions are provided to prompt for a Boolean (true/false), String (text string), Double (decimal number), or Integer (whole number) value. In this example, the *getIntegerFromUser* built-in function will be called.

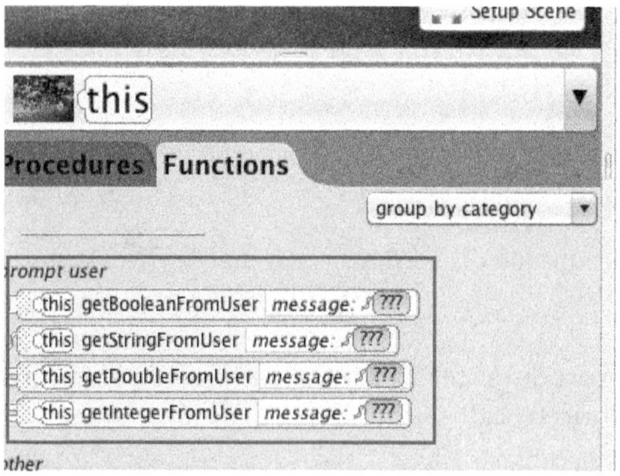

Figure 12.47   *Built-in functions that prompt the user for input*

When an input function is called, the value entered by the user will be returned to the calling statement. The returned value must immediately be used or, it may be stored in a variable for use in a later statement. In this example, the returned number will be stored in the *inputLocation* variable. To create an **assignment statement** (Figure 12.48):

(1) Drag the **assign** tile into the editor.
(2) Select the *inputLocation* variable from the popup menu.
(3) Select 0 as a placeholder value from the cascading menu.

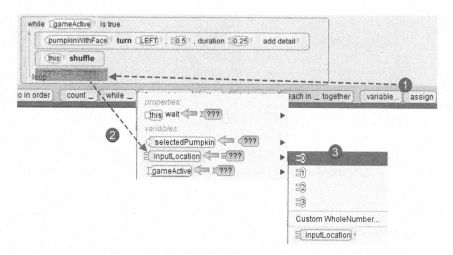

Figure 12.48   *Create an assignment statement*

The resulting assignment statement is shown in Figure 12.49. Note that the 0 value is a placeholder.

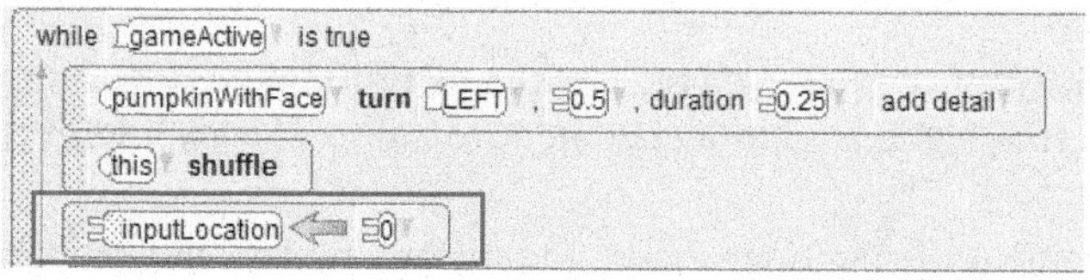

Figure 12.49   *Resulting assignment statement*

To replace the 0 placeholder, (1) select *this* in the Scene editor's Object Selector, then (2) drag the *getIntegerFromUser* tile from the Functions tab into the editor and drop it on top of the 0, as shown in Figure 12.50. From the dropdown menu, (3) select Custom TextString. Alice will automatically display a popup dialog box, where you can enter a text string as the prompt. Type "Enter a guess (1, 2, or 3)" without the quote marks. The resulting statement is shown in Figure 12.51. The text string "Enter a guess (1, 2, or 3)" is the prompt.

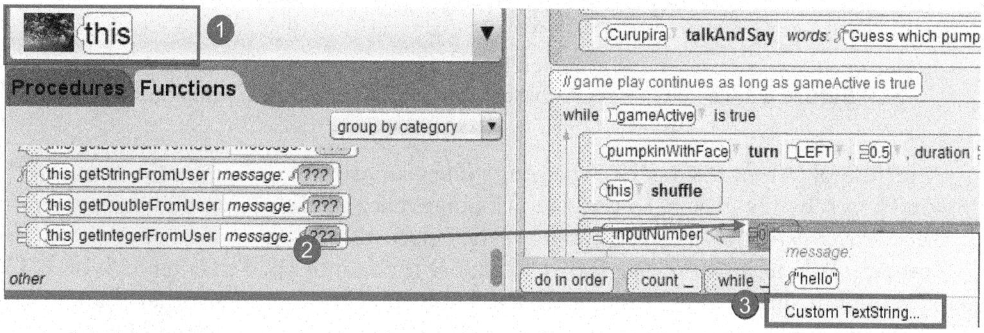

Figure 12.50   *Replace placeholder with* getIntegerFromUser *function.*

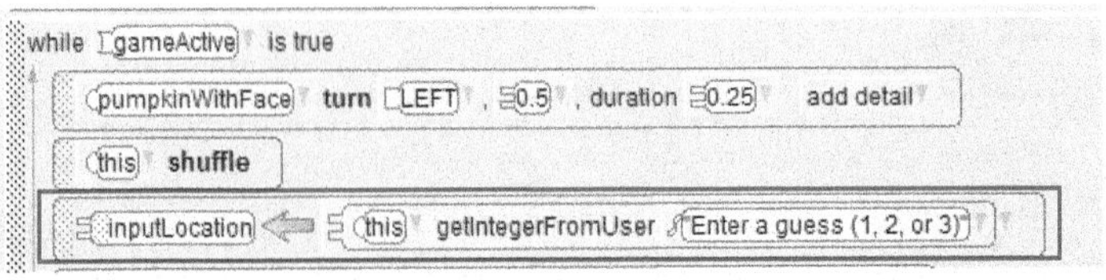

Figure 12.51   *Input will be stored in the* inputLocation *variable.*

Test-run the project. After the *shuffle*, you should see an input box with a keypad where the player is prompted to enter a number. When entered, the number is assigned (stored in) *inputLocation*.

12.10.2 Use the input

The number entered by the player is the location of one of the pumpkins in the row but is NOT the name of the pumpkin as shown in Figure 12.52. Add statements in the segments of the two *if/else* code blocks that call *getPumpkin* and store the returned value in the *selectedPumpkin* variable.

- In the *if* segment of the outer *if/else*, create a conditional expression, "inputLocation equals 1." In this segment, add a statement to call *getPumpkin* with *gameSpot1* as the marker.
- In the *if* segment of the inner *if/else*, create a conditional expression, "inputLocation equals 2." In this segment, add a statement to call *getPumpkin* with *gameSpot2* as the marker.
- In the *else* segment of the inner *if/else*, add a statement to call *getPumpkin* with the *gameSpot3* marker.

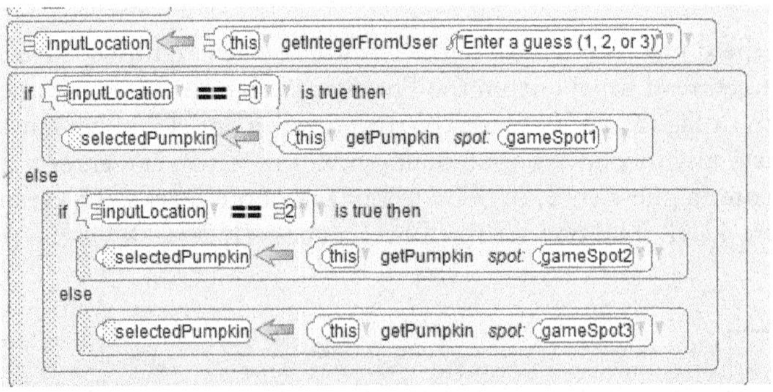

Figure 12.52   *Call* getPumpkin *to identify the selected pumpkin.*

After the player enters a guess, the *selectedPumpkin* variable contains the name of the pumpkin chosen by the player. To provide visual feedback to the player, add a statement to turn the *selectedPumpkin* so its front can be seen (Figure 12.53).

Test-run. When the input box is displayed, use the number pad to enter 1, 2, or 3. The selected pumpkin should turn. Run again, this time entering a number other than 1, 2, or 3. You should see that the pumpkin at position 3 is automatically selected. This avoids a runtime error that would be caused by out-of-range input.

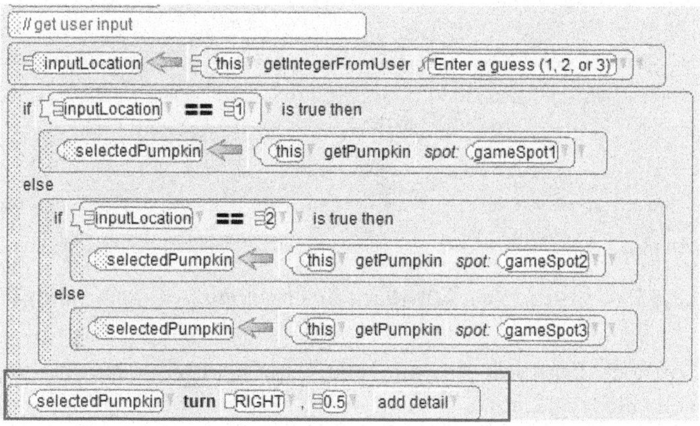

Figure 12.53 • *Provide visual feedback to the player.*

12.11 Check the Game State: End Conditions

Each time the player enters a guess, the **game state** should be updated. The game state includes the values in the tracking variables and the positions of objects in the scene. In this example, the *guessCount* variable (a tracking variable) should be updated by adding 1. After the statement that turns the pumpkin for visual feedback, add a statement to add 1 to *guessCount* (Figure 12.54). Adding 1 to the value in a variable is known as an **increment**. Subtracting 1 is **decrement**.

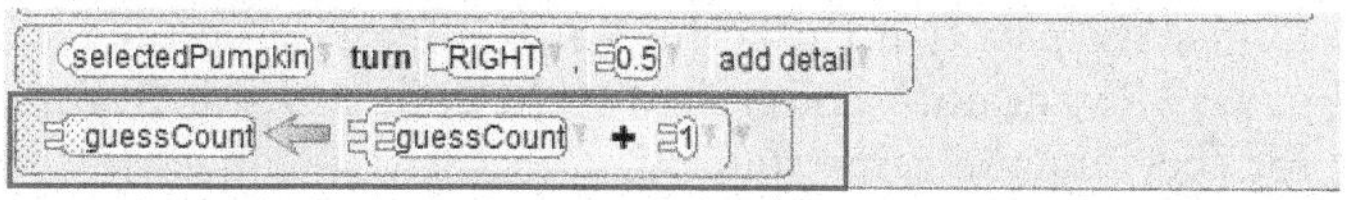

Figure 12.54 • *Increment the* guessCount *tracking variable.*

The game is now in one of three possible states:

(1) The player has guessed correctly.
(2) The player hasn't guessed correctly and has used all three guesses.
(3) The player hasn't guessed correctly but still has one or two guesses remaining.

If the game is in either of the first two states, the game should end and the result (win or lose) should be announced. Otherwise, the game should continue.

To determine the game state, add an *if/else* code block. Create a conditional expression for the *if* part: *selectedPumpkin == pumpkinWithFace*. Add statements in the *if* part that sets *gameActive* to *false* and has Curupira *say* "The pumpkin head is yours" (Figure 12.55).

There are two more possible states, so add a second *if/else* and nest it within the first *if/else*. In the inner *if* part, create a conditional expression: *guessCount ==3* for the second possible state. Add statements in the inner *if* part that sets *gameActive* to *false*, has the

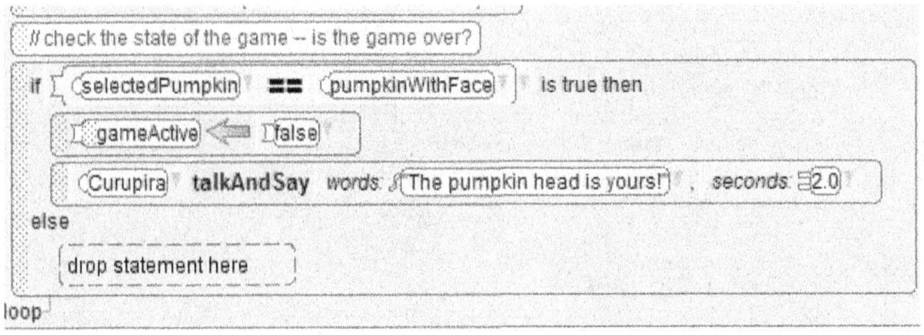

Figure 12.55   *If* pumpkinWithFace *has been guessed, game ends with a win.*

Curupira say "You lost. But, you can play the game again," and *turn* the *pumpkinWithFace* for visual feedback (Figure 12.56).

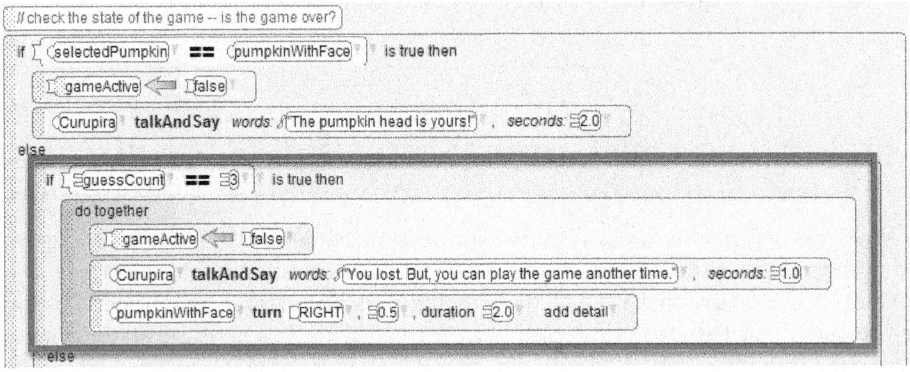

Figure 12.56   *If all three guesses have been made, game ends and player loses.*

If the game isn't in either the first or second state, it must be in the third state. Add statements to the inner *else* part that turns the *pumpkinWithFace* so the face can be seen and have the pumpkin say "Try again." The nested *if/else* code block in Figure 12.57 shows the completed code for checking the game state.

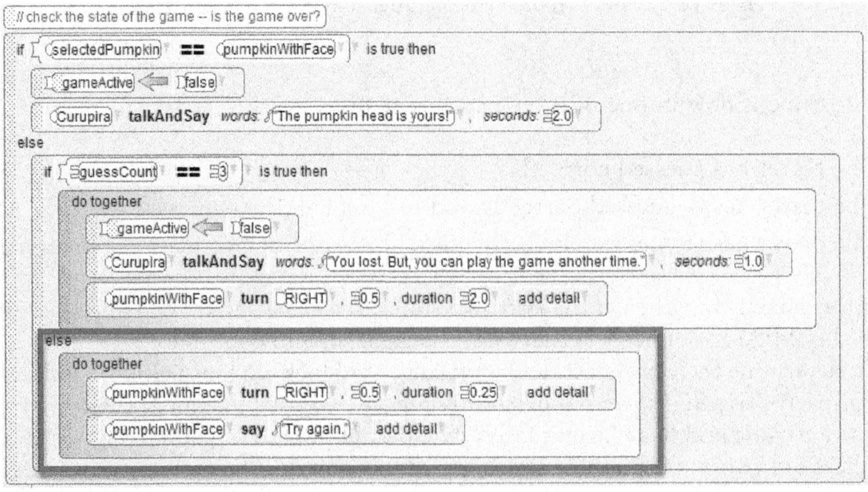

Figure 12.57   *Game is still active; try again*

Test-run the program. Run it several times and make an effort to execute each part of the nested *if/else* code blocks that check the state of the game. In other words, run enough tests so that you win the game at least once and lose the game at least once.

The last step in the algorithm is Larry's request to have *pumpkinWithFace* returned to Nicholas, who is inside the circus wagon. Implementation of this final part of the animation is left as an exercise for you. See the end of chapter exercises for this chapter.

12.12 Generalizing a Game Algorithm

Now that we have created two interactive games (collecting all the tokens in Chapter 11 and the shell game here), it is possible to consider a generalized algorithm for a game. At the beginning of a game, an initial game setup is needed. This includes actions such as initializing important variables, setting up the camera, or moving objects to their initial positions for starting the game. After setup, there is typically a **game loop** that runs the main part of the game where the player makes choices that affect the state of the game. The game state is typically represented by the values stored in tracking variables and the positions of objects in the scene. While the game loop is running, two game components must be conducted by the program code: a Game Update component and a Check Conditions component.

The Game Update component includes

- Updates to the position of game objects
- Responses to player input
- Updates to the UI
- Feedback to the player

It's important to note that the code for some updates is not necessarily contained inside the game loop code block itself. The code for some updates will likely be written in an event listener. Nevertheless, while the game loop is running, events (for example, mouse-clicks and keypresses) cause updates to the game state, handled by the event listeners.

The Check Conditions component evaluates the end conditions of the game. If the game has ended, then the game loop ends. Finally, the game gives the player feedback about if they won or lost.

The generalized algorithm is outlined in Figure 12.58. We will use this algorithm again in later chapters to aid in creating interactive games. You may also find it helpful in designing and creating your game projects.

do in order

do game setup

main game loop

do game update stuff

check if game over

give feedback on game win or loss

Figure 12.58   *A generalized algorithm for a game*

Summary

Alice has built-in procedures for rotational motion, for example, *turn* and *roll*. By default, in a *turn* or *roll* action, the rotation is centered around an internal pivot point at the base of the object. If a different pivot point is needed (for example, for projectile motion) an external pivot marker may be used as an argument to *asSeenBy*, an optional parameter. In this chapter, internal and external pivots were added and used to illustrate swapping and shuffling objects in an ordered row.

The shell game example was used to introduce and illustrate a generalized algorithm for creating an interactive game. As part of the process of designing the game, we first clarified the end conditions and the player's goals in the game. The game setup included declaring and initializing variables to track the game state. The end conditions are needed for creating a game loop that runs continuously while the game is active. In this example, a *while* loop control structure was used for creating the game loop.

While the game loop is running, two major game components must be cared for by the program code: updating the game state and checking for the end of the game. Updating the game state involves updates to the position of game objects, responses to user input, updates to UI, and feedback to the player. Checking for the end of the game is accomplished by evaluating the end conditions. When an end condition is evaluated as *true*, the game is over. At the end of the game, feedback is provided to the player on game win or loss.

In this example, each time the game loop is executed, the player is asked to enter a guess. The player enters a number (1, 2, or 3) to select the pumpkin. The entered number actually selects the location of a marker, not the pumpkin itself. (The pumpkins have been randomly shuffled.) A custom function, named *getPumpkin*, was written to identify which pumpkin was at the selected marker location. A custom function must contain a *return* statement to return a value to the calling statement.

Terms

assign	helper procedure	prompt
assignment statement	high-level algorithm	random selection
custom function	increment	*return* statement
cutscene	input function	shuffle
external pivot	internal pivot	swap
game loop	pivot point	user input
game state	pre-made procedure	*while* loop

Concept Questions

1. All objects in Alice have a *center*, which is the pivot point automatically used for rotations (*turn* and *roll*). Under what circumstances is it useful to add an internal pivot to an object at a location other than the center?

2. In built-in Alice procedures, what optional parameter is used to rotate an object around (a) an internal pivot (other than the object's *center*) or (b) an external pivot?

3. In Alice, an object marker is most commonly used to mark a single target position to which an object will move at some time during the animation. What built-in procedure is typically used to move an object to an object marker?

4. If the following code is executed, the cat does not appear to *move* at all.

```
do together
    cat  move  FORWARD , 1.0   add detail
    cat  move  BACKWARD , 1.0   add detail
```

But in the *swap* procedure in this chapter, the following code actually does *turn* the object (a pumpkin). Explain why.

```
do together
    obj1  turn  RIGHT , 0.5 , asSeenBy  pivot , duration 0.5   add detail
    obj1  turn  LEFT , 0.5 , duration 0.5   add detail
```

5. What are the possible data types that may be used as the *return type* of a custom function? A complete list is not required. Describe as an overview with general categories of data types.

6. The Alice interactive development environment (IDE) does not allow you to write a custom function that does not have a *return* statement. Justify this requirement.

7. When is it appropriate to declare variables as local to a procedure, rather than as property variables in the Class definition?

8. The *GhostTrainHub* project in Chapter 11 introduced events and event listeners for interaction with the user. The *FindingNicholas* project in this chapter, however, calls a built-in function to get the player's input. What is the major difference in the code requirements for these two modes of obtaining input from the user?

9. Think about a game you've recently played, perhaps on a computer or mobile device. Write a short one-paragraph description of the game. Try to create a possible high-level algorithm for the game, using the outline provided in the generalized game algorithm discussed at the end of this chapter. Based on your high-level algorithm, answer the following questions:

   (a) What is done to set up at the start of the game?
   (b) What happens during the main game loop?
   (c) How does the main game loop decide that the game is over?
   (d) What determines if you won or lost?
   (e) What kind of feedback does the game provide?

Exercises

. . . .

If you did not download and implement the code in this chapter, you may be able to obtain a copy from your instructor for Exercises 1 and 2.

1. The *swap* procedure in this exercise always rotates the pumpkins around the pivot marker in the same direction. This is not really a problem, but the animation could be improved by modifying the code so the pumpkins do not always rotate in the same direction. Revise the *swap* procedure so the pumpkin rotates sometimes in one

direction and sometimes in the other direction around a pivot marker. Hint: Alice has a *nextRandomBoolean* function that returns either *true* or *false*. We can interpret *true* as "heads" and *false* as "tails" and use the random value to choose one of two possible actions.

2. Look carefully at the user input code in the shell game. The user was asked to enter a number between 1 and 3, inclusive. The user's entry was then checked to see if it was 1 or 2. If not, the input number was assumed to be 3. Although this technique is effective, it doesn't give the user a chance to correct a typo. Revise the code for the shell game to repeatedly check the user's input until the value entered is in the range of 1 to 3.

3. The last step of the algorithm is to return the *pumpkinWithFace* object to the haunted Nicholas character. Implement this step. Suggestions: Put the *pumpkinWithFace* object on Larry's arm and have Larry take the pumpkin to Nicholas in the circus wagon. When Nicholas receives the pumpkin, position the pumpkin on his head. The starter scene already has an object marker, named *skeletonWagonMarker*, for moving Larry to the wagon. Also, the starter scene has some camera markers for repositioning the camera. For example, *wagonView* is a marker for a close-up view of the exterior of the wagon and *insideWagonShot* for a view of the interior of the wagon.

4. Create an animation for a number guessing game, where a fox has caught a bird and offers to let the bird go if it can correctly guess a selected number between 1 and 10. Randomly generate the number and allow four guesses. Ask the user to enter a guess. If the user correctly guesses the number, the bird flies away. Otherwise, bird is on the menu for the fox.

5. Download the **RollingDie.a3p** project from **www.alice.org/AliceToJava** (or obtain a copy from your instructor). The project contains a cube shape (Box) with small dot shapes attached to the sides, simulating a dice object. If the die is turned forward or backward, it turns into the ground because its center point is on the bottom (the side having six dots). Use an *axes* object to create an internal pivot at the center of mass for the die. Resize the *axes* object, or reset its opacity, so it is not visible outside the die. Write code to test the internal pivot in which the die turns forward four times.

6. Using the *RollingDie.a3p* project from Exercise 5, write a *randomRoll* procedure using the *if/else* logic shown here. The *if/else* code block is repeated a random number of times, within the range of at least 3 times and at most 12 times.

```
if ⌐ nextRandomBoolean ⌐   is true then
    // turn dice forward 0.25 and left 0.5
else
    // turn dice backward 0.5 and right 0.25
```

Test the *randomRoll* procedure by calling it in *myFirstMethod* with a counted loop 30 times. Count the number of times a specific side of the die faces upward. For an even distribution, the side containing 1 dot should be facing upward about 5 out of 30 times. (Note: This is just a quick check.)

Project
....

Create an animation that re-creates a popular TV game show of the 1970's, *Let's Make a Deal*®, in which a contestant is given the choice of selecting a door on the stage. Behind one of the doors is a valuable prize (for example, a new car). Behind the other two doors are less valuable prizes (for example, a television set or a goat). The prizes are placed behind the door randomly, so each play of the game the prizes are in random locations. When the contestant selects a door, the computer selects a door not picked by the contestant and not hiding the valuable prize and that door is opened. The contestant is then asked, "Do you want to keep the door you selected or pick the other closed door?" When the contestant makes a final selection, the contestant wins that prize. **HINT:** Alice 3 does not have a door object. Try using a wall object instead of a door. For example, the small Mars Outpost wall could be used by resizing it (height 2 m).

March 1, 1910: Esther

The Bell

When the avalanche hits, Esther gets caught in the threshold of her house. She finishes helping Larry start the engine and runs to her own train car. Right before Esther closes the door, the train becomes disconnected, and she watches the first two cars leave hers behind. She yells, but by then the noise of the storm is so loud she can't even hear herself. Wet, white snow pelts her face; the sky is opaque. She can hear splintering wood, and she braces herself in the door frame. The ground underneath the house starts sliding and shaking. When the movement finally stops, the snow in the air turns to sand. The grit scrapes her skin raw. And then as suddenly as it started, everything calms, and the dust gradually settles, revealing a bright-orange sunset and flat horizon.

Esther's home is cracked. The entire foundation split in two like a dollhouse. Her furniture is gone, the wardrobe mirror shattered. But Esther doesn't need a mirror to extend her arms and see the leather black wings attached, or feel the pointed ears and sharp fangs on her head. After years of pretending, she's finally real.

When the sandstorm clears, she climbs the tower, each step agony. Her muscles are sore and smaller than she is used to. Esther surveys the desert around her. There's a courtyard at the base of the pavilion her house landed on. Across the courtyard are more stone structures, soaring towers, and an unfathomably deep step-well full of sparkling clear water. Within the perimeter of this walled courtyard is grass, and beyond that, nothing but sand, as far as her considerable eyesight can see.

Bats, apparently, are not blind.

She watches from the tower window as a person emerges from the water tank below. Her high perch gives Esther a good view of the person's odd zigzag walk. As the person gets closer Esther realizes the reason for the slithering motion. The person is half-snake and half-man. The man stops at the edge of the pavilion and stares. Esther panics; she turns her face to the wall and hides. The house is entirely too exposed, sitting in the middle of a pavilion. Esther doesn't want anyone to notice. To her relief, the man leaves. Disappointingly, he returns later, leading an army. They march right up to Esther's doorstep.

The wooden floorboards and old nails of her house start to creak and moan as if from footsteps, and Esther steels herself for the inevitable confrontation. She half-covers her face with her wing and peers down at the crowd. To her surprise, no one comes up the stairs—the stairs themselves start coming up. The wood bends and contorts as it rises from the base floor. Each entire staircase stays connected to the house by the top step but twists into the air, making them inaccessible.

Esther suspects she made the stairs rise, but she has no idea how.

The army retreats in fear. At first Esther believes she's safe. She sleeps better during the day in her current state, so she only ventures outside at night. She

306

nearly doesn't notice when the first inner wall is built because the work happens in daylight. Once she realizes, Esther perches on her chimney at twilight and surveys the construction progress. The army slowly builds an elaborate labyrinth on the pavilion surrounding her house.

Instead of threatening, the maze feels safe. After her strange abilities with the stairs, she starts to experiment on the building supplies. Esther plays harmless pranks to both impede and aid construction progress. The workers discover equipment isn't found where they left it, some supplies disappear altogether, and entire maze walls are rotated. More often than not, though, projects left unfinished mysteriously become complete overnight. The builders begin to look to the tower with as much fondness as fear. The leader, who isn't actively involved with the construction, orders work to continue. And when the maze is complete, great stone statues guard the gates to the labyrinth, and no one is allowed in. For their own protection.

It isn't lonely, being inside a maze. Esther observes the community living in the water tank. She eavesdrops on people's conversations at twilight, learns their familial connections. The leader's firstborn is a daughter being raised in the warrior tradition. The child is popular—everyone talks about her, this girl named Manasha. People expect Manasha to do great things, but before the girl's training is complete, her father dies unexpectedly. And the young warrior becomes obsessed with the maze.

The first night Manasha approaches the edge of the pavilion, she doesn't go in. She sits directly in front of the gates and simply stares, her spear clutched between her hands. This continues for a year until she ventures inside the first corridor. Once she hits a fork in the maze, she turns and runs out. Finally, on the fifth anniversary of her father's death, she ventures deeper into the labyrinth.

And promptly gets lost.

At first Manasha's plight is funny. Esther giggles, watching from above, able to clearly see the path while Manasha goes in circles. The humor subsides when Esther realizes Manasha is making simple mistakes over and over in panic. The longer she runs through endless stone corridors, the more visibly distressed she becomes. When the sun inches over the horizon, the warrior breaks. Manasha drops her spear, falls to the feet of a stone guardian (an elephant), and clings to the pedestal.

Sympathetic, Esther reaches toward the statue in her mind, planning on using it to give directions. Except this time something takes hold and sucks her in. This time, the statue comes awake.

"Left," Esther whispers. The suggestion relays itself from Esther's mind to the statue. The statue swings its long elephant trunk left. Normally, it considers itself above such trivialities as lost children, but it happens to have awoken in an obliging mood.

Manasha follows the left-hand corridor. When she hits the next fork in the maze, Esther awakens the next statue and whispers the correct direction. This process continues slowly, and Manasha emerges from the maze when the sun fully rises over the horizon. She skitters back into the water tank, eager to be out of the forbidden place.

Yet Manasha returns the next night. This time she nearly reaches the center of the maze. Esther blocks off the inner wall, but she rotates the outer walls and gives Manasha progressively more complicated puzzles to solve. To the amusement of the guardians, Manasha explores the maze nightly, and when the warrior reaches a point where she can't continue, the statues guide her back out.

Through all this, Esther looks on from her tower. Then the old tower bell spontaneously reappears. Curiously, when Esther tries to ring the bell, she can't move it. Unnerved, Esther switches her perch from the tower to the chimney. From there she can hear the creak of the moving staircases. But she's so used to the sound, it bothers her less than the constant solid presence of the bell, which only serves to remind her of things she can't control.

The days blur together until one afternoon she hears a soft squeak in the wooden roof right behind her as if someone took a step. On instinct, she stills, her shoulders hunch and her wings squeeze tight to her sides. No one can make it up those stairs.

"Esther?" a quiet voice asks hesitantly.

Esther takes deep breaths, weighing her options quickly in her mind. She turns her head slightly to the side, sizing up the intruder out of the corner of her eye. The little fluffy thing looks fairly innocuous.

"My name is Tashi," it says.

"How did you get here?" Esther asks.

"The stairs," Tashi answers, as if this was a simple question.

"I meant through the maze," Esther retorts, defensively.

"I had help," Tashi explains.

Esther snorts. She knows exactly who from—she doesn't even have to ask. She turns away again, gazing out into the distance, "Then you should have no trouble finding your way back out." Her voice is tired. If she can be reached here, across deserts and through a labyrinth, nowhere is safe.

"But I came to find you," Tashi implores, "Larry sent me!"

Esther jolts in surprise, swivels around to eye Tashi suspiciously, leaps from her perch with a great unfurling of wings, and lands on the roof in front of the baby yeti. Almost immediately after landing, Esther takes a step backward and covers half her face with a wing, "You know Larry?"

"Yes!" Tashi smiles, relieved at having her attention. "I can take you to him."

"Not possible," Esther says sadly. "I don't know how to fly. And the staircases, they move." For the first time since they became uncontrollable, Esther stares down the stairs. She has no idea how the little fluffy thing made it up. Tashi must be extremely quick.

"I'll race you," Tashi says.

Esther glances over at Tashi and grins. Esther never could turn down a challenge. They set off, taking one step at a time. Tashi makes it down the initial flight of stairs first. She briefly turns her head to watch Esther.

"Come on!" Tashi calls encouragement.

Esther shakes her head in refusal. She is poised at the end of the staircase rising higher and higher, frozen in place as the gap between her feet and the floor widens. The staircase twists, and at first she thinks she's going to fall off. She closes her eyes, prepared for the inevitable drop, but it never comes. Instead gravity shifts and her feet become glued to the wooden step. With her eyes closed it feels as if she's standing upright—until she opens them and realizes she's nearly horizontal to the ground. Horizontal to the ground and yet not falling.

Time speeds back to normal, the staircase straightens out with a rush, the base step connects at the bottom, and she stumbles onto the floor. Suddenly everything seems clearer, trepidation drains out of Esther entirely, and her brain feels less like mush. By this time Tashi is long gone down the next stairwell. Esther is losing, but she eagerly follows anyway and makes it to the bottom only minutes after. When she takes her foot off the final step, the staircases slow to a stop, settling into their proper places. The bell inside the top of the tower starts ringing loudly.

Esther tumbles out of the cracked basement of her house while still staring upward, admiring her bell. The minute she looks straight ahead and sees the pinstripe suit and top hat, she doesn't waste a breath. She runs forward, flings her arms around Larry, and nearly knocks him over in a gigantic bear hug.

"Hi," Larry says, laughing.

"Hi," Esther repeats.

She waits a beat, still hanging on him like a bat, and then says, "You're a skeleton."

Larry shrugs.

"And I'm a bat," she grins and lets go. She unfurls her wings so he can see. Next to Larry stands Tashi and the warrior, Manasha.

"Hold up," Manasha interrupts the reunion. "Are you telling me that for nearly one hundred years the only danger behind the labyrinth's walls has been an overgrown bat?"

"Danger?" Esther asks innocently, looking confused. "What danger?"

"One hundred years!" Manasha throws up her hands. "An entire maze built. For no reason." She swivels on the spot and slithers away.

"Wait!" Larry calls. "We need your help getting back!"

"No," Esther says. "You don't." She clasps her hands together dramatically and the maze walls spring backward one at a time, clearing a path from the center to the entrance. Larry stands open-mouthed in shock. But before Esther can explain, the bell overhead stops ringing and when the last note fades, Esther, the house, and her train car disappear with it.

13

Built-in Arrays, Poses, More Events, and Interactive Controls

Concept Objectives

- Writing code to iterate through an array, accessing one item at a time
- Writing code to access all items in an array at the same time
- Declaring and updating tracking variables

- Using a general game algorithm to implement a simple game
- Writing code with nested while loops
- Creating keyPress and scene activation event listeners
- Using Boolean operators in binary conditional expressions

The major focus of this chapter is to introduce built-in arrays and expand the use of event listeners in the context of an interactive game. keyPress and scene activation event listeners and Boolean operations will also be introduced.

An array is an ordered collection of items of the same type. The items in an array may be objects. For example, an array might be nine players on a basketball team, a school of fish, or a group of trees in a forest. An array may also contain items that are all numbers, or all text strings, or other types of values. One of the advantages of using an array of objects is the ability to create code where all objects in the array perform the same action, either one at a time or all at the same time.

Some arrays in Alice are built in, and other arrays are custom-built, created by the programmer. Built-in arrays in Alice consist of a subset of joints in the skeletal system of an object. For example, the elephant's trunk has a built-in array of joints. Built-in arrays in Alice objects allow for creating animation that mimics the motion of an appendage, such as an elephant's trunk or a dog's tail, by applying an animation to each joint in the array.

Joints in 3D Alice models can also be animated by calling a special custom procedure for a pose. A pose is pre-configured arrangement of the position and orientation of some or all of an object's skeletal joints.

13.1 Story Analysis for Demo

To illustrate built-in arrays, poses, and new interactive controls, two programming examples will be presented. The first programming example is a short demo of writing code for built-in arrays. The second programming example uses built-in arrays and poses in an interactive game. The storyline for the game is a selected excerpt from Episode 7, *Esther: The Bell*, in the *Haunted Circus* story. In this episode, Tashi and Larry travel through the portal to find Esther. Esther was the circus singer who pretended to live as a bat. She flapped the arms of her winged dress while running and she slept upside down.

The short demo is inspired by the stone elephant guard in the *Esther* episode, but is not an actual excerpt from the story. In this demo, Tashi and Larry are standing in front of the elephant stables and are asking for help in finding Esther. A summary of the demo example is

Larry asks for help in finding Esther
The elephant lifts its trunk and says "Esther is trapped in the temple"
The elephant returns its trunk to its original state
The elephant lifts its trunk and says "You must find your way through the maze"

13.2 Design for Demo

The elephant's trunk has a built-in array of joints, which will be used to lift and curve the trunk. Because this is a quick demo, there is no need for custom procedures. The code will be implemented in *myFirstMethod*.

13.2.1 Algorithm for demo

An algorithm for the demo is shown in Figure 13.1.

do in order
       Larry says "Please help us find Esther."
      do together
          elephant's trunk curve upward, one joint at a time
          elephant say "Esther is trapped in the inner temple."
      elephant's trunk return to its original state
      do together
          elephant's trunk curve upward, all joints at the same time
          elephant say "You must find your way through the maze."

Figure 13.1 • *Algorithm for demo animation*

13.2.2 Demo starter world

The starter file for this demo world, named *IndiaTempleStarter.a3p*, may be downloaded from **www.alice.org/Alice3ToJava**. Download and open the starter world. If successfully downloaded, the initial scene should appear as seen in Figure 13.2. The temple grounds are widespread, containing many elaborate structures. The initial scene of the demo world is an overview from the water tower area. Through the trees on the right, you can see a courtyard in front of the elephant stables. Larry and Tashi are standing in the courtyard near the elephant stables.

Figure 13.2 • *Initial scene for the demo starter world*

Camera markers have been included in the starter world that will be used for changing the camera viewpoint to other locations in the scene (Figure 13.3).

Figure 13.3   *Camera view markers in the demo starter world*

The Biped class has *talk* and *talkAndSay* procedures, already imported for this project (Figure 13.4).

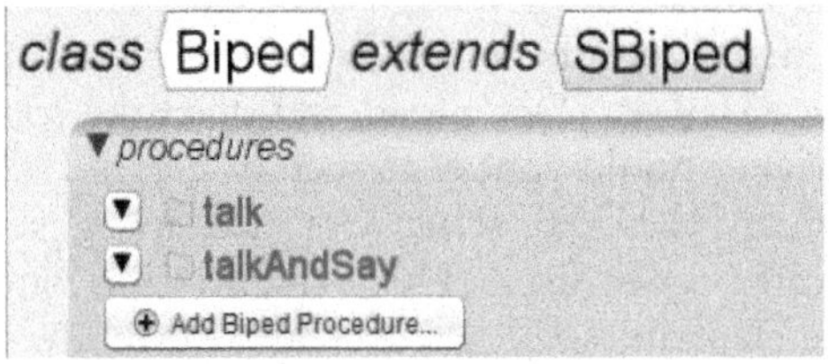

Figure 13.4   *Imported procedures in the Biped class*

13.3 Implement and Test the Demo

In *myFirstMethod*, add comments to document the demo's algorithm (Figure 13.5).

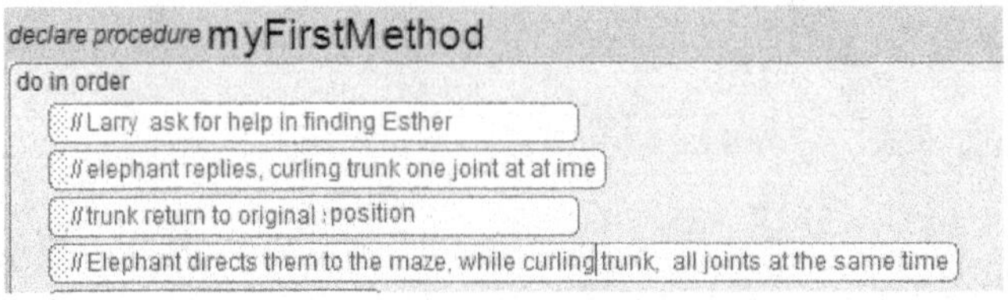

Figure 13.5   *Comments to document the algorithm*

The first algorithm step is Larry asking the elephant to help them find Esther. To view this action, the camera must cut to a view of Larry and Tashi in front of the elephant stables. Add a statement for a short delay; then a statement to cut the camera to the *elephantStableView* camera marker. Next, add a *talkAndSay* statement to have Larry ask for help (Figure 13.6).

declare procedure **myFirstMethod**

do in order

//Larry asks for help in finding Esther

camera **delay** 2.0

camera **moveAndOrientTo** elephantStableView , duration 3.0 add detail

Larry **talkAndSay** words: "Please help us find Esther." , seconds: 2.5

Figure 13.6 ● *Camera zooms in and Larry asks for help in finding Esther.*

13.3.1 Built-in array of skeletal joints

In the next algorithm step, the elephant is to reply and curl its trunk at the same time. The Elephant class does not have a built-in procedure for curling the trunk, so you will have to write some statements to define this action.

An elephant object has a built-in array, named *trunk*[ ]. The brackets at the end of the name is the syntax symbol for an array, in Alice. The trunk array contains six skeletal joints (Figure 13.7). Each joint in *trunk*[ ] is an item of the array. Items of an array are arranged in an **ordered** sequence. The position of each item in an array is identified by a number within the brackets, known as an **index**. In this example, the items in *trunk*[ ] start with *trunk*[0] near the elephant's mouth and end with *trunk*[5] at the extreme tip of the trunk. In Alice, and many other programming languages, the numbering of array items always starts with an index of [0].

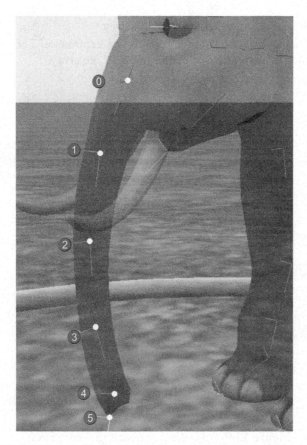

Figure 13.7 ● *Skeletal joints in an elephant's* trunk[] *array*

Take a moment to act out curling an elephant's trunk by miming the action slowly with your arm. Notice that you rotate your shoulder joint, then your elbow joint, then your wrist joint to create a curl motion. A similar motion for the *trunk[]* array may be created by rotating each joint in the elephant's trunk array, in order from one joint to the next.

13.3.2 Iteration with *for each in*

The term iterate means to repeat something. To iterate through an array means to perform some operation with items of an array, either one at a time (starting at index 0 and proceeding through to the last item) or all items at the same time. Alice has two control structures for iterating through an array: *for each in* and *each in together*, as seen in Figure 13.8. These two control structures are often known as *for* loops because we think of them as "for each item in the array ..."

Figure 13.8   *Two controls for iterating through an array*

To create a *for each in* code block, first drag the *for each in* tile into the editor. A dialog box is displayed. In the box, follow these steps (Figure 13.9):

(1) Select the item type. In this example, select *SJoint*.
(2) Enter an item name. In this example, *itemJ* is the item name. The item name is a variable that may refer to any one of the items in the array.
(3) Select CustomArray in the array pulldown menu.

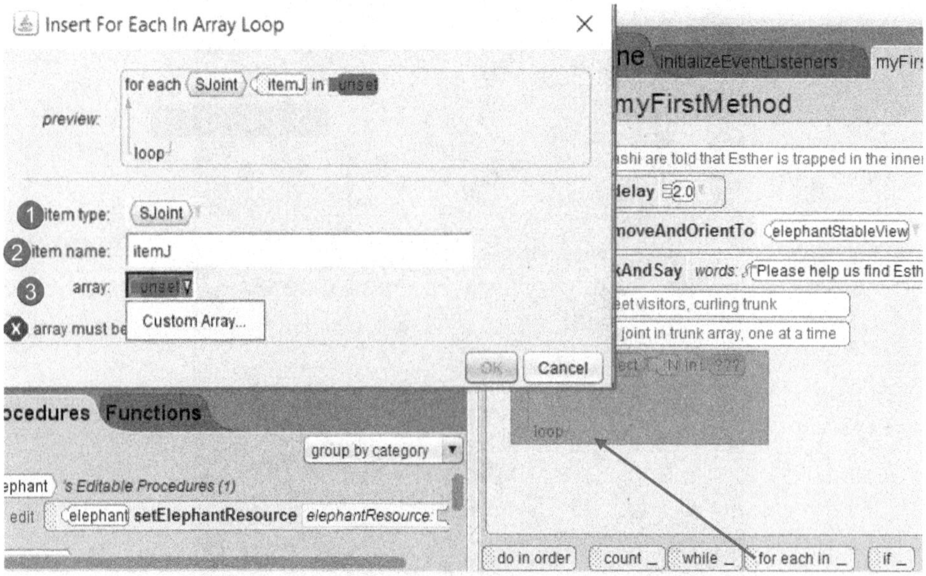

Figure 13.9   *Create a* for each in _ *code block.*

When CustomArray is selected, a second dialog box is displayed (Figure 13.10). In this example, just click the OK button to create an empty array as a placeholder. Then click OK again. The resulting code block, with a placeholder array (*SJoint*[ ]), is shown in Figure 13.11.

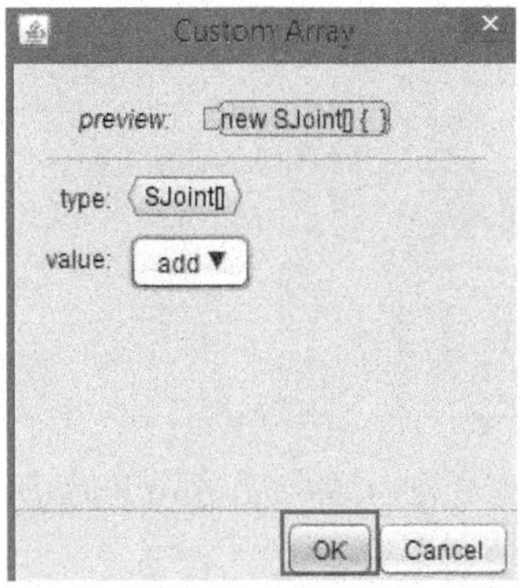

Figure 13.10 • *Create an empty placeholder array.*

Figure 13.11 • For each in *code block with placeholder array*

To replace the placeholder array, first select the elephant object in the Object Selector. In the Functions tab, drag the *getTrunkArray* tile over and drop it on top of the placeholder, as shown in Figure 13.12. The resulting code block is shown in Figure 13.13. In this *for each* loop, *itemJ* represents a joint in the elephant's trunk array, starting with the joint at *trunk[0]*.

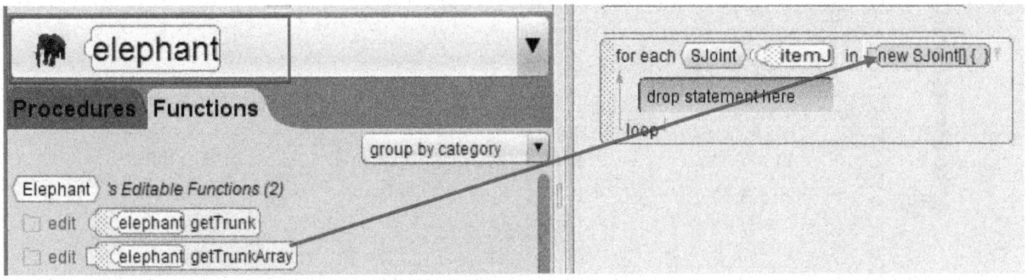

Figure 13.12 • *Replace the placeholder with* getTrunkArray.

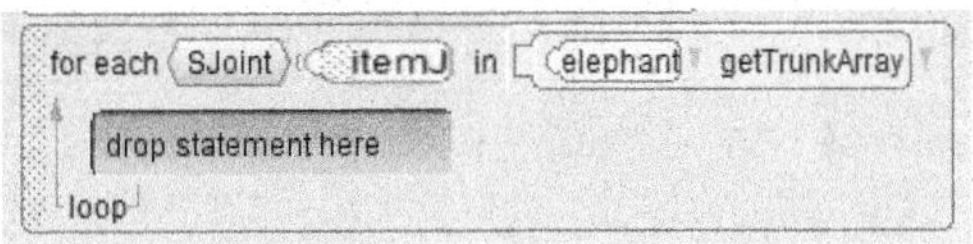

Figure 13.13 • *Resulting* for each in *code block*

Now, a statement must be added to the code block as an instruction for how each joint should rotate (*turn* or *roll*). In the Object Selector, select *itemJ* (Figure 13.14). Then, drag the *turn* tile into the code block to create a statement that turns a skeletal joint backward 0.125 rev in 0.25 seconds.

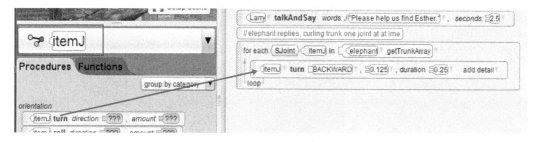

Figure 13.14   *Each item will turn backward, one at a time.*

Test-run the project. Carefully observe the curling of the trunk. Each skeletal joint *turns*, one by one, starting with the item at the base and continuing to the last item at the tip of the trunk. You may notice the *turn* by the last two skeletal joints is not as obvious as turns by the first few joints in the array. This is because the last two skeletal joints are very close together and their turning has less effect on the overall appearance of the trunk.

To illustrate how the *for each in* code block works, we **unrolled** it in Figure 13.15. To "unroll a loop" means to write code that performs the same action, but without the loop. The *do in order* in Figure 13.15 unrolls the action as a sequence of statements, each statement turning one of the joints in the array. In this example, the elephant's trunk has only six joints, so the unrolled *do in order* code block has six statements, to show the sequence of execution by the joints in the array.

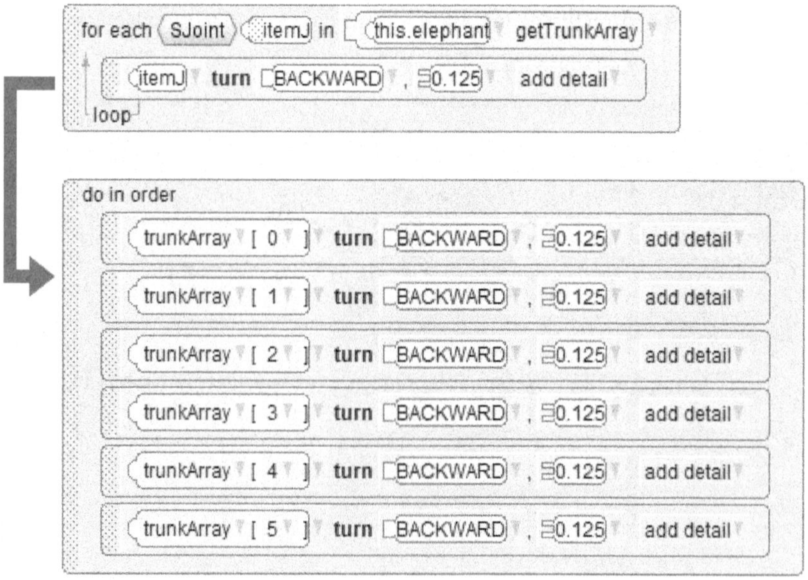

```
for each ( SJoint ) ( itemJ ) in [ ( this.elephant ) getTrunkArray )
    ( itemJ ) turn [BACKWARD) , ≡0.125)  add detail
loop
```

```
do in order
    ( trunkArray [ 0 ] ) turn [BACKWARD) , ≡0.125)  add detail
    ( trunkArray [ 1 ] ) turn [BACKWARD) , ≡0.125)  add detail
    ( trunkArray [ 2 ] ) turn [BACKWARD) , ≡0.125)  add detail
    ( trunkArray [ 3 ] ) turn [BACKWARD) , ≡0.125)  add detail
    ( trunkArray [ 4 ] ) turn [BACKWARD) , ≡0.125)  add detail
    ( trunkArray [ 5 ] ) turn [BACKWARD) , ≡0.125)  add detail
```

Figure 13.15   *An expansion of the* for each in *loop, showing how it works*

At the same time as the elephant's trunk curls upward, the elephant should reply to Larry's request. Add a *do together* code block and drag the *for each in* code block into the *do together*. Then add a *say* statement for the elephant to reply that "Esther is trapped in the inner temple." The resulting *do together* code block is shown in Figure 13.16. Notice the elephant's reply is implemented with a call to *say*, not *talkAndSay*. The *talkAndSay* procedure is defined for a Biped but the elephant is a Quadruped.

Figure 13.16   do together *with nested* for each in *code block and* say *statement*

Once again, test-run the project. Now, you should see the elephant's trunk curl at the same time as the speech bubble is displayed for the elephant's reply.

13.3.3 *straightenOutJoints*

The next algorithm step is to return the trunk to its original position. You could do this by creating another *for each in* code block and writing code to *turn* each joint *forward* the same amount as it was turned backward. An easier technique is to simply call the built-in *straightenOutJoints* procedure. Create the statement as shown in Figure 13.17. Select a *duration* of 1.5 seconds to allow time to watch the trunk slowly straighten.

Test-run the project. You should see the trunk curve upward slowly and then return to its original position.

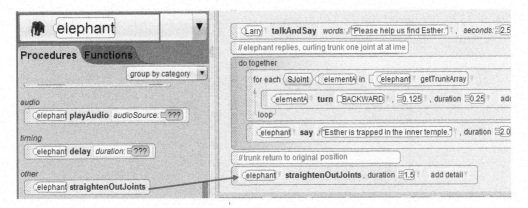

Figure 13.17   *Call* straightenOutJoints *to return elephant's trunk to original position.*

Note that the *straightenOutJoints* procedure is convenient but should be used with caution. When called, *straightenOutJoints* restores all joints in the entire object to their original position. In cases where several actions have been used to move and rotate several different subparts of an object's body, you may want to restore the position of some but not all parts of the body.

13.3.4 Iteration with *each in together*

The next algorithm step is the elephant curling its trunk again and telling Larry and Tashi to find their way to the temple through the maze. For demonstration purposes, use the *each in together* control construct to curl the trunk where all the joints turn at the same time.

Create a second *do together*. This time, drag the *each in together* tile to the editor to create a code block where the joints in the *trunk[]* array will *turn* all at the same time. Enter *itemK* as the item name for the *each in together* control statement. Create a statement in the *each in together* code block to *turn itemK* backward 0.125 with a *duration* of 0.25. Then, add a statement to have the elephant *say*, "You must find your way through the maze." Figure 13.18 illustrates the code block. In this *for each* loop, *itemK* represents each joint in the elephant's *trunk[]* array.

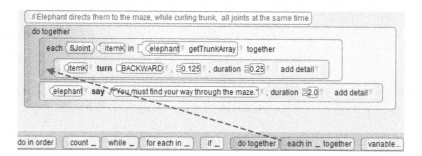

Figure 13.18   do together *with nested* each in _ together *code block*

Once again, test-run the project. As the animation runs, you should see the elephant lift and curl its trunk twice. In the first curl (*for each in*), the trunk lifts slowly, one joint turning at a time. In the second (*each in together*), the trunk lifts rapidly, all joints turning at the same time.

To better describe the rapid execution of the *each in together* loop, we unrolled it in Figure 13.19. To unroll the *for each together*, a *do together* code block is used to contain the statements, which execute all at the same time.

Figure 13.19   *Unrolling an* each in together *loop to show how it works*

The last algorithm step is to cut the camera to view the maze that protects the temple. Add a statement to change the camera's viewpoint to the *mazeView* camera marker. The completed code is shown in Figure 13.20.

Save and test-run the project. After the elephant tells Larry and Tashi that they need to make their way through the maze, you should see the camera viewpoint cut to show the maze and the temple within.

```
declare procedure myFirstMethod
do in order
    // Larry asks for help in finding Esther
    camera delay 2.0
    camera moveAndOrientTo elephantStableView , duration 3.0    add detail
    Larry talkAndSay words: "Please help us find Esther." , seconds: 2.5
    // elephant replies, curling trunk one joint at a time
    do together
        for each SJoint elementA in [ elephant getTrunkArray
            elementA turn BACKWARD , 0.125 , duration 0.25    add detail
        loop
        elephant say "Esther is trapped in the inner temple." , duration 2.0    add detail

    // trunk return to original position
    elephant straightenOutJoints , duration 1.5    add detail
    // Elephant directs them to the maze, while curling trunk, all joints at the same time
    do together
        each SJoint elementB in [ elephant getTrunkArray together
            elementB turn BACKWARD , 0.125 , duration 0.25    add detail
        elephant say "You must find your way through the maze." , duration 2.0    add detail

    camera moveAndOrientTo mazeView , duration 2.0    add detail
```

Figure 13.20 • *Completed built-in array demo*

13.4 Story Analysis for an Interactive Game

The second example in this chapter is an interactive game in which array programming concepts will be applied and expanded. Poses and event listeners will also be introduced. This example is from an excerpt of Episode 7, *Esther: The Bell*. The selected excerpt begins where Tashi finds Esther on the roof of the old manor house, located in the inner temple. A summary of the story excerpt is provided here:

> Tashi has climbed to the top of the haunted manor and encounters Esther on the roof. At first, Esther is suspicious of Tashi. Tashi tells Esther that she can lead

her to Larry, but Esther doesn't believe she can make it down the twisting stair-cases of the haunted manor. Tashi convinces Esther to brave the uncontrollable moving staircases, and together they make it down to the bottom. When Esther walks off the last staircase-step, the school bell in the tower starts ringing. Larry is happy that Tashi was able to help Esther down the twisting staircases.

A possible analysis for this story is:

Tashi meets Esther

Esther confronts Tashi, trying to send her away

Esther confides she can't fly now and the twisting, dizzying stairs keep her trapped

Tashi challenges Esther to try descending the stairs

Esther and Tashi descend the stairs

The bell rings and Larry celebrates finding Esther

13.4.1 Adapting for an interactive game

The selected story segment begins where Tashi meets Esther on the roof of the temple and convinces her to try descending the staircases will be implemented as an opening cutscene. Tashi and Esther's descent (from the roof to the ground level) on twisting, turning staircases can be an interactive game because it has our characters overcoming a challenge (twisting staircases) to achieve a goal (successfully navigating Tashi and Esther down the staircases) and end conditions for win/loss (player wins, if successful in less than 4 missed steps).

In the original story, Tashi challenges Esther to go down the stairs. Esther accepts the challenge and they go down the stairs separately. We have adapted this part of the story to have Tashi offer to help Esther and they go down the stairs together. This adaptation will make it easier to track the game state because the two objects descend the stairs in sync and the end condition can be checked for one object (because the two are together).

With this in mind, the following is a high-level algorithm for the cutscene and the game (Figure 13.21) as well as a storyboard-style sketch (Figure 13.22).

do in order

    //play opening cutscene

        Tashi meets Esther

        Esther jumps down to face Tashi and tells her to go away

        Esther says she can no longer fly and the twisting stairs make her too dizzy

        Tashi challenges Esther to try descending the stairs

    //play game

        player controls Tashi and Esther to get them down the stairs

        if Player Wins:

            bell rings and Larry congratulates Tashi and Esther

        if Player has guessed more than three times:

            player loses and the game ends

Figure 13.21   *Algorithm for cutscene and game*

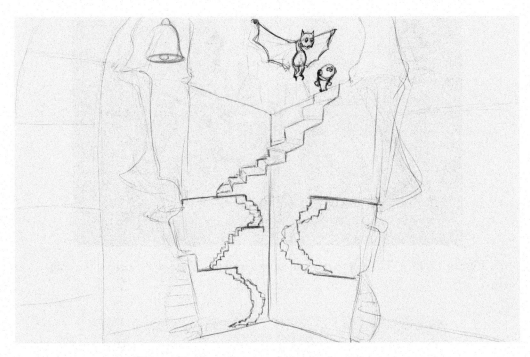

Figure 13.22 • *Storyboard sketch of twisting stairs*

13.4.2 Game starter world

A startup project file, *FindingEstherStarter.a3p*, can be downloaded from **www.alice.org/Alice3ToJava**. Download the file and then open it in Alice 3. Click the Scene Setup button to view the initial scene in the Scene editor. The initial scene is a view of an old manor house (an instance of the HauntedHouse class). The manor house is in the corner of the inner temple, where it crash-landed after the Circus Train's avalanche disaster. Larry is on the ground level. Tashi and Esther are on the roof of the manor house. With Larry on the ground level are Manasha and Nagi. Manasha is a Nagi, a snake-like spirit associated with the protection of water—springs, wells, and rivers. Yali is a mythical beast: half-lion, half-elephant, with greater powers than either one.

The manor house has four staircases between the first and second floors of the house. Another set of stairs has been added in the attic, leading to the temple's roof (Figure 13.23). The manor's built-in staircases, named *stairsW*, *stairsX*, *stairsY*, and *stairsZ*, are curved. The added staircase in the attic is a straight up/down staircase, but has been curved by calling a custom *curve* procedure.

Select *camera* in the Toolbox and view the object and camera markers (Figure 13.24). The object and camera markers in this scene are used to manage views and positions on the roof and the ground level of the manor house.

Figure 13.23   *The manor has four staircases plus an added staircase in the attic*

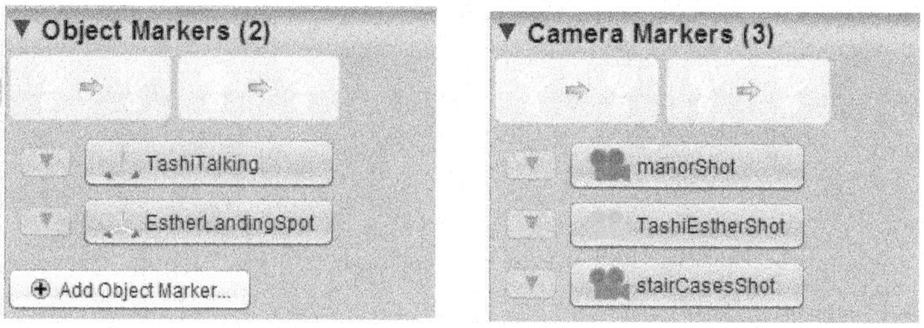

Figure 13.24   *Object and camera markers in the starter scene*

13.4.3 Pre-made custom procedures

Three classes in the starter world have pre-made custom procedures to speed the development of the opening cutscene (Figure 13.25). The Scene class has *TashiMeetsEsther* and *EstherTrapped*. The Bat class has *lookDownAndRight*, *nod*, *sigh*, *glanceLeft*, and *glanceRight*. The StaircaseDown class has *curve*. Each of these procedures is discussed, as needed, in the chapter sections.

Figure 13.25   *Pre-made procedures in the starter world*

13.5 High-Level Structure

The first thing we will do is create the high-level structure for the game. Then, we will implement the detailed steps in each. Referring back to the algorithm in Figure 13.21, it includes two high-level steps:

> play opening cutscene
> play game

   Declare two new procedures in the Scene class: *playOpeningCutscene* and *playGame*. Add a call to each inside *myFirstMethod* (Figure 13.26).

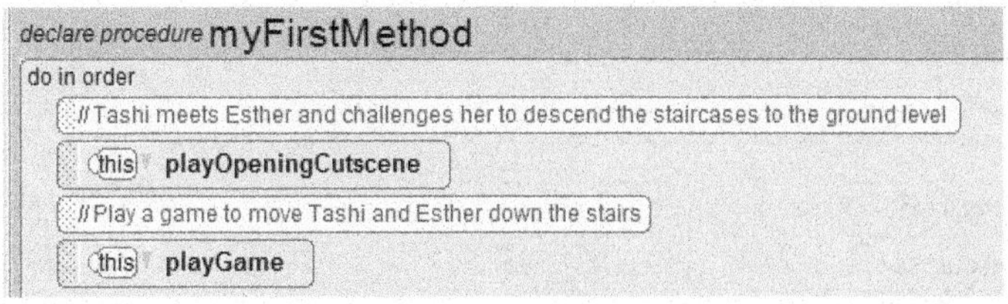

Figure 13.26 • *Implementation of the high-level algorithm in* myFirstMethod

13.6 Opening Cutscene

Begin filling in the details of our program, starting first with the opening cutscene. Open the *playOpeningCutscene* tab. Refer back to our algorithm in Figure 13.21, and create comments for each step in the cutscene procedure (Figure 13.27).

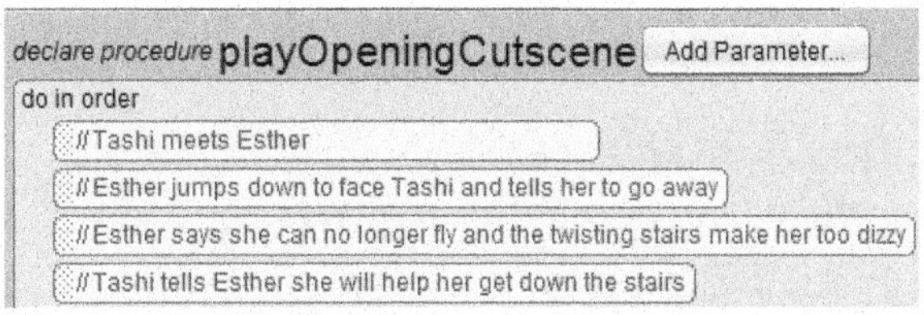

Figure 13.27 • *Comments to document the overall algorithm*

   The first step in the cutscene is Tashi meeting Esther on the roof of the manor house. The Scene class has a pre-made procedure, named *TashiMeetsEsther*, that implements this action (Figure 13.28). When Esther and Tashi meet, Esther is surprised by Tashi's appearance on the roof, but she doesn't want to talk to Tashi. Esther's pre-made procedures, *lookDownAndRight*, *nod*, and *sigh*, animate body language that conveys Esther's sadness and her unwillingness to talk. Red boxes in the image shown in Figure 13.28 highlight the calls to Esther's pre-made procedures (defined in the Bat class).

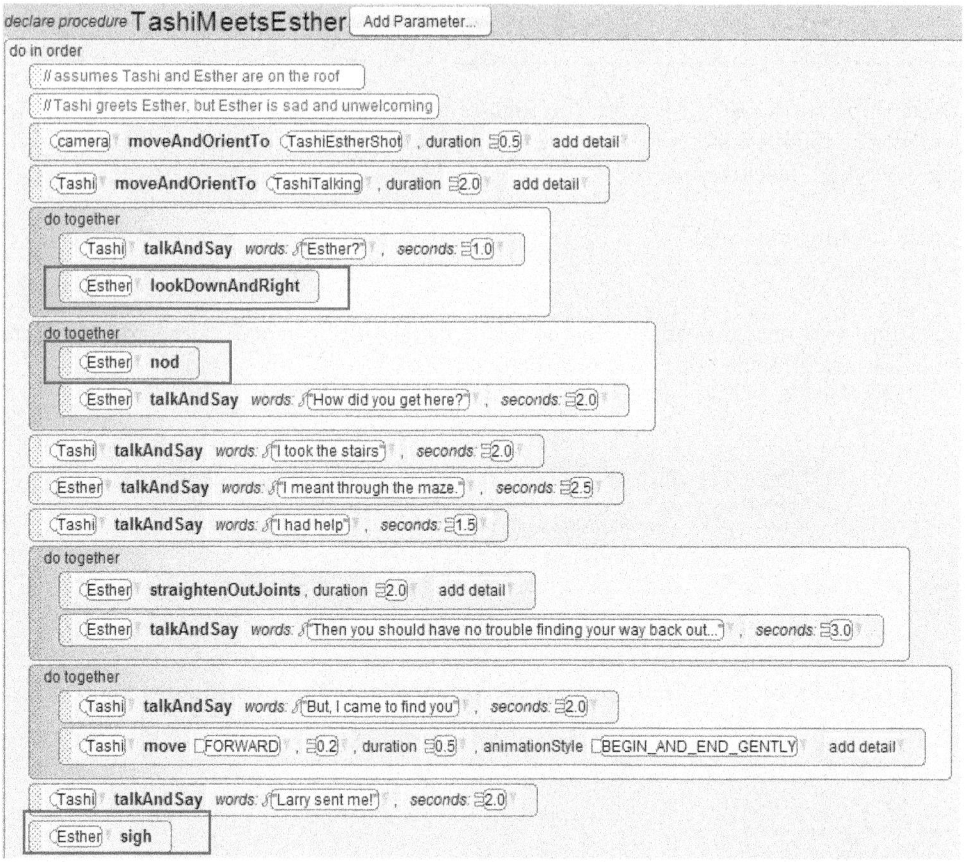

Figure 13.28   *Pre-made* TashiMeetsEsther *procedure*

To test the *TashiMeetsEsther* procedure, add a delay statement in *playOpeningCutscene* and then a statement to call *TashiMeetsEsther* (Figure 13.29). Test-run the project. You should see the camera move to the scene on the roof and Tashi's opening conversation with Esther.

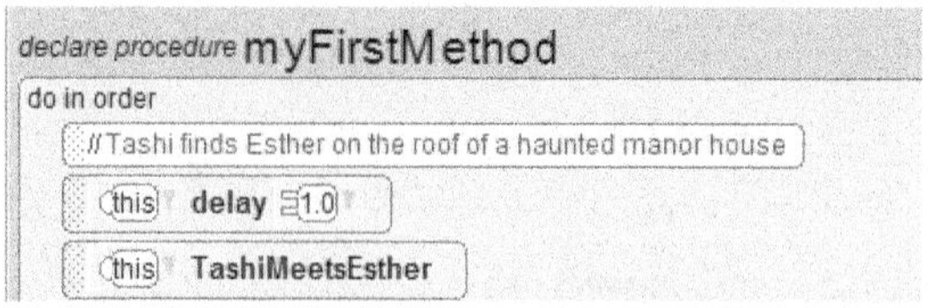

Figure 13.29   *Call and test-run* TashiMeetsEsther.

13.7 Animating with Poses

Esther is intrigued that Tashi has claimed, "Larry sent me!" Reluctantly, Esther jumps down to confront Tashi face to face. To perform the jump, Esther might be expected to spread her wings and then refold them close to her body as she lands.

A Bat object's wings have a complex set of joints with specific orientations around an axis for flexing and folding the skin on the wings. Writing a procedure for a flying object's wing action is a time-consuming task requiring patience and experience. For this reason, Alice provides built-in procedures utilizing poses for many of the 3D models that have wings. A pose is a preset arrangement of specific joints for an object.

A pose may be animated by calling a built-in procedure for arranging a set of skeletal joints in a specific configuration. In fact, we've already used a pose during the opening demo exercise with the *straightenOutJoints* procedure. This procedure arranges the entire set of an object's joints to their default, upright position. Esther has three built-in procedures for arranging her skeletal joints into a pose: *vampirePose*, *spreadWingsPose*, and *foldWingsPose* (Figure 13.30).

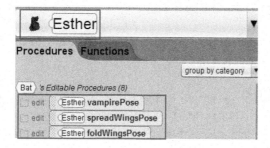

Figure 13.30   *Built-in procedures for poses*

A wing jump action can be easily implemented by calling the procedures for poses. A decomposition for *wingJump* is shown in Figure 13.31. The decomposition calls *spreadWingsPose* and *foldWingsPose*.

do in order

    do together

        turn right

        spread wings (pose)

    move up

    move to a marked location in front of Tashi (marker)

    fold wings (pose)

Figure 13.31   *Decomposition for* wingJump

Declare a new *wingJump* procedure in the Bat class. In the *wingJump* Editor tab, enter code statements to implement the design. Figure 13.32 illustrates example code for the procedure. Note the procedure has a marker parameter to specify a target location where the bat will land when it jumps.

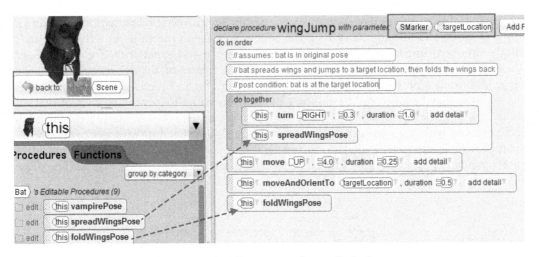

Figure 13.32   wingJump *procedure calls built-in poses.*

Return to *playOpeningCutscene* and add a statement to call *wingJump*. Then, create a *do together* code block with statements that have Tashi back away at the same time as Esther intuitively creates a barrier with a *vampirePose* (Figure 13.33). Test-run.

Figure 13.33   *Calling* wingJump *in* myFirstMethod

Poses are a great feature, saving much programmer time and effort. When using poses, however, it is often important to return the object or the object's subpart to its original pose. Returning to the original pose is not always needed, but is a good rule of thumb. In this example, the *wingJump* procedure spreads the bat's wings and then returns the wings to their original pose. When *wingJump* is called, Esther is positioned in a *vampirePose* but code was not written to return to her original pose. In this example, Esther will stay in the vampire pose as she continues to talk with Tashi but will be returned to her original pose before the procedure ends.

In the next step, Esther confides to Tashi that she can no longer fly and the twisting motion of the staircases makes her dizzy. The Scene class has a pre-made procedure named *EstherTrapped* that implements this step in the algorithm (Figure 13.34).

Figure 13.34 • EstherTrapped *procedure*

Note the *EstherTrapped* procedure calls *glanceRight* and *glanceLeft* (custom procedures in the Bat class) to turn Esther's eyes left and right, following the motion of the twisting staircases in the haunted manor house. Also, notice the built-in *straightenOutJoints* procedure is called to return Esther to her original pose.

Add a statement in *playOpeningCutscene* to call *EstherTrapped*, as shown in Figure 13.35. Test-run the project. You should see Esther end her dialogue and then straighten her wings.

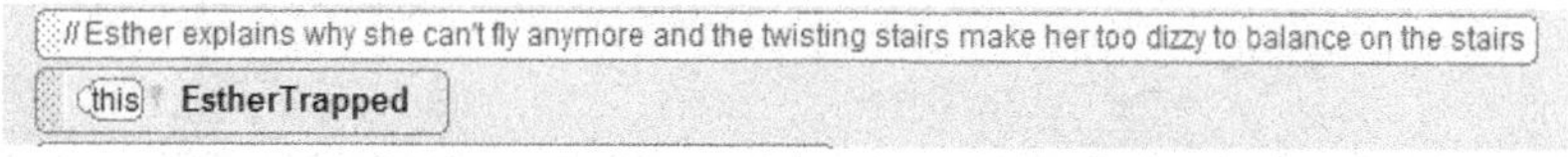

Figure 13.35 • *Call* EstherTrapped *in* playOpeningCutscene

After Esther straightens her wings, Tashi's challenge to Esther includes an offer to put her wings around Tashi's shoulders so they can move down the staircases together. Esther accepts the offer. The Scene class has a pre-made procedure named *TashiOffers* that implements this step in the algorithm (Figure 13.36).

Add a statement in *playOpeningCutscene* to call *TashiOffers*. The completed procedure is shown in Figure 13.37. Test-run. You should see Esther move to hold onto Tashi's shoulders, in preparation for the game.

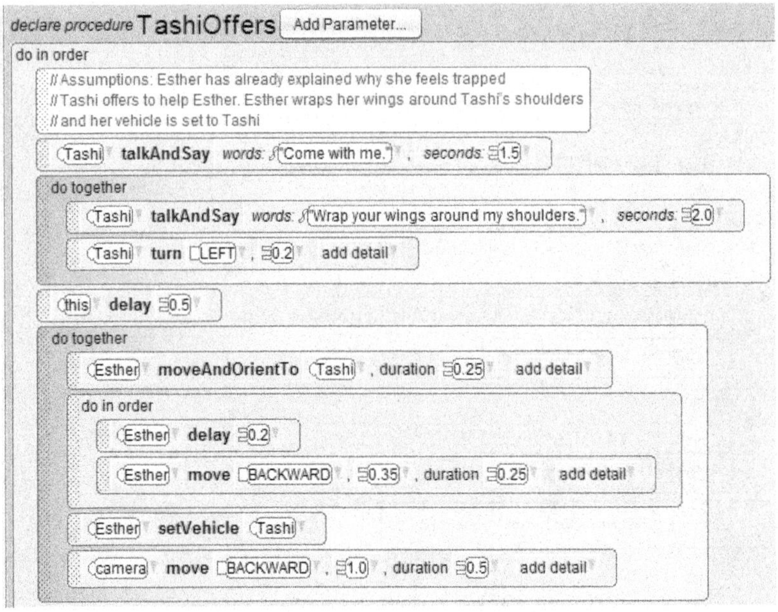

Figure 13.36   TashiOffers *procedure*

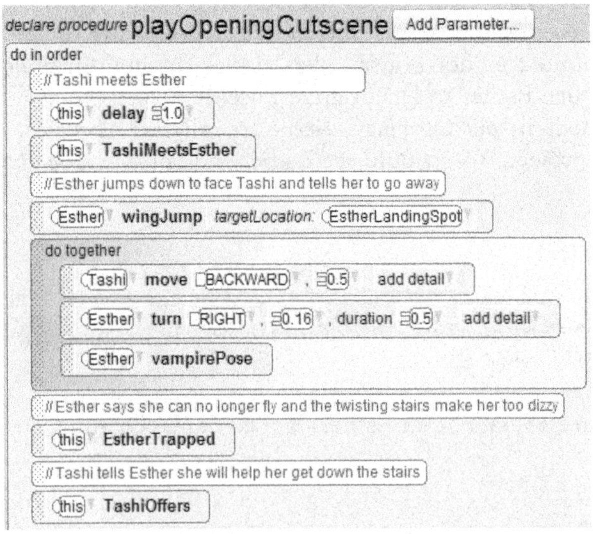

Figure 13.37   *Completed* playOpeningCutscene *procedure*

13.8 Play Game Decomposition

Now we are ready to turn our attention to the game. Up to now, our task description, design analysis, and algorithm have not provided much detail about the game portion of our program. A game description, including the player's goals and the end conditions, is

The player's goal is to navigate Tashi and Esther down the moving staircases of the manor to reach the ground. While the game is active, the manor's staircases are constantly twisting up and down. When on a staircase, Tashi and Esther will automatically travel from the top of a staircase to its bottom. As the staircase is twisting and curving up and down, the bottom of the staircase may be suspended in mid-air, a dangerous distance from the floor. Tashi and Esther must wait until the staircase twists back down so the bottom of the staircase is close to the stair's base on the floor. The player controls the navigation by pressing the SPACEBAR to tell Tashi to jump from the staircase bottom to the base on the floor. The player must time the jump so that the staircase bottom (where Tashi is standing) is very close to the staircase base on the floor. If Tashi is too far away, she will not jump and the player has missed. If the player misses four times, Esther will give up, the game stops, and the player loses. If Tashi and Esther reach the ground level, the player wins. The bell rings and Larry congratulates Tashi and Esther. The bell continues to ring and Esther and the manor house disappear.

Earlier, a *playGame* procedure was declared for the Scene class, and a call to *playGame* was created in *myFirstMethod*. The *playGame* procedure will contain the code that controls the game. Other procedures will be called to carry out specific parts of the game. Event listeners will also be needed. Read the game description again. Pay special attention to the words **while, when** and **if**. In general, these words indicate where to use events and conditionals in programming the action of the game. Let's pull out these instances:

- While the game is active, the manor's staircases are constantly twisting up and down
- When on a staircase, Tashi and Esther will automatically travel from top ... to bottom
- When the player presses the SPACEBAR (event)
  - If Tashi is at the bottom of the staircase, (conditional)
    - If Tashi is close enough to the stair base, (conditional)
      Tashi and Esther make the jump
    - Else (conditional) player gets a miss (feedback)
  - Else Tashi says "Can't jump yet" and player gets a miss
- If the player misses more than three times (conditional)
  - Esther gives up and the player loses the game (fail condition)
- If Tashi and Esther reach the ground level (conditional)
  - The player wins (win condition)

In this game, the movement of the staircases of the manor is controlled through code that is looping throughout the duration of the game. This is the first time that we are creating a game where the game world is constantly changing, independent of player input. In addition to the moving staircases, the program must listen for the player to use the SPACEBAR to control when Tashi attempts to jump off the bottom of a staircase to its base on the floor.

If we reorganize our game description to separate these two constantly-executing pieces (**Stairs animation** and **Controls**) from the main game flow, we have the following:

- **Stairs animation:** While the game is active, the staircases are twisting.
- **Controls:** The player can use the SPACEBAR (event) to tell Tashi to jump

- If Tashi is at the bottom of the staircase when the player presses the SPACEBAR, (conditional)
  - If Tashi is close enough (conditional)
    Tashi makes the jump
  - Else (conditional)
    The player gets a miss (feedback)
- Else Tashi says "Can't jump yet" and player gets a miss (conditional)
- **Main flow of the gameplay:** While the game is active,
  - When Tashi is at the top of a staircase, she will automatically travel to the bottom
  - If the player misses more than three times (conditional)
    - Tashi gives up and the player loses the game (fail condition)
  - If Tashi and Esther reaches the ground level (conditional)
    - The player wins the game (win condition)

13.9 Implementation: Stairs Animation

Let's begin the game implementation by creating the looping staircase animation that must run throughout the game. A *sceneActivated* event listener will be used. This will allow the staircase animation loop to run independent of other parts of the game. To start, click the *initializeEventListeners* tab and then the Add Event Listener button. Select Scene Activation/ Time and then addSceneActivationListener in the cascading menus (Figure 13.38).

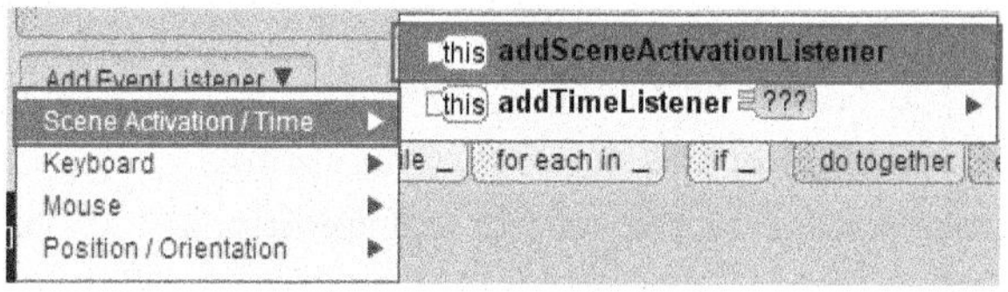

Figure 13.38 *Add a* SceneActivation *listener.*

Alice already has a *sceneActivated* listener, but creates a second *sceneActivated* code block in the event listener's tab. Add a comment to the new code block, describing the movement of the stairs (Figure 13.39).

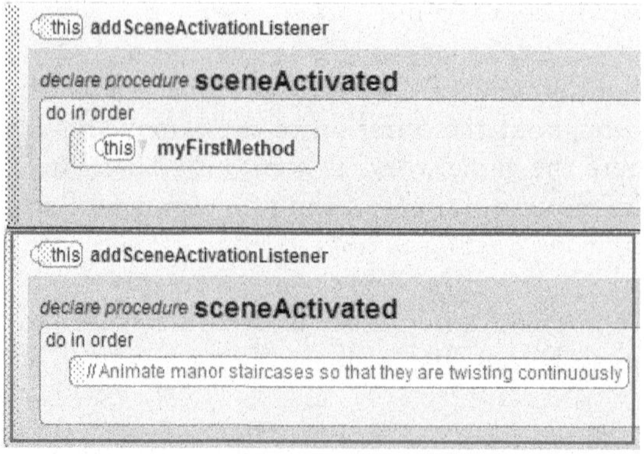

Figure 13.39 *A new* sceneActivated *listener for twisting stairs*

Now it is time to create the code to twist the stairs. Figure 13.40 is a close-up shot of a staircase object. The staircase is a sequence of steps—an array of skeletal joints with a joint on each step.

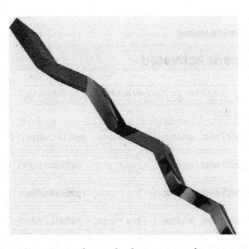

Figure 13.40   *A staircase has a built-in array of joints, one on each step.*

13.9.1 Stair-twisting helper procedure

Because the manor has several staircases, it will be convenient to have a helper procedure that can be used to twist any staircase object. Declare a new *twistStairs* procedure in the Scene class. In the *twistStairs* editor tab, enter code statements to twist the joints in each step of a built-in *stairs[]* array (Figure 13.41). Declare two parameters: *anArray* for an array of skeletal joints in a staircase, and *timing*, which specifies a duration.

Turning the joints is implemented using an *each in together* code block so that all joints are turning backward at the same time. The second *each in together* code block turns all joints forward, thereby returning the steps to their original position.

```
declare procedure twistStairs with parameters: ( SJoint[] ( anArray ,  ( DecimalNumber )  timing )
do in order
    // assumes: stairs are in original position
    // turns all joints in the joints array at the same time
    // returns the stairs to the original position

    each ( SJoint )( stepI in ( anArray )  together
        ( stepI )  turn ( BACKWARD ) , ( 0.05 ) , duration ( timing )   add detail

    each ( SJoint )( stepJ in ( anArray )  together
        ( stepJ )  turn ( FORWARD ) , ( 0.05 ) , duration ( timing )   add detail
```

Figure 13.41   twistStairs *procedure*

13.9.2 Using an infinite *while* loop

The *twistStairs* procedure will animate the stairs up and down once. To make this animation repeat endlessly, we will call it from within a *while* loop code block with *true* as the *while* conditional. Because *true* is always true, the loop will continue without stopping.

13.10.1 Set up the game

Code statements in the *playOpeningCutscene* procedure have already positioned Tashi and Esther on the roof of the temple, near the top of the attic stairs. The camera still needs to be repositioned to provide a clear view to the player for Tashi and Esther descending all the staircases. Write a code statement to change the camera viewpoint to the *stairCasesShot* camera marker (Figure 13.47). This will give the player a view of the entire manor during the game. Test-run.

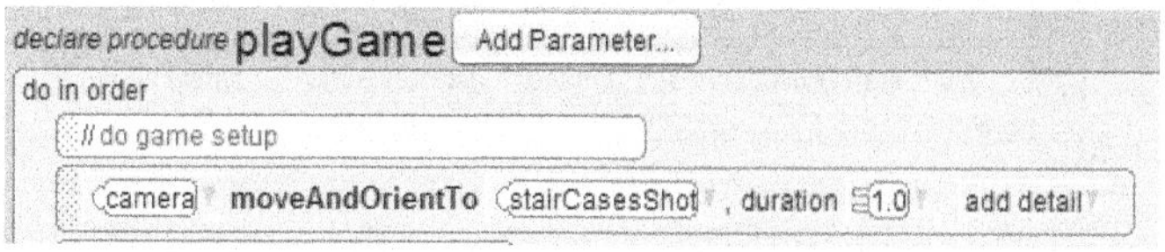

Figure 13.47   *Position the camera for viewing the staircases.*

Tracking variables are needed for each of the following:

- the count of the number of times the player has missed (*misses*)
- determining if Tashi and Esther are on the bottom step of a staircase (*onBottomStep*)
- determining if the game is active (*gameActive*)
- the base of the current staircase (*baseOfStairCase*)
- the number of the current staircase (*stairCase*)

Tracking variables are typically checked and/or updated in more than one procedure while the game is running. For this reason, tracking variables are often declared and initialized in the Scene class. In the Scene class tab, declare the four tracking variables in Properties and initialize, as shown in Figure 13.48.

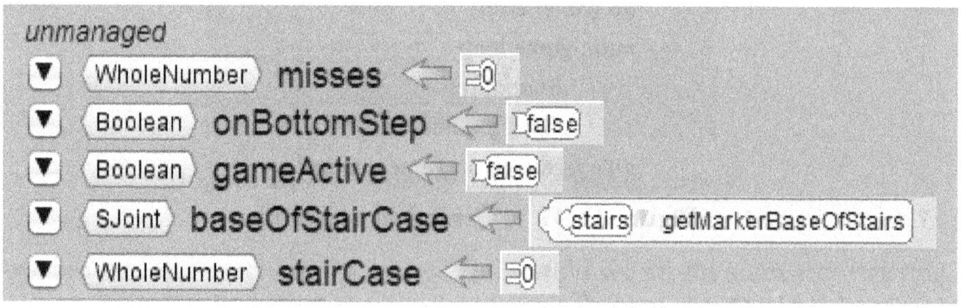

Figure 13.48   *Declare the tracking variables in the Scene class.*

13.10.2 The main game loop

The next step is a main game loop. Return to the *playGame* tab. Add a statement to set the *gameActive* tracking value to *true*. Then, below the comment *//main game loop*, add a *while* loop. Select *gameActive* as the loop condition. Figure 13.49 shows the code that should be in the *playGame* procedure so far.

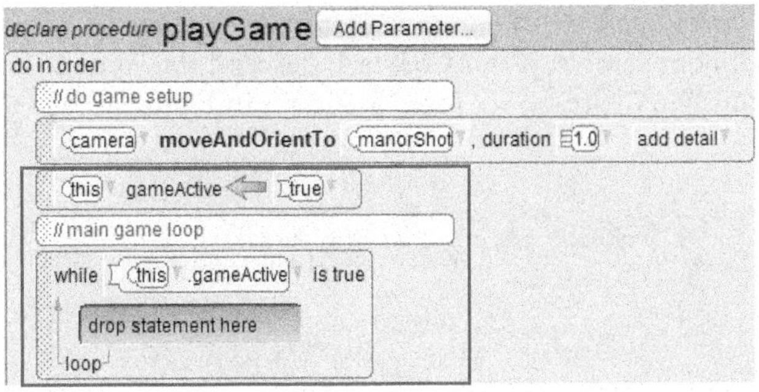

Figure 13.49 *Use* gameActive *as the condition for the main game loop.*

If you test-run the program at this time, you will see the attic staircase still moves into camera view while Tashi and Esther are talking. We can now use the *gameActive* tracking variable to fix this issue. Return to the *sceneActivated* event listener. Inside the first *while true* loop, add an *if/else* control structure. Use *this.gameActive* as the condition. Then, move the call to *stairTwist* inside the *if* part of the *if/else* code block (Figure 13.50).

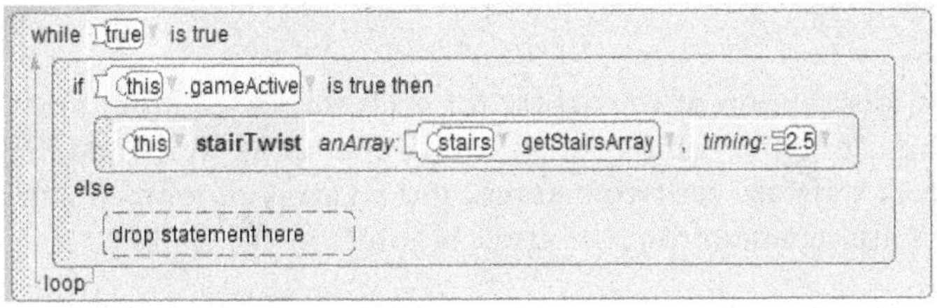

Figure 13.50 *Using* gameActive *in the* sceneActivated *listener to control twisting stairs*

Test-run. The attic stairs will only twist if the game is active.

13.10.3 Updates

The main game play loop has two basic components: *do updates* and *check end conditions*. In this example, updates are primarily dependent on Tashi and Esther's descent on the staircases and the player pressing the SPACEBAR to signal a jump. Tashi and Esther will descend four staircases, in sequence: *stairs, stairsW, stairsX,* and *stairsY*. The staircases have varying numbers of steps and different names, so the *stairCase* tracking variable will be used to track the current staircase. Initially, the *stairCase* tracking variable was assigned 0. On each iteration of the *while* loop, Tashi will descend the next staircase. This means that every time through the loop, the *stairCase* tracking variable must be updated by adding 1. Add a statement inside the *while* loop to add 1 to *stairCase* (Figure 13.51).

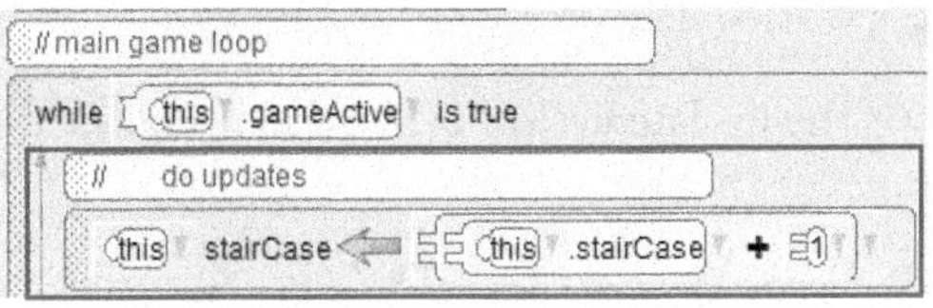

Figure 13.51 *Increment* stairCase *by 1 with each loop repetition.*

The number in *stairCase* will be used to determine which set of stairs that Tashi and Esther will descend. For example, if *stairCase* is 1, descend the stairs in the attic. If *stairCase* is 2, descend the *stairsW*. A bare-bones logic is shown in Figure 13.52.

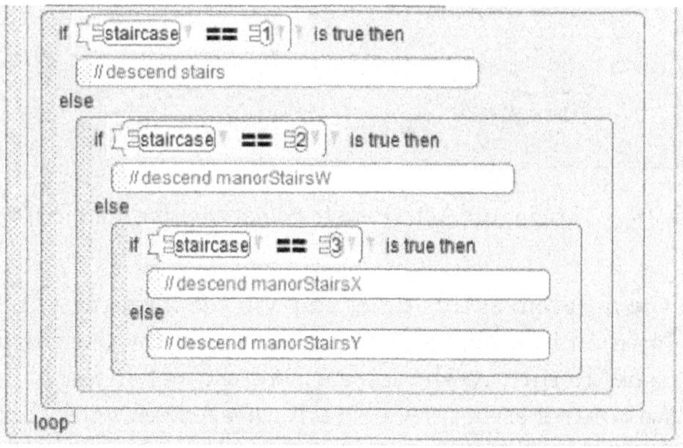

```
if    staircase    ==    1    is true then
      // descend stairs
else
      if    staircase    ==    2    is true then
            // descend manorStairsW
      else
            if    staircase    ==    3    is true then
                  // descend manorStairsX
            else
                  // descend manorStairsY
loop
```

Figure 13.52   *Bare-bones logic of* updateTashiPosition

A high-level description of the action for each staircase is the same: descend a staircase. To break this action into simpler steps, think about how Tashi and Esther will descend a single staircase. A staircase has two markers and an array of joints (Figure 13.53). The top and base markers are separate from the array of joints in the stairs.

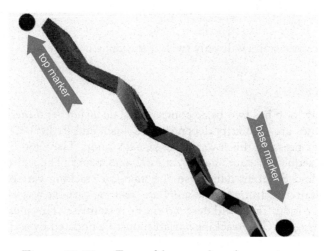

Figure 13.53   *Top and base markers for a staircase*

A decomposition for the update action is shown in Figure 13.54.

do in order

> Tashi and Esther move and orient to top marker
> Tashi and Esther descend a staircase
> update *baseOfStairCase* (tracking variable)

Figure 13.54 ● *Decomposition for update action*

Tashi and Esther will first move to the top marker. Then, descend the stairs, one step at a time. Finally, they will wait for the player's keypress before attempting a jump to the base marker. We don't know exactly when the player will press the SPACEBAR, so the *baseOf-StairCase*, tracking variable should be updated for use, when needed. To implement the update action, declare a custom procedure named *updateTashiPosition* in the Scene class.

Add comments to document the precondition, action, and postcondition. Then, add statements in nested if/else code structures to have Tashi and Esther descend the current set of stairs (Figure 13.55).

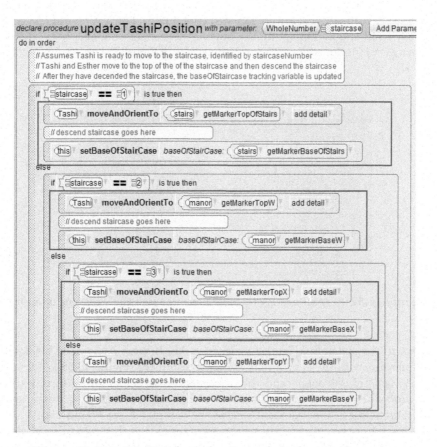

Figure 13.55 ● *Updates for each staircase have the same three steps.*

Each *if/else* code segment is basically the same, except that the actions are performed with a different staircase. A comment in each code block indicates the code for descending the steps one by one is yet to be added. Once again, this is the same code in each code block. This is an example of a good place to use a helper procedure. A helper procedure will allow us to write the code once and call it four times. A decomposition for a helper procedure to descend a staircase is shown in Figure 13.56.

do in order

    Tashi and Esther move down the steps, one at a time

    // Tashi and Esther are on the bottom step

Figure 13.56   *Decomposition for* descendStaircase

Declare a new procedure, named *descendStaircase*, for the Scene class. The helper procedure must be sent the name of the staircase to be descended. So, add a parameter, named *staircase*, of type *SJoint[]*. Add comments to document any assumptions, actions, and post-conditions.

Create a *for each in* code block to move Tashi (and Esther) through the sequence of steps one at a time. Then set Tashi's vehicle to the step. (Otherwise, when the twisting staircase moves away, Tashi and Esther are left suspended in mid-air.) When the *for each in* loop is completed, Tashi and Esther are on the bottom step of the stairs array for that staircase. After the *for each in* loop, add a statement to set the *onBottomStep* tracking variable to *true* (Figure 13.57).

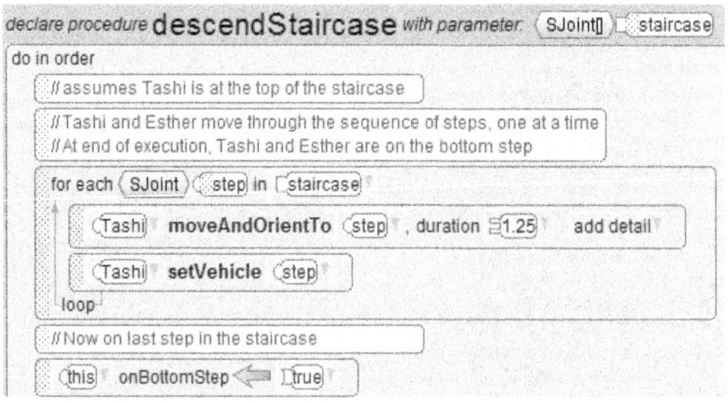

Figure 13.57   *Tashi and Esther move down the staircase steps, one at a time.*

Return to the *updateTashiPosition* procedure tab. In each *if/else* code block, add a call to *descendStaircase*, with the appropriate staircase argument (Figure 13.58).

To test *updateTashiPosition* and the *descendStaircase* helper procedure, return to the *playGame* procedure tab and add a statement to the main game loop that calls *updateTashiPosition*. Use *stairCase* as the argument sent to the parameter, see Figure 13.59.

Test-run. After the cutscene animation, you should see Tashi and Esther descend the staircases. Tashi and Esther proceed from one staircase to the next, starting with the stairs in the attic. Tashi and Esther do not hesitate between staircases because, as of yet, no code has been written to have them wait for the player's SPACEBAR keypress. And a keypress event listener has not yet been implemented. These actions will be implemented next.

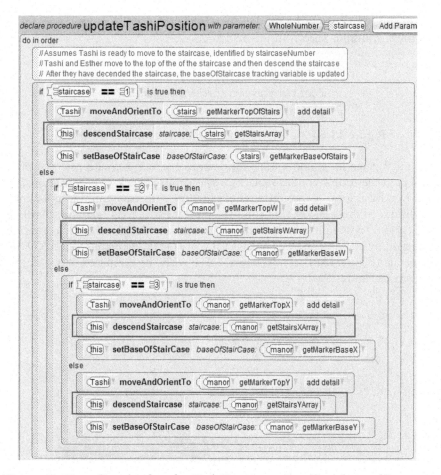

Figure 13.58 *Completed* updateTashiPosition *with calls to* descendStaircase

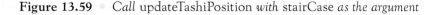

Figure 13.59 *Call* updateTashiPosition *with* stairCase *as the argument*

13.10.4 Interactive control with Binary Operators

After *updateTashiPosition* has executed, Tashi and Esther are on the bottom step of one of the staircases (*onBottomStep* is *true*). The player will now have control of the jump from the bottom step to the base marker on the floor. Tashi and Esther will wait for the player to press the SPACEBAR, a signal to Tashi that she should attempt to jump to the base of the stairs. When the player presses the SPACEBAR, Tashi will either jump (if she is close enough to the base) or reject the jump (in which case, the player misses). The player only gets three misses.

Because more than one jump attempt may be needed, a loop control structure is needed to allow repeated keypresses and track the number of misses. We don't know how many attempts and misses will be needed, so a *while* loop will be used. A decomposition for controlling the jump is shown in Figure 13.60.

> *while onBottomStep* is *true* and *misses* is less than 4
> > wait for the player to press the spacebar
> > attempt jump

Figure 13.60   *Decomposition for player control of the jump*

In the main game loop, add a *while* loop control structure, with *true* as a placeholder condition. The *while* loop's conditional expression must check two conditions, either of which would end the loop. A conditional expression with two conditions is known as a **binary condition**. In this case, BOTH conditions must be *true*: (1) Tashi must still be on the bottom step, and (2) *misses* must be less than four. Replace the placeholder condition with a binary condition by clicking on *true* and selecting BOTH *this.onBottomStep* AND *true* in the cascading menus (Figure 13.61). Then, replace *true* with the condition *this.misses < 4*. The result is shown in Figure 13.62.

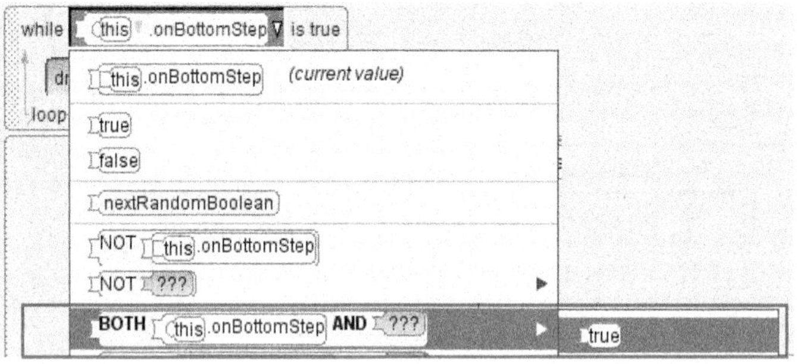

Figure 13.61   *Select BOTH ... AND as the binary condition.*

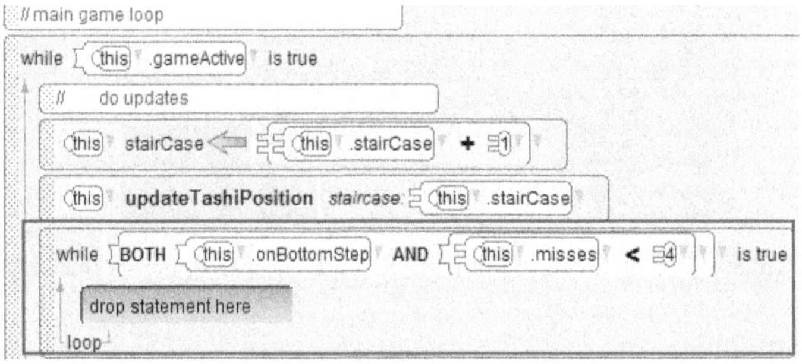

Figure 13.62   *While Tashi is still on the bottom step and number of misses is less than 4*

The **AND** in this binary condition is a **Boolean operator**. A Boolean operator is a symbol that connects two or more conditions to form one complex condition. Alice, like most other programming languages, has three Boolean operators: NOT, AND, and OR.

- **NOT**—The opposite of a truth value.
  - If "hungry" is *true*, NOT "hungry" is *false*.

- **AND**—If BOTH of two truth values are *true*, *true*. Otherwise, *false*.
  - If "hungry" is *true* AND "enough money" is *true*, the result is *true*.
- **OR**—If at least one of two truth values is *true*, *true*. Otherwise, *false*.
  - If "hungry" is *false* OR "enough money" is *true*, the result is *true*.

Within this inner *while* loop, the player must be given control of the jump. Two code elements are needed: a tracking variable that will lock (prevent) a jump, and a keypress event that will unlock (allow) a jump. To create a lock tracking variable, return to the Scene class tab and add a Boolean property, named *locked*. Initialize to *true* (Figure 13.63).

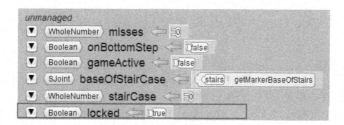

Figure 13.63 ◦ *Declare a tracking variable to lock and unlock attempted jumps.*

Add a *while* loop nested within the first, and select *this.locked* as the condition (Figure 13.64). No statement is needed within this inner *while* loop. Tashi is just patiently waiting on the bottom step.

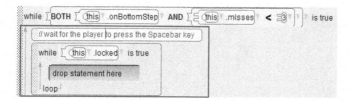

Figure 13.64 ◦ *An inner* while *loop to have Tashi wait until the* SPACEBAR *is pressed*

Now, an event listener is needed to watch for the player to press the SPACEBAR. The listener will unlock the jump (by changing *locked* to *false*). Return to *initializeEventListeners* editor tab and click the Add Event Listener button. Select Keyboard and then *addKeyPressListener* from the cascading menus (Figure 13.65).

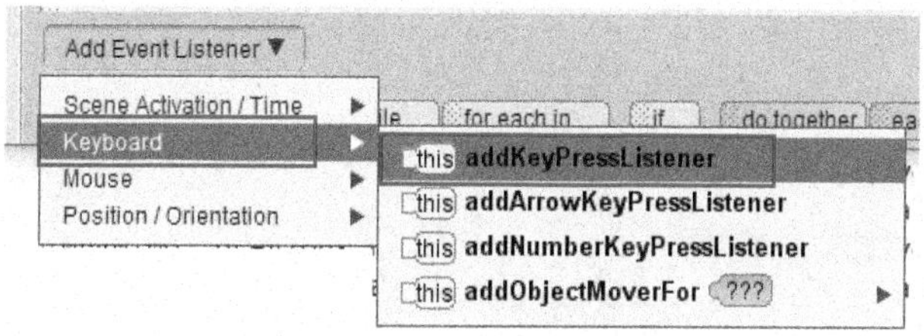

Figure 13.65 ◦ *Adding a KeyPressListener*

In the header for the new *keyPressed* listener code block, click on *multipleEventPolicy* and select IGNORE from the pull-down menu (Figure 13.66). The IGNORE setting tells Alice to ignore repeated SPACEBAR clicks until the current response is completed.

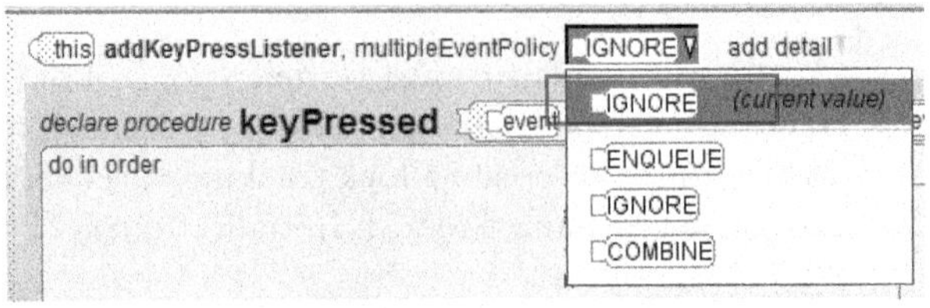

Figure 13.66   *Select the IGNORE multiple event policy.*

A *keyPressed* listener is alert to any key that is pressed on the keyboard. We want only the SPACEBAR, so add an *if/else* control structure to the listener and select *true* as a placeholder condition. Then, drag the *isKey* tile and drop it on top of *true*. Select *Custom Key* from the dropdown menu. A dialog box pops up where you can press the SPACEBAR (Figure 13.67). The resulting *if/else* code block is shown in Figure 13.68.

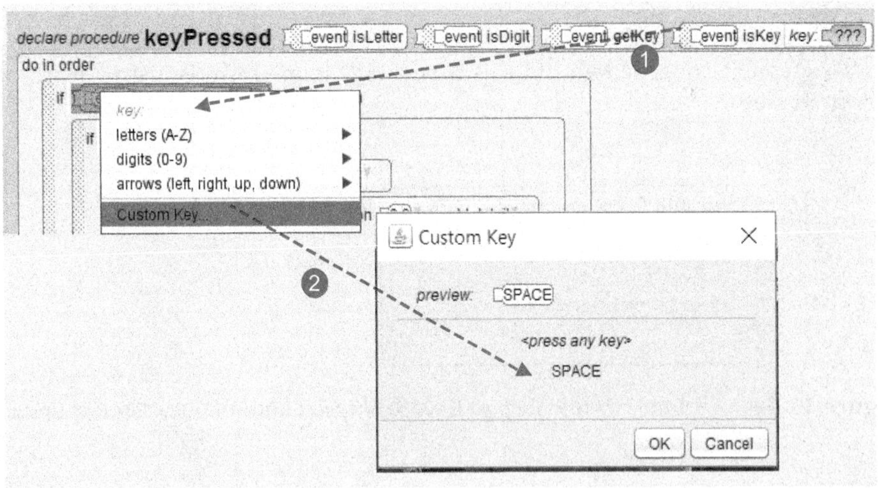

Figure 13.67   *Select the SPACEBAR as the key.*

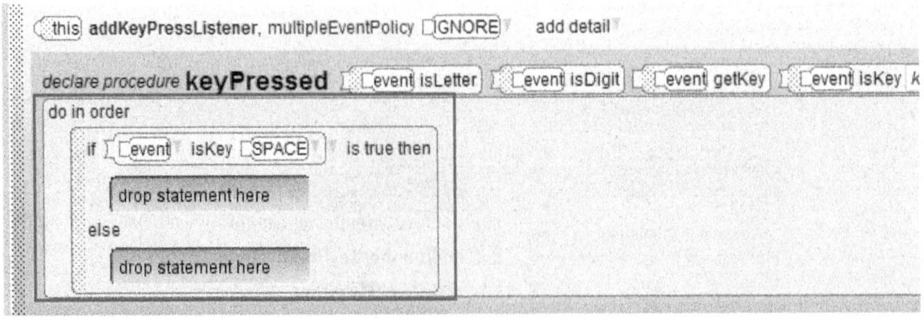

Figure 13.68   *Resulting condition for the space keypress*

It is possible for the player to press the SPACEBAR at any time, even when Tashi and Esther are not on the bottom step in the staircase. To avoid responding to this situation, modify the conditional expression by adding a second condition that requires *onBottomStep* is also *true* (Figure 13.69). Now, pressing the SPACEBAR will only work when Tashi is on the bottom step of a staircase.

Finally, add a statement that sets the *locked* tracking variable to *false* (Figure 13.70).

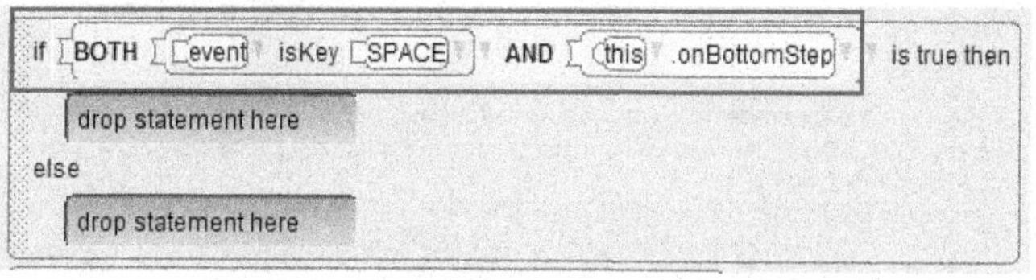

Figure 13.69 • *Binary condition,* SPACEBAR *press AND* onBottomStep

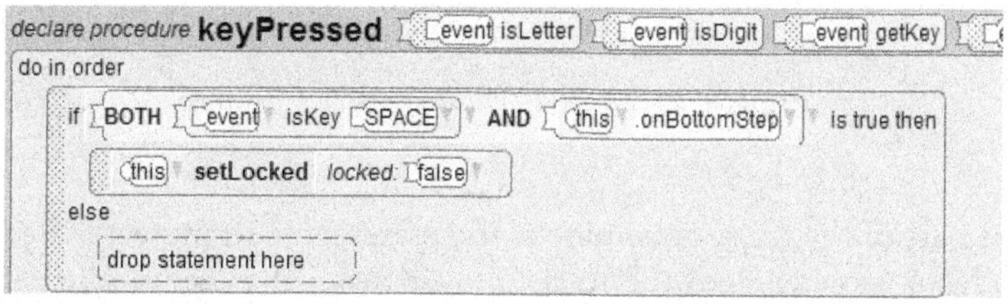

Figure 13.70 • *When* SPACEBAR *is pressed, set* locked *to* false

The *locked* tracking variable and *keyPressed* event listener are now in place, giving the player control of timing for the jump. When the player presses the SPACEBAR, the jump is unlocked and the *while locked* loop ends. Tashi and Esther are free to jump. A decomposition for a jump attempt is shown in Figure 13.71.

> do in order
>
> > if Tashi is close enough to the base marker
> > > Tashi jump to the *base*
> > > Tashi set *vehicle* to *base*
> > > reset *onBottomStep* to *false*
> > else
> > > Tashi say "Too far to jump"
> > > add 1 to *misses*

Figure 13.71 • *Decomposition for a jump attempt*

Declare a new procedure in the Scene class named *attemptJump*. The procedure must be sent the name of the target base marker. Add a parameter, named *base*, of type SJoint. Add comments to document any assumptions, actions, and post conditions. The first step in the *attemptJump* procedure is a check of the distance between Tashi and the base marker. In this example, we selected a distance less than 0.075 meters. You may adjust this distance, if you wish. Add an *if/else* code block to the procedure. In the *if* segment of the *if/else* code block, add statements to move Tashi and set her vehicle to the base. Then, add a statement to reset the *onBottomStep* tracking variable to *false* (Figure 13.72).

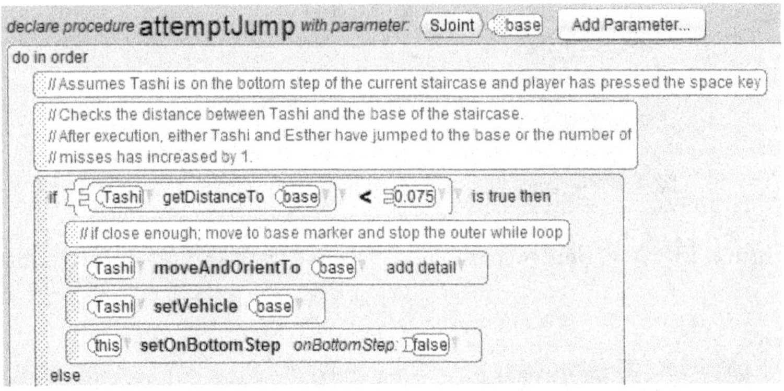

Figure 13.72   *If within 0.075 m., jump*

In the *else* part of the *if/else* code block, add statements to increase the count of misses by 1 and have Tashi provide feedback to the player regarding the number of misses (Figure 13.73).

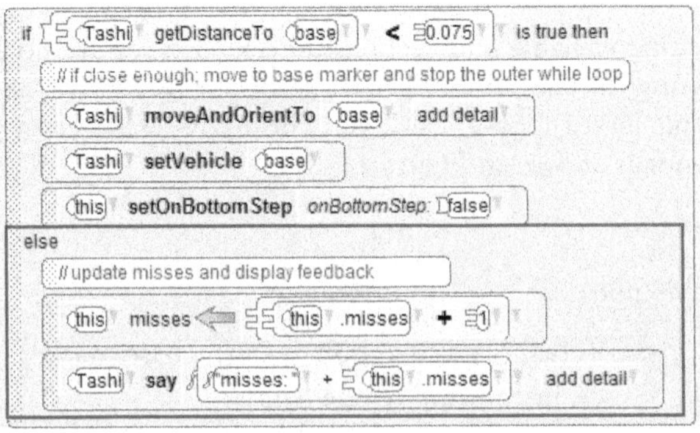

Figure 13.73   *Otherwise, increase misses count and provide feedback.*

Return to the playGame editor tab. After the *while locked* loop, add a statement to call *attemptJump* and send the *baseOfStairCase* tracking variable as an argument to the *base* parameter. Then, add a statement to reset *locked* to *true* (Figure 13.74).

13.10.5 Testing and debugging interactivity

Test-run. You should see Tashi and Esther remain on the bottom step until you press the SPACEBAR. Your testing efforts should include several possibilities:

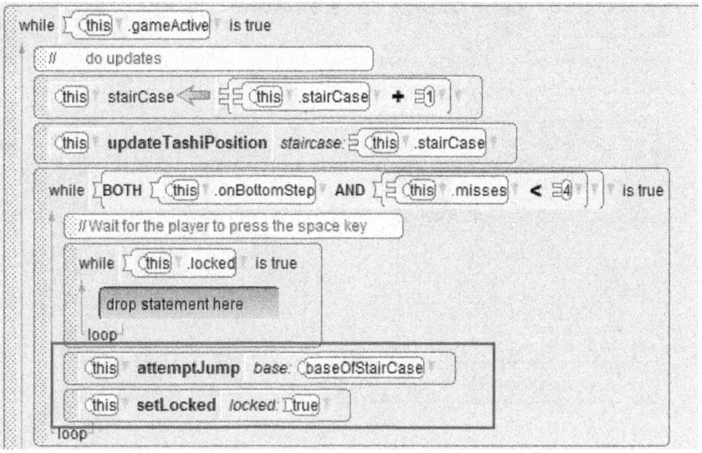

Figure 13.74   *Add statements to attempt a jump and reset the locked tracking variable.*

- Try pressing the SPACEBAR when you are sure they are on the bottom step.
- Try pressing the SPACEBAR when they are on the bottom step but not close enough to jump.
- Try missing four times, to see if the loop ends and no more jumps are allowed.
- Try pressing the SPACEBAR while they are descending the staircase but aren't at the bottom.

You may have discovered the count of misses does not increase when the SPACEBAR is pressed while they are still descending the staircase. This is a bug in the *keyPressed* event. Fixing this bug requires a tracking variable for the *descending* action and added code for the *keyPressed* event. Begin by returning to the Scene class tab and adding a tracking variable, named *descending*, of type Boolean. Initialize to *true* (Figure 13.75).

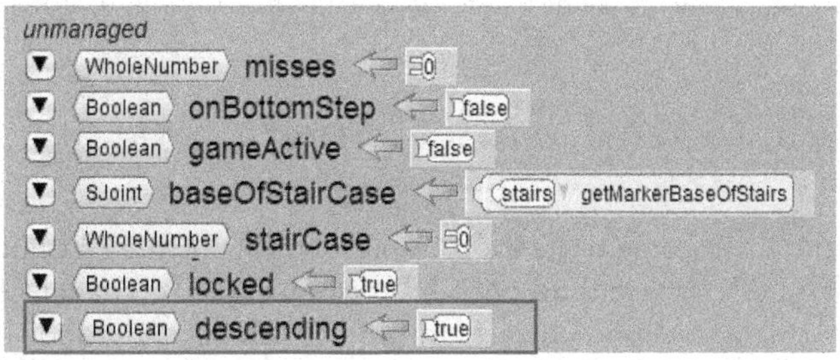

Figure 13.75   *Add a tracking variable, descending.*

Now, return to the *descendStaircase* procedure and add statements to set descending to true at the beginning and reset it to false at the end of the code block (Figure 13.76).

Finally, return to the *keyPressed* event listener. Add a second *if/else* code block, nesting it within the *else* segment of the first *if/else*. Create a binary condition expression for the

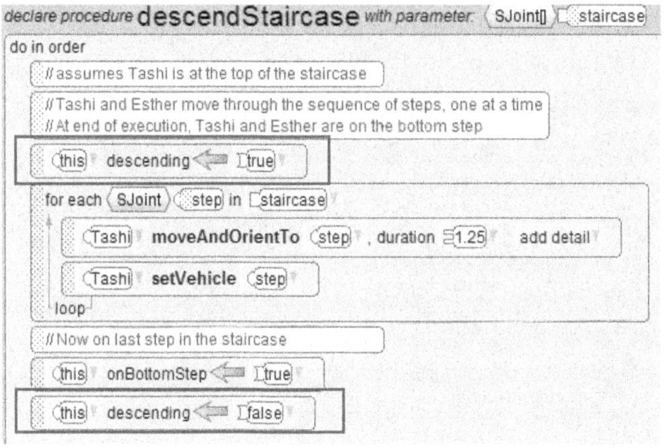

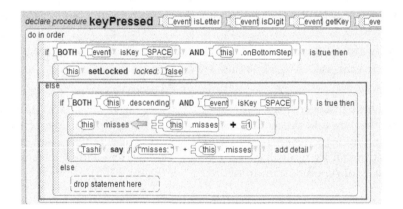

Figure 13.76   *Add statements to set* descending *at beginning and end of the code block.*

inner *if* statement that checks BOTH descending and SPACEBAR press (Figure 13.77). Then, add statements within the inner *if* segment to increase the count of misses and display feedback to the player. Test-run again.

Figure 13.77   *If the* SPACEBAR *is pressed while descending, a miss is counted.*

13.11 Check Game End Conditions

As written so far, the main game *while* loop in *playGame* is infinite because the *gameActive* condition was initialized to *true* and no code has been written to change *gameActive* to *false*. The value of *gameActive* should be changed to *false* when an end condition has been met. The game has two end conditions, one win and one fail. If Tashi and Esther have successfully descended all four staircases, the game is over and the player wins. Or, if the number of misses is greater than three, the game is over and the player loses.

Add an *if/else* code block in the main game loop with *true* as a placeholder condition. Replace the placeholder condition with a binary condition using the OR binary operator. The first condition is *staircaseNumber* equals 4 and the second condition is misses >= 3. In either case, the game is over. So, add a statement in the *if* part to set *gameActive* to *false* (Figure 13.78).

Test-run. You should see the game end if you are able to navigate Tashi and Esther to descend all four staircases. Or, if you have more than three misses, the game should end.

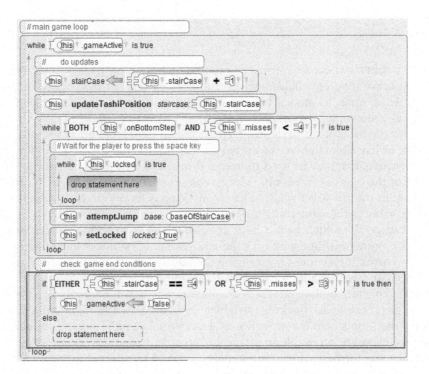

Figure 13.78 • *Completed main game loop with a check on end conditions*

13.12 Feedback for Win or Loss

When the *while* loop ends, it is time to give feedback to the player for win or loss. In the *playGame* procedure, add an *if/else* control construct after the main game *while* loop. Create a binary condition expression that evaluates whether *misses* is less than or equal to 3 and staircase equals 4. In the *if* segment, add statements that have Esther and Tashi turn to face Larry. Also add statements to have Esther and Larry greet one another (Figure 13.79). The *else* segment handles a loss, which means Tashi and Esther did not make it to the ground level. Add statements to the *else* segment to set Tashi's vehicle to *this* scene and have Esther say she can't make it to the ground level.

```
// feedback
if [BOTH [ (this) .misses  ≤ ⋮3 ]  AND [ (this) .stairCase  == ⋮4 ]]  is true then
    do together
        (Tashi)  turnToFace  (Larry)   add detail
        (Esther)  turnToFace  (Larry)   add detail
        (Esther)  moveToward  (Larry)  ⋮1.0   add detail
    (Larry)  talkAndSay  words: ♪"Esther! You did it." , seconds: ⋮4.0
else
    (Tashi)  setVehicle  (this)
    (Esther)  say  ♪"We'll never make it! I give up!" , duration ⋮5.0   add detail
```

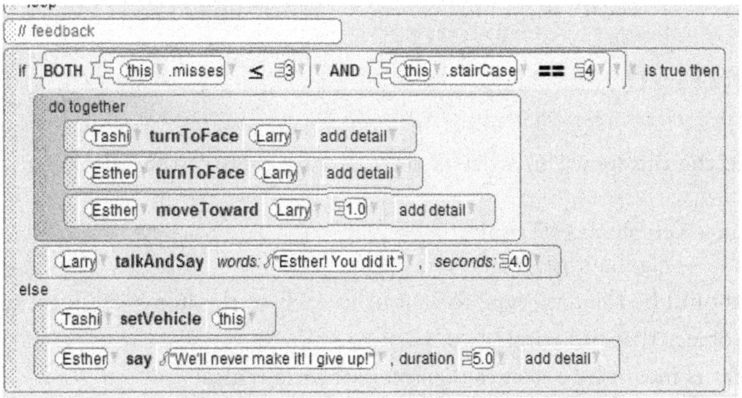

Figure 13.79 • *Display feedback for win or lose.*

Summary

An array is a data structure that stores an ordered collection of items of the same type. The items in an array may be values such as numbers or text strings, or the items may be objects. In Alice, some 3D models have a built-in array of skeletal joints, which is useful for programming animation subparts, for example, an elephant's trunk.

We use the term *access* to describe retrieving an item from an array, storing an item in the array, or having an item in the array perform some action. Alice provides two special *for loop* constructs that may be used to iterate through an array and access the items in the array. One of the loops is *for each in*, which accesses one item at a time in succession from the first item in the array to the last. The second loop is *for each together*, which accesses all items in the array at the same time.

Some Alice 3D models have a built-in pose, which is a specific pattern or configuration of a set of joints within the object's skeletal system. A pose may be animated by calling a built-in or custom procedure for arranging the skeletal joints in a given configuration. For example, the Bat class has a built-in pose for spreading its wings.

In this chapter, built-in arrays were illustrated in the context of a cutscene and interactive game example. Tracking variables were used in the main game loop and in procedures that implement the sequence of actions in a game. Tracking variables declared in the Scene class are accessible in all procedures defined in the Scene class. A *keyPress* event listener was introduced to give the player control of selected actions while the game is running. A Scene activation event listener was introduced as a technique for initiating an action that occurs at the beginning of the game and continues while the game is being played. In games programming, end conditions must be evaluated to determine win or loss. Often more than one condition must be evaluated in order to determine the flow of the game. In such cases, Boolean operators (NOT, AND and OR) may be used to create binary expressions for evaluating the conditions.

Terms

array	*for each in*	*keyPress* event listener
binary condition	index	ordered array
Boolean operator	items in an array	pose
each in together	iterate through an array	unrolled code structure

Concept Questions

1. Indicate the difference in what is retrieved by each of the following statements (be specific):
   (a) snout ← elephant.getTrunk
   (b) snout ← elephant.getTrunkArray
2. What should be the data type for snout in each of the items in Question 1, above?
3. For an object that has wings:
   (a) What is meant by a *joint configuration* for the wings?
   (b) What kind of built-in procedure is designed to change a joint configuration for the wings?

4. Each of the following describes a programming task involving multiple joints. Indicate which control structure is most likely appropriate for implementing the task: (A) *for each in*, (B) *each in together*, (C) Both A and B, (D) Neither A nor B. Justify your answer.

   (a) A falcon turns its neck to view a mouse that is running on the ground
   (b) A mother bird wraps a wing around a new hatchling
   (c) A train follows a path of joints on a railroad track
   (d) A *longNeckSnail* slowly turns its shell

5. What is meant by the phrase, "An array contains an ordered sequence of items"?

6. Up to now, two event listeners have been introduced to work with keys on the keyboard: an *ObjectMover* (Chapter 11) and a *keyPress* listener (this chapter). Briefly compare the expected actions when these event listeners fire.

Exercises
....

1. Re-create the example game project presented in this chapter (or obtain a copy from your instructor.) In the final scene, if Tashi and Esther have successfully descended all four staircases to the ground floor of the manor, the bell (hanging on the rooftop) should start ringing. Import a bell-ring sound clip as a resource for the project. Then, create a *ring* method for the Bell class. To test, in *myFirstMethod* add a counted loop control structure at the end that rings the bell five times. Set the fog density to slowly fade the scene as the bell rings.

2. Modify the game animation to make it more challenging for the player. Instead of having Tashi say "Too far to jump" and allowing Tashi and Esther to stay on the bottom step until the player presses the SPACEBAR again, Tashi and Esther fall off the stairs and tumble to the ground. Then, reposition Tashi and Esther at the top of the first set of stairs to continue the game. In order to win the game, the player will need to press the SPACEBAR at just the right time for all four staircases in sequence.

The remaining exercises are practice for working with poses and built-in arrays.

3. Create a world containing two peacocks (Flyer). The dominant peacock uses his tail to intimidate the younger peacock. Create an animation where one peacock spreads his tail plumage and the other peacock bows his head. Use a *pose* procedure for spreading the tail plumage and a *for each in* loop control to bow the head using the array of joints in the peacock's neck. Add a *count* variable that counts the number of iterations in the *for each in* loop. Then have the peacock say the number of iterations, which is the number of joints in the neck array.

4. Create a world with a *longNeckSnail* and a snail house, as shown here. Create an animation where the snail turns to look at the camera and the camera zooms in for a close-up shot of the snail. Then, use an *each in together* loop control to have the snail's eyes turn curl inward, creating a parentheses-like effect. Then, use a *straightenOut-Joints* to return the eyes to their original pose. Run to test the code.

    Next, create a copy of the *each in together* loop and paste it below the *straightenOut-Joints* statement. Add a *moveToward* camera (0.25 m) statement for each eye in this second *each in together* code block. Create a second *straightenOutJoints* to return the eyes to their original pose after the second *each in together* loop. Run again. What is different?

5. Create a world with three quadrupeds (cat, dog, and squirrel), as shown here. The three quadrupeds have tails of varying lengths. Write a procedure in the Quadruped class to wag a tail. Then test the procedure with each animal. Adjust the number of revolutions for the *turn* of the tail joints so the wagging tail has a reasonable swing, regardless of which animal is wagging its tail.

6. Create a world using the Fantasy Template and add a baby dragon to the scene, as shown next. Create a *wrapTail* procedure for the BabyDragon class. The *wrapTail* procedure should curl the tail around to one side of the dragon. In *myFirstMethod*, write code to pose the dragon in a sitting position and wrap its tail around.

Project (Open Ended)

Create your own interactive animation for a story segment you have selected from another source. Your project should make use of built-in joint arrays and poses. Use at least two objects with different joint arrays and at least one *keyPress* event listener (not an *Object-Mover* event listener).

EPISODE 8

March 1, 1910:
Adelaide

••

The Reanimated Zombie Kittens

Adelaide knows the avalanche is coming before it does. Usually her cats seek shelter from a storm—the first sign of a change in weather. Now that she's alone she expected no warning. But her own hair is standing on end, and she can't seem to relax. There's an ache in her bones, and she doesn't smell snow. She smells warm rain. Something isn't right. She goes to the engine to warn Larry and tells him to take the train into the tunnel. She doesn't wait while he and Esther get the train running; instead she returns directly to her passenger car.

She never makes it. Right before she opens the door, she sees the silent wall of white approaching. It's nearly eight feet tall, and she barely has time to take a breath or yell a warning before the snow hits. The avalanche knocks her off her feet, and she clings to the railing for as long as she can. When Adelaide's strength gives out she's flung backwards away from the train, and is suddenly falling. In a flash of white she passes backwards through a hole in the ground and she's surrounded by rock walls. Down and down she goes until finally she flips right side up and lands, lightly, on all four of her feet.

It takes her a moment to comprehend that she has four feet. She bends her legs, the front ones and the back ones. She flexes what used to be her hands and discovers claws. And covering her skin from head to toe is fur.

Looking around, she sees nothing but sand and boulders and a small pool of water inside a large circular cave. The air is hot and smells of the ocean. Adelaide pads over to the water and leans forward over it until she can see her reflection. Big yellow eyes blink back at her. She wrinkles her little pink nose, and whiskers move along with it.

She's as much a cat as her own kittens.

A potion bottle from her magic act is deposited on the sand next to her paw. More bottles litter the pool of water. Surprisingly none of them are broken—the various liquids, herbs, and lotions are still safe inside. At first she wonders how the bottles got there, but then she watches one pop out from an underwater channel and float to the surface of the small pool, and her question is answered. There must be another way out of this cave through the water.

She dips a paw into the pool and shudders, as if every instinct is holding her back. When she puts an entire arm in, she quickly takes it out. The fur on her skin goes soggy and thick when wet. It weighs her down and makes movement slow. She shakes her paw and puts a decent amount of distance between herself and the pool.

She's not going to venture underwater to try and escape. She tells herself it's because she doesn't know for certain how long she would need to hold her breath before reaching the other side. Glass bottles don't need to breathe after all, so aren't a good test case. But really, she just has a strong aversion to wet.

Which means she's stuck in a 15-foot-high cave with nothing but useless bottles of "potion" ingredients.

She assumes she's alone until she hears the pitiful cries of another creature in the center of the cave. A cheeping baby ostrich lies twitching in the ray of light cast down from the hole in the roof.

Adelaide slowly steps forward. She tries to appear as unthreatening as possible, which is hard to do, being a cat approaching an injured bird.

"You fell, didn't you?" Adelaide coos and crouches down next to it.

The little ostrich nods. Its leg is turned in a completely wrong angle.

Adelaide gingerly rolls the ostrich over, "Your leg is broken. I can't ..."

"Oh my god!" A panicked cry from overhead startles Adelaide. A small pebble pings off Adelaide's forehead and scatters into the recesses of the cave.

Adelaide looks up and sees the long neck and head of an older ostrich and a hippo glaring down at her from the cave opening.

"Get away from my baby!" the ostrich screeches.

Adelaide complies momentarily to collect a few of the bottles from the sand. She then convinces the parent ostrich to allow her to apply a salve over the baby's injuries and to set the broken leg. When the parent is placated, Adelaide carefully starts to feel the ostrich's leg to find the broken point.

Oddly, the baby ostrich relaxes at Adelaide's touch and stops the tiny cheeps of pain. The minute Adelaide takes her hand away, the ostrich springs to his feet with a happy peep and runs off to investigate the cave.

The parent ostrich thanks Adelaide enthusiastically and introduces himself, "My name is Filbert. And this is Tumbo." The hippo waves silently. Filbert continues to fret nervously. Now, about safely getting his son, Mosi, out of the cave, "He can't fly. We need to haul him up somehow, do we have any rope?"

Tumbo promptly disappears for 10 minutes and comes back with a frayed bundle of rope and a bucket. "From the pirate ship," Tumbo offers as explanation.

Hauling Mosi out is the easy part. The tiny ostrich fits in the bucket perfectly. But when they drop the bucket back down and Filbert yells at Adelaide to get in, she can barely fit both feet inside. She ends up sitting awkwardly on the bucket's rim, clinging to the rope. Which snaps when she's halfway up to the cave opening.

Luckily, she lands on her feet again, being a cat.

Tumbo searches, but it turns out there is no more rope. Adelaide is well and truly stuck. She paces in circles around the light from the sun high overhead.

"We'll *bring* you food instead. It's the least we can do. And water. Do you drink water?" Filbert announces and turns to his partner, "We should get it water; it might drink water. Tumbo, you know water, where do we get water?"

Adelaide tries to explain that she's under a curse and has no need to eat or drink, but neither listen and instead send copious amounts of food down by bundling it in leaves and dropping it. Adelaide lets them without fuss. She keeps track of the passing days on the walls, and as the years go on, life trapped in an underwater cave would get lonely if it weren't for her adopted ostrich and hippo family and the gossip they bring along with the food.

"Think nothing of it," says Filbert, "We live on a deserted island, what else is there to do?"

The island becomes a lot less deserted on the 36,500th day when her kittens show up.

A small clowder of black cats appears amidst shimmering light in the middle of the cave. Adelaide almost believes the sight to be a mirage at first, a hallucination brought about by being alone so long. Adelaide stalks around them, examining the ragged, patchy fur and bits of peeling skin. When she reaches out to touch them, their necks and legs are stiff, as if forced into one position for too long. None of the cats move.

Adelaide fixes them. Filbert throws down a sailor's old sewing kit, and Adelaide stitches her kittens back together. When she finishes the first one, and pets its raggedy fur, its eyes turn luminous. The cat stretches and pushes against Adelaide's paw. One by one, the fixed cats take on a life of their own. The reanimated zombie kittens are perhaps not the prettiest creatures, but they're unusually friendly for cats, and they are incredibly loyal. Their knees are stiff and they walk like peg-legged pirates, but they follow Adelaide everywhere and she finds she can communicate with them telepathically.

The zombie kittens are also fiercely protective. Perhaps because, on some molecular level, they understand their existence hinges on Adelaide. So when a swirling vortex of wind opens at one end of the cave and a gigantic train slides through with squealing breaks and sparking wheels, and the zombie kittens take cover behind boulders, they make sure Adelaide hides too.

The tunnel disappears as quickly as it arrived, leaving one section of an engine embedded in the cave wall and still spewing steam. Adelaide sticks her head above the rock and stares. Around her she can sense the zombie kittens doing the same. A skeleton trips down from the cab of the train followed by a miniature yeti. Adelaide immediately recognizes the suit and hat as belonging to her old circus leader. But that was years and years ago, according to her scratched calendar.

"We're alive!" the yeti exclaims gleefully.

The skeleton groans, leaning his head against the train and gasping for breath.

"Hey!" the yeti says again, "Look!" She disappears from sight and quickly reappears holding a black kitten even tinier than herself.

"One of the dead kittens!" the skeleton exclaims.

"Meow," says the kitten.

The skeleton jumps back, startled. As if on cue, the entire cave starts to echo with meows and cat heads of all sizes start popping up from behind the rocks. The cats drop to the floor and start to advance ominously on the train. The movement of their stubby legs is robotic, as if they're a bunch of wind-up toys let loose. Their little cat bodies sway side to side as they teeter along on their tiny paws. The zombie kittens reach the train and form a threatening ring around the intruders. They look ready to pounce, but Adelaide gets there first. She jumps from behind the rock and bounds forward.

"Larry?" Adelaide asks, breathlessly.

Larry's jaw drops open,. "Adelaide?"

The cat smiles in a grin that stretches from ear to ear and starts bouncing in place, emitting excited squeaks, "I can't believe it's you!"

"I know!" Larry exclaims, equally as excited.

The two friends begin talking simultaneously. Tashi stands awkwardly to the side, unable to understand a word.

"A touching reunion, but don't forget we're trapped," Tashi says after the conversation calms down.

"Trapped?" Adelaide asks, confused.

"Our train is stuck and any tunnel will take us back underwater," Larry explains, "Tashi can't breathe underwater. We nearly died getting here. There's no way out."

"Yes, there is! With the help of my friends, we can escape," Adelaide grins and gestures to the kittens surrounding them.

"Your friends the cats ...?" Larry asks skeptically.

"Reanimated stuffed zombie kittens," Adelaide corrects, "Much easier to herd than live cats."

Adelaide spins around and claps her hands, "Okay everyone, line up!"

The kittens hastily make an extremely disorganized line.

"No, not like that," Adelaide chides gently, "In order."

The kittens swap places with each other until the line neatly runs from smallest kitten to tallest.

"Now," Adelaide says, immensely proud, "stack!"

The kittens jump on top of one another, starting from the largest and going down the line. Finally, the tiniest kitten claws her way to the top and the wobbling tower of reanimated zombie kittens reaches the opening in the cave ceiling.

Tashi and Adelaide climb the cats like a ladder and escape through the cave roof. Filbert and Tumbo help pull them to safety at the top. Adelaide then orders the kittens, who are zombies and therefore impervious to drowning, onto the train. Larry, who also doesn't need to breathe underwater thanks to his skeletal state, rings the train bell. Two tunnels open, one behind the train and one in front. Larry pilots the train through the water, and up the ocean floor onto the beach.

Triumphant, Adelaide sends the kittens back into her old train car. An enterprising young ostrich sneaks in with the herd. And when the car disappears and reappears in Adelaide's forest cabin, Adelaide swears she can hear Filbert's anxious cries still echoing off the walls.

snore

14

Custom Arrays and Functions

Concept Objectives

- Creating and initializing a custom array of objects
- Iterating through a custom array
- Accessing a specific item in an array
- Using random access for an item in an array
- Writing and calling a procedure with an array parameter
- Writing a procedure with an array where no parameter is needed
- Writing code for a linear search of an array
- Writing code that calls a *compareTo* function

The programming example in the previous chapter illustrated how to use built-in arrays of skeletal joints. In this chapter, the programming example will illustrate how to define your own **custom array**. In a built-in array, all items in the array are skeletal joints. Similarly, a custom array is composed of items that are all of the same data type.

The items in an array must have some common properties and be able to perform at least some of the same actions. For example, you could create a custom array of Bipeds, all knowing how to *talk*. As with built-in arrays, *for each in* and *each in together* loops are used to iterate through custom arrays.

Two examples will be used in this chapter to illustrate custom arrays and writing program code to animate items in an array. The first example is a quick demo that will illustrate the basic operations for creating and using an array. The second program example will apply these operations and concepts in a more complex animation. The program example animates a selected excerpt from Episode 8, *Adelaide: The Reanimated Zombie Kittens*, in the *Haunted Circus Train* story. In this episode, Tashi and Larry travel through a portal to find Adelaide, the nine-lifed circus enchantress, known for her magical spells and death defying stunts. In her personal train car, Adelaide spent her time rescuing discarded kittens.

14.1 Demo: Basic Operations with a Custom Array

Download *Demo.a3p* from **www.alice.org/Alice3ToJava**. The scene has the theme of the *Adelaide* episode, but is "bare bones" with only a few objects as needed to provide a quick demo of basic operations (Figure 14.1). The scene contains a few flat rocks on a sandy ground surface in a cave. Four StuffedZombieKitten objects, named *kit0*, *kit1*, *kit2*, and *kit3*, have been added to the scene. The kittens are arranged in a row, starting with *kit0* on the

Figure 14.1   *Four zombie kittens on a sandy surface*

left and ending with *kit3* on the right of the screen. The kittens have different heights and eye colors.

Begin by writing code in *myFirstMethod* to have each kitten turn one complete revolution (Figure 14.2). Test-run. You should see each kitten turn around, in the order in which the statements are written.

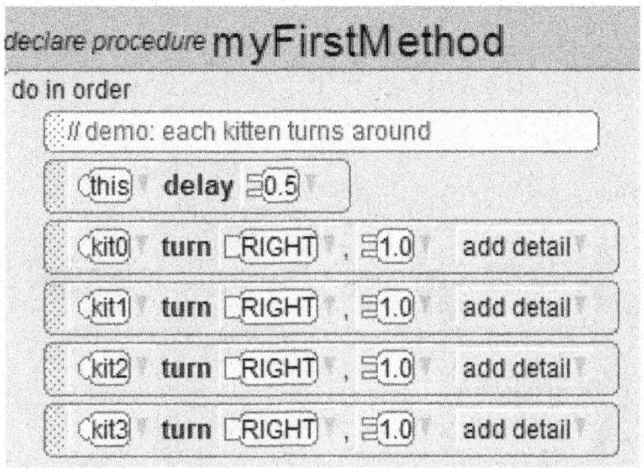

Figure 14.2 • *Each kitten turns one complete revolution.*

This example code is quick and easy to write because there are only four kittens. If there were 20 or 30 kittens, it would be tedious to create statements for each kitten to perform some complex action, such as a dance step in a dance line. In cases where many items are needed, a custom array is a useful **data structure**. A data structure contains a collection of **items** (also known as **elements**) and is stored in some organized format in the computer's memory. This demo will show how to create an array of kittens and write code statements using the array, instead of statements for each individual.

14.1.1 Create and initialize a custom array of objects

As was illustrated with built-in arrays, an array data structure is an **ordered** format. That is, each item is arranged in an indexed position, starting with an index of 0, the next item at index 1, and so forth, to the last item in the array. To create a custom array, begin with a declaration statement for the array name and a data type for the items it will contain. Follow these steps (Figures 14.3 and 14.4):

(1) Drag and drop the variable tile into the editor.
(2) In the Insert Variable dialog box, select the value type (*StuffedZombieKitten*).
(3) Check the *is array* box.
(4) Enter a name for the array (*kittens*).
(5) Click the initializer box.
(6) In the Custom Array dialog box, add objects in the desired sequence.

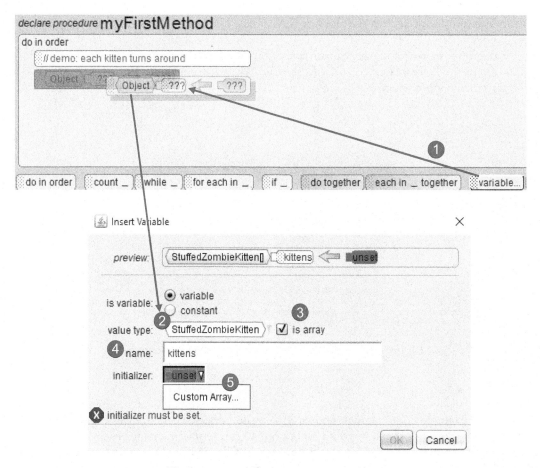

Figure 14.3   *Create a custom array.*

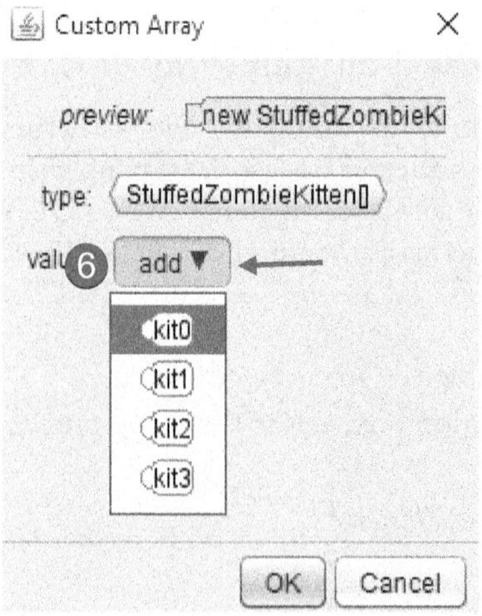

Figure 14.4   *Click the value menu to add objects to the array.*

Figure 14.5 shows the custom array after all four kittens have been added. Note that each kitten's index is displayed in brackets [ ]. When all kittens have been added to the array, click OK.

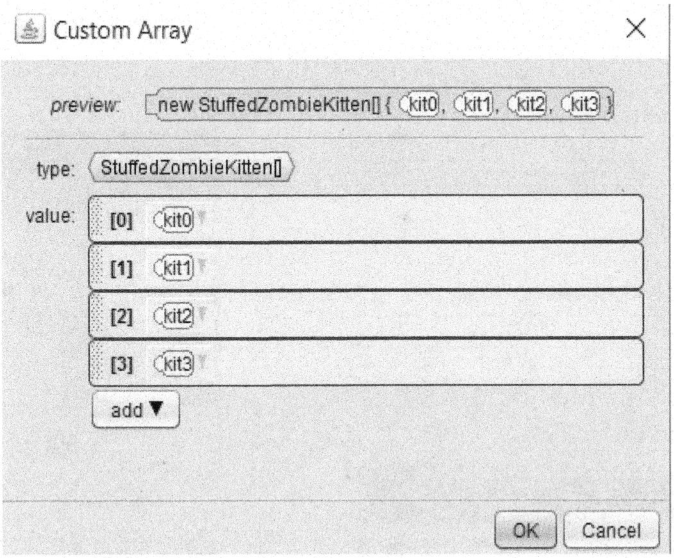

Figure 14.5   *Four kittens added to the array*

The array declaration statement should now be in *myFirstMethod*, as shown in Figure 14.6. (The previously written statements for turning the kittens have been deleted.) Note the pair of brackets in the name, *StuffedZombieKitten*[ ]. As with built-in arrays, the brackets are a syntactic symbol used to write code for an array. As a result of the declaration statement, the four kittens are now organized in an ordered data structure, with kit0 in kittens[0], kit1 in kittens[1], kit2 in kittens[2], and kit3 in kittens[3].

Figure 14.6   *Custom array declaration statement*

In Alice, the length of an array is the number of objects in that array. In this example, the length of the array is 4. Note: Because the index numbering begins at 0, the last item in the array is at index 3.

14.1.2 Iterate through a custom array

Now that we have an array, code can be written for the entire array of kittens. A *for each in* loop structure will iterate through the *kittens* array and turn each kitten around one complete revolution. Create a *for each in* loop structure for a custom array by following these steps (Figure 14.7):

(1) Drag a *for each in* tile into the editor.
(2) In the popup dialog box, select *StuffedZombieKitten* as the item type.
(3) Enter *kit* as the item name.
(4) Select *kittens* as the array and then click OK.

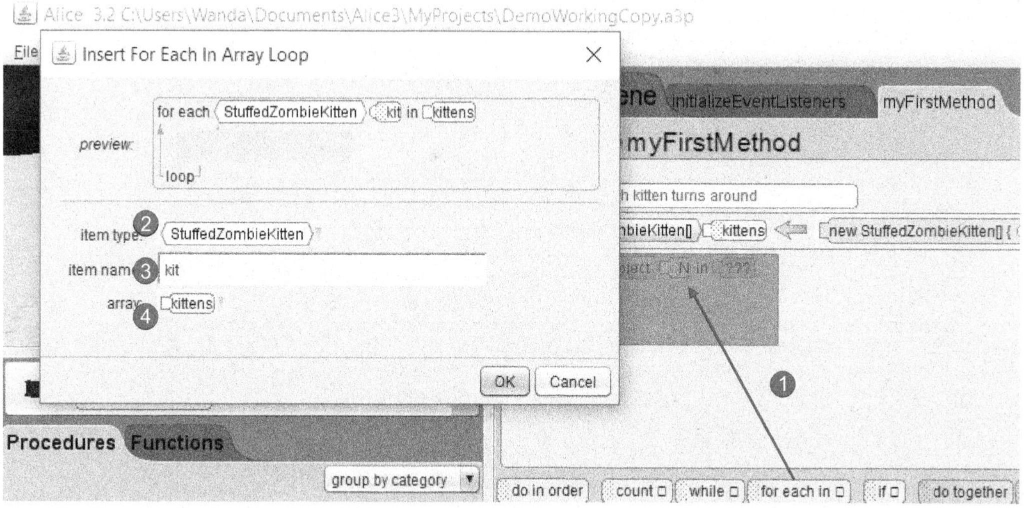

Figure 14.7   *Create a* for each in *loop.*

The "item name" is a variable that will refer to any one of the items in the array. In this example, *kit* is the item name. This means that *kit* may be used as a general reference to any one of the kittens in the array. In *myFirstMethod*, select *kit* in the Object Selector and then drag the *turn* tile to the code block (Figure 14.8). Select RIGHT as the direction and 1.0 as the amount.

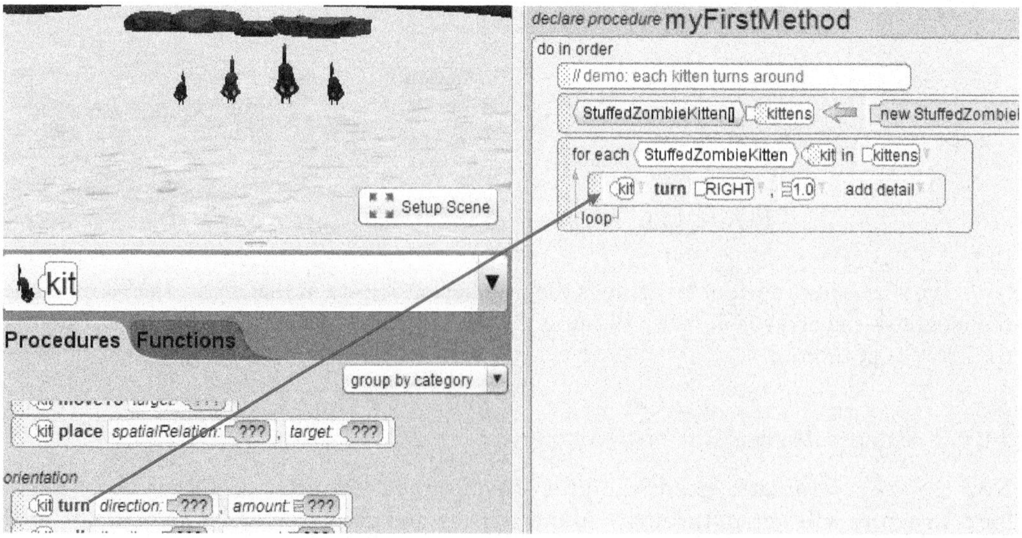

Figure 14.8   *Each* kit *in the* kittens *array turns right, one at a time.*

Test-run the project. When the *for each in* loop executes, the item name *kit* refers to one of the kittens in the *kittens* array, starting with the kitten at index 0 and progressing in order through the array, one kitten at a time. So, as you watch the animation, you should see each kitten turn around, in order, from left to right on the screen.

An *each in together* loop may also be used with a custom array to have all objects in the array perform the same actions at the same time. Use the same set of steps as shown earlier, but drag in an *each in together* loop tile to create a second code block. This time, use the *kittens* array but enter *cat* as the item name. Then create a statement within the *each in together* code block to have the *cat* turn right (Figure 14.9).

Note: Although not required, it is good practice to use a different item name for each loop. Using different item names in different loops makes the code easier to read and debug.

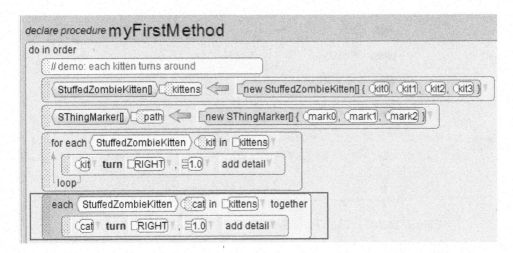

Figure 14.9   *Each cat in the* kittens *array turns right, all at the same time.*

Test-run the program again. Now the kittens each turn right, one at a time (in the *for each in* loop structure), and then all kittens turn right at the same time (in the *each in together* loop).

14.1.3 Access an item in an array

The built-in *for each in* and *each in together* loop are convenient for iterating through all the items in an array. However, as you write code to work with an array of items, you will sometimes want to **access** (retrieve, give an instruction to, or modify) one specific item in the array. To illustrate how to access a single item in an array, let's write a statement to have the last kitten in the array turn left after all the kittens have turned right. (The last kitten is a contrarian and likes to do things her own way.)

First, click the Object Selector to view the list of objects in this scene (Figure 14.10). The Object Selector contains *this* (the scene) and a list of the individual objects within this scene. There is no mention of the *kittens* array because the Object Selector lists individual objects, only.

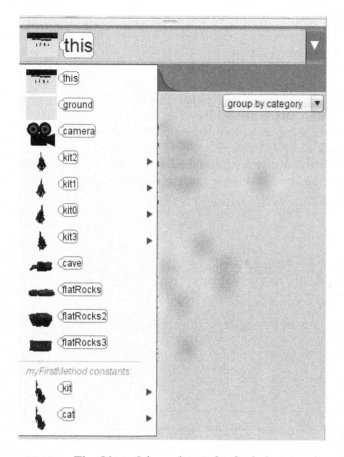

Figure 14.10 *The Object Selector lists individual objects in this scene.*

To work around this issue, just choose one of the kittens as a placeholder object. In the example shown in Figure 14.11, kit0 was selected. Kit0 is not a preference—we just selected one of the kittens. Then, drag kit0's *turn* tile into the editor and drop it to create a statement that turns kit0 left, one revolution.

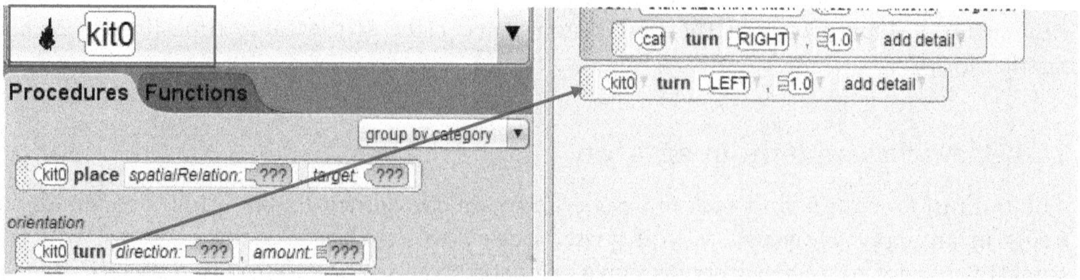

Figure 14.11 *Create a turn statement for kit0.*

Now, to replace the placeholder (kit0) with an item from the *kittens*[] array: Click the object name in the *turn* statement. Then, select the *kittens*[] array and the index, 3, in the cascading menus (Figure 14.12).

The resulting statement is shown in Figure 14.13. The kitten at index 3 in the *kittens*[] array is accessed and given an instruction to *turn* LEFT 1.0 revolution. Test-run. At the end

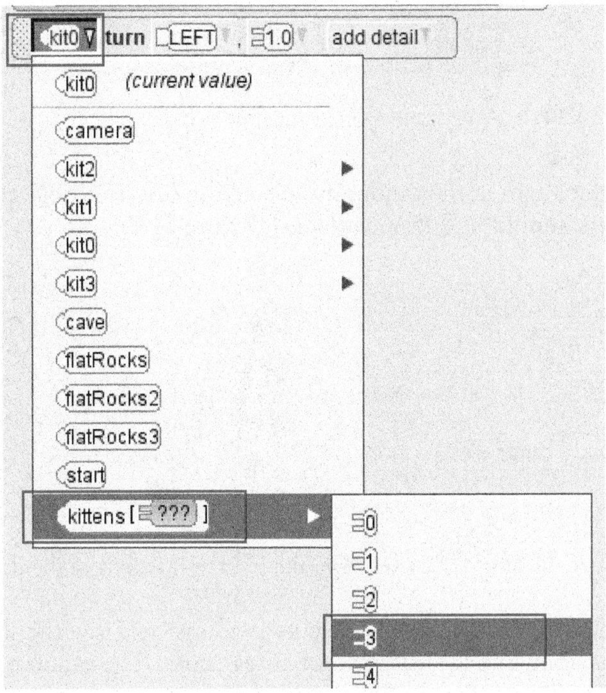

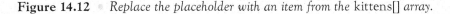

Figure 14.12 ● *Replace the placeholder with an item from the* kittens[] *array.*

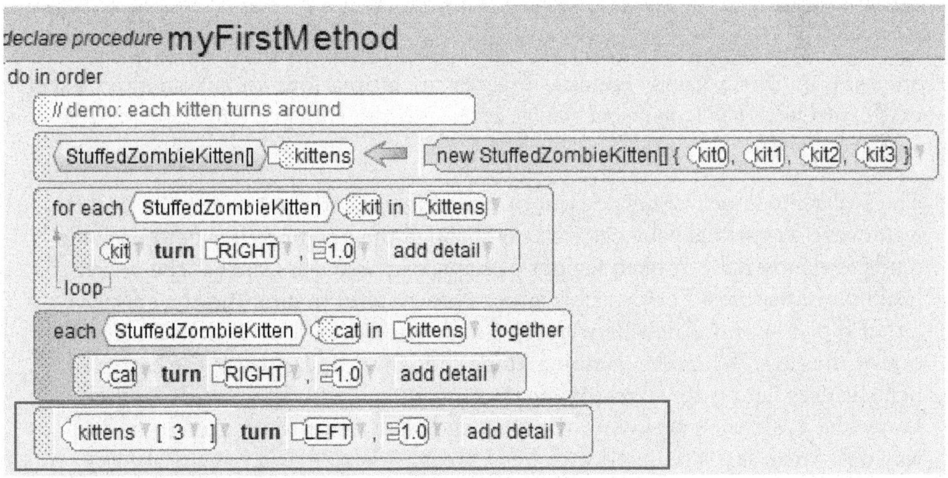

Figure 14.13 ● *Access the kitten at indexed position 3.*

of the animation, after the kittens have each turned right one at a time and then turned right all together, you should see the last kitten turn to her left.

The example statement to access an item in a custom array is purposely simplistic for demonstration purposes. To provide a quick example of the power that item access provides, let's write a couple of lines of code to randomly turn kittens in the array. First, declare a new variable, named *randIndex*, of type WholeNumber. Initialize *randIndex* to 0 (Figure 14.14).

Now, add a *count* loop that will repeat 10 times. Inside the count loop, add a statement to set *randIndex* to a random number in the range of 0 to 3, inclusive. Then, add a second

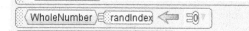

Figure 14.14   *A variable to hold a random index for the* kittens *array*

statement to turn the kitten at the randomly selected index. The object name at the beginning of the statement should be *kitten[randIndex]* (Figure 14.15).

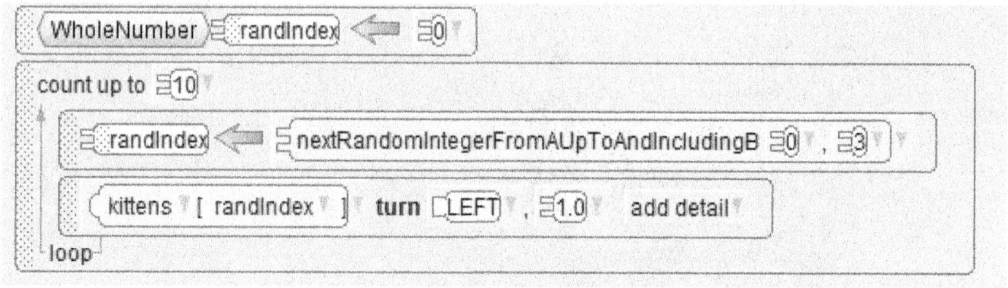

Figure 14.15   *Use a random index to turn kittens in the array.*

Test-run. When the count loop is executed, you should see the kittens turn in random order. Run the animation at least two or three times. The random order of the turns should be different with each run.

14.2 Program Example Story Analysis and Design

The program in this second example creates an animation for an adapted excerpt of Episode 8, *Adelaide: The reanimated zombie kittens*, in the *Haunted Circus* story. The episode is summarized here:

> The avalanche knocks Adelaide out of her train car and drops her in an underwater cave. A curious baby ostrich falls through the opening after her. Adelaide tends to the ostrich's broken leg out of habit and discovers she has the power to heal living creatures. The ostrich's father is so grateful that he and the adoptive father hippo supply Adelaide with food and water, even though they can't get her out of the cave. When the zombie kittens suddenly appear inside the cave with her, she uses her power to reanimate them, fueling life back into their bodies. Larry and Tashi then crash into the cave, and all three of them need to find a way out. Since she is reunited with her kittens, Adelaide now has the ability to escape the cave. Tashi and Larry watch as Adelaide lines up the kittens and orders them to sort themselves from tallest to smallest. She then tells the kittens to start stacking on top of each other, creating a wobbling tower to reach the hole in the ceiling. Adelaide, Tashi, and Larry climb the cats like a ladder and are helped out of the hole by Filbert and Tumbo. Adelaide finally orders the kittens to drive the train through the tunnel, back into the water, and onto the beach. When the kittens and Adelaide climb into her train car, it disappears.

To turn the story into a short animation, we selected an excerpt starting where Larry and Tashi have crashed into the cave and the engine is stuck in the wet sand. One analysis of the excerpt could be

Larry and Tashi talk about the cave, the creepy feeling of the zombie kittens looking at them, and seeking a way out

Adelaide jumps into the scene and tells Larry and Tashi she has a plan for escaping from the cave

Adelaide arranges the kittens in a row

The tallest kitten moves to an anchor position to start a tower

The kittens, one at a time, pile on top of one another, resulting in a wobbly, ladder-like tower that extends to the hole at the top of the cave

14.2.1 Design

The next step is design. A storyboard may be used to figure out the composition of the scene, the camera motions, and the flow of the story (Figure 14.16). The major action in the storyboard centers on the need to find a way out of the cave. Even if they can remove the wet sand from around the wheels of the train, Larry fears that Tashi will drown if they ride the engine back out of the underwater cave. Tashi had almost drowned on their way in. Adelaide has an escape plan. She will line up the kittens and then have them stack on top of one another, the tallest kitten at the bottom. The stack of kittens will form a tower, a ladder-like structure for climbing out of the cave.

As with previous program examples, some details of the story excerpt have been omitted or modified. Of particular interest in this example is the arrangement of kittens in

Figure 14.16 ◦ *Storyboard for the Adelaide episode*

a row (a visualization of the custom array of kittens). In the original story, the kittens are arranged in a row, by height, from shortest to tallest. In our program example, the kittens will be arranged in a row, but not by height. Then, we will search through the array for the tallest kitten and move it to the anchor position. (Sorting the array of kittens by height will be performed in the following chapter of this textbook.)

A possible algorithm for this example is shown in Figure 14.17.

do in order

    do together

        Larry and Tashi talk about their current situation

        Larry and Tashi look at the kittens that surround them

        Random kittens turn their heads, curiously watching Larry and Tashi

    Adelaide jumps into the scene and greets Larry

    Tashi tells Adelaide they are trapped

    Adelaide says she has a plan to escape

    Adelaide tells the kittens to line up, in a horizontal row

    The tallest kitten takes an anchor position on top of a rock

    The kittens pile on top of one another, in a vertical column, one at a time

    The tower wobbles and Tashi says she won't be the first one going up the tower

Figure 14.17   *Algorithm for Adelaide example program*

14.2.2 Starter world

A starter world, *FindingAdelaideStarter.a3p*, has been prepared and is available for download from **www.alice.org/Alice3ToJava**. Download the *FindingAdelaideStarter* file. Then, start Alice and open the downloaded world. Click the Scene Setup button to obtain a larger view of the initial scene in the Scene editor. If successfully downloaded, the initial scene should appear as shown in Figure 14.18. The train engine has rematerialized inside an underwater cave. Larry and Tashi have already disembarked from the train and are standing in the dark cave. Twenty-one stuffed zombie kittens have gathered around and are watching Larry and Tashi.

The starter world contains six object and eight camera markers that may be used to reposition objects or to change the camera's viewpoint (Figure 14.19).

Figure 14.18 • *Opening scene in the Scene editor*

Figure 14.19 * *Object and camera markers for FindingAdelaide*

The interior of the cave is the setting for the animation illustrated in this chapter. You may find it interesting to click the camera marker named *islandView*. When the camera changes viewpoint to the *islandView* marker, you will see the exterior of the cave. The cave is located at the water's edge of a tropical island, as shown in Figure 14.20. A portal tunnel leads into the cave, which is where the train engine, Tashi, Larry, and the zombie kittens are located in the initial scene.

Figure 14.20 * *Camera view of the tropical island in the FindingAdelaide project*

If you have not already done so, return the camera to the initial scene viewpoint by clicking the *start* camera marker.

Return to the Code editor and then click the Scene class tab. Scroll to the bottom of the Scene class tab. The Scene already has a custom array named *cats*, initialized with the 21 *StuffedZombieKitten* objects (Figure 14.21). Note: The image in Figure 14.21 does not show the entire declaration—it is too wide for the printed page width in this textbook.

unmanaged
▼ | StuffedZombieKitten[] | **cats** ⇐ | new StuffedZombieKitten[] (stuffedZombieKitten, stuffedZombieKitten2, stuffedZombieKitten3, stuffedZombieKitten4, stuff

Figure 14.21   *The cats[ ] array, declared in the Scene class has 21 stuffed zombie kittens.*

The Scene class has four pre-made procedures: *openingConversation, AdelaideJumpsIn, conversationWithAdelaide,* and *escapePlan* (Figure 14.22, top). The pre-made procedures implement several of the steps in the algorithm. The code in these procedures uses programming concepts and techniques covered previously in other chapter examples and can be used here with little explanation. The Biped class has *talk* and *talkAndSay* procedures imported for this project (Figure 14.22, bottom left). The BlackCat class has *run* and *wideEyeExpression* procedures (Figure 14.22, bottom right).

Importantly, all procedures that involve writing code for the custom *cats* array have not yet been implemented but will be illustrated in the remainder of this chapter.

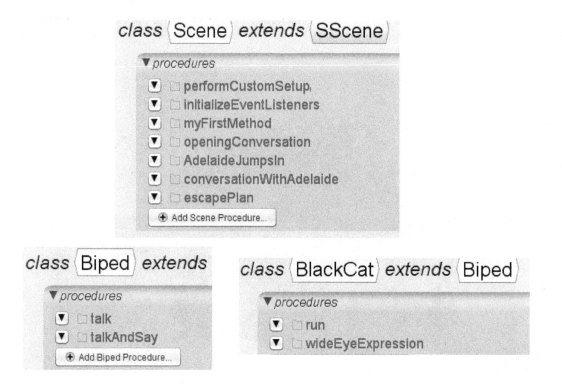

Figure 14.22   *Pre-made and imported procedures in* FindingAdelaideStarter

14.3 Implementation with a Custom Array

In the Code editor, click the *myFirstMethod* tab. You will see that comments have already been added (Figure 14.23).

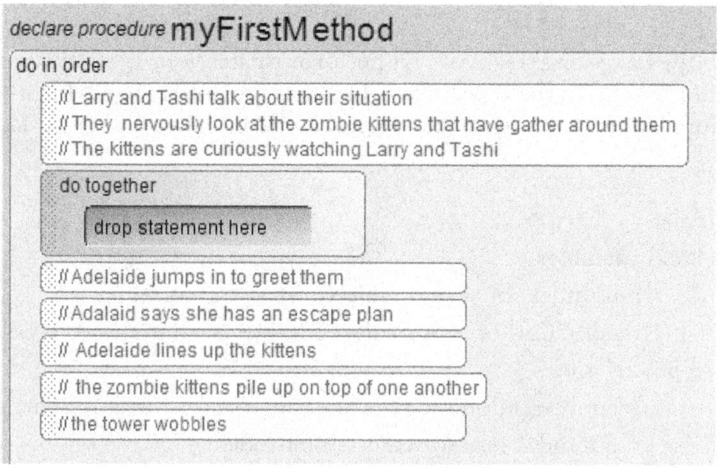

Figure 14.23 • *Comments document the FindingAdelaide algorithm.*

The first step of the algorithm is a *do together* that has three actions executing at the same time. One of the actions is Larry and Tashi's opening conversation, where they realize they are trapped in the cave. While they are talking, they start looking around at lots of little zombie kittens. Likewise, the kittens are curiously watching Larry and Tashi.

One of the three actions in the *do together* has already been implemented in the Scene class as a pre-made procedure: *openingConversation*. Create a statement inside the *do together* code block that calls *openingConversation* (Figure 14.24). Test-run the project. You should see Larry and Tashi talking for several seconds.

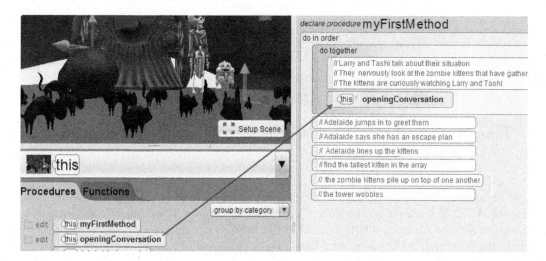

Figure 14.24 • *A call to the pre-made* openingConversation *procedure*

14.3.1 Writing a procedure with an array parameter

The second action in the *do together* is Larry and Tashi anxiously looking at the different zombie kittens that have gathered around them. Because they are talking for several seconds and becoming more and more anxious about their situation, they should each look at several different kittens during the time they are talking. We will write a procedure for Larry and Tashi to look at randomly selected kittens in the array of kittens that surround them.

Because both Larry and Tashi are to perform this action, it makes sense to write a procedure, named *lookAt*, in the Biped class. This way, both Larry and Tashi will be able to call the procedure. A decomposition for the procedure is shown in Figure 14.25.

do in order
> **local variables**
>> randIndex, of type WholeNumber, initialized to 0
>> randomCat, of type StuffedZombieCat, initialized to cats[0]
> repeat 12 times
>> generate randomIndex in the range of 0 ... length of array
>> randomCat is assigned cats[randIndex]
>> this Biped turn head to look at randomCat

Figure 14.25   *Decomposition for* lookAt

Declare a procedure for the Biped class and name it *lookAt*. Add comments to document assumptions and actions. Then, declare the first variable, *randIndex* of type Whole-Number and initialize it to 0 (Figure 14.26).

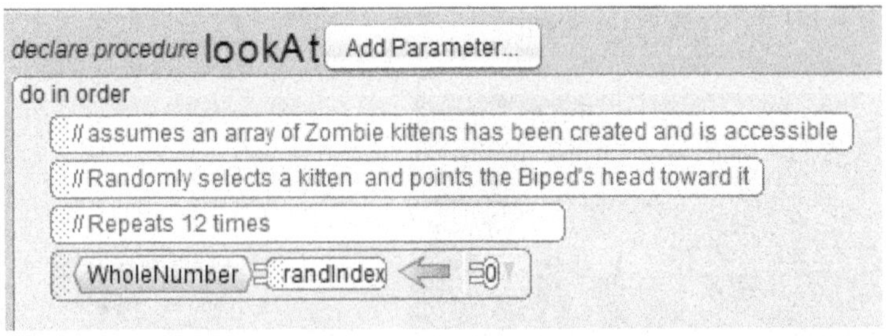

Figure 14.26   *Declare the* lookAt *procedure, add comments, and a add local variable.*

Now declare the second variable, *randomCat* of type *StuffedZombieKitten*. In the variable declaration dialog box, Alice will notify you that "No suitable fillins were found." (Figure 14.27). This message is because any object that is not a Biped object is **out of scope** in a procedure or function that is defined in the Biped class. In this case, it means no zombie kitten is accessible in this procedure.

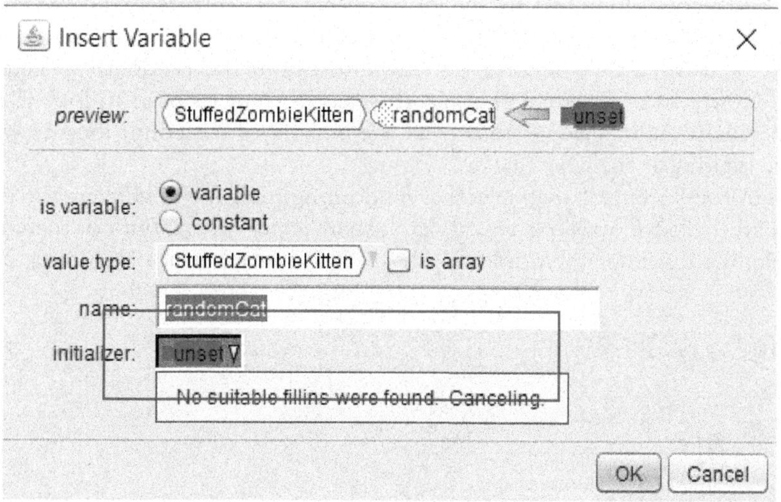

Figure 14.27   *No zombie kitten objects are available as an initial value for* randomCat.

The way to make the zombie kittens available in the *lookAt* procedure is to create a parameter for an array of zombie kittens (Figure 14.28). In this example, the parameter is named *kits*.

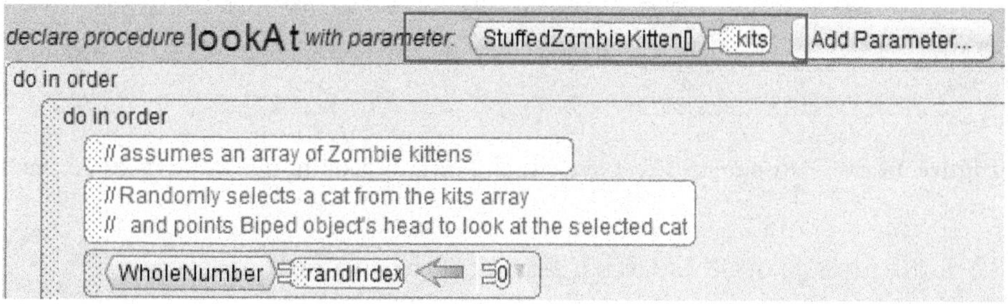

Figure 14.28   *Declare a parameter for the* StuffedZombieKitten *array.*

The *randomCat* variable can now be declared and initialized with a kitten from the *kits* array (Figure 14.29). In this example, we selected *kits*[0] as the initial value.

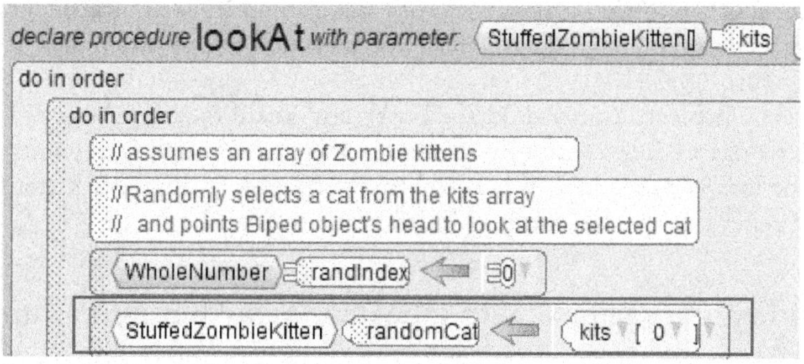

Figure 14.29   *Declare* randomCat *variable and initialize to* kits*[0]*

Now, add a count loop and set the loop control to 12 (Figure 14.30). Within the count loop, add a statement to generate a random index in the range of 0 to the length of the array (*kits.length*), exclusive. Add a second statement to assign the randomly selected kitten to *randomCat*. Now, add a statement that has this Biped point its head to look directly at the *randomCat*. Finally, add a *delay* statement at the bottom of the count loop to wait two seconds before looking at the next cat.

Note: In the statement that selects a random number for *randIndex*, the random generator with an exclusive option is called. Exclusive means "up to, but not including." So, in this example, the range for the random index is 0 ... up to, but not including, 21.

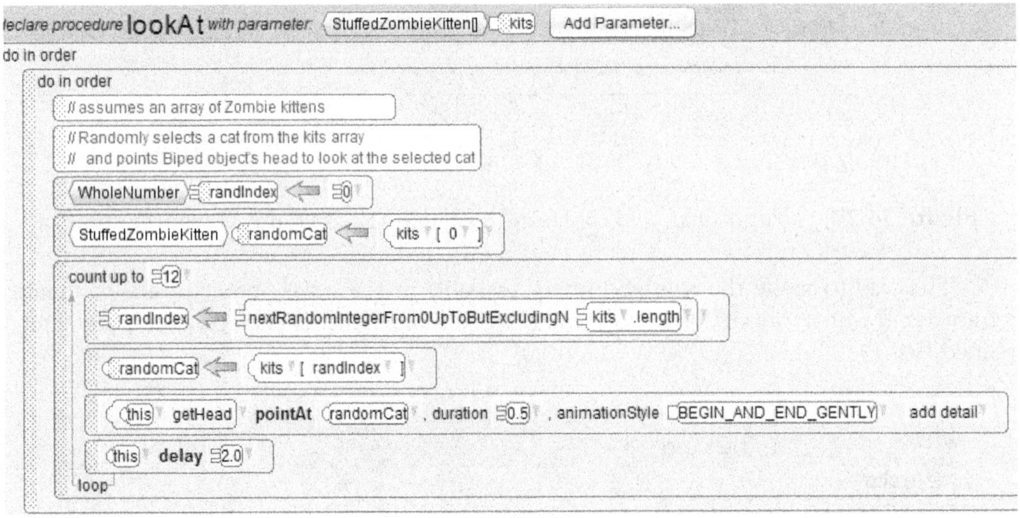

Figure 14.30   *Randomly select one cat and turn to point at that cat; repeat 12 times.*

14.3.2 Calling a procedure with an array argument

Now the *lookAt* procedure can be used to have Larry and Tashi look at randomly selected zombie kittens. Return to *myFirstMethod*. Select Larry in the Object Selector. Drag the *lookAt* procedure tile to the editor and drop it inside the *do together*. Select *this.cats*[ ] as the argument for the *kits* parameter (Figure 14.31).

When *lookAt* is called, the *kits* parameter receives a reference to the argument, which is the *cats*[ ] array in this example. At runtime, statements in *lookAt* that use the *kits*[ ] array will actually execute with the *cats*[ ] array that was passed in as an argument to *kits*[ ].

Add another statement that calls *lookAt*, this time to have Tashi *lookAt* kittens in the *cats*[ ] array (Figure 14.32).

Test-run the project. You should see Larry and Tashi talking. At the same time, their heads should be pointing at randomly selected kittens. Although Larry and Tashi are each performing the *lookAt* procedure, it is likely they will look at different kittens because each call to *lookAt* generates its own random index value.

14.3.3 Writing a procedure with a custom array but no parameter

The *do together* code block in *myFirstMethod* is still not complete. The third action in the *do together* is the zombie kittens watching Larry and Tashi with typical kitten curiosity. To give

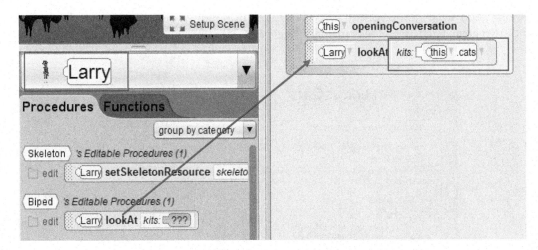

Figure 14.31 • *Call* lookAt *procedure with* this.cats[ ] *as the argument.*

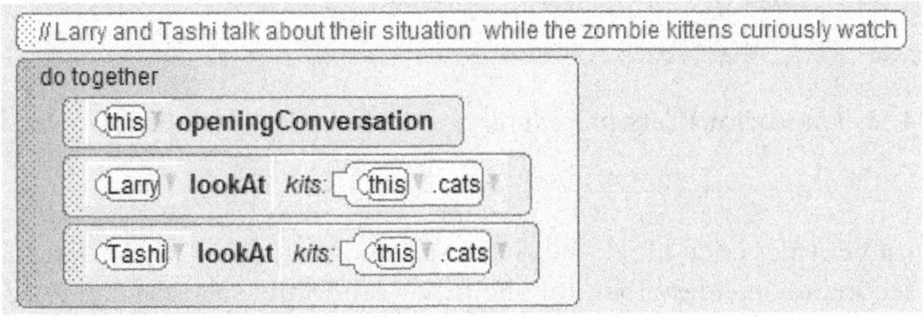

// Larry and Tashi talk about their situation while the zombie kittens curiously watch

do together

    this   openingConversation

    Larry   lookAt   kits: this   .cats

    Tashi   lookAt   kits: this   .cats

Figure 14.32 • *Larry and Tashi anxiously look at the zombie kittens.*

some variety to the kittens' actions, let's have two kittens in the *cats*[ ] array turn their necks at the same time. Two random indexes will be needed. A decomposition for a procedure is shown in Figure 14.33.

do in order

    repeat 20 times

        do together

            do in order

            generate randomIndex1 for first kitten

            cat[randomIndex1] turn neck

            do in order

            generate randomIndex2 for second kitten

            cat[randomIndex2] turn neck

Figure 14.33 • *Decomposition for kittens watching Larry and Tashi*

The actions are performed only by kittens in the *cats*[ ] array. So declare a new procedure in the Scene class and name it *curiousCats*. No parameter is needed because the *cats*[] array is accessible in Scene class procedures. Add comments to document assumptions and actions. Add a *count* loop control structure that will repeat 20 times and nest a *do together* with two *do in order* code blocks inside it (Figure 14.34).

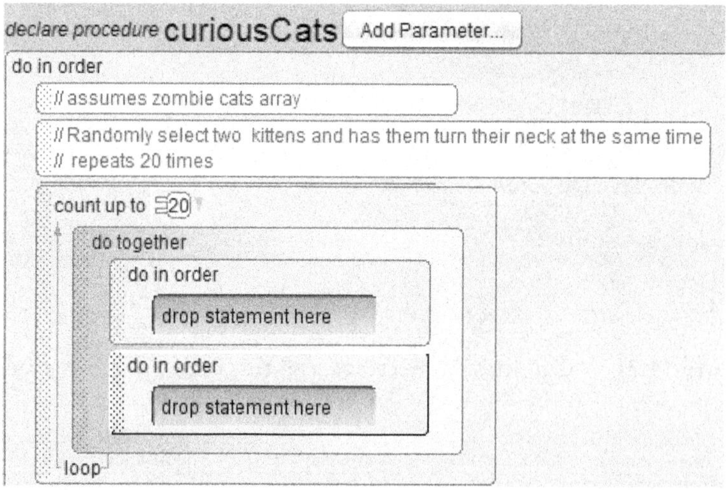

Figure 14.34   *The* curiousCats *procedure; two* do in order *blocks nested in a* do together

The first *do in order* code block will have statements for one of the randomly selected cats, and the second *do in order* block for the other randomly selected cat. Add a statement to the first *do in order* code block to generate a random number in the range of 0 ... to length of *cats*[ ] array, exclusive. Then, add a statement to have the randomly selected cat turn its neck left and right (Figure 14.35).

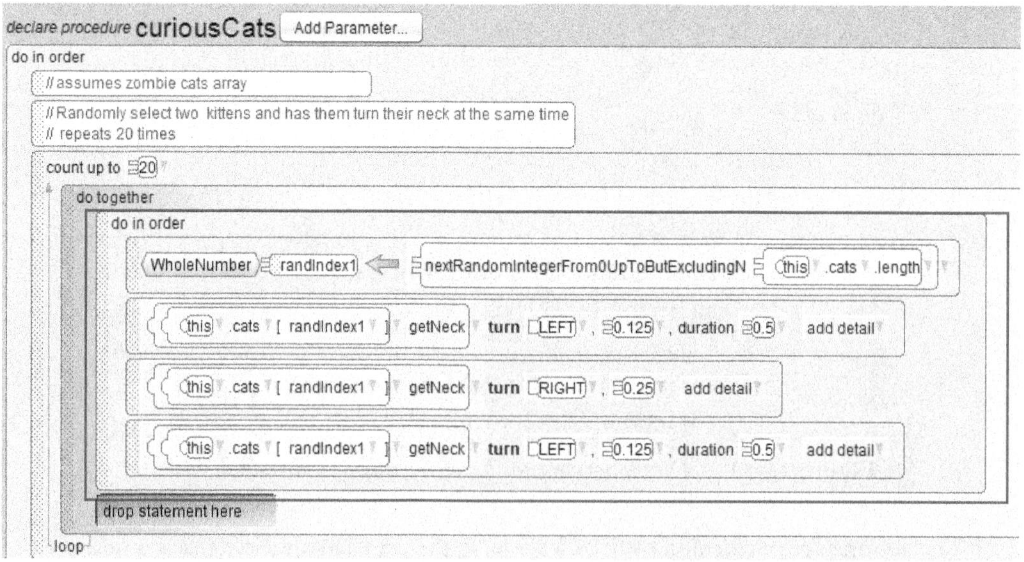

Figure 14.35   *A randomly selected cat turns its neck left and then right.*

Now, add statements for another randomly selected kitten the second *do in order*. The completed *curiousCats* procedure is shown in Figure 14.36.

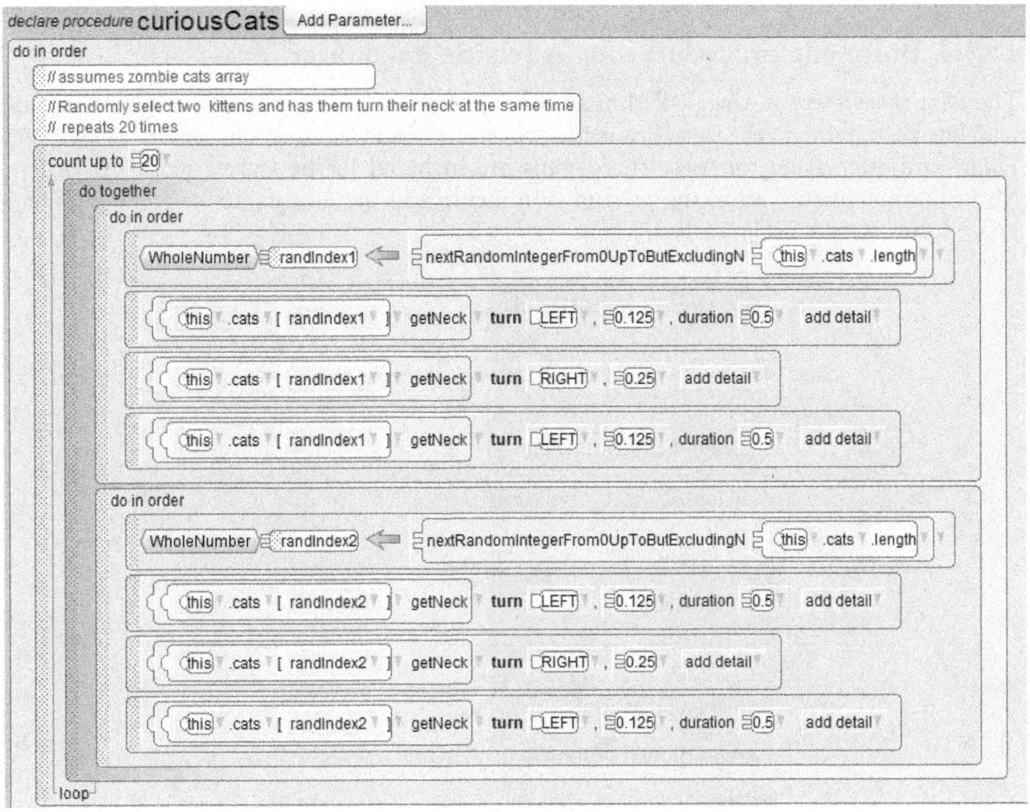

Figure 14.36 *Completed* curiousCats *procedure*

Return to *myFirstMethod* and add a statement in the *do together* code block that calls *curiousCats* (Figure 14.37). The *do together* code block is now complete.

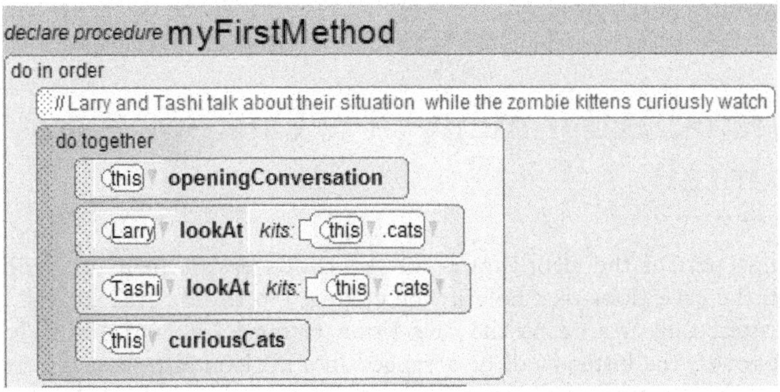

Figure 14.37 *Completed* do together *in* myFirstMethod

Test-run the project. You should see Larry and Tashi talking and turning their heads to look at randomly selected zombie kittens. At the same time, two randomly selected kittens should be turning their necks as they watch Larry and Tashi.

14.3.4 Pre-made procedures for Adelaide encounter

The next three steps in the algorithm animate Larry and Tashi's encounter with Adelaide, who has been living in the cave. Pre-made procedures (*AdelaideJumpsIn*, *conversationWithAdelaide*, and *escapePlan*) for these three steps are included in the starter world. In *myFirstMethod*, immediately after the second comment, add statements to call the pre-made procedures, in order (Figure 14.38).

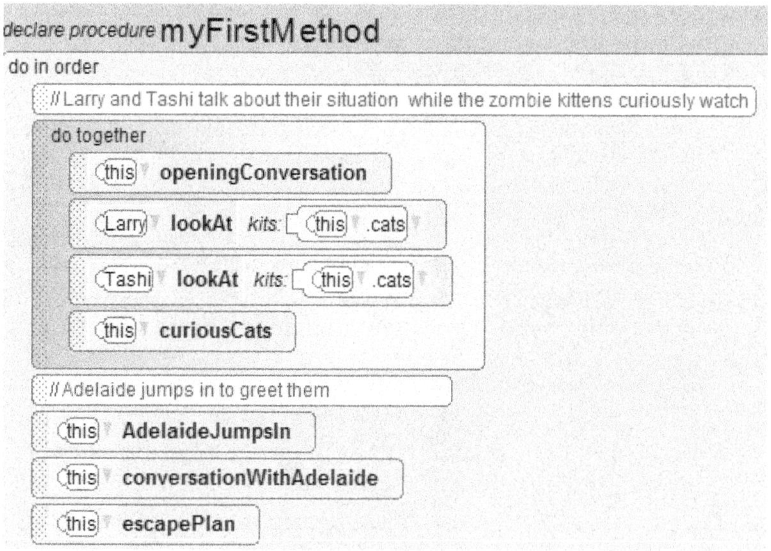

Figure 14.38   *Add calls to pre-made procedures for the encounter with Adelaide.*

The *AdelaideJumpsIn* and *conversationWithAdelaide* procedures call the *run* and *wideEyeExpression* pre-made procedures, defined in the BlackCat class. All pre-made procedures in this example are composed of code similar to previously presented procedures. However, you may wish to view the pre-made procedures in the BlackCat class, particularly for Adelaide's wide-eyed expression.

14.4 Visual Alignment of a Custom Array (Horizontal)

The remaining part of the algorithm is for Adelaide's escape plan—to build a tower of kittens from the cave floor to a hole in the ceiling. Up to now, the kittens have been in locations scattered all around on the cave floor, facing Larry and Tashi. To prepare for building the tower, the kittens will be arranged in a horizontal row on the ground, in the same order as they are indexed in the *cats*[ ] array. This action provides a visual representation of the kittens in a custom array.

The technique for aligning the kitten objects, side by side in a row, is to position the first kitten at a marker for the beginning of the row. Next, move the second kitten to the same position as the first kitten and then slide the second kitten to its left. Then, mark the second kitten as the "previous kitten." With the first two kittens in position, we can now iterate through the remaining kittens in the array. With each iteration, the next kitten will be moved to the previous kitten's position and then slide down the row. That kitten becomes the previous kitten, and the loop moves on to the next kitten. When the loop ends, all the kittens will be in a horizontal row across the ground.

Using this technique, a decomposition for aligning the kittens in a row is shown in Figure 14.39. Two local variables are declared, *first cat* (Boolean) and *prevCat* (StuffedZombieKitten).

do in order
local variables
    Boolean firstCat, initialize to true
    StuffedZombieKitten prevCat, initialize to cats[0]

camera move to catLineShot (marker)
for each kit in cats array
    if firstCat is *true*
        kit move and orient to catLine (marker)
        set firstCat to *false*
    else
        kit orient to prevCat
        kit slide left (place left of prevCat)
    set prevCat to kit

Figure 14.39   *Decomposition for aligning the kittens in a row*

The first local variable, *firstCat*, is a Boolean. When *true*, the *firstCat* is yet to be positioned in the row. Once the first kitten has been positioned in the row, it no longer needs to be positioned so *firstCat* is changed to *false*. The second local variable, *prevCat*, is used like a sticky note that is moved from kitten to kitten in the array to keep track of the most recent kitten positioned into the row.

In the Scene class tab, add a new procedure named *alignInRow*. Because this procedure is declared in the Scene class, no parameter for the *cats*[ ] array is needed. Add comments that document any assumptions, actions, and post conditions (Figure 14.40).

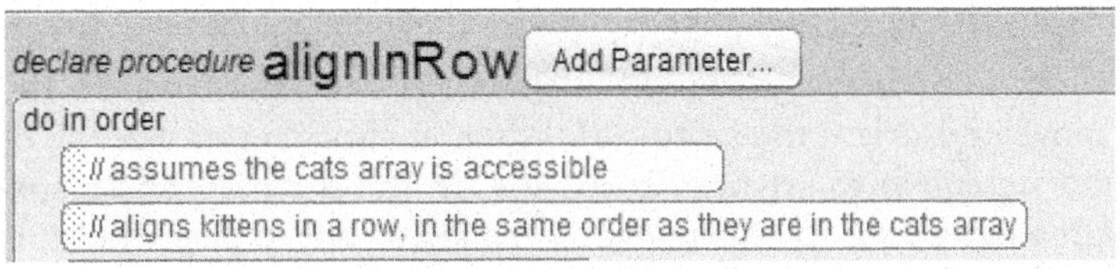

declare procedure **alignInRow** Add Parameter...
do in order
    // assumes the cats array is accessible
    // aligns kittens in a row, in the same order as they are in the cats array

Figure 14.40   *Add alignInRow procedure to Scene class*

First, declare the local variables *firstCat* of type Boolean and *prevCat* of type Stuffed-ZombieKitten, as shown in Figure 14.41. Initialize *firstCat* to *true* and *prevCat* to *cats*[0] (the first kitten in the *cats*[ ] array).

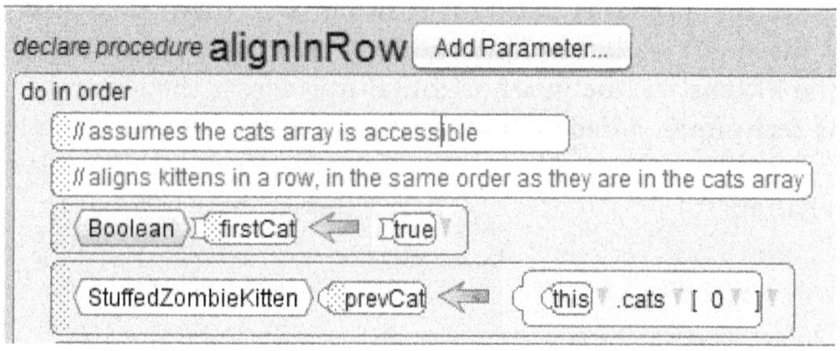

Figure 14.41   *Reposition camera and declare tracking variables.*

The camera needs to change viewpoint so the kittens can be seen as they reposition into the row, one at a time. Add a statement to have the camera *moveAndOrientTo* the *cat-LineShot* camera marker. Next, create a *for each in* loop to iterate through the *cats*[ ] array and name the array item *kit* (Figure 14.42).

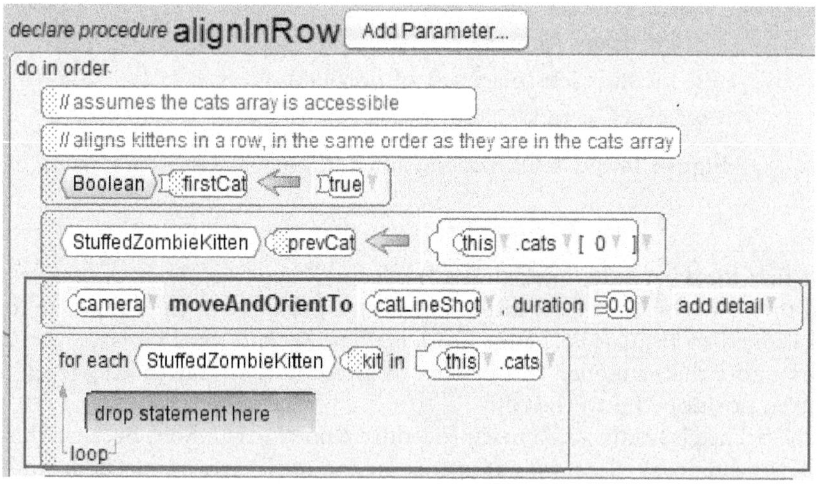

Figure 14.42   *Iterate through the array with a* for each in *loop.*

Within the *for each in* code block, add an *if/else* control structure, as shown in Figure 14.43. Add a condition in the *if* statement: if *firstCat* is *true*. In the *if* part, add a statement to move and orient the *kit* to *catLine* (an anchor marker for the beginning of the row) and then a statement to set *firstCat* to *false*. In the *else* part, add a statement to *orient* the *kit* to the previous kitten (*prevCat*) and then a statement to *place* the *kit* to the left of the previous kitten. Below the *if/else* code block, add a statement to set *prevCat* to the current *kit* (in preparation for the next kitten in the array).

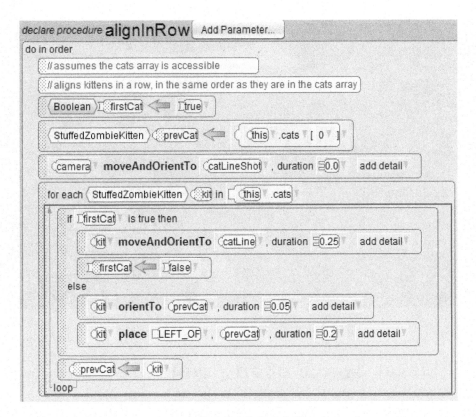

Figure 14.43 — *Completed* alignInRow *procedure*

Return to *myFirstMethod* and add a statement to call *alignInRow*, below the call to *escapePlan*, as shown in Figure 14.44.

Figure 14.44 — In myFirstMethod, *add a statement to call* alignInRow.

Test-run the program. After Adelaide's conversation with Larry and Tashi, the kittens should be lined up, all in a row on the ground, as shown in Figure 14.45.

Figure 14.45   *Zombie cats, aligned in a row*

14.5 Linear Search of an Array

Now that the kittens are all in a row, we can search for the tallest kitten to take the anchor position and then start building the tower. One way to search for the tallest kitten is to perform a linear search. A linear search starts at the beginning of an array and moves sequentially through the array from item to item, looking for an item that meets a specific requirement. The search continues until a match is found or all items have been checked.

We will begin our search by assuming the first kitten in the cats array is the tallest. (Not likely, but a possible choice.) We will use a tracking variable to tag it as the tallest. (You might think of the tag as similar to a collar that can be placed around the kitten's neck.) Then we will walk through the array, one kitten at a time, and compare the next kitten's height to the height of the one currently tagged. If a kitten is found that is taller than the one currently tagged, the tag will be changed to the taller kitten. When all kittens in the array have been checked, we know the tallest kitten in the row is the one currently tagged.

In *myFirstMethod*, immediately beneath the comment to "find the tallest kitten in the array," add a statement to declare a tracking variable for the tag, named *tallestCat*, of type Stuffed-ZombieKitten. Initialize the variable to *stuffedZombieKitten* (the first kitten in the array). Then, add a *for each in* loop for the *cats[]* array with *nextCat* as the loop's item name (Figure 14.46).

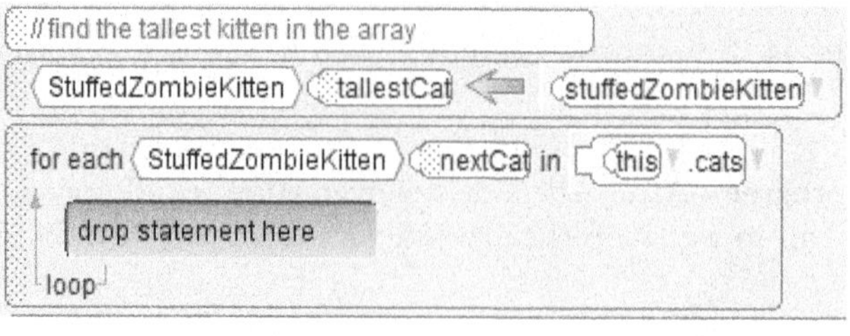

```
// find the tallest kitten in the array
StuffedZombieKitten  tallestCat  ⬅  stuffedZombieKitten

for each  StuffedZombieKitten  nextCat  in  this .cats
    drop statement here
loop
```

Figure 14.46   *A loop to search for the tallest cat in the cats[ ] array*

Now, add an *if/else* statement within the *for each in* code block, with *true* as the placeholder condition (Figure 14.47).

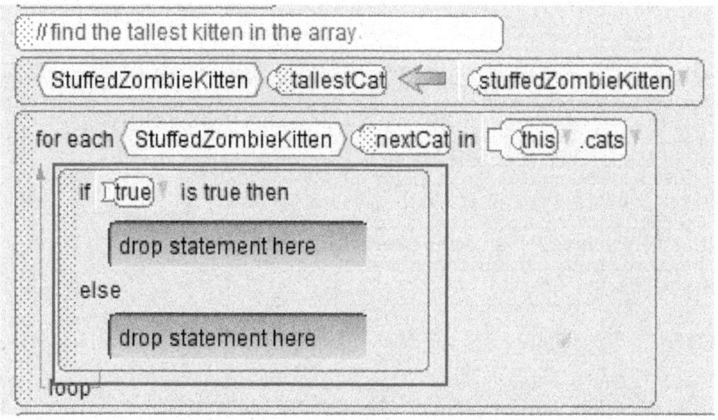

Figure 14.47 • *An if/else code block to check for a taller kitten*

14.5.1 A *compareTo* Custom Function

The *true* placeholder in the *if/else* statement must be replaced with an expression to determine which of two kittens is the tallest. It would be convenient to just call a function that compares the height of two kittens. The StuffedZombieKitten class does not have such a function, so we will build our own custom function with an expression to determine which of two kittens is the tallest.

The function will be a *compareTo* function, a well-known **standard function** for comparing two objects of the same class. A standard function is not part of the programming language but is often custom-written by professional programmers. As a standard function, a *compareTo* function is expected to compare two objects (*this object* and *other object*) of the same class, using a property or value that the two objects have in common. Then, *compareTo* will return one of three possible values:

- A number greater than 0 if *this object's* value is greater than the *other object's* value
- A number less than 0 if *this object's* value is less than the *other object's* value
- 0 if the two objects' values are the same

In this example, the heights of the two kitten objects (*this kitten* and *other kitten*) will be compared. The function will return a number greater than 0 (in this example, it returns 1) if *this kitten* is taller than *other kitten* and returns a number less than 0 (in this example, −1) if *this kitten* is shorter than *other kitten*; otherwise, it returns 0.

Open the StuffedZombieKitten class tab in the Code editor and click the Add StuffedZombieKitten function button. Name the function *compareTo* and select *WholeNumber* as the return type. Add a parameter named *otherKitten* of type StuffedZombieKitten. Then add comments to document the standard features (Figure 14.48).

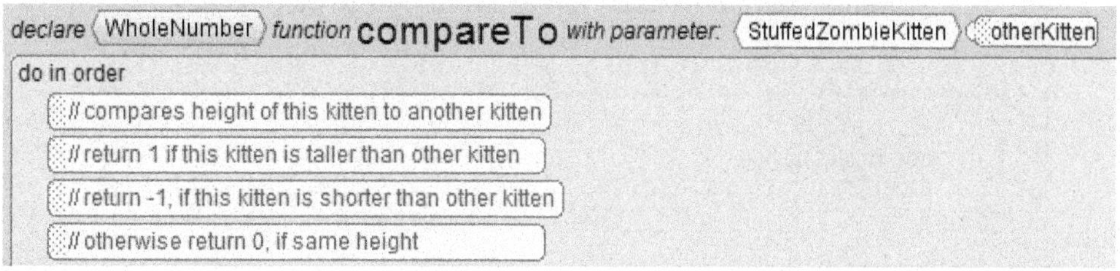

Figure 14.48 • *A custom* compareTo *function declaration*

Declare local variables for the height of each object and then use an *if/else* control structure to compare and return the result (Figure 14.49).

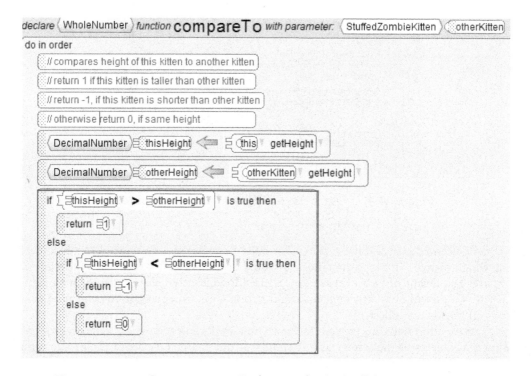

Figure 14.49   *Custom* compareTo *function for the StuffedZombieKitten class*

Now, the *compareTo* function can be used to replace the *true* placeholder in the *if/else*. Return to *myFirstMethod* and call the *compareTo* function to compare the height of *nextCat* to the previous *tallestCat* (Figure 14.50). If *compareTo* returns a number greater than 0, then *nextCat* is taller than the previous *tallestCat*, so update *tallestCat* to *nextCat*. Note: The scope of this textbook does not allow enough time and space for numerous in-depth examples that reflect the high-level usability of the *compareTo* function. However, the *compareTo* procedure will be used again in Chapter 15.

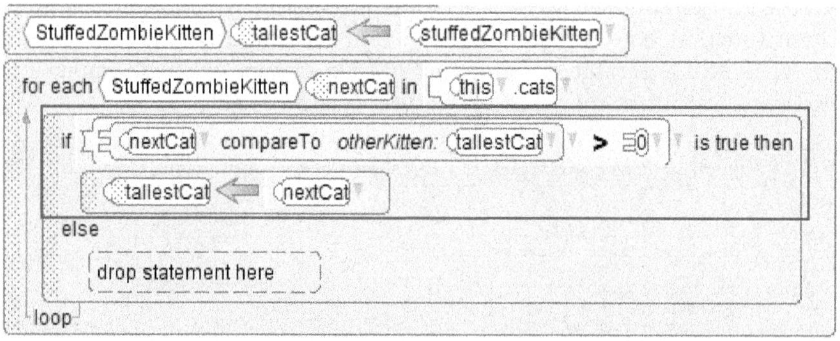

Figure 14.50   *Call* compareTo *with* nextCat *(this cat) and* tallestCat *(other cat).*

14.6 Visual Alignment of an Array (Vertical)

The next step in the algorithm is to stack the kittens in a tower (a vertical column that will act as a ladder to the top of the cave). The tallest cat will be the anchor for the tower. The technique for stacking the kittens is very similar to aligning the kittens in a row. The major difference is the tallest kitten will be positioned at a marker for the anchor position and the remaining kittens stacked on top of it. A decomposition for a procedure to stack the kittens to create a tower is shown in Figure 14.51.

do in order

    Parameter

        StuffedZombieKitten *tallest*

    Tracking variable

        StuffedZombieKitten *prevCat*,

    camera move to *leaningTowerOfCatsShot* (camera marker)

    Larry, Tashi and Adelaide turn to look at *catLadderStart* (object marker)

    tallest move and orient to *catLadderStart* (object marker)

    stack kittens on the tower, using a *for each in* loop

        if kit is tallest

            do nothing (already in the tower)

        else

            kit orient to *prevCat*

            kit place above *prevCat*

            kit move down (to put feet on back of prevCat)

                kit set vehicle to prevCat

    prevCat is assigned kit

Figure 14.51   *Decomposition for a* stack *procedure*

In the Scene class, declare a new procedure named *stack*. Create a parameter of type StuffedZombieKitten named *tallest*. Add comments to document assumptions and actions (Figure 14.52).

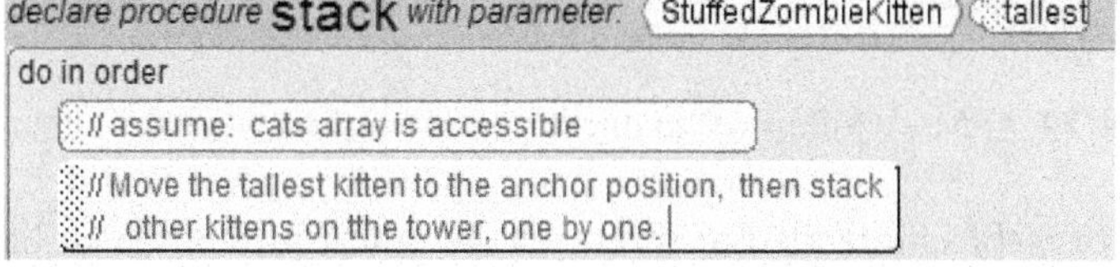

Figure 14.52   *Declaration of* stack *procedure with parameter* tallest

Add a statement for the *prevCat* tracking variable and initialize it to *tallest*. Next, add statements to move and orient the camera's viewpoint to the *leaningTowerOfCatsShot* camera marker. Then add statements to turn Larry, Tashi, and Adelaide to face the *catLadderStart* object marker, which is located on the top of the rock (Figure 14.53).

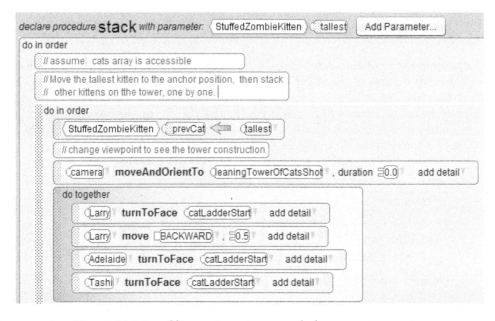

Figure 14.53   *Change viewpoint to watch the tower construction*

Now the tower construction begins. First, add a statement to move and orient the *tallest* kitten to the top of the rock, marked by *catLadderStart*. Next, add a *for each in* loop for the *cats*[ ] array, using *kitten* as the item name. Create an *if/else* code block within the *for each in* loop (Figure 14.54).

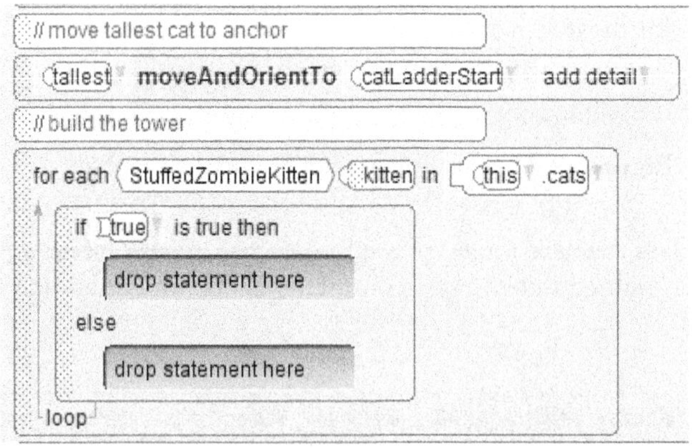

Figure 14.54   *Move tallest cat to anchor position, then pile each kitten on top.*

The *if* part of *if/else* is intended to filter out the tallest kitten, which has already been positioned at the anchor of the tower. If the kitten is the tallest kitten, skip it—we don't want to move it twice. Otherwise, *place* the next kitten above the previous kitten, and then move it down so its feet are standing on the back of the previous kitten. The distance the kitten moves down is computed by dividing the height of the previous kitten by 2.5 (a factor that was determined relative to *place* procedure's built-in distance for positioning one object above another). Then, set the kitten's vehicle to the *prevCat* and reset *prevCat* to this kitten (Figure 14.55).

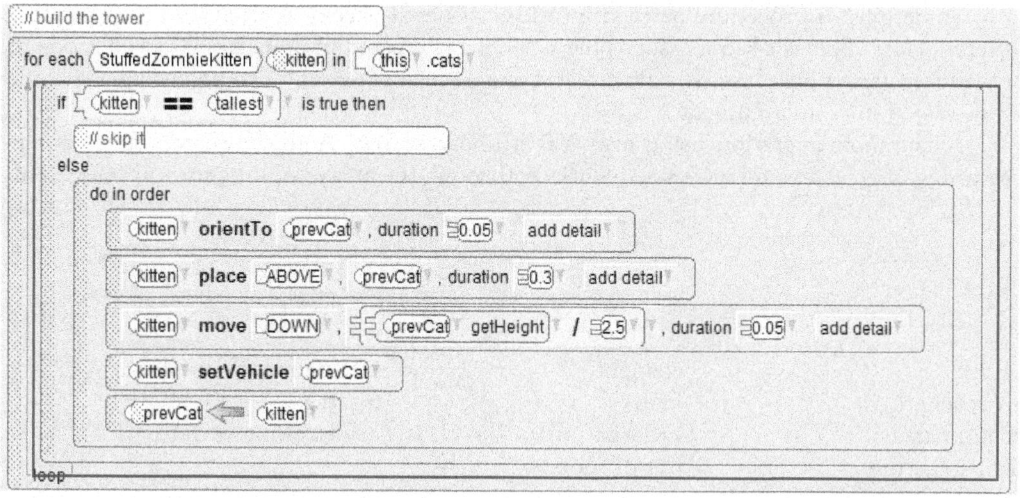

Figure 14.55 • *If kitten is tallest, skip the positioning. Otherwise, stack it on the tower.*

Return to *myFirstMethod* and add a statement to call *stack* with *tallestCat* as an argument to the parameter (Figure 14.56). Test-run the project. Near the end of the animation, you should see the largest kitten move into position as the anchor and the other kittens stack on top, one at a time, to create the tower.

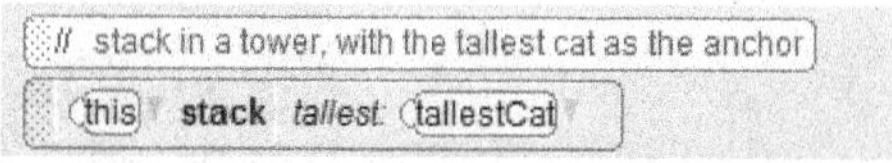

Figure 14.56 • *In* myFirstMethod, *add a statement to call* stack *with* tallestCat *argument*

The tower should "wobble" a bit. This is left as an exercise for you. See the exercises at the end of this chapter.

Summary

An array is a data structure used for storing and organizing items of the same data type. The items, also known as elements, are stored in an ordered sequence. The ordering is implemented using an index, starting with the first item at index 0, the next at index 1, the next at index 2, and so on through the last item in the array. The length of an array is the number of items in the array, which is one more than the index of the last item.

A custom array may be created by declaring the array as a property of a class or it may be declared locally, within a procedure. In this chapter, the *cats*[ ] array was declared as a property of the Scene class. The advantage of declaring an array in a class is that it can be accessed by any procedure or function defined for that class, without using a parameter.

Writing code that works with an array typically involves using a loop construct such as *for each in* to iterate through the array one item at a time or *each in together* to access all items in the array at the same time. Individual items in an array may be accessed using the syntax arrayName[*index*], where *index* is the position of the item in the ordered array.

Sometimes, a procedure defined in one class needs access to an array belonging to a different class. This is a scope issue. That is, an array created in one class is out of scope to procedures in another class. To bridge the scope issue, a parameter can be declared and the array passed in as an argument.

A common operation using arrays is a linear search. A linear search starts at the beginning of an array and moves sequentially through the array, looking for a specific item.

Terms

access	element	standard function
array length	item	tag
custom array	ordered	tracking variable
data structure	out of scope	

Concept Questions

1. What is meant by describing an array as an *ordered* data structure?
2. An Alice world has a cat, gopher, bear, fox, cow, dog, and lion objects in the scene. Write a code statement to create an array named *animals* of type Quadruped. The objects in the array should be in the same order as shown in this screen capture:

Questions 3–6 assume the animals array has been properly declared, as described in Question 2 above.

3. Would it be possible to modify the program to add a Cheshire Cat object to the scene and include it in the *animals* array? Why or why not?
4. Which animal, if any, is located at (a) animals[0], (b) animals[7], and (c) animals[3]?
5. Describe the animation that occurs when the following code block is executed:

```
for each ( Quadruped )( mammal ) in ( animals )
    do together
        mammal  move  FORWARD , 1.0   add detail
        mammal  say  "hello"   add detail
    loop
```

6. Compare the result of executing the following code block to the code block in question 5:

```
each (Quadruped) (mammal) in (animals)  together
    (mammal)  move  [FORWARD] , [1.0]   add detail
    (mammal)  say  [hello]   add detail
```

7. In many computer science instructional materials, diagrams are used to illustrate arrays of data. The diagrams may be drawn as either a horizontal row or a vertical column of boxes, with the data written in each box. An example of a horizontal array illustration is shown here:

kittens	[0]	[1]	[2]	[3]
	kit0	kit1	kit2	kit3

In the *FindingAdelaide* example, which procedure provides a visual representation of an array as: (a) a horizontal row, and (b) a vertical column?

8. Two variables, *firstCat* and *prevCat*, are used in the *alignInRow* procedure. Briefly describe the purpose of each.

Exercises

1. Add a *wobble* procedure to the *FindingAdelaide* animation presented in this chapter. A *wobble* procedure should have each of the kittens roll left and right a very small amount (in the range of 0.0 to 0.001 revolutions). To test, use a *count* loop in the *stack* procedure to call wobble four or five times, at the same time as the tower is being built.

2. Create a *talkAndSay* procedure for the Quadruped class in the *FindingAdelaide* project. Then modify Adelaide's *say* statements to call *talkAndSay*.

3. The *FindingAdlaide* animation presented in this chapter ends when the tower of kittens has been constructed to escape the cave. Let's assume Adelaide and Tashi escape but Larry, the train engine, and the kittens remain in the cave. Add code to end the episode, where Larry and the kittens board the train engine, the bell rings, and Larry pilots the train through the mouth of the cave onto the island's beach.

4. Create a scene containing eight bell objects, as shown here. Create an array of type Bell and add the bell objects to the array. Add the smallest bell as the 0th item and continue adding bells of gradually increasing sizes such that the last bell is the largest. Add a procedure for "ringing" a bell object to the Bell class. (You may wish to use the *ringBell* procedure originally written in Chapter 6.)

5. For the array of Bells created in exercise 2, use a *for each in* loop to ring the bells in order, from smallest to largest. Then, use an *each in together* loop to ring all the bells at the same time.

6. Add a mouse-click on an object event listener for the array of bell objects. When the user clicks on one of the bells in the array, play the bell sound. If you have access to sound equipment to create your own sound files, add a set of different bell-ring audio files to represent an octave of sounds and have each bell play its own sound.

7. Create a scene containing at least 10 Biped objects of at least three different classes in the Biped family. Size the objects so that some are more and others are less than one meter in height. Create an array of type Biped and add the objects to the array. Write a procedure for the Biped class to have a Biped object kick the right leg, as if kicking a ball, and then put the leg back into its original position. Then, write code that uses a *for each in* loop to have each object in the array kick, if its height is more than one meter. If the object doesn't kick, have it turn to look away from the camera.

8. Using the scene created for exercise 7, write a linear search that has the tallest object in the array turn around. Then, write a linear search for the shortest object and have the shortest object move forward.

9. Create a simulation of a Magic 8 ball. The user will ask a "yes" or "no" question out loud and then click the ball (a black sphere from Shapes). For example, the user could ask "Will I be selected for the basketball team?" When the ball is clicked, the response will be randomly selected from an array of possible responses. Responses in the array could be something like "Of course!" or "No way!"

Projects

1. The *FindingAdelaide* example presented in this chapter begins with the zombie kittens all gathered around Larry and Tashi in the cave setting. Take a step back in time to when the train first pulls into the cave. The arrival of the train has alarmed the kittens, and they have hidden behind the rocks and stones around the edge of the cave. Once the dust settles, the kittens' curiosity will take over, and they will walk out to observe the arriving passengers. The task in this project is to create a creepy walk animation, where the kittens gradually emerge from their hiding places. Each kitten walks a path of markers (a custom array) from their hiding place to a target location on the ground. Together, the kittens gradually surround Larry and Tashi.

   A project starter world named *CreepyWalkProjectStarter.a3p* captures the moment where the kittens are hidden behind the rocks and stones. The CreepyWalk starter world is available for download at **www.alice.org/Alice3ToJava**. Download and open the starter world. You will find the initial scene has numerous markers scattered on the ground around Larry and Tashi. The markers you see in the initial scene are the target locations in the paths the kittens follow as they emerge from their hiding places and walk toward Larry and Tashi.

The StuffedZombieKitten class in the starter world declares a *path* property, which means each kitten has a *path* array variable. Also, the Scene class has a procedure named *setPathArrays*. In this procedure, each kitten's path variable has been set to four or five markers that define the path that kitten will walk. The first marker in each path has the kitten emerge from its hiding place; the remaining markers define the path the kitten will walk.

You may write other code to make your project more creative, but the required code for this project includes

- A *walk* procedure in the StuffedZombieKitten class. The walk should rotate the joints (roll and turn clavicle and hip joints) in each of the four legs to create a walking motion. Remember that the kittens are stuffed zombies, however, so the walking motion does not need to be graceful.

- A *creepyWalk* procedure in the Scene class. The *creepyWalk* procedure should have each kitten walking its own individual path, but all kittens walking at the same time. Be aware that the distance between markers in a path varies. This means the number of times a kitten should perform the *walk* animation between one marker and the next depends on the distance. To avoid "sideways" walks, have the kitten *turn to face* the next marker before walking toward it, and then orient to the target marker after arriving at it.

- An event listener to allow the user to press the left and right arrow keys to turn the camera and left or right. This will allow the person viewing the animation to see the kittens as they are walking.

2. Create an underwater scene with an array that represents a school of PajamaFish. In the PajamaFish class, write a procedure for *swim*. Write code to have all the fish in the array turn and swim in the same direction at the same time. Then, write a procedure to have the school of fish swim into a pattern, for example, the letter "A." Hint: One way to create a pattern is to first create an array of markers. Each marker remembers a specific location in the pattern for one fish object. Then have each fish swim to its corresponding marker location in the pattern.

15

Java: Custom Arrays and Sort

Concept Objectives

- Declaring and initializing a Java array
- Writing and calling a search function in Java
- Writing and calling a swap procedure in Java
- Using a custom *compareTo* function in Java
- Using the built-in *compareTo* function (from Java's Integer class)
- Sorting an array in Java
- Creating an algorithm visualization for sorting an array

The purpose of this chapter is to continue an exploration of arrays, this time in Java. We will do this by illustrating a sort with the *cats*[] array that was created in the *FindingAdelaide* animation, presented previously in Chapter 14. To sort an array means to rearrange the order of the elements (items) in an array. In the world of Java, "element" is commonly used to describe an item in an array. The new ordering is based on some characteristic property, such as name, height, or age, of the elements in the array. Along the way, we will explore Java's syntax requirements for arrays and build a custom function with parameters in Java.

A modified version of the *Finding Adelaide* project has been prepared especially for the program example in this chapter. *FindingAdelaideToNetBeansSetup.a3p* may be downloaded from **www.alice.org/Alice3ToJava** or you may obtain a copy from your instructor, if you are taking a course.

Start NetBeans, and import *FindingAdelaideToNetBeansSetup.a3p* as a new Java project from an existing Alice project (Figure 15.1).

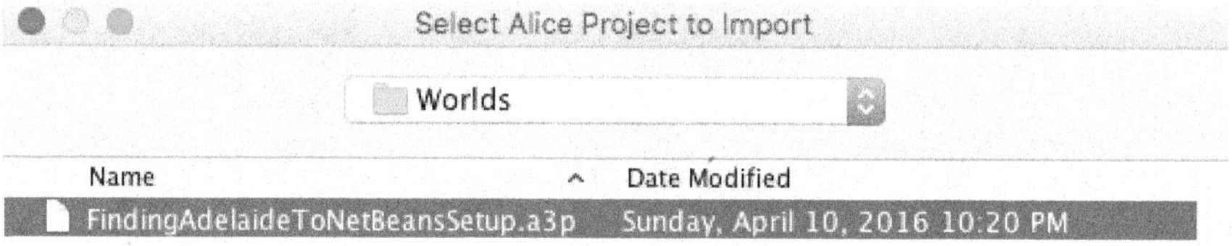

Figure 15.1   *Import* FindingAdelaideToNetBeansSetup.a3p

After successfully importing the project, the display in NetBeans should look something like that shown in Figure 15.2. In the image shown here, the StuffedZombieKitten class tab is active in the editor, but you may have a different active class tab displayed on your computer. As you view the code in NetBeans, remember the **//** symbol is often used to comment out (disable) a single line of code in both Alice and Java. Also, Java has a **/* */** notation that can be used to comment out either a single line or multiple lines of code between the beginning **/*** symbol and the closing ***/** symbol.

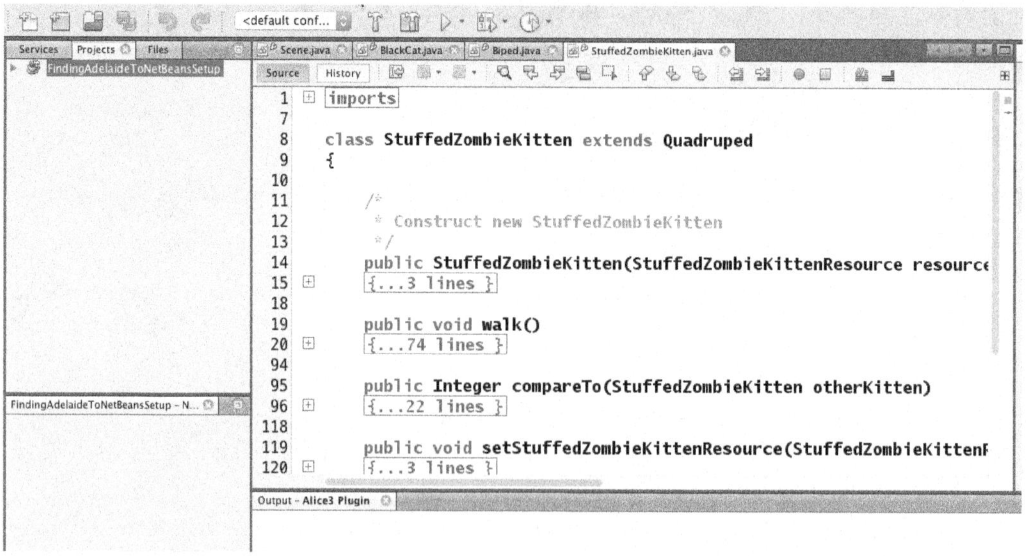

Figure 15.2   FindingAdelaideToNetBeansSetup *project in NetBeans.*

Click on Run to test that the import was successful. You will see much of the same animation as in the previous *FindingAdelaide* project (Figure 15.3).

Figure 15.3   *Imported* FindingAdelaide *project running in NetBeans*

Several key elements of the animation are purposely changed or missing in the imported version. For example, the conversation between Larry and Tashi and then between Larry and Adelaide are disabled and the code statements that find the tallest kitten have been removed.

Writing code for a Java array will first be demonstrated by writing code in Java that you have previously written in Alice. This is a useful technique for using what you already learned in Alice as a basis for learning how to write the same program code with Java syntax. Then, we will write Java code to sort the array. Writing code to sort an array is a concept not covered in previous Alice examples, so this chapter will explore programming concepts beyond what you learned in Alice.

15.1 Arrays in Java

In Alice, creating an array is a two-step process: First, an array is declared (given a data type and a name that identifies the array). In the *FindingAdelaide* example, we declared an array of type *StuffedZombieKitten*[] and named it *cats*. Second, the array is initialized by adding (assigning) objects to the array. The array declaration and initialization statement for the *cats*[] array is shown in Figure 15.4. The *cats*[] array length is 21. In Alice, this means there are 21 kittens in 21 positions, indexed from 0 to 20.

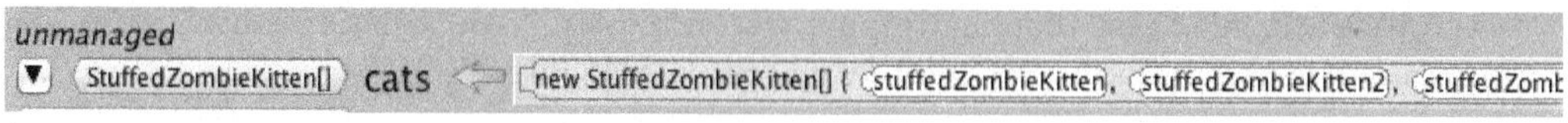

Figure 15.4   *The* cats *array declaration in the Scene class, Alice version*

15.1.1 Java array declaration

Creating an array in Java involves the same two steps: First, the array is declared by specifying a data type and given a name and then elements are added to the array. In Java, the general syntax form for an array declaration looks like this:

```
<data type>[] <identifier>
```

Where `<data type>` generically represents the type of date for the elements in the array, the [] brackets symbol is an **index operator,** and `<identifier>` is a generic representation of the name of an array.

When you imported the *FindingAdelaideToNetBeansSetup* project into NetBeans, the array declaration statement that was created for the *cats*[ ] array in Alice was automatically translated into Java syntax. To view the *cats*[ ] array declaration statement in NetBeans, click on the Scene class tab and find the section labeled /* *Scene fields* */ (Figure 15.5). (Hint: You may need to click on the + expansion box in NetBeans to view this code section.)

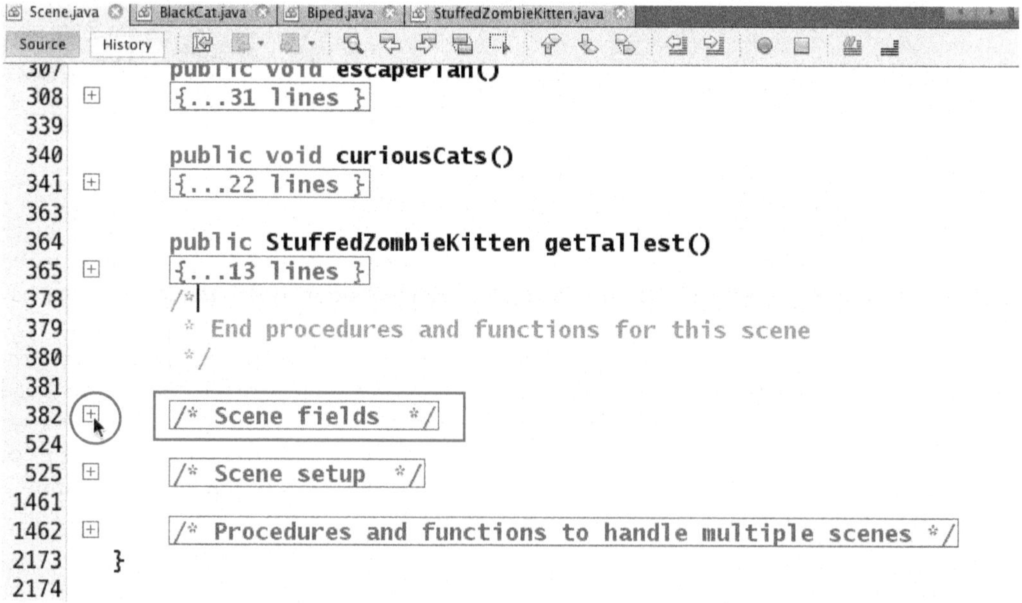

Figure 15.5   *Scene fields section of the Scene class*

In the Scene fields section, find and examine the declaration for the *StuffedZombieKittens* array, *cats* (Figure 15.6). The array declaration looks like this:

```
StuffedZombieKitten[] cats
```

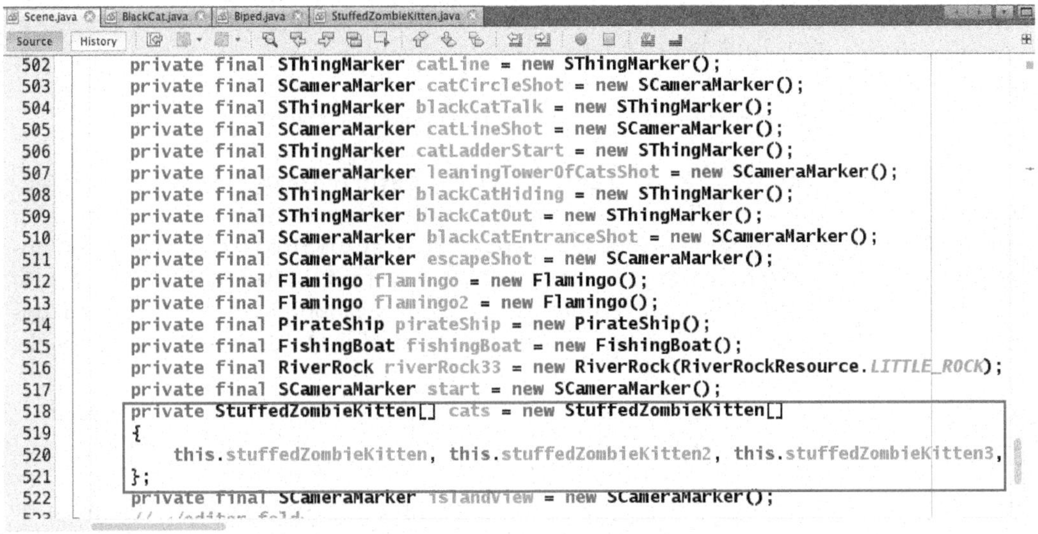

Figure 15.6 • cats*[ ] array declaration, as translated to Java*

15.1.2 Java array initialization

After the array data type and name (identifier) are declared, the second step is to initialize the array by adding elements to the array. Adding elements to an array may be done in two different program styles. We will illustrate both styles.

The first array initialization style is to extend the declaration statement with a specification of the length of the array and then, later in the program, write a statement (or statements) to add the elements. The extended declaration statement general syntax form looks like this:

```
<data type>[] <identifier> = new <data type>[size]
```

The = symbol is the assignment operator in Java (equivalent of the ← symbol, in Alice). After the assignment operator is the word *new*. The term *new* is a reserved word that tells the system to create a new object or data structure. In this case, a new data structure is created—an array of a given length. In our *FindingAdelaide* example, the statement

```
StuffedZombieKittens[] cats = new StuffedZombieKittens[21];
```

creates the array data structure and sets aside 21 positions for stuffed zombie kitten objects.

Each position in the array is actually a reference to a memory cell (a space in the memory of the computer) where one object or value of a particular type may be stored. In this initialization style, no kittens have yet been assigned to the memory cells. That is, the array length is 21—there are 21 spaces where a kitten object could be held, but the number of kittens actually assigned (number of elements in the array) is zero.

Kittens are assigned to the array by writing statements to assign a specific kitten to a specific indexed position in the array, as in:

```
cats[0] = stuffedZombieKitten;
cats[1] = stuffedZombieKitten2;
cats[2] = stuffedZombieKitten3;
```

The second initialization style does not specify the length of the array. Instead, an **initializer list** (a list of elements to be added to the array) immediately follows the declaration statement with a list of values/objects. The list is enclosed in curly braces. In this example, the declaration and initialization looks like this:

```
StuffedZombieKittens[] cats = new StuffedZombieKittens[]
{
StuffedZombieKitten, StuffedZombieKitten1, StuffedZombieKitten2, Stuffed-
ZombieKitten3, StuffedZombieKitten4, StuffedZombieKitten5, StuffedZombieKitten6,
StuffedZombieKitten7, StuffedZombieKitten8, StuffedZombieKitten9, StuffedZom-
bieKitten10, StuffedZombieKitten11, StuffedZombieKitten12, StuffedZombieKitten13,
StuffedZombieKitten14, StuffedZombieKitten15, StuffedZombieKitten16, StuffedZom-
bieKitten17, StuffedZombieKitten18, StuffedZombieKitten19, StuffedZombieKitten20
}
```

15.1.3 Access an individual element in an array

Once an array is declared and initialized, code statements may be written for the purpose of retrieving, giving an instruction to, or modifying an array element. In Alice, we wrote code to access an individual array element by using the index. For example, the Alice statement in Figure 15.7 tells the zombie kitten at index position 3 in the *cats[]* array to turn left.

Figure 15.7   *Access a zombie kitten at index-position 3 in the* cats[] *array.*

The same index syntax is used in Java for accessing objects and values stored at a specific position in an array. For example, the Alice statement in Figure 15.7 above would be written in Java as:

```
cats[3].turn(TurnDirection.LEFT, 1.0);
```

An array has an integer (whole number) property named *length*. The *length* property is often used in writing code for accessing array elements. *Length* is the capacity of the array—the number of buckets for holding elements. In the Alice IDE, a new array is declared and initialized in a dialog box (Figure 15.8). In Alice, the array *length* is automatically determined by the number of objects that were added in the dialog box.

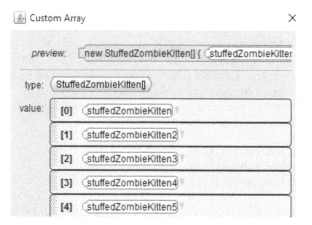

Figure 15.8   *In Alice, a new array is declared and initialized in a dialog box.*

The number of elements an array may hold cannot be changed while the program is running. We say an array "has a fixed length." In Alice an array is always full (no empty buckets). This means you can confidently write an Alice statement to access the last kitten in an array using an index of *cats.length-1* (Figure 15.9).

Figure 15.9 *Access the last kitten in the* cats[ ] *array using an index of* length-1.

If an initializer list is used to declare and initialize the array (see Figure 15.6, earlier), the same indexing technique may also be used in Java. In Java, the code statement would look like this:

```
cats[cats.length-1].turn(TurnDirection.LEFT, 1.0);
```

Be aware, however, that Java arrays may not necessarily be full. For example, the code in Figure 15.10 shows a *cats* array declaration and initialization in the style that declares the array and then initializes the array by adding elements to the array in individual statements. Note that the array is declared with a length of 21 (21 buckets, with an index of 0 to 20) but only four elements have been added. This means 17 buckets in the array are empty (do not yet hold a kitten object). When writing code with this initialization style, you need to be careful about using *length* to access elements in the array. The last statement in the example shown in Figure 15.10 is an error. There is no kitten in the last bucket of the array.

```
StuffedZombieKitten[] cats = new StuffedZombieKitten[21];
cats[0] = kit0;
cats[1] = kit1;
cats[2] = kit2;
cats[3] = kit3;

//error
    cats[cats.length-1].turn(TurnDirection.LEFT, 1.0);
```

Figure 15.10 *Initialization with individual statements*

Consider writing code to randomly select one of the kittens in in the *cats[]* array, as defined in Figure 15.10, above. Suppose we declare and initialize a Random object, *rand*, using the Random class in the Java Class Library. Then declare a new variable, named *randIndex*, of type Integer and initialize to 0.

```
Random rand = new Random();
Integer randIndex = 0;
```

Next, add a statement to set *randIndex* to a random number using the *length* of the array to specify the range.

```
// generate a random index in the range of 0 to length-1
randIndex = rand.nextInt(cats.length);
```

Finally, add a statement to turn the kitten at the random index position.

```
cats[randIndex].turn(TurnDirection.RIGHT, 1.0);
```

If this code were executed, it would work sometimes but crash other times. This is because it will sometimes generate a random index value for an empty bucket. If the bucket is empty, access to an element fails.

15.2 Sorting an Array

Sorting is the process of arranging a collection of elements in a specific order based on some criteria. We have been describing an array as an ordered collection of elements. But collections of elements can be, and often are sorted in such a way that the elements re-ordered. There are many reasons for sorting. Think of the song list in your music player application. Initially, the ordering may be based on when the song was added to the list. To make it easier to find the song you want, you have most likely reordered the list of songs, based on the artist's name, the album name, or the genre.

In the *FindingAdelaide* project, the tower of kittens was originally built starting with the tallest kitten. However, the rest of the kittens were just piled on top of one another in whatever order they were in the array. When you look at this tower, it's easy to realize that it might not be the most stable arrangement. The tower might gain some stability if it were built with the tallest kitten on the bottom, and then the next tallest, and so forth with successively shorter kittens, ending with the smallest kitten on the top. We are going to sort the array in order, from tallest to shortest, and then build the tower.

15.2.1 The selection sort algorithm

There are many different algorithms for writing code to sort an array. Some sort algorithms are very easy to implement but are generally inefficient to use with large amounts of data. Other sort algorithms can be very efficient with large amounts of data but are very complex to implement. The sort algorithm we will demonstrate here is known as the **selection sort**. The selection sort works well for small to moderate numbers of elements, and it is relatively easy to implement.

The selection sort uses a loop to iterate through the array, from one index position to the next. At each index position, a search is called to find an element from that position to the end of the array. The search seeks an element that meets a given criteria from that position to the end of the array. After the search, a swap is used to move the found element to the current index position. The general algorithm, shown in Figure 15.11, assumes the array has no empty buckets and uses *length-1* to control the number of loop iterations.

*for every **index position** in the array, up to but not including *length-1**
    find an element <meeting criteria> in the array AFTER the **index position**
    swap the found element with the element at the **index position**

Figure 15.11   *Selection sort algorithm*

Think through how this algorithm works. For example, imagine the following array of numbers (Figure 15.12). The index of each position is listed in the bottom row. The top row shows the integer value stored at each index position. Let's use the selection sort algorithm to sort the values in **descending order**, from largest to smallest.

13	41	54	27
0	*1*	*2*	*3*

Figure 15.12   *Initial array*

The loop begins at index position 0.

At index position 0, the value is 13. Search the remaining elements in the array to find the largest value greater than 13. The found element is 54, at index position 2 (Figure 15.13).

13	41	54	27
0	*1*	*2*	*3*

Figure 15.13   *Search for the largest value after index position 0*

Swap the found element at index position 2 with the element at index position 0. The result is in Figure 15.14.

54	41	13	27

Figure 15.14   *Array after swapping values at index positions 0 and 2*

The loop now goes to the next index position, index 1.

For index position 1, the value is 41. Search the remaining elements in the array to find the largest value greater than 41. There is no value greater than 41, so the array remains unchanged (Figure 15.15).

54	41	13	27
0	*1*	*2*	*3*

Figure 15.15   *No swap for index position 1*

The loop now goes to the next index position, index 2.

For index position 2, the value is 13. Search the remaining elements (only one element). We find that 27 is a greater value than 13 (Figure 15.16).

54	41	13	27
0	1	2	3

Figure 15.16 *Find the largest value after index position 2.*

Swap the found element at index position 3 with the element at index position 2. The result is in Figure 15.17.

54	41	27	13
0	1	2	3

Figure 15.17 *Array after swapping values at index positions 2 and 3*

The loop stops at the last element. The array is now sorted in decreasing order from largest to smallest. If an array is sorted from smallest to largest, we say it is in **ascending** order.

15.2.2 Implementation: select sort

To sort the *cats*[] array, the criterion we will use is *height*. The array will be sorted in decreasing height, from the tallest to the shortest. Using this criterion with the selection sort algorithm, the decomposition is shown in Figure 15.18.

*for every **index position** in the cats[] array, up to but not including length-1*
    *find the tallest kitten in the array **AFTER the index position***
    *swap the found kitten with the kitten at the **index position***

Figure 15.18 *Decomposition for* sort *procedural method*

Click the Scene class tab in the *FindingAdelaide* NetBeans project. Immediately after the *myFirstMethod* code block, declare a *swap* procedural method (Figure 15.19).

```
/*
 * Procedures and functions for this scene
 */
public void myFirstMethod()
{...22 lines }

public void sort() {
    /*
     * Arrages the ordering of the cats array from largest by height
     * to smallest
     */
}
```

Figure 15.19 *Declaration of sort in the Scene class*

Inside the *swap* code block, create a *for* loop that will move through every index position in the array except the last, at *length-1* (Figure 15.20). Notice that the loop counter variable is *index* and the repetitions expression is *index < cats.length - 1*.

```
public void sort() {
    /*
     * Arrages the ordering of the cats array from largest by height
     * to smallest
     */

    for (Integer index = 0; index < cats.length - 1; index ++) {

    }

}
```

Figure 15.20 for *loop to check every index position but the last*

Two actions must take place in the *for* loop: a *search* and a *swap*. We will write a helper method for each of these actions. The first helper method will be a function method, named *findLargestAfterIndex*, and the second will be a procedure method, named *swap*.

15.2.3 A function helper method: *findLargestAfterIndex*

In the Alice version of *FindingAdelaide*, a linear search was written to find the tallest kitten in *cats[]*. But it was not written as a procedure or function. The code was executed only once and was written as part of *myFirstMethod*. The selection sort algorithm performs a linear search over and over again. So for sorting purposes, we will write a linear search function method named *findLargestAfterIndex*.

When *findLargestAfterIndex* is called, we expect it to find the tallest kitten from the current index to the end of the array. The tallest kitten found by the search will then be swapped with the kitten at the current index. In order to perform a swap, the index position of the found kitten will be needed. So, *findLargestAfterIndex* will be written as a function method that returns the index of the tallest kitten found.

After the *sort* code block, declare *findLargestAfterIndex*. Enter the word *public*, then the word *Integer* to indicate that this method will contain a *return* statement and an Integer value will be sent back to the calling statement (Figure 15.21). The search will start from the current index position in the loop. Therefore, add a parameter, named *startIndex* of type Integer. Add comments in the code block to document the action performed by the function.

```
⊞    public void sort() {...11 lines }

⊟    public Integer findLargestAfterIndex(Integer startIndex) {
         /*
          * Searches the array cats from startIndex + 1 to the end
          * for the largest cat, as defined in the StuffedZombieKitten
          * compareTo method
          */

     }
```

Figure 15.21 *Declare a* findLargestAfterIndex *function method of type Integer*

Immediately after the comments, add a statement to declare a tracking variable, named *tallestCatPosition*, of type Integer. Initialize *tallestCatPosition* to *startIndex*. Then, add a *for* loop. Within the *for* loop parentheses, name the loop control variable *position* and initialize *position* as *startIndex* + 1. Enter *position* < *cats.length* as the repetitions expression, and then *position*++ (Figure 15.22).

```java
public Integer findLargestAfterIndex(Integer startIndex) {
    /*
     * Searches the array cats from startIndex + 1 to the end
     * for the largest cat, as defined in the StuffedZombieKitten
     * compareTo method
     */

    Integer tallestCatPosition = startIndex;
    for (Integer position = startIndex + 1; position < cats.length; position ++){

    }

}
```

Figure 15.22   *A loop to search for the tallest kitten, beginning at* startIndex + 1

Next, add an *if/else* statement. The condition for the *if/else* will make use of the *compareTo* custom function. This *compareTo* function was written as part the *FindingAdelaide* project in Chapter 14. Remember that a *compareTo* function is a well-known standard function for comparing two objects of the same class. As in Alice, the heights of the two kitten objects (*this kitten* and *other kitten*) are compared. We are satisfied that the function returns a value greater than 0 if *this kitten* is taller than *other kitten*, returns a value less than 0 if *this kitten* is shorter than *other kitten*, and otherwise returns 0.

Create a conditional expression in the *if* part of the *if/else* control structure. Compare *cats[position]* to *cats[tallestCatPosition]* (Figure 15.23).

```java
public Integer findLargestAfterIndex(Integer startIndex) {
    /*
     * Searches the array cats from startIndex + 1 to the end
     * for the largest cat, as defined in the StuffedZombieKitten
     * compareTo method
     */

    Integer tallestCatPosition = startIndex;
    StuffedZombieKitten currentTallest = cats[tallestCatPosition];
    for (Integer position = startIndex + 1; position < cats.length; position ++){
        if (cats[position].compareTo(cats[tallestCatPosition]) > 0) {

        }

    }

}
```

Figure 15.23   *Using the* compareTo *function in the if statement*

If *compareTo* returns a value greater than 0, then the kitten at *cats[position]* is taller than the current tallest, so update the tracking variable, *tallestCatPosition*, to the *position* index (Figure 15.24).

```java
public Integer findLargestAfterIndex(Integer startIndex) {
    /*
     * Searches the array cats from startIndex + 1 to the end
     * for the largest cat, as defined in the StuffedZombieKitten
     * compareTo method
     */

    Integer tallestCatPosition = startIndex;
    StuffedZombieKitten currentTallest = cats[tallestCatPosition];
    for (Integer position = startIndex + 1; position < cats.length; position ++){
        if (cats[position].compareTo(cats[tallestCatPosition]) > 0) {
            tallestCatPosition = position;
        }
    }
}
```

Figure 15.24 *Update the* tallestCatPosition *tracking variable.*

After the loop is finished, the variable *tallestCatPosition* contains the index position for the tallest kitten from the *startIndex* position to the end of the array. Add a *return* statement to send this index value back to the *sort* method (Figure 15.25).

```java
public Integer findLargestAfterIndex(Integer startIndex) {
    /*
     * Searches the array cats from startIndex + 1 to the end
     * for the largest cat, as defined in the StuffedZombieKitten
     * compareTo method
     */

    Integer tallestCatPosition = startIndex;
    StuffedZombieKitten currentTallest = cats[tallestCatPosition];
    for (Integer position = startIndex + 1; position < cats.length; position ++){
        if (cats[position].compareTo(cats[tallestCatPosition]) > 0) {
            tallestCatPosition = position;
        }
    }

    return tallestCatPosition;
}
```

Figure 15.25 *Return the index value* tallestCatPosition.

15.2.4 Calling the helper function

The returned index will be an Integer value. In the sort method, declare a variable of type Integer and name it *tallestCatPosition*. Assign it a value by calling *findLargestAfterIndex* with *index* as the argument (Figure 15.26).

15.2.5 A procedure helper method: *swap*

After the tallest kitten has been found, the tallest kitten will be swapped with the kitten at the current *index* position. Think about exchanging the location of two books on a

```
public void sort() {
    /*
     * Arranges the ordering of the cats array from largest by height
     * to smallest
     */

    for (Integer index = 0; index < cats.length - 1; index ++) {
        // find the tallest cat in the remainder of the array
        Integer tallestCatPosition = findLargestAfterIndex(index);
    }

}
```

Figure 15.26   *A variable receives the returned value of a call to* findLargestAfterIndex.

bookshelf. In order for the second book to be placed into the position of the first book, you would first take one of the books and hold it in your hand (or put it on a table), then place the second book where the first book had been, and finally place the book from your hand (or from the table) into the position left open by the second book. This same process is used to swap two elements in an array, as shown in Figure 15.27.

parameters
  firstPos, of type Integer
  secondPos, of type Integer
local variable
  StuffedZombieKitten *temp*

first kitten is held by *temp*
second kitten moves to *firstPos* (position where the first kitten was)
first kitten moves to *secondPos* (position where the second kitten was)

Figure 15.27   *Decomposition for* swap

Declare the *swap* procedural method after the *findLargestAfterIndex* code block (Figure 15.28). This is a procedure method (does not have a *return* statement), so enter void as the data type. Add two Integer parameters, *firstPos* and *secondPos*. When *swap* is called, we expect two arguments will be sent to the parameters, specifying the index positions of the two kittens to be swapped.

```
public Integer findLargestAfterIndex(Integer startIndex) {...17 lines }

public void swap(Integer firstPos, Integer secondPos) {
    /*
     * Exchanges the elements in array cats so that the element in the
     * secondPos is located in the firstPos, and the element in the
     * firstPos is located in the secondPos.
     */

}
```

Figure 15.28   swap *procedural method with two Integer parameters*

In the *swap* code block add a statement to create a local *StuffedZombieKitten* variable, named *temp*, and initialize with *cats[firstPos]*. Now, add a statement to move the kitten currently at *secondPos* to *firstPos*. Finally, add a third statement to move the kitten being held by *temp* into *secondPos* (Figure 15.29).

```
public void swap(Integer firstPos, Integer secondPos) {
    /*
     * Exchanges the elements in array cats so that the element in the
     * secondPos is located in the firstPos, and the element in the
     * firstPos is located in the secondPos.
     */

    StuffedZombieKitten temp = cats[firstPos];
    cats[firstPos] = cats[secondPos];
    cats[secondPos] = temp;
}
```

Figure 15.29 *Implementation of the* swap *procedure method*

15.2.6 Using the Integer class *compareTo* function

Now that *swap* is implemented, a statement can be added to *sort* to call *swap*. However, remember the possibility that a swap is not always needed. Actually, *cats[]* is a small array, and there is a good chance that a kitten will already be in an appropriate position in the array. Only if the *index* loop control variable is not the same as the *tallestCatPosition* tracking variable should *swap* be called.

The Integer data type has a **natural ordering**, that is, elements of the Integer class can be compared based on the value of that type. As such, the Integer class has a built-in *compareTo* method that behaves in the same way as the custom *compareTo* method we wrote earlier. For the Integer class, the built-in *compareTo* returns a value greater than 0 if *this* Integer is greater than *other* Integer, returns a value less than 0 if *this* Integer is smaller than *other* Integer, and otherwise returns 0.

We will use the Integer class's built-in *compareTo* function to check whether the *index* loop control variable and the *tallestCatPosition* tracking variable are different. Add an *if* statement that compares *index* to *tallestCatPosition* and calls the *swap* procedure only if 0 is not returned (Figure 15.30).

```
public void sort() {
    /*
     * Arrages the ordering of the cats array from largest by height
     * to smallest
     */

    for (Integer index = 0; index < cats.length - 1; index ++) {
        // find the tallest cat in the remainder of the array
        Integer tallestCatPosition = findLargestAfterIndex(index);

        if (tallestCatPosition.compareTo(index) != 0) {
            swap(index, tallestCatPosition);
        }
    }
}
```

Figure 15.30 *Using* Integer's *built-in* compareTo *to decide whether a* swap *is needed*

15.2.7 Calling *sort*

Now, the array of kittens can be sorted by height, before the tower is built. In NetBeans, scroll to *myFirstMethod* in the Scene class. Just before the statement that calls *alignInARow*, add a statement to call *sort* (Figure 15.30).

Finally, run the program. The kittens should now line up in descending order (Figure 15.31).

```java
    public void myFirstMethod()
    {
//Larry and Tashi talk about their situation  while the zomb

        /*
         * disabled
         * doTogether(()->{this.openingConversation();}, ()->
         */
//Adelaide jumps in to greet them
        this.AdelaideJumpsIn();
        /*
         * disabled
         * this.conversationWithAdelaide();
         */
        this.escapePlan();
// Adelaide lines up the kittens
        this.sort();   ←
        this.alignInRow();
//
//sort the array of ZombieKittens

//  stack in a tower, with the tallest cat as the anchor
        this.stack(this.cats[0]);
```

Figure 15.30   *Add a statement to call* sort *in* myFirstMethod.

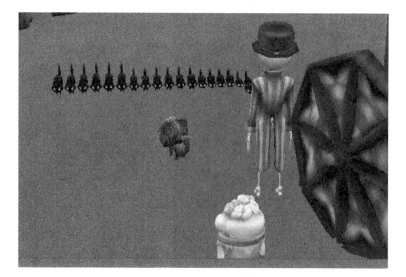

Figure 15.31   *Kittens aligned in tallest to shorter order*

15.3 Visual Representation of the Sort Mechanism

Watching the animation run, you can see that *sort* has performed its job because when the kittens line up, the ordering is from tallest to shortest. This shows the end result of the *sort*, but it doesn't really show how *sort* did its work.

It would be interesting if we could actually watch the swapping that takes place as the *sort* method executes. An animation that allows the viewer to actually watch the steps as an algorithm is performed is known as **algorithm visualization**.

A visual representation of *sort* can be created with two minor modifications to our code. The first involves modifying the *swap* routine. The second is to change the order in which the *sort* and *alignInRow* procedures are called in *myFirstMethod*.

15.3.1 Modifying the *swap* procedural method for visualization

Two object markers, named *firstPosition* and *secondPosition*, are already in the *FindingAdelaide-ToNetBeansSetup* project that you imported from Alice into NetBeans. Note the corresponding names: *firstPos* index and *firstPosition* marker, *secondPos* index with *secondPosition* marker. The markers will be used as trackers for the objects located at the index positions.

Add a statement to *moveAndOrient* the *firstPosition* marker to the kitten in *cats[firstPos]*. Then, add a statement to *moveAndOrient* the *secondPosition* marker to the kitten in *cats[secondPos]* (Figure 15.32). In each statement, set the duration to 0.

```
public void swap(Integer firstPos, Integer secondPos) {
    /*
     * Exchanges the elements in array cats so that the element in the
     * secondPos is located in the firstPos, and the element in the
     * firstPos is located in the secondPos.
     */

    firstPosition.moveAndOrientTo(cats[firstPos], MoveAndOrientTo.duration(0));
    secondPosition.moveAndOrientTo(cats[secondPos], MoveAndOrientTo.duration(0));

    StuffedZombieKitten temp = cats[firstPos];
    cats[firstPos] = cats[secondPos];
    cats[secondPos] = temp;
}
```

Figure 15.32 *Setting up the tracking object markers before the* swap

Now immediately below the statements just added, insert a *do together* code block from the palette and enter 2 as the number of "things" that will be executed together (Figure 15.33).

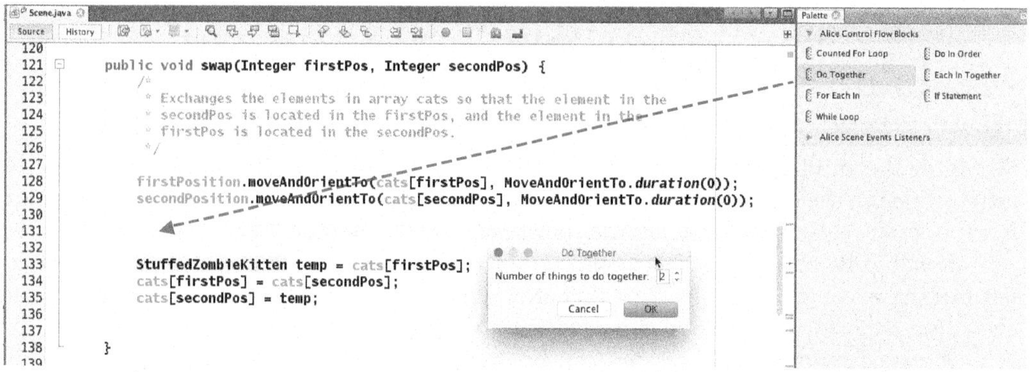

Figure 15.33   *Insert a* do together *code block into* swap.

Within the *do together* are two threads. In the first thread, add a statement to *moveAndOrient* the kitten at *cats[firstPos]* to the *secondPosition* marker. In the second thread, add a statement to *moveAndOrient* the kitten at *cats[secondPos]* to the *firstPosition* marker (Figure 15.34).

```java
public void swap(Integer firstPos, Integer secondPos) {
    /*
     * Exchanges the elements in array cats so that the element in the
     * secondPos is located in the firstPos, and the element in the
     * firstPos is located in the secondPos.
     */

    firstPosition.moveAndOrientTo(cats[firstPos], MoveAndOrientTo.duration(0));
    secondPosition.moveAndOrientTo(cats[secondPos], MoveAndOrientTo.duration(0));

            //start a Thread for each Runnable and wait until they complete
    doTogether(() ->
    {
        cats[firstPos].moveAndOrientTo(secondPosition);   <—
    }, () ->
    {
        cats[secondPos].moveAndOrientTo(firstPosition);   <—
    });

    StuffedZombieKitten temp = cats[firstPos];
    cats[firstPos] = cats[secondPos];
    cats[secondPos] = temp;

}
```

Figure 15.34   *The* do together *code block with two threads*

15.3.2 Modify the call to *sort*

Finally, return to *myFirstMethod* and modify the code so that the cats line up first and then sort into decreasing order (Figure 15.35).

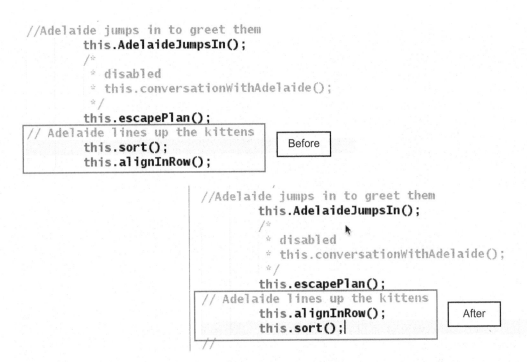

```
//Adelaide jumps in to greet them
        this.AdelaideJumpsIn();
        /*
         * disabled
         * this.conversationWithAdelaide();
         */
        this.escapePlan();
// Adelaide lines up the kittens
        this.sort();
        this.alignInRow();
```
Before

```
//Adelaide jumps in to greet them
        this.AdelaideJumpsIn();
        /*
         * disabled
         * this.conversationWithAdelaide();
         */
        this.escapePlan();
// Adelaide lines up the kittens
        this.alignInRow();
        this.sort();
//
```
After

Figure 15.35 *Rearrange the calls to* sort *and* alignInRow *in* myFirstMethod.

Test-run. You should now be able to watch the operation of the *sort* as kittens rearrange themselves in order, tallest to shortest (Figure 15.36).

Figure 15.36 *Kittens rearranging their lineup*

Summary

In this chapter, the *FindingAdelaide* project from Chapter 14 was imported into NetBeans and used as an example for illustrating how to create and write code for custom arrays in Java. In particular, the declaration of the *cats*[] array was used to illustrate Java syntax for declaring and initializing an array. Then, custom procedure and function methods were written to demonstrate writing code that modifies the composition of an array.

Arrays are of fixed length, meaning that once an array is declared and initialized, the number of buckets cannot be changed while the program is running. Still, modifications may be made to the composition of an array. For example, elements may be swapped within an array.

A common operation that changes the composition of an array is sorting. Sorting is the process of arranging a collection of elements in a specific order based on some criteria. There are many algorithms for implementing a sort, which vary in terms of ease of implementation and efficiency in working with large amounts of data. The sort used in this chapter is the *selection sort*, which works well for small to moderate amounts of data and is relatively easy to implement. The selection sort iterates through an array and performs two major actions in each iteration: a search and a swap.

A critical component of a search is the ability to compare two objects of the same class. A custom *compareTo* function method was used to compare two zombie kittens in terms of height. A built-in *compareTo* was used to compare to Integer index values, which have a natural order. A *compareTo* function is expected to return a value greater than 0 if this source object has some property that is greater than the target object, returns a value less than 0 if the source object property is smaller than the target object, and otherwise returns 0.

Swapping the position of elements in an array usually involves using a temporary element to hold the first element while the second is moved into the original position of the first. Then the element with a temporary hold is put into the location vacated when the other element was moved. In this example, *swap* was modified to create an algorithm visualization to allow the *swap* operation to be viewed as the *sort* was performed.

Terms

algorithm visualization	fixed length	selection sort
array buckets	index operator	sort
ascending order	initializer list	void
descending order	natural ordering	

Concept Questions

1. What is the difference between the meaning of "item" and the meaning of "element" when talking about an array?

2. A statement in this chapter indicates that an array has a fixed length. When can the length of an array be changed?

3. The assignment operator in Alice is a back arrow (<–). What is the assignment operator in Java?

The following statements are taken from a NetBeans project that imports the Alice gallery. Use these statements for questions 4–10.

```
Biped[] cast = new Biped[10];
Quadruped[] zoo = new Quadruped[]
   {this.camel, this.elephant, this.bison, this.tiger, this.fox};
```

4. (a) What is the length of the cast array?
   (b) How many buckets are in the cast array?
   (c) How many objects are in the cast array?

5. (a) What is the length of the zoo array?
   (b) How many buckets are in the zoo array?
   (c) How many objects are in the zoo array?

6. Write statements to add each of the following objects to the cast array, in the order listed.

   ghost, of type Ghost

   Jamie, of type IceSkater

   monkey, of type GoldenMonkey

   Harry, of type MarchHare

7. After the objects in question 6 have been added to the cast array,
   (a) What is the index position of the monkey in the array?
   (b) What is the index position of the camel in the zoo array?

8. Which object does this code fragment access in the zoo array?

   ```
   zoo[length -2]
   ```

9. Is there a bug in the following Java statement? Explain your answer.

   ```
   cast[4] = zoo[2];
   ```

Exercises

1. In the *FindingAdelaide* example in this chapter, the *cats*[] array is sorted in descending order based on height. Modify the project to sort the array in ascending order, based on width.

2. Do some research (online or in your local library) to find a bubble sort algorithm specifically designed for Java. Using the bubble sort algorithm, add a second *sort* procedure method, named *bubbleSort*, to the *FindingAdelaide* example of this chapter. Implement the *bubbleSort* algorithm. In *myFirstMethod*, write a statement to call *bubbleSort* and use a comment to disable the statement that calls the selection *sort* method. Test-run.

March 1, 1910: Gideon

The Oven Mitts

Gideon sleeps through the avalanche. All those jokes everyone used to make about how he could sleep through anything turn out to be true.

It's peaceful. In the uncertain period between waking and sleeping, Gideon feels nothing but calm and a gentle rising and falling motion, as if the train is very slowly chugging along a series of smooth bumps. He opens his eyes. And wonders if he is still dreaming. Because the stone mausoleum is gone. He is alone, with nothing around him but twisted, strange trees. The trunks of the trees split off like spider webs and extend down deep into murky water. Gideon looks below himself and sees nothing but the same water.

He is floating on air.

His skin is thin, and translucent, and blue, and when he tries to feel the top of his head his hands go straight through. He, too, seems to be made of nothing but air.

He moans. And what comes out is a thin, echoing sound, like his normal voice but as if he was walking through a tunnel.

It sounds quite good. Which is surprising.

A soft wind filters through the trees, and he finds himself drifting along with it. He can't walk like normal people; when he tries he just ends up moving his arms and legs while remaining in one place. Instead, he picks up the air currents and uses them to drift between trees. Everywhere in the swamp looks identical. Each tree is a slight variation of the others, not a single landmark in sight and he fears he is going in circles. Eventually Gideon gives up. He stops trying to control the direction he goes and lets the wind take him where it wills. He floats through the swamp, wailing in despair and frustration, and rather enjoying himself.

Until the dragon finds him.

When a gigantic purple beast swoops down from above and lands on a tree root directly in front of him, Gideon's first reaction is fear. But the dragon crouches low and hesitates, and Gideon realizes the creature is as nervous about him as he is afraid of it.

"I followed your voice," the dragon booms.

The dragon's own voice is so loud it reverberates through Gideon, and for a second afterwards his hearing goes quiet as if plugged.

"Okay," Gideon replies coolly, as if this is a normal conversation. After all, what could a dragon possibly do to threaten a ghost?

The dragon blinks, as if slightly thrown off by Gideon's reaction. "I am Tuonela," the dragon says majestically, "The gatekeeper of this forest."

"I'm Gideon," says Gideon, "The phantom of this forest."

Tuonela eyes Gideon curiously. "I was . . . wondering," the dragon looks as if the words pain them, "I was wondering if you would consent to sing for me and my daughter."

"Okay," Gideon shrugs.

"You agree?" Tuonela asks warily.

"I agree," Gideon smiles, "Unless you need me to travel anywhere, because I can't move unless the wind is blowing."

Tuonela solves the drifting problem. Tuonela's wings flap heavily towards Gideon, and the gust of air sends the ghost spiraling in whatever direction the dragon chooses. Soon, Gideon can see Tuonela's tower in the distance above the trees. The tower appears closer than it is because the stone levels grow larger as it gets taller, throwing off Gideon's sense of perspective. When they finally reach the tower, the very base of it is miniscule. It has one tiny human-sized door, useless to dragons. Tuonela leaves Gideon on the ground and launches upward, circling the tower to gain height. Gideon watches the dragon disappear underneath the rooftop. The top of the tower looks big enough to hold at least two dragons.

Gideon hums and looks around, not able to do much else since the wind is unusually still in this place. Beside the tower base, slowly sinking into the muck, is his old mausoleum.

"You found it!" Gideon exclaims when Tuonela returns with a smaller dragon in tow. Gideon points to the mausoleum.

Gideon reveals the secret compartment, once used for coffins and now used for storing the Prenderghast circus tent. Gideon tries to help set up the tent but his hand goes straight through the object as if he was nothing. Tuonela eyes Gideon expertly and then dumps a scrap of canvas over the ghost's head.

"There, now you're like a balloon," Tuonela says with certainty.

The extra fabric works. Gideon can touch things again, and he directs the dragons in constructing the circus tent. They even unfold the bleachers, despite being in an isolated swamp with a scant audience.

Tuonela smiles at Gideon when the tent is complete, "And now, you will sing so Celeste can dance."

The tent becomes the dragonette's practice space. Celeste dances, Tuonela's tail thumps out a beat, and Gideon sings. Neither dragon seems to care what Gideon sings, so long as it follows the tempo. He slowly starts to figure they must be tone deaf.

That's not to say Gideon doesn't enjoy the enthusiasm, he does. The dragons are demanding in their music needs, and Gideon eagerly rises to the occasion.

The blissful storybook fantasy quickly fades when the first soldier arrives. He doesn't look particularly brave or well equipped. When he points threateningly at Tuonela, his arm shakes from nerves.

He's dead in under a minute.

The body mysteriously disappears, and Gideon discovers he'd rather not ask questions. The second person is a little more self-sure. She yells a lengthy speech about the dragons' tyranny over their village coming to an end. She manages to shoot Tuonela's upper arm before she's toasted to a crisp.

"Do you terrorize the village?" Gideon asks.

"Nonsense," Tuonela says haughtily, "We take what we need, no more."

By then the dragons have a system down. Tuonela captures the interlopers, puts them in the tent, and forces them to watch Celeste's dance performance. Each guest claps enthusiastically at the end, but Gideon suspects it's for the wrong reasons. After they've watched the show, the guests all disappear. Tuonela carries each to the top of the tower. Gideon suspects they get eaten. He doesn't eat, his body lacks substance so doesn't need it. But Celeste complains regularly about being hungry. And sometimes Tuonela will disappear for days on end with no explanation.

"I want a real audience," Celeste confesses to Gideon while Tuonela is off on a hunt, "I want people to watch me dance and come for no other reason but that."

"I watch you dance," Gideon offers.

"Yes but you only watch because you want to sing," Celeste says, "Don't you want someone to listen to you, too?"

No audience actually isn't Gideon's growing problem. Gideon doesn't admit it, but he is bored. He sings the same songs repeatedly or invents new ones. The new ones all start to sound the same eventually, too. He starts thinking about leaving. He can't move forward or backward without help, but he can float. He tests how high he can go. But he never dares go beyond experimenting.

Fittingly, it's a living skeleton who interrupts their routine. The skeleton blunders into a practice session as if pushed, trips, and falls flat on his face in front of Celeste. Celeste screams and hops away. The skeleton screams in return and scrambles backwards on his hands and knees. The skeleton tries to run but Tuonela launches into the air, soars forward, and blocks the tent entrance. The dragon's tail curls around the skeleton's body and lifts it into the air.

"You interrupted my daughter's practice," the dragon growls.

"Did I?" the skeleton smiles beautifully, "So sorry."

In a flash of recognition, Gideon accidentally blurts out the skeleton's name, "Larry!"

Still in the dragon's clutches, Larry turns to look behind him. His head rotates all the way backwards at an unnatural angle that would have snapped any living person's neck. Larry's face lights up, "Gideon! I followed the sound of your singing."

Gideon's face drains of color. He looks as if he's seen a ghost instead of become one.

"Another fuzzy creature is behind the entrance flap!" Celeste interrupts, pointing.

Everyone turns to look. The tuft of hair on a creature's head disappears from sight behind the canvas. With a few short wing blasts, Tuonela suddenly fills the entire space between the entrance flaps. The dragon dives, scoops a small furry creature into its talons, and soars out of the tent.

"I'll be right back," the dragon calls, sounding tired.

Larry stands in haste, but stops when the little dragon swivels her eye to watch him.

"I wouldn't leave, if I were you," Celeste says sweetly.

Larry sits defeated. Gideon hovers next to him.

"What are they going to do with Tashi?" Larry asks.

"Throw your friend in a pot, boil it, eat it . . .," Gideon says mournfully, "Happens to everyone."

"Is that what they did to you?"

"No," Gideon sighs, "I stay willingly. I sing so Celeste can dance."

After a few short minutes Tuonela swoops through the entrance and orders Gideon to continue.

Gideon takes a deep breath and starts to sing again.

Larry makes a move to cover his ears before he realizes he doesn't have any.

"Wait, wait!" Larry cries, stumbling forward and holding out his hands, "Your daughter is clearly a very good dancer naturally. But has she had any formal training? I am a circus ringmaster; this tent you are using is actually my old venue. Give me back my friend — alive!" he holds up a finger for emphasis, "and I'll teach Celeste."

The little dragon gasps with delight, "We had a traveling circus for dinner once!" She turns and whines to the large dragon, "Please?"

"Very well," the large dragon says warily, "Teach my daughter to dance in your circus, and I'll allow you to collect your friend." There's a duplicitous smile on the dragon's face, and it makes Gideon nervous about the outcome of the bargain.

Larry glances at Gideon, gulps nervously, and agrees. He does his best to teach Celeste. He invents the dances as he goes. Thankfully the dragons are clueless about proper form. When Larry runs out of ideas, he pronounces Celeste fit for the stage. Years of overselling underwhelming acts in the large circus prepared Larry well for this moment.

Tuonela leads Larry and Gideon out of the tent ominously.

"Your friend is at the top of the tower," Tuonela bellows, "If you can reach them, you may collect them. There are no stairs, as we do not need them."

Larry stares at the tower and his bones tremble. It does not look structurally sound.

"I'll go," Gideon says quietly, but bravely, "I'm heavier than air. I can't float very high on my own, but if I hit clouds, they push me higher so I think I can make it."

He does make it. Gideon hits the top of the tower, and finds Tashi huddled, terrified in a corner. The baby yeti jumps into Gideon's arms, and they float back down together. Tashi leaps onto the ground and runs straight for Larry.

"Larry!" Tashi cries, "I'm so sorry I tried to eat you when we first met. I promise not to try ever, ever again. They had a gigantic pot, with seasoning. And old skeletons, actual dead dormant skeletons were scattered on the floor. I much prefer walking, talking skeletons."

"Don't worry, I'll cook for everyone," Gideon reassures Larry, "No eating fellow circus troupe members on our train."

"You can," Larry says, "But I've been thinking . . . I have an idea for a new theme to our circus that would suit your talents perfectly."

Gideon's eyes go wide and a yellow glow lights his cheeks, "I can keep singing?" He swoops towards the railroad tracks, where the dragons have already packed the tent and reassembled Gideon's train car. Gideon flies through the marble pillars and stops abruptly when he sees his mitts lying on the tile. He slides his hands into them, and they fit as perfectly as the canvas sheet. For one minute Gideon, the mitts, and the train car shine brilliantly as if one object, and then zip into a puff of smoke.

16

Event-Driven Programming and Advanced Game Controls

Concept Objectives

- Using a *keyPress* listener with a COMBINE multiple event policy
- Using a *collisionStarted* detection event listener
- Using a *timeElapsed* event listener
- Using a *viewExited* event listener
- Using a 3D text object to provide feedback for debugging and game state
- Implementing a main game loop with event listeners

Interactivity and event-driven programming were introduced in previous chapter examples. In this chapter, more advanced, challenging aspects of event listeners and event-driven programming will be used to implement the main game flow. Event listeners are used for player controls, governing the speed of an object's motion, and checking game end conditions.

To illustrate event-driven programming with collision detection, timing components, and text output, the programming task in this chapter will continue with Episode 9, *Gideon: The Oven Mitts*, from the *Haunted Circus*. In this episode, Larry and Tashi find Gideon, the shy circus cook who always wears oven mitts to hide his disfigured hands (the result of a horrible baking accident when he was young). Gideon loves to sing and he also performs as a trapeze aerialist in the big circus tent.

16.1 Analyze the Story

Begin by reading and analyzing the story to determine the background components, and select the objects and actions for an animation script. A summary of the episode is

> Gideon sleeps through the avalanche and wakes up floating disembodied in a swamp. He is basically a ghost who can only move with the air currents, and so he starts drifting and singing. A helicopter-parent dragon finds him and convinces Gideon to sing while the dragon's child, Celeste, dances. Celeste and Gideon perform for fighters who come to kill the dragons and are eaten instead. Similarly, Larry and Tashi almost end up in the dragon's soup. Larry confronts the dragons, and Tashi is kidnapped because she interrupted Celeste's performance. As repayment, Larry has to teach Celeste how to dance. The dragon then tells Larry where Tashi is. But the tower has no stairs and can only be reached by flight. Gideon offers to go in his place. Gideon rises to the top of the tower, hitting clouds as he goes. He carries Tashi down to the base of the tower, much to the dragons' surprise. Larry hugs the floating, ghostly shape hovering near the circus tent. Larry thanks him and says that Gideon's unique singing talent might be exactly what the new circus show needs. The dragons help pull Gideon's mausoleum train car out of the mud, and when Gideon finds his oven mitts and pulls them back on, the entire train car disappears.

For animation, we selected a segment of the episode that begins after Larry and Tashi have blundered into Celeste's practice space and frightened the young dragon. Tuonela has captured Tashi and whisked her away to the top of a tower. Fearing for Tashi's life, Larry has negotiated a deal for Tashi's release in exchange for dancing lessons for Celeste. The dragon challenges Larry to climb the tower. Gideon volunteers to rescue Tashi.

To turn this segment of the *Gideon* episode into a cutscene and an interactive game, one analysis of the episode could be

> Tuonela tells Larry he must rescue Tashi from the tower
> Larry is astonished by the height of the tower that has no stairs
> ghost (Gideon) volunteers to rescue Tashi
> ghost floats upward to rescue Tashi
> ghost carries Tashi down to the base of the tower

16.2 Design
....

In this example, the conversation between Tuonela, Larry, and Gideon (a ghost) can be presented in an opening cutscene. The cutscene can animate the conversation between Tuonela, Larry, and the ghost where Tuonela challenges Larry to rescue Tashi from the tower, but the tower has no stairs. Gideon volunteers to rescue Tashi. A possible algorithm for the cutscene is shown in Figure 16.1.

do in order

> Tuonela agrees that Larry can rescue Tashi (at the top of a tower that has no stairs)
> Larry drops his jaw in astonishment at the height of the tower
> ghost volunteers to rescue Tashi

Figure 16.1 • *Algorithm for cutscene*

The part of the story where the ghost attempts to rescue Tashi offers a challenge and possible end conditions for implementing a game. We could just write code to have the ghost float up to the top of the tower. But, it would be a lot more fun to create a game in which the player's goal is to interactively guide the ghost to the top of the tower for rescuing Tashi.

The game can be made challenging by varying the speed at which the ghost floats upward. For example, the ghost's upward float speed could gradually slow down. Also, we could include a way for the player to speed up the float. For example, guiding the ghost into a collision with a cloud would increase the float speed.

The end conditions should plan for both win and loss. If the player succeeds in reaching the top of the tower, the player would win the game. If the ghost's float speed slows too much, so the ghost falls back to the ground, the player would lose the game.

Other game details will be needed for implementing the game. For now, our general game description provides a basis for a high-level algorithm (Figure 16.2).

do in order

> play game
>> game setup
>>> move ghost into start position
>>> display instructions
>> main game loop
>>> do updates
>>> check if game over
> give feedback on game win or loss

Figure 16.2 • *Algorithm for an interactive game*

A startup project file, named *FindingGideonStarter.a3p*, may be downloaded from **www.alice.org/Alice3ToJava**. Download the file and then open it in Alice. Click the Scene Setup button to view the initial scene in the Scene editor (Figure 16.3). Larry and the ghost (Gideon) are standing in a clearing, facing the dragon. The circus tent is in the background.

Figure 16.3   *Initial scene for the* FindingGideon *project*

Select *camera* in the Toolbox and then view the object and camera markers (Figure 16.4). The object and camera markers are used to manage views and positions near the tower and on the ground level near the old circus tent.

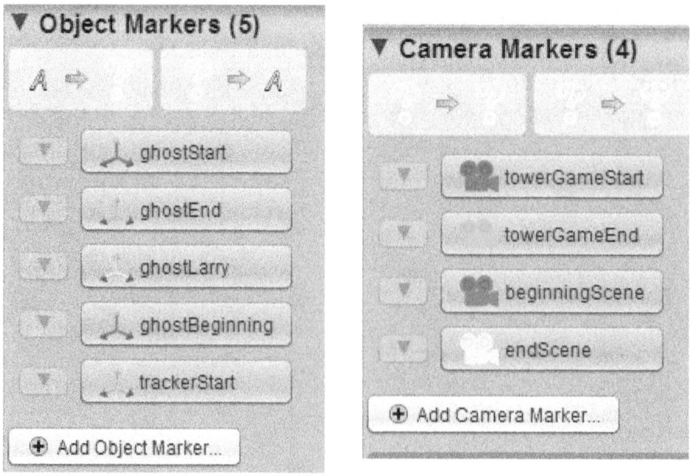

Figure 16.4   *Object and camera markers in the starter world*

Five classes in the starter world have pre-made custom procedures, most of which were especially written for a quick implementation of the cutscene (Figure 16.5). Note that *dragonMessage* and *volunteer* are in the Scene class. The Biped class has *eyesLookRight*, *eyesLookLeft*, and *eyesLookUp*, written specifically for this episode, but also has *talk*, *talkAndSay*, and *blinkEyes*, imported from previously saved class files. The Quadruped class has *talk* and *talkAndSay*, similar to the Biped's *talk* and *talkAndSay*. The Skeleton class has *gapeUpward* and the Ghost class has *nodHead*.

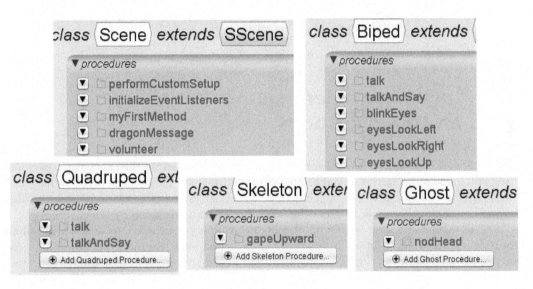

Figure 16.5   *Pre-made custom procedures in five of the class files*

16.3 Implementation: The Opening Cutscene

Return to the Code editor and view *myFirstMethod*. Comments have already been added to *myFirstMethod* to document the algorithm steps. The first three steps in the algorithm implement the cutscene between Larry, Tuonela, and the ghostly Gideon. Statements that call the pre-made custom procedures (*dragonMessage*, *gapeUpward*, and *volunteer*) procedures have already been entered (Figure 16.6).

The concepts and techniques used for implementing the code in the *dragonMessage*, *gapeUpward*, and *volunteer* procedures are the same as those discussed and demonstrated in previous chapters. The procedures are provided in the starter world to allow focus on the new programming concepts. In any case, we suggest you open the procedures and view the code to gain perspective on the conversation, which tells the story and "sets the stage" for playing the game.

Test-run the project to view the conversation in the opening cutscene.

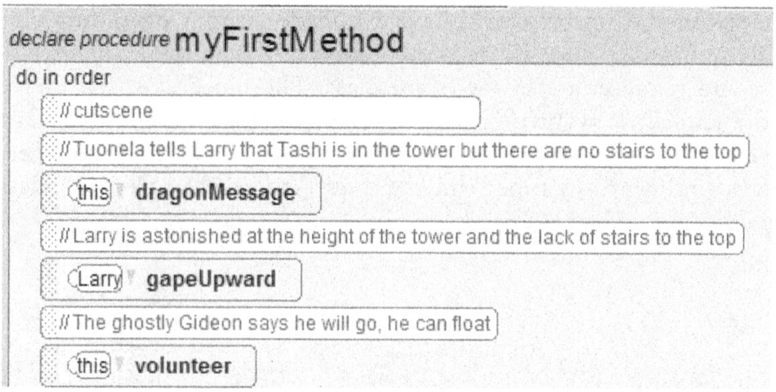

```
declare procedure myFirstMethod
do in order
    // cutscene
    // Tuonela tells Larry that Tashi is in the tower but there are no stairs to the top
    (this)  dragonMessage
    // Larry is astonished at the height of the tower and the lack of stairs to the top
    (Larry)  gapeUpward
    // The ghostly Gideon says he will go, he can float
    (this)  volunteer
```

Figure 16.6   *Implementation in* myFirstMethod

16.4 Implementation: Game with an Implied Loop

The high-level steps in our general game algorithm are: first, set up the game; then, perform the main game loop. In this example, the setup will include moving the camera and ghost into starting positions and initializing tracking variables. Instructions will then be displayed to prompt the player to press the SPACE key to start the game.

The main game loop will be implemented using event listeners to create an **implied loop** (NOT a main loop in *myFirstMethod*). The implied loop technique is commonly used by professional game developers. Implementing the game loop with event listeners has two advantages: an event listener can end the game immediately when an end condition is reached (not waiting for a main loop control structure to end), and an event listener can easily restart the game (instead of closing and restarting the entire program.)

A more detailed description of the play of the game is needed to determine which event listeners are needed and how they will create and control a game loop. The following is a description of the play of the game, including the player's interactions with the game and actions that occur independent of the player:

> The game begins with the ghost in a start position in front of the tower. The ghost gives instructions to the player on how to play the game. The player presses the space key to start the game. The ghost starts floating upward, but the speed of upward movement slows with each passing second (the effect of gravity). The player can use the left and right arrow keys to move the ghost left or right for collision with a cloud. If a collision occurs, the cloud provides an updraft so the ghost's upward floating speed increases.
>
> As the ghost floats upward, the camera also moves upward. Although the ghost's upward speed can increase or decrease, the camera's upward speed is constant. If the ghost's float speed is too slow, the camera can move high enough so the ghost is no longer in view. If the float speed is too fast, the ghost can float out of the camera's point of view. At any time, if the ghost goes out of the camera's view, the game is over and the ghost will fall back to the ground, the game is over and the player loses. The game will reset.
>
> If the ghost reaches the top of the tower (collides with an endLine marker), the ghost rescues Tashi and the player wins the game.

16.4.1 Game analysis and design

A quick analysis of the game description yields a list of the player's controls and other events that may occur as the game is played:

- **Player's controls:**
  - The player can press the space key to start the game.
    - The ghost starts floating, continuously.
    - The camera starts moving upward, continuously.
  - The player can press the left or right arrow key to guide the ghost to collide with a cloud.
- **After the game starts:**
  - A timer is counting, in seconds
    - With every passing second, the ghost's float speed is decreased.
  - The ghost can collide with a cloud.
    - The ghost's float speed increases.
  - The ghost can collide with the top of tower marker (endLine).
    - Rescue Tashi and the player wins.
  - The ghost can float out of the camera's view
    - The player loses this round and the game resets.

Game design diagrams will help in selecting event listeners for the player's controls and other events. A *keyPress* listener will watch for the player to press the SPACE, LEFT ARROW, or RIGHT ARROW keys (Figure 16.7). Note that arrow keys will move the ghost to its left or right (the opposite of your left/right, as you view the scene).

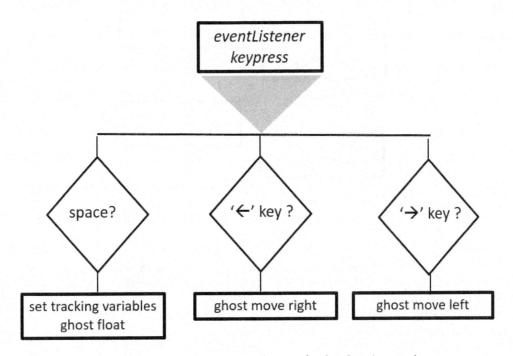

Figure 16.7   *Keypress event listener for the player's controls*

Two event listeners are needed to govern the ghost's float speed (Figure 16.8). A timeElapsed listener will automatically trigger every second to decrease the ghost's float speed. A collisionStarted listener will watch for the ghost to collide with one of the clouds.

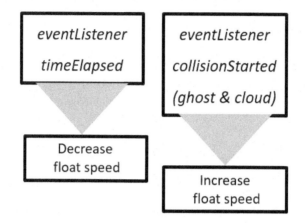

Figure 16.8   *Events that govern the ghost's float speed*

Two event listeners are needed to watch for an end condition, one for win and one for loss (Figure 16.9). A *collisionStarted* listener will watch for the ghost to collide with the end-Line marker (marks the top level of the tower, where Tashi is held). A **viewExited** listener will watch for the ghost to float out of the camera's view.

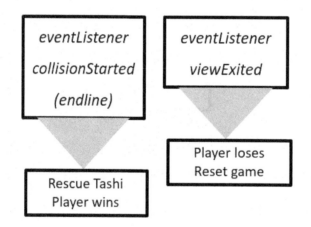

Figure 16.9   *Event listeners for end conditions, win and loss*

16.4.2 Game setup

To set up for playing the game, the ghost must move to a game-start position, near the tower. At the same time, the camera must be positioned to view the ghost and the tower. We know the float speed is going to change as the game is played. So, a tracking variable is needed for the ghost's float *speed*. We also know the ghost will not start floating until the player presses the SPACE key to begin the game. A tracking variable will be used to track whether the ghost is *floating*. A decomposition for the game setup procedure is shown in Figure 16.10.

do in order

Tracking variables

Decimal number speed

Boolean floating

camera move and orient to *towerGameStart* (camera marker)

ghost move and orient to *ghostStart* (object marker)

ghost set *speed* at 0.0

ghost set *floating* to false

Figure 16.10 • *Decomposition for setting up the game*

Declare a new procedure in the Scene class, and name it *gameReset*. We selected the name *gameReset* because it is possible the player may lose the game and this procedure can be called again to restart the game. In the new *gameReset* editor tab, add comments for the assumptions and actions. Then, add statements to move and orient the camera to the *towerGameStart* camera marker and the ghost to the *ghostStart* object marker (Figure 16.11).

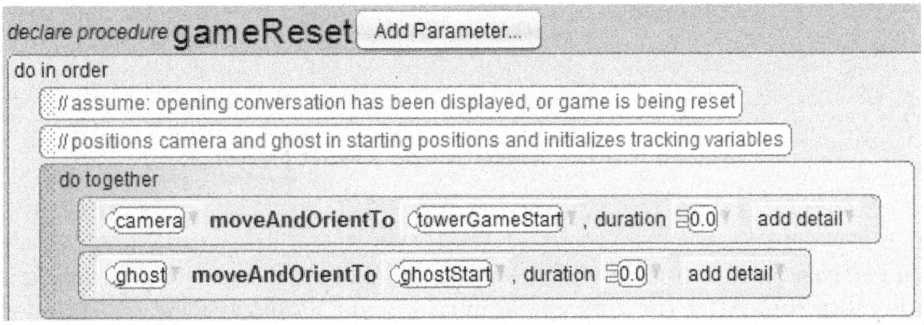

Figure 16.11 • *Move and orient the camera and ghost to marked game start positions.*

The *speed* (DecimalNumber) and *floating* (Boolean) variables both track the state of the ghost. Declare the tracking variables as properties of the Ghost class (Figure 16.12). Initialize *speed* to 0.0 and *floating* as *false*.

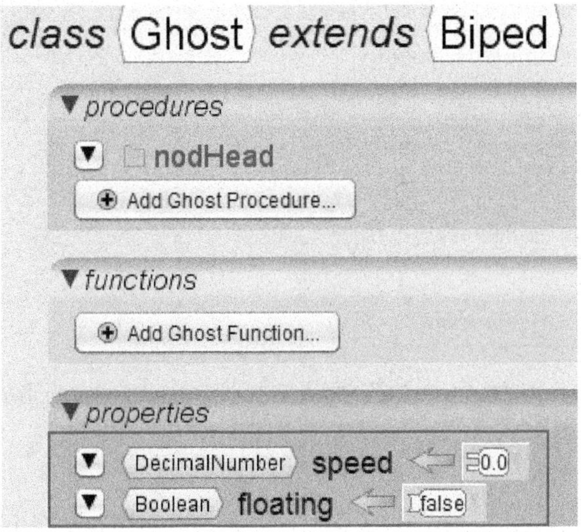

Figure 16.12 • *Declare tracking variables as properties of the Ghost class.*

Even though *speed* and *floating* are initialized in the declaration statements in the Ghost class, we know the *gameReset* procedure may be called several times as the player learns to play the game. For this reason, *gameReset* should also have statements that set the tracking variables to their initial values each time it is called. Figure 16.13 shows the completed *gameReset* procedure.

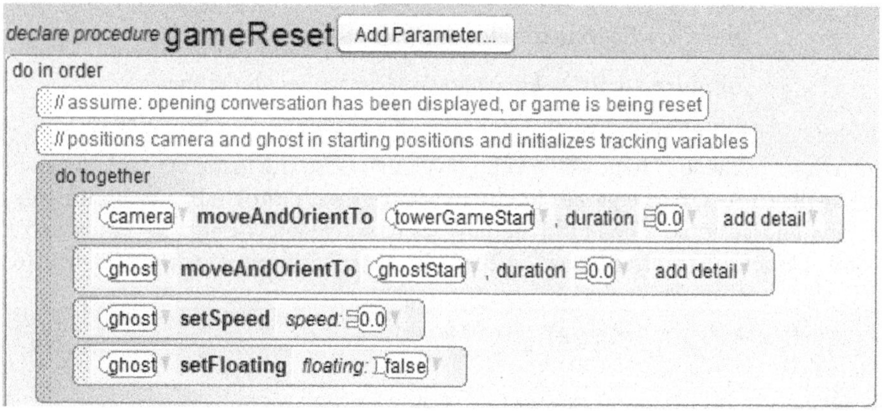

Figure 16.13   *Completed* gameReset *procedure*

To test *gameReset*, return to *myFirstMethod* and add a statement to call *gameReset* (Figure 16.14). Test-run. After the cutscene animation, you should see the ghost and camera positions update to their game-play positions near the tower (Figure 16.15).

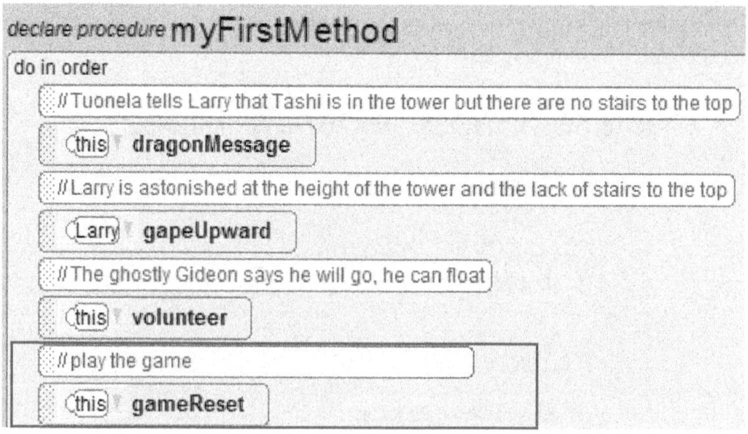

Figure 16.14   *Call* gameReset *from* myFirstMethod.

Note the game does NOT automatically start. The player must press the SPACE key to start the game. In *myFirstMethod*, add a statement to display instructions that prompt the

Figure 16.15 • *Game start scene*

player to press the SPACE key, saying "Press space key to start. Use arrow keys to move left or right" (Figure 16.16). Test-run, again.

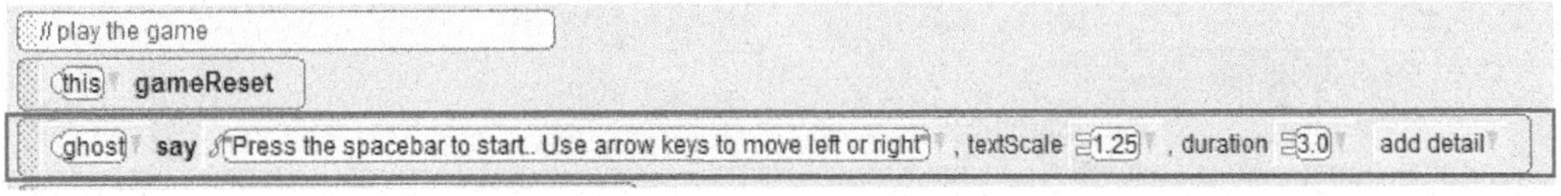

```
// play the game
this   gameReset
ghost   say  "Press the spacebar to start.. Use arrow keys to move left or right"  , textScale 1.25  , duration 3.0   add detail
```

Figure 16.16 • *Display instructions*

16.5 Event Listener: keyPress

When the player presses the SPACE key, the ghost should start to float and the camera should start its constant upward motion. We could write a *keyPress* listener for the SPACE key and a second *keyPress* listener for the left and right arrow keys, but a single *keyPress* event listener can handle all three keys. A design for a single *keyPress* event listener was illustrated earlier in Figure 16.6. Now, write code in the event listener to identify which key was pressed (SPACE, LEFT ARROW, or RIGHT ARROW) and then take appropriate action for that key.

Return to the *initializeEventListeners* editor tab and click the Add Event Listener button. In the dropdown menu, select Keyboard and then addKeyPressListener in the cascading menu (Figure 16.17).

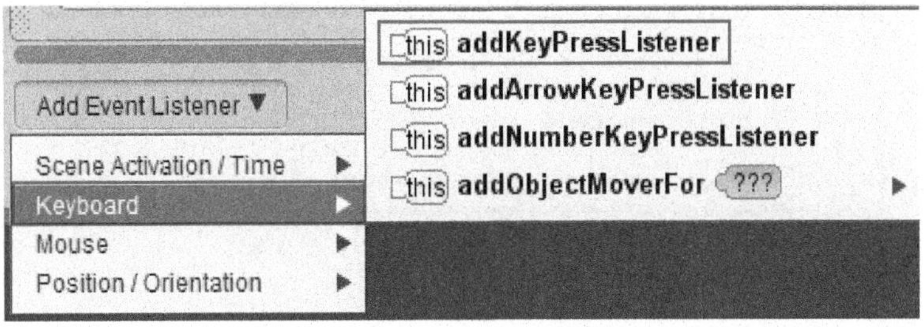

```
Add Event Listener ▼              this  addKeyPressListener
                                  this  addArrowKeyPressListener
  Scene Activation / Time   ▶     this  addNumberKeyPressListener
  Keyboard                  ▶     this  addObjectMoverFor  ???   ▶
  Mouse                     ▶
  Position / Orientation    ▶
```

Figure 16.17 • *Add a* keyPress *event listener.*

To handle a *keyPress* event, we need to check which of the three keys the player has typed. In the *keyPressListener* code block, create three *if/else* control structures, as shown in Figure 16.18. The *if/else* control structures are not nested. Each *if/else* statement will check the event signal for a specific key.

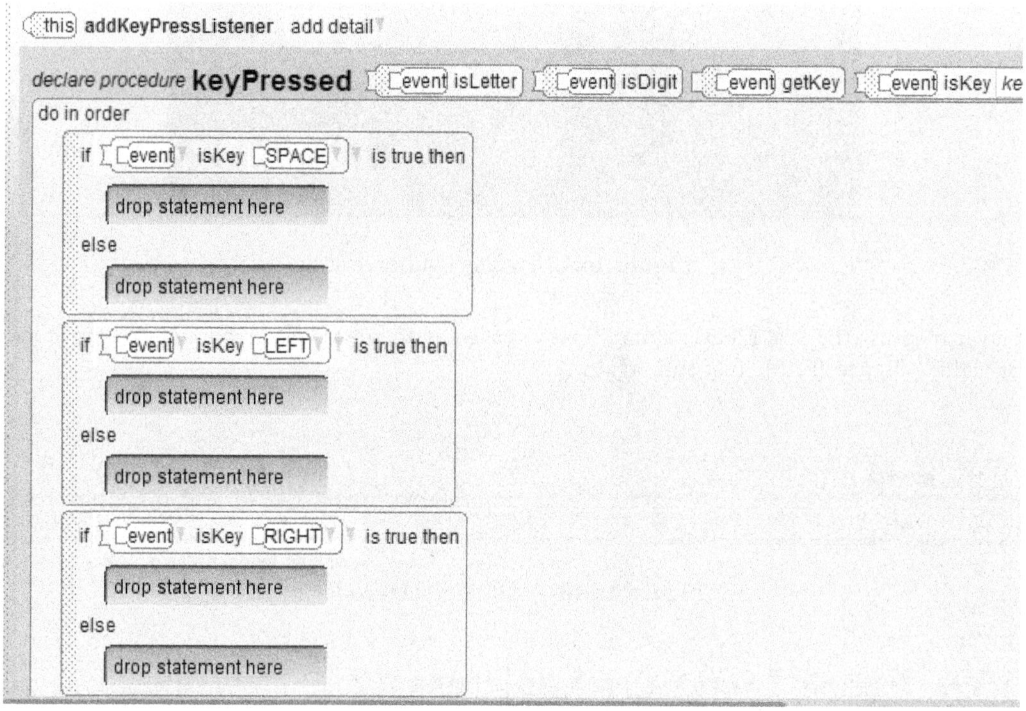

Figure 16.18   *Three if/else code blocks to identify which key was pressed*

First, implement the response to the SPACE key press. The response to a SPACE press has two parts: initialize the tracking variables and start the ghost's float. Add statements in the SPACE key's *if/else* code block to set *speed* to 1.25 m/sec and *floating* to *true*, as shown in Figure 16.19. This is a gentle floating speed, based on repeated trials of game play, but may be adjusted as you develop your own version of the game.

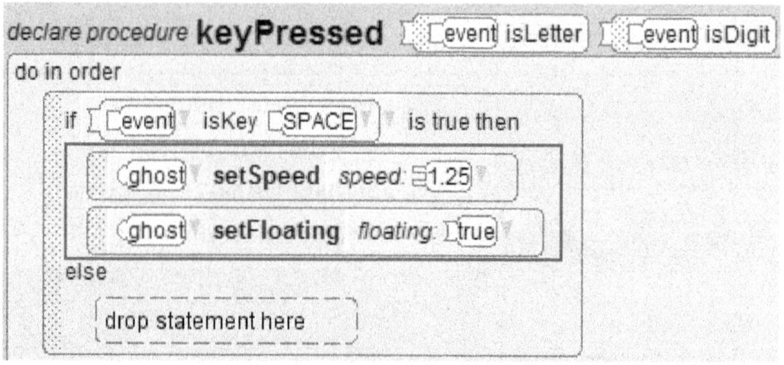

Figure 16.19   *Set tracking variables to game-active values.*

The ghost is to continue floating until Tashi is rescued or the game is reset. To allow for continuous floating, create a *float* procedure, that can be called from the *keyPressed* event listener. Return to the Scene class tab and add a procedure named *float*. In the new *float* editor tab, create a *while* loop, as shown in Figure 16.20. The condition for the *while* loop checks the value of the *floating* tracking variable. While *floating* is *true*, the ghost and the camera will keep moving upward. The camera moves up a consistent 1.25 m/sec (the same as the ghost's initial float speed). The ghost's *move* distance is determined by calling the ghost's *getSpeed* function. Notice the BEGIN_AND_END_ABRUPTLY optional argument is used in both statements for a smooth *float* animation.

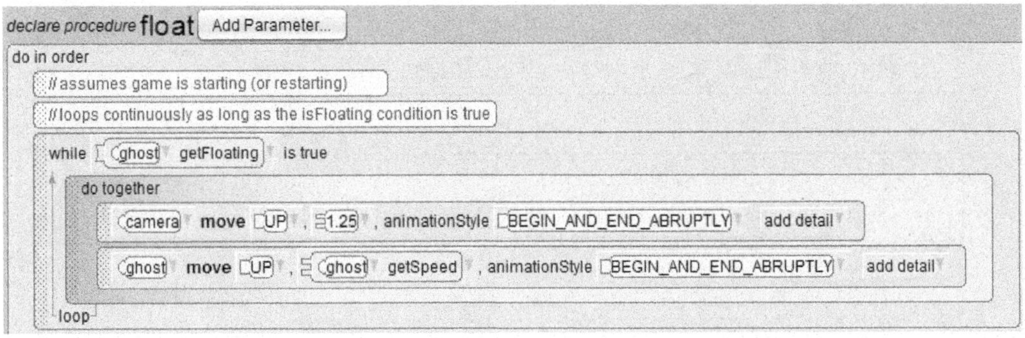

Figure 16.20 • *The float procedure*

Now, call the *float* procedure from the SPACE key's *if/else* code block (Figure 16.21). Run to test. When prompted to start the game, press the SPACE key. You should see the ghost floating upward at a gentle pace. When the player presses the SPACE key and the ghost starts floating the main game loop is active.

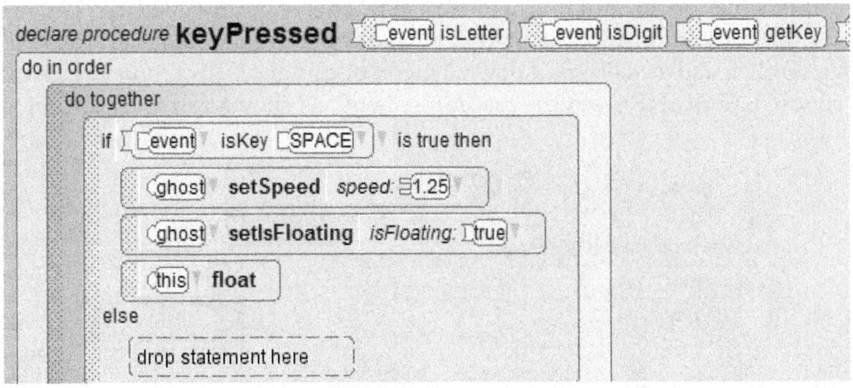

Figure 16.21 • *Call float.*

The left and right arrow *keyPress* event handler code is shown in Figure 16.22. Once again, notice the BEGIN_AND_END_ABRUPTLY optional argument in each *move* statement.

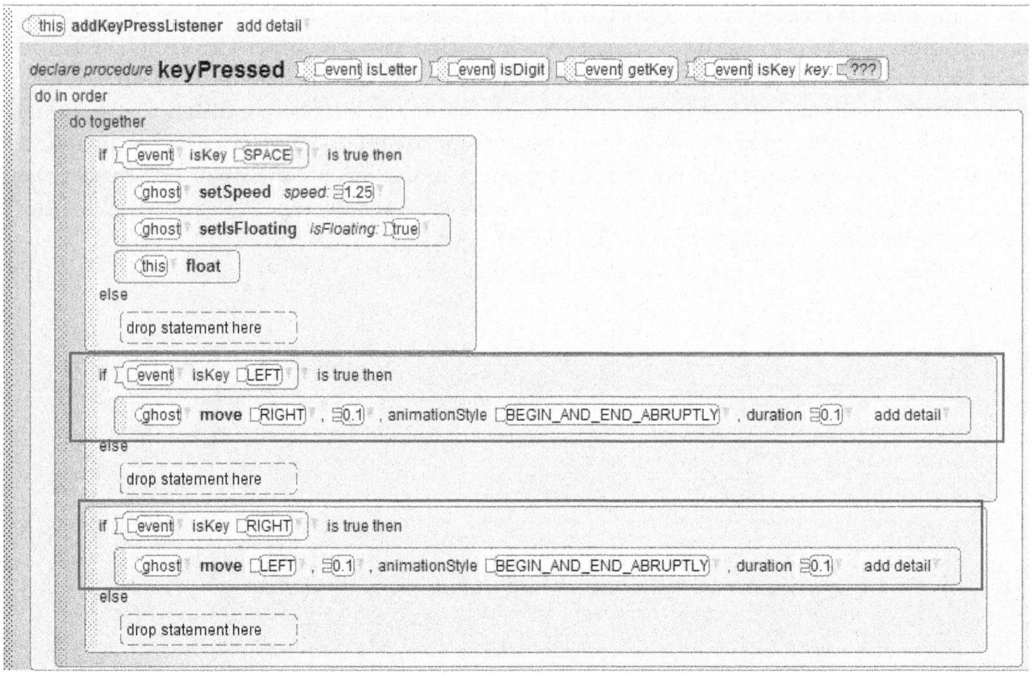

Figure 16.22   *Coded* if/else *statements to handle arrow keys*

Now that code has been written for all three *keyPress* events, run the project again and test for the left and right arrow key actions while the ghost is floating. What happens—or doesn't happen—may be a surprise. The ghost does not respond to the arrow *keyPress* events.

The problem is a *keyPress* listener responds, by default, to only one event at a time. In this example, the SPACE *keyPress* happens first and calls the *float* procedure. The *float* procedure has a *while* loop that takes over and runs continuously. As a result, the arrow *keyPress* handler code is not executed.

With this situation in mind, Alice's software engineers designed the *keyPress* event listener with optional arguments that care for handling multiple events. In the *keyPressListener* header, (1) click *add detail* to pull down a menu of options, select **multipleEventPolicy**, and then choose COMBINE from the cascading menu, as shown in Figure 16.23.

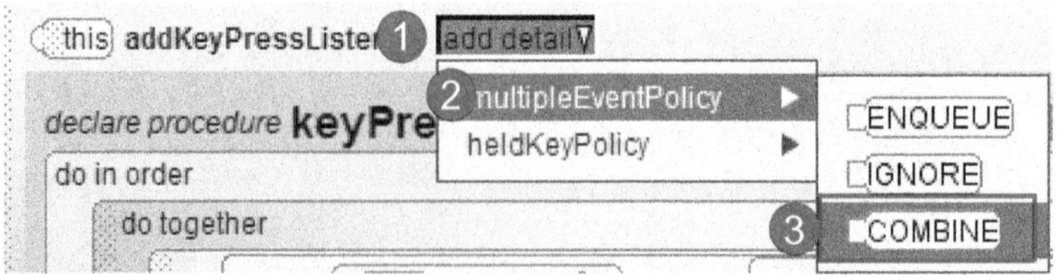

Figure 16.23   *Select the COMBINE multiple event policy.*

Now, test-run the project. Run it at least two or three times. Your testing should show that after the SPACE keypress starts the game, a left or right arrow keypress works to move the ghost left or right, as expected. You are also likely to see that the ghost's float *speed* is faster than when previously tested. The increase in float *speed* is a bug, because no code statements have yet been written to increase the ghost's float *speed*.

16.6 Debugging: TextString Output for Feedback

....

Although we know the increased float speed is a bug, figuring out where the bug is and why things aren't working as expected is sometimes a challenge in interactive programs. The challenge is that the values in the tracking variables are stored in the computer's memory but are not visible to the programmer who is viewing the game play and trying to find a bug.

One way to make debugging easier is to provide feedback that displays the value stored in a tracking variable. A 3D text object may be used to display the value stored in the *speed* tracking variable.

Open the Scene editor. In the Gallery, (1) click on the Shapes/Text tab and (2) select *TextModel*, as shown in Figure 16.24. In the popup dialog box, (3) enter the name *speed-Tracker*. (4) Note the initial value is "hello." Click OK to create a text string object.

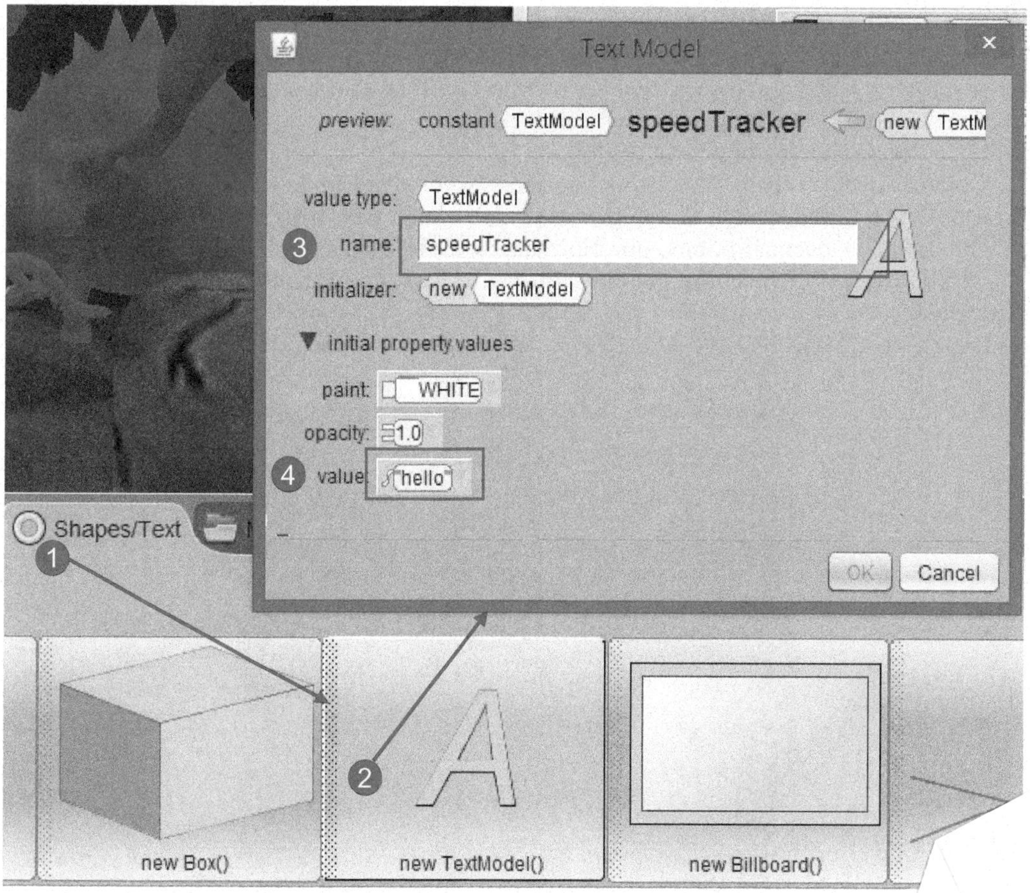

Figure 16.24 • *Create a 3D text object.*

The *speedTracker* text string object should now be visible in the scene, Figure 16.25. (The actual location of the text object in the scene may be diff computer. This is okay—its location will be changed later.)

Figure 16.25 *The* speedTracker *text string object in the scene*

16.6.1 Setup for text display

In the Scene Editor's Toolbox, select the *speedTracker* object, as shown in Figure 16.26. *Text* is the property that contains the text string that is displayed. Change the *Text* property to "0.0". You should see the *speedTracker* object no longer displays the default "hello" string. Now, it displays a string of characters "0.0".

   Note: The text string "0.0" is not a numeric value that can be used in arithmetic computations. The text display is a string of keyboard characters, which may include the digit keys (0, 1, 2 ... 9), decimal points, question marks, alphabetic letters, and other keys.

   Now, reduce the height of the *speedTracker* to 0.25. Note that width and depth automatically change in proportion to the change in height. (On most computer monitors, the resulting text size will be large enough to read but not distracting to the animation.)

Figure 16.26 *Adjust the values of Text, Vehicle, and Height.*

For debugging purposes, the *speedTracker* must be in a position where it can be seen while the game is running. A marker has already been placed in the starter world as a location for repositioning the 3D text object. Follow these steps to position the text at the marker (Figure 16.27):

(1) In the list of Object markers, click *trackerStart*.
(2) At the top of Object markers list, click the leftmost object-shift button.

You should see the text immediately reposition to the *speedTracker* marked position.

Now that the *speedTracker* is in position, hide it by setting its opacity to 0.0 (Figure 16.28). If not hidden, the *speedTracker* will be visible in the cutscene animation. The opacity can be set back to 1.0 when the game starts. Lastly, set the text object's vehicle to the *ghost*. This will enable the *speedTracker* object to float with the *ghost*, where it will provide feedback for debugging. It can also provide feedback to the game player.

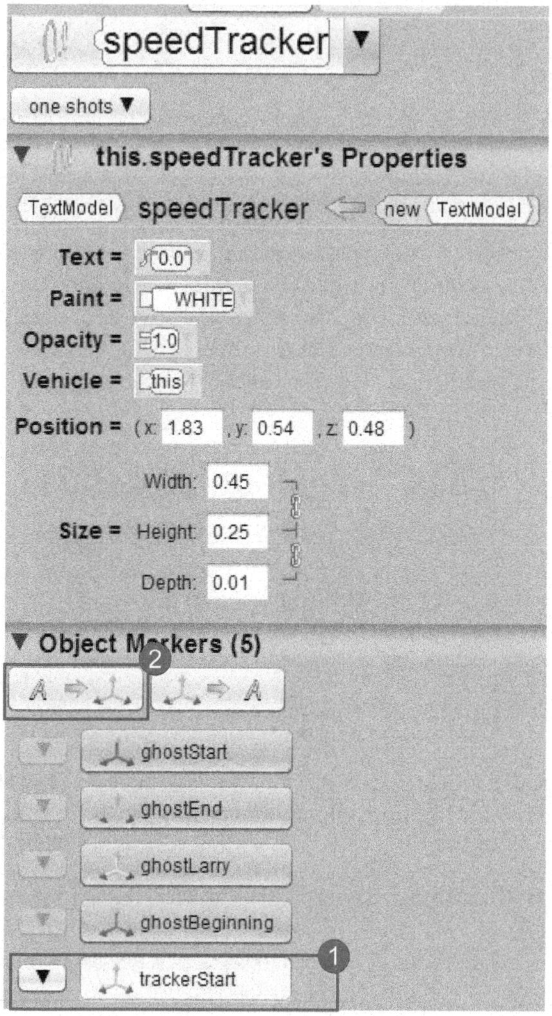

Figure 16.27 ◦ *Reposition the text object to the* trackerStart *marker.*

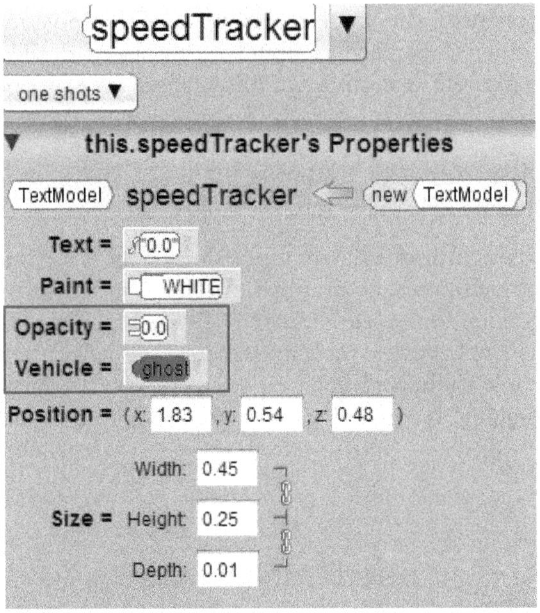

Figure 16.28   *Set the* speedTracker's *opacity to 0.0 and its vehicle to* ghost.

16.6.2 Tracking and updating the text string display

The next step should be to test the *speedTracker*. The *speedTracker* displays a text string. But the ghost's float *speed* is a decimal number. To display the speed, the decimal number value must be (1) updated to the latest value and then (2) converted to keyboard characters in a text string. Write a procedure to update and convert the speed for display as a text string. Declare a procedure, named *update*, for the TextModel class (Figure 16.29).

Figure 16.29   *Declare an* update *procedure.*

In the *updateSpeed* procedure, create a parameter named *floatSpeed* of type Decimal-Number. Add comments for assumptions and actions (Figure 16.30).

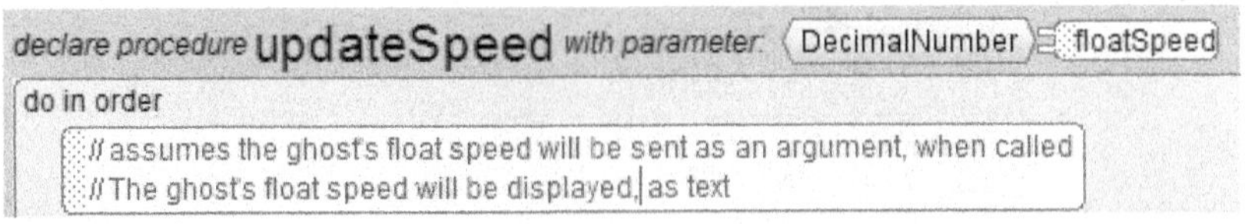

Figure 16.30   updateSpeed *procedure with parameter and comments*

To set the text *value* property to the *floatSpeed*, select the *setValue* tile in the procedures tab and drag it to the *updateSpeed* procedure, as shown in Figure 16.31a. Select *Custom
TextString* from the menu. In the popup window, enter a blank space in the text box and
click OK. The resulting statement has a **blank string** tile, which looks like an empty speech
bubble because it contains only a space (Figure 16.31b).

With the blank string in place, the *setValue* procedure can **concatenate** (append) other
characters to the string. To concatenate *floatSpeed* to the blank string, follow these steps
(Figure 16.32):

(1) Select the blank string tile in the *setValue* statement.
(2) In the pulldown menu, select the blank string + *???* option.
(3) Select *DecimalNumber* in the cascading menu.
(4) Select *floatSpeed* from the last cascading menu.

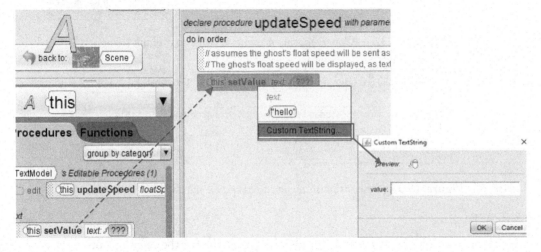

Figure 16.31a   *Setting the text value property to a blank string*

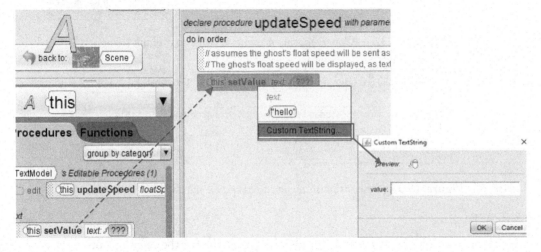

Figure 16.31b   *Resulting statement with a blank string tile*

The concatenation operation forces a conversion of *floatSpeed's* numeric value to a
text string that can be displayed by the *speedTracker* text object. The resulting statement is
shown in Figure 16.33.

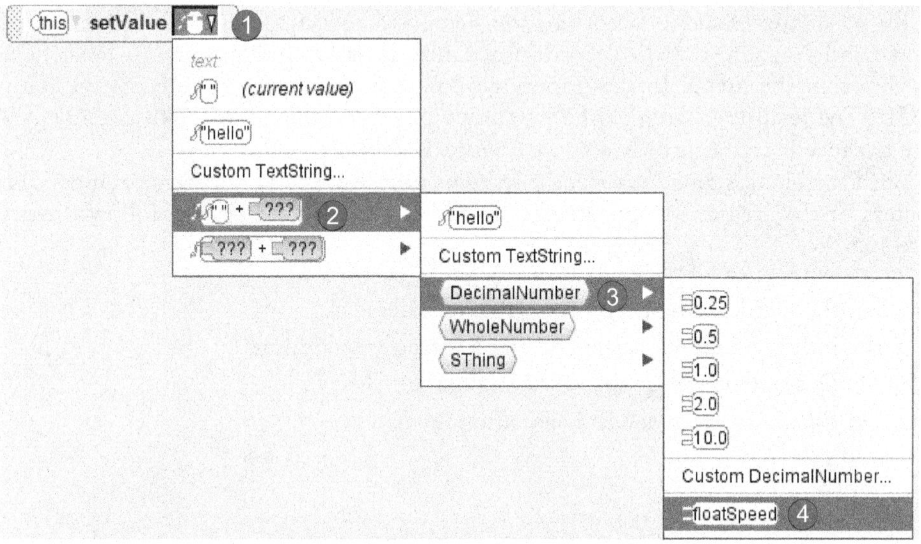

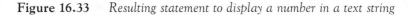

Figure 16.32   *Concatenating a numeric value to a blank string*

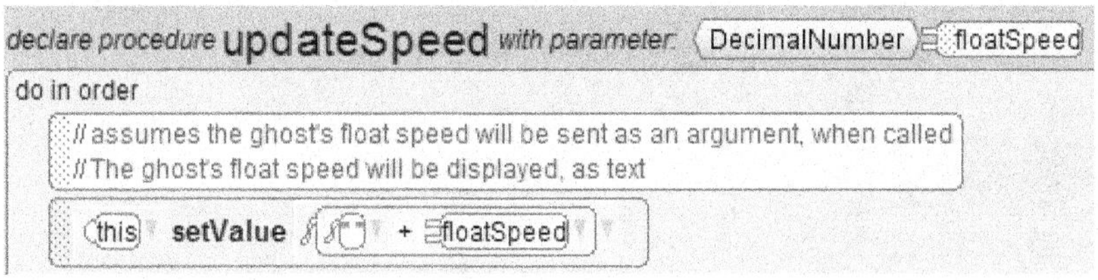

Figure 16.33   *Resulting statement to display a number in a text string*

16.6.3 Testing

We hid the *speedTracker* object so it wouldn't be visible during the opening cutscene. When the game starts, it must be made visible for testing and debugging. Return to the *gameReset* procedure tab. Add statements to set the *speedTracker's* opacity to 1.0 and update the text display to 0.0 (matching the ghost's float *speed*) (Figure 16.34).

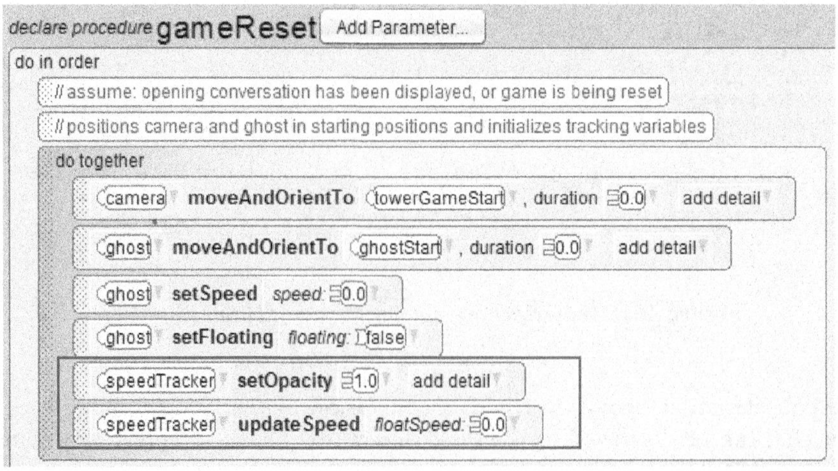

Figure 16.34   *Modify* gameReset *to show the* speedTracker *object and update its value.*

Next, return to the *keyPressed* event listener and add a statement to update the *speedTracker* value when the SPACE key is pressed (Figure 16.35). The argument for *floatSpeed* is a call to the ghost's *getSpeed* function. In this way, we know the *speedTracker* is displaying the current ghost's speed.

```
declare procedure keyPressed    event isLetter    event isDigit    event getKey    event
do in order
    if  BOTH    event  isKey  SPACE    AND  NOT    ghost  getFloating         is true then
            ghost  setSpeed  speed: 1.25
            ghost  setFloating  floating: true
            speedTracker  updateSpeed  floatSpeed:  ghost  getSpeed
            this  float
    else
            drop statement here
```

Figure 16.35   *Call* updateSpeed *from within the* keyPressed *event listener.*

Now, test-run. Figure 16.36 illustrates a sample run. Run it several times. You will likely see somewhat different speeds each time the project runs, even though the ghost's *speed* is specifically set to 1.25 in the SPACE key's *if/else* code block.

Figure 16.36   *Ghost speed feedback*

As you think about why this is happening, recall that we set the *multipleEventPolicy* for the *keyPress* event listener to COMBINE. When the SPACE key is pressed, the player is likely to hesitate slightly before releasing the key. This allows the event to trigger multiple times— a desired effect for the arrow keys but not for the SPACE key. Multiple triggering by the SPACE key combines the speeds. The longer the user holds down the SPACE key, the greater the ghost's *speed*.

16.6.4 Debug to restrict multiple event triggers

The space *keyPress* event should trigger only once at the beginning of the game and not trigger again unless the game resets. To prevent multiple event firings when the SPACE is pressed, add a second condition in the *if/else* code block for the SPACE key. As illustrated in Figure 16.37, (1) click the *isKey SPACE* condition, then (2) select the BOTH ... AND expression, and (3) *true* from cascading menus.

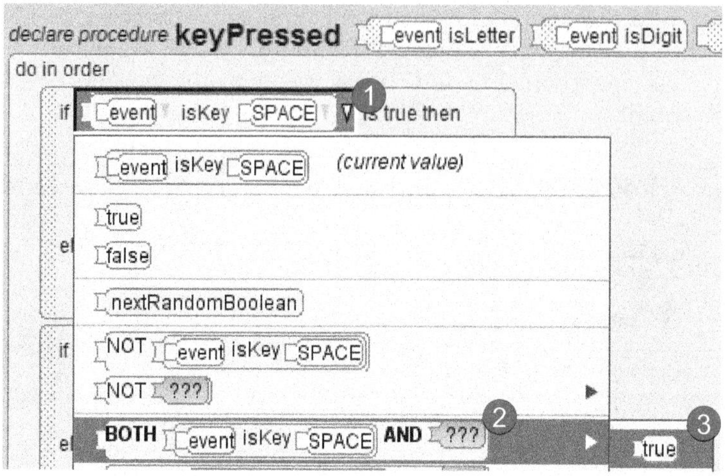

Figure 16.37   *Add a second condition to the* if/else *statement.*

If the ghost is already floating, we don't want to increase the speed. So, the second condition should be something like, "ghost is NOT already floating." To represent this condition, replace *true* with *NOT ghost.getFloating*, as shown in Figure 16.38.

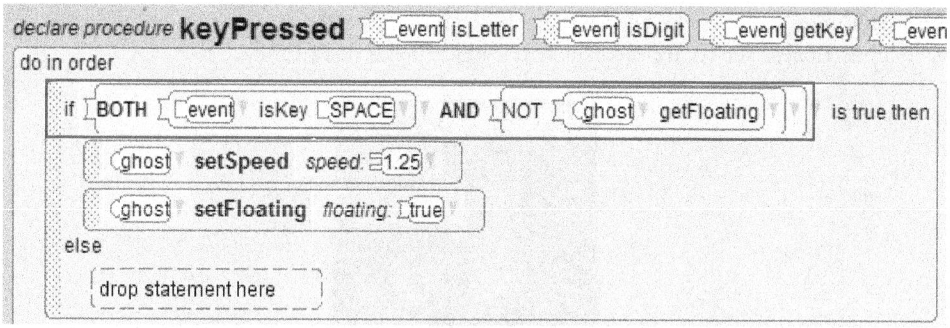

Figure 16.38   *Replace* true *with* NOT ghost.getFloating.

Now, test-run the project and watch the *speedTracker* output. The ghost's *speed* should begin at 1.25 when the SPACE key is pressed and should not change, even if the SPACE key is held down an extra second.

At this point, the game setup, instructions, and the player's controls (*keyPressed* event listener) have been implemented. The rest of this chapter will focus on implementing the event listeners that update the ghost's *speed* and check for end conditions.

16.7 Event Listeners for Speed Updates

One of the specifications in the game description is that the ghost's float *speed* should slow down with every passing second. A time-elapsed listener may be used to implement this feature of the game.

16.7.1 Time-elapsed event

To create a time-elapsed event listener, return to the *initializeEventListeners* editor tab and, (1) click the Add Event Listener button, then (2) select Scene Activation/Time, and (3) *addTimeListener* from the cascading menus (Figure 16.39).

Figure 16.39 ● *Create a time-elapsed event listener.*

In the *addTimeListener* code block header, select 1.0 second as the time-elapse that will trigger the event Figure (16.40). A 1.0 second time-elapsed segment means the event listener will trigger once every second.

Figure 16.40 ● *Select an amount for the time-elapsed segment.*

To implement a response to the time-elapsed trigger, add an *if/else* code block. The condition is that the ghost is floating, determined by calling the ghost's *getFloating* function (Figure 16.41). This condition is necessary to keep the clock from ticking while the cutscene is animating. This condition also keeps the clock from ticking when the game is reset.

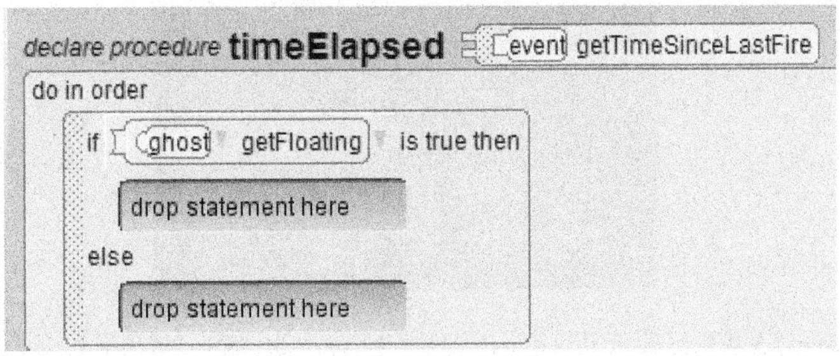

Figure 16.41 ● *Only trigger this response if the ghost is floating.*

Within the *if/else* code block, add a *do together* code block that contains statements to decrease the ghost's speed by 0.075 and update the *speedTracker* display at the same time (Figure 16.42). Notice that the *setSpeed* statement subtracts 0.1 from the ghost's current float *speed*. Then, the ghost's *getSpeed* function is called as the argument for updating the *speedTracker*.

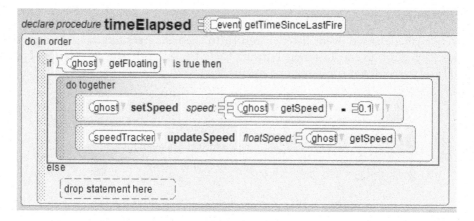

Figure 16.42   *Completed* timeElapsed *event listener*

Test-run. The ghost should start floating at 1.25 m/sec, as indicated by the *speed-Tracker*. After 1 second, the speed should decrease to 1.15. After 2 seconds the speed should be 1.05 seconds and become progressively smaller with every second.

16.7.2 Rounding error

You may notice after a few updates that the speed is displayed as a number having many, many digits to the right of the decimal point, similar to the number shown in Figure 16.43. This is because value of type DecimalNumber is stored in the computer's memory as binary digits. After several subtractions, a **rounding error** may occur due to the binary representation. A rounding error means that if this computation were done with pencil and paper, the digits to the right of the decimal point would be different than the value stored in the computer's memory. In the example shown in Figure 16.43, about 16 digits to the right are "off"—that is, not quite what we expected.

Figure 16.43   *Rounding error 16 digits to the right of the decimal point*

16.7.3 Format output to display with two decimal places

In this example, the rounding error isn't really a problem, but it is a distraction to the player. One way to resolve this issue is to **format** the output to a specific number of places to the right of the decimal point. Open the TextModel class tab in the Code editor and declare a new function, named *twoDecimalPlaces*, of type *DecimalNumber*. In the function header, declare a parameter of type *DecimalNumber* and name it *number* (Figure 16.44).

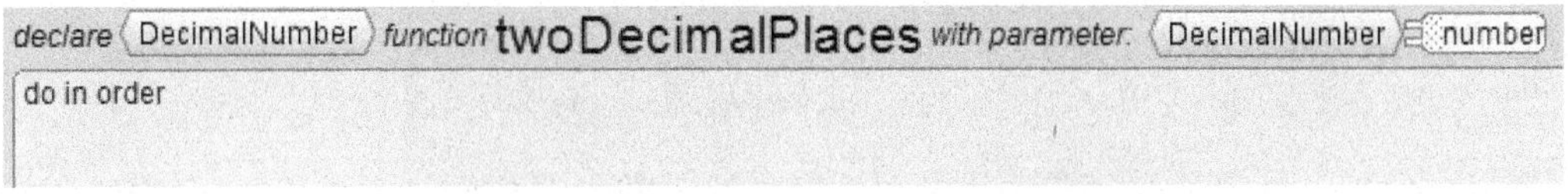

declare (DecimalNumber) *function* **twoDecimalPlaces** *with parameter:* (DecimalNumber)≡(number)

do in order

Figure 16.44 ● twoDecimalPlaces *function header*

Add a *return* statement that multiplies the number by 100, rounds it to the nearest whole number, and then divides by 100 (Figure 16.45).

declare (DecimalNumber) *function* **twoDecimalPlaces** *with parameter:* (DecimalNumber)≡(number)

do in order

return ≡≡ round ≡≡number ⊤ * ≡100.0 ⊤ ⊤ / ≡100.0 ⊤

Figure 16.45 ● *Round the number to two decimal places.*

Now, reopen the TextModel's *update* procedure in the editor. Modify the *setValue* statement to apply the *twoDecimalPlaces* custom function to the *floatSpeed* parameter value (Figure 16.46).

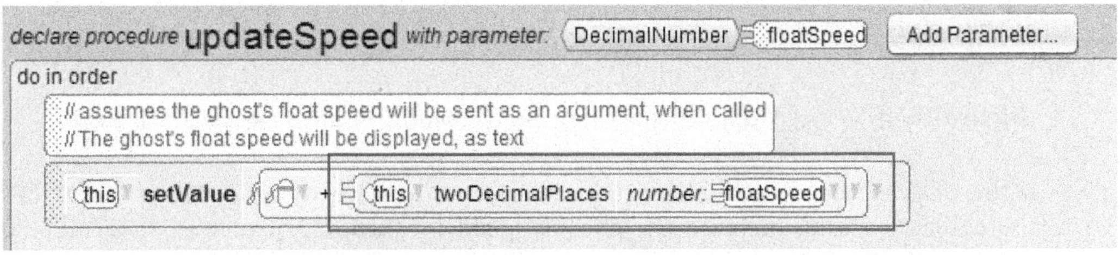

declare procedure **updateSpeed** *with parameter:* (DecimalNumber)≡(floatSpeed)   Add Parameter...

do in order

// assumes the ghost's float speed will be sent as an argument, when called
// The ghost's float speed will be displayed, as text

(this) **setValue** ⌐ + ≡ (this) twoDecimalPlaces *number:* ≡floatSpeed

Figure 16.46 ● *Apply the* twoDecimalPlaces *function to* floatSpeed.

Test-run, again. The ghost's speed should steadily decrease and the *speedTracker's* display should never show more than two digits to the right of the decimal point.

16.7.4 Collision Event Listener

The second event that governs the ghost's float *speed* is a collision with a cloud. Although a *keyPress* listener has been added to allow the game player to steer the ghost toward a cloud, no code has yet been written to detect when a ghost-cloud collision occurs. A *collision start* event listener will be used to implement this feature of the game.

To create a *collision start* event listener, (1) click the Add Event Listener button in the *initializeEventListeners* editor tab, then (2) select Position/Orientation, and (3) *addCollisionStartListener* from the cascading menus (Figure 16.47). At the far right of the cascading menus, select (4) Custom Array for *setA* and (5) Custom Array for *setB*.

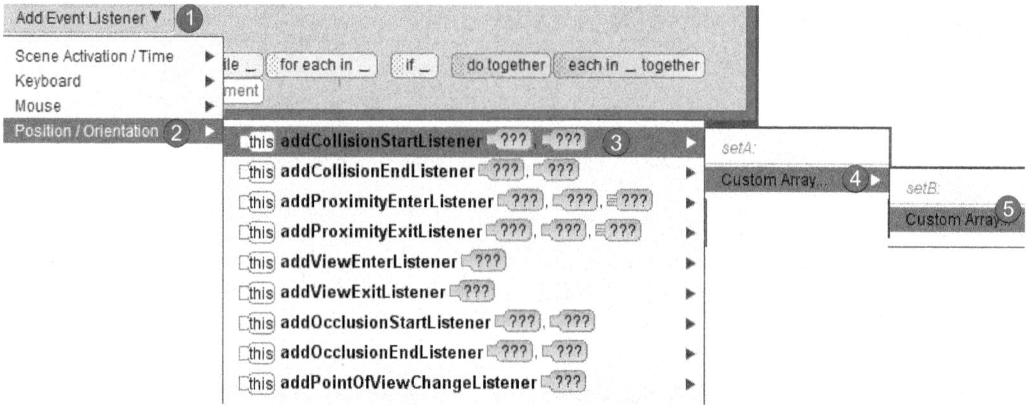

0

Figure 16.47   *Create a collision start listener with two arrays of objects.*

Notice the header for the collision event listener code block has two custom arrays: *setA* and *setB*. The event listener will automatically watch for a collision of any object in *setA* with any object in *setB*. Click on *setA*. In the popup window, select only the *ghost*. Next, click on *setB*. In the popup window, select each of the 14 clouds in the scene, one at a time, to add them to *setB*. The resulting code block is shown in Figure 16.48.

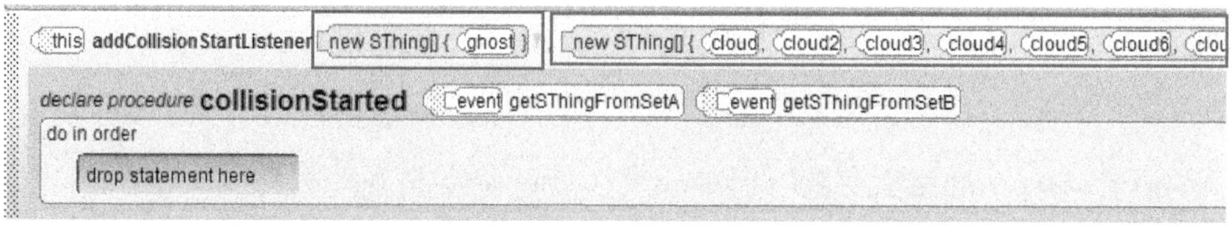

Figure 16.48   *SetA contains the ghost; SetB contains 14 different cloud objects.*

In the *collisionStarted* code block, add statements to have the ghost say "CLOUD" when the collision starts, increase the ghost's speed by 0.25, and call the *speedTracker's* *updateSpeed* procedure with *ghost.getSpeed* as the argument (Figure 16.49).

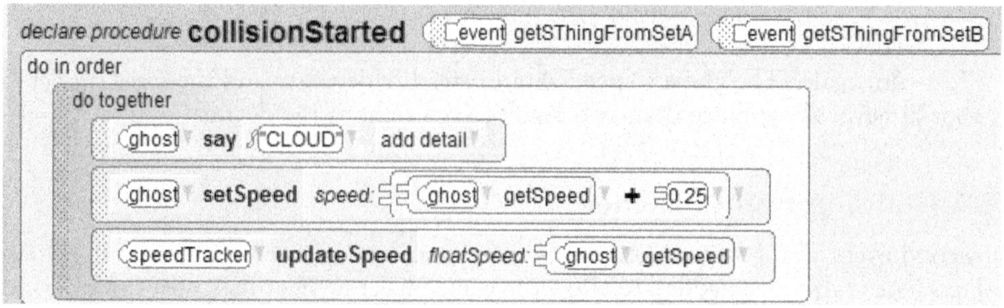

Figure 16.49   *Completed collision start event listener*

Test-run the project. You should see the ghost say "CLOUD" when colliding with a cloud. This is intended as visual feedback that a collision has occurred. You should also see the *speedTracker* show an increase in speed.

16.8 Event Listeners for End Conditions

Two events are needed for checking end conditions, one for win and one for loss. In this game, the win condition is similar to games where the goal is to cross a "finish line." In the initial scene for the Tower game, a box shape (*endLine*) was created and positioned in horizontal alignment with the plane of the floor at the top level of the tower (see Figure 16.50). Unlike a camera or object marker, the box shape marks a wide space for a possible collision. A wide line is needed because the ghost is floating left and right in response to arrow keypresses. Note: By default, the endLine box is hidden in the scene, but we made its opacity 1.0 to capture this image.

Figure 16.50 endLine *object at the top of the tower*

16.8.1 Win condition: collisionStarted event listener

In this game, a second *collisionStarted* listener will be created to watch for the ghost to collide with the *endLine* object. Create a second *collision start* event listener. For this collision listener, *setA* should be the ghost and *setB* the *endLine* object (Figure 16.51).

Figure 16.51 *Collision event listener for ghost and* endLine *objects*

When the ghost collides with *endLine*, the game is over and the player has won. Add a statement to reset *floating* to *false* and *speed* to 0.0, Figure 16.52. Then hide the *speedTracker's* display by setting its opacity to 0.0.

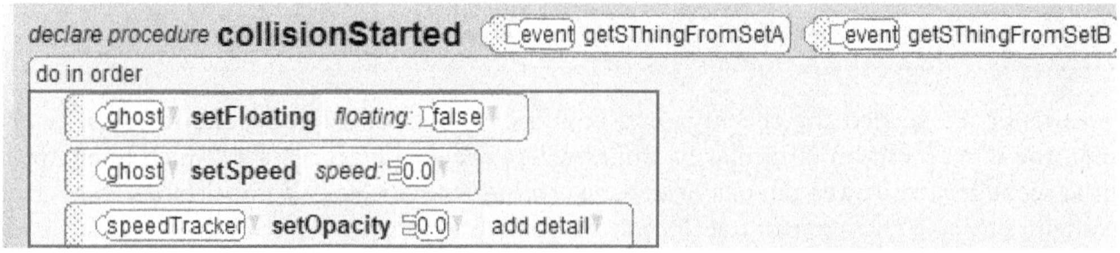

Figure 16.52 *Reset tracking variables to end the game when the player wins.*

When the player wins the game, the ghost should rescue Tashi from the tower. Writing and calling a *rescue* procedure is left as an exercise for you. See the exercises at the end of this chapter.

16.8.2 Loss condition: viewExited Listener

At any time in the game, if the ghost floats out of the camera's view, the game is over and the player loses the game. The game should reset to allow the player to try again. A *viewExited* event listener watches for a specified object within the camera's viewpoint. If the object cannot be found within the camera's view, the listener triggers the *viewExited* procedure.

To create a *viewExited* event listener, (1) click the Add Event Listener button in the *initializeEventListeners* editor tab, then (2) select Position/Orientation, and (3) *addViewExitListener*, and (4) Custom Array for *set* from the cascading menus (Figure 16.53).

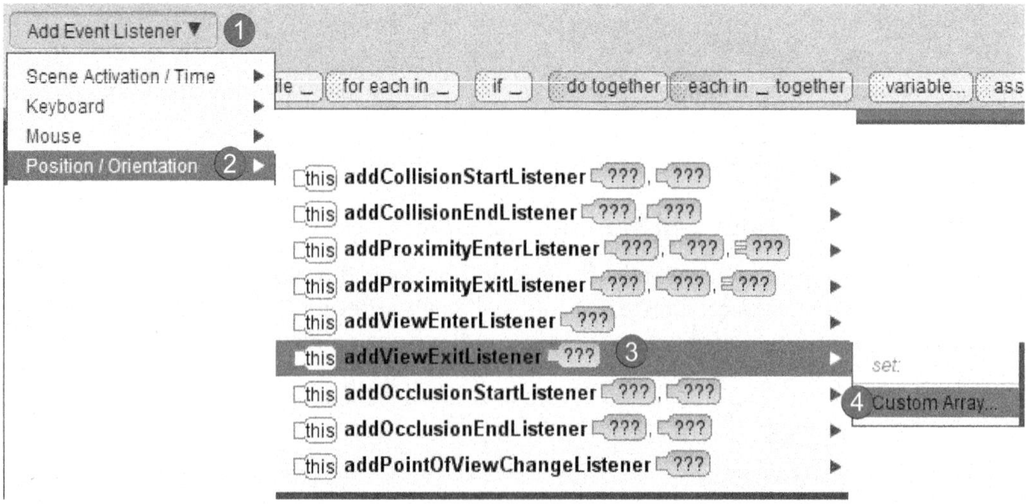

Figure 16.53 *Create a* viewExited *event listener.*

In the *addViewExitListener* code block heading, select the *ghost* as the only object in the custom array. The resulting code block is shown in Figure 16.54.

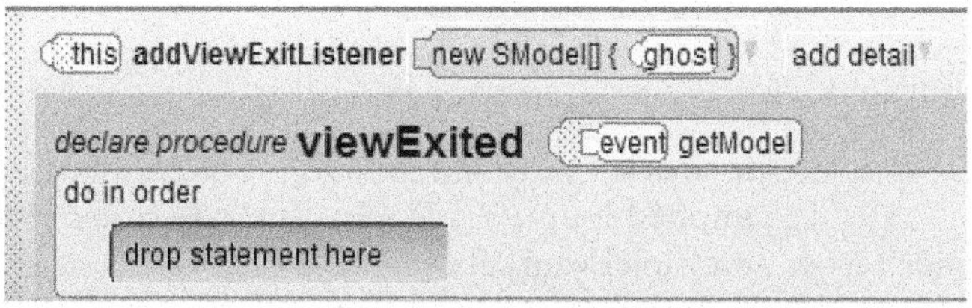

Figure 16.54   viewexit *event listener code block*

To respond to the *viewExited* event, add a statement in the *viewExited* code block to call the Scene's *gameReset* procedure (Figure 16.55). Test-run the game several times, and purposely try to have the ghost's pace be too fast or too slow so the ghost floats out of the camera's view.

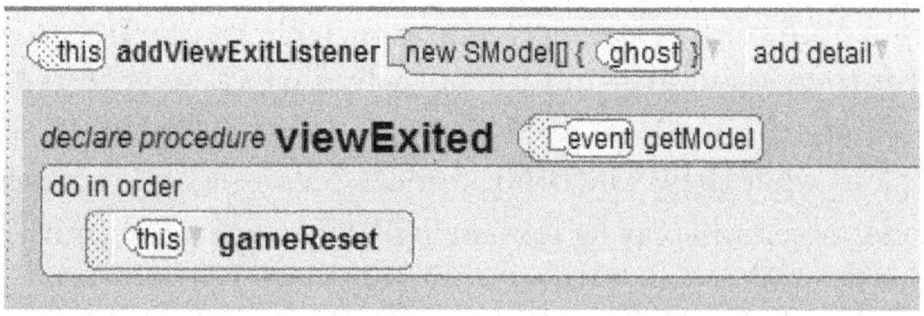

Figure 16.55   *Call* gameReset.

The timing elements in this game have been purposely selected to provide a reasonable pace for the novice player, but slow enough to allow for debugging the code. You may wish to adjust the float speed and the amounts of increase/decrease to provide a greater challenge for the more experienced player. (See the exercises at the end of this chapter.)

Summary

In this chapter, more advanced, aspects of event listeners and event-driven programming are presented in the context of creating a game with more challenging interactive features than in previous examples. A *keyPress* event listener has options that affect how multiple presses of the same key are handled. Also the COMBINE policy allows a listener to listen for a keypress on more than one key. The collision of one object with another object may be detected using a *collisionStart* listener. The *collisionStart* listener requires two custom arrays of objects, *setA* and *setB*, and detects the collision of any object in *setA* with any object in *setB*. The use of tracking components for game state may include tracking the state of a specific object. In the Tower game, we tracked the ghost's floating speed.

In the Tower game the ghost's floating speed is affected by gravity (the speed slows with every passing second) and collision with a cloud. As in many games, timing is a factor. In the Tower game, the timing is related to the ghost maintaining a float speed that keeps the ghost within view of the camera. Tracking the game state (speed, game score, game active) is easier with some visual feedback. A 3D text object is one way to create feedback because the text output may be updated as the value of a tracking variable changes. Feedback helps the programmer debug the code and helps the player during the play of the game.

Terms

3D text

blank string

collisionStarted listener

concatenate

format

implied loop

multipleEventPolicy

rounding error

timeElapsed listener

viewExited listener

Concept Questions

1. In the Tower game, why is the game setup procedure named *gameReset*?

2. Describe the purpose of the *speed* tracking variable in the Tower game, not only in terms of what it tracks, but also in terms of why that value is tracked.

3. Describe the purpose of the *floating* tracking variable in the Tower game, not only in terms of what it tracks, but also in terms of why that value is tracked.

4. In the Tower game, the *keyPress* event listener uses a COMBINE *multipleEventPolicy* argument. Explain what the COMBINE option does in a *keyPress* event listener.

5. A 3D TextModel object displays a text string. What operation must be performed in order to display a number value using a 3D TextModel object?

6. In a computer program, arithmetic operations with decimal numbers may result in a rounding error. What is the cause of such an error?

7. Many event listeners have a custom array where one or more objects are specified as the target object(s) for the listener. A *collisionStarted* event listener, however, has two custom arrays. Explain why two arrays are needed for a *collisionStarted* listener.

8. Why is a box shape, instead of an object marker, used to mark the finish line in the Tower game?

Exercises

1. When the player wins the Tower game, the ghost should rescue Tashi. The rescue procedure, however, still needs to be written. If you have not already done so, download the project file, *FindingGideonStarter.a3p*, and implement the code presented in this chapter. (Or obtain a copy from your instructor.) Then, create a *rescue* procedure. Two camera markers, named *towerGameEnd* and *endScene*, and an object marker, named *ghostEnd*, are already in the starter world and may be helpful for writing code for the rescue.

2. The ghost's speed in the Tower game is purposely gentle and the amount of decrease each second is small. A slow speed allows the programmer to more easily debug the game and is also good for a novice player. However, after playing the game a few times, you may want the game to be more challenging. Increase the ghost's speed and the amount subtracted each second. Be sure to play the game several times to be sure it is still possible to win the game.

3. In exercise 2, the ghost's speed and the amount subtracted each second were modified in the code. Instead of just modifying the code and having only one speed level, ask

the user to select a level of play (Novice, Medium, or Experienced) and then adjust the speed and timed subtraction based on the user's selection.

4. In the Tower game, each time the ghost exits the camera view, the game automatically resets to play again. Modify the game to ask the user if they want to play again. If yes, play again. If not, allow the program execution to stop.

Open-Ended Project

1. Design and build a game of your own. The game must include tracking variables and a 3D TextModel object that displays some form of game feedback (speed, score, time, or some other factor), and make use of at least three different kinds of event listeners. Implement the main game loop using event listeners instead of a main *while* loop. The event listeners must include some form of collision detection.

Epilogue

On the night of the avalanche, the storyteller climbs the tallest tree in the valley to watch. It's one of the few old-growth trees left from the ghost town's logging days. A harsh wind is blowing the storm in from the east and hasn't reached the valley yet, but she sees lightning around the mountain. The storm is so intense the flashes happen in quick succession and light the sky like day. A hazy, purple daylight feels dry and dusty despite the sleeting rain in the distance. It's a summer storm come early. No one could have predicted it.

Clinging to the mountain slope on tracks that seem to be made of stilts are three trains. A single bolt hits the mountain peak above the tracks. After a thunderous rumble, the entire side of the mountain collapses. Precarious snow pack breaks loose and starts a long series of explosions strong enough to snap sturdy tree trunks. When the avalanche hits the trains, the entire world turns blinding white, even without the help of a lightning strike. The storyteller can't see a thing—it's as if her eyes are squeezed shut though she's holding them wide open. The scene then falls dark, until another strike hits and reveals the circus train to be missing, although the wreckage of the other two trains remains.

Raindrops fall on the storyteller's face, alerting her that the storm hit the valley. She climbs down from the tree and goes inside to prepare a cup of tea. She hadn't expected Prenderghast and his troupe to be taken so suddenly. She thought they'd have more time to prepare. She doesn't know what is going to happen now. All she can do is wait. She sighs, sets her tea down briefly, and retrieves her gigantic record book. She searches the harsh winds for memories of the people on the other two trains. And she starts recording the names of the dead.

During the waiting years, she entertains other travelers. She finds their innermost ambition and exploits them by fulfilling wishes, re-creating daydreams, or simply recalling the dead. "If you could wish for one thing forever, what would it be?" she asks. Some guests don't take her seriously; they see a 13-year-old in petticoats and lace dresses and laugh.

"Leave tokens, the darkest, most important bits of yourself here and you will go on to do great things," she says, "I will turn you into legends." People come and go, but no one stays. On the days when she's alone, she sits and listens. Moss grows on her skin as it would a tree. She keeps the objects inside her cabin pristine, but she doesn't notice her own body decaying.

Decades later, just as she's about to lose hope that her gamble will pay off, Lawrence Prenderghast returns with a yeti in tow. The storyteller hastily sends him on his way, as she should have done years ago. By then she's grown old, her bones creak when she walks through the woods with her cane and cleans each of the cabins meticulously. She is grateful to discover the troupe's objects have disappeared. It means five fewer things to dust. She remembers the day they arrived in town—the five friends: one who wants to keep the troupe together forever because it's all he has; one who wants to separate a sense of self from people's perception; one who wants wealth, prestige, and to prove the world wrong; one who wants recognition and to be needed; and one who wants to settle down and be normal.

She returns to her cabin and naps in her chair. She's exhausted all the time now, as if her body knows 113 years is too long to live.

The storyteller wakes with a start. She's no longer in her tiny cabin. The wooden boards are the same, and the door frame is still narrow and empty, but the room has elongated and grown three feet in height. She hobbles outside and immediately recognizes the building. It's the old Royal Hotel, built during this ghost town's boom, torn down after the bust, the place where her father and she first stayed when they immigrated. Her earliest memories happened here, where he told her she was named after a girl who went through a rabbit hole and then harnessed the portal's power into a looking glass. They're all dead now; the town and her father.

She ducks back inside and discovers another change. The table she sat at for so many years is now a long banquet table with many place settings.

She makes a larger pot of tea.

She almost misses their return. She catches the five of them readying the train on the tracks outside her house. They didn't even stop in for a welcome. "You can't leave yet. Where are you going?" Alice exclaims, panic gripping her.

Larry smiles beautifully at her. "We'll be back. We just have a number of new friends we have to go pick up now."

"That's not how this works. You can't bring them all back here."

"Well, we're going to. Would you like to come with us? Aren't you tired of this forest?"

"No! And no," Alice says, and bundles herself back inside her hotel.

She waits for a minute before sticking her head out the door and calling, "If you must go, be sure to drag the liminal spaces together using the tracks. Imagine the land like an island, where each slice is a different area and the tunnels connect it. It'll be quicker."

She waits again. A pain pulled taut like a string from the base of her neck down to her wrist throbs with worry. There's a great deal of noise when the train returns—talking, laughing, various animal noises, and a strange grinding of stone. It fills the forest and interferes with the voices in Alice's mind. Suddenly, she can't hear the ghosts. She steps outside her door to quiet the crowd, but they push past her into the hotel. She stands, outlined in the doorway, and watches them pass her teapot around the table.

"So, Alice," Larry says, "we've all shared what we asked for now. I wanted to travel freely, Nicholas wanted uninterrupted study time, Esther wanted an escape from the spotlight, Adelaide wanted independence, and Gideon wanted to be heard. But what did you wish for?"

"I don't want to be forgotten," she says quietly. "I don't want them to be forgotten."

"You mean this?" Tashi slides teacups out of the way and heaves the record book onto the table.

Alice nods, her breath going short again at seeing her life's work handled roughly.

"I wrote your name in, see?" Tashi flips pages and points proudly.

Alice nods again and smiles timidly. She turns and walks away from the wooden porch, her cane sticking in the thick pine needle carpet.

Larry quietly follows. He catches up to her when she's halfway up the mountain path out of the forest. "The circus is going to stay together," he says. "I talked it over with the troupe and everyone's decided."

Alice smiles and nods. She sniffs, and her breath shakes a little when the skeleton stoops to put his arms around her. When he breaks the hug, she presses a pocket watch into his hand.

"The watch stopped at 1:42 a.m. that night," she says, "and I knew."

"Thank you for returning it," Larry says kindly. He laughs, "When I left the watch and asked for the circus to stay together forever, I didn't exactly expect this."

"I kept my promise." Alice presses down on her cane to try and stand straight, holding her head high. "Technically, your wish came true, but because everyone wanted to go separate ways, everyone was flung separate ways. You always needed to be the one to complete it. I was powerless with you all stuck betwixt and between."

Larry nods. "We're going to keep traveling. We'll be the most haunted sideshow in the world. Maybe even galaxy, if we can figure out how. Tashi will stay here, hold down the fort, so to speak. Her new friends will help when they visit. Did you know there's some hairy creature around this area that Tashi introduced me to the other day? Like the forest equivalent of the yeti. Anyway, Tashi's excited. She'll handle any hikers who might blunder into this town from now on."

Alice keeps smiling, trying very hard to be more happy than despondent. "Keep it growing," she says insistently, "The mythological world and reality are linked like two sides of a looking glass. Some things can go through and some can't. You can see the other side if you look out of the corner of your eye or catch a glimpse of it in the mirror. Don't let it fade."

"Never," Larry grins. With a tip of his hat, he turns and runs back down to the hotel.

Alice turns towards the mountain. She starts up the hill again. Her mind is quiet, and there is no sound on the trail except for her cane pattering along the packed dirt. If she walks all evening she will hit the base of the tunnel, and from there, who knows, maybe the abandoned switchbacks to the peak.

She's so tired. She might even stop for a rest.

Epilogue Capstone Project

E.1 Epilogue Starter World

An epilogue world has been created as a starter for a capstone project. Download *EpilogueStarter.a3p* from **www.alice.org/Alice3ToJava** or obtain a copy from your instructor if you are taking a course. Start Alice and open the *EpilogueStarter* world. If the file has downloaded without corruption, you should see the initial scene in the code editor, as shown in Figure E.1.

Figure E.1 • *Initial scene view in downloaded starter world*

In *myFirstMethod* a statement has been added to move and orient the camera to a camera marker for an overview of the scene (Figure E.2). The comment in *myFirstMethod* documents the intent to demo writing code for running the circus train on the railroad tracks in this world.

```
declare procedure myFirstMethod
do in order
    // Short demo of running the train on the tracks
    camera  moveAndOrientTo  overhead , duration 0.0    add detail
```

Figure E.2 • myFirstMethod *in the starter world*

Run the starter world. Be patient—this world has hundreds of objects and takes a few seconds to load in the runtime window. You will see an overview of the epilogue scene (Figure E.3), that encompasses worlds from each episode of the *Haunted Circus*: snowy ice-covered mountains, Pacific Northwest forest, Amazon rainforest, Southeast Asian temple with a maze, a swamp with a dragon's tower, and an island with a cave.

Figure E.3   *Overview of Epilogue scene*

The scene contains 37 individual railroad track objects, connected end to end to create a complete circuit that meanders around the scene. The old Prenderghast Circus train has been assembled on the tracks, starting with the *trainEngine*, followed by *trainCarFlat1*, *trainCarFlat2*, *trainCar*, and *trainCarFlat3*. The flat cars carry a mausoleum, a haunted house, a train car, and a circus wagon, respectively (Figure E.4).

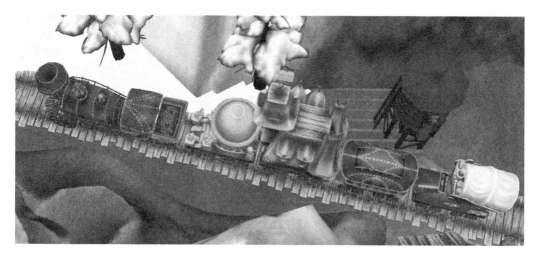

Figure E.4   *Close-up view of the Prenderghast train on the railroad tracks*

The starter world has three camera markers: *overhead*, *bellTowerView*, and *start* (Figure E.5).

Figure E.5 ⬦ *Camera markers in starter world*

The Scene class has two pre-made procedures that will help you in writing code to run the train on the railroad tracks (Figure E.6).

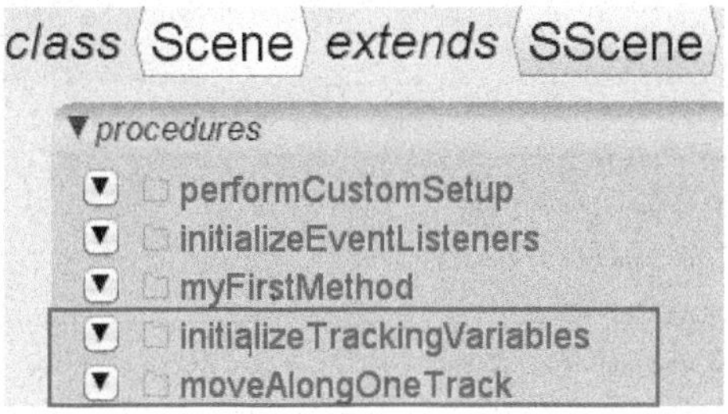

class Scene *extends* SScene

▼ *procedures*
▼ ☐ performCustomSetup
▼ ☐ initializeEventListeners
▼ ☐ myFirstMethod
▼ ☐ initializeTrackingVariables
▼ ☐ moveAlongOneTrack

Figure E.6 ⬦ *Pre-made procedures in the Scene class*

E.1.1 How the train is built

Writing code to run the train on the tracks requires some knowledge of how the train cars are connected to one another as well as how the tracks are connected to one another to build the railroad. This section illustrates building the train.

Each train car has a *nextCarLocation* marker that trails along behind it as shown in Figure E.7. Note the *nextCarLocation* marker (green arrow) is about 2 meters behind the engine's coal car in this example.

Figure E.7 ⬦ *The* nextCarLocation *marker trails behind a train object.*

To create a train with a chain of cars, each car after the engine is positioned at the *nextCarLocation* of the car in front of it. For example, in Figure E.8, a one-shot is used to *moveAndOrient* a *trainCarFlat* to the train engine's *nextCarLocation* marker. The result is shown in Figure E.9. The gap between the two cars is where (in real life) a coupling mechanism is used to create a link between the cars.

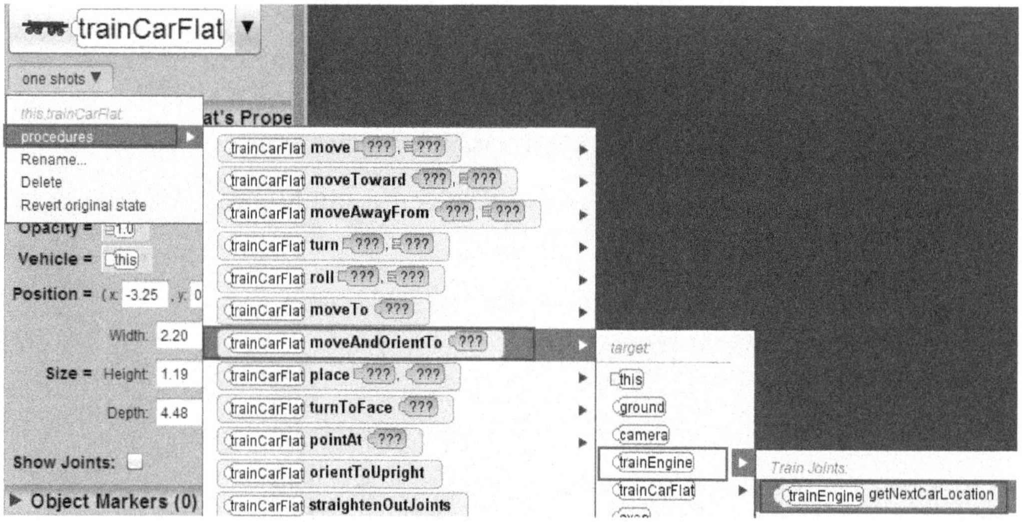

Figure E.8   *Using a one-shot to position one car behind another, using* nextCarLocation

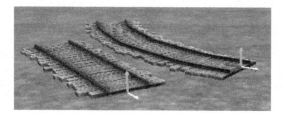

Figure E.9   *Result of positioning one car behind another*

E.1.2 How the railroad is built

A railroad is built by connecting individual track segments, end to end. Similar to the train cars, each track has a *nextTrackLocation* marker (Figure E.10). Note that the track's marker is at one edge of the track.

Figure E.10   *Each track has a* nextTrackMarker.

To connect one track to another, a second track is positioned at the *nextTrackMarker* of the track in front of it. In Figure E.11, a one-shot is used to *moveAndOrient* one track behind another track at the *nextTrackMarker* marker. The result is in Figure E.12. Note there is no gap between one track and the next.

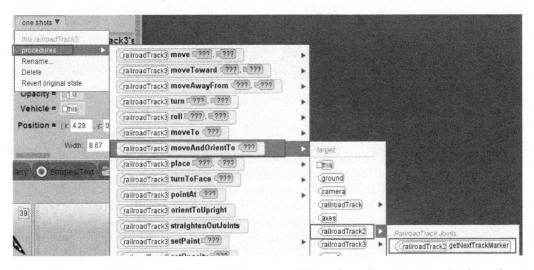

Figure E.11 • *Using a one-shot to position one track behind another, using* nextTrackMarker

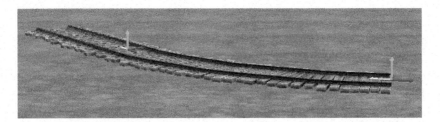

Figure E.12 • *Result of positioning one track behind another*

E.2 Setup: An Array of Tracks and Tracking Variables

Each railroad track has a built-in array of joints that mark positions along the track. The array of joints may be used as a marker path for moving the train across a track. The number of marked positions on a track depends on the length and curvature of the track. The Alice Gallery has a straight track with an array of two markers, a slightly curved track with an array of three markers, and a long, curved track with an array of six markers (Figure E.13). (The curved tracks have both left- and right-curve versions in the Gallery.)

It is easy enough to think about writing code to move a single train car along a track—just move the car from one marker to the next in the built-in array path. But the action becomes more complicated with a train (a chained sequence of an engine and four cars) and a railroad consisting of a sequence of 37 tracks that run through tunnels and around curves.

Figure E.13 *Built-in arrays of markers on the tracks*

Writing code to run the train along the tracks is easier if we set up an array for organizing the sequence of the tracks. The Scene class in the starter world already has an array of tracks, named *tracks* (Figure E.14). The remainder of this section illustrates how to write code to have the engine run by moving along the tracks, from one track to the next track in the array.

Writing code to have the four cars follow the engine is easier if we set up tracking variables that remember where the engine has just traveled. In addition to the *tracks* array declaration, Figure E.14 shows the declaration of four tracking variables. The tracking variables (*prevPosition0*, *prevPosition1*, *prevPosition2*, and *prevPosition3*) will track markers the engine has most recently moved through. Four trackers are needed, one for each train car that follows the engine.

Figure E.14 *Declaration of an array of tracks and tracking variables in the Scene class*

The tracking variables are intended to be used for moving the four cars forward to markers that the engine has previously visited. However, the variable declaration statements initialize the markers to a placeholder value. The tracking variables will be updated in *myFirstMethod*.

To replace the placeholder value (and properly initialize) the tracking variables, let's pretend the train engine has just moved to the first track, named *railroadTrack*. If the engine has just moved to the first track, then the engine has just moved across the last two tracks (*railroadTrack37* and *railroadTrack36*) in the circuit (Figure E.15). This means the four cars that follow along behind the engine are now on tracks 37 and 36 (left to right, on screen).

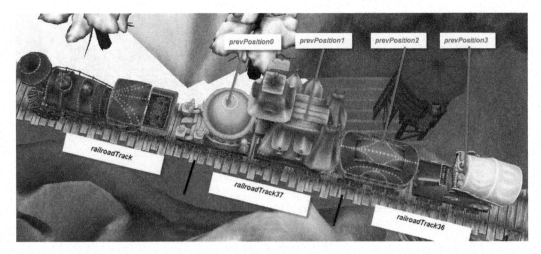

Figure E.15 • *The engine on the first track; the four cars on tracks 37 and 36*

To properly initialize the tracking variables, access is needed to the markers in path arrays belonging to tracks 37 and 36. Return to *myFirstMethod*. Immediately after the camera positioning statement, add statements to declare variables that access the path arrays in these two tracks (Figure E.16).

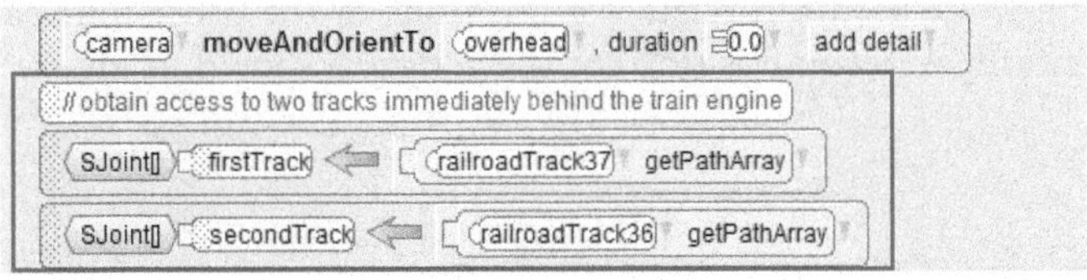

```
camera  moveAndOrientTo  overhead , duration  ≡0.0    add detail
// obtain access to two tracks immediately behind the train engine
SJoint[]  firstTrack  ⟸   railroadTrack37  getPathArray
SJoint[]  secondTrack  ⟸   railroadTrack36  getPathArray
```

Figure E.16 • *Variables to access path arrays in the two tracks behind the engine*

Now, initialize the tracking variables by calling the *initializeTrackingVariables* pre-made procedure (Figure E.17) with *firstTrack* and *secondTrack* as arguments. Figure E.18 is a copy of the code in the *initializeTrackingVariables* procedure, in which the tracking variables are assigned markers from the first and second track (tracks 37 and 38) path arrays.

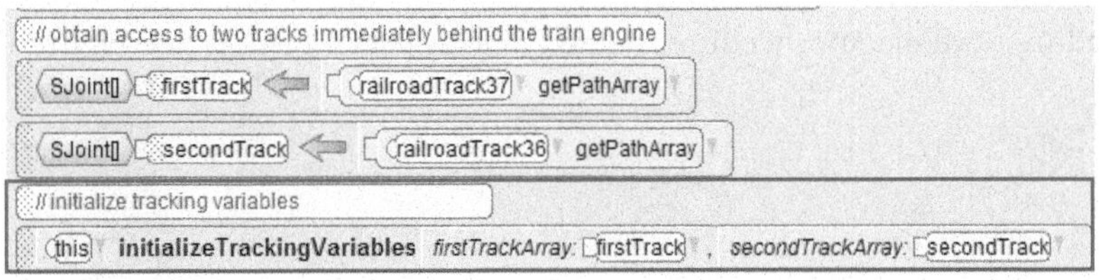

```
// obtain access to two tracks immediately behind the train engine
SJoint[]  firstTrack  ⟸   railroadTrack37  getPathArray
SJoint[]  secondTrack  ⟸   railroadTrack36  getPathArray
// initialize tracking variables
this  initializeTrackingVariables  firstTrackArray: firstTrack , secondTrackArray: secondTrack
```

Figure E.17 • *Call the pre-made initialization procedure.*

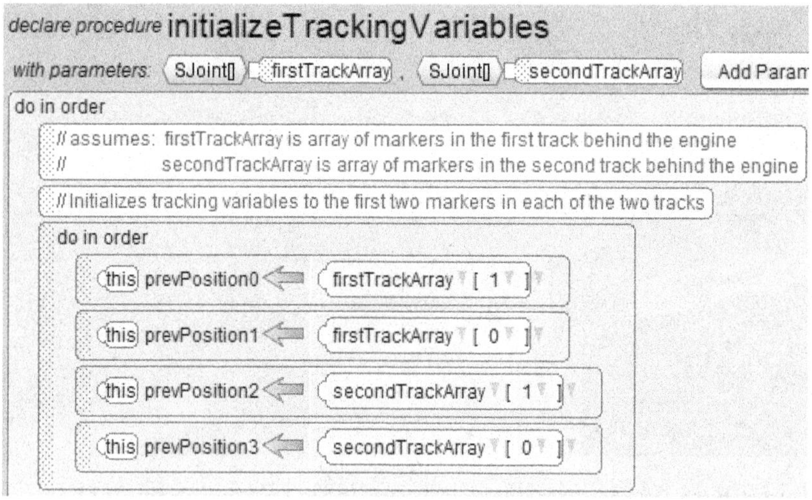

Figure E.18   *Pre-made* initializeTrackingVariables *procedure*

E.3 Writing Code to Run the Train

The joint markers in a track can be used to move the engine along the track and the tracking variables can now be used to update the positions of the other four cars each time the engine moves forward. A decomposition for the action is shown in Figure E.19.

for each marker in the track, one-by-one
      do together
            train engine move and orient to the next marker
            other train cars move along behind the train engine
      update tracking variables

Figure E.19   *Decomposition for running the train along one track*

For convenience, the code for running the train along one track has already been implemented in a pre-made procedure, named *moveAlongOneTrack*. See Figure E.20.

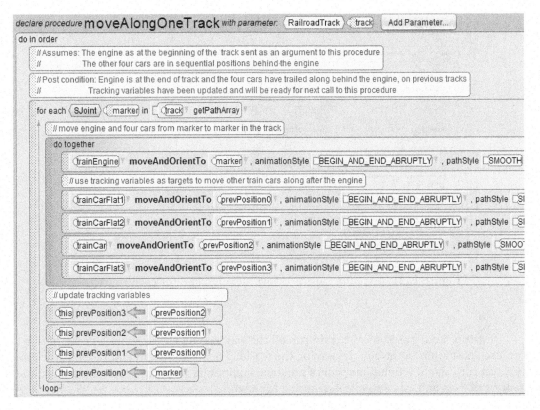

Figure E.20 • *The* moveAlongOneTrack *procedure*

The *moveAlongOneTrack* procedure has a parameter for the current *track*. A *for each in* control structure is used to loop through each *marker* in the current *track* path array. Within the loop, a *do together* code block contains statements to move the *trainEngine* to the marker and the other four cars to the markers specified by the tracking variables.

The tracking variables are used to have each train car move to a different marker. After the engine and four cars have all progressed to their targeted marker, the tracking variables are updated and the loop moves on to the next marker.

Supposedly, when the *moveAlongOneTrack* procedure finishes execution, the engine will have moved through every marker in a track's path array and the four cars have followed the engine but remain in their respective positions behind the engine. The easiest way to test the *moveAlongOneTrack* procedure is to call it from *myFirstMethod*. But, calling the procedure just once results in an animation that is difficult to observe because the camera is relatively far away from the train. Let's just go ahead and write code to run the train around the entire railroad circuit.

Return to *myFirstMethod*. Add a statement for a delay of 1.5 seconds. Then, add a *for each in* control structure, with *track* of type *RailroadTrack* as the item name and *tracks* as the array. Within the loop, add a statement to call *moveAlongOneTrack* with *track* as the argument (Figure E.21).

```
declare procedure myFirstMethod
do in order
  // Short demo of running the train on the tracks
  camera  moveAndOrientTo (overhead), duration ⊟0.0   add detail
  // obtain access to two tracks immediately behind the train engine
  SJoint[]  firstTrack  ⟸  [ railroadTrack37  getPathArray ]
  SJoint[]  secondTrack  ⟸  [ railroadTrack36  getPathArray ]
  // initialize tracking variables
  this  initializeTrackingVariables  firstTrackArray: ⌷firstTrack  ,  secondTrackArray: ⌷secondTrack
  this  delay ⊟1.5
  // run around the entire railroad circuit
  for each RailroadTrack  track in [ this .tracks ]
    this  moveAlongOneTrack  track: track
  loop
```

Figure E.21   *Call the* moveAlongOneTrack *in a* for each in *loop*

Test-run. You should see the train run all the way around the track with no hesitation. If you see hesitation in the run, try saving the world. Then, shut down and reopen Alice to try a test-run, again. (Hesitation occurs on some computers when an Alice scene has hundreds of objects and Alice has been running for a while.)

Capstone Project

Use the Epilogue starter world to create your own animation, with the train running around the track. Add event listeners for starting and stopping the train, and switch the camera viewpoint. (You may wish to create additional camera markers for this option.) Allow the user to use the arrow keys to turn and move the camera. Use your imagination to add features and functionality. Some interesting ideas include the following:

1. Stop the train engine near the water tower and refill the train's water supply.
2. Use the circus tent, which has full functionality, with the trapeze and a working trampoline.
3. Explore the swamp in a boat.
4. Expand the island world/have characters walk across the bridge.
5. Play a soccer game in the Amazon rainforest.

Index

Page numbers in bold indicate definitions

A
····

access, **367**
  element in Java array, 402–404, 402f, 403f
  items in custom array, 367–370, 368f, 369f, 370f
  value stored in a variable, 199–201, 217f
actions, identifying in a story, 9–11
activate scene, **43**
active class, **39**
active method, **39**
addMouseClickOnObjectListener event, 239f
Adelaide episode, 352–387
  algorithm, 372f
  object and camera markers for, 373f
  pre-made procedures for, 382, 382f
  starter world for, 372
  story analysis for, 370
  storyboard for, 371f
algorithm, **14**
  bubbleSort in Java, 417
  documenting with comments, 51–54f
  example development of, 18–19, 18f
  game, 232f, 335f
  generalized game, 299, 299f, 335f
  high-level for a game, **271**
  Selection sort in Java, 404–406
  translating to code of, 54–59, 55f, 56f, 57f, 58f, 59f
algorithm visualization, **413**
Alice. *See also* Code editor; Scene editor
  Blank Slates tab, 30
  class, **21**
  class hierarchy, 21
  class menus in, 40, 155, 155f
  class tab in, 39, 155–156, 156f
  Code editor in, 36, 39–40, 39f, 40f
  code display using Java syntax, 46–47, 46f, 47f
  data types in, 202–203, 202f, 203f, 211–214
  edit tabs in, 39, 155–156, 156f
  File menu, New Project in, 135, 135f
  Methods panel, Procedures and Functions tabs in, 41, 41f
  method tab in, 39, 155–156, 156f
  move, turn, and *roll* in, 50
  naming convention of, 82–83
  Procedures and Functions tabs, 41, 41f
  run program in, 43–46, 43f, 44f, 45f, 46f
  Scene class in, 39, 157f
  Scene editor in, 20–21, 20f, 21f
  side-by-side panel with Java, 150–151, 151f
application logic, **139**
args parameter, 144, 144f
argument, **42, 56**
  calling a procedure with, 42, 56, 378, 378f
  for optional (detail) parameter, 44, 161–163, 44f, 162f, 163f
  null placeholder in Java, 162, 162f
arithmetic expressions, **178,** 204
  compute value using, 195–198, 196f, 197f, 198f
  creating, 197, 198f
  in Java, 215–216, 216f
  order of operations, 201
array, **240, 312,** 387. *See also* **built-in arrays; custom array**
  access individual element in, 402–404, 402f, 403f
  ascending order values, **406,** 417
  buckets, **402**
  calling procedure with argument for, 378, 378f
  descending order values, **405**
  empty placeholder, 317f
  initializer list for (Java), **401**
  iterate through, 384f
  Java, 399–404, 400f, 401f, 403f
  Java declaration of, 400, 400f, 401f
  Java initialization of, 401–402
  length, **365**
  select sort for (Java), 406–407, 406f, 407f
  swap method for elements in (Java), 409–411, 410f, 411f
assignment
  operator, **158,** 417
  statement, 294–295, 295f
  value to variable, **294**
assumed pre-conditions, **84**
audio
  resource, 128f
  source file, import of, 127–128, 128f

B

background information, 10, 11
"belongs to," 23
Billboard, 235–238
    creating new, 236f
    front paint image for, 236f
    hiding, 241f
    import image for, 235f
    instructions displayed on, 238f
    listen for mouse-click on, 240f
    name for, 236f
    paint color for, 237f
binary condition, 342
binary operators, interactive control with,
        341–346, 342f, 343f, 344f, 345f, 346f
Biped class, 122–124, 122f, 123f, 124f, 187–188,
        187f, 188f
bit, 213
Blank Slates tab, 30
blank string, 443
blinkEyes, 429
body language, 89
Boolean data type, 202, 203f, 211, 211t
Boolean expression, 220
    relational operators used in, 220f
Boolean operators, 312, 342
bubbleSort, 417
bug, 59, 60–64, 60f, 61f, 62f, 63f, 64f
build, 143
built-in array, 311–353
    demo of, 321f
    each in together in demo illustrating, 320–321,
        320f, 321f
    iteration with for each in, 316–319, 316f, 317f,
        318f, 319f
    skeletal joints in, 315–316, 315f
    starter world for demo illustrating, 313–314,
        313f, 314f
    story analysis for demo illustrating, 312–314,
        313f, 314f
    straightenOutJoints in, 319–320, 319f
    testing for demo illustrating, 314–321, 314f,
        315f, 316f, 317f, 318f, 319f, 320f, 321f
byte, 211t, 213

C

call a method (procedure or function), 43
    with argument for detail parameter, 44, 44f
camelCase, 82, 93
camera cut, 178
camera illusion technique

    decomposition using, 182f
    implementation of, 182–183, 182f, 183f, 184f
camera marker, 102
    in a scene, 104–105, 105f
    view objects with, 107–109, 108f, 109f
    walking path with, 181f
camera view panel, 20–21
change in state, 246
child class, 122
class, 21. *See also* Scene class; Program class
    active, 39
    child, 122
    custom procedure, adding to, 81–82, 82f
    Enum, 163, 203
    family of, 121
    Gallery collection of, 21
    main, 136, 136f, 145f, 147, 148
    parent, 122–126, 122f, 123f, 124f, 125f
    wrapper, 212
Class Hierarchy tab, 22, 22f
Class menu, 170
    in Alice and Java projects, 155, 155f
    including Program class in, 44, 44f
Class tab, Alice and NetBeans, 155–156, 156f
coatTransformation procedure, 249–250
code block, 66, 66f
    collapse by default in Java, 154, 154f
    Java, 139–142, 139f
code completion, 140, 162
    argument to optional parameter with,
        161–163, 162f, 163f
    menu list of optional parameters, 162f
    statements with required parameter with,
        163–165, 164f, 165f
Code editor, 20, 43
    Display *"this"* word in, 83–84, 83f, 84f
    Edit Code button for, 39
    initializeEventListeners tab in, 39, 39f
    myFirstMethod tab in, 39, 39f
    Object selector box in, 39, 39f
    Scene class tab in, 39, 40f
code palette (NetBeans), 165
    control statements, 165f
    NetBeans, 165–167, 165f, 166f, 167f
code reuse, 87
    implementation intended for, 185–189, 185f,
        186f, 187f, 188f, 189f
    previously saved code imported for, 187–188,
        187f, 188f
code statement, 23
    creating, 40–42, 40f, 41f, 42f
    translating algorithm into, 54–59, 55f, 56f, 57f,
        58f, 59f
collision event listener, 449–450, 450f
collisionStarted listener, 425, **432**, 450, 454

command lines, **142**
    Run button compared to, 142–143, 143f
    text string containing (Java), 144f
comments, **52**
    creating documentation with, 52–53, 53f, 54f
    custom procedure with, 84, 85f
    documenting algorithm with, 53, 54f
    implementation using stepwise refinement
      with, 105, 106f
    in myFirstMethod, 80f, 182f
    in syntax-sensitive text editor (NetBeans), 138f
    not executable code, 67
    symbol for, 53
compareTo function, 387–388, 411, 411f, 416
computer programming, **8**
    problem-solving approach of, 8–9, 8f, 11
concatenation, **443**
conditional expressions, **230**
    built-in functions with, 246–249, 247f, 248f, 249f
    if-else with, 249f
constant, **158**
controls, **230**
control structure, **52**
copy-and-paste keyboard shortcut for, **87**, 87f
Counted For loop (Java)
    doTogether with, 219f
    loop control variable for, 219–220, 219f, 220f
    Template for, 221, 221f
count loop, 90, **178**, **199**
    design for animation example using, 179–180,
      179f, 180f
    talkAndSay procedure with, 199, 199f
    variable as control, 199–201, 199f, 200f, 201f
curly braces (Java code block), 139–140, 139f
custom array, 361–395, **362**
    access item in, 367–370, 368f, 369f, 370f
    add objects to, 364f, 365f
    algorithm for program example illustrating,
      372f
    basic operations with, 362–370, 362f, 363f,
      364f, 365f, 366f, 367f, 368f, 369f, 370f
    calling procedure with argument for, 378, 378f
    create, 362f, 363–365, 363f, 364f, 365f
    declaration statement in myFirstMethod for,
      365f
    design for program example illustrating,
      371–372, 371f, 372f
    for each in loop structure with, 365–367, 366f,
      367f
    implementation with, 375–382, 375f, 376f,
      377f, 378f, 379f, 380f, 381f, 382f
    initialize, 362f, 363–365, 363f, 364f, 365f
    iterate through, 365–367, 366f, 367f
    Java, 397–417

    linear search of, 386–388, 386f, 387f, 388f
    Object Selector to view objects in scene with,
      367–368, 368f
    starter world for program example illustrat-
      ing, 372–374, 372f, 373f, 374f
    story analysis for program example illustrat-
      ing, 370–374, 371f
    storyboard for program example illustrating,
      372f
    visual alignment of (horizontal), 382–385,
      383f, 384f, 385f, 386f
    visual alignment of (vertical), 389–391, 389f,
      390f, 391f
    writing procedure with no parameter for,
      378–382, 379f, 380f, 381f
    writing procedure with parameter for, 375f,
      376–378, 376f, 377f, 378f
custom function, 269–303, **270**, **291**
    compareTo (example), 387–388, 387f, 388f, 416
    declaration steps for, 291f
    writing, 291–294, 291f, 292f, 293f
custom procedure, **78**
    adding to a class, 81–82, 82f
    calling, 85–86, 85f, 86f
    comments for documenting of, 84, 85f
    declaration of, 81–84, 82f, 83f, 84f
    naming, 82–83, 82f, 83f
    with parameter, 190–194, 190f, 191f, 192f,
      193f, 194f, 195f
    pre-made with built-in arrays, 324, 324f
    reuse, 87, 87f, 88f
    "this" word with, 83–84, 83f, 84f
    writing code to define, 84–85, 85f, 92
cutscene, **270**

D
••••

data, **41**
data structure, **363**
data types
    Alice, 202–203, 202f, 203f, 211–214
    Boolean (Alice and Java), 202, 203f, 211, 211t
    char (Java), 210
    Character (Java), 210
    DecimalNumber, 193, 193f, 202, 203f, 211
    Double (Java), 211, 211t, 213
    int (Java), 210
    Integer (Java), **201**, 211t
    Java, 211–214, 211t, 212f, 213t, 214f, 222, 223
    primitive (Java), **212**
    String (Java), 215, 215f
    TextString, 190–192, 191f, 192f, 202, 203f, 211
    WholeNumber, 202, 203f, 211

data value, 178, 209–211

debug, **59**, 60–64, 60f, 61f, 62f, 63f

    design revision following, 64–66, 64f, 65f, 66f, 67f

debugging

    game interactivity example of, 346–348, 347f, 348f

    multiple event triggers example of, 445–446, 446f

    testing, 444–445, 444f, 445

    text display setup for, 440–442, 440f, 441f, 442f

    TextString output for feedback with, 439–446, 439f, 440f, 441f, 442f, 443f, 444f, 445f, 446f

DecimalNumber, 202, 203f, 211

    add parameter of type, 193, 193f

declaration, **22**

    custom array, 363–365

    custom function, 387–388

    custom procedure, 81–83

    in Scene class, 109–110

    object, 23

    parameter, 190–192

    property, 158

    statement, 23

    variable, 195–197

decomposition, **55**

    stepwise refinement with repeated, 106–107, 106f, 107f

decrement, **220**

default, **22**

    parameters with, 69

default location, **23**

design, 13–33

    in Alice programming, 15f

    comments that reflect, 106f

    event-driven programming example, 427–429, 427f, 428f, 429f

    game, with event listener, 232f, 258f

    game with implied loop, 431–432, 431f, 432f

    set design, 15–18, 16f, 17f–18f

    stepwise refinement in, 119f

    stepwise refinement diagram, 106f

    story analysis as start for, 78–80, 79f, 80f

    storyboard in, 78–79, 79f, 102–103, 103f

    thinking, 14–15, 14f, 15f

design revision, 64–67

    cyclic nature of, 64f

detail parameters, **44**, 44f

dialog, 121, 121f, 130

    synchronizing, 126f

    writing code for, 126

direction, possible values for, 58, 58f

documentation

    creating, with comments, 52–53, 53f, 54f

do in order, **43**, 52

    Java default, 168, 168f

do together, **78**–79

    creating code block for, 86–87, 86f, 87f

    each in together code nested with, 320f

    for each in code nested with, 319f

    nested code block, 88–89, 89f

doTogether (Java version of Alice's *do together*), **165**

    code template, 165–167, 165f, 166f, 167f

    Counted For loop with, 219f

    do in order with, 168, 168f

    Lambda expressions with, 167–168, 167f, 168f

    NetBeans template for, 165–167, 165f, 166f, 167f

    writing Java code with, 216–218, 217f, 218f

dot operator, **139**

Double, 211, 211t, **213**

duration, **44**

    adding, 44, 44f, 192–194, 193f, 194f

    default, 44

E
• • •

each in together, **316**

    custom array with, 367

    do together nested with, 320f

    iteration with, 320–321, 320f, 321f

    unrolling loop of, 320f

Edit Code button, 39

edit tabs

    Alice and NetBeans, 155–156, 156f

elements, **363**, 416

encapsulation, **212**

end conditions, **230**

    game state, 297–299, 297f, 298f

Enum classes, **163**, 203

Epilogue capstone project, 461–470

    how railroad is built in, 464–465, 464f, 465f

    how train is built in, 463–464, 463f, 464f

    markers on tracks, 466f

    pre-made procedures with, 463f

    starter world for, 461–465, 461f, 462f, 463f, 464f, 465f

    tracks and tracking variables array for, 465–467, 466f, 467f, 468f

    writing code to run train for, 468–470, 468f, 469f, 470f

Epilogue story, 457–459

Episodes
  Adelaide (Reanimated Zombie Kittens), 356–359
  Esther (Bell), 306–309
  Gideon (Oven Mitts), 420–423
  Larry (Ice Block), 4–6
  Nicholas (Pumpkin Head), 264–267
  The Forest Cabin, 174–176
  The Ringmaster Coat, 226–228
  The Train Engine, 71–74
  The Tunnel, 98–100

Esther episode, 306–309
  algorithm for, 313, 313f
  design for, 312–314, 313f, 314f
  starter world for, 313
  story analysis for, 312

event, 230

event-driven programming, 425–455
  collision event listener with, 449–450, 450f
  collisionStarted event listener in, 451–452, 451f, 452f, 453f
  design example, 427–429, 427f, 428f, 429f
  event listeners for speed updates with, 446–450, 447f, 448f, 449f, 450f
  game analysis and design with, 431–432, 431f, 432f
  implied game loop with, 430–435, 431f, 432f, 433f, 434f, 435f
  keyPress event listener for, 435–438, 435f, 436f, 437f, 438f
  opening cutscene with, 429, 430f
  restrict multiple event triggers with, 445–446, 446f
  text display setup for, 440–442, 440f, 441f, 442f
  TextString output for feedback with, 439–446, 439f, 440f, 441f, 442f, 443f, 444f, 445f, 446f
  time-elapsed event listener with, 447–448, 447f, 448f
  updating text display for, 442–443, 442f, 443f, 444f
  viewExited listener in, 452–453, 452f, 453f

event handler, 232

event listener, 230
  collision, 449–450, 450f
  collisionStarted, 451–452, 451f, 452f, 453f
  implementation of, 238–242, 239f, 240f, 241f
  keyPress, 435–438, 435f, 436f, 437f, 438f
  mouse-click on object, 234
  mouse-click with multiple target objects, 251–254, 251f, 252f, 253f, 254f
  object mover, 238

  pointOfViewChange, 244f
  preventing repeated firing of, 250, 250f, 251f
  speed updates with, 446–450, 447f, 448f, 449f, 450f
  timeElapsed, 447–448, 447f, 448f
  viewExited, 452–453, 452f, 453f

execution, 18, 52. *See also* run program

export, 126
  name and save file for, 127, 127f
  talk procedure example, 126, 126f

external pivot, 270

F
...

Facebook™, 8

fail conditions, 230

family of classes, 121

feedback to game player, 230
  debug with TextString output for, 439–446, 439f, 440f, 441f, 442f, 443f, 444f, 445f, 446f
  game win or lose, 349, 349f

File menu, New Project in, 135, 135f

final keyword, 158

fire, 245

fixed length of array, 403

float, 211, 211t

follow camera, 241

for each in, 316
  custom array with, 365–367, 366f, 367f
  do together with nested, 319f
  unrolling loop of, 318f
  iteration with, 316–319, 316f, 317f, 318f, 319f

Forest Cabin episode, 174–175, 205
  algorithm for, 180f
  design for, 179–180, 179f, 180f
  story analysis for, 178
  storyboard for, 180f

for loop (Java), 90, 219, 221f
  limit, usage of variable as 219–221, 219f, 220f, 221f

format, 448
  two decimal places display, 448–449, 449f

FORWARD
  skeletal joint, 62, 62f
  move direction, 58, 58f

frames, storyboard, 15, 16

function, 39, 230. *See also* custom function
  built-in, 246–249, 247f, 248f, 249f
  compareTo, 387–388, 411, 411f, 416
  getDistanceTo, 248, 248f
  getPumpkin, 291–292, 292f, 296, 296f
  input, 294
  Procedures and Functions tabs, 41, 41f

G
••••

Gallery, 20–22, 21f
  3D model classes from, 21
  Class Hierarchy tab in, 22, 22f
  tabs in, 22, 22f
game, 259. *See also* game controls; interactivity
  adapting story for, 230–234, 233f, 234f
  algorithm for, 232f, 283, 299, 299f, 322f, 335f
  checking end conditions for, 348, 349f
  collision event listener with, 449–450, 450f
  collisionStarted event listener in, 451–453, 451f, 452f, 453f
  comments, 335f
  debugging interactivity for, 346–348, 347f, 348f
  decomposition, 283–285, 284f, 285f
  decomposition for play of, 330–332
  design with event listener, 232f, 258f
  feedback for win or lose for, 349, 349f
  generalized algorithm for, 299, 299f, 335f
  goals, **230**
  high-level structure for, 325, 325f
  interactive control with binary operators, 341–346, 342f, 343f, 344f, 345f, 346f
  loss condition in, 452–453, 452f, 453f
  main loop for, 336–337, 337f
  player's controls for implied loop, 431, 431f
  restrict multiple event triggers with, 445–446, 446f
  time-elapsed event listener with, 447–448, 447f, 448f
  tracking variable for condition of, 254–257, 255f, 256f, 257f
  win conditions in, 451–453, 451f, 452f, 453f
game controls. *See also* game
  event listeners for speed updates with, 446–450, 447f, 448f, 449f, 450f
  game loop, **299**, 300
  implied loop for, 430–435, 431f, 432f, 433f, 434f, 435f
  interactive control, 341–346, 342f, 343f, 344f, 345f, 346f
  keyPress event listener for, 435–438, 435f, 436f, 437f, 438f
  main loop for, 336–337, 337f
  player's controls, 431, 431f
  reset, 433–434
  viewExited event listener in, 452–453, 452f, 453f
game state, **297**
  checking, 297–299, 297f, 298f
  end conditions in, 297–299, 297f, 298f
  win conditions in, 451–453, 451f, 452f, 453f
getDistanceTo function, 248, 248f

GhostTown animation, 205
  object and camera markers in, 181f, 234f
  scene for, 180f
  starter world for game adaptation from, 233–234, 233f, 234f
GhostTownExportToNetbeans.a3p
  import of, 210f
  in NetBeans, 210, 210f, 211f
Gideon episode, 420–423
  design for, 427
  story analysis for, 426
graphics-based editor, **136**
  text-based comparison with, 144–146, 145f, 146f

H
••••

HelloWorld project
  Alice to Java import of, 150, 152, 161
  main method header in, 144, 144f
  in NetBeans, 137f
helper procedure, **287**
high-level algorithm, **271**
high-level structure, 325, 325f

I
••

IDE. *See* Alice; NetBeans; interactive development environment
if-else control structures, **230**, 259
  code block with, 245f
  code block with conditional expression, 249f
  creating, 245f
  if and else segments of, 249, 249f, 250f
  keyPress identified with, 436, 436f
implementation, 35–72, **36**
  camera and object markers, 104–105, 105f
  camera illusion technique, 182–183, 182f, 183f, 184f
  camera marker, 107–109, 108f, 109f
  Code editor for, 36, 39–40, 39f, 40f
  code reuse in, 185–189, 185f, 186f, 187f, 188f, 189f
  code with Java syntax in, 46–47, 46f, 47f
  comment documentation with, 105, 106f
  creating code statements, 40–42, 40f, 41f, 42f
  custom array, 375–382, 375f, 376f, 377f, 378f, 379f, 380f, 381f, 382f
  custom procedure, 80–81, 80f, 81f
  cutscene, 277–283, 277f, 278f, 279f, 280f, 281f, 282f, 283f
  cyclic nature of, 64f
  debugging with, 60–64, 60f, 61f, 62f, 63f, 64f

with incremental development, 51, 51f, 52f
in Java, 133–148
problem-solving approach step, 36
stepwise refinement in, 104–116, 104f
syntax-sensitive text editor in Java, 137–139, 138f
testing with, 54, 54f
three typical operations used in, 52f
TODO note comment for (Java), 138–139, 138f
translating algorithm to code with, 54–59, 55f, 56f, 57f, 58f, 59f
implicit *this*, 163
implied loop, 430
analysis and design for game with, 431–432, 431f, 432f
example game implementation with, 430–435, 431f, 432f, 433f, 434f, 435f
player's controls for game with, 431, 431f
import, 126
Alice 3 to Java, 149–172
Alice project into NetBeans, 151–154, 152f, 153f, 154f, 171
audio source file, 127–128, 128f
image in Resource Manager, 235f
previously saved code, 187–188, 187f, 188f
increment, 220, 297, 297f
incremental development, 51
cyclic nature of, 51f
implementation with, 51, 51f, 52f
index of array item/element, 315
index operator, 400
infinite while loop example, 332–334, 332f
inheritance, 101–131, 102
parent class custom procedure for, 122–126, 122f, 123f, 124f, 125f
initializeEventListeners tab, 39, 39f
initializer list for array (Java), 401
input built-in functions, 294
instructions, 18
int, 213
Integer, 202, 211t
interactive development environment (IDE), 20.
See also Alice; NetBeans
interactivity, 229–261, 230
adapting story for, 322–323, 322f, 323f
built-in functions in conditional expressions with, 246–249, 247f, 248f, 249f
game control, 341–346, 342f, 343f, 344f, 345f, 346f
if/else control structure with, 245–250, 245f, 246f, 247f, 248f, 249f, 250f, 251f
implementation of event listener for, 238–242, 239f, 240f, 241f

implementation of UI to display instructions for, 235–238, 235f, 236f, 237f, 238f
mouse-click with multiple target objects, 251–254, 251f, 252f, 253f, 254f
object mover listener for, 242–243, 242f, 243f
preventing repeated event listener firing with, 250, 250f, 251f
troubleshooting code for, 254, 254f
internal pivot, 270
creation of, 272–274, 273f, 274f, 275f
items in array, 312
access, 363, 367–370, 416, 368f, 369f, 370f
iterate through array, 316
with *for each in*, 316–319, 316f, 317f, 318f, 319f
with *for each in together*, 316

J
..

Java
arithmetic expressions in, 215–216, 216f
arithmetic operators, 213t
array access of individual element in, 402–404, 402f, 403f
array declaration in, 400, 400f, 401f
array initialization in, 401–402
arrays in, 399–404, 400f, 401f, 402f, 403f
array sorting, 404–412, 404f, 405f, 406f, 407f, 408f, 409f, 410f, 411f, 412f
capitalization and naming in, 140
class menus in, 155, 155f
code completion, 161–165, 162f, 163f, 164f, 165f
compareTo function for array sort in, 411, 411f, 416
custom array in, 397–417
data types in, 211–214, 211t, 212f, 213t, 214f, 222, 223
default *do in order* in, 168, 168f
doTogether in, 165–168, 165f, 166f, 167f, 168f, 216–218, 217f, 218f
importing Alice 3 to, 149–172
Lambda expressions in, 167–168, 167f, 168f
for loop used in, 219–221, 219f, 220f, 221f
NetBeans IDE, 134–135, 134f, 135f, 141, 141f, 142f
NetBeans code palette, 165–167, 165f, 166f, 167f
new project creation in, 135–137, 135f, 136f, 137f
preference settings for, 150f
primitive data types in, 212–213, 212f, 213t
side-by-side panel in Alice, 150–151, 151f

Java (*continued*)

    sort for custom array written in, 413–415, 415f

    swap method written in, 409–411, 410f, 411f

    syntax, 46–47, 46f, 47f

    System.out in, 140–141, 140f, 141f

    testing code in, 221–222, 221f, 222f

    TODO note in implementation of, 138–139, 138f

    variables in, 215–216, 216f

    writing code in, 139–142, 214–218, 139f, 214f, 215f, 216f, 217f, 218f

joint-reference, **62**

K
••••

keyboard shortcuts, 87, **141**

    copy-and-paste (Alice), **87**, 87f

    writing code in NetBeans IDE, 141, 141f, 142f

keyPress, **312**

    event listener for, 435–438, 435f, 436f, 437f, 438f

    handle arrow keys with, 438f

    if/else code blocks to identify key, 436, 436f

keyword, **22**, **39**, 139

L
•••

lambda code block, **167**

lambda expression, **168**

    doTogether with, 167–168, 167f, 168f

Larry episode, 4–6

    algorithm for, 15

    set design for, 15

    story analysis for, 10–11

legal operators for primitive data types, **213**

Let's Make a Deal® animation, 303

loop control value, 90, **199**

loop control variable, **219**

    Counted For loop, 219, 220f

    initialized, 220f

M
••••

main class, 136, 136f, 145f, 147, 148

main method, 136–137, 139, 144, 147, 148

markers, **20**, **104**

    camera and object, in scene, 104–105, 105f, 181f, 273f, 301, 314f, 324f, 373f, 428f

    pivot, 287–289, 287f, 288f, 289f

    view objects with camera, 107–109, 108f, 109f

methods, **40**. *See also* myFirstMethod

    active, **39**

    calling with detail parameter, 44, 44f

    main, 136–137, 139, 144, 147, 148

    tiles for built-in functional, 246–247

    tiles for built-in procedural, 54, 55f

Methods panel, Procedures and Functions tabs in, 41, 41f

method tabs, Alice and NetBeans, 155–156, 156f

modifiers, **144**

modulus, **213**

mouse-click event listener, **238**

    listener with multiple target objects, 251–254, 251f, 252f, 253f, 254f

move, 50–68, 163–165, 165f

    arguments in, 58, 58f

    default value for duration of, 69

    object, 68

    statement, 163–165, 165f

moveAndOrientTo, 111, 111f

multipleEventPolicy, **438**

myFirstMethod, 39, 39f

    calling, 85–86, 86f

    comments in, 80f, 182f

    display in Java mode of, 160f

    editor tab of, 42

    execution of, 43, 43f

N
••••

naming convention, **82**

    Alice, 82–83

natural ordering, **411**

nested code block, **88**

    do in order in, 88, 88f, 91

    do together in, 88–89, 89f, 90f, 91

NetBeans IDE, 134–135

    Alice project import into, 151–154, 152f, 153f, 154f, 171

    classes and code organization in, 155–156

    Class tab in, 155–156, 156f

    code palette, 165–167, 165f, 166f, 167f

    doTogether code template, 165–167, 165f, 166f, 167f

    edited code for, 153

    edit tabs in, 155–156, 156f

    filename extension for, 153

    keyboard shortcuts in, 141, 141f, 142f

    methods tab in, 155–156, 156f

    panels, 135f

    Run button in, 142, 142f

    Scene class in, 157f

start page of, 134f

transfer of hidden code from Alice to, 160–161, 160f, 161f

transfer of procedure component to, 158–160, 159f, 160f

transfer of properties component to, 157–158, 158f

New Project, File menu selection of, 135, 135f

Nicholas episode, 264–267

    algorithm for, 271f

    design for, 271, 271f

    story analysis for, 270–271

    storyboard for, 271f

non-editable code in Alice, **157**

null placeholder, argument with, 162, 162f

O
....

object, 9–11, **21**

    add to custom array, 364f

    add to scene, 21

    positioning of, in scene, 24–26, 25f, 26f

object marker, 301

    in scene, 104–105, 105f

Object mover event listener, 242–243

Object selector, view of objects in scene with, 367–368, 368f

Object selector box, 39, 39f

Object tree, 21, 21f

one-shots, **24**

    menu, 26, 26f

    object positioning using, 24–26, 25f, 26f

optional parameter, **161**

    code completion menu list of, 162f

    code completion to add argument for, 161–163, 162f, 163f

options settings, collapse by default/code blocks option, 154, 154f

ordered sequence in array, **315**, **363**

out of scope, **376**

The Gideon (Oven Mitts) episode, 420–423

    design for, 427

    story analysis for, 426

P
...

palette, **165**. *See also* code palette

parameter, **42**

    add duration as, 192–194, 193f, 194f

    adding to header, 215, 215f

    add two different data types, 194, 194f, 195f

    args, 144, 144f

    code completion statements with required, 163–165, 164f, 165f

    custom procedure with, 190–194, 190f, 191f, 192f, 193f, 194f, 195f

    default values for, 69

    detail (having default value), optional, **44**, 44f, **161**, 161–163, 162f, 163f

    required, 161, 163–165, 164f, 165f

    writing Java code with, 214–216, 214f, 215f, 216f

    writing a procedure with array, 375f, 376–378, 376f, 377f, 378f

parent class, **122**

    writing custom procedure for, 122–126, 122f, 123f, 124f, 125f

parentheses, 140

path of markers, **178**

pivot markers, swap with, 287–289, 287f, 288f, 289f

pivot point, **273**, 300

    external, 279, 279f, 280f

    internal, 272–274, 273f, 274f, 275f, 280–281, 280f, 281f

playAudio, 119–120, 120f

    audio source file import for, 127

player in a game, **230**

    game controls, 431, 431f

player input. *See* user input

pointOfViewChange, 243–244

    select options for, 244f

pose, **312**

    animating with, 326–329, 327f, 328f, 329f, 330f

    built-in procedures for, 327f

post-conditions, **84**

pre-made procedures in starter worlds, **276**

Prologue Prenderghast Haunted Circus story, 1–2

primitive data types, **212**

    in Java, 212–213, 212f, 213t

    legal operations on, 213–214, 213t

println (Java), 141

private, **158**

problem, **8**

problem-solving approach, 8–9, 8f, 11

    implementation in, 36

procedure header, **81**

procedures, **39**. *See also* custom procedure; pre-made procedures

    alignInRow, 383, 383f, 384f, 385f

    array parameter in writing, 375f, 376–378, 376f, 377f, 378f

    audioDialog, 131

    calling with array argument, 378, 378f

    coatTransformation, 249, 249f, 250f

procedures (*continued*)

creepyWalk, 395

CurupiraKickPumpkin, 278, 278f, 279f

declare and implementation of, 109–112, 110f, 111f, 112f

declaring, guidelines for, 110

default duration of, 44

departure, 131

descendStaircase, 340, 340f

dialog, 121, 121f, 124–126, 125f, 126f, 130

EstherTrapped, 328–329, 329f

findLargestAfterIndex, 407–409, 407f, 408f, 409f

float, 437, 437f

foldWingsPose, 327, 327f

fromCoalBox, 109–112, 110f, 111f, 112f

gameReset, 433–434, 433f, 434f, 453, 453f

helper, **287**

initializeTrackingVariables, 467, 467f, 468f

jump procedure, 93

lookingForPumpkinWithFace, 277, 277f

moveAlongOneTrack, 468–469, 469f, 470f

moveAndOrientTo, 111, 111f

openingConversation, 375, 375f

playAudio, 119–120, 120f, 127

playGame, 335, 335f

playOpeningCutscene, 325–326, 325f, 326f

pre-made, **276**, 277f

pressureBuilds, 118, 118f

println, 141

revealTrek, storyboard for, 186f

ringBell, 118–120, 119f, 120f

say, 42, 87, 87f

self-documenting name of, 82

setVehicle, 56, 56f, 57, 57f

shuffle, **270**, 289–293, 290f, 291f

sneakPeek, 184–185, 184f, 185f

specialEffect, 261

spin, 204

spreadWingsPose, 327, 327f

stack 389f, 390f, 391f

stair-twisting helper procedure, 333, 333f

talk, 81f, 85f, 86f, 87, 87f, 88f, 122, 122f, 187–189, 187f, 188f, 189f, 429

talkAndSay, 190–191, 190f, 191f, 199, 200f, 214f, 215f, 216–218, 217f, 218f, 429

TashiMeetsEsther, 325–326, 325f, 326f

TashiOffers, 329, 330f

tiles for built-in procedural methods, 54, 55f

toFirebox, 114–116, 115f, 116f

turn, 59, 59f

turnTowardFirebox, 112–114, 113f, 114f

twistStairs, 333, 333f

unlockAndDepart, 256–257, 256f, 257f

updateTashiPosition, 339, 339f, 340–341, 341f

walk, 395

walkPath, 182–183, 183f

wingJump, 327–328, 327f, 328f

wobble, 393

wrapTail, 353

writing for parent class, 122–126, 122f, 123f, 124f, 125f

Procedures tab, 54, 55f

program, **8**

run, 43–46, 43f, 44f, 45f, 46f

Program class

in Class menu, 44, 44f

enable display of, 45, 45f

tab, 45f

program task, 8

analyzing and understanding, 9–10, 10f

task description, 10, 11

first programming task, 9–10

programming language preference, 46, 46f

prompt, **294**

Prop category button, 22, 22f

properties, 39–40

property, **21**, **23**

vehicle, 55

public, **144**

R

randomly selected objects, **270**

shuffle with, 289–290, 290f, 291f

real value, **202**

relational operator, **220**

Boolean expressions use of, 220f

repetition, **178**

count loop, **90**

Counted for loop (Java), 169, 219–220

while loop, 286

required parameter, **161**

code completion to write statements with, 163–165, 164f, 165f

Resource Manager

dialog box, 235, 235f

import audio in, 127–128, 128f

import image in, 235f

resources for object's skin, **22**, **116**

return data type, **291**

Ringmaster Coat episode, 226–228

changing point of view for, 243

design for, 231

story analysis for, 230–231

roll, 50

RollingDie.a3p project, 302

Rotation of an object or joint
   turn, 4, 62
   roll, 62, 65
rounding error, **448**
Run button, 43, 43f
   compare command lines with, 142–143, 143f
   in NetBeans IDE, 142, 142f
   what happens with, 142–144, 143f, 144f
   behind scene look at, 44–46, 44f, 45f, 46f
runtime window, **43**

S
...

say, 42
   duration, 81f
   modified duration, 163f
scene
   adding object in, 21–26
   positioning objects in, 24–26
sceneActivated listener, 332, 332f
scene activation, **312**
Scene class, 39, 40f, 109–112, 110f, 111f, 112f
   code component organization in, 156–161, 157f, 158f, 159f, 160f, 161f
   tab in Code editor, 39, 40f
Scene editor
   Camera Markers menu in, 108f
   Camera view in, 20, 21f
   Class Hierarchy tab in, 22, 22f
   close-up camera shot in, 109, 109f
   Gallery in, 20–22, 21f, 22f
   Prop category button in, 20–22, 21f, 22f
   properties section in, 40
   reset camera in, 108f
   Setup Scene button for, 20, 20f
   snap grid in, 65, 65f
   three panels of, 20, 21f
   toolbox in, 20–21, 21f, 55, 65
   vehicle property in, 55
Scene tab in Code editor, 39
selection sort, **404**
Select Project dialog box, 19, 19f
   Blank slates tab in, 30
   open saved project in, 36–37, 37f
self-documenting procedure names, **82**
semicolon in Java code, 140
sequence, **43**
setActiveScene event listener, 46
set design, 15–18, **18**
   purpose of, 30
   sense of place in, 27–29, 28f, 29f
   storyboard frame for, 15, 16f, 17f–18f

translation into Alice scene, 19–26, 19f, 20f, 21f, 22f, 23f, 24f, 25f, 26f
Setup Scene button, 20, 20f
setVehicle, 56–57, 57f
short data type (Java), 211t, **213**
shuffle with random selection of objects, 289–290, 290f, 291f
skeletal hierarchy, orientation of joint in, 62f
skeletal joint, 61f
   actions of, 62, 62f
   built-in arrays of, 315–316, 315f
   creating new statement for, 63f
skin (object appearance), **116**
sort, **398**
   array in Java, 404–412, 404f, 405f, 406f, 407f, 408f, 409f, 410f, 411f, 412f
   selection, **404**
   selection sort algorithm for Java, 404–406, 404f, 405f, 406f
   swap method in, 409–411, 410f, 411f
   visual representation of mechanism for, 413–415, 413f, 414f, 415f
source code, **143**
speed updates
   collision event listener with, 449–450, 450f
   event listener for, 446–450, 447f, 448f, 449f, 450f
spine bending animation technique, implementation of, 184–185, 184f, 185f
standard function, **387**
starter worlds, 50, 50f, 180–182, 180f, 181f, 182f
   DemoStarter.a3p, 313
   CreepyWalkProjectStarter.a3p, 394
   EpilogueStarter.a3p, 461
   Episode1Starter.a3p, 50
   FindingAdelaideStarter.a3p, 372, 374f
   FindingAdelaideToNetBeansSetup.a3p, 398
   FindingEstherGameStarter.a3p, 323
   FindingGideonStarter.a3p, 429
   FindingNicholasStarter.a3p, 272
   FirstWorldStarter.a3p, 27
   GhostTownStarter.a3p, 180
   GhostTownExportToNetBeans.a3p, 210
   GhostTrainHubStarter.a3p, 233
   HelloWorld.a3p, 150
   HelloWorldImportToNetBeans.a3p,
   IndiaTempleStarter.a3p, 313, 313f
   PortalStarter.a3p, 104
   ThawExportToNetBeans.a3p, 222
   ThawStarter.a3p, 80
state, 246, 259
statements, **18**. *See also* code statement; declaration
   assignment, 294–295, 295f

statements (*continued*)
  code completion with required parameter, 163–165, 164f, 165f
  debugging with, 60–61, 61f
  test with temporary, 275–276, 275f
static, **144**
stepwise refinement, 101–131, **102**
  comment documentation with, 105, 106f
  design diagram that represents, 106f
  design using, 102–104, 103f, 104f, 119f
  repeated decomposition with, 106–107, 106f, 107f
  using, 116–120, 117f, 118f, 119f, 120f
stepwise refinement diagram, **106**, 106f
story analysis, 78
  adapting story for interactive game, 322–323, 322f, 323f
  design based on, 78–80, 79f, 80f
storyboard, **15**
  background scene details in, 17f–18f
  character placement and action of, 16f
  design with, 78–79, 79f, 102–103, 103f
  example algorithm derived from, 79, 79f
  frames of, 15, 16
  level of detail in, 16
straightenOutJoints, 319–320, 319f, 352
String, **141**. *See also* TextString
  blank, **443**
  command lines with, 144f
  parameter with, 215, 215f
swap, **270**, 301
  Java array sort method using, 409–411, 410f, 411f
  modifying for visualization of sort, 413–414, 413f, 414f
  pivot markers used in, 287–289, 287f, 288f, 289f
  shuffle with, 289–290, 290f, 291f
symbol, **53**
"//" symbol, 53
syntax, **42**, **143**
  Java, 46–47, 46f, 47f
syntax-sensitive text editor, 137–139, 138f
  comments in, 138f
  TODO note in, 138–139, 138f
system, **140**
System.out, text output with, 140–141, 140f, 141f

T
• • •

tag, **386**
task. *See* program task
task description, **10**, 11
testing, 54, 54f

  custom procedure with, 80–81, 80f, 81f
  Java code, 221–222, 221f, 222f
  runtime window with, 54
  temporary statement for, 275–276, 275f
text-based editor, **136**
  graphics-based comparison with, 144–146, 145f, 146f
text output, System.out for, 140–141, 140f, 141f
TextString, 202, 203f, 211
  add parameter of type, 190–192, 191f, 192f
  output for feedback with debug, 439–446, 439f, 440f, 441f, 442f, 443f, 444f, 445f, 446f
  setup for display of, 440–442, 440f, 441f, 442f
  tracking and updating display of, 442–443, 442f, 443f, 444f
this keyword
  class dependence of, 84f
  Code editor panels with, 83–84, 83f, 84f
  preference settings for, 150f
thread, **168**, **233**
  do in order assumed within, 168, 168f
3D graphics animation, Java code for, 161–165, 162f, 163f, 164f, 165f
3D models, **20**
  Gallery objects of, 21
  internal skeletal joint system, 127
3D text object, 425, 439, 439f, 441, 454, 455
timeElapsed listener, **432**, 447–448, 447f, 448f
TODO note, **138**
  Java implementation with, 138–139, 138f
Toolbox, 20–21, 21f
  snap grid in, 65, 65f
  vehicle property in, 55
toRoundedInteger, **200**
tracking variables, 386
  declaration of, 466f
  game setup with, 433f
  set to game-active values, 436f
Train Engine episode, 74–75
  algorithm for, 79f
  design for, 78–80, 79f, 80f
  story analysis for, 78
  storyboard for, 79f
  Thaw animation for, 79f
troubleshooting. *See also* debugging
  interactivity code, 254, 254f
Tunnel episode, 98–100
  algorithm for, 104
  story analysis for, 102
  storyboard in, 102–103, 103f
turn, 50, 59, 59f
Twitter™, 8

U

••••

UIs. *See* user interfaces
unrolled code structure, **318**
    each in together, 320f
    for each in, 318f
update text display, 442–444
user (player), 230
user input, 230, 294
    built-in functions that prompt, 294f
    getting, 294–296, 294f, 295f, 296f
    using, 296, 296f, 297f
    visual feedback with, 297f
user interfaces (UIs), **230**
    implementation of instructions display in,
        235–238, 235f, 236f, 237f, 238f

V

••••

vampirePose, 327, 327f
variables, **178**, **195**, 204
    assigning a value to, **294**
    as count loop control, 199–201, 199f, 200f,
        201f
    compute value using, 195–198, 196f, 197f, 198f
    declaring, 195–197, 196f, 197f, 255, 255f
    initializing, 195–197, 196f, 197f

    in Java, 215–216, 216f
    writing Java code with, 214–216, 214f,
        215f, 216f
vehicle, **55**
    code statement to set, 57f
    default, 55
    object moving with its, 55–58, 55f, 56f, 57f,
        58f
viewExited listener, 425, **432**
visualizing
    array (horizontal), 378f
    array (vertical), 385–386
    array sort mechanism, 413f
    invisible data, 117–118
void (Java), **144**, **410**

W

•••••

while loop, **270**
    repetition with, 286–287
    stairs animation with infinite, 333–334, 334f,
        335f
WholeNumber, 202, 203f, 211
win condition, **230**
    in game controls, 451–452, 451f, 452f, 453f
wrapper classes, **212**
wrist joint, rotational action of, 60